ON THIS DAY

ON THIS DAY

THE HISTORY OF THE WORLD IN 366 DAYS

METRO BOOKS
New York

METRO BOOKS
New York

An Imprint of Sterling Publishing
387 Park Avenue South
New York, NY 10016

ISBN 978-1-4351-5900-6

For information about custom editions, special sales, and premium and corporate purchases, please contact Sterling Special Sales at 800-805-5489 or specialsales@sterlingpublishing.com.

Manufactured in Hong Kong

2 4 6 8 10 9 7 5 3 1

www.sterlingpublishing.com

WHAT IS *On This Day?*

Is this book an encyclopedia, a history book, a book of trivia, a book of days, a source of quirky anecdotes or a serious reference work? In fact, it can be used as all of these. With an entire page for each of the 366 days of the calendar year, it describes in a lively and accessible way, many of the major events (and a lot of the minor ones) that have happened throughout history.

However *On This Day* doesn't just tell you when an event happened. In many cases, it also sets that event in context. The announcement of the death of Galileo on January 8, for example, provides an opportunity for a biography of the Italian astronomer

May 25, 1935 Athlete Jesse Owens sets five new world records.

and explains how he came to renounce his scientific theories about the universe. The book can also be used as a source of background information on areas such as the history of space travel, recent developments in Eastern Europe, the American Civil War, or the women's liberation movement.

On This Day is wide ranging both in terms of time span and subject matter. From Julius Caesar to the present day, it covers over 2000 years of history and a multitude of subjects including sporting records, exploration, film and entertainment, music and literature, fashion, scientific achievements, politics, inventions, quotations, birthdays, wars, and royalty. As well as providing factual information, the book can be dipped into as a fun source of trivia.

August 6, 1945 The *Enola Gay* drops an atom bomb on Hiroshima.

December 25, 440 AD Christ's birth date becomes official.

January 17, 1912 Captain Scott reaches the South Pole.

JANUARY

AMERICAN SLAVES "MUST BE UNCHAINED"

1863 As civil war rages in America, President Abraham Lincoln today declared freedom for all slaves in the southern states that have rebelled against his government. In Washington huge crowds of emancipated slaves celebrated the announcement, which honours a pledge made by the president before the war began. "The old South must be destroyed and replaced by new propositions and new ideas," said Lincoln in a speech. But his order does not apply

to slaves in border states fighting on the Union side against the South, nor does it affect slaves in southern areas already under Union control – and, of course, the rebel Confederates will not act on Lincoln's order. What the proclamation does show is that the Civil War is really being fought to end slavery. The issue has dominated the election campaign, with Democrats claiming that the Northern states will be overrun with "semi-savages".

Men their rights and nothing more; women their rights and nothing less.
Susan B. Anthony, American feminist – motto of the first issue of the suffragette journal *The Revolution*, 1868.

---

44 BC Julius Caesar, founder of the Roman Empire, introduces the Julian calendar.

1538 German and Swiss states introduce the Gregorian calendar.

1600 Queen Elizabeth I grants a charter establishing the British East India Company.

1804 Haiti declares independence from France, becoming the first Latin-American state to gain its freedom.

1901 The Commonwealth of Australia is established.

1958 The European Economic Community comes into being.

1990 Romania abolishes the death penalty.

BIRTHDAYS

E. M. Forster 1879, British novelist, whose works include *A Passage to India* and *Howard's End*.

J. Edgar Hoover 1895, American founder and head of the FBI.

Harold 'Kim' Philby 1912, British traitor who spied for Russian intelligence.

J. D. Salinger 1919, American author whose novels include *Catcher in the Rye*.

CASTRO TOPPLES CUBAN DICTATOR

1959 Cuban dictator Fulgencio Batista has fled from his war-torn island after failing to secure the support of the US in his struggle against the revolutionary forces of Fidel Castro. Castro, 32, is expected to declare Santiago de Cuba, from where he commands his rebel army, Cuba's provisional capital. Dr Manuel Urrutia is to be the new president and will fly to Havana, bringing to a formal end Castro's 25-month struggle against the hated Batista regime.

• 1961 – ADIEU TO THE BRITISH FARTHING • 1999 – THE EURO BECOMES LEGAL TENDER

BLACK HOLE OF CALCUTTA AVENGED

1757 Robert Clive's forces have recaptured Calcutta and avenged the infamous "Black Hole" incident when, last year, the Nawab of Bengal captured the city and imprisoned the British defenders in a tiny airless room, where 123 died. Calcutta was founded by the British East India Company, which bought the villages of Sutanati, Kalikata, and Govindapur in 1698. Its recapture now was seen as essential to British prestige in India. Clive went to India as a clerk in 1743 and joined the company's army four years later. He was appointed lieutenant governor of Fort St David, near Madras, in 1755. Now Clive is expected to challenge the Nawab in an attempt to bring Bengal under British rule. If he succeeds, Clive can expect to become governor of Bengal, known for its vast wealth.

MUSLIMS LOSE GRIP ON SPAIN

1492 Seven hundred years of Arab rule in Spain ended today when Granada, the last Spanish Muslim stronghold, fell to the army of Spain's Christian queen. Muslims are regarding this as Islam's worst-ever catastrophe, while Christians hail it as "the most blessed day in Spain's history". With today's Reconquest, Muslim invasions from North Africa are no longer a threat. The final ousting of the Moors is the work of a gifted royal pair, Isabella I of Castile and Ferdinand II of Aragon, who married in 1479. Their kingdoms have been fighting the Moors for centuries, in what finally became a crusade.

Army fiasco triggers Boer War

1896 The three-day raid by Starr Jameson and 500 British soldiers into the Boer republic of the Transvaal, purportedly in support of British settlers, has ended in defeat, capture and humiliation with 17 men killed and 55 missing. The Parliaments in both Cape Town and London are in an uproar over what is being termed "a colossal folly". Jameson, a close associate of British imperialist and Prime Minister of the Cape Colony Cecil Rhodes, had planned to overthrow the Boer government of President Paul Kruger. Instead, he and his men are today languishing in a Pretoria jail. Jameson's folly could now tip Britain into war with the Boer republics. Rhodes' political career can hardly survive this disaster – questions are being asked about whether the raid was his idea and just how much Colonial Secretary Joe Chamberlain knew about it.

Pharaoh's treasures may unleash curse

1924 British archaeologist Howard Carter has made a dazzling discovery in Egypt's Valley of the Kings – a pharaoh's tomb filled with treasure, including a solid gold coffin, a gold mask, jewellery and other artifacts. The tomb is that of Tutankhamen, a pharaoh of the 18th dynasty who died 3276 years ago. Egyptologists say this is by far the richest of the few royal burial chambers that survived comparatively intact. More than 60 royal tombs have been discovered in the Valley of the Kings, including that of Ramses VI.

Human law is law only by virtue of its accordance with right reason, and by this means it is clear that it flows from eternal law. In so far as it deviates from right reason it is called an unjust law; and in such a case, it is no law at all, but rather an assertion of violence.

Thomas Aquinas, who died today in Rome, 1274.

LUTHER PROVOKES PAPAL WRATH

1521 A Papal bull from Pope Leo X has ordered the excommunication of Martin Luther after a deadline for him to recant his heretical views expired. In 1520, Luther completed three celebrated works in which he stated his views: in his *Address to the Christian Nobility of the German Nation*, he invited the German princes to take the reform of the church into their own

hands; in *A Prelude Concerning the Babylonian Captivity of the Church*, he attacked the papacy and the current theology of sacraments; and in *On the Freedom of a Christian Man*, he stated his position on justification and good works. Luther's dispute with Rome began when he challenged the doctrine of Indulgences (the remission of punishments for sins confessed) and their sale to raise funds for the church. The rift widened in 1517 when Luther posted his famous "95 Theses" on the door of the castle church at Wittenberg in Saxony-Anhalt.

1777 George Washington defeats the British at the Battle of Princeton.

1918 New Zealand-born scientist Ernest Rutherford announces he has split the atom.

1958 British explorer Sir Edmund Hillary reaches the South Pole.

1959 Alaska becomes the 49th state of the USA.

1962 Pope John XXIII excommunicates Cuban premier Fidel Castro.

1967 Jack Ruby, killer of Lee Harvey Oswald and alleged assassinator of John F. Kennedy, dies.

1980 British naturalist Joy Adamson, author of *Born Free* is murdered in a Kenyan game park.

BIRTHDAYS

Marcus Tullius Cicero 106 BC, Roman statesman and orator.

Clement Attlee 1883, Labour Prime Minister 1945–51.

J. R. R. Tolkien 1892, South African-born novelist and author of *The Lord of the Rings*.

Michael Schumacher 1969, German champion Formula One driver.

• 1870 – WORK BEGINS ON BROOKLYN BRIDGE • 1961 – USA SEVERS LINKS WITH CUBA

1884 The Fabian Society is formed in London to promote socialist ideals.

1885 The first successful appendix operation is performed in Iowa.

1896 Utah becomes the 45th state of the Union.

1936 *Billboard* publishes the first-ever pop chart in New York.

1948 Burma leaves the British Commonwealth to become fully independent.

1972 Rose Heilbron becomes the first British female judge at London's Old Bailey.

1990 Russian President Gorbachev tells Lithuania's communists that they are allowed to leave the Soviet Communist party.

BIRTHDAYS

Sir Isaac Newton 1643, British physicist and mathematician.

Jakob Grimm 1785, eldest of the two brothers who wrote *Grimm's Fairy Tales*.

Louis Braille 1809, French inventor of an alphabet system for the blind.

Grace Bumbry 1937, American opera singer who was the first black singer to take the stage at Bayreuth.

REBEL ELVIS GETS GI SHOW ROLLING

1957 Two days before what is being billed as his final appearance on the *Ed Sullivan Show*, rock star Elvis Presley today underwent his pre-induction army medical check-up at the Kennedy Veterans' Hospital in Memphis. Though his formal drafting is some months off Presley's willingness to serve his country has already done much to tame the image of a rock'n'roll rebel that has entranced youngsters and maddened parents. Since his debut in July 1954 he has proved a brilliant investment for promoter Colonel Tom Parker; last year

his "Hound Dog" became the fastest-selling single ever. His appearances on the *Ed Sullivan Show* have helped generate an adoring fan club that sends him 3000 letters a week.

TRAGIC END FOR SPEED CHAMPION

1967 A 300-mph (482-kph) somersault has ended the career of British speed king Donald Campbell, whose jet-powered speedboat *Bluebird* went out of control today on Coniston Water in northern England as he tried to beat his own record of 276 mph (444 kph). He made a good first run and then turned for a second attempt without stopping to refuel. The end came when the boat ran into its own wake at full speed and lifted out of the water. Divers searching for Campbell's body found only his helmet and teddy bear mascot.

• 1944 – GERMANS DRAFT CHILDREN INTO ARMY • 1965 – DEATH OF POET T. S. ELIOT

Farewell to Shackleton

1922 The British polar explorer, Sir Ernest Shackleton, has died at sea while on his way to lead a fourth expedition to the Antarctic. His 1914 expedition to cross the Pole collapsed when his ship, *Endurance*, became trapped in ice. Shackleton led his men to the edge of the ice and then sailed hundreds of miles in an open boat – an extraordinary feat during which no lives were lost.

KHMER ROUGE BLITZ CAMBODIAN CAPITAL

1975 The Cambodian capital Phnom Penh today came under direct siege by Khmer Rouge communist rebels using heavy rocket and artillery attacks. The Khmer Rouge advance has been relentless, in spite of massive economic and military aid from the United States to Lon Nol's government. Military experts predict the capital can hold out for no more than four months. North Vietnam and the Viet Cong have helped the Khmer Rouge in their war against the government of Prince Norodom Sihanouk and Lon Nol. Their sanctuaries in the mountains of southern Cambodia have been the subject of massive bomb attacks by US planes, but by 1970 the Khmer Rouge already controlled about two-thirds of Cambodia. Their leader is Pol Pot, a shadowy figure who joined Ho Chi Minh's Indo-Chinese Communist party in the 1940s.

X-RAY VISION

1896 A German physicist, Wilhelm Roentgen, today demonstrated what he calls the X-ray. This is a form of high-energy radiation that allows him to see through solid objects. The technique may prove useful in medicine. Roentgen discovered the new ray last year, by accident.

How could they tell?
Dorothy Parker, US writer, on being told John Calvin Coolidge, 30th US president, had died today, 1933.

1066 Death of Edward the Confessor, the English king renowned for his piety.

1589 Death of Catherine de Medici, Italian wife of Henry II of France.

1818 First regular trans-Atlantic service between New York and Liverpool.

1925 Mrs Nellie Taylor Ross of Wyoming becomes first US woman governor.

1930 Joseph Stalin collectivizes Soviet farms, forcing wealthy peasants off their land.

1964 Pope Paul IV meets the Ecumenical Patriarch of Constantinople in Jerusalem, the first meeting between the heads of Catholic and Orthodox churches in 500 years.

1971 England play Australia in the first-ever one-day cricket match in Melbourne.

BIRTHDAYS

John Burke 1781, British genealogist and founder of *Burke's Peerage*.

Robert Duvall 1931, US film actor who appeared in *To Kill a Mockingbird*.

King Juan Carlos of Spain 1938.

Diane Keaton 1946, US film actress.

• 1919 – HITLER FORMS NAZI PARTY • 1989 – US FIGHTERS CLASH WITH GADDAFI JETS

1066 Harold II of England is crowned.

1884 Gregor Mendel, the Austrian botanist who discovered the principles governing the inheritance of characteristics in living things, dies aged 62.

1916 The British government institutes conscription to replace the many thousands of fighting men killed in the trenches in France.

1930 Australian cricketer Don Bradman scores 452 not out against Queensland in his first innings as he bats for New South Wales.

1931 New Sadler's Wells Theatre opens in London.

1988 La Coupole, the famous Parisian brasserie, is sold to be turned into an office block.

1995 Death of South African communist leader Joe Slovo.

BIRTHDAYS

King Richard II of England 1367 son of Edward the Black Prince.

Joan of Arc 1412, French heroine and saint.

Anthony Minghella 1954, English Academy Award-winning director of *The English Patient*.

THEODORE ROOSEVELT DIES

1919 Theodore Roosevelt, the American president who occupied the White House for two terms died today at Oyster Bay after a life dedicated to politics, literature and adventure. He once said, "I wish to preach . . . the doctrine of the strenuous life." He will be remembered as the president who restrained big business, pushing through anti-Trust legislation which discouraged market control and price rigging. In international affairs he won a Nobel Prize for mediating peace between Russia and Japan, and was responsible for widening America's international influence; in the Roosevelt Corollary to the Monroe Doctrine, he also enshrined America's right to interfere in Latin America. Roosevelt began his career running the New York police, then became state governor. First taking power after the assassination of William McKinley in 1901, he was elected in his own right in 1904, serving until 1909.

HENRY VIII – FOURTH TIME LUCKY?

1540 King Henry VIII of England married his fourth wife, Anne of Cleves, today in an alliance that could secure the king both an heir and powerful friends – though it has deepened his rift with Catholic Rome. Anne's brother, the Duke of Cleves, is a powerful German Protestant prince with whom Henry shares political interests. Henry's chief minister, Thomas Cromwell, negotiated the marriage, gaining Lutheran support to counter a Catholic alliance against England. The king's marital affairs have so far been disastrous: he divorced Catherine of Aragon and had Anne Boleyn executed, while Jane Seymour died. When Henry first saw his fourth wife at the wedding today, he bellowed: "You have sent me a Flanders mare!"

Breakthrough in Communications

1838 Samuel Morse today demonstrated a revolutionary electromagnetic telegraph that promises to open up a new world in long-distance communications. The device sends a pulse of current down a line, energizing an electromagnet at the receiving end which pulls an iron armature attached to a pencil. The pulses are short or long, producing "dots" or "dashes" which can be used as a code to represent the letters of the alphabet.

• 1928 – RIVER THAMES BURSTS ITS BANKS • 1945 – LAST-DITCH NAZI ASSAULT FAILS

HERO WASHINGTON IS FIRST US PRESIDENT

1789 George Washington, hero of America's revolutionary wars, has been unanimously elected as the first president of the United States. Members of the electoral college in New York gave an overwhelming vote to the hero of Yorktown, who is expected to take office on April 30. Washington was closely involved in drafting the constitution two years ago. Despite his audacity in the war against England, Washington is expected to move cautiously. He is acutely aware of the need to build an executive structure that can accommodate future presidents.

1536 Death of Catherine of Aragon, King Henry VIII of England's first wife.

1610 Galileo Galilei announces his discovery of four moons circling Jupiter.

1785 Dr John Jeffries and Jean-Pierre Blanchard cross the English Channel in a hot-air balloon.

1905 The first government appointment of a black man – as head of South Carolina customs services.

1927 A transatlantic telephone link between London and New York is opened.

1975 The Organization of Petroleum Exporting Countries raises the price of crude oil by 10 per cent.

1990 The Leaning Tower of Pisa is closed to the public as its rate of movement accelerates.

LAST RITES FOR EMPEROR WHO WAS LAST OF THE GODS

1989 Hirohito, the Japanese emperor who disavowed his ancient claim to divinity in an act of contrition for World War II, died today after a 62-year reign. He is succeeded by Crown Prince Akihito. After the 1946 constitution stripped him of all but ceremonial powers, he devoted himself to ceremonial duties and his pet subject, marine biology. Hirohito opposed war with the US in the 1930s, including Japan's invasion of Manchuria and her alliance with Nazi Germany, but was powerless to restrain the generals. In 1941 he favoured peace with Washington, but was convinced that a pre-emptive strike at Pearl Harbor was necessary. Hirohito's broadcast confirming Japan's surrender after the destruction of Hiroshima and Nagasaki tested the post-feudal fabric of Japanese society: many believed surrender impossible for a Japanese emperor.

BIRTHDAYS

Joseph Bonaparte 1768, Corsican, eldest brother of Napoleon Bonaparte and King of Naples and Spain.

Gerald Durrell 1925, British author and naturalist.

Lewis Hamilton 1985, English Formula One racing champion.

• **1927 – HARLEM GLOBE TROTTERS FOUNDED • 1945 – NEW BURMA ROAD COMPLETED**

794 Danish Vikings attack Lindisfarne Island off the northeast coast of England.

1889 New Yorker Dr Herman Hoperith patents the first computer.

1941 Robert Baden-Powell, founder of the Boy Scouts, dies.

1942 German troops begin the retreat from Leningrad.

1948 Richard Tauber, the much-loved Austrian tenor, dies in Australia.

1976 Zhou En-Lai dies, Chinese Communist premier 1949–76.

1979 Vietnamese troops crush the Khmer Rouge and occupy Phnom Penh, capital of Cambodia.

1996 Death of French socialist president François Mitterrand, aged 80.

BIRTHDAYS

Solomon Bandaraike 1899, Prime Minister of Sri Lanka 1956–59.

Elvis Presley 1935, first American rock'n'roll icon.

Stephen Hawking 1942, English theoretical physicist and author of *A Brief History of Time*.

David Bowie 1947, British rock musician and actor.

DEATH OF GALILEO

1642 Galileo Galilei, the mathematician and astronomer, has died at Arcetri. Galileo rose to prominence as professor of mathematics at the University of Padua, where he challenged key assumptions in Aristotelian physics. He was the first to exploit the telescope to gaze on lunar mountains and the moons of Jupiter and became convinced that Copernicus had been right: the earth rotates around the sun, not vice-versa. The Holy Office at Rome issued an edict against Copernicanism and in 1632 Galileo was called to Rome by the Inquisition. He was condemned to life imprisonment for heresy and forced to recant. Even so, he said under his breath, "But still it moves."

Jackson leads US forces to victory

1815 US forces led by Major General Andrew Jackson have crushed an invading British army at New Orleans in an engagement that could be the last of this war. Now English diplomats have begun to negotiate a peace settlement. It was British insistence on the right to commandeer US vessels and their men that originally sparked off the conflict in 1812.

How can you govern a country that produces 265 different kinds of cheese?

General Charles de Gaulle, on his appointment as French premier, 1958.

• 1963 – EMPIRE STATE BUILDING ABLAZE • 1973 – ELVIS DIVORCES WIFE PRISCILLA

UNWELCOME COST OF WAR WITH FRANCE

1799 William Pitt the Younger introduced income tax in Britain today, at two shillings in the pound (10 per cent). This unpopular move is to pay for the war against Napoleon's France. Pitt, Prime Minister since he was 24, is a liberal reformer who revived Britain's economy following the American Revolution, but the French Revolution has brought different pressures; radical groups inspired by France have found the ear of disgruntled workers and troops have been called out as mass meetings demanding change have led to rioting. War has turned

Pitt the reformer into an oppressor: he has enforced summary trial for trade unionists, banning and arrest of radical workers, and total press censorship. The new income tax is being seen as part of the same unwelcome parcel.

WAVE OF IMMIGRATION HITS BRITAIN'S SHORES

1955 A ship with 400 Jamaican immigrants aboard docked in Britain today – the latest in a growing influx of West Indians arriving to help in the reconstruction of Britain's war-ravaged cities. Conservative politicians are pressing for legislation to control the numbers of immigrants.

1806 Lord Nelson, naval commander and hero of the Battle of Trafalgar, is buried at St Paul's Cathedral in London.

1811 The first women's golf tournament takes place in Scotland.

1878 Death of Victor Emmanuel, first King of Italy.

1909 Ernest Shackleton's polar expedition is forced to turn back just 11 miles from the South Pole.

1920 Alexander Fleming pioneers the use of penicillin at St Mary's Hospital in London.

1951 *Life After Tomorrow*, the first film to receive an 'X' rating in Britain, opens in London.

1972 British miners strike for the first time since 1926.

1996 Rebels seize 3,000 hostages in Chechnya.

BIRTHDAYS

George Balanchine 1904, Russian-born choreographer and co-founder of the New York City Ballet.

Simone de Beauvoir 1908, French novelist, critic and early feminist.

Richard Nixon 1913, 37th President of the USA.

• 1957 – BRITISH PM, ANTHONY EDEN, RESIGNS • 1980 – SHI'ITE EXTREMISTS EXECUTED

1645 William Laud, Archbishop of Canterbury and supporter of English King Charles I, is beheaded in London.

1840 The Penny Post is introduced to Britain.

1870 William and John D. Rockefeller found the Standard Oil Company of Ohio.

1920 The League of Nations is inaugurated in Geneva, Switzerland.

1946 The League of Nations is dissolved and replaced by the United Nations.

1957 Sir Harold Macmillan becomes Prime Minister of Britain.

1984 General Zia of Pakistan frees Benazir Bhutto, daughter of former prime minister Zulfikar Ali Bhutto who was executed in 1979.

1985 Clive Sinclair launches the C5, a battery-operated tricycle.

BIRTHDAYS

Dame Barbara Hepworth 1903, British sculptor.

Gustáv Husák 1913, First Secretary of the Czechoslovakian Communist Party 1969–87.

GOVERNMENT SAYS BRITONS CAN'T JOIN ANTI-FRANCO FORCES

1937 Britain has announced a ban on its nationals joining the International Brigades gathering in Spain to defend the Constitutionalist Republican forces against General Franco's Nationalists in the civil war that has erupted there. The US is to impose a ban on Americans joining the fighting. 59,000 idealists from all countries have flocked to Spain to join the "fight for liberty". The eight-month-old conflict has gained international overtones with Nazi and fascist troops fighting for Franco, while the USSR has sent weapons and military advisers to the Republicans. The Comintern, the international communist brotherhood, has organized thousands of liberals and leftists from 53 countries into volunteer International Brigades to fight fascism.

THE VOTE FOR WOMEN AT LAST

1918 Women's rights took a huge stride forward today when legislatures in London and Washington gave women the right to vote. In Britain, the House of Lords gave its approval to the Representation of the People Bill, which gives women over 30 the vote. In Washington the House of Representatives also voted in favour of suffrage for women.

IT'S ALL CHANGE IN LONDON

1863 London's first underground railway, the Metropolitan, opened today, inaugurating a new era in city travel that could do much to help clear the congested roads of carriages and pedestrians. Passengers are delighted with the new service, but some foresee problems because of the smoke the trains spew from their chimneys.

You're lucky I don't shove your beard down your gullet! … Get out, viper! … Sheer off, filibuster! Out of my sight, you gallows bird! … Baboon! … Carpet-seller! … Pockmark! … Cannibal! … Er.

Captain Haddock, irate, sees off a slave-trader in *The Red Sea Sharks* – Hergé's Tintin first appeared today, 1929.

• **1949 – FIRST VINYL RECORD LAUNCHED IN USA • 1971 – COCO CHANEL DIES**

Hong Kong talks overshadowed by Tianenmen memories

1990 China today lifted martial law, seven months after the horrific military massacre of 2600 pro-democracy demonstrators in Peking's Tianenmen Square. The troops withdrew from Tianenmen Square in honour of Hong Kong's governor, Sir David Wilson, who arrived for talks with the Peking regime on the colony's future. In 1997 the colony reverts to Chinese control as Britain's 99-year lease runs out. Sir David is to meet Chinese premier Li Peng, who praised the withdrawing troops for their role in "crushing the emerging anarchy", as he put it. "For this, the people will never forget them," he added. There were huge turnouts in Hong Kong in support of the pro-democracy demonstrators. Confidence died, the economy stumbled, and an exodus began – led by the skilled professionals the colony will desperately need if Hong Kong is to survive into the future.

IT'S A ZOG'S LIFE

1946 King Zog, the colourful monarch who started life as Ahmed Zogu, a conservative northern tribal chief in Albania, has been dethroned and the country declared a republic again. Zog elevated himself to the monarchy after seizing power in 1925 in the turbulent period following the collapse of Ottoman Turkish rule. Allying himself with Italy, Zog carried out some modernizations, but his entanglement with Italy's fascist dictator, Benito Mussolini, backfired; in 1939 Italian fascist forces invaded Albania and Zog was forced into exile. During the war he was unable to exploit a power struggle between the communist and non-communist liberation forces to his advantage and when the communists won, Zog lost.

1569 The first state lottery is held in England.

1867 Mexican president Benito Juarez returns to Mexico City following the defeat of French forces.

1891 Baron Georges-Eugène Haussman, architect who replanned Paris as a city of long boulevards, dies in poverty.

1922 Insulin is first used with success in the treatment of diabetes.

1954 All Comet aircraft are grounded following a mysterious crash off the island of Elba.

1959 Pakistani cricketer Hanif Mohammad hits a record-breaking 499 runs.

1970 Nigerian civil war reaches a bitter end.

1989 US president Ronald Reagan bids goodbye to the American people after two terms in office.

2014 Death of Israeli prime minister, Ariel Sharon, born in 1928.

BIRTHDAYS

Ezra Cornell 1807, American founder of Cornell University, New York.

Sir John Alexander 1815, Canada's first Prime Minister.

• 1892 – 13-YEAR-OLD BRIDE FOR GAUGUIN • 1963 – WHISKY A GO-GO CLUB OPENS IN LA

1519 Maximilian I, King of Germany and Holy Roman Emperor from 1493, dies.

1879 The British-Zulu War begins in South Africa.

1957 President Eisenhower urges the Soviet Union to agree a ban on space warfare.

1964 The Sultan of Zanzibar is banished and the country becomes a republic.

1970 A Boeing 747 jet makes the maiden transatlantic flight.

1989 Former Ugandan leader Idi Amin is expelled from Zaire.

2010 The first criminal trial without a jury for 400 years opens in London.

BIRTHDAYS

Charles Perrault 1628, French writer and collector of fairy tales.

Johann Pestalozzi 1856, Swiss founder of a new principle of teaching.

John Singer Sargent 1856, American painter best-known for his portraits of society figures.

Hermann Goering 1893, commander of the German Air Force during World War II.

PEACE IN BIAFRA BUT FAMINE LOOMS

1970 The secessionist Nigerian state of Biafra today surrendered to Nigerian federal troops after a disastrous three-year war likely to be even more catastrophic in its aftermath as starvation grips the population. As the last Biafran airstrip was taken by federal troops, reports began to emerge of rape and pillage by the victors on a horrifying scale. During its brief existence, the oil-rich state of Biafra covered 44,000 sq miles. It was created by the Ibo, the dominant ethnic group in Nigeria, and led by Lt Col. Chukwuemeka Odumegwu Ojukwu. He is said to be demanding political asylum in nearby Ivory Coast.

HAITI DEVASTATED BY MASSIVE QUAKE

2010 An earthquake, measuring 7.0 on the Richter scale, hits the Caribbean country of Haiti, killing around 230,000 people and leaving over one million homeless. The quake was the country's most severe in 200 years and devastated the capital city, Port au Prince, destroying the Presidential palace, Parliament and other important buildings, along with countless homes and businesses. Aid efforts are hampered by damage to the port and airport. Homeless refugees are housed in tents, creating an ongoing humanitarian crisis.

In a hierarchy, every employee tends to rise to his level of incompetence. Work is accomplished by those employees who have not yet reached their level of incompetence.

Peter Lawrence, Canadian author of *The Peter Principle*, who died today, 1990.

• 1959 – $400 MILLION CONTRACT FOR MERCURY SPACE PROGRAMME

DREYFUS VICTIM OF RACISM SAYS NOVELIST ZOLA

1898 The distinguished novelist Emile Zola today stunned the Parisian literary and political world with an open letter on the front page of *L'Aurore* entitled "J'accuse", which makes a blistering attack on the French army over the affair of Captain Alfred Dreyfus. His letter forces simmering conflicts between the republicans and right-wing pro-monarchists into the open, showing just how deeply rooted anti-semitism is in French society. Officials are now examining the letter for a possible libel action, which could force Zola, one of France's leading literary figures, to flee the country. Meanwhile Captain Dreyfus, an Alsatian Jewish officer on the French general staff, has been sent to prison charged with giving information to the German military attaché in Paris. However, there is new evidence – which is supported by Zola's letter – that suggests the charges are false and Dreyfus should be pardoned.

Labour Party Born: Socialism Gets Serious

1893 James Keir Hardie, the new member of parliament for West Ham who last year arrived to take his seat at Westminster dressed in yellow trousers and to the tune of the Marseillaise, has fathered an organization that could in time shock Britain's frock-coated Tories even more deeply than his dress sense. It is called the Labour Party and results from an alliance of British trade union and socialist movements. The Fabian Society, the newly-formed Independent Labour Party, and Keir Hardie's own Scottish Labour Party will all be united under the Labour Representation Committee. Hardie, who started work as a miner at the age of 10 and educated himself at night school, secured election as an independent socialist, but now he has a party to back him.

1599 Death of Edmund Spenser, English poet who wrote *The Faerie Queene*.

1910 Caruso is broadcast by radio singing at the New York Metropolitan Opera House.

1915 South African troops occupy Swakopmund in German South West Africa.

1941 Irish author James Joyce, whose book *Ulysses* caused outrage because of its sexual frankness, dies after surgery in Zurich.

1957 Elvis Presley records the hit "All Shook Up" in a Hollywood studio.

1974 The world's largest airport opens in Dallas, TX.

1979 Concorde begins flights from Washington D.C. to Dallas.

1988 Death of Chiang Ching-kuo, President of the Republic of China of Taiwan since 1978.

1990 Twenty-four people die in riots in Baku, Soviet Azerbaijan.

BIRTHDAYS

Sophie Tucker 1884, Russian-born singer and vaudeville star in America.

Michael Bond 1926, creator of the much-loved children's character Paddington Bear.

• 1964 – BEATLES TOP US CHARTS • 2012 – *CONCORDIA* CRUISE SHIP CAPSIZES

MARILYN MONROE BECOMES MRS DIMAGGIO

1954 Marilyn Monroe, the screen star of *How to Marry a Millionaire*, has followed her own advice and found herself a wealthy new husband. This time it's 1940s baseball hero Joe DiMaggio. After a checkered start to her career, actress Norma Jean Baker (her real name) has nowhere to go but up, as Hollywood vies for the talents of this new international sex goddess. DiMaggio, now 40, led the New York Yankees to 10 pennants and nine World Series titles. In 1941 he hit safely in 56 consecutive games, an all-time record. Soft-spoken and courteous, DiMaggio has endeared himself to the American public – and now wed one of America's most desirable women.

Bradford book burnings as Rushdie takes cover

1989 British Muslims today burned copies of Salman Rushdie's book *The Satanic Verses* in public. Rushdie has been catapulted to the centre of an international furore over the book, which has caused fury throughout the Islamic world for its alleged blasphemies against the Prophet Mohammed. Muslim communities in Bradford publicly supwport Iranian leader Ayatollah Khomeini's call for the author's assassination. Rushdie has gone into hiding and is under British police protection. The issue has caused Muslim indignation that Western blasphemy laws only apply in a Christian context.

FAR-FLUNG URANUS

1986 *Voyager 2*, the only spacecraft to reach the planet Uranus, today passed within 50,625 miles of the planet's cloud tops. *Voyager 2* has been collecting data on Uranus and its rings and satellites for four months. Suprsingly, the planet's rings were only discovered in 1977. Uranus, the seventh planet from the sun, is about four times the size of the Earth. *Voyager 2* has detected an ocean perhaps 6000 miles deep.

• 1858 – ITALIAN ASSASSIN MISSES NAPOLEON III • 1957 – HUMPHREY BOGART DIES

Irish glimpse independence

1922 The Provisional Irish Parliament, Dail Eireann, is tonight debating a treaty proposal that could finally make Ireland an independent nation. The Irish Free State proposal has split Ireland's nationalist politicians: Foremost nationalist Eamon de Valera has refused to sit in the proposed new chamber because an oath to the British Crown is required. But the IRA's Michael Collins – reported to have been holding secret talks with British Home Secretary Winston Churchill – insists Ireland must accept the flawed treaty.

PLANE CRASHES INTO NEW YORK'S HUDSON RIVER

2009 US Airline flight 1549 landed on the icy waters of the Hudson River shortly after take-off, when birds collided with both engines. All 155 passengers and crew survived as Captain Sullenberger steered the aircraft onto the water. Mayor Bloomberg described the crew as "five real American heroes".

1559 Elizabeth I is crowned queen of England.

1790 Fletcher Christian and other mutineers from the *Bounty* land on Pitcairn Island in the South Pacific.

1797 James Hetherington is fined £50 for wearing the first bowler hat.

1878 Women receive degrees for the first time at London University.

1880 The first telephone directory is published in London.

1971 President Sadat of Egypt officially opens the Aswan High Dam on the River Nile.

BIRTHDAYS

Jean-Baptiste Poquelin, (Molière) 1622, French satirical dramatist.

General Gamal Nasser 1918, first president of the republic of Egypt.

Martin Luther King 1929, American clergyman, leader of the civil rights movement in the 1960s and winner of the Nobel Peace Prize in 1964.

Margaret O'Brien 1937, American child actress who won a special Academy Award in 1944, at just seven years old.

NIXON HALTS US BOMBING OF VIETNAM

1973 US President Richard Nixon today ordered a halt to all bombing of Vietnam by American warplanes, less than one month after the massive US "Christmas bombing" raids hit North Vietnam's capital, Hanoi. This initiative comes as the Paris peace conference opens, with a cease-fire to end the conflict believed to be imminent. The Christmas bombing had been planned by White House strategists as a means of forcing Viet Cong leaders to moderate their demands at the Paris negotiating table.

• 1759 – BRITISH MUSEUM OPENS • 1971 – BRITAIN EMBRACES DECIMAL CURRENCY

1547 Ivan the Terrible is crowned the first Tsar of Russia.

1780 British forces defeat the Spanish at Cape St Vincent and relieve Gibraltar.

1891 Death of French composer Léo Delibes, best-known for his ballet *Coppélia.*

1932 Duke Ellington records "It Don't Mean a Thing" in New York.

1944 General Eisenhower is appointed Supreme Commander of the Allied Forces in Europe.

1957 The Cavern Club opens in Liverpool as a venue for rock groups.

1957 Italian conductor Arturo Toscanini dies.

1970 Colonel Gaddafi becomes Chairman of the Revolutionary Command Council in Libya.

1979 The Shah of Iran dies in exile in Egypt.

BIRTHDAYS

André Michelin 1853, French manufacturer of rubber tyres.

Lord Thomson of Fleet 1921, Canadian newspaper magnate.

USA BANS BOOZE

1920 With heavy hearts, party-going Americans raised their glasses for the last time today in the final hours before the 18th Amendment to the Constitution came into force, banning the consumption of alcohol in the United States. Many foresee trouble and lawlessness as the price of restraining individual liberty with the "Noble Experiment". New York's police chief says 250,000 extra officers will be needed to enforce the ban, though the provisions planned in the new Volstead Act should do much to stop contraband liquor entering the country. America is not going dry overnight: liquor

has been banned in some states since before the Civil War and the Prohibition Party fielded a presidential candidate 50 years ago. Today's legislation is the culmination of a long temperance battle.

An ally has to be watched just like an enemy.

Leon Trotsky, who was today removed from the leadership of the Communist Party by Joseph Stalin and placed under house arrest – 1925.

DESERT STORM BREAKS WITH BOMBS ON BAGHDAD

1991 Allied jets bombed Baghdad as war broke out early today. In spite of desperate last-minute peace efforts, the UN deadline for Iraq's Saddam Hussein to withdraw his troops from Kuwait expired at midnight without an Iraqi response. The action started when US warships in the Gulf launched Cruise missiles at Iraqi targets. In the next four hours allied aircraft flew 400 missions against 60 targets in Iraq. UN Secretary General Perez de Cuellar, President Mubarak of Egypt and King Fahd of Saudi Arabia all sent urgent appeals to Iraqi strongman Saddam Hussein yesterday, but so far these appeals have been fruitless.

• 1919 – RED ROSA LUXEMBOURG MURDERED • 1937 – DU PONT CO. PATENTS NYLON

Shah of Iran out, Khomeini in

1979 In one of recent history's most extraordinary reverses, the once-mighty Shah of Iran has fled at the command of an aged, exiled priest. Jubilant Iranians danced for joy when Tehran Radio announced today that the Shah was unable to resist mounting opposition masterminded by Ayatollah Ruholla Khomeini. The crowds lost no time in toppling surviving statues of the Pahlavi dynasty begun by the Shah's father. The deposed ruler's armed forces, his grandiose plans to restore Persia's former greatness, his modernizations using oil revenues and US support all counted for nothing in the face of discontent at his regime's corruption and brutality.

SCOTT REACHES SOUTH POLE BUT NORWEGIANS WERE FIRST

1912 Britain's polar explorers completed a terrible overland journey to reach the South Pole today – only to find they were not the first. A Norwegian tent at the pole showed that Roald Amundsen and his team had beaten Captain Robert Falcon Scott's party by one month. "Great God, this is an awful place," wrote Scott in his diary as his party swallowed their disappointment at their discovery. Poor logistics and unreliable equipment hampered the expedition from the start, and resulted in the ill-equipped party travelling far more slowly than the Norwegians. Amundsen men had reached the South Pole racing along behind dog-sleds.

1773 Captain Cook's *Resolution* crosses the Antarctic Circle, the first ship ever to do so.

1827 Duke of Wellington is appointed Commander-in-Chief of the British Army.

1852 The British recognize the independence of the Transvaal Boers.

1961 Patrice Lumumba, first president of the Democratic Republic of the Congo, is assassinated.

1995 5,000 die in an earthquake that strikes Kobe, Japan. It is Japan's biggest in 47 years.

2008 Bobby Fischer, American former world chess champion, dies aged 64.

BIRTHDAYS

Benjamin Franklin 1706, American statesman who helped draft the Declaration of Independence.

David Lloyd George 1863, British prime minister 1916–1922.

Molra Shearer 1926, British ballerina and star of the film *The Red Shoes*.

Muhammad Ali 1942, American three-time world heavyweight boxing champion.

• 1934 – 500-CARAT DIAMOND FOUND IN PRETORIA • 1983 – BBC PIONEERS BREAKFAST TV

BIRTHDAYS

Peter Mark Roget 1779, British lexicographer whose *Thesaurus* remains indispensable for writers.

A. A. Milne 1882, British author who created Winnie the Pooh.

Thomas Sopwith 1888, British aircraft designer best-known for the World War I biplane the Sopwith Camel.

Cary Grant 1904, British actor and Hollywood star.

RUSSIAN FORCES BREAK SIEGE OF LENINGRAD

1943 The Red Army has broken the 890-day siege of Leningrad and re-established land communications with the city, which since September 1941 has been subject to terrible air and artillery bombardment from German forces. During the siege the city received only irregular supplies over the frozen Lake Ladoga and its inhabitants consumed everything near-edible they could lay their hands on. The city's relief is the high point of the current massive Soviet counter-offensive which moved into top gear as the roads and waterways froze. The Red Army is now moving toward Voroshilovsk and its divisions are threatening the main German invading force at Stalingrad, where a battle is expected.

DOPING SCANDAL

2013 After years of denial, cyclist Lance Armstrong has admitted to doping in all of his seven Tour de France victories. Those titles have been stripped from the Texan. In a frank interview with Oprah Winfrey, Armstrong confessed to using performance-enhancing drugs, but denied that he had masterminded what has been described as the most sophisticated doping enterprise in sport.

Though I've belted you an' flayed you, By the livin' Gawd that made you, You're a better man than I am, Gunga Din!

Rudyard Kipling, novelist, poet and chronicler of imperial Britain, who died today aged 70 – 1936.

• 1878 – COOK DISCOVERS HAWAII • 1843 – VERDI'S *I LOMBARDI* OPENS IN MILAN

PALACH REMEMBERED

1989 Police today used tear gas, water cannon and baton charges to break up a huge demonstration taking place in the centre of Prague. The demonstrators were commemorating the 20th anniversary of the death of Jan Palach, the Czechoslovak student who burned himself to death in Jan Palach Square in violent protest against the Soviet invasion of 1968. The demonstration today was led by dissident writer Vaclav Havel of the Charter 77 human rights movement.

INDIRA GANDHI IS INDIA'S FIRST WOMAN PM

1966 Indira Gandhi today became India's first woman leader, following in the footsteps of her father, Jawaharlal Nehru, India's first prime minister. Mrs Gandhi, a widow, was sworn into power today following the sudden death last week of Prime Minister Lal Bahadur Shastri as he was signing a peace pact with Pakistan. She has been president of the ruling National Congress Party since 1959. She follows Sri Lanka's Mrs Sirimavo Bandaranaike, the world's first woman prime minister in 1960.

1853 Verdi's *Il Trovatore* premiers in Rome.

1884 Massenet's opera *Manon* receives its first performance in Paris.

1942 The Japanese invade Burma.

1966 Sir Robert Menzies resigns as Prime Minister of Australia.

1988 Severely disabled Irish writer Christopher Nolan wins the Whitbread Book of the Year Award at the age of only 22 for his autobiography *Under the Eye of the Clock*

1995 Russian troops seize the presidential palace in Grozny, Chechnya.

BIRTHDAYS

James Watt 1736, inventor of the steam engine.

Robert E. Lee 1807, American general and Confederate Commander-in-Chief in the US Civil War.

Edgar Allan Poe 1809, American writer of the macabre.

Paul Cézanne 1839, French Post-Impressionist painter.

Janis Joplin 1943, American rock singer.

Dolly Parton 1946, American country singer.

WASHINGTON MAYOR STUNG IN CRACK BUST

1990 FBI agents using an attractive black actress as bait have caught Washington's mayor Marion Barry red-handed as he smoked a cocaine-laced cigarette in a hotel room. The "sting" operation came as Barry – long suspected of illegal drug consumption – accepted a "crack" cigarette from the police informer while hidden FBI video cameras recorded the event. Seconds later one of America's best-known black leaders was under arrest.

• 1793 – KING LOUIS XVI OF FRANCE IS SENTENCED TO THE GUILLOTINE

1892 The first baseball game is played in Springfield, Massachusetts.

1944 The RAF drop 2300 tons of bombs on Berlin.

1958 Edmund Hillary reaches the South Pole, the first explorer to do so since Captain Scott.

1964 The Great Train Robbers go on trial in Britain.

1971 Four die as RAF Red Arrows collide mid-air.

1981 Ronald Reagan is inaugurated as President of the USA, the oldest candidate to take office.

1981 Iran releases 52 American hostages.

1988 Palestinians begin the intifada (uprising) in protest against Israeli occupation of the West Bank.

BIRTHDAYS

George Burns 1896, American comedian and film actor.

Federico Fellini 1920, Italian film director whose works include *La Strada*.

Edwin "Buzz" Aldrin 1930, American astronaut and second man on the moon.

ENGLAND'S FIRST PARLIAMENT TO MEET AT WESTMINSTER

1265 A new era in relations between the English king and his people opened today with the summoning of a parliament in London that includes both gentry from the shires and burgesses from the towns. For the first time, the whole country is represented in a single chamber at Westminster Hall. The parliament was convened by the Earl of Leicester, Simon de Montfort, the king's troublesome brother-in-law. Since his return to this country in 1262, de Montfort has built a hegemony of power. His military victory over King Henry III at Lewes last year in the Barons' War gives the tired king (Henry has been on the throne since he was nine) no option but to acquiesce to the new parliament.

PARLIAMENT

We stand on the edge of a new frontier.

John F. Kennedy, on his inauguration as US president, 1961.

ROOSEVELT DOES IT AGAIN

1937 Franklin Delano Roosevelt took office today for a second presidential term after the most outstanding victory ever in an American election. Roosevelt took all the states except Maine and Vermont in a glittering referendum on the results of his "New Deal" programme of relief, recovery and reform after the Depression of the early 1930s. Although his schemes have brought agricultural recovery, Roosevelt still faces determined opposition from the Supreme Court to his Agricultural Adjustment Act that raises farm prices and pays farmers more for producing less. If the Court rules these government plans unconstitutional, Mr Roosevelt has threatened to nominate another six judges to wrest majority control from the conservatives blocking him. The election shows that the United States is solidly behind him.

• 1841 – HONG KONG CEDED TO BRITAIN FROM CHINA • 1936 – BRITAIN MOURNS GEORGE V

America's Tehran hostages go free

1981 America's 444-day agony over the hostages held in Iran ended today as the 52 diplomats landed safely in Algiers. Looking exhausted but still smiling, the senior US diplomat Bruce Laingen stepped to freedom from the aircraft, flanked by the two women hostages, Kathryn Koob and Elizabeth Ann Swift. Iran's ruler, Ayatollah Khomeini, at first insisted that the students who took over the US embassy in Tehran were beyond his control. He has now doubly humiliated US President Jimmy Carter by releasing the captives just hours after Carter handed over the presidency to Ronald Reagan. No one knows what concessions Reagan, who triumphantly announced the resolution of the crisis, has had to make. The crisis was sparked by the decision to allow the ailing and exiled Shah of Iran into the US for medical treatment.

1846 The first edition of the *Daily News*, edited by Charles Dickens, is published in London.

1907 Taxi cabs are officially recognized in Britain.

1935 Snowdonia, Wales, is designated a national park.

1951 Atomic bombs are tested in Nevada for the first time.

1954 The USA launches *Nautilus*, its first nuclear submarine.

1976 British and French Concordes make their inaugural commercial flights.

1988 Briton Brian Milton lands his microlight aircraft in Darwin after a 51-day flight from London.

BIRTHDAYS

Thomas "Stonewall" Jackson 1824, American general who commanded Confederate forces in the Civil War.

Christian Dior 1905, French fashion designer.

Paul Schofield 1922, British stage and film actor.

Jack Niklaus 1940, American champion golfer.

Placido Domingo 1941, Spanish operatic tenor.

LENIN DIES

1924 Vladimir Ilyich Lenin, the Father of the Russian Revolution, who started out as a country lawyer but went on to topple an emperor and shake the world with a new creed, has died at the age of 53. In the Communist pantheon he was second only to Karl Marx, and a special mausoleum is being built in Moscow's Red Square where his embalmed body will be on display in a glass coffin.

FRENCH ROYAL BEHEADED

1793 France is today without a monarch and the Revolution has blood on its hands. At 10.30 this morning the head of Louis Capet – as King Louis XVI is now known – rolled into a waiting basket as the guillotine claimed its most illustrious victim yet. He had been found guilty of treason. The crowds who had assembled to watch the spectacle cheered as he died.

• 1911 – FIRST MONTE CARLO CAR RALLY • 1959 – DEATH OF CECIL B. DE MILLE

BLOOD OF MASSACRE STAINS TSAR'S HANDS

1879 Zulus massacre British forces at Isandlwana.

1901 Queen Victoria dies, ending a 64-year reign.

1924 Ramsay MacDonald becomes Britain's first Labour Prime Minister.

1941 The British capture Tobruk from the Germans.

1964 Kenneth Kaunda is the first Prime Minister of Northern Rhodesia.

1972 The UK, Denmark and the Irish Republic join the EEC.

1973 Death of Lyndon B. Johnson, 36th US president.

2008 Australian actor Heath Ledger dies, aged 28.

BIRTHDAYS

Francis Bacon 1561, English statesman, philosopher and Lord Chancellor of England.

August Strindberg 1849, Swedish playwright and novelist.

Beatrice Webb 1858, British founder member of the Fabian Society.

D. W. Griffith 1875, American film director whose pioneering works include *Birth of a Nation.*

John Hurt 1940, British actor.

1905 A mass march to the Winter Palace in St Petersburg today turned into a horrifying slaughter as Cossack troops fired salvo after salvo into the crowd at close range, leaving the snow red with the blood of at least 500 people. This "Red Sunday" massacre of strikers could ignite the long-simmering discontent with the rule of Tsar Nicholas II. His regime is weakened by the turmoil of military defeat at the hands of Japan, and today's massacre could lead feuding liberal and radical groups to unite against the government. The outrage is all the greater because the peaceful march of 1000

demonstrators was led by a St Petersburg priest – Father Gapon – while other marchers carried crosses, icons, and even the Tsar's portrait.

Mao's peasant army marches into Peking

1949 Chinese leader Mao Tse-Tung marched into Peking today at the head of a battle-hardened guerrilla army to make the Communists virtual masters of China. The vanquished Nationalist leader Generalissimo Chiang Kai-shek appealed for immediate peace talks, but Mao contemptuously dismissed the appeal. The guerrillas crossed the Yangtze to defeat a huge Nationalist army at Huai Hai north of the capital, taking over 300,000 prisoners. Mao now plans to march on to Shanghai to mop up Chiang's fleeing forces, completing the task he began in 1935.

• 1666 – MOGUL EMPEROR SHAH JAHAN DIES • 1983 – BJORN BORG RETIRES

THE WAR IN VIETNAM IS OVER, SAYS NIXON

1973 US President Richard Nixon tonight told American TV viewers his government has achieved an agreement that will bring "peace with honour" and an end to the war in Vietnam. Negotiators in Paris are hammering out the final text of a peace treaty to be signed in the next few days. Its central provision is a ceasefire that must hold long enough for the Americans to withdraw. Though Nixon, buoyed up by his massive election victory, claims the peace agreement will preserve the principle so many Americans and Vietnamese have died for – the right of the South Vietnamese to settle their own political future – the draft text does not actually say what will happen to South Vietnam's President Thieu. He is refusing to sign it because Viet Cong troops will remain inside his country, but US troops will get out and prisoners of war will be exchanged. Ominously, Hanoi's chief negotiator Le Due Tho concluded, "Right has triumphed over wrong."

SALVADOR DALI FAILS TO LIVE FOREVER

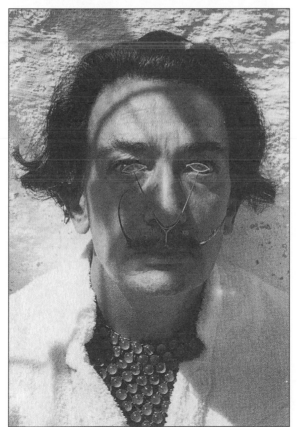

1989 "Geniuses don't die, I'm going to live forever," the Spanish surrealist painter Salvador Dali is on record as saying. Nevertheless, he died today, at his Spanish castle in Figueras. He was 78. Famed for his varnished moustache, flowing capes and outrageous behaviour, Dali had been a recluse since the death of his wife, Gala, in 1982. Dali was a technical virtuoso and his dreamlike scenes – melting watches and painstakingly detailed beauties supported by fantastical crutches – commanded huge prices. He once said his paintings were motivated by his megalomania. The art world was angered by recent confirmation that he had been signing blank canvases for others to paint.

1571 Queen Elizabeth I opens the Royal Exchange in London.

1713 Treaty of Utrecht redraws map of Europe.

1823 The US recognizes Argentina and Chile.

1849 British-born Elizabeth Blackwell qualifies in the USA as the first woman doctor.

1908 A 7000-mile telegraph from London to India is introduced.

1955 Spanish dictator General Franco decides to reinstate the monarchy.

1968 North Korean patrol boats attack and capture a US Navy intelligence ship in the Sea of Japan, killing several of its crew.

2004 The *Mars Express* orbiter detects evidence of frozen water molecules at Mars's south pole.

BIRTHDAYS

Edouard Manet 1832, French Impressionist painter.

Sergei Eisenstein 1898, Russian film director who made *The Battleship Potemkin*.

Jeanne Moreau 1928, French actress whose films include *Jules et Jim*.

• 1943 – BRITISH CAPTURE TRIPOLI FROM THE GERMANS

JANUARY
24

1236 King Henry III of England marries Eleanor of Provence.

1915 The British fleet defeats the Germans at the Battle of Dogger Bank.

1916 Conscription is introduced in Britain.

1935 Canned beer is sold for the first time in Richmond, Virginia.

1961 A US B-52 bomber breaks up in mid-air, killing three crew and releasing two 24-megaton nuclear bombs.

1976 The *Olympic Bravery*, a 270,000 ton oil tanker, runs aground off France.

1976 A Russian satellite crashes near Yellowknife in north-west Canada.

2001 20 million Hindus attend the Maha Kumbh Mela at Allahabad, India, to bathe in the River Ganga at dawn.

BIRTHDAYS

Hadrian 76 AD, Roman emperor and builder of Hadrian's Wall.

Desmond Morris 1928, British zoologist and writer, author of *The Naked Ape*.

Neil Diamond 1941, American singer and songwriter.

GOLD STRIKE IN CALIFORNIA

1848 What could turn out to be the greatest gold rush in the history of the United States began today when James Marshall made a rich strike at Sutler's sawmill on the American River in northern California. It is several years since farmer Francisco Lopez found traces of gold on a freshly-dug onion nearby, but the stampede is now just beginning. The government of the Mexican-owned territory is spreading the news of the find in the hope of increasing the population of California, which now has just 14,000 inhabitants. A gold strike of this magnitude will bring fortune-hunters from all over the world.

WAITE MISSION ENDS IN KIDNAP

1987 Terry Waite, the special representative of the Archbishop of Canterbury, has been kidnapped in Beirut. Hoping to negotiate the release of hostages held by Islamic extremists, he left five days ago for a meeting with Shi'ite Muslims, followers of the Ayatollah Khomeini, believed to be holding the hostages. Waite's bodyguards say he dismissed them and then vanished. He may have opted for silence because he is near to a breakthrough in releasing the captives.

FRENCH BANK'S HUGE DECEPTION

2008 Société Général, one of France's most prestigious financial institutions, revealed the biggest bank deception in history as rogue trader Jerome Kerviel cost the bank 4.9 billion euros through risky trading Kerviel was arrested following an internal investigation which identified his 50 billion euro trading position, and accused of breach of trust, falsifying documents and unauthorised computer use. Société Général was fined 4 million euros for control failures that allowed Kerviel's actions to go undetected.

• 41 AD – ROMAN EMPEROR CALIGULA MURDERED • 1965 – WINSTON CHURCHILL DIES

MANSON GUILTY OF SHARON TATE MURDERS

1971 Cult leader Charles Manson was found guilty today of murdering actress Sharon Tate and four others in a ritual slaughter in August 1969. Satanist Manson, who led a drug-ridden Californian commune of disturbed women, warned the judge, "You won't outlive this, old man," as the court took legal steps to have him and his accomplices sent to the gas chamber. The trial was punctuated by Manson's outpourings about race, war and Satan. The death penalty has been suspended in California, so Manson and his co-convicts face life terms instead.

There's no starvation in Uganda. If you get hungry you can go into the forest and pick a banana.

Idi Amin Dada, who seized power in Uganda today, 1971.

FIRST WINTER OLYMPICS UNDER STARTER'S ORDERS

1924 The first Winter Olympics are being held in the shadow of Mont Blanc at Chamonix in France, despite the reluctance of the International Olympics Committee to give them their full title. Competitors from 18 countries are taking part, and the Scandinavians are seizing the lion's share of the medals. Ski-jumping, cross-country skiing and speed skating are among the new sporting categories being inaugurated this week, although it is still felt in some quarters that the traditional Nordic Games would be a more suitable recipient of the Olympic title.

1327 Edward III accedes to the English throne.

1832 The state of Virginia rejects abolition of slavery.

1878 A Russian boat fires the first torpedo used in war and sinks a Turkish steamer.

1944 In Macao, the Reverend Florence Tim-Oi Lee becomes the first woman Anglican priest.

1952 Vincent Massey is first Canadian-born Governor-General of Canada.

1957 The UN orders Israel to quit Aqaba and Gaza.

1981 Roy Jenkins, Dr David Owen, Shirley Williams and Bill Rodgers form the Social Democrats.

2004 Scientists discover the fossil of the oldest known land creature, a 428-million-year-old millipede.

BIRTHDAYS

Robert Burns 1759, Scottish poet who wrote many poems in dialect.

Virginia Woolf 1882, British novelist, critic and leading member of the Bloomsbury Group.

Edvard Schevardnadze 1928, Russian politician and former foreign minister under Gorbachev.

• 1533 – HENRY VIII MARRIES ANNE BOLEYN • 1917 – USA BUYS VIRGIN ISLANDS

1500 Explorer Vicente Yáñez Pinsón claims Brazil for Portugal.

1827 Peru ends its union with Chile and declares independence.

1828 The Duke of Wellington becomes prime minister of Britain.

1871 The Rugby Football Union is formed in London.

1931 Mahatma Gandhi is released from prison for talks with the British government in India.

1939 In Spain, General Franco's rebel troops capture Barcelona.

1950 India becomes a democratic republic within the Commonwealth.

2001 Thousands die in a powerful earthquake that strikes Western India and parts of Pakistan.

BIRTHDAYS

Douglas MacArthur 1880, American general and Supreme Commander of the Allied Forces in the Pacific during World War II.

Stephane Grappelli 1908, French jazz violinist who played in the Hot Club of France quintet.

Paul Newman 1925, American actor, director and producer.

OVER HERE AGAIN:
US troops back in Europe

1942 For the first time since American "doughboys" left France soon after the 1918 Armistice, US ground troops arrived in Europe today to join the struggle against Adolf Hitler's Nazis. Sir Archibald Sinclair, Britain's Minister for Air, was in Northern Ireland to welcome the shipload of American soldiers as they stepped ashore to the tune of "The Star-Spangled Banner" – played by a British military band who hadn't known to rehearse it because the arrival of the American troops was kept secret. But not everyone welcomed them: the Dublin government said the troop landings violated Eire's neutrality.

GORDON KILLED AS KHARTOUM FALLS TO DERVISHES

1885 In a stunning reverse for the British government, the Mahdi Muhammad Ahmad is today master of Khartoum. The British commander General Charles Gordon is dead, killed by a dervish spear and decapitated, his forces overrun even as a British force speeds to relieve the beleaguered city. Disobeying Prime Minister Gladstone's orders to evacuate, Gordon held the city for almost a year against the Mahdi's army, showing himself to be almost as fanatical as his charismatic Muslim foe.

FLICKERING THREAT TO SILVER SCREEN

1926 Members of the Royal Institution in London today peered at crude and flickering images of a ventriloquist's doll as electrical engineer and inventor John Logie Baird unveiled his new "television" machine. Baird's home-made equipment successfully transmitted a radio signal from a camera that is partly mechanical and partly electrical. The resulting image was sent electrically to a small screen. Two years ago Baird was able to transmit

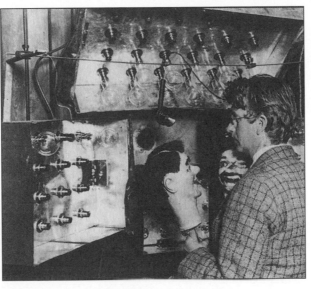

the outline of shapes, and he has progressed from there. The Scottish inventor's far-fetched idea is that his device could one day provide every home with a substitute for the cinema.

1822 Greece declares independence following her war against Turkey.

1868 Dr Livingstone is found in Africa by Sir Henry Morton Stanley.

1901 Death of Giuseppe Verdi, Italian composer.

1923 Adolf Hitler holds the first congress of the National Socialist Party in Munich.

1943 The US Air Force bombs Germany for the first time.

1969 Flooding in California leaves thousands homeless.

1967 Round-the-world yachtsman Francis Chichester is knighted on the quay at Greenwich by Queen Elizabeth II.

BIRTHDAYS

Wolfgang Amadeus Mozart 1756, Austrian composer and child prodigy.

Charles Dodgson 1832, British mathematician who, as Lewis Carroll, wrote *Alice in Wonderland* and *Alice Through the Looking Glass*.

Kaiser William II 1859, third German emperor and grandson of Queen Victoria.

MURDOCH TAKES OVER TIMES

1981 Australian press baron Rupert Murdoch has bought 'The Thunderer' – the *Times* of London, Britain's most venerated newspaper – and the *Sunday Times*. Murdoch first bought into the British press in 1969 when he acquired the *News of the World* – more in keeping with his sensationalist style than the august *Times*. He has overcome considerable British opposition to the takeover with the clearance of the purchase today by the Monopolies Commision.

EXILED LEADER RETURNS

1980 Robert Mugabe, the leader of Rhodesia's guerilla army, has returned to Salisbury after five years of exile to take part in forthcoming elections that will transfer the country to majority rule. Mugabe is tipped to win the election, after which the country will be renamed Zimbabwe.

It could never be a correct justification that, because the whites oppressed us yesterday when they had power, the blacks must oppress them today when they have power.
Robert Mugabe, guerrilla chief, on return from exile, 1980.

• 1973 – A CEASEFIRE IN VIETNAM • 2010 – J. D. SALINGER DIES

814 Death of Charlemagne, Holy Roman Emperor.

1547 King Henry VIII of England dies in London after a 38-year reign.

1725 Peter the Great, Tsar of Russia 1682–1721 and Emperor of Russia since 1721, dies aged 53.

1855 The Panama railway is completed, linking the Atlantic and Pacific oceans.

1935 Iceland becomes the first country to make abortion a legal operation.

1982 Italian troops storm an apartment in Padua and free kidnapped US Brigadier-General James Dozier, who has been held by terrorists for 42 days.

BIRTHDAYS

Ernst Lubitsch 1892, German-born film director who made many films in Hollywood, including *Heaven Can Wait.*

Jackson Pollock 1912, American Abstract-Expressionist painter.

Mikail Baryshnikov 1948, Russian ballet dancer who defected to the West in 1974 while on tour with the Kirov ballet in Canada.

MILLIONS SEE SPACE SHUTTLE EXPLODE

1986 America's space shuttle *Challenger* exploded in a ball of fire today soon after blasting off for its tenth flight, killing all seven aboard instantly. Millions of viewers saw the televised launch turn to tragedy as the space shuttle's fuel tanks, containing liquid hydrogen and oxygen, exploded 10 miles from the ground. The crew included Christa McAuliffe, a high school teacher who had won her place on the flight in a nationwide competition. It is unlikely that the "citizen in space" programme involving congressmen, teachers and journalists will continue. *Challenger* itself seemed reluctant to undertake its final mission: the launch was postponed five times and only went ahead after unseasonal ice was chipped from the skin of the shuttle.

I don't know anything about music. In my line you don't have to.
Elvis Presley, who made his first TV appearance today, 1956.

JAPAN OCCUPIES SHANGHAI IN CHINA INVASION

1932 Japanese troops have occupied Shanghai. This follows Japan's seizure last year of Manchuria, the former Chinese province, as the first step in its drive to create a new Asian empire. Fighting continues on the northern front in Manchuria, as well as close to Nanking, in a full-scale invasion of China. Attempts to bring peace have been fruitless: Tokyo has paid no attention either to the League of Nations or to the overtures of US Secretary of State Henry Stimson.

• 1807 – LONDON LIT BY GAS LIGHTS • 1939 – OTTO HAHN SPLITS THE ATOM

STEM CELL DEVELOPMENT

1986 A radical and remarkably easy way to make cells that can grow into any tissue in the body has been developed by scientists in Japan. The feat has been hailed as a major discovery, and if it can be repeated in human tissue, could lead to cheap and simple procedures to make patient-matched stem cells capable of repairing damaged or diseased organs.

If with me you'd fondly stray,
Over the hills and far away.
John Gay, from *The Beggar's Opera*, first performed today – 1728.

MARCOS SUPPORTERS THWARTED BY AQUINO

1987 President Corazon Aquino of the Philippines put down another attempted coup against her two-year-old administration today, forcing rebels to abandon the Manila television station they seized two days ago. Loyal troops stopped the rebels broadcasting to the nation by cutting off power to the transmitters, but another rebel force attacked the Villamor air base near the capital. Once again, supporters of exiled and ailing ex-dictator Ferdinand Marcos and his wife Imelda are behind the troubles.

1820 King George III of England dies at 81, having reigned for over 59 years.

1856 Britain's highest military decoration, the Victoria Cross, is instituted by Queen Victoria.

1861 Kansas becomes the 34th US state.

1916 German Zeppelins bomb Paris for the first time.

1947 Buckingham Palace is lit by candles as lowest-ever temperatures cause nationwide power cuts.

1960 President de Gaulle of France makes a TV address attacking Algerian rebels planning civil war.

1978 Sweden bans the use of ozone-depleting aerosol sprays.

BIRTHDAYS

Thomas Paine 1737, English philosopher and writer famed for his "Give me liberty or give me death" speech, given in pre-Revolutionary America.

Germaine Greer 1939, Australian feminist writer best known for *The Female Eunuch.*

Oprah Winfrey 1954, American television host, actress, producer and philanthropist, known for her eponymous talk show.

KARL BENZ PATENTS FIRST PETROL-DRIVEN CARRIAGE

1886 Three German engineers are vying to perfect a horseless carriage driven by petroleum spirit. Nikolaus August Otto has just patented his "Silent Otto" gas engine, with four cycles: intake, compression, stroke, and exhaust. His design is a considerable improvement on Jean-Joseph Etienne Lenoir's noisy two-cycle engine introduced in 1862. But the new motor needs something to drive, and Karl Benz today patented his design for an automobile to be powered by Otto's engine. Gottlieb Daimler, a younger engineer, is meanwhile working on a high-speed internal-combustion engine.

• 1596 – FRANCIS DRAKE BURIED AT SEA • 1987 – GORBACHEV CALLS FOR DEMOCRACY

1606 Four conspirators involved in Guy Fawkes' Gunpowder Plot are hanged, drawn and quartered in London.

1948 Orville Wright, one of the Wright brothers who made the first powered flight, dies.

1961 The contraceptive pill goes on sale in the UK.

1965 Winston Churchill is buried after a full state funeral.

1973 Watergate conspirators Gordon Liddy and James McCord are convicted of spying on Democratic headquarters.

1983 A massive exodus begins as Nigeria expels Ghanaians living within its borders.

BIRTHDAYS

Anton Chekhov 1860, Russian playwright whose plays include *The Seagull*.

John Profumo 1915, British cabinet minister caught up in a scandal involving Christine Keeler.

Harold Prince 1928, American stage producer/director of *West Side Story*.

Gene Hackman 1931, American actor who won an Oscar for *The French Connection*.

"TRAITOR" CHARLES BEHEADED

1649 King Charles I of England, Scotland and Ireland today stepped on to the scaffold in front of the Banqueting House in Whitehall to deliver his final words. Liberty and freedom, said the monarch who had levied taxes without parliamentary consent, ruled for 11 years without any parliament, and refused to recognize the court that condemned him, consisted of having a monarch like a loving father to run the government, not in having any share of that government. A subject and sovereign were "clear different things", he said. Then he placed his head on the block and the axe came down. Since his army's defeat at Naseby by Oliver Cromwell's Roundheads three years ago, Charles had manoeuvred desperately to escape this fatal day, offering Ireland, Rome, and even Scotland incentives to aid him. But the courts deemed him a "tyrant, traitor, murderer and enemy of the people".

Mahatma Gandhi gunned down

1948 Mahatma Gandhi, India's "Great Soul" and prophet of non-violence, has been assassinated. Still weakened from a lengthy fast to urge peace between Muslims and Hindus, Gandhi was walking through a New Delhi garden on his way to prayer when a Hindu fanatic stepped from the crowd and fired three shots into his emaciated body. Gandhi's last words were "Ram, Ram", meaning "Oh God, Oh God". His killer, Nathuram Godse, made no attempt to flee and was saved from a lynching at the hands of the furious crowd by air force officers. It was Gandhi's fervent opposition to the painful partition of India on independence in 1947 that brought about his death: his Hindu killer thought Gandhi's anti-partition sentiment was pro-Muslim and pro-Pakistan. Tomorrow his body will be cremated and its ashes cast into the Jumna River.

How pleasant to know Mr Lear!
Who has written such volumes of stuff!
Some think him ill-tempered and queer,
But a few think him pleasant enough.
Edward Lear, on himself – the "laureate of nonsense" died today, 1888.

• 1933 – HITLER BECOMES CHANCELLOR • 1958 – YSL HOLDS 1ST MAJOR FASHION SHOW

MORE THAN A MILLION DIE IN BLOODY STALINGRAD

1943 The Red Army has captured Stalingrad in the greatest – and bloodiest – land battle of this war. The German army is believed to have lost 850,000 troops and the Soviets almost as many in the seven month struggle that has destroyed most of this strategic city on the Volga. The capture of German commander Von Paulus – who twice rejected Russian General Zhukov's surrender terms – came as he was promoted to Field Marshal by Hitler in a desperate attempt to stop him capitulating. But Hitler failed to live up to a promise to relieve the city with air drops and thousands of German soldiers starved to death in the bitter cold.

Viet Tet offensive may turn war

1968 Strategic buildings in Saigon came under surprise attack today as Viet Cong troops broke a truce and launched a major offensive. The so-called Tet Offensive shows the determination and audacity of North Vietnam's general. Although the Communists are losing large numbers of men, they have proved their ability to strike even at supposedly secure cities. With American casualties now exceeding 1000 per day, domestic American hostility to the war is burgeoning. Tet could prove the turning-point in the war.

DR DEATH

2000 Family GP Dr Harold Shipman has been sentenced to life for murdering 15 of his female patients, making him Britain's worst convicted serial killer. He is also suspected of killing more than 100 other patients. In court, the judge, Mr Justice Thayne Forbes, said: "You brought them death, disguised by the attentiveness of a good doctor."

1788 Bonnie Prince Charlie, the Jacobite pretender to the English throne, dies in exile in Rome.

1876 All American Indians are ordered to move on to reservations.

1910 Dr Crippen poisons his wife then chops her into bits and buries her.

1917 The US enters World War I after Germany torpedoes American ships.

1955 RCA introduces the first musical synthesizer.

1956 The creator of Winnie-the-Pooh, A. A. Milne, dies.

1958 The first satellite to orbit the earth, *Explorer I*, is launched from Cape Canaveral.

BIRTHDAYS

Franz Schubert 1797, Austrian composer whose work includes Unfinished Symphony.

Anna Pavlova 1885, Russian ballerina who came to London and formed her own company which travelled worldwide.

Norman Mailer 1923, American writer and novelist whose career spans 40 years with books like *The Naked and the Dead*.

• 1950 – US PRESIDENT TRUMAN GIVES GO AHEAD FOR HYDROGEN BOMB

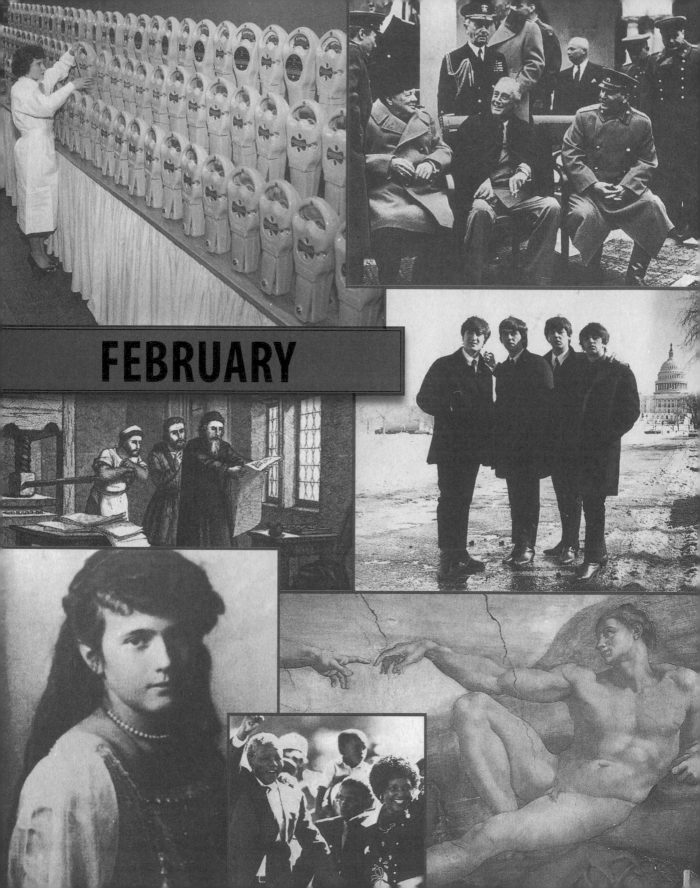

FEBRUARY

DE KLERK TAKES APARTHEID APART

1990 South African President F.W. de Klerk today knocked out the main props of the racist apartheid system that has held the white minority in power for the last 42 years. In an epoch-making speech to parliament in Cape Town today he said it was now time to get rid of the cornerstones on which the apartheid system is based. He also announced the end of the 30-year ban on the African National Congress, the South African Communist Party and other anti-apartheid organizations, and promised that Nelson Mandela, a political prisoner for 27 years, would be free within a fortnight. In the Johannesburg townships blacks demonstrated joyfully at the news, but white conservative groups are accusing de Klerk of betraying his people.

SPACE SHUTTLE DISINTEGRATES

2003 The US space shuttle *Columbia* broke up as it re-entered the earth's atmosphere, killing all seven astronauts on board. This marks a major setback for the US space program and has left the nation stunned. This is the first time an accident has occurred on landing in the 42 years of American space flight. The shuttle disintegrated 16 minutes before it was due to land at Cape Canaveral in Florida.

AYATOLLAH BACK IN TRIUMPH

1979 Iran's religious leader Ayatollah Khomeini ended 16 years of exile today, returning to a frenzied welcome at Tehran airport. A huge crowd of supporters hailed the old man who has forced the Shah of Iran to flee. Much of Khomeini's success was due to his command of the media – when international radio stations denied him airtime, his supporters flooded Iran with audio cassette tapes of his speeches. Today the 79-year-old Ayatollah promised to intensify the struggle against the enemies of his radical Shi'ite Islamic sect.

FEBRUARY 1

1650 Death of French philospher René Descartes.

1790 US Supreme Court meets for the first time.

1896 Puccini's opera *La Bohème* premiers in Turin.

1908 Portuguese King Carlos I and Prince Luiz are killed by soldiers after a failed revolution.

1944 Dutch abstract painter Piet Mondrian dies in New York.

1966 The silent screen actor Buster Keaton dies.

1977 The Pompidou Centre opens in Paris.

1981 Norway elects its first woman prime minister, Gro Harlem Brundtland.

1985 Twenty-six alleged killers of Filippino opposition leader Benigno Aquino, gunned down as he stepped from the plane on his return from exile, go on trial in Manila.

BIRTHDAYS

John Ford 1895, American film director, best known for western classics including *Stage Coach*.

Clark Gable 1901, American film actor and international heart throb.

Boris Yeltsin 1931, Russian president 1991–1999.

• 1893 – EDISON OPENS FIRST FILM STUDIO • 1958 – US LAUNCHES FIRST SATELLITE

1801 Ireland is represented for the first time in British parliament.

1870 Press agencies Reuters, Havas and Wolff sign an agreement that enables them to cover the whole world.

1914 The first pack of Cub Scouts is formed in Sussex, England.

1915 Germany begins U-boat blockades of British waters, while the US warns Germany against attacking American ships.

1970 English philosopher and Nobel Prize winner Bertrand Russell dies.

1986 Liechtenstein women gain the vote.

2014 US actor Philip Seymour Hoffmann dies.

BIRTHDAYS

Nell Gwynn 1650, English actress and mistress of King Charles II.

Charles Maurice de Talleyrand-Périgord 1754, French foreign minister to Napoleon Bonaparte.

James Joyce 1882, Irish novelist whose *Ulysses*, was banned.

Stan Getz 1927, American jazz tenor saxophonist.

Eva Cassidy 1963, singer.

Soviet army finally quits Afghanistan

1989 The Soviet Union's nine-year military occupation of Afghanistan ended today as the final armoured column of Red Army forces set off home from the capital, Kabul. The USSR agreed two years ago as part of the Geneva accords that the last of its forces would be gone by February 15 this year. These last 120,000 troops are now making their way up the Salang Highway, watchful for ambush by US-backed mujahideen guerrillas. The Russians have left large amounts of arms behind for the government forces. Afghan President Najibullah, who continues to rule under emergency powers, said today that a life-or-death struggle with the guerrillas would now begin.

NEW AMSTERDAM GETS YORKED

1665 A British fleet today captured New Amsterdam, the centre of the Dutch colony in North America. The British force outnumbered and outgunned the Dutch garrison, and Dutch governor Peter Stuyvesant, under pressure from anxious civilians not to open fire, finally surrendered without a fight. The flourishing trading settlement on the island of Manhattan is to be called New York in honour of the Duke of York, its new governor and the younger brother of England's King Charles II. The Dutch bought the island from the Manhattan Indians in 1626 for a few dollars' worth of trinkets, and made it a base for Dutch settlement. The colony thrived under Peter Stuyvesant's iron rule, but the settlers are relieved to see the last of their evil-tempered governor. Stuyvesant had lost a leg to a Portuguese cannonball, and replaced it with a wooden peg bound with silver. He was a puritanical tyrant, given to punishing offenders for such moral crimes as playing tennis while religious services were being held. The English style is rather different – last year the continent's first race course opened at Newmarket in British-held Long Island.

• **1878 – GREECE AT WAR WITH TURKEY • 1943 – GERMANS SURRENDER AT STALINGRAD**

FATHER OF PRINTING DIES IN POVERTY

1468 Johann Gutenberg, a blind, impoverished German goldsmith from Mainz, has died in obscurity. It was he who developed the letterpress printing method and oil-based inks that are now making a fortune for Johann Fust and his son-in-law, Peter Schoffer. They have used Gutenberg's techniques to mass-produce copies of the Bible. Gutenberg had also transformed a wine press into a press capable of printing pages of his Gothic type. In 1450 he borrowed a large amount of money from Fust to develop his system of movable type cast in lead. Five years later Fust foreclosed on the mortgage and took possession of the type and presses, setting himself up as a printer. Despite Gutenberg's personal failure, his cheap method of mass-producing printed pages has freed the written word from the jealous monopoly of the monasteries.

1399 Death of John of Gaunt, father of King Henry IV of England.

1488 Portuguese explorer Bartolomeu Dias becomes the first European to land on African soil.

1730 The London *Daily Advertiser* publishes first stock exchange quotations.

1966 A Soviet unmanned spacecraft, *Luna IX*, achieves the first landing on the moon.

1969 Yasser Arafat becomes the leader of the Palestine Liberation Organization.

1969 English actor Boris Karloff dies aged 82.

2006 1,300 people drown when an Eygptian ferry sinks in the Red Sea.

MACMILLAN PREDICTS "WIND OF CHANGE"

1960 A "wind of change" is blowing through Africa, bringing a new national consciousness, Britain's prime minister warned South Africa's whites-only parliament today. Harold Macmillan told the astonished white politicians in the Cape Town parliament they should accept racial equality. Britain is trying to establish racial equality throughout the Commonwealth, but Macmillan's speech has raised a storm of criticism from white South Africans resentful of British meddling. Macmillan forecast that the coming challenge was whether the emergent nations of Africa and Asia would align themselves with the ex-colonial powers of the West or with the communist Eastern bloc.

There will certainly be no one to blame if I should kill myself, even if the immediate cause should for instance appear to be F.'s behaviour. I can find no other solution. I can't live without her and must jump, yet – and this F. suspects – I couldn't live with her either.

Franz Kafka,
novelist, writes in his diary, 1914.

BIRTHDAYS

Felix Mendelssohn-Bartholdy 1809, German composer of *Midsummer Night's Dream*.

Gertrude Stein 1874, American writer and critic living in Paris.

James Michener 1907, American author of blockbuster novels that include *Hawaii*.

Simone Weil 1909, French writer whose work was published posthumously.

• 1919 – WOODROW WILSON CHAIRS FIRST LEAGUE OF NATIONS MEETING

1793 Slavery is abolished in all French territories.

1920 South African aviators Pierre van Ryneveld and C. J. Quinton take off from Brooklands on the first flight from England to Cape Town, South Africa.

1926 Malcolm Campbell tops 174 mph (280 kph) in Wales to break the world land speed record.

1938 Joachim von Ribbentrop becomes foreign minister of Germany while Hitler takes control of the army.

1948 Ceylon gains independence from Britain.

1983 American singer Karen Carpenter dies of anorexia nervosa.

BIRTHDAYS

Fernand Léger 1881, French Cubist painter who also designed ballet sets, tapestries and ceramics.

Charles Lindbergh 1902, American aviator who made the first solo flight over the Atlantic.

Byron Nelson 1912, American golf champion who won the first two US Masters titles.

Alice Cooper 1948, American rock singer.

LINCOLN'S UNION LOSES SOUTHERN STATES

1861 In an atmosphere of looming conflict with American President Abraham Lincoln and his Northern Republicans, delegates from seven Southern states met today in Montgomery, Alabama, to draft a separate constitution for what they are now calling the Confederate States of America. Led by South Carolina, which seceded from the Union last year, Mississippi, Florida, Alabama, Georgia, Louisiana and Texas have all formally broken ties with Washington in the last three weeks. Lincoln's convincing election victory in the rapidly industrializing North and his implacable opposition to slavery in the rural South tipped the scales towards secession. The South says it cannot survive without its slaves. The Confederates face the choice of abandoning their almost feudal way of life or fighting to defend it. Jefferson Davis is to be their first president.

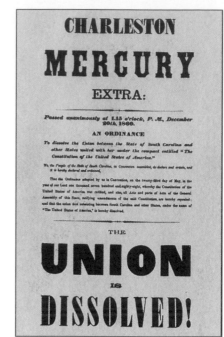

PRESIDENT FOR POST-SHAH IRAN

1980 Revolutionary Iran today installed its first elected president. However, President Abolhassan Bani-Sadr will follow the line of the country's de facto ruler, religious leader Ayatollah Khomeini. Bani-Sadr is a moderate economist who, like Khomeini, spent a long exile in Paris. Though he was elected president last month with as much as 75 per cent of the popular vote, Bani-Sadr does not command a majority in the Iranian parliament, where fundamentalist Shi'ite Muslim clerics are firmly in control. However, Khomeini is now planning to strengthen Bani-Sadr's powers in order to deal with the crisis of the US hostages held captive in the Tehran embassy by Revolutionary Guards. Meanwhile, in New York, the United Nations is preparing to mount a commission of inquiry into the exiled Shah of Iran's affairs.

If a woman like Eva Peron with no ideals can get that far, think how far I can go with all the ideals that I have.

Margaret Thatcher in a *Sunday Times* interview – she became head of Britain's Conservative Party today, 1975.

Germany refuses to pay war debts

1920 Just a month after signing an agreement to pay its former enemies £10 billion over the next 40 years as reparation for the Great War, Germany says it cannot afford to make the payments. Government spokesmen have captured German popular feelings of "indignation" over the conditions imposed as part of the Peace of Versailles, and are trying to avoid coming up with the cash. Today's debate in the Reichstag heard that the agreement would lead to "economic and political pauperization" and could drive Germans to extreme nationalism. Meanwhile, in Britain, post-war economic gloom has put a million people out of work.

METERS HIT TOWN

1958 London's exclusive Mayfair is no place for squatters – or their cars. From today motorists had to pay for the privilege of parking in a Mayfair street. In a trial scheme to ease the city's endemic traffic congestion, each kerbside space now has a parking meter. Feeding coins into the slot buys parking time, registered on a dial. When the dial runs out, the car is illegally parked, and its owner liable to a fine. Drivers greeted the new arrangement with suspicion today and many metered spaces stayed empty while cars jostled for parking in unmetered streets nearby. The meters were first used in America in 1935. The fines are nothing new, however – Mr William Marshall earned the first parking summons in 1896 after leaving his car awkwardly parked in a street in London's City.

1782 Spain captures Minorca from British troops.

1935 Boxing authorities in New York rule that no fight can exceed 15 rounds.

1945 General MacArthur and US troops enter Manila.

1953 Walt Disney's *Peter Pan* goes on general release.

1957 Rock group Bill Haley and the Comets take London by storm.

1974 Patti Hearst, granddaughter of multi-millionaire William Randolph Hearst, is kidnapped.

1983 Nazi war criminal Klaus Barbie faces a war crimes trial.

1989 An unknown Mozart symphony is discovered in Odense, Denmark.

2004 20 Chinese cocklepickers are drowned in UK's Morecambe Bay.

BIRTHDAYS

Sir Robert Peel 1788, British PM and founder of the Metropolitan Police.

William Burroughs 1914, American novelist who wrote *The Naked Lunch*.

Bob Marley 1945, Jamaican reggae composer and performer.

• 1922 – *READER'S DIGEST* MAGAZINE LAUNCHED • 1989 – SATELLITE SKY TV LAUNCHED

1493 Maximilian I of Germany takes the title Holy Roman Emperor.

1515 Death of Aldus Manutius, the first publisher of paperbacks.

1788 Massachusetts becomes sixth state in the Union of American States.

1804 The first locomotive converted from a steam-hammer power source runs in Merthyr Tydfil, Wales.

1804 Joseph Priestley, discoverer of oxygen, dies.

1865 Robert E. Lee becomes commander of the Confederate Armies.

1917 British women over 30 get the vote.

1952 Death of British monarch, King George VI.

2000 Grozny in Chechnya, falls to Russian troops.

BIRTHDAYS

Queen Anne 1665, last Stuart ruler of Britain.

Christopher Marlowe 1664, English poet and playwright.

George Herman (Babe Ruth) 1895, American baseball player with a tremendous batting record.

François Truffaut 1932, French director of fine films including *Jules et Jim*.

IS THE TSAR'S DAUGHTER STILL ALIVE?

1928 Reporters and curious onlookers crowded round the gangplank of a disembarking liner at New York to catch sight of a 25-year-old woman who may be the murdered Russian Tsar's youngest daughter. Anastasia Chaikovsky claims to be the only member of Russia's imperial Romanov family to survive the revolution. In 1918 the Tsar and his whole family were shot in a cellar at Ekaterinburg by Bolshevik soldiers. Mrs Chaikovsky says she hid under their bodies after being struck in the face with a bayonet, which broke her jaw. A sympathetic Russian soldier later took her to the frontier. The son of the Tsar's former physician said today that she really is the Grand Duchess he played with when they were children.

BUSBY'S BABES DIE IN TRAGIC CRASH

1958 British sports fans are in mourning tonight for the Manchester United football team, which has been virtually wiped out in an air crash at Munich. The team had just qualified for the European Cup semi-finals in a match at Belgrade, and was returning home via Munich when their plane crashed on its second attempt to take off from the snowbound runway. Seven players were killed, including four full British internationals. Other players and officials are gravely injured, among them Matt Busby, the Scottish manager who forged his "Babes" into one of the best teams in Europe.

LONG TO REIGN OVER US

2012 Queen Elizabeth II marks her 60th anniversay as Britain's Monarch. She is only the second monarch ever to do so. In a message to the nation, the queen said she and her husband have been "deeply moved" to receive so many kind messages about her Diamond Jubilee. The record for the longest-reigning British monarch is held by Queen Victoria, who reigned from 1837 to 1901. Queen Elizabeth looks set to break that record in just three years, during September 2015.

• 1840 – NZ MAORIS UNDER BRITISH RULE • 1926 – YEHUDI MENUHIN DEBUTS, AGE 6

Gold struck in South Africa's Transvaal

1886 An English carpenter, George Walker, struck gold today in the Transvaal in South Africa while building a cottage for a prospector. Walker's shovel uncovered a clear gold streak when he started digging the foundations. His discovery has geologists looking at the Boer republic's Witwatersrand Ridge with growing excitement. Specks of the coveted metal have been found in nearby rivers for the last 30 years, but it is now thought that the whole ridge may be one massive field of gold.

VIETNAM HEADS FOR WAR

1950 East and West have backed rival factions in the French colony of Vietnam in Indochina, fanning the flames of civil war. Last week the Soviet Union granted formal recognition to the provisional government of Marxist guerrilla leader Ho Chi Minh. Today the United States and Britain endorsed the French-backed government of Emperor Bao Dai. This is no surprise: the US has been discreetly funding Paris in its battle against Ho's Viet Minh communists since fighting broke out in 1947. Ho declared Vietnam's independence from France at the end of World War II. He is a founder member of both the French Communist Party and the Comintern.

IRA STRIKES AT NO. 10

1991 In its most daring daylight raid yet, the IRA today fired three mortar bombs at the British Prime Minister's residence at No. 10 Downing Street. One bomb landed in the garden and a second shattered the windows of the room where John Major and his war cabinet were discussing the Gulf crisis, but nobody was seriously hurt. The mortars were hidden inside a commercial van parked nearby and fired through its roof by remote control. Prime Minister John Major said that such terror tactics would not change Britain's Northern Ireland policy "one iota".

1792 Austria and Prussia sign a military pact against France.

1863 One hundred and eighty-five people die as HMS Orpheus is wrecked on the coast of New Zealand.

1959 Death of Daniel F. Malan, prime minister of South Africa 1948–54 and architect of apartheid.

1971 Switzerland finally allows women to vote.

1990 The Central Committee of the Soviet Communist Party votes for a package of reforms that will end its monopoly of power.

1999 Death of King Hussein of Jordan, a symbol of stability in the Middle East, aged 64.

2001 Ariel Sharon elected Prime Minister of Israel.

BIRTHDAYS

Sir Thomas More 1478, English Lord Chancellor, executed by Henry VIII.

Charles Dickens 1812, great English author of many well-loved novels.

Alfred Adler 1870, Austrian psychoanalyst who introduced the concept of the inferiority complex.

• 1685 – ENGLISH KING CHARLES II DIES • 1960 – DEAD SEA SCROLLS UNEARTHED

FEBRUARY

8

1725 Peter the Great of Russia dies and is succeeded by his wife Catherine.

1872 Indian viceroy Lord Mayo is assassinated by nationalists.

1886 The unemployed demonstrate in Trafalgar Square and looting and rioting break out on Oxford Street and Pall Mall.

1924 The gas chamber is used for the first time in Carson City, Nevada to execute Chinese gang-member Gee Jon.

1974 Skylab space station astronauts return safely after 85 days in space.

1990 American pop singer Del Shannon shoots himself.

BIRTHDAYS

John Ruskin 1819, English writer and art critic.

William Sherman 1820, American Union general during the Civil War.

Jack Lemmon 1925, American film actor noted for both comedy (*Some Like it Hot*) and dramatic parts (*Save the Tiger*).

James Dean 1931, American film actor and cult hero who died young in a road accident.

JAPANESE CATCH RUSSIANS OFFGUARD

1904 The Russian imperial fleet anchored at Port Arthur in Manchuria has been crippled by a surprise night attack by Japanese warships, plunging the two countries into war. The Japanese sank two Russian battleships and a cruiser in the port, trapping the rest of the fleet. Tokyo now claims it has captured seven warships. Only after the battle did the Japanese emperor inform the Russians they were at war. Hostilities were sparked by mounting Russian ambitions in Korea and Manchuria – areas that rapidly-industrializing Japan sees as its spheres of interest.

A dead woman bites not.

Lord Gray, calling for the execution of Mary Queen of Scots, 1587.

MARY QUEEN OF SCOTS BEHEADED

1587 Mary Queen of Scots was beheaded today on the orders of her cousin, England's Queen Elizabeth I. She had been found guilty of plotting to assassinate the queen and restore England to Catholicism, believing that Henry VIII's marriage to Elizabeth's mother Anne Boleyn was illegal. Mary inherited the throne of Scotland at the age of six. In her teens she married the French Dauphin, and was Queen of France for a year until he died. Later she married Lord Darnley. After Darnley's murder – in which Mary may have been implicated – the Earl of Bothwell became her third husband. In 1568, defeated in battle in Scotland, Mary fled to England, but the jealous Elizabeth had her jailed for nearly 19 years. Witnesses at her execution told of Mary's fortitude in the face of death. It took the axeman two blows, and Mary's lips continued to move for 15 minutes afterwards. Her pet dog was found hiding in her skirts.

• 1906 – TAHITIAN TYPHOON KILLS 10,000 • 1910 – US BOY SCOUTS INAUGURATED

FAB FOUR SWEEP AMERICA

1964 The US crime rate plunged dramatically tonight as 73 million Americans cancelled everything to watch four lads from Liverpool appear on the *Ed Sullivan Show*. Six weeks ago nobody in America had ever heard of The Beatles. One week ago their single "I Wanna Hold Your Hand" hit the top of the US hit parade, and yesterday the British pop group arrived in New York for a 10-day US tour to meet scenes of mass hysteria and near-riot, with police out in force to keep the peace. Radio stations

broadcast the progress of their trans-Atlantic jet as thousands of teenagers – mostly female – packed the airport to greet the "fab four" and follow them through the city. The Beatles swept to the top of the charts in Britain six months ago with a string of best-ever sellers, riding an unprecedented tide of mass adulation.

It's easy, you turn left at Greenland.

John Lennon, when asked how he found America, 1964.

MASSACHUSETTS ON VERGE OF ARMED RISING

1775 Hostilities are imminent between Britain and the American colony of Massachusetts. In London today parliament announced that there is rebellion, and approved new laws to control the situation. Dissatisfaction over British rule has been mounting for the last 10 years, and now it threatens to spill into war. The situation has deteriorated rapidly in the 14 months since American rebels disguised as Indians destroyed cargoes of British tea in Boston harbour in protest against British taxes. The hated Tea Tax was imposed to save the British East India Company, which had built up a crippling surplus of tea in London. Settlers swore to pay no further taxes to Britain, and there has been sullen opposition to the laws Britain imposed to restore order – oppressive measures the colonists are calling the Intolerable Acts. Since late last year an illegal assembly known as the First Continental Congress has urged Americans to boycott British goods and to arm themselves.

1799 The US Navy draws first blood in a war with France.

1825 John Quincy Adams is elected US president ending a two-month impasse.

1881 Fyodor Dostoevsky, the great Russian novelist who wrote *Crime and Punishment*, dies at the age of 60.

1971 The first British soldier is killed in Ulster as nationalist troubles mount.

1972 The third month of the miners' strike causes Britain's prime minister Edward Heath to declare a state of emergency.

1981 Musician Bill Haley, famous for "Rock Around the Clock", dies.

1996 The IRA admits planting a bomb in the Docklands area of London, ending a 17-month ceasefire.

BIRTHDAYS

Carole King 1941, American songwriter and singer who wrote many hits for other people before recording any of her own.

Mia Farrow 1945, American actress who made many comedies with Woody Allen.

• 1801 – HOLY ROMAN EMPIRE DISSOLVED • 1958 – BECKETT'S *ENDGAME* BANNED

1354 Students in Oxford cause death and mayhem in a running street battle with locals.

1840 Britain's Queen Victoria marries her first cousin, Prince Albert.

1840 French-speaking Lower Canada and English-speaking Upper Canada are reunited after 50 years of division.

1889 The use of the revised Bible is authorized by the Church of England.

1923 Death of William Röntgen, German physicist who invented the X-ray.

2005 US playwright Arthur Miller dies aged 89.

2014 Death of Shirley Temple, American actress and diplomat, age 85.

BIRTHDAYS

Boris Pasternak 1890, Russian author famed for his prize-winning novel *Doctor Zhivago*.

Jimmy Durante 1893, American comedian and vaudeville star.

Berthold Brecht 1898, German Marxist poet and playwright.

Greg Norman 1958, Australian golfer dubbed "The White Shark".

POWERS FREED IN BERLIN BRIDGE SWAP

1962 In an exchange worthy of a thriller, captured US spy-plane pilot Gary Powers tonight started walking from the Communist side of a Berlin bridge, while the highest-ranking Russian spy ever caught, KGB Colonel Rudolf Abel, set off from the American side. The two men passed in silence in the middle of the bridge, and walked on to freedom. Powers thus escaped the 10-year prison sentence imposed on him two years ago by a Soviet court following his high-altitude spying mission on Soviet military installations. His U-2 spy-plane could fly higher than the Russian jet fighters, but a Soviet surface-to-air missile brought it down near Sverdlovsk. The incident soured relations between the two superpowers and wrecked the "Big Four" summit meeting in Paris a few days later between Eisenhower, Khrushchev, Macmillan and de Gaulle. The US was finally forced to admit it had been spying. Colonel Abel was captured in New York five years ago and sentenced to 30 years for spying.

JOHANNESBURG POLICE DRIVE 60,000 BLACKS OUT OF HOMES

1955 Thousands of armed South African police have begun evicting 60,000 blacks from their homes in Sophiatown near Johannesburg, with bulldozers flattening the township in their wake. They are forcing the angry Africans to move to a new settlement called Meadowlands, where there are no land rights — most of the residents owned their land. The African National Congress is staging a series of protests against the all-white government's latest imposition of its racist apartheid policies.

SWING HIT STRIKES GOLD

1942 American bandleader Glenn Miller was today presented with a special pressing of his hugely popular record "Chattanooga Choo Choo" – the pressing was made of solid gold. The swing hit has officially sold a million copies, the first record ever to do so.

• 1763 – THE TREATY OF PARIS ENDS SEVEN YEARS OF WORLDWIDE WAR

MANDELA FREE – AT LAST

1990 Nelson Mandela was freed today after 26 years in jail for his opposition to South Africa's white racist regime. President F.W. de Klerk unconditionally revoked the 72-year-old black leader's life sentence for treason and sabotage. Met at the prison by his wife Winnie and a crowd of supporters, Mandela set off to address a jubilant crowd in front of Cape Town's city hall. His message was one of "peace, democracy and freedom" – but he also endorsed the African National Congress's "armed struggle". In jail, he had refused offers of freedom in exchange for renouncing violence. Mandela, a lawyer, became an ANC leader in 1949, working under Nobel Peace Prize-winner Albert Luthuli. The ANC, founded in 1912, was committed to peaceful resistance for 48 years, in spite of the brutal official response to black protest. But when white police massacred black protestors at Sharpeville in 1960, Mandela started a sabotage campaign. In jail he became the symbol of freedom in the black struggle that has now forced de Klerk's government to renounce apartheid.

1810 French emperor Napoleon I marries Marie Louise, daughter of the first emperor of Austria.

1858 Benito Juarez is declared constitutional President of Mexico.

1929 The Vatican City becomes an independent sovereign state.

1976 Ice skater John Curry wins Britain's first-ever gold medal for figure skating.

1990 James "Buster" Douglas defeats heavyweight boxing champion Mike Tyson after a controversial late count in round eight when Douglas was floored.

2012 Death of Whitney Houston, one of the biggest female pop stars of all time.

ALLIED VICTORS CARVE UP POST-WAR EUROPE

1945 With victory in the war with Germany virtually assured, the three allied leaders, Winston Churchill, Franklin D. Roosevelt and Joseph Stalin, have mapped out Europe's future at a secret meeting in the Black Sea resort of Yalta. The three leaders agreed that Adolf Hitler's Nazi forces must accept an unconditional surrender. Post-war Germany will be split into four occupied zones, with Russia in control of the whole of eastern Germany. A deadlock over Berlin – which will be in the Russian zone – is still

to be resolved. They also planned the invasion of Japan, and Stalin agreed to declare war on Japan once Germany surrenders. After the war the old League of Nations will be replaced by a new organization to be called the United Nations. The "Big Three" leaders will meet again later this year to complete their plans for the new world body.

Henry Fox Talbot 1800, British physicist best known for his pioneering techniques in photography.

Thomas Edison 1847, prolific American inventor whose "firsts" include the electric light bulb.

Mary Quant 1934, English major fashion innovator of the 1960s.

Burt Reynolds 1936, American actor noted for his tongue-in-cheek style.

• **1975 – THATCHER BECOMES FIRST WOMAN TO LEAD BRITAIN'S CONSERVATIVE PARTY**

1688 William of Orange and his wife Mary take the English throne.

1804 German philosopher Immanuel Kant dies.

1894 Death of Hans von Bulow, outstanding conductor.

1898 A Brighton resident is the first British motorist to die in a car crash.

1929 Lillie Langtry, British actress, and one-time mistress of King Edward VII, dies aged 76.

1935 The airship *Macon* crashes in America.

1948 The ashes of Mahatma Gandhi are placed in the holy waters of the Ganges at Allahabad.

1990 Dr Carmen Lawrence becomes the first woman premier of an Australian state.

2002 An Iranian airliner crashes, killing 117 on board.

BIRTHDAYS

Charles Darwin 1809, British naturalist and author of *The Origin of Species*.

Abraham Lincoln 1809, US president who was assassinated a few days after the end of the American Civil War.

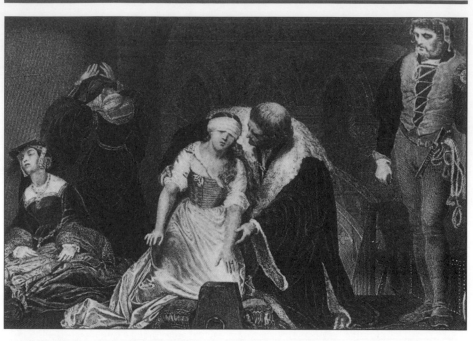

MARY TUDOR EXECUTES COUSIN

1554 The "nine days queen", Lady Jane Grey, lost her head today at the Tower of London. She was 16. The execution was ordered by her cousin Mary Tudor, the present queen. The protestant King Edward VI had proclaimed his cousin Jane, fifth in line to the throne, as his successor above his half-sister Mary, a Catholic, since Jane would keep England beyond the reach of Catholic Spain. Jane ascended the throne in July last year with her husband Lord Guildford Dudley. Mary deposed them nine days later and condemned them to death for treason.

Child emperor gives up dynasty

1912 China's five-year-old boy-emperor Pu Yi listened in his court in Peking today as his aunt read out a letter. He could not have understood that it was his abdication, marking the end of the 267-year rule of the Qing dynasty and 3000 years of monarchy. The Manchurian Qing tribe conquered China during the chaos following the fall of the Ming Dynasty. Their rule has declined through 70 years of foreign wars and insurrection. The current uprising began on October 10 when an army revolt in the south became a full-scale nationalist rebellion. The revolutionary leader Dr Sun Yat-sen was made president of the new republic last month but, to avoid civil war, he has given up the presidency to General Yuan Shih-k'ai – suspected of planning to usurp the throne.

. . Any man's death diminishes me, because I am involved in mankind. And therefore never send to know for whom the bell tolls; it tolls for thee.

John Donne, writing about a distant funeral bell in 1624.

• 1831 – RUBBER GALOSH INVENTED • 1861 – UK'S FIRST INTERCLUB FOOTBALL MATCH

CAMPBELLS KILL SLEEPING HOSTS AT GLENCOE

1692 The chief of the Macdonald clan and 36 of his warriors were murdered in a treacherous pre-dawn attack at their Glencoe stronghold today – by their guests. Robert Campbell of Glenlyon and his 128 men were acting under English orders. Clan chief Maclain was slain in his bed; 36 of his men and a number of women and children were killed. The rest of the clan escaped into the hills. The Macdonald chiefs supposed crime was that he had not signed allegiance to the new king, William of Orange. In fact he had signed, though late, having been delayed by blizzards. Dalrymple deliberately suppressed the fact, wanting to make an example of a Jacobite clan for supporting the exiled King James II.

LINDBERGH BABY KILLER GOES TO CHAIR

1935 A New Jersey jury today found Bruno Hauptmann guilty of kidnapping and murdering flying ace Charles Lindbergh's infant son three years ago. The judge sentenced him to die on the electric chair. Hauptmann is an illegal immigrant who fled from a life of crime in Germany. Lindbergh, who made the first solo flight across the Atlantic in 1927, paid a $50,000 ransom after his son was snatched, but the baby's body was found two months later. Hauptmann was caught late last year spending ransom money, and more of it was found in his cellar. There was scientific evidence that he had made the ladder used in the kidnapping, and the ransom note contained spelling mistakes Hauptmann commonly made.

1542 The faithless wife of English king Henry VIII, Catherine Howard, is beheaded for treason.

1866 The James Younger gang robs a Missouri bank of $60,000.

1883 Death of German composer Richard Wagner.

1917 Dutch spy and *femme fatale* Mata Hari is arrested by the French.

1958 British suffragette Dame Christabel Pankhurst dies.

1960 The French test their first atomic bomb.

1971 South Vietnamese troops aided by US aircraft and artillery enter Laos.

1991 Germany's Red Army Faction carry out a gun attack on the US Embassy in Bonn, claiming a link with the Gulf War.

BIRTHDAYS

Georges Simenon 1903, Belgian crime novelist and creator of Maigret.

George Segal 1934, American film actor and star of many comedies, including *A Touch of Class*.

Peter Gabriel 1950, British musician and member of Genesis; influential in popularizing "World Music".

• 1941 – PENICILLIN USED FOR FIRST TIME • 2002 – MILOSEVIC ON TRIAL FOR GENOCIDE

1797 British naval forces defeat the Spanish fleet off Cape St Vincent.

1852 Great Ormond Street Children's Hospital opens in London.

1906 Fifty-four people are arrested as suffragettes battle with police outside the British Parliament.

1973 An Israeli fighter shoots down a Libyan passenger plane killing 74 passengers and crew.

1979 The US ambassador to Afghanistan is kidnapped in Kabul.

1984 British ice dance partners Torvill and Dean win the gold at the Winter Olympics in Sarajevo.

2013 South African Paralympic star Oscar Pistorius is arrested after the shooting of his girlfriend Reeva Steenkamp.

BIRTHDAYS

Christopher Scholes 1819, American inventor of the typewriter.

Carl Bernstein 1944, American journalist who, with Bob Woodward, exposed the Watergate scandal.

Alan Parker 1944, British film director whose films include *Bugsy Malone*.

HAWAIIAN SPEAR KILLS CAPTAIN COOK

1779 The explorer Captain James Cook is dead, killed by a native spear in Hawaii. Cook was a peaceful man, not given to brutalizing the native peoples he encountered on his epic voyages – but some of his men had started trouble with a local chief. The villagers retaliated by stealing the ship's cutter. Cook took 12 armed marines ashore to take a hostage to swap for the cutter. But the villagers had never seen guns and were not afraid of Cook's men. They attacked, felling the Captain.

RUSHDIE MUST DIE

1989 Iran's religious leader Ayatollah Khomeini has condemned the Anglo-Indian writer Salman Rushdie to death for blasphemy in his book *The Satanic Verses*. The book has provoked uproar in the Islamic world. In London, Rushdie went into hiding under police guard.

ELEGANT DRESDEN DESTROYED BY BOMBS

1944 Dresden, one of Germany's most graceful cities, has been destroyed in a firestorm by the most destructive bombing raid of the war. Nearly 2000 RAF and US bombers laden with high explosives and incendiaries pounded the city mercilessly in three waves over 14 hours. Dresden was considered safe since it was not a war target, and was crammed with refugees. At least 130,000 civilians died in the raid, and many more were injured. Most of Dresden's public buildings were themselves art treasures, including superb examples of 17th- and 18th-century baroque and rococo architecture, while the city's famous galleries housed major collections of the Italian, Flemish and Dutch masters. Today Dresden is a pile of smoking rubble. Air Chief Marshall Arthur "Bomber" Harris, head of RAF Bomber Command, is facing a storm of criticism over the raid, both on humane grounds and strategically – senior Allied planners wanted to attack military targets. But Harris claims his "terror bombing" tactics will destroy the German will to fight.

• **1400 DEATH OF ENGLISH KING RICHARD II** • **1929 – ST VALENTINE'S DAY MASSACRE**

AGEING ALI LOSES TITLE

1978 Muhammad Ali lost his world heavyweight title to Leon Spinks in a 15-round decision at Las Vegas tonight. Ali first won the title in 1964, but was stripped of it for refusing to fight in Vietnam. He started fighting again in 1970 and won the title a second time when he beat the fearsome George Foreman in a sensational upset in 1974. Ali is 36, and after tonight's defeat punters are saying he is past it – but he is a superb athlete with enormous staying power. Spinks is only the third fighter ever to beat Ali. Joe Frazier did it in 1971, but Ali later beat him twice. Ken Norton defeated Ali in 1973, but Ali won the return bout. Now Ali wants a return match against Spinks. If Ali wins, he'll be the only man to hold the title three times.

1882 New Zealand cargo ship *Dunedin* sails with the first consignment of frozen meat for the British market.

1922 The Permanent Court of International Justice holds its first session in the Hague.

1942 Singapore falls to Japanese forces.

1944 The Allies begin to bomb German-held Monte Cassino in Italy.

1945 British forces reach the River Rhine in their advance to Berlin.

1974 A battle rages on the Golan Heights between Israeli and Syrian forces.

1982 Eighty-four die as a storm wrecks an oil rig off the coast of Newfoundland.

BIRTHDAYS

Galileo Galilei 1564, Italian mathematician, astronomer and physicist.

Jeremy Bentham 1748, English philosopher and pioneer of utilitarianism.

Charles Tiffany 1812, American jeweller and founder of Tiffany's, NY.

Ernest Shackleton 1874, British explorer.

Matt Groening 1954, American creator of *The Simpsons*.

BATTLESHIP BLAST EDGES US AND CUBA CLOSE TO WAR

1898 The US battleship *Maine* exploded and sank in Havana harbour today with the loss of 260 lives. She had been sent to Havana to protect American citizens during the current Cuban rebellion against Spanish rule. The US says today's tragic explosion was caused by a floating mine. The incident has brought the two countries to the brink of war. The American press is holding Spain responsible and demanding revenge.

Clash at Wapping

1986 London police faced 5000 union pickets trying to stop distribution of the *Sunday Times* and *News of the World* newspapers. Press baron Rupert Murdoch moved the papers to the new computerized plant at Wapping in London's docklands to outflank the 2000 print union strikers who'd brought production to a halt.

• 1933 – US PRESIDENT FDR ESCAPES ASSASSINATION • 1971 – BRITAIN GOES DECIMAL

1834 Lionel Lukin, the British inventor of the lifeboat, dies.

1887 The jubilee of British Queen Victoria is celebrated in India with the freeing of 25,000 prisoners.

1945 US forces capture Bataan in the Philippines.

1972 A miners' strike plunges Britain into darkness as electricity supplies are cut.

1983 Arson is suspected as fire devastates South Australia, leaving 8,500 homeless.

1989 The police announce that the Pan Am plane crash at Lockerbie in Scotland is the result of a bomb.

1991 During the Gulf War, two Scud missiles hit Israel.

BIRTHDAYS

Robert Flaherty 1884, US documentary film maker and former explorer.

John Schlesinger 1926, British film director whose films include *Midnight Cowboy*.

John McEnroe 1959, American tennis player famed as much for his temper as his fine stroke.

COCO KILLS THE CORSET

1923 Let women rejoice – the corset is dead. That is the clear message of the new haute couture collection shown in Paris today by the High Priestess of Style, Coco Chanel. Coco's New Woman of the Twenties is young and free, and will have no truck with the fussy fashions still lingering from the last century. Gone forever are the corsets, ruffles and cloying drapes, giving way to bobbed hair, low heels, shorter skirts and sweaters – and freedom. Coco Chanel opened a milliner's shop in Paris in 1909, and five years later she added clothes to her line. She sees fashion as architecture: "It's a matter of proportions," she says. Her new clothes are classics – simple and chaste, with an austere, youthful look.

AMIN SECRET POLICE MURDER ARCHBISHOP

1977 Ugandan dictator Idi Amin has murdered the country's Archbishop, the Most Reverend Janani Luwum. The Archbishop and two cabinet ministers were arrested at an opposition rally in Kampala by troops. Amin announced today that they had died in a car crash, but there is no doubt that they were murdered by Amin's notorious State Research Bureau secret police. Tens of thousands of people are known to have been murdered and many terribly tortured since Amin's coup in 1971.

SHOULD GULF WAR GO NUCLEAR?

1991 One in three people in a poll of seven of Europe's largest cities, published today, wants the allies to use nuclear weapons if Saddam Hussein uses chemical weapons in the Gulf War over Iraq's invasion of Kuwait. It is well known that Iraq has chemical weapons, and Saddam says he will use them in the ground war that now seems imminent.

• 1659 – FIRST CHEQUE SIGNED IN ENGLAND • 1959 – CASTRO IS CUBA'S NEW LEADER

CND AIMS TO BAN THE BOMB

1958 Spurred by the threat of having American nuclear weapons on British soil, a new pressure group was formed in London today to demand that Britain "Ban the Bomb". The Campaign for Nuclear Disarmament (CND) chose veteran peace campaigner Bertrand Russell as its president and other notable supporters include the writer J B Priestly and the former MP, Michael Foot. CND is demanding that Britain take the initiative in stopping the arms race and abandon nuclear weapons – unilaterally if need be.

1855 The imperial Chinese army ousts the Small Sword Triad gang from Shanghai.

1880 Tsar Alexander II narrowly escapes an assassination attempt by Russian Nihilists.

1962 After the longest murder trial in British legal history, James Hanratty is found guilty of the murder of Michael Gregston in a layby on the A6 and is sentenced to hang.

1982 Martial law is imposed in Poland.

1982 Death of Lee Strasburg, founder of the New York Actors' Studio.

1982 Death of Jazz great Thelonius Monk.

2008 Kosovo declares independence from Serbia.

BIRTHDAYS

Andrew "Banjo" Paterson 1864, Australian poet and journalist and author of "Waltzing Matilda".

Alan Bates 1934, British stage and film actor whose notable successes on *The Go-Between*.

Michael Jordon 1963, American, widely regarded as the greatest ever basketball player.

Chinese attack former allies in Vietnam

1979 Months of border skirmishes erupted into war today as Chinese forces poured into Vietnam. China had backed North Vietnam during the Vietnam War, but since Hanoi's victory in 1975 Vietnam has turned to the Soviet Union, causing tensions with China. Last month Vietnam invaded Cambodia and drove out Pol Pot's murderous Khmer Rouge regime – which China supports. There is rising panic among Vietnam's ethnic Chinese population as rumours of anti-Chinese purges spread, and thousands of refugees are fleeing to China or taking to small, crowded boats for a perilous voyage to freedom.

It is a great shock at the age of five or six to find that in a world of Gary Coopers you are the Indian.

James Baldwin, black US writer, in a speech at the Cambridge Union, 1965.

MONGOL LEADER WAS RUTHLESS BUT LOVED ART

1405 Timur the Lame, the Mongol conqueror who built pyramids of skulls all over Central Asia, is dead – laid low by disease during an expedition to conquer China. He was 68. Timur (called Tamerlane in Europe) carved out a vast empire by the sword, stretching from Mongolia to India, from Baghdad to Egypt – although he was crippled in his youth and often had to be carried into battle on a litter. Claiming direct descent from Genghis Khan, Timur routed the Golden Horde, conquered the Turks, Anatolians, Mamelukes, Arabs and Persians, and sacked Delhi, Damascus and Baghdad. His four sons now stand to inherit the empire.

• 1909 – DEATH OF WARRIOR CHIEF, GERONIMO • 1972 – VW BEETLE OUTSELLS FORD MODEL T

1455 Death of Fra Angelico, Florentine painter and Dominican friar.

1855 Russian autocrat, Tsar Nicholas I, dies.

1876 A direct telegraph link is established between Britain and New Zealand.

1967 The father of the A-bomb, American physicist Robert Oppenheimer, dies.

1990 Demonstrators storm the headquarters of Romania's provisional government and demand its resignation.

1991 The US assault ship *Tripoli* and the guided missile cruiser *Princeton* are damaged by mines in the Persian Gulf during the Gulf War.

BIRTHDAYS

Mary Tudor 1517, English queen known as "Bloody Mary" because of her persecution of Protestants.

Niccolò Paganini 1782, Italian virtuoso violin player and composer.

Yoko Ono 1933, Japanese-American artist and performer.

John Travolta 1954, American film actor who made his name in *Saturday Night Fever*.

A LIFE OF GENIUS

1564 Michelangelo Buonarotti, the artistic paragon of the Renaissance Age and Italy's finest creative genius, has died in Rome at the advanced age of 89. He was still working at the end. Michelangelo was equally at ease with sculpture, painting, architecture, even poetry, but his first love was for marble and the chisel. The *Pietà* and the colossal *David*, both carved when he was in his twenties, are masterpieces, although the extraordinary frescoes of the Book of Genesis that adorn the ceiling of the Sistine Chapel are arguably his greatest work. They were commissioned by Pope Julius II, and took four years to complete. Twenty years later he returned to the Sistine Chapel to paint the famous *Last Judgement* on the wall behind the altar for Pope Clement VII. The sack of Rome and the destruction of the Florentine Republic left Michelangelo disillusioned, and his later works show a deep spiritual sorrow. His last sculpture, a second *Pietà*, was intended for his own tomb. He mutilated it in a fit of dejection, and never finished it. The figures are as powerful as ever, but filled with suffering – and with a passionate faith. It is an inspired portrait of the dead Christ, yet to rise again.

CASTRO STEPS DOWN

2008 One of the most distinctive icons of the 20th century, 81-year-old Cuban president Fidel Castro announced his retirement, ending his 49-year reign. Castro had been in power since he led the 1959 revolution, deputized by brother Raul and Che Guevara. He established the first Marxist-Leninist state in the Western hemisphere, almost within sight of US soil, yet outlasted nine US presidents and numerous CIA assassination plots. Raul Castro was selected to succeed his brother by Cuba's National Assembly. Fidel stepped down leaving a failing economy, but also a legacy of free healthcare and an admirable education system, which has supplied doctors to the developing world.

• 1546 – DEATH OF MARTIN LUTHER • 1678 – PUBLICATION OF *PILGRIM'S PROGRESS*

SPINNING ROTORS LIFT NEW CRAFT

1921 Etienne Oehmichen, a French engineer, has built a helicopter with two huge rotors powered by a mere 25-horsepower motor – and today it made a successful test flight in Paris. Oehmichen's secret is the craft's lightweight construction – it weighs only 220 lbs (100 kg). Helicopters built by other pioneers have been much too heavy. Though Oehmichen's helicopter takes off successfully, he admits he does not yet know how to keep it stable, nor can he control its direction.

Vital Dardanelles under attack

1915 A Franco-British fleet today began shelling Turkish fortifications along the strategic Dardanelles waterway in a bid to defeat Turkey and reopen the critical Black Sea supply route to Russia. The Russians desperately need war supplies from Britain and France, who in turn need the Ukraine's grain. Sixteen allied battleships are bombarding the Turkish forts at long range, for fear of mines. The big guns are being directed by spotter aircraft from the new aircraft carrier HMS *Ark Royal*.

HIGH PRICE FOR FREEDOM

1861 Tsar Alexander II today signed a proclamation setting free 20 million serfs – almost a third of Russia's population. But the emancipation has strings attached: to become owners of the land they till, serfs must pay a redemption tax to the government and a fee to their former landlords. Very few have the means to do so.

Genius is one per cent inspiration, ninety-nine per cent perspiration.

Thomas Edison,
American inventor, who was granted a patent for his phonograph today, 1878.

WhatsApp?

2014 Facebook announces the purchase of the mobile messaging service WhatsApp in a $19bn deal that represents the social media company's biggest acquisition to date. Mark Zuckerberg, founder of Facebook, described WhatsApp as an "incredibly valuable" service that was well on its way to connecting 1 billion people around the world. WhatsApp allows unlimited free text messaging and picture sending between users and is currently among the world's most downloaded mobile apps.

FEBRUARY
19

1800 Napoleon Bonaparte becomes First Consul of a new French dictatorship.

1855 Bread riots break out in Liverpool, England.

1909 US president Theodore Roosevelt calls for a world conference on conservation.

1914 British explorer Campbell Besley announces his discovery of lost Inca cities.

1937 Italian forces begin the pillage of Addis Ababa, capital of Ethiopia.

1942 The Japanese air force bombs the Australian city of Darwin.

1959 Britain, Greece and Turkey guarantee the independence of the island of Cyprus.

BIRTHDAYS

Nicolas Copernicus 1473, Polish astronomer who propounded the theory of the earth and other planets revolving round the sun.

Carson McCullers 1917, American writer whose works include *The Ballad of the Sad Cafe*.

Lee Marvin 1924, American film actor who played tough-guy roles.

• 1897 – WOMEN'S INSTITUTE FOUNDED IN CANADA • 1906 – CORNFLAKES GO ON SALE

FEBRUARY
20

1513 Pope Julius II, patron of Michelangelo, dies.

1677 Death of Benedict Spinoza, Dutch philosopher.

1811 Austria declares itself bankrupt.

1938 British Foreign Secretary Anthony Eden resigns over Prime Minister Neville Chamberlain's decision to hold talks with the Italian Fascist dictator Benito Mussolini.

1985 Contraceptives go on sale in the Irish Republic for the first time.

1997 Death of Deng Xiaoping, China's reformist and paramount leader, aged 92.

2006 A court in Austria sentences British historian David Irving to three years in prison for Holocaust denial.

BIRTHDAYS

Voltaire 1694, French man of letters, philosopher, scientist and moralist.

Robert Altman 1925, American film director who sprang to prominence with the film *M*A*S*H*.

Sidney Poitier 1927, American actor and the first black person to win an Oscar, for *Lilies of the Field*.

MOUNTBATTEN FINAL VICEROY FOR INDIA

1947 Britain's Labour government has given Lord Louis Mountbatten the task of supervising a peaceful transition to independence for India after centuries of British rule. The government also announced that Britain will leave India by June next year. As the last viceroy, Mountbatten will try to negotiate agreement between the divided Hindus and Muslims, whose leaders are said to be considering partitioning the country. Mountbatten, a great-grandson of Queen Victoria, was Supreme Allied Commander for Southeast Asia during the War and recaptured Burma from Japan. His appointment is controversial: his predecessor, Field Marshall Lord Wavell, was dismissed from his post and opposition leader Winston Churchill (who had refused to free India) has demanded an explanation.

King of Scotland murdered in sleep

1437 Scotland's King James I has been assassinated by a group of nobles seeking to place a rival on the throne. He was 42. James was staying at the Dominican friary at Perth. His assassins, led by Sir Robert Graham, have failed in their plans since James's son is to succeed him.

LAST OF THE MOGULS

1707 Aurangzeb, the sixth and perhaps the last of the great Mogul emperors of India, died today at 88, his empire crumbling about him. Aurangzeb seized the throne at Agra from his father, Shah Jahan, 49 years ago, killing two of his brothers and jailing the third to secure the succession. He moved his capital to Delhi, and his rule was stable until his third son backed a revolt by the Rajputs – the Hindu warriors of Rajasthan. Aurangzeb was at continuous war with the Hindu kingdoms ever after. His military excesses have brought the empire close to bankruptcy, his subjects taxed to starvation. He destroyed hundreds of Hindu temples, and his religious persecutions will leave a long and bitter legacy.

• 1962 – US ASTRONAUT ORBITS PLANET EARTH • 2001 – FOOT AND MOUTH HITS UK

MALCOLM X GUNNED DOWN IN NEW YORK

1965 The American Black Muslim leader Malcolm X was shot dead today while addressing a meeting in New York. A rival sect is suspected of the killing. Malcolm X once preached black violence, but he converted to orthodox Islam after a pilgrimage to Mecca last year and abandoned his extreme, separatist stance for a more optimistic socialism. Born Malcolm Little, Malcolm X had a violent youth; his father was killed for backing black revolutionary Marcus Garvey. Malcolm drifted to New York in his teens, fell into a life of crime in Harlem and served six years for burglary. In jail he read the works of Black Muslim leader Elijah Muhammad, and once freed he joined the sect and changed his name to Malcolm X. Intelligent and articulate, he was soon the chief Black Muslim spokesman. But he proved too radical for the Muslims, and split with them two years ago.

NIXON IN CHINA

1972 US President Richard Nixon landed in Peking today, extending the hand of friendship to Communist China. Speaking at a state banquet in the Great Hall of the People, Nixon invited Prime Minister Chou En-lai to join him in a new "long march" to world peace. Nixon and national security adviser Dr Henry Kissinger, who arranged the visit, were met by Chou En-lai at the airport. They then visited Chairman Mao Tse-tung in the Forbidden City. Nixon's visit reverses the hardline US policy on Communist China – it is the first exploratory step towards full diplomatic recognition of the regime which is backing the other side in the Vietnam War. A major stumbling-block is US support for the Nationalist regime in Taiwan: Peking insists that the US must choose between the two Chinas before relations can be normalized between Peking and Washington.

President Nixon's motto was, if two wrongs don't make a right, try three.
Norman Cousins of the *Daily Telegraph*, on President Richard Nixon, 1979.

1849 The end of the Second Sikh War, sees the Punjab annexed by Britain.

1858 First electric burglar alarm installed in Boston.

1957 Israel defies a UN deadline and holds on to the Gaza Strip.

1960 Castro nationalizes private businesses in Cuba.

1969 The US Patents Office grants a patent to King Hassan of Morocco for his device to monitor human heart function.

1986 Shigechiyo Izumi, the world's oldest man, dies in Japan, age 120.

1989 Two of Winnie Mandela's bodyguards are charged with the murder of Stompie Mocketsi, age 14.

1989 Czech writer Vaclav Havel goes to jail for initiating demonstrations.

BIRTHDAYS

Antonio Lopez de Santa Anna 1794, Mexican revolutionary.

August von Wasserman 1866, German bacteriologist who invented a test for detecting syphilis.

W. H. Auden 1907, Anglo-American poet.

Nina Simone 1934, American jazz musician.

• 1916 – GERMAN GUNS BATTER VERDUN • 1991 – DAME MARGARET FONTEYN DIES

BIRTHDAYS

George Washington 1732, first president of the USA.

Sir Robert Baden-Powell 1857, British founder of the Boy Scouts.

Luis Buñuel 1900, Spanish surrealist film director whose films include *The Discreet Charm of the Bourgeoisie.*

Niki Lauda 1949, Austrian motor racing champion.

THE FIVE AND DIME MONEY MACHINE

1879 American storekeeper Frank W. Woolworth opens a 5 and 10 Cent Store in Lancaster, Pennsylvania. The area's conservative Amish and Mennonite communities apparently approve of this aid to thrifty living and have given Woolworth's new venture a warm welcome. If the store succeeds, Woolworth's plan is to open a growing chain of 5 and 10 cent stores – he reckons centralized purchasing will help him keep prices down, and profits up.

The latest definition of an optimist is one who fills up his crossword puzzle in ink.
Clement King Shorter, in the *Observer*, 1925.

CHRISTCHURCH EARTHQUAKE

2011 A major earthquake in Christchurch, New Zealand, left 185 people dead, hundreds more injured and toppled buildings in what the country's prime minister described as "New Zealand's darkest day". The magnitude 6.5 earthquake caused the centre of Christchurch to crumble; several large buildings were reduced to piles of twisted debris, pipes burst across the city and large holes appeared in roads. The city's hospital and airport were evacuated and dozens of shocked and injured residents gathered in open spaces as sirens sounded across the city. The earthquake also caused a 30 million-tonne chunk of ice to break off from the Tasman Glacier, more than 150 miles away on the West Coast.

• 1819 – SPAIN CEDES FLORIDA TO THE US • 1940 – NEW DALAI LAMA IS 5 YEARS OLD

Cabinet bomb plot foiled by police

1820 Only a few days after the Prince Regent acceded to the throne as King George IV, London police have foiled a plot to murder his Cabinet. The plot was uncovered when a revolutionary group led by London estate agent Arthur Thistlewood was infiltrated by a police informer. Thistlewood had stored a cache of arms in the hay-loft at a house in Cato Street, West London. The plan was to plant a bomb at a house in Grosvenor Square where the Cabinet was to meet tonight for dinner. With the ministers despatched, the prisons were to be thrown open and London set afire. Police raided the house today and arrested Thistlewood and his followers.

US FLAG FINALLY FLIES OVER IWO JIMA

1945 The Stars and Stripes is flying over Iwo Jima, a strategic island 750 miles (1200 km) from Tokyo, but the invading force of 30,000 US Marines still has a fight on its hands. The Japanese garrison, numbering 23,000, is fighting without quarter. They are still defending a network of deep underground bunkers. Once conquered, the island-fortress will serve as an Allied air base for the final assault on Japan.

1732 Handel's *Oratorio* is performed for the first time in Britain.

1836 The Mexican army lays siege to the Alamo in San Antonio, Texas.

1898 Emile Zola is imprisoned for his letter *J'accuse*, which accused the French government of anti-Semitism and of wrongly imprisoning Captain Dreyfus.

1917 French actress Sarah Bernhardt has her right leg amputated.

1924 Death of Thomas Woodrow Wilson, 28th president of the USA.

1931 Death of Australian opera star, Dame Melba.

1968 Theatre censorship ends in Britain.

BIRTHDAYS

Samuel Pepys 1633, English civil servant who wrote the famous Diary.

Meyer Rothschild 1743, German banker who founded a dynasty.

Victor Fleming 1883, American film director best-known for *The Wizard of Oz*.

Erich Kästner 1899, German author who wrote the children's book *Emil and the Detectives*.

• 1987 – DEATH OF ANDY WARHOL • 1991 – BLOODLESS COUP IN THAILAND

1582 Pope Gregory XIII introduces the Gregorian calendar.

1887 Paris and Brussels establish a telephone line, the first cities to do so.

1920 The National Socialist German Workers Party announces its programme for establishing the Third Reich.

1932 Speed king Malcolm Campbell beats his own land speed record, reaching 253.96 mph at Daytona Beach.

1946 Juan Perón is elected President of Argentina.

1989 Fifty-one die when a cargo door drops off a Boeing 747 over the Pacific.

1999 Thirty-eight people are killed in twin avalanches which hit the small town of Galtuer in the western Austrian Alps.

BIRTHDAYS

Wilhelm Grimm 1786, German philologist and folklorist.

Michel Legrand 1932, French composer noted for his film scores, which included the Oscar-winning *The Summer of '42.*

Steve Jobs 1955, co-founder of Apple Inc.

STEAMING AHEAD

1923 The 400-mile (640 km) journey from London to Edinburgh shrank to a mere day trip today as the "Flying Scotsman" set off to inaugurate the London and North Eastern Railway's (LNER) new scheduled train service between the two cities. Designed by H N Grelsey, the locomotive built for LNER at Doncaster Works, South Yorkshire. The powerful new steam engine is said to be capable of pulling its line of carriages at 100 mph (160 kph).

MISSING LINK FORGED

1961 British anthropologists Louis and Mary Leakey have found a second "Missing Link" in the ancient evolutionary chain between apes and men. Two years ago, after a painstaking 28-year search in East Africa's Olduvai Gorge, Mary Leakey uncovered the 1¾ million-year-old fossilized skull of the most ancient pre-human creature yet found, Australopithecus. Today the Leakeys uncovered another skull, that of a child, along with a collarbone and parts of a hand. This pre-human's brain was twice the size of the first skull and half the human size, with smaller teeth, and opposable thumbs. Stone tools were found near the skull. The Leakeys are calling it *Homo habilis* – "handy man". They say it is the earliest toolmaker, and a direct human ancestor.

AMERICAN ASTOR FIRST WOMAN MP

1920 American-born Nancy Astor was today the first woman to speak in Britain's House of Commons. Her husband, Conservative MP Waldorf Astor, succeeded his father as Viscount Astor last year and moved to the House of Lords. Lady Astor won his seat in the Commons in a by-election two months ago. Today she took her place in the Mother of Parliaments, and rose to speak in opposition to a proposal to abolish the Liquor Control Board. Lady Astor has strong opinions on temperance, and on women's rights and child welfare.

• 1848 – FRANCE BECOMES A REPUBLIC FOR THE SECOND TIME • 1966 – ARMY COUP IN GHANA

GUERILLA WARFARE LANDS SUFFRAGETTE IN COURT

1913 Emmeline Pankhurst, the founder of Britain's suffragette movement, went on trial near London today accused of bombing Chancellor of the Exchequer David Lloyd George's villa in Surrey a week ago. Nobody was hurt in the explosion. Mrs Pankhurst described it today as "guerrilla warfare" and accepted responsibility for this and various other violent acts. She and her daughters Christabel and Sylvia have been jailed several times for inciting riots. Mrs Pankhurst founded the Women's Social and Political Union (WSPU) in 1903 to press for voting rights for British women – rights already established in the British colonies of New Zealand and Australia. Women of all classes joined in massive demonstrations, civil disobedience and hunger strikes – and have been harassed, jailed, and thrown bodily out of Parliament. It is the WSPU's militant tactics that have brought the suffragettes growing public hostility in this divisive issue.

He who begins by loving Christianity better than Truth will proceed by loving his own sect or church better than Christianity, and end by loving himself better than all.

Samuel Coleridge Taylor, Romantic poet, son of an English clergyman, 1825.

THIRD OSCAR FOR DAY-LEWIS

2013 Actor Daniel Day-Lewis has become the first man in history to win three Best Actor Oscars. Having previously won for his roles in *There Will Be Blood* and *My Left Foot*, his performance in *Lincoln* has cemented his place in the pantheon of acting legends.

1308 King Edward II of England is crowned.

1570 Queen Elizabeth I of England excommunicated by Pope Pius V.

1913 Federal income tax comes into force in the US.

1932 Austrian-born Adolf Hitler becomes a German citizen.

1939 The first Anderson bomb shelter is built in Britain.

1983 Death of Tennessee Williams, American dramatist.

1989 American heavyweight boxer Mike Tyson defeats British champion Frank Bruno.

2001 Death of Sir Donald Bradman, the Australian cricketer who shot to fame in 1930 for scoring 334 runs against England.

BIRTHDAYS

Pierre-Auguste Renoir 1841, French Impressionist painter.

Enrico Caruso 1873, Italian operatic tenor, the greatest of his time.

Anthony Burgess 1917, English writer and author.

George Harrison 1943, British pop musician and former Beatle.

• 1862 – DOLLAR BILL GOES GREEN • 1997 – CLONING OF DOLLY THE SHEEP

1791 The Bank of England issues the first ever pound note.

1815 Napoleon Bonaparte escapes from his exile on the island of Elba.

1935 Radar demonstrated for the first time.

1951 The 22nd Amendment is passed, limiting US presidents to two four-year terms.

1980 Diplomatic relations are established between Israel and Egypt.

1991 Saddam Hussein orders Iraqi troops to retreat from Kuwait.

1993 A car bomb planted by Muslim fundamentalists explodes under the World Trade Center in New York.

1995 Barings Bank in London goes into receivership after the Nick Leeson scandal.

BIRTHDAYS

Victor Hugo 1802, French novelist whose books include *Les Miserables*.

Richard Gatling 1903, American gunsmith.

Fats Domino 1928, American jazz musician.

Johnny Cash 1932, American country and western musician.

BOXER LEADERS BEHEADED

1901 Two leaders of China's Boxer Rebellion were publicly beheaded by a court executioner in Peking today, ending the two-year uprising against the presence of foreigners in China. Japanese soldiers led the condemned rebels to their deaths while a combined foreign force guarded the route. Last August 10,000 allied troops captured Peking and ended a 56-day Boxer siege of the European legations. The Empress Dowager Tz'u-hsi, who shared the beliefs of the secret society, the "Righteous Harmony Fists", and refused to act against the Boxer rebels, had fled the capital. She has not yet dared to return. Western diplomats say the Chinese government will be forced to pay indemnity for the death of 1500 foreigners in the rebellion and that Western troops will be permanently stationed in Peking.

HITLER LAUNCHES PEOPLE'S CAR

1936 A new family car intended to rival American Henry Ford's famous Model T has been unveiled in Germany. Chancellor Adolf Hitler today opened a factory in Saxony that will mass-produce a small, cheap, family saloon. This Volkswagen – literally, the "people's car" – has been designed by Ferdinand Porsche of Auto Union, better known for more luxurious models. The new Volkswagen is streamlined in design, and has a revolutionary four-cylinder, air-cooled engine mounted over the rear axle. Adolf Hitler hopes the new car will do much to transform the German economy.

SOVIETS OUT

1990 Playwright Vaclav Havel, Czechoslovakia's new president, announced in Moscow today that all Soviet troops will leave Czechoslovakia by July, ending 21 years of armed occupation. Most of the troops are expected to be gone by June, when elections are to be held.

If people behaved the way nations do, they would all be put in straitjackets.
Tennessee Williams, American playwright, who died today, 1983.

• 2012 – *THE ARTIST*: FIRST SILENT FILM TO WIN AN OSCAR SINCE 1927

GULF WAR OVER

1991 The Gulf War ended today. Saudi forces entered Kuwait City at first light as the Iraqi army fled northward, only to be cut off by allied forces which had moved behind them in a lightning strike. Later in the day the Iraqi government announced its unconditional acceptance of the UN resolutions on Kuwait, and US president George Bush announced tonight that the war is over. All allied military action will cease from tomorrow morning. No chemical weapons were used during the four-day ground battle which has ended the war, and allied casualties were light. The US lost 184 men in the war. The allies have taken 80,000 Iraqi prisoners, and allied leaders calculate that 85,000 to 100,000 Iraqis have been killed. Initial estimates are that Iraq's destroyed infrastructure will take $200 billion and a generation to repair, and that Kuwait's reconstruction will cost $50 billion.

God grant that this is the work of the Communists. You are witnessing the beginning of a great new epoch in German history. This fire is the beginning.

Adolf Hitler, German Chancellor, speaking to a foreign correspondent as the Reichstag burns, 1933.

Freed slaves get the vote – in theory

1869 Four years after the Civil War, the last of three amendments to the US Constitution enshrining the rights of freed slaves as full US citizens was passed by the US Congress today: the new 15th Amendment prevents state governments denying the vote to anyone "on account of race, colour, or previous condition of servitude". The defeated rebel states of the South must ratify it before they can be readmitted to the Union – but they can still use poll tax and literacy rules to stop blacks voting. For many blacks, very little has changed; the 15th Amendment is only a piece of paper.

1557 The first Russian embassy in London opens.

1782 British parliament votes to abandon the American War of Independence.

1939 General Franco's rebel Nationalist government is recognized by Britain and France.

1952 The new United Nations building in New York sees its first session.

1980 Michael Jackson is awarded his first Grammy.

1989 Emergency powers are introduced in Kosovo, Yugoslavia, as Serbians attempt to assert rule over ethnic Albanians.

2010 Chile is struck by one of the strongest earthquakes ever recorded.

BIRTHDAYS

Constantine the Great 274 AD.

Rudolf Steiner 1861, Austrian philosopher and educationist.

John Steinbeck 1902, Pulitzer Prize-winning author who wrote *The Grapes of Wrath*.

Elizabeth Taylor 1932, English Hollywood star.

Antoinette Sibley 1939, British prima ballerina.

• 1879 – SACCHARINE DISCOVERED • 1948 – COMMUNISTS TAKE POWER IN PRAGUE

1784 John Wesley, founder of the Wesleyan faith, signs its deed of declaration.

1922 Princess Mary, daughter of King George V, marries Viscount Lascelles in London.

1966 The Cavern Club, the venue where the Beatles made their mark, goes into liquidation.

1972 In Marseilles, French police seize 937 lb (425 kg) of pure heroin.

1975 Thirty-five die when a London Underground train accelerates into a dead-end tunnel at Moorgate.

1989 In Venezuela, President Peres faces riots as food prices rise.

1991 Khaleda Zia, widow of President Rahman of Bangladesh, wins the first national election in the country's history.

BIRTHDAYS

Professor Linus Pauling 1909, American chemist, physicist and Nobel Prize winner.

Sir Stephen Spender 1909, British poet and critic.

Brian Jones 1942, founding member of the Rolling Stones.

POPE RESIGNS!

2013 After eight years in the role, Pope Benedict XVI has resigned, the first Pope to do so in 600 years. Citing ill-health as a reason for his departure, Pope Benedict described himself as "simply a pilgrim who is starting the last phase of his pilgrimage on this earth." Having been elected in 2005 Pope Benedict oversaw a traumatic period in the Catholic Church's history, with allegations of sexual abuse by priests and internal feuding and corruption revealed in leaked documents.

Arms alone are not enough to keep the peace – it must be kept by men.

J. F. Kennedy,
US president, 1962.

"KILL US AGAIN" DARE INDIAN ACTIVISTS

1973 Militant American Indian activists seized the Sioux village of Wounded Knee in South Dakota today, and challenged the government to repeat the Indian massacre that happened there more than 80 years ago. The militants are holding 10 hostages. They are demanding free elections of tribal leaders, a review of all Indian treaties and full investigation of the Bureau of Indian Affairs – whose Washington headquarters were occupied for a week last November by protesting Indians. The militants are members of the American Indian Movement (AIM), formed five years ago. In December 1890, in the last clash between US troops and Indians, the US Seventh Cavalry opened fire on Sioux Chief Big Foot and his followers at Wounded Knee, killing 300 men, women and children.

• 1574 – SPANISH INQUISITION TAKES FIRST VICTIMS • 1896 – SWEDISH PM SHOT DEAD

NOBEL-WINNER TUTU ARRESTED

1988 South Africa's Anglican Archbishop Desmond Tutu was arrested today for demonstrating outside the parliament building in Cape Town in defiance of a ban on political activity by the white minority government. He was leading a protest against the death sentence imposed on the "Sharpeville Six" for killing a black townships councillor. Archbishop Tutu is a focus for resistance to the apartheid system and a well-known figure worldwide. He won the Nobel Peace Prize in 1984, the second South African to do so (Albert Luthuli, president of the African National Congress, was the first). In a nation riven by strife, Tutu preaches non-violence. He has condemned the state of emergency in force since June 1986 and defies the emergency laws in calling for economic sanctions against South Africa and for foreign disinvestment. Archibishop Tutu is not likely to be held for long – jailing him would cause the government even more trouble than freeing him.

New Home for Jewish People: His Majesty's Government view with favour the establishment in Palestine of a national home for the Jewish people, and will use their best endeavours to facilitate the achievement of this object, it being clearly understood that nothing shall be done which may prejudice the civil and religious rights of existing non-Jewish communities in Palestine.

Arthur Balfour, British foreign secretary, in a letter to Lord Rothschild, 1917.

BUNNY GIRLS LET LOOSE

1960 Hugh Hefner opens his new Playboy Club in Chicago, in which "Bunny Girls" in scanty black swimsuits with a fluffy white tail stitched on to their behinds and big Bugs Bunny ears, are strictly for looking at. Hefner, who was brought up in a strict Methodist home, started his magazine *Playboy* seven years ago with only $10,000 (£5,500), and is now a very wealthy man. He said tonight that the new club is just the first of a worldwide network of Playboy Clubs.

642 St Oswald, bringer of Christianity to north-east England, is killed in battle.

1880 The St Gotthard tunnel, providing a rail link between Switzerland and Italy, is completed.

1908 Onnes, a scientist from the Netherlands, succeeds in liquefying helium.

1960 An earthquake in Morocco destroys much of Agadir and kills about 12,000 people.

1984 Death of Roland Culver, British stage and film actor who appeared *The Yellow Rolls-Royce*.

2004 President Jean-Bertrand Aristide of Haiti is ousted in a military coup.

BIRTHDAYS

Anne Lee 1736, British-born founder of the American Society of Shakers.

Gioacchino Rossini 1792, Italian composer who wrote *The Barber of Seville*.

John Holland 1840, Irish-American inventor of the submarine.

Ranchhodji Morarji Desai 1896, Indian prime minister imprisoned with Mahatma Gandhi.

• 1956 – RACIAL TURMOIL SPLITS ALABAMA • 2004 – *LORD OF THE RINGS* WINS 11 OSCARS

MARCH

NEW DISCOVERY LEIGH PICKS UP TOP OSCAR

1940 English actress Vivien Leigh has won an Oscar for her role as Scarlett O'Hara in the film *Gone with the Wind*, now breaking all box-office records in America. The film won five Oscars in all. Miss Leigh was a young unknown when Hollywood producer David Selznick chose her for the part coveted by every female star in Hollywood. She had only one obscure British film to her credit – though she won a record £50,000 movie contract five years ago following a successful stage debut in London. Miss Leigh plays a proud Southern belle fighting to regain what her family has lost in the Civil War, using and discarding men along the way. She meets her match in the unscrupulous Rhett Butler, played by Hollywood king Clark Gable – but it is Miss Leigh who has won the Oscar. The film, a marathon four hours long, cost more than $2 million to make. It is based on the Pulitzer Prize-winning novel by Margaret Mitchell.

RIDDLE OF NOSTRADAMUS'S FUTURE IMPERFECT

1555 A "Book of Centuries" consisting of cryptic four-lined rhymed verses has been published in France by Michel Nostradamus, a provincial doctor. The book's 900 "Centuries" contain a series of prophecies about future events. Predictions include a massive fire in London in the year 1666, global war erupting twice in the far-distant 20th century, the coming of an anti-Christ from the deserts of Persia later in the same century and, most absurd of all, a revolution that will overthrow the mighty French monarchy before the 18th century is over. Snatches of Hebrew, Latin and Portuguese, and the use of anagrams, make the book very difficult to understand fully yet it is impossible to dismiss.

1875 The US Congress passes the Civil Rights Act.

1880 Pennsylvania becomes the first US state to abolish slavery.

1934 Peking's "Last Emperor" is crowned.

1946 Bank of England goes into public ownership.

1949 Boxer Joe Louis retires at the age of 35.

1959 Archbishop Makarios returns to Cyprus after three years in exile.

1961 President Kennedy forms the Peace Corps of volunteers to work in Third World Countries.

2001 The Taliban demolish Buddhist statues in Afghanistan.

BIRTHDAYS

Frédéric Chopin 1810, Polish composer and pianist.

Oskar Kokoschka 1886, Austrian-born Expressionist painter who became a British citizen in 1947.

Glenn Miller 1904, American band leader and composer.

Ron Howard 1954, American director and producer. His works include the Oscar-winning *Cocoon* and *A Beautiful Mind*.

• 1912 – FIRST-EVER PARACHUTE JUMP • 1932 – AVIATOR LINDBERGH'S BABY SNATCHED

1864 President Lincoln rejects Confederate General Lee's call for peace talks.

1882 An unsuccessful attempt to assassinate Queen Victoria is made.

1949 In Fort Worth, Texas, Captain James Gallagher completes the first round-the-world flight.

1955 Floods in Australia kill 200 people and leave 400,000 homeless.

1958 A British team under Sir Vivian Fuchs is first to cross the Antarctic.

1990 Nelson Mandela is elected deputy president of the African National Congress.

BIRTHDAYS

Sam Houston 1793, American soldier and first president of the Republic of Texas.

Kurt Weill 1900, German composer who collaborated with Bertolt Brecht on such works as *The Threepenny Opera*.

Lou Reed 1944, American singer whose best-known recording is "A Walk on the Wild Side".

Dame Naomi James 1949, New Zealander who sailed single-handed round the world in 1977–8.

SUPERSONIC BEAUTY TAKES TO THE SKY

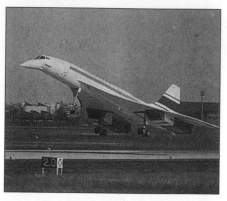

1969 Concorde, the supersonic Anglo-French airliner, roared off the runway, straightened its pointed nose and took to the skies today, carrying with it the promise of space-age air travel for the common man. Today's successful maiden flight at Toulouse of the French prototype 001 brought to fruition the £360 million agreement between France and Britain to build a jetliner that will travel at twice the speed of sound. The five-year venture has produced an elegant aircraft: it has delta wings with subtly curved leading edges and a streamlined nose-cone that slopes down in a distinctive droop to give the pilot better visibility on takeoff and landing. The plane will seat 125 passengers. Initially, commercial service will be limited to first-class only, for businessmen in a hurry. Concorde will halve the flying time between London and New York.

The whole commerce between master and slave is a perpetual exercise of the most boisterous passions, the most unremitting despotism on the one part, and degrading submissions on the other.

Thomas Jefferson, today Congress banned the import of slaves to America, 1807.

AUSTRALIA GOES IT ALONE

1986 Queen Elizabeth II today signed the Australia Bill, severing Britain's formal ties with its former colony almost two centuries after British convicts were shipped to Botany Bay in 1788. Australia has been virtually self-governing since the 1901 constitution was introduced; but in 1975 Sir John Kerr, Governor General, caused a furore by dismissing Labour leader Gough Whitlam. Outraged Australians decided that the Queen should have less to do with their government.

TEX-MEX TROUBLES

1836 American settlers in Texas have declared their independence from Mexico and set up a new state with a new flag – the Lone Star. Mexican dictator General Antonio Lopez de Santa Anna has invaded Texas to reassert control and the Texan rebels are currently in retreat, but the matter is far from settled.

• 1791 – SEMAPHORE MACHINE UNVEILED • 1972 – *PIONEER 10* BLASTS OFF FOR MARS

COMMUNISTS GO INTERNATIONAL

1919 Plans to set Europe ablaze with Communist revolution were announced today by Russia's Bolshevik leader Vladimir Ilich Lenin. A new organization, the Communist International or "Comintern", has been set up to dictate policies to Communists in other countries. It is a more radical offshoot of the three Internationals that have existed since the Socialist movement started 35 years ago. Lenin believes he has a greater chance of establishing control if the Socialist creed spreads to neighbouring countries.

SCARGILL'S ARMY RELUCTANTLY ADMITS DEFEAT

1985 Britain's coal miners finally bowed to the inevitable today, voting to return to work after a year-long strike. Mrs Thatcher is claiming a "famous victory" over the National Union of Mineworkers' leader Arthur Scargill, who has long been a thorn in the side of the Conservative Party leadership. The strike was sparked by Mrs Thatcher's government insisting on closing loss-making pits. The miners' delegates today voted 98-91 to return to work, despite insistence by the National Coal Board management that they would have to accept financial penalties for their actions, and that those dismissed will not be reinstated. The bitter dispute leaves the state-owned National Coal Board facing a record £2.2 billion loss this year.

1802 Beethoven publishes "Moonlight Sonata".

1857 Britain and France declare war on China.

1924 President Kemal Atatürk abolishes the Caliphate and disestablishes the Islamic region in Turkey.

1931 "The Star Spangled Banner" is adopted as America's national anthem.

1950 The US Congress votes to admit Alaska as the 49th state.

1974 A Turkish Airlines DC10 crashes into a wood near Paris, killing 344.

1990 Venezuela suspends foreign debt payments after widespread rioting.

2010 Former UK Labour Party leader and writer Michael Foot dies, aged 96.

BIRTHDAYS

George Pullman 1831, American industrialist and inventor of the luxury railway carriage.

Alexander Graham Bell 1847, Scottish inventor who emigrated to the USA and invented the telephone.

Jean Harlow 1911, American actress and platinum blonde sex symbol.

EUROPE UP IN ARMS

1848 Revolution is sweeping across Europe, spurred by hunger, economic depression and the political demands of the growing middle classes. During a public outbreak of fury in Paris last month, King Louis Phillippe fled while a mob wrecked his palace then formed a government and "national workshops" for the jobless. Now the flames have spread to the Austrian empire, with demonstrations raging in both Vienna and Hungary. In Vienna, conservative statesman Klemens von Metternich has been driven from office. Hungary has declared its autonomy, while Croatia is in turn demanding its freedom from Hungary. Elsewhere, Venice has renounced Austria's authority and proclaimed a republic. Serfdom in the Austrian empire is crumbling; there is no proper constitution. In Germany, unrest may cause the Prussian king to call a constitutional assembly.

1193 Saladin, legendary Muslim commander dies in Damascus.

1634 Samuel Cole opens the first tavern in Boston.

1824 The Royal National Lifeboat Institution is founded in Britain.

1873 The New York *Daily Graphic* becomes the first illustrated daily newspaper.

1980 Robert Mugabe becomes the leader of newly independent Zimbabwe.

1989 Pope John Paul II brands Salman Rushdie novel *The Satanic Verses* blasphemous.

BIRTHDAYS

Prince Henry the Navigator 1394, Portugese patron of explorers under whose auspices Madeira, the Azores and the Cape Verde Islands were colonized.

Antonio Vivaldi 1678, Italian composer best known for *The Four Seasons*.

Alan Sillitoe 1928, British author and playwright whose books *Saturday Night and Sunday Morning* and *The Loneliness of the Long Distance Runner* were both turned into films.

CHARLES II GIVES QUAKER NEW START IN AMERICA

1681 King Charles II has given his authorization for what promises to be a bold social experiment in his American colonies. Today, by Royal Charter, he granted William Penn, a Quaker, the right to set up a new colony at West Jersey. The King also paid off £16,000 of Penn's family debts. The Charter gives the 38-year-old Penn near-dictatorial powers over the new colony, its Indian population and its surroundings, which he proposes to name Pennsylvania.

LINCOLN INHERITS COUNTRY IN TURMOIL

1861 Abraham Lincoln was sworn in today as the 16th president of a Federation of States united only in name: the country is divided and on the threshold of civil war. Lincoln's inaugural address did little to alter matters in the southern states where his hostility to slavery is well-known. Lincoln, a prosperous lawyer and congressman, was about to give up politics when the issue of extending slavery into Kansas and Nebraska fired him to carry on. In 1856 he joined the Republicans but failed to get into the senate: last year he only narrowly secured his party's presidential nomination. His first challenge comes from Fort Sumter in South Carolina, which is being deprived of supplies by forces loyal to Jefferson Davis, the Confederate President.

Let me assert my firm belief that the only thing we have to fear is fear itself.

Franklin D. Roosevelt, on his inauguration as US president during a period of chaos; American banks closed down as he took the oath in 1933.

• 1789 – FIRST US CONGRESS HELD • 1882 – FIRST ELECTRIC TRAMS RUN IN BRITAIN

BRITISH TROOPS FIRE ON AMERICAN DEMONSTRATORS

1770 British troops opened fire on an unruly crowd in Boston today, killing five Americans. The incident has been dubbed the "Boston Massacre". It follows 18 months of simmering tension since they arrived in Massachusetts in a show of force to quell American resentment over the Stamp Act, which taxes all legal or printed documents. Massachusetts was said to be "on the brink of anarchy". The Americans saw the troops as oppressors, and there have been fights between soldiers and citizens ever since. Today a crowd gathered at the Customs House became unruly, and a squad led by Captain Thomas Preston opened fire, killing three men and mortally wounding two others. All troops were immediately withdrawn from the town and Preston and six soldiers are under arrest.

THE KRAYS BEHIND BARS

1966 The criminal overlords of London's East End, 35-year-old twins Ronald and Reginald Kray, were today jailed for 30 years for murder. Four of their underworld gang were also convicted. As they were led away, one of the Krays told the judge menacingly: "I'll see you later!" It was the longest murder trial ever held at London's famous Old Bailey, lasting 39 days.

MAN OF STEEL DIES

1953 Joseph Stalin, who forged the Soviet Union into a global superpower at the cost of oppression by which millions were killed, has died of a brain haemorrhage. His body is lying in state in Moscow. No clear successor has yet emerged. Stalin, the son of a Georgian shoemaker, started his career robbing banks to raise Bolshevik funds. He seized power after Lenin's death in 1929. During World War II he broke Hitler's military power at Stalingrad – earning him the title of the country's saviour. On equal terms with Churchill and Roosevelt, he demanded their acquiescence in the Soviet domination of Eastern Europe after the war.

1461 Henry VI of England is deposed by the Duke of York in the course of the Wars of the Roses.

1856 The Covent Garden Opera House in London is destroyed by fire.

1926 The Shakespeare Memorial Theatre in Stratford-on-Avon is engulfed by flames.

1933 In Germany, the Nazis win almost half the seats in the elections.

1991 Baghdad Radio announces that the Iraqi government has annulled the annexation of Kuwait and promised that Kuwaiti assets will be restored.

1991 The last Cruise missile leaves Greenham Common airbase in Berkshire to be dismantled in Arizona as part of the INF disarmament treaty.

BIRTHDAYS

King Henry II 1133, first Plantagenet king of England.

Rosa Luxemburg 1871, German socialist leader and founder of the left-wing Spartacus movement.

Elaine Page 1952, British musical star who shot to fame in the Lloyd Webber musicals *Evita* and *Cats*.

• 1930 – BIRDSEYE FREEZES PEAS • 1936 – BRITAIN LAUNCHES SPITFIRE AIRCRAFT

1901 An anarchist fails in his attempt to assassinate Kaiser Wilhelm of Germany.

1932 John Philip Sousa, US composer of military marches, dies aged 78.

1944 Daylight bombing raids on Berlin begin.

1971 In London, 4000 women's libbers march from Hyde Park to 10 Downing Street.

1983 Australian Christopher Massey sets a water skiing record of 143.08 mph (228.9 kph).

1992 American boxer Mike Tyson is found guilty of rape.

BIRTHDAYS

Savinien Cyrano de Bergerac 1619, French novelist and playwright.

Elizabeth Barrett Browning 1806, British poet.

Oscar Straus 1870, Viennese-born composer who wrote *The Chocolate Soldier.*

Ronald Reagan 1911, former American Republican president.

Dame Kiri Te Kanawa 1944, New Zealand soprano.

Mexican massacre of Alamo resistance

1836 The heroic stand by a small band of Texan rebels at the old Alamo mission was today crushed. The 187 besieged Texans have been slaughtered. After a continuous 12-day artillery bombardment, 6000 Mexican troops under General Antonio Lopez de Santa Anna stormed the crumbling mission and massacred the defenders. Santa Anna had the bodies burned as a warning to Texas never again to challenge Mexican rule. One of the few survivors, Susanna Dickinson, a blacksmith's wife, was set free with a message from Santa Anna to Texan General Sam Houston that further fighting would end the same way. Among the dead was the famous frontiersman Davy Crockett, who had only just returned to Texas after two terms in Washington as a US congressman. The Alamo rebels' commander, Colonel Travis, had refused to obey Houston's orders to withdraw to a less vulnerable position.

It takes people a long time to learn the difference between talent and genius, especially ambitious young men and women.

Louisa May Alcott, author of *Little Women*, died today, 1888.

WONDER DRUG KILLS HEADACHE PAIN

1899 A new pain relief drug was patented today, and pharmacists are claiming it has almost magical properties. The drug, called aspirin, is said to relieve even severe pain, particularly headaches, muscle aches and joint pains. It acts within minutes. The patent for aspirin, or acetylsalicylic acid, is held by the chemist Felix Hoffmann, who synthesized the drug in his laboratory. Aspirin's active ingredient occurs in nature in the willow and other plants, and has been known for its medicinal properties since ancient times – but this will be the first time a cheap, reliable pain-killer is made universally available. Aspirin has shown itself to be relatively safe in tests so far. Plans are going ahead for its large-scale manufacture and distribution.

• 1853 – VERDI'S *LA TRAVIATA* PREMIERES IN VENICE • 1900 – GOTTLIEB DAIMLER DIES

BELL RINGS FOR TELEPHONE

1876 A revolutionary new device was patented today – the electric voice telegraph or telephone. Its Scottish-born inventor, Alexander Graham Bell, teaches vocal physiology at Boston University and is an expert on communication with the deaf. He discovered the principle behind his machine last year. The telephone converts sound waves into electrical oscillations, which can then be transmitted long distances via a cable. It is possible it could be used on a commercial scale.

1912 Henri Seimet flies from Paris to London – the first aviator to make the journey non-stop.

1984 Donald Maclean, British Foreign Office official and Russian secret agent who fled to the Soviet Union, dies aged 70.

1988 Death of American transvestite actor Divine, who starred in the cult film *Pink Flamingoes*.

BIRTHDAYS

Joseph Niepce 1765, French doctor who produced the first photograph from nature.

Edwin Henry Landseer 1802, English painter and sculptor of the lions in London's Trafalgar Square.

Piet Mondrian 1872, Dutch abstract painter famed for his geometric compositions.

Maurice Ravel 1875, French composer whose works include *Bolero*.

Lord Snowdon (Anthony Armstrong Jones) 1930, British photographer and former husband of Princess Margaret.

Viv Richards 1952, Antiguan cricketer and former captain of the West Indies cricket team.

CHINESE SHOOT TIBETAN REBELS

1989 Chinese security forces opened fire on Tibetan monks and civilians in Lhasa today. Officially, 12 "agitators" were killed, but Tibetan sources claim there are many more dead and wounded. A Western businessman in the city reports seeing "piles of bodies", and some estimates put the number of deaths in the hundreds. Hundreds more Tibetans have been arrested. The shootings started two days ago during a demonstration to mark the first Tibetan uprising against China 30 years ago. The strife continues as Chinese forces search for demonstrators, while rioting Tibetans have wrecked Chinese-owned shops and offices. China invaded Tibet in 1950, claiming it as a Chinese province, but Tibetans have been pressing for independence since 1985, thwarted by Peking. Today's show of force is by far Peking's most brutal response yet. It does not bode well for the Chinese pro-democracy movement in Peking.

ALLIES CROSS THE RHINE INTO GERMANY

1945 Nine years to the day after Hitler's troops occupied the Rhineland, making war inevitable, American troops have seized a strategic bridge over the Rhine and have crossed into Germany. Tonight troops poured across the bridge at Remagen and are now securing other crossings for heavy armour. While Soviet troops are advancing on Berlin, the US is concentrating on southern Germany.

• 1838 – JENNY LIND DEBUTS IN STOCKHOLM • 1917 – FIRST-EVER JAZZ RECORDING

1702 Queen Anne accedes to the British throne after the death of William III.

1790 The French Assembly votes to continue slavery in the colonies.

1952 An artificial heart is used for the first time on a male patient, keeping him alive for 80 minutes.

1917 Count Ferdinand von Zeppelin, inventor of the Zeppelin airship, dies at 79.

1983 Sir William Walton, British composer who wrote the film scores for the films *Hamlet*, *Henry V* and *Richard III*, dies.

1988 Police in a south Indian village enforce a government ban on the nude worship of a Hindu god.

2001 Donald Campbell's boat, *Bluebird*, is recovered from Coniston Water, Cumbria, 34 years after he died trying to break the water speed record.

BIRTHDAYS

Kenneth Grahame 1859, Scottish author of the children's book *Wind in the Willows*.

Otto Hahn 1879, German who won the Nobel Prize for chemistry in 1944 and discovered nuclear fission.

TSAR'S TIME SHORT AS REVOLT GROWS

1917 There have been widespread street demonstrations in Petrograd, provoked by food shortages. This is nothing new for the turbulent Russia of today, but for the first time the Tsar's soldiers have refused to fire on the crowds or suppress the uprising. The army, which has suffered terrible casualties at the German front, now seems more an ally of the people than the increasingly isolated Tsar Nicholas II, who left Petrograd's garrison commander General Khabalov with the hard task of maintaining order. The moderate parliament, or Duma, which began its new session last week, senses matters are moving to a head as revolutionaries and defecting soldiers roam the streets. The Tsar's days of absolute power are clearly numbered.

LOST IN FLIGHT

2014 A Malaysia Airlines aircraft carrying 227 passengers and 12 crew has vanished during a flight from Kuala Lumpur to Beijing. The airline said the pilot last had contact with air traffic controllers 120 nautical miles off the east coast of the Malaysian town of Kota Bharu. The mysterious disappearance has prompted the most expensive search effort in history.

IRAN-CONTRA TRIAL KICKS OFF

1990 In a damning White House scandal, a former National Security Adviser has gone on trial on charges of conspiracy, obstructing Congress and lying to the nation. Admiral John Poindexter, President Ronald Reagan's top security adviser

in 1985, became embroiled in the Iran-Contra affair as a consequence of secret agreements made by the Reagan administration to secure the release of US hostages in Iran in 1981. A covert arms sales fund of $30 million was diverted to finance right-wing guerillas fighting Nicaragua's Sandinista government. In 1986 Poindexter resigned, and later told Congress he was to blame and that President Reagan had known nothing of the dealings.

• 1910 – FIRST PILOT'S LICENCES GRANTED • 1989 – CHINA DECLARES MARTIAL LAW IN TIBET

BONEY'S MME

1796 Napoleon Bonaparte, the brilliant French officer who has just been made commander of the Army of the Interior, today married Josephine, a Creole divorcée and famous society beauty. A widow since her first husband the Vicomte de Beauharnais was guillotined in 1794, Josephine, 33, sought the marriage with Napoleon to protect her reputation after the two commenced a passionate affair which soon became very public.

CHOLESTEROL KID BURSTS BACK

1987 Ex-world heavyweight champion George Foreman is making a comeback. He knocked out Steve Zouski in the fourth round tonight. Since nobody's ever heard of Steve Zouski, so what? This is what – it is 16 years since Foreman lost the crown to Muhammad Ali in Zaire. He's now 42 and bigger than ever before: he weighed in at an immense 263 lb or 18st 31b (down from 320lb) – a flabby, unpenitent, non-dieting heavy-eater. "I'm comfortable at 255," he says. The fans have dubbed him the Cholesterol Kid. But he won in a style that commands notice – in fact he looked unstoppable. The man himself is determined to get a shot at the title. In 1977 Foreman had a religious experience in his dressing room after losing a fight to Jimmy Young. He retired from the ring and took to the pulpit. Now he's back – with conviction.

1864 General Ulysses Grant is made General-in-Chief of the Union Forces in the American Civil War.

1918 Frank Wedekind, German dramatist, poet and essayist, dies aged 54.

1923 Vladimir Ilich Lenin suffers a massive stroke and retires from leadership.

1932 Eamonn de Valera is elected president of Ireland.

1946 Thirty-three English football fans are killed when barriers collapse at Bolton Wanderers' ground.

1967 Svetlana Alliluyeva, daughter of Joseph Stalin, defects to the West.

BIRTHDAYS

Amerigo Vespucci 1454, Italian navigator who discovered the mouth of the Amazon and gave his name to America.

André Courrèges 1913, French couturier and inventor of the miniskirt in 1964.

Yuri Gagarin 1934, Soviet astronaut and the first man in space.

Bobby Fischer 1943, American chess champion who won the world title from Boris Spassky in 1972.

RIOTS AS POLL TAX PROTEST SWEEPS ENGLAND

1990 Six hundred years after England last saw popular unrest over government attempts to impose an unpopular poll tax, prime minister Margaret Thatcher is facing nationwide protest against her own version of the tax. This week there have been a number of violent demonstrations as left-wing protesters sought to disrupt meetings in provincial cities where the tax was being set. Today dozens were arrested in south London as riot police broke up demonstrations. Mrs Thatcher claims the new tax, charged on all adults regardless of circumstance, is fairer than the old system of property rates. She also believes it will help ensure that local government gives tax-payers better value for local services. Her opponents say she has abused civil liberties.

• 1831 – FRENCH FOREIGN LEGION FOUNDED • 1888 – KAISER WILHELM I OF PRUSSIA DIES

1661 Death of Cardinal Jules Mazarin, French statesman.

1968 In Wellington Harbour, NZ, a car ferry capsizes in a severe storm, drowning 200.

1981 Death of Sir Maurice Oldfield, the British intelligence chief.

1985 Death of Konstantin Chernenko, General Secretary of the Soviet Communist Party.

1988 The Chinese army occupies Lhasa, in Tibet, after Tibetans demonstrate against Chinese rule.

BIRTHDAYS

Tamara Karsavina 1885, Russian ballerina and co-founder of the Royal Academy of Dancing in London.

Arthur Honegger 1892, French composer who was one of Les Six, a group of composers who united against Romanticism and Impressionism.

Prince Edward 1964, youngest son of Queen Elizabeth II of the UK.

Sharon Stone 1958, American actress nominated for a Best Actress Oscar for her performance in *Casino*.

CHARLES JUST AVOIDS KILLER AVALANCHE

1988 Prince Charles narrowly avoided disaster today on a skiing holiday in the Swiss Alps when a freak avalanche swept off two members of his royal party, killing one of them. The dead man was named as Major Hugh Lindsay, a member of the royal household. Mrs Palmer-Tomkinson, a close friend of the heir to the British throne, was injured. The Prince had been enjoying skiing off-piste in an area where rescue teams would have had difficulty in rescuing him had disaster struck. He is badly shaken by the incident.

You expect your party to stay with you when the going gets tough. They got scared – so be it, so be it.
Margaret Thatcher, 1991.

SOLDIER IN HIDING

1974 A Japanese soldier was today found in hiding on Lubang Island in the Philippines. He believed World War II was still being fought, and was waiting to be relieved by his own forces. Told the good news, he is now awaiting a potentially massive payoff from his war pension.

We don't want apartheid liberalized. We want it dismantled. You can't improve something that is intrinsically evil.
Bishop Desmond Tutu, South African clergyman, 1985.

US WINS EX-MEX STATES

1848 The United States is today a million square miles larger thanks to the addition of California, New Mexico and parts of Texas – the spoils of victory in the war with Mexico. By today's congressional vote, reluctantly approving the terms of the Treaty of Guadalupe Hidalgo, Washington gains control of these lands but must pay their Spanish-speaking settlers $15 million compensation. The treaty ends a period of political hostility almost as bitter as the fighting: one group wanted to annex the whole of Mexico and throw it open to slavery. The abolitionists succeeded in banning slavery in new territories. The war has hardly been glorious – though casualties were light, almost a third of the 100,000-strong American volunteer army has succumbed to disease.

• 1969 – JAMES EARL RAY PLEADS GUILTY TO THE MURDER OF MARTIN LUTHER KING, JR

MADRID SHAKEN BY BOMB BLASTS

2004 Ten bombs ripped apart trains at three stations in Madrid during the morning rush hour, killing 190 and wounding 1,200. It was originally thought that the Basque separatist group ETA planted the bombs. However, an Islamic tape found with the detonators suggest that the Islamic militant group al-Qaeda is responsible. Al-Qaeda has threatened revenge on Spain for backing the American-led invasion and occupation of Iraq.

US lifeline for warring allies

1941 America has handed a financial lifeline to nations fighting Hitler by allowing President Franklin D. Roosevelt to apply US economic muscle without declaring war. Congress today approved the Lend-Lease Act, which will allow Britain, China, the USSR and others to receive tanks, ships and munitions on preferential credit terms. The Allies cannot otherwise afford to keep fighting the war.

1682 The Royal Hospital in Chelsea is founded to care for soldiers.

1702 The first daily paper in England, the *Daily Courant*, is published.

1844 New Zealand Maoris rise up against the British.

1926 Eamonn de Valera resigns as leader of Sinn Fein in Ireland.

1955 Death of Sir Alexander Fleming, discoverer of penicillin.

1988 The Bank of England pound note ceases to be legal tender.

2011 The HMS *Ark Royal*, former flagship of the British Navy is decommissioned after nearly 30 years of service.

Earthquake sends Tsunami Japan's way

2011 An earthquake, measuring 8.9 on the Richter scale, struck northeast Japan, triggering a tsunami which swept away cars, ships and buildings in Japan's Miyagi and Fukushima prefectures, damaging dozens of coastal communities. The wave was up to 15 metres high and left 12,000 people unaccounted for. It was Japan's most powerful earthquake since records began, the fifth largest in the world since 1900. The earthquake caused the Fukushima Daiichi nuclear power plant to shut down and the electric pumps which cool the fuel rods to cut out. The back-up diesel generators kicked in as planned and continued to cool the fuel rods, but when the tsunami hit an hour later the generators were damaged and radiation leaked from the plant.

BIRTHDAYS

Sir Malcolm Campbell 1885, British holder of the world speed records on land and sea.

Harold Wilson 1916, British Labour Prime Minister 1964–70 and 1974–6.

Douglas Adams 1952, British author of the cult radio serial *The Hitch-Hiker's Guide to the Galaxy*.

Rupert Murdoch 1931, Australian media tycoon.

• 1985 – GORBACHEV IS NEW SOVIET LEADER • 2006 – MILOSEVIC DIES FACING TRIAL

604 AD Death of St Gregory, the Pope who initiated the Anglo-Saxons' conversion to Christianity.

1507 Cesare Borgia dies at the siege of Viana in Navarre.

1881 Tunisia is made a protectorate of France.

1912 Juliette Gordon Low founds US Girl Guides.

1913 Canberra is made capital of Australia.

1940 The Russo-Finnish War is brought to an end.

1945 Young Jewish diarist Anne Frank dies in a German concentration camp.

1999 Death of violinist, Yehudi Menuhin.

BIRTHDAYS

John Aubrey 1626, English antiquary whose novel *Brief Lives* was published 201 years after his death.

Kemal Atatürk 1881, Turkish statesman and soldier.

Vaslav Nijinsky 1890, Russian dancer and choreographer.

Jack Kerouac 1922, American author of *On the Road*.

Liza Minnelli 1946, US singer, dancer and actress.

NAZIS ANNEXE AUSTRIA

1938 Adolf Hitler's troops marched into Austria today, making the country a German province. But Austrians, who have watched Hitler's plans for integrating the country into his Third Reich since the murder of Chancellor Engelbert Dollfuss in 1934 in an abortive Nazi putsch, are ecstatic. Cheering crowds greeted the jack-booted troops as they poured in, and a massive welcome is being prepared for Hitler himself – he is expected in Vienna within 48 hours. The pretext for the *Anschluss* was the resignation of Austrian premier Kurt von Schuschnigg, who had been forced to include Nazis in his cabinet. Hitler is already turning his eye on Czechoslovakia, where oppressed native Germans in the Sudetenland seek integration with Germany.

TRUMAN LAUNCHES COLD WAR BY WARNING US OF COMMUNIST THREAT

1947 Americans are coming to terms with a new piece of political jargon – "the Cold War". Financier Bernard Baruch borrowed the term from columnist Herbert Bayard Swope to describe the power struggle between Washington and Moscow. Now President Truman has put the Cold War at the top of the political agenda with a speech to the US Congress in which he urged the country to mobilize in a global crusade against expanding communism – a policy he is calling the Truman Doctrine. The US would give economic and military aid to countries deemed to be under Soviet threat, such as Greece and Turkey, he said. Washington would also "support free peoples who are resisting attempted subjugation by armed minorities or by outside pressures".

• **1789 – US POST OFFICE ESTABLISHED** • **1955 – JAZZ GREAT CHARLIE PARKER DIES**

AMATEUR STARGAZER SPOTS NEW PLANET

1781 A new planet unknown to the ancient astronomers has been discovered by a German stargazer. William Herschel, an organist by profession, has a passion for grinding lenses and building telescopes with which to survey the heavens. He noticed that one of the stars in the constellation of Gemini had the characteristics of a planet. Today it was confirmed that a seventh planet in addition to Earth does indeed exist. The new planet, which is even further from the sun than Saturn, has yet to be named, but a possibility is Uranus, after the Greek god of the sky. Herschel is at work compiling a star catalogue.

1894 The first professional striptease takes place at the Davan Fayoneau Music Hall in Paris.

1900 British forces under Field Marshal Roberts take Bloemfontein in the second Boer War.

1906 American feminist Susan B. Anthony dies.

1926 The first commercial air route is established across Africa.

1928 Four hundred and fifty people are drowned when a dam near Los Angeles bursts.

1977 Czech secret police torture to death the leader of the Charter 77 movement, Jan Potocka.

1974 The Charles de Gaulle airport in Paris is opened.

1978 Moluccan terrorists hold 72 people hostage in government buildings in Assen, Holland.

TSAR MURDERED BY EXTREMIST BOMB

1881 Tsar Alexander II has been murdered by extremists on the very day he had finally agreed to implement democratic reforms. Two bombs were thrown at the Tsar in St Petersburg. The first exploded harmlessly, but as the Tsar stood in the street asking questions about the attack a member of the *Narodniks* extremist organization threw a second bomb that killed him. Alexander survived a string of assassination attempts after his proclamation ordering the emancipation of the serfs in 1861, but the *Narodniks* were determined to eliminate him. This group of populist intellectuals condemned Alexander to death two years ago for refusing to summon a popular assembly. Ironically, Alexander signed a manifesto that would have created a national consultative assembly just before his death. The assassination itself will now postpone such a step.

BIRTHDAYS

Dr Joseph Priestley 1733, English chemist who discovered oxygen in 1774.

Neil Sedaka 1939, American singer-songwriter.

Joe Bugner 1950, Hungarian-born British heavyweight boxing champion.

• 1930 – **PLANET PLUTO DISCOVERED** • 1961 – **37-YEAR-OLD BRIDE FOR PICASSO, 79**

MARCH 14

1869 The third Maori rebellion in 15 years ends with the defeat of the guerrilla leader Titokowaru.

1891 The first underwater telephone cable is laid on the bed of the English Channel.

1900 President McKinley puts America on the Gold Standard.

1915 The German cruiser *Dresden* is sunk.

1953 Nikita Krushchev becomes First Secretary of the Communist Party of the Soviet Union.

1991 Death of Howard Ashman, American lyricist, director and playwright.

2014 Death of Tony Benn, British politician and diarist, born in 1925.

BIRTHDAYS

Victor Emmanuel II 1820, first king of a united Italy.

Albert Einstein 1879, German-born physicist and mathematician.

Quincy Jones 1933, American composer *(In the Heat of the Night)* and producer (Michael Jackson's album *Thriller).*

Michael Caine 1933, English actor whose films include *The Ipcress File.*

THE KALEIDOSCOPE CHOREOGRAPHER

1976 Busby Berkeley, high priest of the Hollywood musical extravaganza, died today. His influence was greatest in the 1930s, when kaleidoscopic patterns of intertwining lines of massed dancers kicking their legs up – often filmed from above – became his trademark of thinly-repressed eroticism. On both stage and screen Berkeley went for grandiose choreography even when the intimate would have sufficed. At the time, films like the "Gold Diggers" series and *Footlight Parade* were big hits, but fashions – and society's perceptions of women – changed. Berkeley's overblown chorus-lines stepped back out of the limelight, and he had no choice but to follow them.

SPAIN EXPELS 150,000 JEWS

1492 Queen Isabella of Castile has ordered the 150,000 Jews in Spain to accept Christian baptism or face immediate expulsion. Most of the Jews are planning to leave rather than betray their faith. To Isabella and her husband Ferdinand, both devout Catholics, the offence of the Jews is twofold – in the past they were an important part of the Arab cultural renaissance in Iberia, contributing to the body of Spanish-Arab work on science and philosophy and other subjects that is proving a vital influence in today's Europe. Now the royals, who have forced the Arabs from Granada, are eager to sweep away the Jews, too.

RUBY GUILTY OF OSWALD MURDER

1964 Dallas night-club owner Jack Ruby has been found guilty of killing Lee Harvey Oswald, the presumed murderer of President John F. Kennedy. Two days after Kennedy's death last year, as Oswald was being taken from Dallas police headquarters to prison, Ruby shot him at close range. Now Ruby, 52, has been sentenced to death for silencing the only man who might have proved whether or not a wider conspiracy to kill Kennedy existed. The Warren Commission is investigating Oswald's motives and whether he had links with Ruby.

• 1883 – DEATH OF KARL MARX • 1961 – NEW ENGLISH BIBLE PUBLISHED

STALIN PURGES ON

1938 The Soviet dictator Joseph Stalin's infamous purges of the Communist Party reached their peak today with the execution of 18 senior figures, several of them Lenin's favourites. Among those shot at Lubyanka prison, after "confessing" extraordinary crimes against the state, was Nikolai Bukharin. Bukharin's revolutionary credentials appeared even more respectable than Stalin's – which perhaps contributed to his fate. The trials have also seen a former premier and an ex-head of the secret police confessing to the most improbable plots to overthrow the Soviet state.

CAESAR SLAIN

44 BC Julius Caesar should have listened to his fortune-teller. "Beware the Ides of March", he was told, but instead he insisted on attending a meeting of the Senate in Pompey's theatre today. Caesar has recently compared himself to Alexander the Great, and was planning the conquest of Parthia. Many Romans were convinced he had to be stopped and the dictator was brutally attacked. Stabbed by Marcus Brutus, he fell with the words, "You too, Brutus?"

1584 The Russian tsar, Ivan the Terrible, dies.

1820 Maine becomes the 23rd state of the Union.

1933 Adolf Hitler proclaims the Third Reich in Germany.

1937 Bernard Faustus sets up America's first blood bank.

1975 The death is announced of the Greek shipping tycoon Aristotle Onassis.

1989 The Hungarian city of Budapest fills with rival demonstrators who voice their opposition to the Communist government.

1990 Farzad Bazoft, a British journalist is hanged as a spy in Iraq.

1991 Albania and the United States restore full diplomatic relations after a gap of 52 years.

BASEBALL GOES PRO

1869 The Cincinnati Red Stockings are professionals, and out of their first 92 baseball games this season they have won 91. Their success as the first truly professional team is encouraging others to follow suit in the organized league, the National Association of Baseball Players. Baseball has come of age. It first appeared in the Eastern United States in the 1820s as a development of rounders. In 1845 the rules were laid out, and in 1857 they were amended by a convention of baseball clubs. Now the whole game is going professional.

Andrew Jackson 1767, who became seventh president of the United States in 1828, served two terms and finally retired in 1837.

David Wall 1946, British dancer, formerly with the Royal Ballet company, latterly director of the Royal Academy of Dancing.

1802 US military academy at West Point established.

1815 William of Orange is made King of the United Netherlands.

1930 The Spanish leader Miguel Primo de Rivera y Orbaneja dies.

1937 British statesman Sir Joseph Austen Chamberlain dies.

1973 British monarch Queen Elizabeth II opens the new London Bridge.

2012 Indian batsman Sachin Tendulkar is the first to score 100 international centuries.

BIRTHDAYS

James Madison 1751, fourth US President, who was first elected in 1809 and retired at the end of his second term, in 1817.

Georg Simon Ohm 1787, German physicist who in 1827 discovered the basic law of electric current, later known as Ohm's law.

Jerry Lewis 1926, American film star famous for his zany roles and partnership with singer-actor Dean Martin.

Bernardo Bertolucci 1940, Italian film director whose films include *Last Tango in Paris*.

India's most powerful sultan surrenders

1792 Tippoo Sahib, the most powerful Indian sultan still resisting the advance of British imperialism, has finally been beaten in battle. His defeat ends the third war fought over Mysore and means he will be forced to give up half his immense lands to the administration of the British East India Company. Tippoo's secret was that he studied western military operations and was able until now successfully to second-guess British moves. But against General Charles Cornwallis he did not fare as well as the American colonists, who soundly beat the British commander at Yorktown. After this defeat Cornwallis was sent to India as governor-general with the mission of crushing Tippoo Sahib. While the sultan has been beaten, he is still far from crushed.

EVANS FINDS ANCIENT HOARD AT KNOSSOS

1900 Just days after he started digging at what he suspected was the site of a Cretan Bronze Age palace, the British archaeologist Sir Arthur Evans today struck an incredible hoard of antiquities dating from the 16th century BC. Sir Arthur has named the civilization whose ruins he is excavating at Knossos, on the Greek island of Crete, the Minoan culture – a reference to the mythical Cretan Minotaur. Sir Arthur says there are signs the Minoans worshipped bulls; he believes the sprawling palace may contain the labyrinth built by Daedalus described in the ancient tale. He has also uncovered the earliest known writing.

US troops massacre 300 villagers in ditch

1968 Reports are reaching Saigon of a massacre of 300 unarmed villagers by American troops in the South Vietnamese village of My Lai. Soldiers under the command of Lt William L. Calley were flown in to break a rebel stronghold. More than 300 women, children and elderly men were herded into ditches and riddled with automatic fire. Calley and his men were apparently not shamed by this mass murder, since it was carefully photographed. There are also reports of another horrifying mass killing of civilians by US troops at My Khe.

• **1899 – AUBREY BEARDSLEY DIES** • **1935 – HITLER RENOUNCES TREATY OF VERSAILLES**

BIRTH CONTROL CLINIC OPENS FOR LONDON'S POOR

1921 A British campaigner today opened a clinic to advise mothers on how to avoid having more children. The Mothers' Clinic in North London has been set up by Dr Marie Stopes, the author of the widely publicized *Married Love* – one of the first books to discuss sexual relations in a straightforward manner. Dr Stopes, a well-known womens' rights campaigner, is facing stiff resistance to her new clinic from church leaders and doctors who insist that by making contraceptives freely available to poor women, immorality will increase.

USSR VOTES ON UNITY

1991 Soviet voters have gone to the polls to decide whether or not their vast country will remain a single unit. President Mikhail Gorbachev has been passionately campaigning for a "yes" vote in the nationwide referendum, while his rival Boris Yeltsin has been urging a "no". Six breakaway republics have refused to participate because they are convinced the draft of the new Union Treaty being proposed by Gorbachev would undermine their freedom. Three have announced they will run their own referendum.

1337 Edward, the Black Prince, is made first Duke of Cornwall by his father, King Edward III of England.

1782 Swiss physicist Daniel Bernoulli dies.

1848 Violence breaks out in Berlin against Prussian ruler Frederick William IV.

1899 A merchant ship run aground off the English coast sends the first radio distress call.

1958 Australian-born polar explorer Sir George Wilkins dies.

1959 The US submarine *Skate* surfaces after completing an historic under-ice voyage to the North Pole.

1983 British PM Margaret Thatcher is the target of an IRA letterbomb campaign.

1992 South Africa's white population votes in favour of constitutional change.

BRITAIN REPEALS TAX TO SAVE AMERICAN COLONIES

1766 Parliament in London is voting on the repeal of the controversial Stamp Act. The Act, passed last year as a means of paying for the cost of maintaining troops in the colonies, required Americans to pay a tax on all legal or printed documents and newspapers. Instead of helping to keep order, it gave the colonists – who have no voice in parliament – a rallying-cry: "Taxation without representation is tyranny." A boycott of British goods and refusal to buy the hated stamps has mushroomed into an organization called the Stamp Act Congress, which recently issued a bill of American rights. A simple repeal of the Act may come too late to stifle the rebellion.

• 1845 – RUBBER BAND PATENTED • 1978 – *AMOCO CADIZ* OIL SPILL

978 Edward, King of England, is murdered at Corfe Castle.

1455 Religious painter and Dominican monk Fra Angelico dies.

1745 Britain's first PM, Robert Walpole, dies.

1850 The American Express Company is set up in Buffalo, New York.

1891 The first London-Paris telephone link is opened.

1931 The American company Schick Inc. starts to manufacture electric razors.

1950 British athlete Roger Bannister runs the first four-minute mile.

BIRTHDAYS

Nikolai Rimsky-Korsakov 1844, Russian composer.

Rudolf Diesel 1858, German engineer and pioneer of the modern car engine.

Neville Chamberlain 1869, British prime minister from 1937 until 1940.

Wilfred Owen 1893, English World War I poet.

John Updike 1932, American novelist.

KAISER SACKS BISMARCK

1890 Otto von Bismarck, the mighty chancellor who has governed Prussia and later Germany with a policy of "blood and iron" since 1862, was today summarily dismissed from his post by Kaiser Wilhelm II. Despite his ability to build a huge empire, the strong-willed Kaiser wanted none of the old politician's advice. Even Bismarck's social welfare legislation, which in 1889 provided Germans with insurance against illness, accident, and old age, could not deflect the enmity of the socialists whom the 31-year-old Kaiser is trying to befriend. Bismarck seemed to court dismissal: he has often failed to turn up in Berlin, spending his time in the country nursing grievances or giving warnings of anarchist plots.

Pakistan court condemns Bhutto to death

1978 An army judge in Lahore today condemned Pakistan's former prime minister, Zulfikar Ali Bhutto, to death after finding him guilty of ordering the murder of a political opponent in 1974. Last July Bhutto's government was overthrown by the army chief of staff, General Muhammad Zia Ul-Haq. Zia stepped in after an allegedly rigged election victory for Bhutto was followed by rioting. In place of Bhutto's free-wheeling and often questionable political methods at the head of his Pakistan Peoples' Party (PPP), the anti-communist Zia has imposed Islamic rule and a political clamp-down. Bhutto's lawyers have promised to appeal, but as the final decision rests with General Zia himself clemency is not expected.

RUSSIAN SPACEMAN TAKES A WALK OUTSIDE

1965 Soviet cosmonaut Aleksei Leonov today became the first man to walk in space as he danced and somersaulted in orbit hundreds of miles above the earth, secured only by a slender lifeline. As co-pilot of the Soviet Union's *Voshkod II* craft, 31-year-old Colonel Leonov left the craft to take the first hand-held film images of the earth during his 15-minute adventure.

• 1662 – PARIS RUNS FIRST PUBLIC BUS SERVICE • 1940 – NATO IS BORN

WORLD'S LONGEST SINGLE-SPAN ARCH BRIDGE

1932 Sydney Harbour Bridge in New South Wales, Australia, was opened today, the world's longest single-span arch bridge. It has a 1650 ft (503 m) span, carries four railway tracks, a 56 ft (17 m) wide road and two footpaths.

721 BC The Babylonians make the first-ever record of an eclipse of the sun.

1791 Equal rights are granted to French and English-speaking settlers in Canada.

1853 Chinese peasants led by the rebel Hong Xiu Quan capture Nanjing.

1930 Former British prime minister Arthur Balfour (1902–6) dies.

1976 Princess Margaret, sister of the Queen of England, separates from Lord Snowdon, after 15 years of marriage.

2008 British science fiction writer Arthur C. Clarke dies, aged 90.

BIRTHDAYS

Dr David Livingstone 1813, Scottish missionary and explorer.

Wyatt Earp 1848, American lawman famed for bringing order to Tombstone, Arizona.

Adolf Eichmann 1906, German SS colonel and war criminal.

Philip Roth 1933, American author best known for *Portnoy's Complaint.*

TOLPUDDLE MARTYRS TRANSPORTED

1834 As punishment for trying to set up a rural trade union, six southern England farmworkers have been sentenced to seven years' transportation to Australia. The punishment – effectively a death sentence because of the harsh conditions in the colony – has brought a huge public outcry. The convicts are being called the Tolpuddle Martyrs, after the name of their Dorset village. The men wanted to set up a branch of the Friendly Society of Agricultural Labourers. At the same time the Whigs are proposing the abolition of wage subsidies to help low-paid farmworkers like the Tolpuddle Martyrs stay out of the workhouses. Britain's harsh treatment of its poor is in stark contrast with its international campaign against slavery.

TV preacher resigns in sex and corruption scandal

1987 TV evangelist Jim Bakker has been forced to resign from his very lucrative Praise the Lord religious network in the southern United States after confessing a string of sexual adventures unfitting for a man of the cloth. Bakker and his wife Tammy Faye were well-known on hundreds of religious networks in dozens of countries, exhorting viewers of the "Jim and Tammy Show" to follow their spiritual example. An extramarital group sex scandal dating from 1980 could now also force his unfrocking as a minister of the Assembly of God. In addition, Bakker is under investigation for having pocketed church funds donated by supporters.

• 1920 – US SENATE VOTES AGAINST JOINING LEAGUE OF NATIONS

1653 Oliver Cromwell, Lord Protector of England, dissolves the Long Parliament.

1792 The French Legislative Assembly approves the guillotine.

1934 Radar is first demonstrated in Kiel harbour, Germany.

1980 British radio pirate ship Radio Caroline sinks.

1995 More than 5,500 people are rushed to hospital and 12 die when sarin nerve gas is released on the Tokyo subway by the Aum Shinrikyo cult.

2003 The US launch missiles at Baghdad, marking the start of a campaign against Saddam Hussein.

BIRTHDAYS

Ovid 43 BC, Roman poet best-known for the *Metamorphoses*.

Sir Isaac Newton 1727, English scientist who discovered the law of gravitation.

Henrik Ibsen 1823, Norwegian dramatist and poet.

Dame Vera Lynn 1917, British singer dubbed the "Forces sweetheart" during World War II.

FIRST DETECTIVE NOVEL: POE DUNNIT

1841 The poet and literary journalist Edgar Allan Poe has today published a horrifying yet fascinating work of fiction that critics are citing as the first example of a new style – the detective story. *The Murders in the Rue Morgue* challenges the reader to exercise the deductive powers of a detective and discover who is really the villain before the final page. Until recently he was editor of the *Southern Literary Messenger*, which has published much of his criticism, poetry and prose fiction.

ASH CLOUD CHAOS

2010 The Icelandic volcano Eyjafjallajoekull erupted for the first time since 1823. The eruption continued into April with a brief pause before a second more violent eruption on 22 April when lava broke out through a new conduit under the ice on the summit of the mountain. Contact between the hot lava and the ice produced an explosive cocktail, as the ice turned to steam and gas escaped from bubbles in the molten rock. This caused a massive ash cloud which disrupted air travel over Europe for weeks on end amid fears that the tiny particles of rock and glass in the cloud could affect the aeroplanes' engines. Flights were grounded across much of Europe as the cloud drifted with the prevailing winds. Millions of passengers were affected and many were left stranded in different parts of the world.

PRINCESS ANNE SHOT AT IN KIDNAP ATTEMPT

1974 Princess Anne, the daughter of Britain's Queen Elizabeth II, escaped unhurt today after an armed man tried to kidnap her in London. The attempt was part of a bizarre bid to draw attention to declining public health services for mental patients in Britain. The gunman, Ian Ball, ambushed the princess's car close to Buckingham Palace and fired six shots into it. After blocking the royal car with his own, Ball tried to drag out the princess but was beaten off by bodyguards and a passerby. He escaped into nearby St James Park but was soon hunted down and caught. Police are enquiring into Ball's psychiatric history.

• 1602 – DUTCH FORM EAST INDIA COMPANY • 1815 – NAPOLEON RETURNS FROM EXILE

MASSIVE GERMAN ATTACK AT THE SOMME

1918 Germany's field commander General Erich Ludendorff has launched a massive offensive on the Somme in a bid to break the Allied line before American reinforcements arrive. Crack German troops are advancing rapidly along a 60-mile front and the Allies have already been forced back several miles. British troops are bearing the brunt of the attack, which is the Germans' first major breakthrough since the early days of the war.

RUSSIA ANNEXES CRIMEA

2014 President Vladimir V. Putin of Russia has formally completed the annexation of Crimea, signing into law bills passed by Parliament reclaiming the contested province from Ukraine. Hours earlier, the acting prime minister of Ukraine signed a political association agreement with the European Union, a pact bitterly opposed by Moscow. As he cemented Russian control of Crimea, Mr Putin declared a temporary ceasefire in a tit-for-tat battle of economic and political sanctions between Moscow and the West. The European Union and the United States have frozen assets and limited the travel of a number of close associates of Mr Putin's for their part in Crimea's annexation.

LEWIS AND CLARK CHART THE WILD WEST

1806 The Lewis and Clark expedition that is charting the unexplored territory between the Mississippi River and the Pacific Ocean has turned homeward. The expedition has proved there is no easy water route across the continent. Army captains Meriwether Lewis and William Clark started out from St Louis almost two years ago. They travelled up the Missouri as far as the Rocky Mountains, crossed over to the Columbia River and thence to the Pacific coast. The plan was to explore the newly acquired territories of Louisiana in a single year, but difficult navigation, hostile Indians and other hardships caused delays. After a second winter in the wilderness by the Pacific shore, the party has split into two groups; one is exploring the Yellowstone River before they rendezvous at the Missouri River for the home leg of their 8,000-mile journey.

1804 A new civil code, the Code Napoleon, comes into force in France.

1871 A commune is declared in the French city of Lyons.

1871 Chancellor Otto von Bismarck opens the first parliament of the newly declared German Reich.

1896 Britain's first cinema opens in London's Piccadilly Circus.

1933 The first parliament of Nazi Germany, with Hitler as Chancellor, is proclaimed in the garrison church at Potsdam.

1946 British minister Aneurin Bevan announces Labour's plans for a National Health Service.

1963 The notorious Alcatraz prison in the bay of San Francisco closes.

1989 Australian PM Bob Hawke breaks down on TV as he admits to adultery.

BIRTHDAYS

Johann Sebastian Bach 1685, German composer and organist.

Benito Pablo Juarez 1801, Mexican president who was deposed by colonial powers Britain and France before being re-elected as head of state.

• 1556 – THOMAS CRANMER BURNED AT THE STAKE • 1908 – WORLD'S FIRST AIR PASSENGER

MARCH 22

BIRTHDAYS

Sir Anthony van Dyck 1599, Flemish artist who became portrait painter to the English court and was knighted by Charles I.

Marcel Marceau 1923, French mime artist.

Stephen Sondheim 1930, American composer of musicals such as *A Little Night Music* and *Sweeney Todd*.

ALDRICH BOWS OUT WITH PANACHE

1981 "Rudy, if you ever need a friend, buy a dog," says fast-talking women's wrestling promoter Harry Sears in Robert Aldrich's final movie, *California Dolls*, released today. The movie is violent, indecent, sexist and disreputable – and it's also terrific, red-blooded fun, with a right rousing climax when the good guys (or rather girls) finally triumph, having had the daylights thumped out of them by a pair of wicked nasties – who are black. It's no surprise that the film is anathema to the critics. Aldrich is perhaps the most forceful American film director to emerge in the 1950s, with a string of hits such as *Whatever Happened to Baby Jane?* His later films brought increasing hostility as he trampled on society's corns, but none can deny their sheer power. With this last film Aldrich has retired, at the age of 63.

FINAL WORDS OF GOETHE THE GREAT THINKER

1832 Johann Wolfgang von Goethe, one of the greatest thinkers of his age, has died at the age of 82. Characteristically, his last words were "More light!" Goethe was a literary giant, philosopher, pioneering scientist and political councillor. Many of his works are seen as high points of literature. At his death he was finishing the second part of his dramatic poem "Faust: A Tragedy", a modern version of the European myth of Dr Johann Faustus.

MOSCOW ORDERS LITHUANIA BACK INTO LINE

1990 Moscow has warned the rebel republic of Lithuania it would act against its declaration of independence – announced just 10 days ago – if the new country does not disband the forces now coalescing into a small army. President Mikhail Gorbachev gave Lithuania 48 hours to remove roadblocks and military posts on its border. Moscow fears the spread of propaganda from the state-owned publishing house. The new government, however, insists that it will obey the restored 1938 Lithuanian constitution, not the Kremlin.

• 1933 – NAZIS OPEN CONCENTRATION CAMP AT DACHAU • 1945 – ARAB LEAGUE SET UP

DRUNKEN OFFICERS STRANGLE MAD TSAR

1801 In a brutal Kremlin coup tonight, the mentally unbalanced Tsar Paul I was strangled in his bed by a group of drunken Russian army officers. They then proclaimed his son Alexander the new emperor. The Tsar's harsh rule, as well as his alliance with Austria against Napoleon (although he later changed sides), alienated the military. He also alienated his people by repealing a law confining corporal punishment to serfs. Paul I's life was fraught with argument and instability. He fought bitterly with his mother, Catherine the Great; she isolated him from his sons and tried to disinherit him. After her death five years ago, he decreed that no woman could ever rule again.

PATIENT DIES – ARTIFICIAL HEART STILL "A SUCCESS"

1983 Retired American dentist Barney Clark has died after gaining a three-month lease of life when an artificial heart was implanted in his chest. Clark's worn-out heart was replaced by a polyurethane and aluminum "Jarvik-7" artificial heart last December at the University of Utah Medical Center in the first operation of its kind. He died of circulatory collapse and other problems associated with the new heart. Doctors claim the trial was a success, nevertheless.

TENNESSEE OUTLAWS THEORY OF EVOLUTION

1925 Charles Darwin's theory of evolution was today outlawed in the southern US state of Tennessee. Governor Austin Peay signed a statute forbidding Darwin's work to be taught in state schools on religious grounds.

1752 Canada's first newspaper, the *Halifax Gazette*, hits the streets.

1765 The Stamp Act comes into force in British colonies.

1861 The first tramcars run in London's Baywater.

1918 Big Bertha, a giant German gun, shells Paris from 75 miles away.

1966 In Rome, the first official meeting for 400 years between the heads of the Catholic and Anglican churches takes place.

2011 Academy Award-winning actress Elizabeth Taylor dies in LA, aged 79.

MUSSOLINI FOUNDS FASCIST PARTY IN MILAN

1919 In Milan, a group of disillusioned former socialists and Italian war veterans has formed a political party inspired by the most authoritarian period of the Roman Empire. Led by Benito Mussolini, the editor of *Il popolo d'Italia*, the group is called the Fasci di Combattimento, after the fasces, the axe that was the symbol of ancient Roman authority. The "Fascists" are both revolutionary and nationalistic. In the current postwar economic and social turmoil, Mussolini and his new party are attacking both communism and liberal business. Their answer for Italy's problems is a strong state.

BIRTHDAYS

Joan Crawford 1908, American film actress whose many films include *A Woman's Face*, *Mildred Pierce* and *Whatever Happened to Baby Jane?*

Akira Kurosawa 1910, Japanese film director whose *Seven Samurai* inspired Hollywood's *The Magnificent Seven*.

Donald Campbell 1921, British world speed record-breaker.

Roger Bannister 1929, British sportsman who ran the world's first sub-four-minute mile in 1954.

• 1933 – HITLER BECOMES DICTATOR • 1983 – PRESIDENT REAGAN PROPOSES "STAR WARS"

1877 The Cambridge and Oxford boat race ends in a dead heat for the first time.

1905 Jules Verne, French author of *Around the World in Eighty Days*, dies aged 77.

1922 Only three out of 32 horses finish at the Grand National at Aintree.

1976 Argentinian president Isabel Peron is deposed by the army.

1976 Death of Viscount Montgomery of Alamein, Commander of the Eighth Army in World War II.

1988 Mordecai Vanunu is found guilty of revealing Israel's nuclear secrets to the *Sunday Times*.

1990 Indian peacekeeping troops pull out of Sri Lanka.

2002 Halle Berry becomes the first black woman ever to receive an Oscar.

BIRTHDAYS

William Morris 1834, British designer, artist and poet who was associated with the Pre-Raphaelite Brotherhood.

Steve McQueen 1930, American film actor whose first major film was *The Magnificent Seven*.

CHINA CRACKS DOWN ON OPIUM TRADE

1839 Chinese troops blockaded the foreign traders' warehouses in Canton today as the Peking court's continued struggle to suppress the opium trade moves toward outright war. Commissioner Lin Ze-xu, the Emperor's special envoy, has surrounded the warehouses with me and has ordered the foreign merchants to give up more than 20,000 chests of the illegal drug, worth about $12 million. The merchants have little choice but to comply and the opium will be destroyed forthwith. The drug – first imported from India in the 17th century – is ruining China morally and financially, says Peking, while filling the coffers of the Scottish, English and American trading houses that have various entrepot facilities at Canton.

ELIZABETH'S GLORIOUS REIGN ENDS

1603 Elizabeth I, England's virgin queen for 45 years, died today. So ends a reign that made England the leading Protestant and maritime power of Europe – and one in which the arts have flourished as never before. Heirless, she is succeeded by the son of Mary Queen of Scots, uniting the thrones of England and Scotland; he will be James I of England and James VI of Scotland.

MADONNA'S MANTEL-PIECE FULL TO BURSTING

1991 Madonna sang her hit "Sooner or Later" from the movie in which she starred, *Dick Tracy*, at the Academy Awards ceremony in Los Angeles tonight – and won an Oscar for it. But she'll hardly be able to find room for it on her mantelpiece. Earlier this month she won *Rolling Stone*'s Best Single, Best Video, Best Tour, Best Dressed Female Artist, Sexiest Female Singer, Best Video and Hype of the Year awards. Three days earlier her single "Vogue" won the International Single of the Year award, and the day before "Rescue Me" was the highest-debuting single by a female artist in history. Madonna has sold more than 80 million albums worldwide; at one time she had a No. 1 hit in 28 countries simultaneously. Only Elvis and the Beatles beat her chart success.

• 1999 – NATO LAUNCHES AIR STRIKES AGAINST MILITARY TARGETS IN YUGOSLAVIA

BIRTH OF A EURO-VISION

1957 Six European countries – France, West Germany, Italy, the Netherlands, Belgium and Luxembourg – took a historic step towards guaranteeing a future of peace and prosperity for their continent today when, via a transcontinental TV link-up broadcast, they signed the Treaty of Rome and formed the European Economic Community. The new EEC aims to create free movement of people, goods and money to generate an economic boom. Tariffs between member states will disappear, common policies will be developed and the first steps towards a European political union will be taken.

ALASKAN OIL DISASTER AS GROUNDED TANKER SPLITS

1989 The worst oil spill in US history was today threatening to decimate marine life over a wide area as 11 million gallons of crude oil poured uncontrolled into the open sea. The 987-ft super tanker *Exxon Valdez* ran aground and split open on a reef in Prince William Sound, Alaska, yesterday, releasing an oil slick into an area rich in marine wildlife and fishing stock. The cause of the accident has not been revealed but the US Coastguard has subpoenaed the tanker's captain and two crew to face federal investigators. There are rumours that the crew had been drinking. The ship's owners, Exxon Shipping, have promised to pay for the gigantic, months-long clean-up that will be necessary.

1609 English navigator Henry Hudson sets off on his third attempt to find the North-West Passage.

1807 The British parliament abolishes the slave trade.

1815 Britain, Austria, Prussia and Russia form a new alliance against Napoleon Bonaparte.

1918 Claude Debussy, French composer of *Pelléas et Mélisande* and *La Mer*, dies aged 55.

1999 A fire in the Mont Blanc tunnel between France and Italy kills 40 people.

2002 A powerful earthquake hits Afghanistan causing 1,800 deaths.

Arturo Toscanini 1867, Italian conductor who refused to conduct in Italy or Germany when they were ruled by the Fascists and the Nazis respectively.

Béla Bartok 1881, Hungarian composer and virtuoso pianist whose music blends East European folk music with dissonant harmonies.

Aretha Franklin 1942, American singer dubbed the "Queen of Soul".

ROBERT THE BRUCE CROWNED KING OF SCOTS

1306 The eighth Earl of Carrick, Robert the Bruce, was today crowned King of Scotland at Scone, becoming Robert I. Bruce's grandfather lost his claim to the throne in 1292; Bruce won back the crown after murdering his rival John Comyn last year. Comyn was backed by the English under King Edward I. After a decade when his allegiance to the cause of Scottish nationalism was wavering, the murder and his accession to the throne have now committed Bruce to the fight to restore national independence to Scotland.

• 1949 – OLIVIER'S HAMLET SWEEPS 5 OSCARS • 1975 – SAUDI KING FAISAL MURDERED

1878 The Sabi Game Reserve in South Africa is the world's first.

1892 American poet Walt Whitman dies.

1936 New Zealand radio begins live broadcasts from the nation's parliament.

1945 David Lloyd George, former Liberal PM of Britain, dies aged 82.

1973 The first woman stockbroker sets foot on the floor of the London Stock Exchange.

1973 British dramatist Noel Coward dies.

2000 Vladimir Putin replaces Boris Yeltsin as President of Russia.

BIRTHDAYS

Chico (Leonard) Marx 1891, American film comedian and member of the famous Marx Brothers family of comic actors.

Tennessee Williams 1914, American playwright, screen writer and novelist.

Diana Ross 1944, American singer and former member of the Tamla Motown all-girl group The Supremes.

Keira Knightley 1985, English actress, star of *Atonement*.

EGYPT AND ISRAEL SIGN PEACE ACCORD

1979 Hopes of a lasting peace in the strife-torn Middle East were given a major boost today when the leaders of Israel and Egypt signed a historic peace treaty in the presence of US President Jimmy Carter. The agreement between Israeli Prime Minister Menachem Begin and Egyptian President Anwar Sadat to restore diplomatic relations opens a new era: 30 years of conflict between the two nations may now be solved. The treaty crowns two years of patient diplomacy following Sadat's surprise journey to Jerusalem to open peace negotiations. Both leaders face domestic problems getting today's bold step accepted. For Carter, the treaty will restore much of the prestige he lost during the Iranian revolution.

NORTHERN IRELAND REACH AN AGREEMENT

2007 Northern Ireland's two opposing parties, Sinn Fein and the Democratic Unionist Party, signed a power-sharing agreement after their first-ever direct talks held at Stormont, the province's parliament. In these historic talks, rival leaders Gerry Adams of the mainly Catholic Sinn Fein and Ian Paisley of the DUP agreed to form a joint executive to run the province from 8 May.

ENGLAND MONARCHY CERTAIN TO RETURN

1660 The return of the monarchy to England is now all but certain after the longest Parliament in the country's history dissolved itself today. The so-called Long Parliament survived for 20 years through the Civil War. A new Parliament will be elected to prepare the way for the restoration of King Charles II, who has promised to rule as a constitutional monarch. The country is now looking forward to peace.

• 1827 – BEETHOVEN DIES • 1920 – "BLACK & TANS" ARRIVE IN IRELAND TO FIGHT THE IRA

Strike brings Poland to a halt

1981 Millions of Polish workers today staged a general strike in protest at police harassment of activists belonging to the trade union Solidarity. They were urged to do so by union leader Lech Walesa. The strike is a show of strength against hard-line communists trying to reclaim concessions made last year when mass strikes won Solidarity recognition as the Warsaw Pact's first independent trade union. The union wants the hard-liners forced out of power. Walesa would be willing to make deals with the communist rulers to secure the union's position, but union militants are pressing for a more political line. Poland's new party leader, General Jaruzelski, is under pressure to declare martial law and ban Solidarity.

FATAL JUMBO COLLISION

1977 The worst accident in flying history shocked the world today when two Jumbo jets collided, claiming 574 lives. The two Boeing 747s, belonging to KLM and Pan Am, crashed on the runway at Tenerife on the Canary Islands, sending huge jets of flame and smoke into the air. The accident happened when the American plane turned on to the runway where the Dutch Jumbo was about to take off. Both had been diverted from nearby Las Palmas because of a bomb threat. All 248 KLM passengers perished in the ensuing fire, while some 70 Pan Am passengers were tonight being treated in hospital for horrific burns.

US TROOPS ROUT CREEK INDIANS

1814 Troops under General Andrew Jackson today inflicted an overwhelming defeat on the Creek Indians at the Battle of Horseshoe Bend in eastern Alabama. More than 800 Indians lost their lives in the battle, which marks the end of a year-long war. Much of the Creek territory in Alabama and Georgia will now be brought into the United States.

MARCH
27

1802 Britain and France sign the Peace of Amiens.

1835 Texan rebels are massacred by the Mexican army at Gohad.

1958 Soviet prime minister Marshal Nikolai Bulganin is ousted by Nikita Kruschev in a Kremlin power struggle.

1964 Britain's Great Train Robbers are sentenced to a total of 307 years imprisonment.

2002 Death of Billy Wilder, director of films such as *Some Like it Hot* and *Sunset Boulevard*.

BIRTHDAYS

Baron Georges Haussmann 1809, French town planner, responsible for transforming Paris into a city noted for its long, wide boulevards.

Sir Henry Royce 1863, British engineer and co-founder, with C. S. Rolls, of the Rolls-Royce motor company.

Gloria Swanson 1898, American star of silent films remembered for her role in *Sunset Boulevard*, as a faded movie star.

Quentin Tarantino 1963, American film director known for his distinctive, often violent films.

• 1794 – US NAVY ESTABLISHED • 1914 – FIRST SUCCESSFUL BLOOD TRANSFUSION

1910 The first seaplane takes off in France.

1941 The British Navy sinks seven Italian warships for no loss at the Battle of Matapan.

1943 Russian emigré composer and pianist Sergei Rachmaninov dies in California.

1945 Germany mounts its last V2 rocket attack against Britain.

1969 Former US Republican President Dwight D. Eisenhower dies.

1979 British PM James Callaghan falls over Home Rule for Ireland.

1985 Russian-born painter Marc Chagall dies.

BIRTHDAYS

Raphael (Raffaello Sanzio) 1483, great Italian painter of the Renaissance.

Aristide Briand 1862, French socialist statesman and, with the German statesman Gustav Stresemann, joint winner of the Nobel Peace Prize in 1926.

Dirk Bogarde 1921, British film actor and writer who starred in films such as Joseph Losey's *The Servant*.

KING AND QUEEN OF HOLLYWOOD WED

1920 Douglas Fairbanks and Mary Pickford married today surrounded by friends. Their marriage comes just one year after they broke away from the big Hollywood companies and formed United Artists with Charlie Chaplin. Fairbanks, 35, has had a meteoric rise to fame with productions such as *The Mask of Zorro*. Pickford, 26, became one of the movie industry's first true stars under the direction of D. W. Griffith in *Pollyanna* and *Rebecca of Sunnybrook Farm*. This is her second marriage.

Meltdown in US nuclear reactor

1979 A meltdown in the nuclear reactor core of the Three Mile Island power station at Harrisburg in Pennsylvania caused panic in the eastern United States today. Experts are warning that the reactor core may release radioactive clouds through the region but there are no facilities for a general evacuation of the immediate area. The accident appears to have been caused by the failure of valves controlling cooling water, followed by operator mistakes. Staff at the plant are trying to limit the inevitable release of radioactivity. Local residents are already demanding stricter controls.

RADICALS PROCLAIM PARIS A COMMUNE

1871 Patriotic French radicals buoyed the Revolution of 1789 today proclaimed Paris a "commune of the people". They are seeking to turn France's lost war against the Prussians into a triumph for Jacobin-style socialism by installing proletarian rule. Led by intellectuals and backed by a reformed National Guard, the "communards" aim to set up a municipal government independent of the national government, which has fled to Versailles. The communards are incensed that the government has accepted the humiliating peace terms imposed by the Prussians, including the loss of Alsace and Lorraine. But no one is predicting how long the Commune will last.

• 1912 – FIRST OXFORD–CAMBRIDGE BOAT RACE • 1939 – SPANISH CIVIL WAR ENDS

IDI AMIN FLEES UGANDAN CAPITAL

1979 Uganda's bloody dictator Idi Amin Dada has been driven from the capital, Kampala, and is hiding in the interior. His army is rapidly being worn down by Tanzanian forces sent by President Julius Nyerere to aid Ugandan rebels. Amin's invasion of Northern Tanzania late last year has been his undoing. International quiescence to the excesses of his rule, during which an estimated 300,000 Ugandans have been killed, finally ended when Nyerere struck back. Kampala has been besieged by Tanzanian forces and the Uganda Liberation Front, and even last-minute support for Amin from the Libyan leader Colonel Gaddafi has not helped his retreating army.

1792 Enlightened Swedish King Gustavus III is gunned down at a masked ball.

1871 British monarch Queen Victoria opens the Royal Albert Hall in London.

1891 George-Pierre Seurat, developer of the style of painting known as Pointillism, dies.

1912 British explorer Robert Falcon Scott dies in Antarctica after reaching the Pole.

1970 Peace campaigner and writer Vera Brittain dies.

1989 Space Services Inc of Texas becomes the first private company to make a commercial space launch, sending aloft an instrument package.

COCA-COLA – A TONIC FOR THE BRAIN

1886 A new fizzy drink went on sale at a pharmacy today in Atlanta, Georgia. Coca-Cola, an "Esteemed Brain Tonic and Intellectual Beverage", will cure anything from hysteria to the common cold, claims its inventor, Dr John Pemberton. The non-alcoholic but nonetheless stimulating drink is made from a secret recipe including syrup, caffeine from the cola nut and a tincture of coca leaves. Dr Pemberton's brew faces stiff competition from other elixirs, such as Imperial Inca Cola.

When the white man came, we had the land and they had the Bibles; now they have the land and we have the Bibles.

Dan George,
Canadian Indian chief, 1952.

SOVIET'S FIRST REAL ELECTION SINCE 1917

1989 Communist candidates have been humiliatingly defeated in yesterday's elections for a new-congress – the first contested multi-party election in Soviet history, and the first real choice Soviet citizens have had since the 1917 revolution. Soviet general secretary Mikhail Gorbachev has unleashed a whirlwind with his *perestroika* policy of openness – in Moscow Gorbachev's rival, Russian president Boris Yeltsin, won 90 per cent of the votes, and there were solid opposition gains in the Ukraine and in Leningrad. The Communists have not, of course, lost power – a proportion of the seats in the new assembly were reserved for Party members.

BIRTHDAYS

Edwin Lutyens 1869, British architect known as the last English designer of country houses and for his work on the vice-regal palace of New Delhi.

Pearl Bailey 1918, American jazz singer noted for her role in the all-black version of *Hello Dolly*.

John Major 1943, Former Conservative British Prime Minister 1990–97.

• 1827 – 10,000 ATTEND BEETHOVEN'S FUNERAL • 1973 – US TROOPS LEAVE SOUTH VIETNAM

1855 Afghan leader Dost Mohammed ends 12 years of hostilities by signing a peace treaty with the British.

1950 Léon Blum, French statesman, dies.

1978 British Conservatives hire leading ad agency Saatchi and Saatchi.

1980 Twenty are killed as the funeral of the murdered Salvadorean rebel archbishop Oscar Romero turns into a bloodbath.

1986 James Cagney, US film actor, dies aged 87.

2004 Journalist Alistair Cooke dies, aged 95.

BIRTHDAYS

Francesco Goya 1746, Spanish court painter.

Vincent van Gogh 1853, Dutch Post-Impressionist painter who sold only one of his paintings during his lifetime.

Sean O'Casey 1884, Irish playwright whose best known works were written for the famous Abbey Theatre in Dublin.

Warren Beatty 1937, American film actor and director, brother of Shirley MacLaine.

Eric Clapton 1945, British rock guitarist.

REAGAN SURVIVES ASSASSIN'S BULLET

1981 President Ronald Reagan was seriously wounded today in an assassination attempt as he walked out of a Washington hotel. He was rushed to George Washington Hospital, where a bullet, which passed inches from his heart, has been removed from his lung. The 70-year-old president is reported to have survived the operation well. His assailant, John Hinckley, Jr., fired six shots with a small .22 calibre pistol.

Three other men were wounded: presidential press secretary Jim Brady received a head wound. Hinckley, 25 dropped out of Yale University to work as a disc-jockey. In 1980 he was arrested with a gun at Tennessee airport when former president Jimmy Carter was arriving.

GLORY OF WAR DIES IN CRIMEA

1856 The Crimean War ended today, with the signing of the Treaty of Paris. The devastating power of modern weaponry has shattered any illusions of the glory of arms. Russia has been forced to agree to the demilitarization of the Black Sea and will demolish four of its naval bases there. Russia loses access to the Danube River and must give up claims to Rumanian territory. The European powers – Britain, France, Austria, Prussia and Piedmont – are guaranteeing the Ottoman empire against future Russian expansionism or any claims to the loyalty of Orthodox Christians living in Turkish lands. Britain rules the East Mediterranean once sagain.

AMERICA BUYS ALASKA FROM RUSSIA

1867 "An awful lot of ice for an awful lot of dollars," is how senators in Washington are describing the American proposal to pay $7.2 million to Russia for the frozen wastes of Alaska. An impassioned debate about the merits of buying Alaska is reaching its peak as the Senate votes on the issue. Today the two governments signed a treaty of cession, but the US Senate must now authorize payment. Secretary of State William Seward is adamant that the price is a bargain that will handsomely repay investment when the potential for gold and other minerals is exploited.

• 1842 – FIRST USE OF ETHER AS AN ANAESTHETIC • 2002 – BRITISH QUEEN MOTHER DIES

DALAI LAMA FLEES TIBET

1959 The ruler and spiritual leader of Tibet, the Dalai Lama, has fled to safety in India after Chinese military occupation of his country has made his position in Lhasa impossible. He slipped quietly away on horseback, narrowly escaping capture by the Chinese. On his arrival in West Bengal the young priest-king was welcomed by thousands of Tibetans now also in exile. He was careful to avoid overt criticism of Chinese troops who are reported to be using force in their efforts to eradicate the country's ancient Buddhist faith. Tibet was an independent nation until 1951, when China's People's Liberation Army invaded, crushing all resistance, imposing Chinese law, language and customs. Resentment at the communist suppression of religious customs boiled up into violent protests earlier this year, which were harshly put down. According to Tibetan sources an estimated 65,000 Tibetans lost their lives, while an equivalent number fled to safety in India. The Chinese have installed Panchen Lama in the Dalai Lama's place.

Eiffel changes Paris skyline

1889 Opened in Paris today, the soaring Eiffel Tower is the tallest man-made structure in the world. Only the revolutionary engineering in Alexandre Eiffel's design makes the tower possible: its pylons are curved so precisely that the high wind pressure at the top of the tower is subjected to compress the structure on to its base rather than weakening it. Completed in time for this year's Paris Exposition, which celebrates the centenary of the French Revolution, the 984 ft (300 m) tower is a monument to the achievements of modern engineering.

1820 US missionaries arrive in Honolulu to spread the Word.

1913 New York's Ellis Island receives a record 6745 immigrants in one day.

1939 The British government pledges to defend Poland under the terms of a new tripartite UK/French/Polish treaty.

1985 The British National Coal Board announces a record annual loss of £2225 million.

1989 The master of the *Exxon Valdez* tanker responsible for polluting a vast stretch of Alaskan waters is sacked for drunkenness by the Exxon company.

BIRTHDAYS

René Descartes 1596, French philosopher.

Franz Joseph Haydn 1732, Austrian composer.

Nikolai Gogol 1809, Russian writer whose novel *Dead Souls* is considered one of the finest ever.

Robert Bunsen 1811, German physicist and chemist and inventor of the Bunsen burner.

Al Gore 1948, US Vice-President under Clinton.

• 1855 – CHARLOTTE BRONTË DIES • 1980 – DEATH OF JESSE OWENS

APRIL

LATEST PARIS FASHIONS

1867 Twelve years after staging her first great exhibition – in emulation of the London Exhibition of 1851 – France is again showing off her achievements to the rest of Europe. This year's star attraction at the Paris World Fair is the capital itself, which has been transformed by the rebuilding programmes of Baron Georges Haussmann. The remodelled capital has 85 miles (137 km) of new streets with wide roadways and pavements fringed with trees. The height and façade of all houses and shops along these boulevards have been subject to approval by M. Haussmann

and his inspectors. The city also boasts a new drainage and water system and a landscaped park, the Bois de Boulogne. The finest gem in Paris's refurbished crown will be the luxurious new opera house, which is currently under construction.

April Fool's Day: This is the day upon which we are reminded of what we are on the other three hundred and sixty-four.

Mark Twain, in *Pudd'nhead Wilson's Calendar*, 1894

1204 Death of Eleanor of Aquitaine, wife of Henry II of England.

1795 Martial law is declared in France as food shortages spark riots.

1891 A telephone link between London and Paris comes into operation.

1924 HMV introduces the first gramophone to change records automatically.

1945 US invades Japanese island of Okinawa.

1976 Death of Max Ernst, German-born Surrealist artist and leader of the Cologne Dada group.

1988 Iraq is accused of using poison gas on Kurdish villagers.

2001 Slobodan Milosevic, former Yugoslavian president, is arrested.

BERLIN BLOCKADE SEGREGATES SOVIETS

1948 Relations between former wartime allies are strained following tough Soviet checks on all Western transport entering Berlin. The city, divided into four occupation zones administered by France,

Britain, the US and the Soviet Union – is isolated within Soviet-controlled east Germany, and the western Allies fear the Soviets are planning a complete blockade of the former capital. The Soviets say they are only responding to the Allies' decision to unify their three zones into one West German zone.

BIRTHDAYS

William Harvey 1578, British physician and anatomist who discovered the circulation of the blood.

Prince Otto Eduard Leopold von Bismarck 1815, Prussian statesman and first chancellor of the German Empire.

Sergei Rachmaninov 1873, Russian composer whose works include *Rhapsody on a Theme by Paganini*.

• 1984 – MARVIN GAYE SHOT DEAD • 1960 – US LAUNCHES 1ST WEATHER SATELLITE

1810 Napoleon Bonaparte marries Marie Louise, daughter of the Austrian emperor.

1860 The first Italian parliament meets in Turin.

1921 The IRA first obtain Tommy guns from two gunsmiths in Hartford, Connecticut, USA.

1974 Death of Georges Pompidou, President of France.

1979 Prime Minister Menachem Begin is the first Israeli leader to make an official visit to Egypt.

2005 Pope John-Paul II dies, aged 84.

BIRTHDAYS

Hans Christian Andersen 1805, Danish writer of fairy tales.

Émile Zola 1840, French realist novelist whose books included *Nana*, *Germinal* and *La Terre*.

Sir Alec Guinness 1914, British actor who won an Oscar for *The Bridge on the River Kwai*.

Sir Jack Brabham 1926, Australian world champion motor racing driver.

Marvin Gaye 1939, American soul singer and one of the foremost Tamla Motown artists.

ARGENTINA'S JUNTA SNATCHES FALKLANDS

1982 The British South Atlantic dependency of the Falklands Islands is now in the hands of Argentinian military forces. Falklands governor Rex Hunt ordered the company of British Marines stationed in the island's capital, Port Stanley, to surrender when it became clear that they were massively outnumbered by the invasion force. Fears were raised last week when a party of Argentinian "scrap metallers" landed on the sparsely populated British island of South Georgia, 150 miles (240 km) away. Observers believe that the military junta in Buenos Aires, led by President Leopoldo Galtieri, may have read the British Foreign Office's silence on this as a sign that Britain is prepared to give up her costly commitment to the 2000 islanders, the vast majority of whom reject Argentina's claim to their homeland. The British government is now discussing the possibility of sending a task force to eject the invaders.

I never heard tell of any clever man that came of entirely stupid people.
Thomas Carlyle, Scottish historian, in a speech in Edinburgh, 1886.

KHMER ROUGE GENOCIDE EXPOSED

1979 Vietnamese soldiers now occupying Cambodia are showing the world the unspeakable brutality of Khmer Rouge leader Pol Pot's ousted communist regime. Mass graves containing piles of skulls and bones of at least 2000 people have been found near the town of Stung Treng in north-eastern Cambodia. The new Vietnamese-backed administration in the Cambodian capital Phnom Penh estimates that one million people may have perished during Pol Pot's three-year experiment to take his people back to "Year Zero". A member of Ho Chi Minh's Indo-Chinese Communist Party in the 1940s, Pol Pot committed his Khmer regime to a programme of enforced collectivization, involving the mass evacuation of city-dwellers to the Cambodian countryside. Many of the victims of this radical policy were either worked to death or murdered for resisting the Khmer Rouge's chilling brand of ideological purism.

• 1792 – US STRIKES 1ST SILVER DOLLAR • 1991 – SOVIET COAL MINERS GO ON STRIKE

JUSTICE FOR LINDBERGH

1936 German-born carpenter Bruno Hauptmann today went to the electric chair for the kidnap and murder of the 20-month-old baby son of aviation hero Charles Lindbergh and his wife Anne. The execution had been delayed pending an appeal, which was turned down. Hauptmann proclaimed his innocence throughout the trial last year and denied receiving a $50,000 ransom and bludgeoning the child to death.

Jesse James bites the dust

1882 The notorious outlaw Jesse James, head of the James Gang and mastermind of countless bank and train robberies, was gunned down today at his home in St Joseph, Missouri. Neighbours were shocked to learn that the man they knew as Thomas Howard had a $10,000 price tag on his head. James met his end at the hands of a new recruit to the gang, Bob Ford, who was staying with James, his wife and two children. James's 20-year life of crime began at the end of the Civil War after an apprenticeship with the pro-Confederate band of guerrilla fighters led by William Quantrill. After the war, James and his brother Frank founded their own gang. But in 1876 an attempted bank raid in Northfield, Minnesota went wrong and the gang was decimated.

WINDSOR JEWELS FETCH £31 MILLION

1987 Jewellery worn by the woman who once charmed a British king off his throne was snapped up today. The auction in Geneva included rings, necklaces and brooches belonging to the Duchess of Windsor, who died a year ago. The £31 million raised will go to medical research. Observers believe that buyers, including Elizabeth Taylor and Joan Collins, were more interested in the "Edward and Mrs Simpson" connections than the real worth of the items.

1862 Death of Sir James Clark Ross, English explorer.

1922 In Russia, Joseph Stalin is appointed General Secretary of the Communist Party.

1982 Buenos Aires celebrates the invasion of the Falkland Islands while the UN says Argentina must withdraw.

1991 Graham Greene, author, dies aged 86.

1991 Death of Martha Graham, dancer, choreographer and pioneer of contemporary dance in the USA.

BIRTHDAYS

Henry Luce 1898, American publisher who founded *Time, Life* and *Fortune* magazines.

Marlon Brando 1924, American Method actor who won Oscars for *On the Waterfront* and *The Godfather*.

Doris Day 1924, American actress and singer who delighted audiences with musicals such as *The Pajama Game* and *Calamity Jane*.

Helmut Kohl 1930, German statesman twice elected chancellor.

• 1784 – INDIA ACT PASSED IN BRITAIN • 1897 – DEATH OF GERMAN COMPOSER BRAHMS

1687 James II of England issues a Declaration of Indulgence.

1774 Death of Oliver Goldsmith, English dramatist, poet and novelist whose work includes *She Stoops to Conquer*.

1849 Prussia's Frederick William IV is elected Emperor of Germany but refuses to take the crown.

1963 The Beatles snatch the first five places in the US singles charts with "Can't Buy Me Love", "Twist and Shout", "She Loves You", "I Want to Hold Your Hand" and "Please Please Me".

1979 Zulfikar Ali Bhutto, the ousted prime minister of Pakistan, is hanged by the military regime for the alleged murder of a political opponent.

1981 Cancer-sufferer Bob Champion wins the Grand National on Aldaniti.

BIRTHDAYS

Muddy Waters 1915, American blues singer and guitarist whose hits include "I've Got My Mojo Working" and "Mannish Boy".

Heath Ledger 1979, Australian actor who won a posthumous Oscar for *The Dark Knight* in 2009.

DREAM-MAKER KING SHOT DEAD

1968 Civil rights leader Dr Martin Luther King, the man who inspired black and white Americans with his eloquence, vision and compassion, was today shot dead by an unidentified white assassin at a motel in Memphis, Tennessee. The son of a preacher, Dr King became world famous in 1963 for his "I have a Dream" speech in which he spelt out his vision for America's poor, both black and white. Dr King first played a major role in the civil rights movement in 1955 when he led a year-long bus boycott in protest against segregation on public transport in Montgomery, Alabama. Afterwards he established the South Christian Leadership Conference, which used non-violent marches and protests as a way of drawing attention to the issues of black rights and poverty. At the time of his death, King was planning a multi-racial Poor People's March.

MURDOCH TRIES TO END UGLY WAR IN WAPPING

1986 Media mogul Rupert Murdoch is ready to make peace with the workers who have been trying to disrupt operations at his new factory at Wapping in London's docklands. The plant's new technology has been installed at the expense of compositors, now out of work. Murdoch is hoping that the offer of giving the old Gray's Inn Road plant, in central London, to the printers' union will bring the acrimonious dispute to an end. The strike, involving some 2000 print workers, has affected production of a number of Murdoch's papers, which are being produced by management while journalists — traditionally allies of the printers — have been told they will be fired if they fail to cooperate.

If a man hasn't discovered something he would die for, he isn't fit to live.

Martin Luther King, who died today, 1968.

• **1896 – GOLD DISCOVERED IN THE YUKON** • **1949 – NORTH ATLANTIC TREATY SIGNED**

SOLIDARITY TURNS THE CORNER

1989 The end of communist rule in Poland is in sight after today's historic political pact between the independent trade union federation Solidarity and the government of Wojciech Jaruzelski. After weeks of negotiations, Solidarity has finally won the right to contest partially free elections and to publish its own newspaper. The pact also provides for a democratically elected senate and president. Opinion polls will be held in June. Solidarity has been banned by the Polish authorities since 1982. Its re-legalization is well overdue, since martial law was finally lifted in the middle of 1983. However, throughout the ban, the organization continued to receive widespread support among a Polish population that is desperate for saviours. Many hopes are now riding on Solidarity and its charismatic leader, Lech Walesa. The current regime's apparent willingness to allow Solidarity to take part in the political process is widely acknowledged to be an indication of its own inability to provide answers to Poland's mounting economic problems in the absence of popular support.

Power tends to corrupt, and absolute power corrupts absolutely. Great men are almost always bad men . . . there is no worse heresy than that the office sanctifies the holder of it.

Lord Acton, British historian, 1887.

WILDE ABOUT THE BOY

1895 A trial has opened at the Old Bailey. Playwright Oscar Wilde, the author of the highly successful plays *The Importance of Being Earnest* and *Lady Windemere's Fan*, is suing the Marquess of Queensberry for libel. The Marquess is alleged to have left a note at Mr Wilde's club accusing him of sodomy. Now the Marquess is threatening to produce an impressive list of witnesses to testify in support of his allegation. Insiders claim that the temper of the boxing-mad Marquess has been sorely tried by his son, Alfred, who has made no secret of the intimate nature of his relationship with Mr Wilde.

1874 Johann Strauss's *Die Fledermaus* receives its premiere in Vienna.

1944 The Germans begin the deportation of the Jews from Hungary.

1960 The film *Ben Hur* wins 10 Oscars.

1964 General MacArthur, commander of the Pacific forces in World War II, dies.

1975 Nationalist Chinese leader Chiang Kai-shek dies in Taiwan aged 87.

1989 Vietnam announces it will withdraw its troops from Cambodia by September 1989.

1991 President Bush orders US Air Force transport planes to drop supplies to Kurdish refugees in northern Iraq.

BIRTHDAYS

Herbert von Karajan 1908, Austrian conductor noted for his association with the Berlin Philharmonic Orchestra.

Bette Davis 1908, American actress best-known for *Whatever Happened to Baby Jane?*

Gregory Peck 1916, American actor noted both for his fine film performances and his work for humanitarian causes.

• 1793 – WASHINGTON TO BECOME US CAPITAL • 1955 – WINSTON CHURCHILL RESIGNS

1199 Richard I of England dies from an infected wound while on Crusade.

1520 Raphael, Italian Renaissance painter and architect, dies.

1830 The Church of the Latterday Saints is founded.

1843 English poet William Wordsworth is appointed Poet Laureate.

1944 Pay As You Earn Income Tax is introduced in Britain.

1965 The US launches the first commercial communications satellite, *Early Bird*.

1968 Pierre Trudeau is Prime Minister of Canada.

2009 Italian earthquake kills 294 people.

2014 US actor Mickey Rooney dies, aged 93.

BIRTHDAYS

Harry Houdini 1874, American magician and escapologist.

Anthony Fokker 1890, Dutch aircraft designer.

Sir John Betjeman 1906, British Poet Laureate loved for his gentle social satire.

Pete Tosh 1945, Jamaican reggae artist and founder member of the Wailers.

BONAPARTE ABDICATES

1814 French emperor Napoleon Bonaparte was today forced to abdicate unconditionally. The beginning of the end for the ambitious Corsican was his defeat last October at the so-called "Battle of the Nations", where he lost a third of his half-million troops. Bonaparte refused to negotiate and in an audacious manoeuvre inflicted reverses on the advancing allied armies. However, it soon became apparent that the allies could outwit him by quickly reaching Paris and setting up a new government. From his headquarters at Fontainebleau, Napoleon received news of the French people's enthusiasm for the return of the Bourbons and had to step down.

OLYMPICS ANEW

1896 A modern version of the ancient Olympic Games was opened today in Athens, initiated by French aristocrat Baron Pierre de Coubertin, who hopes to stimulate interest in physical fitness and promote understanding between nations. The first record of the Games dates from 776 BC, although it is thought that they were already 500 years old by then. The venue was Olympia, home of the Greek god Zeus in whose honour they were held every four years – until Greece lost its independence and the Christian Roman emperor, Theodosius, abolished them to discourage paganism, in AD 394.

African presidents shot down

1994 The presidents of the African states of Rwanda and Burundi were killed when their plane crashed near Kigali, Rwanda. Some observers say the aircraft was brought down by rocket fire. Juvenal Habyarimana and Cyprian Ntayamira were returning from a meeting of African leaders in Tanzania, set up to discuss ways of ending the ethnic violence in their countries. Violent clashes between the Hutu tribe and the minority Tutsis has plagued both states for centuries. The deaths of the presidents could worsen the situation. Heavy fighting has already been reported around the presidential palace in Rwanda and explosions have taken place in Kigali.

• 1580 – **LONDON'S ST PAUL'S DAMAGED BY EARTHQUAKE** • 1917 – **THE US ENTERS WWI**

VESUVIUS KILLS HUNDREDS

1906 Hundreds of Italians living in the vicinity of Mount Vesuvius have been killed in a cataclysmic volcanic eruption. Lava from the volcano has devastated the nearby town of Ottaiano and in Naples, some nine miles away, buildings have collapsed under the weight of the debris from the eruption. The volcano has been active since AD 79 when, after years of lying dormant, it erupted with spectacular, and tragic, effect. The thriving towns of Pompeii and Stabiae were buried under ash and the city of Herculaneum under a mud flow. The smoking giant has frequent outbursts, usually harmless. This latest is one of the most destructive in its fractious history and many are wondering how long they can go on living in its unpredictable shadow.

You have a row of dominoes set up; you knock over the first one, and what will happen to the last one is that it will go over very quickly.

President Dwight D. Eisenhower on the "domino effect", during the Battle of Dien Bien Phu, 1954.

TURPIN HANGS

1739 Travellers in northern England may once more sleep easily in their beds after the hanging today of notorious highwayman Dick Turpin. The innkeeper's son from Essex had been operating in the area for about two years, after working on the fringes of London with his then partner-in-crime Tom King. The duo, whose haunts included Hampstead Heath, built on the myth of highwaymen started by the dashing French rascal Claude Duval. A mob took away Turpin's body for burial after it was cut down from the Mount, outside the walls of York city.

1614 El Greco, Cretan-born painter, sculptor and architect, dies in Spain.

1862 General Ulysses Grant's troops win the Battle of Shiloh.

1943 Chemist Albert Hoffman synthesizes the drug lysergic acid diethylamide (LSD).

1943 British economist John Maynard Keynes launches a plan for post-war reconstruction.

1947 Death of Henry Ford, American car manufacturer.

1971 Nixon promises to withdraw 100,000 troops from Vietnam by Christmas.

1978 President Carter backpedals on building the neutron bomb.

BIRTHDAYS

Ole Kirk Christiansen 1891, Danish toymaker who invented Lego.

Billie Holiday 1915, American jazz singer.

Ravi Shankar 1920, Indian sitar player.

David Frost 1939, British television presenter and producer.

Francis Ford Coppola 1939, American film producer best known for *The Godfather*.

• 1948 – WORLD HEALTH ORGANIZATION FOUNDED • 1958 – 3,000 MARCH FOR CND

217 AD Roman emperor Caracalla is assassinated.

1513 Spanish explorer Juan Ponce de Léon discovers Florida.

1904 Britain and France sign the Entente Cordiale.

1925 The Australian government and the British Colonial Office offer low-interest loans to encourage 500,000 Britons to emigrate to Australia.

1904 Russian ballet dancer, Vaslav Nijinsky, dies.

1962 Cuban leader Fidel Castro offers to ransom prisoners held since the invasion of the Bay of Pigs.

1990 British golfer Nick Faldo wins his second successive US Masters.

BIRTHDAYS

Mary Pickford 1893, Canadian-born actress who became known as "America's Sweetheart".

Sir Adrian Boult 1889.

Ian Smith 1919, Rhodesian prime minister who unilaterally declared independence from Britain in 1965 in the interests of retaining white supremacy.

Dorothy Tutin 1930.

Julian Lennon 1963.

PICASSO DRAWS LAST BREATH

1973 Spanish painter Pablo Picasso died today at his chateau at Mougins after suffering a heart attack. He was 91. His genius began to flower after he moved from his native Barcelona to Paris in 1904. Stimulated by the unique intellectual and

artistic climate of the French capital, he threw off his "blue period" of limited colour variation and gloomy subject matter to concentrate on a lighter style, known as his "rose period". Picasso's early spirit of artistic adventure led him to originate the abstract style that became synonymous with his name – Cubism. His legacy consists of 140,000 paintings and drawings, 100,000 engravings, 300 sculptures and thousands of other documents, such as the menu cards he illustrated to pay for his dinners in the early days in Paris. Nevertheless, he still found the time for enjoying the good life, beautiful women and bullfighting.

Thatcher dies in hotel

2013 The first lady Prime Minister of Britain and one of the most controversial leaders of recent times, Margaret Thatcher, has died, aged 87. The Iron Lady was staying at the Ritz hotel in central London, recovering from the latest in a series of strokes that had drastically reduced her health in recent years. Thatcher divided opinion during her Premiership, leading the country into war with Argentina in 1982 over the Falkland Islands and breaking the union powers during the Miners' Strikes of 1984-5. She has been granted a ceremonial funeral with full military honours.

Whoso, therefore, ill-treats, beats or pushes any of the natives, whether he be in right or wrong, shall, in their presence, be scourged with 50 lashes, in order that they may perceive that such conduct is against our will; and that we are desirous to deal with them in all love and friendship, according to the order of our superiors.

Commander Jan van Riebeeck's orders to his men before they disembark from three Dutch East India Company ships to found a settlement at the Cape of Good Hope, 1652.

• **1838 – BON VOYAGE TO THE *GREAT WESTERN*!** • **1953 – KENYA JAILS KENYATTA**

1963 The British film *Lawrence of Arabia,* starring Peter O'Toole, won seven Oscars in Los Angeles tonight, including Best Picture, Best Director, for David Lean, and Best Score, for composer Maurice Jarre.

1553 Death of François Rabelais, the French satirical writer.

1869 The Hudson Bay Company cedes its territory to Canada.

1882 Death of Dante Gabriel Rossetti, English painter and poet who co-founded the Pre-Raphaelite Brotherhood.

1940 The Germans invade Norway and Denmark.

1945 Dietrich Bonhoeffer, German theologian involved with anti-Hitler conspirators, is hanged In Flossenbürg concentration camp.

1960 An assassination attempt on South African president Vorwoerd fails.

1981 *Nature* magazine publishes the longest-ever scientific word, which boasts 207,000 letters.

The physician can bury his mistake, but the architect can only advise his client to plant vines.

Frank Lloyd Wright, American architect, died today, 1959.

SADDAM STATUE TOPPLES WITH BAGHDAD

2003 Scenes of joy greeted US tanks as they rolled into the Iraqi capital Baghdad, confirming that Saddam Hussein is no longer in power. In the main square, a group of Iraqis tried to pull down a statue of Saddam Hussein in a show of contempt for their former leader. They climbed the statue to secure a noose around its neck but were unable to topple it. US troops joined in, using an armoured vehicle to gradually drag down the statue. Just before the statue was down, a US soldier covered the face with a US flag. This was not well received so it was quickly removed and replaced by the old Iraqi flag, to roars of approval. As the statue fell, the crowd jumped on it, chanting as they danced on the fallen effigy, in a symbolic gesture of contempt as it was torn to pieces. They then cut off the head, tied chains around it, and dragged it through the streets. The US military campaign in Iraq is set to continue, although a US Army spokesman has made a very upbeat assessment of the gains made so far in Iraq.

Isambard Kingdom Brunel 1806, English engineer.
Charles Baudelaire 1821, French poet.
Hugh Hefner 1926, American publisher of *Playboy* fame.
Jean Paul Belmondo 1933, French actor who made his name in the films of the 1960s.

• 1865 – END OF BLOODSHED IN US CIVIL WAR • 2005 – CHARLES MARRIES CAMILLA

1809 Austria declares war on France.

1820 British settlers arrive at Algoa Bay, South Africa.

1858 Chinese governor-general Ye Mingchen of Canton dies in Calcutta, a prisoner of the British.

1864 Archduke Maximilian of Austria becomes Emperor of Mexico.

1921 Sun Yat-Sen is elected president of China.

1960 The US Senate passes the Civil Rights Bill.

1974 Golda Meir resigns as Israeli prime minister.

1989 Riots rock Tiblisi, capital of Georgia, USSR.

1989 Nick Faldo becomes the first Briton to win the US Masters.

BIRTHDAYS

William Hazlitt 1778, English critic and essayist.

Joseph Pulitzer 1847, American newspaper proprietor who founded the Pulitzer Prize.

Max von Sydow 1929, Swedish actor who found success at home in Ingmar Bergman films.

Omar Sharif 1932, Egyptian actor whose many films include *Lawrence of Arabia* and *Doctor Zhivago*.

ZAPATA ZAPPED

1919 People's champion Emiliano Zapata was today cut down in a hail of bullets after being ambushed by soldiers of the Carranza regime. Zapata took his first step along the revolutionary path in 1910 when the policies of dictator Porfirio Diaz ensured that land appropriated from the peasants remained in the possession of the wealthy. Power changed hands several times in quick succession, as first Diaz, then Francisco Madera, then Victoriano Huerta were unseated. Throughout this time Zapata fought for acceptance of his plan to return to a communal system of land ownership, under the slogan "Land and Liberty". An alliance with the unpredictable Pancho Villa brought some military successes but eventually ended when Villa's army was defeated. Essentially a man of principle, Zapata died untainted by the desire for power and money evident in some of his lieutenants.

PLANE CRASH KILLS LEADING POLISH DELEGATION

2010 Polish President Lech Kaczynski and other senior Polish figures were killed in a plane crash near Smolensk in Russia. All 95 passengers, including Poland's army chief, its central bank governor, MPs and leading historians were killed as the plane hit trees on its approach to the airport in thick fog. The Polish delegation was flying to Russia to mark the 70th anniversary of the Katyn massacre of Poles by the Soviets during World War II. Aviation experts were split on the issue of blame. Russia blamed the crash on pilot error, saying the crew were ordered to land despite bad weather. Polish experts say Russian air traffic control gave the pilot poor advice.

NORTHERN IRELAND PEACE DEAL

1998 Peace talks between British Prime Minister Tony Blair and the Republic of Ireland's leader Bertie Ahern have ended in an historic agreement on the future of Northern Ireland. Dubbed The Good Friday Agreement, the plan is the result of nearly two years of negotiations. Tony Blair said the accord marked a new beginning: "Today I hope the burden of history can at long last start to be lifted from our shoulders." The agreement includes plans for a Northern Ireland Assembly and cross-border institutions involving the Irish Republic. The proposals will be put to a referendum in May. Bertie Ahern said he hoped now a line could be drawn under Ireland's "bloody past".

• 1841 – *NEW YORK TRIBUNE* FIRST PUBLISHED • 1849 – SAFETY PIN PATENTED

NAZI EICHMANN FINALLY FACES TRIAL

1961 Alleged Nazi war criminal Adolf Eichmann today entered a Jerusalem court to hear the 15 charges against him, 12 of which carry the death penalty. As head of the Gestapo's Jewish section, Adolf Eichmann is said to have been responsible for sending millions of Jews to their deaths during the Second World War. Eichmann fled to Argentina after the war in an attempt to evade capture but was eventually tracked down by the Vienna-based Nazi-hunter Simon Wiesenthal. Wiesenthal then tipped off the Israeli secret service. A team of secret service agents kidnapped Eichmann last year and brought him back to their own country to face a long overdue trial.

GREEN LIGHT FOR ORANGE

1689 The coronation of William III, Prince of Orange, champion of Protestantism, and his wife Mary, Protestant daughter of the deposed Stuart king James II, sets the seal on a remarkable transition of power in Britain. Since arriving last November, William has been involved in negotiations with the Lords and Commons over the future rule of the country. A Bill of Rights that excludes Roman Catholics from the throne, gives political and civil rights to the people and supremacy to parliament, is expected to reach the statute books later in the year. Meanwhile, the nation is breathing a collective sigh of relief at seeing the back of James II, whose obsession with promoting the Catholic cause brought about his downfall.

1713 France cedes Newfoundland and Gibraltar to Britain.

1919 The International Labour Organisation is founded in affiliation with the League of Nations to improve living standards and working conditions.

1951 World War II hero General Douglas MacArthur is stripped of his command by US President Truman, following a disagreement over the Korean War.

1961 Bob Dylan makes his first live appearance when he opens for John Lee Hooker at Gerde's Folk City in Greenwich Village.

1977 Death of Josephine Baker, black American singer and dancer.

2006 Iranian president Mahmoud Ahmadinejad announces that Iran has "joined the club of nuclear countries".

Sir Charles Hallé 1819, German pianist and conductor who emigrated to England and founded the Hallé Orchestra in Manchester.

Joel Grey 1932, American actor and singer who stole the show in the film *Cabaret*.

More pain for the Dust Bowl

1935 Disaster has already struck the hard-pressed folk of America in the shape of the Depression. Now dust storms are threatening half the country. The worst-hit areas are the so-called "Dust Bowl" states of Kansas, Colorado, Wyoming,

Oklahoma, Texas and New Mexico. In the 1920s much of the vast prairie was planted with crops of wheat which degraded the topsoil, leaving the land dusty and arid, ideal for the turbulent prairie winds to whip up into a huge black destructive mass that can devastate homes and crops. The government is being urged to declare the affected area a disaster zone.

• 1929 – CARTOON CHARACTER POPEYE MAKES HIS FIRST APPEARANCE

1817 Death of Charles Messier, French astronomer.

1838 English settlers in South Africa vanquish the Zulus in the Battle of Tugela.

1877 Britain annexes the Transvaal.

1954 Bill Haley and the Comets record "Rock Around the Clock".

1960 Ray Charles wins the Best Male Vocalist Grammy Award.

1981 Death of boxing champion, Joe Louis.

1989 Death of boxing champion, Sugar Ray Robinson.

2004 Cricketer Brian Lara achieves 400 runs, the highest ever score in test cricket.

BIRTHDAYS

Bobby Moore 1941, British footballer who played for England 108 times.

Tom Clancy 1947, American thriller and espionage writer.

Alan Ayckbourn 1949, British dramatist whose plays combine farce with minute observation of British class structure.

David Cassidy 1950, American teenybopper idol.

CONFEDERATES CHALLENGE LINCOLN

1861 Confederate forces today threw down the gauntlet to Republican president Abraham Lincoln by firing on Fort Sumter in Charleston Harbor. The fort has been under threat since the president first took office five weeks ago. Lincoln's opposition to the second Crittenden amendment, which would have allowed states to be either pro-slavery or pro-freedom, resulted in six more states seceding from the Union and joining South Carolina to form the Confederate States of America. Federal troops garrisoned in Fort Sumter and at other military installations within the confederacy are called on to surrender. Lincoln plans to send reinforcements to the beleaguered fort, indicating his determination to bring the rebels to heel. It can only be a matter of time before he mobilizes the vast resources available to his generals. Theoretically outnumbered by a ratio of 2:1 in manpower, and 30:1 in availability of arms, the Confederates can only be hoping that their cause will attract aid from overseas.

RUSSIANS WIN THE HUMAN SPACE RACE

1961 A new phase in the competition for top dog status between the Soviet Union and the United States opened today when Russian cosmonaut Major Yuri Gagarin became the first man in space. The single orbit of the Earth completed by Gagarin in the four-and-a-half ton *Vostok 1* space vehicle took 108 minutes. Gagarin is said to feel fine and shows no immediate signs of the adverse effects that weightlessness and re-entry into the Earth's atmosphere can have on the body.

• 1945 – FRANKLIN D. ROOSEVELT DIES • 1981 – US LAUNCH *COLUMBIA* SPACE VEHICLE

POITIER'S OSCAR BOOST

1964 Sidney Poitier, described as "the world's most handsome black man", won an Oscar tonight for his performance in Ralph Nelson's *The Lilies of the Field*. He is the first black actor ever to receive the award. At a time when the civil rights movement and its white liberal allies seem to be under threat from reactionary forces, Poitier's Oscar is a much-needed morale booster for the black community in America. However, whether Poitier's portrayal of a nice black man with nice wholesome views really deserved the film industry's most prestigious accolade is debatable.

1598 Henry IV of France issues the Edict of Nantes.

1668 John Dryden, British poet and critic, is appointed Poet Laureate.

1829 The House of Commons passes the Catholic Emancipation Act.

1882 The Anti-Semitic League is founded in Prussia.

1904 In the Russo-Japanese War a mine sinks the flagship of the Russian fleet, killing 600.

1935 Imperial Airways and Qantas inaugurate a London to Australia service.

2003 Paula Radcliffe breaks the world record in the London Marathon.

Soviets admit to Katyn massacre

1990 One of the Kremlin's best-kept lies was admitted today after decades of deception: the systematic murder of over 15,000 Polish army officers by the Soviet secret police. This crime, known as the Katyn massacre after the pine forest in Russia where the executions were carried out in the spring of 1940, has always been officially blamed on the Germans, despite evidence to the contrary. The announcement by the Soviet news agency Tass coincides with the visit to Moscow of the Polish leader, General Jaruzelski. The conspiracy of silence over Katyn began as a diplomatic necessity in World War II, when to tarnish the image of "Uncle Joe" Stalin would have spoiled the Allies' propaganda campaign. After the war, western governments preferred to continue the lie rather than admit to their part in the deception.

BIRTHDAYS

Frederick North, Earl of Guildford 1732, English prime minister who introduced the Tea Act that led to the Boston Tea Party.

Thomas Jefferson 1743, American president responsible for drafting the Declaration of Independence and founding the Democratic Party.

Seamus Heaney 1939, Irish poet who won the Nobel Prize in Literature in 1995.

TRIUMPH FOR WOODS

1997 American golfer Tiger Woods has stunned the sporting world and rewritten golf history. He has become both the youngest player (at 21) and the first black player ever to win the US Masters tournament. He also thrilled crowds of supporters by beating the previous record with his 72-hole score of 18-under-par 270, having the widest ever winning margin of 12 strokes, and breaking records with his totals for the last 54 holes, as well as the second and third rounds. His brilliant career is just starting.

• 1860 – US PONY EXPRESS DELIVERS FIRST MAIL • 1939 – MUSSOLINI INVADES ALBANIA

1471 In the English Wars of the Roses, the Yorkists defeat the Lancastrians at the Battle of Barnet.

1759 George Frederick Handel dies in London.

1814 The US repeals its trade embargo with Britain.

1860 Fort Sumter falls to the Confederate Army.

1931 Britain gets its first Highway Code.

1951 Death of Ernest Bevin, British Labour politician and minister of labour during World War II.

1954 Soviet diplomat Vladimir Petrov seeks political asylum.

1983 The first cordless telephone is introduced in Britain.

BIRTHDAYS

Philip II 1527, Spanish king who sent his armada to conquer England in 1588 and met with defeat.

Francis Duvalier 1907, Haitian president and dictator nicknamed "Papa Doc", legendary for his corruption and brutality.

Rod Steiger 1925, American actor who won an Oscar for *In the Heat of the Night*.

DRAMA OFF STAGE AS LINCOLN SHOT

1865 President Abraham Lincoln is failing fast after being shot in the back of the head at point-blank range. The president and Mrs Lincoln were attending a performance of *Our American Cousin* at Ford's Theatre in Washington when the attack occurred. His assailant, John Wilkes Booth, a member of one of America's most distinguished acting families and a Confederate fanatic, then jumped from the box on to the stage, shouting "Sic semper tyrannis! ['Thus always to tyrants'] – The South is avenged". He then ran out of the theatre, limping heavily, mounted a horse and galloped off into the night. Lincoln will go down in history as the man who saved the Union and in the process brought about the emancipation of America's black slaves. In his own words: "If I could save the Union without freeing any slave I would do it; and if I could save it by freeing all the slaves I would do it; and if I could save it by freeing some and leaving others alone, I would also do that." A manhunt is underway to bring the assailant to justice.

NIGHT OF TERROR

2014 Nigeria's militant Islamist group Boko Haram has abducted more than 200 girls from a boarding school in the northern town of Chibok. Reports claim an estimated 200 heavily armed militants arrived at night in 20 vehicles to steal supplies and kidnap the students. Active since 2002, Boko Haram, which wants to set up an Islamist caliphate in Africa's largest economy, has fought back against an army offensive and killed thousands in bomb and gun attacks, striking as far afield as the central city of Jos and the capital Abuja.

• 1903 – TYPHUS VACCINE DISCOVERED • 1986 – FEMINIST SIMONE DE BEAUVOIR DIES

BOMBERS TARGET THE BOSTON FINISH LINE

2013 As runners approached the finish line of the annual Boston Marathon, two bombs exploded, killing 3 people and injuring 264. Two Chechens suspected of the attack were identified. One, Tamerlan Tsarnaev, was shot and killed after a police chase on 18 April. His brother, Dzhokhar, was captured the next day and charged with use of a weapon of mass destruction and malicious destruction of property resulting in death. More than 2000 runners completed the final mile of the course a month after the bombings as a tribute to the victims of the attack.

MUTINY AT SEA

1797 Revolutionary fever has spread across the Channel and infected the Royal Navy's fighting men at Spithead and Nore. The mutinies in the Channel fleet are caused by arrears in pay, bad food, ill treatment, lack of leave and arduous blockade duty. The unrest could not have come at a worse time, with Britain at war with Revolutionary France. Admirals Jervis and Howe are threatening draconian measures if order is not quickly restored.

1753 Dr Samuel Johnson publishes his Dictionary.

1764 Death of Madame de Pompadour, powerful mistress of King Louis XVI of France.

1865 President Andrew Johnson is sworn in as American president.

1925 John Singer Sargent, American painter specializing in society portraits, dies in London.

1945 Looted Nazi art treasures, including paintings by Rubens, Goya, Raphael and Leonardo da Vinci are recovered.

1988 Greta Garbo dies in New York. She was 84.

1998 Death of Pol Pot, aged 70, cruel dictator of Kampuchea (now Cambodia).

THE UNSINKABLE DOES THE UNTHINKABLE

1912 The British luxury liner the *Titanic* has sunk after hitting an iceberg during her maiden voyage to New York. Over 1500 people are feared drowned in the icy waters of the North Atlantic. The vessel collided with the "skyscraper" sized iceberg shortly before midnight on April 14, causing a 300-foot (91 m) gash in the vessel's right side. Five of the ship's watertight compartments were

punctured, causing the ship to sink at around 2.20 am. The ship's double-bottomed hull, divided into 16 watertight compartments, was said to make her unsinkable. Reports from some of the 691 survivors suggest that there were not enough spaces on the lifeboats for the 2224 people on board. More lives would have been lost if the liner *Carpathia* had not reached the *Titanic* within 80 minutes.

BIRTHDAYS

Leonardo da Vinci 1452, Italian painter, sculptor, architect, scientist, engineer and inventor.

Henry James 1843, American novelist who spent much of his life in England.

Bessie Smith 1894, American singer considered by many the finest female blues singer ever.

• 1793 – £5 NOTES ISSUED IN ENGLAND • 1989 – HILLSBOROUGH FOOTBALL DISASTER

1446 Death of Filippo Brunelleschi, celebrated Florentine architect.

1828 Death of Spanish painter, Francisco de Goya.

1883 Paul Kruger becomes president of the South African republic.

1902 More than 20,000 people rally in Dublin Park to protest against British government legislation.

1917 Vladimir Ilyich Lenin returns to Russia after three years of exile.

1953 The royal yacht *Britannia* is launched.

1975 The communist Khmer Rouge seize Phnom Penh, capital of Cambodia.

BIRTHDAYS

Jules Hardouin-Mansart 1646. French court architect to Louis XIV; who designed the Gallery of Mirrors at Versailles.

Giovanni Batista Tiepolo 1696, Venetian rococo painter.

Sir Charles Chaplin 1889, English-born comedian much loved for his portrayal of a tramp in baggy trousers and bowler hat.

Henry Mancini 1924, American composer responsible for many film scores.

PRINCE CHARLES NOT SO BONNY

1746 The hopes of the grandson of the deposed Catholic king of England, James II, regaining the throne of England for his family were dealt a severe blow today at Culloden Moor in Scotland. It was here that the so-called "Young Pretender", Charles Edward Stuart, decided to take on the might of the British Army under the command of William, Duke of Cumberland, the second son of George II. "Bonnie Prince Charlie" Stuart's 5000 Highlanders were no match for Cumberland's 9000 soldiers, many of them regulars equipped with the latest weaponry. Many are questioning the wisdom of Stuart's decision to make a stand on flat ground which offered every advantage to Cumberland's artillery. Stuart managed to escape the carnage and is thought to be in hiding somewhere in the area.

TRAGEDY ON VIRGINIA CAMPUS AS GUNMAN KILLS 32

2007 Student Cho Seung-Hui went on the rampage at Virginia Tech University in Blacksburg killing 32 students and staff in the US's worst mass shooting in history. At 7.15 in the morning police were called to West Ambler Johnston Hall where they found the bodies of two students – Cho's first victims. Around two hours after the first shootings, Cho opened fire again, this time at Norris Hall, killing a further 30 people. Police arrived at the scene as the last shots were fired and discovered Cho's body among those of his victims. He had turned the gun on himself.

SHOOT TO KILL

1988 The Palestine Liberation Organization's military commander, Khalil al-Wazir, was today mown down by bullets in the Tunisian capital. The PLO say the killing is the work of an Israeli hit squad. Mr al-Wazir was a thorn in the Israelis' sides, masterminding attacks into Israel from Lebanon. He was also thought to have orchestrated the recent Palestinian unrest in the occupied territories.

• 1990 – NELSON MANDELA HOSTS LONDON CONCERT CELEBRATING HIS FREEDOM

LUTHER'S DIET OF WORMS

1521 The congress of church and state heads meeting at Worms to decide the case of the nonconformist German priest Martin Luther has granted him an extra day's grace. At this afternoon's meeting Luther requested time to reflect on the assembly's demand that he acknowledge or deny the vast body of heretical works attributed to him. The 38-year-old firebrand is not without friends in high places, despite the open hostility of the Holy Roman Emperor Charles V. His refusal to accept the authority of the Church of Rome over individual conscience and the Bible has struck a sympathetic chord in many quarters of German society. Luther's supporters fear that any moral triumph will be at the price of a ban on his writings.

CUBA'S BAY OF PIGS INVADED

1961 A small force of about 1300 Cuban exiles has been thwarted in its aim of toppling the Communist regime of Fidel Castro. The invasion force ran into the Cuban army soon after landing in the Bahia de Cochinos (Bay of Pigs) and its members were either captured or shot.

In this world nothing is certain but death and taxes.

Benjamin Franklin, who died today, 1790.

1860 The first match between an American and English boxer.

1924 Benito Mussolini's Fascist party wins the Italian elections.

1970 Country singer Johnny Cash performs for President Nixon in the East Room of the White House.

1982 The Polish Solidarity organization becomes legal after a 10-year ban.

1990 Moscow imposes a blockade upon Lithuania in an attempt to stem demands for independence.

2003 Death of John Paul Getty, aged 84, American oil magnate.

2014 Colombian Nobel Prize winning writer, Gabriel García Márquez dies aged 87.

BIRTHDAYS

Sir Leonard Woolley 1880, British archaeologist most famous for his excavations at Ur in southern Iraq.

Nikita Khruschev 1894, Russian politician, prime minister of the USSR 1958–64.

James Last 1929, German bandleader, composer and arranger of international easy-listening renown.

LIBYAN EMBASSY SNIPERS KILL WOMAN PC

1984 A peaceful demonstration in London's St James's Square turned into a battlefield today when a gunman inside the Libyan embassy opened fire on the protesters. A tragic victim of the outrage was 25-year-old woman police constable Yvonne Fletcher, one of several police officers on duty, who later died of her injuries in hospital. Ten other people were injured, none seriously. The embassy has been sealed off by police while the British government plans its response. Politicians are calling for diplomatic bags to be searched in future to prevent the importation of arms.

• 1790 – BENJAMIN FRANKLIN DIES • 1980 – RHODESIA BECOMES INDEPENDENT ZIMBABWE

1775 Paul Revere rides from Charleston to Lexington to warn US militiamen of the British advance.

1791 William Wilberforce's parliamentary campaign to abolish the slave trade meets defeat in the House of Commons.

1942 US Bomber aircraft attack Tokyo.

1949 The Republic of Ireland Act comes into force.

1954 President Neguib of Egypt resigns.

1968 An American tycoon buys London Bridge for £1 million, confusing it with Tower Bridge.

1991 Publisher Robert Maxwell launches his Mirror Group Newspapers towards public flotation.

BIRTHDAYS

Lucrezia Borgia 1480, Italian illegitimate daughter of Pope Alexander VI who was married three times by the age of 18.

Leopold Stokowski 1882, English-born conductor of America's leading orchestras.

Malcolm Marshall 1958, Barbadian fast bowler who regularly pulverized the English cricket teams.

EINSTEIN DIES

1955 Albert Einstein died in his sleep today at Princeton Hospital, aged 75. Regarded as one of the most creative intellects in human history, Einstein was awarded the Nobel Prize in Physics in 1921, for his photoelectric law and his work in the field of theoretical physics. His theory of relativity was verified by the Royal Society of London in 1919. When Hitler became Chancellor of Germany in 1933, Einstein moved to America, where his recommendation that US scientists develop an A-bomb ahead of the Nazis marked the beginning of the Manhattan Project. The horror of Hiroshima in 1945 shocked Einstein into issuing letters calling for the prevention of the bomb's use in the future.

SAN FRANCISCO TUMBLES IN MASSIVE EARTHQUAKE

1906 At 5.13 this morning San Francisco was hit by the most violent earthquake ever recorded in its history. Worst hit by the earthquake is the central business district, where an estimated 512 blocks are thought to have been either destroyed or to be currently under threat. First estimates suggest that as many as 700 people may be dead and 250,000 made homeless. Earthquakes have hit San Francisco before – in 1864, 1898 and 1900 – but none has wrought such widespread devastation.

• 1934 – WORLD'S FIRST LAUNDRETTE OPENS, IN FORT WORTH, TEXAS

HUGE EXPLOSION SHAKES OKLAHOMA CITY

1995 A lorry packed with 4,000 pounds of explosives has blown up a government building in Oklahoma City, killing 168 people. The blast happened just after 09.00 local time when most workers were in their offices. Chaos ensued as paramedics treated survivors on the pavement and rescue workers dug others from the rubble. The ten-storey Alfred Murrah building housed the Federal Bureau of Alcohol, Tobacco and Firearms, as well as social security offices and a nursery. President Bill Clinton vowed "swift, certain and severe punishment" for those behind the attack. "The United States will not tolerate and I will not allow the people of this country to be intimidated by evil cowards," he said. The attack comes exactly two years after the siege at Waco, Texas and some commentators are linking the two. However, there are also suspicions that right-wing groups, or Middle Eastern terrorists are involved.

1588 Death of Paolo Veronese, Italian painter of the Golden Age of Venice.

1689 Death of Queen Christina of Sweden who abdicated in 1654.

1824 British poet Lord Byron dies.

1933 Britain bans all trade with the USSR.

1948 The US tests a plutonium bomb in the Marshall Islands.

1966 Australian troops leave Sydney to join US forces in Vietnam.

1983 A car bomb destroys the US embassy in Beirut.

1999 The German parliament returns to the newly-renovated Reichstag building in Berlin.

2004 Two fuel trains collide in North Korea, causing 3,000 casualties.

WACO CULT SIEGE ENDS IN INFERNO

1993 At least 70 cult members are feared dead as fire swept through the besieged headquarters of the Branch Davidian sect near Waco, Texas. Cult leader David Koresh is not thought to have survived. White House officials say the fire was started deliberately by cult members when the FBI began a dawn raid. The cult's buildings have been surrounded since February when four agents with the Bureau of Alcohol, Tobacco and Firearms were killed as they tried to arrest Mr Koresh on firearms charges.

No, she will only ask me to take a message to Albert.

Benjamin Disraeli, British politician, on his deathbed today, declines a visit by Queen Victoria, 1881.

BIRTHDAYS

Sir Thomas Hopkinson 1905, British journalist, author, editor of *Picture Post* (1940–50) and *Drum International* (1958–61).

Dudley Moore 1935, British musician and comedian.

Maria Sharapova 1987, Russian two-time Tennis Major winner.

THE PRINCE AND THE SHOWGIRL

1956 The wedding today of Prince Rainier of Monaco and American screen actress Grace Kelly has set the seal on a story that is ripe for turning into a Hollywood movie. The couple met and fell in love last year at the international film festival in Cannes, which is only a few hours' drive from Rainier's home, a pink palace perched on a rock overlooking the Mediterranean. Over 1200 guests attended the televised Catholic wedding ceremony in Monte Carlo. Grace Kelly the film star was widely admired for her cool charm and classy good looks, but it was under the direction of the master of suspense, Alfred Hitchcock, that those attributes were tapped to best effect. Kelly's performance in *To Catch a Thief*, in which she played love scenes opposite Cary Grant, is said to have struck a raw nerve in husband-to-be Rainier, who tried to delay the film's release.

• 1882 – CHARLES DARWIN DIES • 1952 – DALAI LAMA FLEES TIBET AS CHINESE INVADE

1653 Oliver Cromwell dissolves the Long Parliament.

1768 Death of Canaletto, Venetian artist.

1857 West African Muslim leader Ai Hajj Uman lays siege to the French fort of Medine in Senegal.

1883 Edouard Manet, one of the first Impressionist painters, dies.

1929 King Victor III of Italy opens a parliament composed entirely of Fascists under the leadership of Benito Mussolini.

1944 The RAF drops 4,500 tons of bombs on Germany in a single raid.

1989 A gun turret on US battleship Iowa explodes, killing 47 sailors.

BIRTHDAYS

Adolf Hitler 1889, Austrian-born dictator, of Germany and architect of World War II.

Joan Miró 1889, Spanish Surrealist painter, graphic artist and designer.

Ryan O'Neal 1941, American film actor who starred in *Love Story*, *Paper Moon* and *What's Up Doc?* among other movies.

ART NOUVEAU ATTRACTS OLD MONEY

1896 Fashionable Paris is being drawn like a magnet to the gallery opened recently by the well-known connoisseur, dealer and writer on Japanese art Samuel Bing. His "Maison de l'Art Nouveau" is devoted to showing both fine and applied works of art – but with a difference. All the works are examples of the so-called "new art" and owe their inspiration to the present. When M. Bing threw open his doors in the rue de Provence last December he unveiled a vast and bewildering array of paintings and decorative objects, each of them executed as unique items and designed from scratch. This aesthetic ideal is currently in vogue all over Europe, and can be seen in poster and book illustration, glasswork, jewellery, textiles, furniture and architecture. The practitioners of the new art prefer naturalism to the formalized type of decoration seen in the past. The effects can be startling – writhing plant forms as patterns, heart-shaped holes in furniture, cast-iron lilies and copper tendrils.

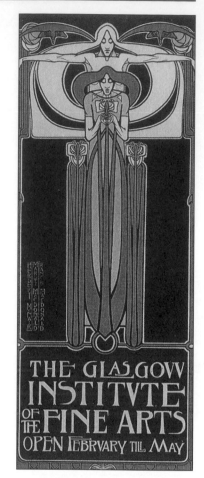

GORBACHEV PLAYS HARDBALL

1990 Mikhail Gorbachev has cut off 85 per cent of gas supplies to the rebellious republic of Lithuania. Shortly before this move, he had ordered that the Baltic state's oil pipelines be shut down. A Soviet foreign ministry spokesman has warned that if Lithuania does not tow the Kremlin line and back down from its declared aim of independence "we may have to take other measures". The Lithuanian president Vytautas Landsbergis remains defiant: "We can hold out for 100 years without gas and oil". Despite pleas from the Lithuanians, the European Community has resolutely stayed outside the quarrel, urging restraint on both sides.

• 1770 – COOK DISCOVERS TERRA AUSTRALIS • 1999 – COLUMBINE HIGH SCHOOL MASSACRE

HEATH GIVEN DOUBLE-EDGED SWORD

1968 Conservative Party leader Edward Heath was today handed a political hot potato by fellow Tory and former Cabinet minister Enoch Powell, who has called for an end to non-white immigration from the Commonwealth. In a highly charged and emotive speech given in Birmingham, Powell likened the Labour government's policy of allowing 50,000 dependents of immigrants into the country each year to that of a people "busily engaged in heaping up its own funeral pyre". The liberal-minded Mr Heath, who has denounced the speech as racist and inflammatory, is expected to take a strong line with Powell, possibly ejecting him from the Shadow cabinet. Ironically, by supporting Powell he could revive his popularity with the British electorate, many of whom are worried by the number of immigrants entering the country.

All you need in this life is ignorance and confidence; then success is sure.

Mark Twain, who died today, 1910.

RIO MIFFED BY BRASILIA

1960 Brasilia, the brain-child of President Juscelino Kubitschek, was today dedicated as the official capital of Brazil. Building work in the new capital is still underway and several of the more ambitious projects planned by architect Lucio Costa and his adviser Oscar Niemayer will take several more years to complete. The new city stands on a plateau some 580 miles (930 km) north-west of previous capital Rio de Janeiro. Miffed at their city's loss of status, and the pouring of huge amounts of money into developing the interior of the country, the citizens of Rio de Janeiro are denouncing the plan. President Kubitscek intends that Brasilia and the region in which it stands should be seen as a symbol of Brazil's future greatness. However, there are also fears that the ambitious programme may bankrupt the country, which has high inflation and has doubled its foreign debt since work began on planning Brasilia in 1957.

APRIL 21

1509 Henry VIII accedes to the English throne.

1699 Death of Jean Racine, French dramatist.

1831 The Texans vanquish the Mexicans at the Battle of San Jacinto.

1898 The US declares war on Spain.

1901 Sculptor Auguste Rodin shocks Paris when his semi-nude statue of Victor Hugo is exhibited.

1910 Mark Twain, American journalist and author dies aged 74.

1914 American troops occupy the Mexican city of Vera Cruz in order to stop German weapons reaching the Mexican command.

1989 More than 10,000 mass in Beijing's Tiananmen Square.

2003 Death of Nina Simone, singer and songwriter of jazz and blues music, aged 70.

BIRTHDAYS

Charlotte Brontë 1816, British novelist, eldest of the three Brontë sisters and author of *Jane Eyre, Villette* and *Shirley*.

Elizabeth II 1926, who became Queen of England in 1952.

• 1828 – WEBSTER'S US DICTIONARY PUBLISHED • 1992 – EURO DISNEY OPENS IN PARIS

1500 Portuguese navigator Pedro Alvarez Cabral discovers Brazil and claims it for Portugal.

1838 The British packet steamer *Sirius* becomes the first steamer to cross from New York to Britain.

1915 The Germans use poison gas for the first time on the Western Front.

1969 British yachtsman Robin Knox-Johnston completes his solo non-stop round-world trip in his ketch *Suhaili* in 312 days.

1972 John Fairfax and Sylvia Cook are the first to row across the Pacific.

1983 £1 coins replace the paper £1 note in Britain.

BIRTHDAYS

Vladimir Ilyich Lenin 1870, Russian leader of the Bolshevik Revolution and first leader of communist Russia.

Vladimir Nabokov 1889, Russian-born novelist and poet, author of *Lolita*.

Robert Oppenheimer 1904, American nuclear scientist.

Jack Nicholson 1937, American Oscar-winning actor, famous for roles in *The Shining* and *One Flew Over the Cuckoo's Nest*.

USA CLEANS UP BASEBALL

1876 The reputation of the fast-growing game of baseball looks set to be saved by the formation of the National League of Professional Baseball Clubs. Most of the teams that made up the now discredited National Association of Professional Baseball Players, formed five years ago, are to join the new league. In five seasons the Association gained an unenviable reputation as a breeding ground for drunkenness, violence and corruption. The league has drawn up a constitution to which each of the eight founder-member clubs must subscribe. Alcohol is banned from sale at all League grounds and no play is allowed on Sundays. Any club which breaches these and other undertakings will be disqualified from the League.

AIDS BREAKTHROUGH

1984 Medical researchers have identified a type of human cancer virus that may be the causative agent in the killer disease AIDS. The virus identified by a team working at the US National Cancer Institute, has been identified as human T-cell lymphotropic virus, Type III. The discovery has raised hopes of finding an anti-AIDS vaccine and the possibility of eventually developing antibodies that could be used to treat patients with full-blown AIDS.

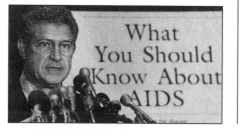

ON YOUR MARKS, GET SET, STAKE THAT CLAIM

1889 An estimated 200,000 people gathered at noon today for the start of a land run in Oklahoma territory. At the crack of the starting pistol the rush was on to stake claims to the two million acres that Congress has agreed should be released for new settlers. Each successful claimant will receive 160 acres of prairie. The race is intended to ensure a fair distribution of the land, but there are reports that some settlers are already in the new territory. The pressure on the US government to allow prospectors into Indian territory has been immense. Organized groups called Boomers, have been settling here illegally since at least 1879. The Indians cannot be sure that today's land race will be the last State-endorsed appropriation of their territory.

• **1971 – DEATH OF HAITI'S HATED LEADER "PAPA DOC"** • **1994 – RICHARD NIXON DIES**

KENNEDY KILLER SENT TO DEATH ROW

1969 A Los Angeles jury decided today that Sirhan B. Sirhan should be sent to the gas chamber for the murder of Senator Robert Kennedy in June last year. Last week the jury rejected psychiatric evidence that portrayed Sirhan as a psychotic mentally incapable of premeditated murder. Sirhan claims to have shot Kennedy to bring attention to the plight of the Palestinian Arabs. He will now join the 80 men already on Death Row in San Quentin prison. State law allows him to appeal.

Hitler's Diaries Found

1983 The German weekly magazine *Stern* announced yesterday that it has in its possession 60 volumes of hitherto unknown diaries kept by Nazi leader Adolf Hitler. The distinguished British historian Lord Dacre (Hugh Trevor-Roper) is convinced that the diaries are genuine. German historians, on the other hand, are expressing extreme scepticism. One, Herr Werner Maser, said that the whole business "smacks of pure sensationalism". Serialization of the diaries in both *Stern* and the London *Sunday Times* is expected.

> *I came, I saw, God conquered.*
>
> **Charles V,** Holy Roman Emperor, after the battle of Muhlberg, 1547.

US HOSTAGE FREED

1990 The release of the US professor Robert Polhill in Beirut last night after 39 months in captivity has raised hopes that more hostages held by Islamic fundamentalist groups may soon be freed. The call by Libya's Colonel Gaddafi for the release of all hostages has been taken as a sign of willingness on the part of the Lebanese kidnap groups to negotiate in earnest. Gaddafi specifically mentioned two Red Cross workers, Emmanuel Christen and Elio Erriquez, held by Abu Nidal's Revolutionary Council, a group with close ties to the Libyan leader.

1616 Death of Miguel de Cervantes, Spanish author of *Don Quixote*.

1661 Charles II is crowned King of England.

1850 British poet William Wordsworth dies aged 80.

1935 Stalin opens the Moscow Underground.

1962 150,000 people rally in London's Hyde Park in the biggest-ever Ban the Bomb demonstration.

1968 The first decimal coins appear in Britain, easing the way to decimalization in 1971.

1990 Death of Paulette Goddard, American actress who starred in Charlie Chaplin's *Modern Times*.

BIRTHDAYS

Joseph Mallard William Turner 1775, English painter and engraver.

Sergei Prokofiev 1891, Russian composer and pianist best-known for *Peter and the Wolf*.

Lester Pearson 1897, Canadian statesman, diplomat and prime minister.

Roy Orbison 1936, American singer and songwriter who had a massive hit with "Pretty Woman".

• 1616 – SHAKESPEARE DIES • 1860 – JOHN STUART EXPLORES AUSTRALIA'S CENTRE

1731 Death of Daniel Defoe, British journalist, novelist and economist.

1895 Captain Joshua Slocum sets forth from Bristol to sail round the world single-handed.

1939 Robert Menzies becomes prime minister of Australia as leader of the United Australia Party.

1967 The Russian spacecraft crashes, killing astronaut Vladimir Komarov.

1986 Wallis, Duchess of Windsor, for whom a British king gave up his throne, dies in Paris aged 89.

1993 The IRA bombs the City of London for the second year in a row.

BIRTHDAYS

William III 1533, king of England.

Philippe Pétain 1856, French general and statesman who signed an armistice with Hitler and led the collaborationist Vichy government.

Shirley MacLaine 1934, American actress, dancer and writer.

Barbra Streisand 1942, American actress and singer.

DISASTER IN THE DESERT

1980 An attempt to rescue the 53 American hostages held in the US embassy in the Iranian capital Teheran since last November has failed. Eight helicopters took off from aircraft carriers in the Gulf of Oman this morning to rendezvous with a 97-man rescue team at a remote area in the desert. Dust storms forced down two of the helicopters short of the target area and a third developed hydraulic problems. The rescue bid had to be abandoned as a result.

WHITE SUPREMACISTS FORM THE KLAN

1866 President Andrew Johnson's programme of reconstruction in the wake of the Civil War is attracting much criticism. In the South a secret society called the Ku Klux Klan has been formed by ex-Confederates dedicated to the principle of "white supremacy". Meanwhile, radical Republicans say that Johnson is allowing provisional governments in the South to undermine blacks' rights.

Any institution which does not suppose the people good, and the magistrate corruptible, is evil.

Maximilien Robespierre,
in the declaration of Human Rights,
on this day, 1793.

BLOODY STRUGGLE FOR IRISH FREEDOM

1916 An uprising against British rule has thrown Dublin into chaos. The day after Easter Sunday, a force of around 2000 Irish para-militaries has succeeded in seizing the General Post Office. Street fighting is continuing as the rebels battle to establish positions in other areas of the city. The leaders of the rebellion have proclaimed a provisional Republican government. Given the military weight against them, however, it can only be a matter of time before they are forced to surrender. The uprising comes two years after the decision by the British Liberal PM Herbert Asquith to suspend implementation of the Home Rule for Ireland bill until hostilities with Germany cease. In this time there has been an increase in support for para-military groups committed to the aim of immediate independence for Ireland.

• 1989 – HERBERT VON KARAJAN RESIGNS AS CONDUCTOR OF BERLIN PHILHARMONIC

SCIENTISTS CRACK THE GENETIC CODE

1953 The world of science moved several steps closer to understanding man's genetic make-up today with the publication of a paper which establishes the structure and function of DNA. DNA stands for deoxyribonucleic acid, the molecules which store an individual's genetic code. British scientist Francis Crick and American biologist James Watson, both of whom work at Cavendish Laboratories in Cambridge, have built a model which shows how the strands of DNA are coiled in a double-helix and connected by hydrogen bonds between the bases.

DNA has thus been identified as the most important substance in the transmission of hereditary characteristics. The finding will undoubtedly help research into the prevention and detection of hereditary diseases. The breakthrough was made possible by the work of the Irish bio-physicist Maurice Wilkins, whose X-ray diffraction studies enabled Crick and Watson to build their model.

US RACE RIOTS

1960 Ten blacks were shot dead in Mississippi today after the latest in a succession of racially inspired incidents. Relations between white and black Mississippians have deteriorated since the Supreme Court's decision in 1954 to declare racially segregated schools unconstitutional. Whites have felt increasingly threatened by the demands for wholesale and immediate change that resulted from the court's decision. More extreme elements within Mississippi white society have resorted to bombing black churches and murdering civil rights workers to prevent the overturn of long-established practices. The black community has retaliated through sit-ins, boycotts and acts of violence.

TROOPS STORM ASHORE AT GALLIPOLI

1915 Over 90,000 allied troops, most of them British and Australian, met stiff resistance from Turkish forces as they stormed ashore on the Gallipoli peninsula this morning. The aim of the landings is to seize the Turkish forts guarding the approaches to Constantinople and open up a route to assist Russian forces. The landings have been described by observers as a triumph of naval improvisation, for no purpose-built landing craft were provided and the troops received no special training for the task.

1660 The English parliament votes to restore the monarchy.

1859 The building of the Suez Canal begins under the supervision of engineer Ferdinand de Lesseps.

1926 Puccini's opera *Turandot*.

1964 The Little Mermaid statue in Copenhagen loses her head to thieves.

2011 At least 300 people are killed in the deadliest tornado outbreak in the Southern United States since 1974.

BIRTHDAYS

King Edward II 1284, English monarch and first heir-apparent to take the title Prince of Wales.

Oliver Cromwell 1599, English soldier and statesman, Lord Protector of England 1653–8.

Guglielmo Marconi 1874, Italian electrical engineer who won the Nobel Prize for physics in 1909 for his work on the transmission and reception of radio waves.

Ella Fitzgerald 1918, American jazz singer.

Al Pacino 1939, American actor who found stardom in *The Godfather*.

• 1719 – *ROBINSON CRUSOE* PUBLISHED • 1990 – HUBBLE SPACE TELESCOPE LAUNCHED

1915 Allied troops land at Cape Helles, in the Dardanelles.

1945 Russian and American forces meet near Torgau in east Germany.

1975 In Portugal's first free elections for 50 years, Mário Soares emerges the victor as leader of the Portuguese Socialist Party.

1984 William "Count" Basie, American jazz pianist and bandleader, dies aged 79.

BIRTHDAYS

Eugène Delacroix 1798, French painter who left more than 9,000 works in his studio upon his death.

Michel Fokine 1880, Russian choreographer who worked with Diaghilev's Ballet Russes in Paris.

Anita Loos 1893, American novelist, poet and screenwriter, best-known for *Gentleman Prefer Blondes*.

Rudolf Hess 1894, German Nazi leader who was Hitler's deputy in the early part of World War II.

Charles Richter 1900, seismologist who created the scale to quantify earthquakes.

FASCISTS UNLEASH TERROR ON GUERNICA

1937 The civil war in Spain took a sinister and devastating turn today with the sudden and horrific bombing by German planes of the medieval Basque town of Guernica. The town was crowded with people who had come in from the surrounding area for market day. Much of the damage was caused by incendiary bombs which exploded into flames on landing. Survivors say that the aircraft also strafed the town with machine-gun fire, causing additional casualties. The attack will inflame Republican sympathizers who allege that the support given by the German and Italian governments to the rebel Nationalist forces of Fascist leader General Franco are in direct contravention of the non-intervention agreement reached by the League of Nations last year. The Soviet Union is the only country to extend a helping hand to the Republican government, although an International Brigade recruited from among opponents of fascism in several European countries has rallied to the Republican cause.

IMPRESSIONS OF IMPRESSIONISM

1874 French art critic Louis Leroy yesterday lampooned a group of artists, whom he terms "impressionists", whose works are currently on show at a studio in the Boulevard des Capucines in Paris. His satirical article appears in the periodical *Charivari* and centres on the lack of precision in the pictures. It seems that the paintings have to be looked at from a distance if the viewer is to perceive the unifying elements in them, namely light and the interplay of coloured reflections. According to Leroy, art-lovers who appreciate classical art would be well advised to retreat as far away as possible – or avoid looking at them at all!

FIRST-EVER MULTI-RACIAL ELECTIONS FOR SOUTH AFRICA

1994 After three and a half centuries of white domination, South Africa has gone to the polls in its first ever multi-racial elections. Millions of black South Africans have voted for the first time after years of negotiations between F.W. de Klerk's National Party and the African National Congress. Nelson Mandela of the ANC is tipped to become president.

There's no such thing as a bad Picasso, but some are less good than others.

Pablo Picasso on Picasso – one of his paintings sold for a record $532,000 today, 1967.

• 1865 – CONFEDERATE GENERAL JOHNSTON SURRENDERS AT DURHAM STATION

NUCLEAR MELTDOWN FEARS COME TRUE AT CHERNOBYL

1986 The nightmare of meltdown in a nuclear reactor has come true. The first sign of trouble was picked up by US spy satellites which detected a fire at the Chernobyl nuclear power station, north of Kiev, Ukraine. Scientists at the Swedish Forsmark nuclear power station next reported a huge rise in radiation levels as fallout spread to Scandinavia. Experts believe the accident may have been caused by catastrophic failure of one of the reactor's welded pressure vessels, allowing melt-down of fuel in the core.

LONDON WELCOMES ITS OWN ZOO

1828 The Zoological Society of London has opened a zoological gardens in Regent's Park almost two years to the day after its founding in 1826. Although today's inauguration was restricted to Fellows of the Society it will not be long before the zoo is welcoming the general public. The Society's aim in opening the zoo is to advance our knowledge of the animal kingdom and introduce "new and curious subjects" to an even more curious human audience.

1521 Portuguese navigator Ferdinand Magellan is killed.

1932 Imperial Airways begin an air service from London to Cape Town.

1968 In Britain, a new Abortion Act comes into force.

1972 Kwame Nkrumah, Ghanaian president who was deposed in 1966 by a military coup while he was in China, dies in Bucharest, Hungary.

1984 The Philadelphia radio station W-WSH has a "No Michael Jackson" weekend.

Triumphant opening of Golden Gate bridge

1937 The new Golden Gate suspension bridge linking the city of San Francisco with Marin County reached completion today after four years. Among its remarkable features are 746-ft (227 m) high bridge towers, the tallest in the world, and 4200-ft (1280 m) span, the longest in the world. Fast-rising tides, frequent storms and fogs and the difficulty of blasting through bedrock 100 ft (30m) below the surface of the water to plant earthquake-proof foundations were among the many problems overcome. Users of the bridge are guaranteed a spectacular view from the six-lane roadway perched 250 ft (76 m) above the surface of the Golden Gate Strait.

BIRTHDAYS

Mary Wollstonecraft 1759, English writer, political radical and feminist whose *A Vindication of the Rights of Women* demanded equal rights in education.

Samuel Morse 1791, American inventor of the magnetic telegraph and the Morse code.

Ulysses S. Grant 1822, American general of the Union army and 18th president of the USA.

Cecil Day-Lewis 1904, Irish-born novelist and Poet Laureate.

1788 Maryland becomes the seventh state of the Union.

1936 King Fu'ad of Egypt dies aged 68.

1953 Japan is finally allowed the self-government of which it had been stripped after World War II.

1977 In Germany, Baader-Meinhof group terrorists Andreas Baader, Gudrun Ensslin and Jan Raspe are jailed for life.

1988 Twenty-eight-year-old Sian Edwards becomes the first woman to conduct at the Royal Opera House, Covent Garden.

2009 Mexico confirms the outbreak of swine flu in humans.

BIRTHDAYS

King Edward IV 1442, English monarch, Yorkist leader during the Wars of the Roses who was crowned after defeating the Lancastrians.

James Monroe 1758, American statesman and fifth president of America.

Kenneth Kaunda 1924, Zambian president who was imprisoned in 1958 for founding the Zambian African National Congress.

"NON" TO DE GAULLE

1969 President de Gaulle has fallen from power over the comparatively uncontroversial issue of regional electoral reform. His decision to resign after his failure to win the referendum of two days ago was inevitable because he had staked his presidency on the issue. De Gaulle will be succeeded by his former wartime aide and prime minister since 1962, Georges Pompidou. "It's like being cuckolded by your chauffeur," was de Gaulle's characteristically blunt comment. By saying "Non" to the 79-year-old de Gaulle, the French people may be signalling their readiness for more liberal government.

MUSSOLINI ASSASSINATED

1945 Italian dictator Benito Mussolini was today shot and strung up head down by his own countrymen. The man once called "Il Duce", the leader, is now seen as little better than a common criminal. The same treatment was meted out to his mistress, Claretta Petacci.

MUTINY ON THE BOUNTY

1789 A mutiny is reported to have broken out on a British armed transport ship in the South Seas. The captain of the 94-ft (29-m) *Bounty*, Captain William Bligh, and 18 loyal crew members have been put in an open boat and are now drifting in

the direction of Timor, near Java. The mutineers, led by master's mate Fletcher Christian, are thought to be returning to Tahiti, where the *Bounty* recently took on board a consignment of 1000 young breadfruit trees which Bligh intended taking to the West Indies as a food source for the African slaves there. The cause of the mutiny is unclear, but Bligh's harshness has been offered as a possible explanation.

• 1770 – CAPTAIN COOK LANDS AT BOTANY BAY • 1919 – GERMANY TO PAY REPARATIONS

PRINCE WILLIAM MARRIES HIS PRINCESS IN FRONT OF WORLDWIDE AUDIENCE

2011 Prince William, second in line for the British throne, married long-term girlfriend Kate Middleton at Westminster Abbey, accompanied by 1,900 guests. Kate's sister Pippa was maid of honour, while Prince Harry was William's best man. The ceremony was followed by a lunchtime reception at Buckingham Palace given by the Queen, and a dinner hosted by The Prince of Wales, with music and dancing. Television and internet coverage of the wedding was watched by millions of people in 180 countries around the world.

1930 A telephone link is established between Britain and Australia.

1945 German plenipotentaries in Italy sign terms of surrender.

1967 In London, 41 groups play at an all-night rave in Alexandra Palace.

1977 Trade unions are declared legal in Spain for the first time since 1936.

1987 The musical *Cabaret* is performed in London without music when the orchestra goes on strike.

2014 British actor Bob Hoskins, star of the film *Mona Lisa* dies, aged 71.

BIRTHDAYS

Arthur Wellesley, Duke of Wellington 1769, English soldier and prime minister who defeated Napoleon at Waterloo.

William Randolph Hearst 1863, American newspaper proprietor.

Duke Ellington 1889, American jazz pianist, composer and bandleader.

Zubin Mehta 1936, Indian conductor and violinist chiefly known for his association with the Israel Philharmonic Orchestra.

HAIR RAISES HACKLES ON BROADWAY

1968 The new musical *Hair* has provoked a mixed reaction from its first-night audience at the Biltmore Theatre, New York. Comments included "vulgar", "dirty" and "juvenile backyard fence graffiti" from the antis and "fresh", "frank" and "the most significant musical of the decade" from those who support the production. Sex, drugs, military service and religion are among the wide range of topics served up for the public's consumption in a number of new songs added since the original production, staged off Broadway last year. A nude scene has added fuel to the charge that *Hair*'s producers are more interested in cheap sensationalism than theatrical values.

BLUE STOCKINGS MAKE STRIDES

1885 The decision to allow women to sit the examinations of Oxford University is further evidence that the door of academe is widening – slowly. This advance is due almost entirely to the efforts of Emily Davies, guiding force behind a committee dedicated to securing higher education for women. Cambridge agreed to open its local examinations to women in 1865 after the success of a pilot project in 1863 when 91 women sat the exams. Four years ago women were allowed to sit the Tripos examination also. However, women are not to be awarded degrees.

• 1842 – CORN ACT PASSED IN BRITAIN • 1980 – DEATH OF ALFRED HITCHCOCK

1803 The US purchases Louisiana and New Orleans from the French.

1900 Hawaii cedes itself to the US.

1912 A second reading of the Irish Home Rule Bill is moved in the House of Commons.

1957 Egypt reopens the Suez Canal to traffic.

1965 Bob Dylan opens his first UK tour in Sheffield.

1968 Frankie Lymon, the American pop star who had a hit at the age of only 14 with "Why Do Fools Fall in Love?" dies of a heroin overdose.

1983 Death of George Balanchine, Russian-born choreographer who was first artistic director to the New York City Ballet.

BIRTHDAYS

David Thompson 1770, English-born Canadian who explored large parts of western Canada.

Franz Lehár 1870, Hungarian composer best-known for *The Merry Widow*.

Jaroslav Hašek 1883, Czechoslovakian novelist who wrote the satirical novel *The Good Soldier Schweik*.

SAIGON FALLS

1975 Communist North Vietnamese forces entered the capital of South Vietnam today, signalling an end to the 15-year Second Indochina War. Despite signing the Paris ceasefire two years ago, the Saigon government had continued its efforts to eliminate Communist power in its territory. However, the withdrawal of US troops in 1973 and Washington's decision to accord the Communist-backed Provisional Revolutionary Government equal status with Saigon signalled to the northern leadership in Hanoi that further American intervention would not be forthcoming. Communist forces in Vietnam have been trying to unite their country under a national government since World War II.

WASHINGTON TAKES THE OATH

1789 George Washington was inaugurated as the first president of the United States of America in a ceremony at Federal Hall in New York today. The 67-year-old Virginian landowner is widely recognized within his own country, and indeed beyond, as the only man capable of giving the new federation the wise and sure leadership it will need in its infancy.

ALI STRIPPED OF HIS TITLE

1967 In a dramatic and unprecedented move, Muhammad Ali has been stripped of his world heavyweight boxing crown for refusing to be conscripted into the US armed forces. Ali's claim that he is exempted from serving in Vietnam on religious grounds has been rejected. The boxing authorities, have promptly taken away his title and revoked his licence. Ali, 25, first won the title as Cassius Clay in 1964. He changed his name to Muhammad Ali after converting to the Muslim faith and becoming a minister. He is expected to appeal.

• 1904 – ST LOUIS EXHIBITION OPENS • 1945 – ADOLF HITLER COMMITS SUICIDE

1983 A poster advertising Sergei Diaghilev's Ballets Russes in 1911 for whom George Balanchine choreographed a number of ballets including *Apollo* and *The Prodigal Son*. Balanchine died this day, aged 79.

• 1948 – THE FIRST LAND ROVER IS EXHIBITED AT THE AMSTERDAM MOTOR SHOW

MAY

EMPIRE STATE SCRAPES THE SKIES OF NEW YORK

1931 US President Herbert Hoover opened the tallest building in the world in New York today – the 102-storey Empire State Building on Fifth Avenue, which stands an incredible 1250 ft (380 m) high. It is the city's third new "skyscraper" in just one year. It went up with lightning speed, the steel framework being finished in less than six months. It met its deadline for completion – today – with no time to spare – the day many New York office leases expire. The Empire State Building has more than 2 million sq ft (609,800 sq m) of office space, much more than the city can absorb with the Depression in full swing. The owners are hoping sightseers to the lofty observation decks will help to pay the taxes.

1707 Union between England and Scotland.

1808 Charles IV of Spain abdicates in favour of Joseph Bonaparte.

1840 The first Penny Black stamps bearing Queen Victoria's head go on sale.

1851 Queen Victoria opens the Great Exhibition in the Crystal Palace in Hyde Park, London.

1862 The Union army occupies New Orleans.

1904 Death of Antonin Dvořák, Czechoslovakian composer.

1989 Anti-government protests in Prague demand the release of jailed playwright Vaclav Havel.

1997 Labour leader Tony Blair is elected UK Prime Minister.

2004 The European Union is enlarged from 15 to 25 states.

BIRTHDAYS

Joseph Addison 1672, English essayist, poet and Whig statesman who co-founded the *Spectator* in 1711.

Joseph Heller 1929, American novelist best-known for his novel *Catch-22*.

THE KING FINDS A QUEEN

1967 Elvis Presley, the King of Rock 'n' Roll and still the world's No. 1 heart-throb, caused widespread female dismay this morning when he married his sweetheart of seven years, Priscilla Beaulieu. The couple wed at the Aladdin Hotel in Las Vegas at a civil ceremony with 100 guests. Priscilla wore a traditional flowing white dress and veil, and Presley a formal suit and black tie. The wedding cake was six tiers high. After the reception they flew to Palm Springs for a two-day honeymoon.

RACING TRAGEDY

1994 Leading Formula One driver Ayrton Senna has been killed on the same stretch of track as fellow driver Roland Ratzenberger was two days earlier at the San Marino Grand Prix.

SOVIETS FIND US SPY

1960 Days before US President Eisenhower and Soviet Chairman Kruschev meet at a Paris summit, an American spy plane has been shot down over the Soviet Union today by a Soviet surface-to-air missile. The pilot, Francis Gary Powers, was captured. The US government has denied Russian accusations that Powers was spying.

• 1873 – DEATH OF DAVID LIVINGSTONE • 1941 – *CITIZEN KANE* PREMIERES IN NEW YORK

1957 Death of Senator Joe McCarthy, who led the communist witch-hunts in 1950s America.

1965 The first satellite TV programme links 9 countries and 300 million viewers.

1972 Death of J. Edgar Hoover, head of the FBI.

1989 China imposes martial law as pro-democracy demonstrators camp in Tiananmen Square.

2012 Lionel Messi breaks Gurd Muller's 39-year old record by scoring 68 goals in a single football season.

BIRTHDAYS

Catherine II 1729, Empress of Russia who gained the throne in 1762 in a coup.

Theodor Herzl 1860, Austrian journalist and first president of the World Zionist Organization in 1897.

Bing Crosby 1904, American singer and actor whose "White Christmas" is the biggest-selling single ever recorded.

Dr Benjamin Spock 1903, American paediatrician whose books influenced generations.

David Beckham 1975, English football player with 115 international caps.

PINK FLOYD'S HIT IS BLACK ANTHEM

1980 British rock group Pink Floyd's hit single "Another Brick in the Wall" was banned by the South African government today. Rebellious black schoolchildren have adopted the song as an anthem. The brutally suppressed nationwide riots of 1976 were started by black schoolchildren rejecting the racist government's education system, which spends six times as much educating a white child as a black child. Now the young protesters chant Pink Floyd's lines: "We don't want no education, we don't want no thought control." Banning the song is not likely to stop them singing it – nor meaning it.

RENAISSANCE MAN MOVES ON

1519 The Florentine painter Leonardo da Vinci has died at Cloux in France at the age of 67. Born in Vinci, the illegitimate son of a notary, he trained in Florence under Verrocchio. His most famous works are the mural *The Last Supper* and the portrait *Mona Lisa*. Leonardo was court artist to the Duke of Milan for 18 years – as well as a civil and military engineer, and an expert mathematician and biologist, a grinder of lenses, a designer of clock mechanisms, of devices for transmitting energy, even of flying machines. In his quest for understanding of the natural world, he studied birds in flight, swirling streams and rock strata, his acute eye freezing motion in sketches and diagrams. To him art and science were one, part of the search for knowledge. Seldom has a search been so rewarded: Leonardo leaves an immensely rich body of work.

DEATH OF OSAMA BIN LADEN

2011 Osama bin Laden, the former head of the Islamist militant group al-Qaeda, and top of the US Most Wanted list, was killed in Pakistan by US forces. The operation, code-named "Operation Neptune Spear", was ordered by United States President Barack Obama and carried out in a Central Intelligence Agency-led operation. The raid on bin Laden's compound in Abbottabad culminated in what was described as "a firefight". U.S. forces took bin Laden's body to Afghanistan for identification, then buried it at sea within 24 hours of his death. Announcing the success of the operation, Mr Obama said it was "the most significant achievement to date in our nation's effort to defeat al-Qaeda". One of bin Laden's sons was also killed in the attack.

• 1952 – FIRST SCHEDULED JET FLIGHT • 1982 – SINKING OF THE *GENERAL BELGRANO*

COLUMBUS CHINA TRIP FINDS JAMAICA INSTEAD

1494 On his second voyage across the Atlantic in search of a westward route to the East, the Italian navigator Christopher Columbus today discovered the tropical paradise of Jamaica. But it is not the fabled Orient, and the fleet is turning back to Isabella, the colony Columbus founded on Hispaniola last month. Columbus returned to Spain last year after his first voyage west, carrying gold and some of the native people, and claiming to have reached islands off the coast of Asia. Encouraged, Queen Isabella funded the second voyage much more generously than the first, providing 17 ships and 1500 men. But Columbus has found no trace of the court of China and its gold. The 39 sailors Columbus left on Hispaniola on the first voyage have been killed by the Indians and the new colony is proving troublesome. Columbus can expect a cool reception when he returns to Spain this time.

BRITAIN FÊTES THE NEW ELIZABETHAN AGE

1951 The South Bank of the River Thames in London lit up this evening as King George VI and Queen Elizabeth opened the Festival of Britain. The five-month festival is designed to disperse the grey post-war cloud with a bright vision of Britain's future. Clusters of illuminations and the revolutionary architecture of the Dome of Discovery and the Festival Hall have drastically changed the South Bank, which was almost entirely destroyed in the London Blitz.

1654 The first toll bridge in America comes into operation in Massachusetts.

1788 The first daily evening newspaper, the *Star and Evening Advertiser*, is published in London.

1917 The first US destroyers join the naval forces ranged against the Germans in World War I.

1958 Death of Henry Cornelius, South African-born British film director whose most notable films are the comedies *Passport to Pimlico* and *Genevieve*.

2008 More than 84,000 people die and many more are left homeless as Cyclone Nargis causes widespread devastation in Myanmar.

BIRTHDAYS

Niccoló Macchiavelli 1469, Italian political theorist who wrote *The Prince* in 1532.

Golda Meir 1898, Israeli politician who became prime minister at the age of 70.

Sugar Ray Robinson 1921, American world boxing champion.

James Brown 1933, American soul singer.

• 1814 – FRENCH MONARCHY RESTORED • 1937 – PULITZER FOR *GONE WITH THE WIND*

1904 Charles Rolls and Henry Royce sign an agreement to collaborate in the production of cars.

1970 Journalist Seymour Hirsch wins the Pulitzer Prize for his reporting of the My Lai massacre by US soldiers in Vietnam.

1983 President Reagan announces his backing for the Nicaraguan Contras in their conflict with the Sandinistas.

1982 HMS *Sheffield* sinks in the Falklands War when hit by an Exocet missile.

2000 The Love Bug virus wreaks havoc with computers all over the world.

BIRTHDAYS

Bartolomeo Cristofori 1655, Italian inventor of the piano.

John Manning Speke 1827, English explorer who identified Lake Victoria as the source of the Nile.

Audrey Hepburn 1929, Belgian-born actress whose most notable films include *Breakfast at Tiffany's*.

Tammy Wynette 1942, American country and western singer best-known for "Stand By Your Man".

BRITAIN COMES TO A STANDSTILL

1926 Britain's workers downed tools today and the country ground to a halt. The first-ever General Strike began at midnight after the general council of the Trades Union Congress voted in favour of supporting the miners' strike which began four days ago in protest at a wage reduction. Talks between the government and the TUC broke down late last night after printers at the *Daily Mail* refused to print an article by the editor, denouncing the TUC as revolutionary. There have been reports of strikers in Glasgow forcing public vehicles off the road, and the army has been put on full alert in Scotland, Yorkshire and South Wales.

MAGGIE JUBILANT

1979 Britain's first woman PM, Margaret Thatcher, moved into 10 Downing Street today after a resounding election win that gives her Conservative government a majority of 43 seats in parliament. Promising a complete transformation of Britain's economic and industrial climate, Thatcher is planning a war on inflation, privatization of the nationalized industries and a curb on trade union power.

Vietnam protesters killed at Kent State

1970 US National Guardsmen shot and killed four students at Kent State University in Ohio today. The dead students were taking part in a massed antiwar protest when the soldiers fired into the unarmed crowd. Nine students were wounded. Two more students were shot dead at Jackson State University, Mississippi. The killings follow three days of student rioting in which the National Guard used bayonets, teargas and finally bullets. The nationwide campus demonstrations erupted after President Richard Nixon sent US troops into Cambodia last week.

When dissent turns to violence it invites tragedy.
Richard M. Nixon, US president, commenting on the shooting of rioting students at Kent State University today, 1970.

RIOTS IN PARIS

1968 Paris was torn by violence today as 30,000 students ripped up the streets to make barricades and student "commando squads" clashed with riot police, answering the police teargas grenades with a hail of bricks and Molotov cocktails. Six hundred and fifty students were injured, and 350 police. The first demonstrations, six weeks ago, were anti-American, but student arrests prompted student leader "Danny the Red" Cohn-Bendit to stage a mass sit-in at the university. Two days ago the riot police broke it up, bringing accusations of police brutality – and today's riots. Tonight the city awaits the mass demonstration planned at the Arc de Triomphe for tomorrow morning. It is unlikely to remain peaceful.

1865 The first train robbery is carried out, near North Bend, Ohio.

1920 Bartolomeo Vanzetti and Nicola Sacco arrested in New York for possession of anarchist literature.

1949 Death of Belgian Count Maurice Maeterlink, leading dramatist of the Symbolist movement.

1955 The World Bank warns that poverty is a greater threat to world peace than the Cold War.

1963 Britain's first satellite is launched.

1967 Flower-power anthem "San Francisco" enters the US singles charts.

1988 Japanese television broadcasts the first transmission from the summit of Mount Everest.

CRUSADERS FLEE FALLEN STRONGHOLD

1291 Egypt's Mamelukes overwhelmed the last Christian stronghold in the Holy Land today. Sultan Qalawun's army battered the Crusader fortress-port of Acre into submission. Giant catapults lobbed bombs over the walls while engineers burrowed under them, and then blew them up with gunpowder. The Egyptian troops poured in, capturing most of the Crusaders as they tried to flee. The sultan attacked Acre because the Crusaders had broken a truce and slaughtered every Muslim in the town. He has sent his captives – 1000 Christian knights, their foot soldiers, women and children – to the slave market at Damascus.

SAS DARES TO STORM EMBASSY

1980 Millions watched live on television as commandos of Britain's secret Special Air Services stormed the Iranian Embassy in London's Knightsbridge to break a six-day terrorist siege. The gang was demanding the release of political prisoners in Iran. The commandos attacked after the terrorists started to shoot hostages. The commandos killed four of the five gunmen and freed 19 surviving hostages. The Embassy building was gutted.

I used to say of him that his presence on the field made the difference of 40,000 men.

Arthur Wellesley, Duke of Wellington, on Napoleon, who died in exile on St Helena today, 1821.

BIRTHDAYS

Søren Kierkegaard 1813, Danish philosopher and prolific writer.

Karl Marx 1818, German philosopher and revolutionary, author of *Das Kapital*.

Michael Palin 1943, British comedian, actor and writer who first became known as a member of Monty Python's Flying Circus.

• 1821 – NAPOLEON BONAPARTE DIES • 1961 – FIRST AMERICAN IN SPACE

MAY
6

1877 The Sioux chief Crazy Horse surrenders and gives up all claim to Nebraska.

1910 King Edward VII of England dies and George V accedes to the throne.

1959 Icelandic gunboats fire live ammunition at British trawlers as the Cod War continues.

1990 P. W. Botha resigns from the ruling National Party in South Africa.

1992 Death of Marlene Dietrich, German actress.

1994 The Channel Tunnel, linking Britain with the Continent, is officially opened by the Queen and President Mitterand.

BIRTHDAYS

Maximilien Robespierre 1758, French revolutionary who instituted the Reign of Terror.

Sigmund Freud 1856, Austrian pioneer of psychoanalysis.

Rudolph Valentino 1895, Italian actor who became a star of Hollywood silent movies.

Orson Welles 1915, American actor, writer and film director.

Tony Blair 1953, former British Prime Minister 1997–2007.

FOUR-MINUTE MILE BARRIER JUST BROKEN BY BANNISTER

1954 Roger Bannister, a 25-year-old British medical student, broke an invisible barrier today when he ran a mile in three-fifths of a second less than four minutes. He was running at the Iffley Road track in Oxford, representing the university against the Amateur Athletics Association, with two fellow students setting the pace. Experts long held that it was impossible for man to run a mile in less than four minutes. Today Bannister took two seconds off the previous record, set by Swede Gunder Hagg in 1945. What will be next – a three-and-three-quarter-minute mile?

DUTCH BUY MANHATTAN FOR A SONG

1626 A Dutch official named Peter Minuit today bought the 22 sq mile (57 sq km) island of Manhattan from local Indians. He certainly got a good deal. The Indians refused his gold and silver – they wanted knives, beads, trinkets, and accepted an offer of them to the value of only 60 guilders (£13/$24). Minuit today named the settlement New Amsterdam and is building a fort there.

HINDENBURG EXPLODES

1937 The German transatlantic airship *Hindenburg* exploded while landing in New Jersey tonight, killing 35 of the 97 aboard and injuring many others. Sailors from the nearby naval base fought to rescue passengers from the burning wreck. The 1000-ft (304-m) airship was delayed by a thunderstorm at the end of her three-day crossing from Frankfurt, and it is thought lightning ignited her 7 million cubic ft of hydrogen gas as her wet mooring ropes touched the ground. This is the fifth airship to crash and today's tragedy must spell the end of the line for them.

• 1851 – YALE LOCK PATENTED • 1983 – HITLER DIARIES ARE FAKE

NAZIS SURRENDER

1945 Nazi Germany surrendered to the Allies early this morning ending the war in Europe. German chief-of-staff General Alfred Jodl signed an unconditional surrender at 2.40 am and delivered his nation "into the victors' hands, for better or worse", as he remarked. Jodl was met by Britain's General Montgomery, US chief-of-staff General Bedell Smith and Soviet General Suslapatov at General Eisenhower's headquarters, a small schoolhouse in Rheims, northern France. The Nazis have collapsed in the last two weeks as the Allies advanced. Adolf Hitler killed himself a week ago as his once-mighty war machine was swept away.

MAY
7

1763 American Indian Chief Pontiac attacks the English garrison at Detroit.

1823 Beethoven conducts the first performance of his "Ninth Symphony".

1832 Greece is declared an independent kingdom.

1918 A peace treaty between Romania and the Central Powers is ratified.

1942 Japanese and American naval forces engage in the Coral Sea.

1943 Allied forces capture Tunis from the Germans.

2010 Tory leader David Cameron forms the first coalition government in the UK since World War II.

BIRTHDAYS

Robert Browning 1812, English poet.

Johannes Brahms 1833, German composer.

Peter Ilich Tchaikovsky 1840, Russian composer chiefly known for his ballets.

Gary Cooper 1901, American actor and heart-throb who won Oscars for *Sergeant York* and *High Noon*.

Eva Perón 1919, Actress, wife of Argentine President Juan Perón and popular 'Spiritual Leader'.

SCIENTISTS CAN CLONE ABE LINCOLN'S GENES

1991 A team of geneticists at Johns Hopkins University was given permission today to clone genes from the remains of US president Abraham Lincoln, assassinated in 1865. They will work with blood stains, bone chips and samples of his hair still preserved. Lincoln is thought to have inherited Marfan's syndrome, characterized by tallness, long arms and a weak heart. The scientists want to test whether Lincoln really had it.

Watergate Pulitzer for Woodstein

1973 The *Washington Post* today won the Pulitzer Prize for the work of investigative reporters Bob Woodward and Carl Bernstein in exposing the Watergate scandal. "Woodstein" have been relentless in exposing the deceit behind the illegal break-in and wire-tapping at the Democratic Party headquarters in the Watergate complex in Washington last June by Nixon re-election campaign members.

• 1847 – AMERICAN MEDICAL ASSOCIATION FOUNDED • 1888 – KODAK CAMERA LAUNCHED

1849 In the first international yacht race, Bermudan beats America.

1876 Death of Tuganini, the last Tasmanian aborigine.

1880 Death of French novelist Gustave Flaubert.

1924 Afrikaans becomes the official language of South Africa.

1955 Hiroshima victims arrive in the USA for plastic surgery.

1961 Former British diplomat George Blake is jailed for 42 years for spying for the Soviets.

1990 Estonia adopts its 1938 constitution and affirms independence.

BIRTHDAYS

Henri Dunant 1828, Swiss philosopher and inspiration behind the Red Cross.

Harry S. Truman 1884, American president who ordered the atomic bombing of Japan.

Sonny Liston 1932, American heavyweight boxing champion.

Sir David Attenborough 1926, English broadcaster and naturalist.

ALEX FERGUSON CALLS TIME AFTER 26 YEARS

2013 Alex Ferguson, the most successful club manager in British football history, has retired after 26 years in charge of Manchester United. He won 25 trophies in his time at Old Trafford, including 13 league titles and two Champions Leagues. Known for his intense competitive streak, Ferguson oversaw a number of winning Manchester United sides, and managed high-profile players such as David Beckham, Cristiano Ronaldo and Wayne Rooney.

PEASANT GIRL RECAPTURES ORLÉANS

1429 France's warrior maiden, Joan of Arc, today led the Dauphin's troops to victory over the English laying siege to Orléans. Clad in full armour, the inspired peasant girl drove the Earl of Salisbury and his 5000 men back over the Loire. The English knights' goal is yet more French land, while Joan's army fought with the religious fervour of crusaders – which is what they are. Since she was 13, Joan has heard holy "voices" giving her the mission to rid France of the English. Today Joan gave thanks to God for her victory, which turns the tide against the enemy from across the Channel.

1200 LOST AS U-BOAT SINKS LUSITANIA

1915 The Cunard transatlantic liner *Lusitania* was sunk today off Ireland by German torpedoes when a U-boat struck without warning. Of the 1924 people aboard, 1200 are feared drowned. The U-boat fired two torpedoes, and the huge ship, queen of the Cunard fleet, sank in 20 minutes. There is widespread outrage at the attack, particularly in neutral America – 120 of those missing are Americans.

I have got an infamous army, very weak and ill-equipped, and a very inexperienced staff.

The Duke of Wellington, in a letter to Lord Stewart at the beginning of the Waterloo campaign today, 1815.

• 1902 – MT PELÉE ERUPTS, KILLING 30,000 • 1921 – SWEDEN ABOLISHES DEATH PENALTY

OSBORNE'S ANGRY REALITY

1956 *Look Back in Anger*, a first play about an angry young man by John Osborne, opened tonight in London to reviews that ranged from indignant through puzzled to dazzled. The critics had lots of nasty things to say about Jimmy Porter, the play's "hero", but he's not supposed to be likeable; Jimmy is an educated working-class youth with a middle-class wife, and his bitter railings at the mindless manners, smug values and entrenched class system bring them both to grief. Heroes are obsolete in Jimmy's grey welfare-state Britain. Critic Kenneth Tynan said Jimmy represents post-war youth "as it really is", and called it "the best young play of the decade".

"GOD" STANDS FOR ELECTION

1991 Despite temperatures of 113°F (45°C), ageing politician N. T. Rama Rao is drawing huge crowds at his campaign meetings in South India. The adoring crowds don't care about the weather, for in the minds of a great many voters Rao is an incarnation of God. This is because Rao, a famous film star, often plays a god – usually Rama, an incarnation of Vishnu, one of the two main Hindu gods. Riding the Rama ticket, Rao swept to power in the opposition Congress Party stronghold of Andhra Pradesh state eight years ago, becoming chief minister. Poor performance lost him the job, but, a string of hit movies later, his popularity is now vast. Rao claims he isn't seeking re-election but only wants to oust the Congress Party from the state.

FLORENCE MOURNS BRILLIANT TYRANT

1492 Lorenzo the Magnificent, Medici ruler of Florence, has died aged 43 after a 23-year reign of unequalled cultural brilliance. Lorenzo, a poet himself, was patron of a circle of influential philosophers and poets such as Luigi Pulci and Politian and artists such as Domenico Ghirlandaio, Fra Filippo Lippi, Andrea del Verrochio, Leonardo da Vinci and Michelangelo; plus musicians and architects – all the great figures of the time. Lorenzo was a undoubtedly a tyrant, but a most refined one, and his city mourns him.

1805 Death of German poet and playwright Friedrich Schiller.

1903 French Post-Impressionist painter Paul Gauguin dies.

1911 The British parliament agrees to Home Rule for Ireland.

1926 US explorer Richard Byrd is the first person to fly over the North Pole.

1946 Victor Emmanuel III of Italy abdicates.

1972 Israeli troops storm a hijacked jet at Jerusalem, freeing 92 passengers held hostage by Palestinian Black September terrorists.

1978 The bullet-ridden body of kidnapped Italian statesman Aldo Moro is found in a car in Rome.

1991 William Kennedy Smith, nephew of Senator Edward Kennedy, is charged with sexual battery.

BIRTHDAYS

John Brown 1800, American abolitionist.

J. M. Barrie 1860, Scottish dramatist best-known for *Peter Pan*.

Pancho Gonzalez 1928, American tennis player who won the US men's singles title eight times.

• 1671 – ENGLISH CROWN JEWELS STOLEN • 1988 – AUSTRALIA OPENS NEW PARLIAMENT

MAY 10

BIRTHDAYS

John Wilkes Booth 1838, American assassin who ended the life of Abraham Lincoln.

Fred Astaire 1899, American actor, dancer and singer.

Paul 'Bono' Hewson 1960, Irish musician with the band U2, and campaigner for African humanitarian issues.

STONEWALL SHOT BY HIS OWN TROOPS

1863 The brilliant commander in the Confederate army General T. J. "Stonewall" Jackson is dead. Shot accidentally by his own troops eight days ago after inflicting a crushing defeat upon the Union army at Chancellorsville in northern Virginia, he developed pneumonia and died today. He was 39. Stonewall Jackson graduated from West Point, distinguished himself in the Mexican War and taught for 10 years at the Virginia Military Institute. He joined the Confederates in 1861. As their outnumbered forces fell back at the battle of Bull Run that July, Jackson stood firm – "like a stone wall", said General Barnard Bee – winning the day for the South. Consistently successful in battle, Jackson's death is a great loss to the South.

CHURCHILL WILL FIGHT

1940 Following furious argument in Parliament over military bungling in Norway, Winston Churchill has replaced Neville Chamberlain as British prime minister and is forming an all-party war government. Meanwhile news came that Adolf Hitler's troops had stormed Holland and Belgium. If Belgium falls, the Maginot Line, the main British defence, will be broken. In Westminster today rebel Tory MPs refused to back Chamberlain unless the opposition Labour and Liberal Parties were brought into an emergency government, but Labour refused to serve under Chamberlain, pre-war champion of appeasement with Hitler. Chamberlain then resigned in favour of Lord Halifax, the foreign secretary. But Labour MPs rejected Halifax in favour of Churchill. With Britain in dire peril, he promised his people nothing but "blood, toil, tears and sweat".

• 1869 – US RAILROAD LINKS EAST AND WEST • 1994 – MANDELA PRESIDENT OF SOUTH AFRICA

BLITZ BATTERS LONDON

1941 A pall of smoke hid the ruins as London emerged this morning from the worst bombing raids yet. At least 1400 people died as 550 German planes unloaded hundreds of bombs and more than 100,000 incendiaries over the city last night. Only 33 bombers were shot down. Many people are still trapped beneath the rubble as rescue teams fight to free them. The damage is immense: the House of Commons, Westminster Hall, Westminster Abbey, the British Museum and all the big railway stations are badly damaged. St Paul's Cathedral was hit, but still stands. German radio announced the raid was a reprisal for the bombing of German cities. London has now lost a total of 20,000 killed in the Blitz and a further 25,000 have been injured.

1812 British prime minister Spencer Perceval is shot dead in the House of Commons.

1824 The British capture Rangoon, using a steamship in war for the first time.

1858 Minnesota becomes the 32nd US state.

1900 World heavyweight champion Jim Jeffries knocks out James J. Corbett after 23 rounds.

1904 Australian diva Nellie Melba signs a recording contract with the Gramophone Company.

1956 Elvis Presley first enters the UK charts with "Heartbreak Hotel".

1985 The main stand at Bradford City football ground in northern England catches fire, killing 40 and injuring more than 170.

1988 Kim Philby, former British intelligence officer who spied for the Soviets, dies in Moscow aged 76.

BIRTHDAYS

Irving Berlin 1888, Russian-born American composer.

Martha Graham 1893, influential American teacher of modern dance.

Salvador Dali 1904, Spanish Surrealist painter.

INDIANS DEFY BRITISH RULE

1857 Britain's Indian sepoy troops have mutinied in Meerut, killing their officers and every European they could find. Thousands are marching to seize Delhi. There is widespread resentment over British rule, which has run roughshod over Indian sensibilities. The British commander at Meerut was warned of today's rebellion but did not believe it could happen and therefore took no precautions.

CYCLONE DEATH TOLL MOUNTS

1991 The death toll from the cyclone that devastated Bangladesh is climbing towards 250,000. The entire coastal plain, millions of acres of fertile rice land, is underwater following fierce floods that swept away whole communities. Supplies are needed urgently – foreign aid has been promised, but not much has arrived, and getting it to those who need it is a massive problem.

• 1981 – *CATS* MUSICAL OPENS IN LONDON • 1981 – BOB MARLEY DIES

1870 Canada purchases the Red River Colony from the Hudson Bay Company.

1932 The kidnapped baby son of aviator Charles Lindbergh is found dead.

1935 Alcoholics Anonymous is founded in Akron, Ohio.

1937 The coronation in London of King George VI and Queen Elizabeth is broadcast live by the BBC.

1943 The Axis powers in North Africa surrender.

1969 The minimum voting age in Britain is lowered from 21 to 18.

1991 The first multi-party general election since 1959 is held in Nepal.

BIRTHDAYS

Edward Lear 1812, English poet who wrote the *Book of Nonsense*.

Florence Nightingale 1820, English nurse and hospital reformer.

Dante Gabriel Rossetti 1828, co-founder of the Pre-Raphaelite Brotherhood.

Burt Bacharach 1929, American composer whose collaboration with Hal David produced hits such as "Walk on By".

GENERAL STRIKE FAILS

1926 Britain's Trades Union Congress has called off the General Strike that has brought the nation to a virtual halt for the last nine days. A bare skeleton of essential services kept the country going after public transport, rail, ports, post, supplies and industry as a whole simply stopped on May 4. Police barricaded vital centres and there were armoured cars on city streets as the army escorted convoys of emergency supplies. Members of the middle classes volunteered at the official Organisation for the Maintenance of Supplies to drive lorries or sort mail. Meanwhile the miners' strike continues with the sympathy of the TUC.

USSR UNBLOCKS BERLIN

1949 The Soviet Union has called off its blockade of Berlin after more than a year. The former capital is entirely surrounded by Russian-occupied Germany. The Russians had closed the roads, stopped the trains and banned food imports from the Soviet sector in protest at the Western Allies' plans to create an independent republic in West Germany. Britain and America beat the blockade with a round-the-clock airlift, with up to 200 flights a day ferrying food and supplies to the city.

SICHUAN PROVINCE SUFFERS HUGE QUAKE

2008 An earthquake measuring 7.9 on the Richter scale hit the Chinese province of Sichuan, leaving 87,000 people dead or missing and around five million homeless. Rescue efforts were hampered by strong aftershocks which claimed more

lives, and heavy rain which caused mudslides. Many children and students were killed. The quake caused 30 lakes to form as landslides blocked rivers. The largest, Tangjiashan Lake, had to be drained by troops as its instability posed a threat to a million homes downstream.

• 1916 – IRISH REBEL LEADERS SHOT • 2000 – INDIA'S POPULATION HITS ONE BILLION

POPE IN VATICAN SHOOTING

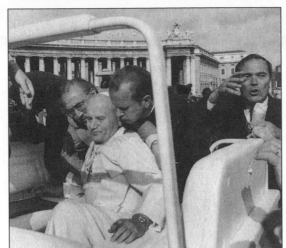

1981 A crowd of 20,000 people in St Peter's Square in Rome today saw Pope John Paul II shot four times by a Turkish gunman. The Pope, in his white open-top jeep, was blessing the crowds during his weekly audience when the gunman opened fire, hitting the Pope and wounding two other people. The gunman was arrested as the jeep sped to safety. After a five-hour operation the Pope was declared out of danger and is expected to recover fully. The gunman, Mehmet Ali Agca, 23, had escaped from Turkey where he was apparently being held for murder. He shot the Pope in protest at "American and Russian imperialism".

I used to say that politics was the second lowest profession and I have come to know that it bears a great similarity to the first.

Ronald Reagan, on the run-up to the presidential campaign trail, on this day, 1979.

MAY
13

1830 The republic of Ecuador is created.

1835 Death of John Nash, English architect.

1958 Right-wing French settlers, backed by the military, seize government buildings in Algiers as 40,000 demonstrators take to the streets to demand independence.

1971 On his 21st birthday, American musician Stevie Wonder receives $1 million as his childhood earnings – he actually earned more than $30 million.

1989 British ex-pilot Jackie Mann is kidnapped in Beirut.

1990 A car bomb in Bogota, Colombia, kills 26.

BIRTHDAYS

Sir Arthur Sullivan 1842, English composer who wrote 16 operettas with librettist W. S. Gilbert.

Georges Braque 1882, French painter who was, with Picasso, the joint creator of Cubism.

Dame Daphne du Maurier 1907, English writer whose novels include *Rebecca* and *Jamaica Inn*.

Joe Louis 1914, American world heavyweight boxing champion.

RIVERA MURAL DRIVES NEW YORK UP THE WALL

1933 A huge mural commissioned for the RCA Building, centrepoint of New York's huge new Rockefeller Center, has been destroyed. The painting, by the renowned Mexican artist Diego Rivera, so outraged New York society that Nelson Rockefeller, who commissioned Rivera, asked him to remove it. He refused, so Rockefeller had the mural scraped off. The painting, *Man at the Crossroads*, showed man's progress through technology to a proletarian Utopia, and included a large portrait of Lenin. New Yorkers say a bastion of capitalism such as the Rockefeller Center is hardly the place for a portrait of the revolutionary leader.

• 1844 – *GUARDIA CIVIL* ESTABLISHED IN SPAIN • 1846 – US AND MEXICO AT WAR

1796 British physician Edward Jenner carries out the first successful vaccination against smallpox.

1801 Pasha Yusuf Karamanli of Tripoli declares war on the US.

1847 HMS *Driver* completes the first round the world voyage by a steamship.

1900 The second modern Olympic Games open in Paris.

1948 Atlantic Records is founded in the USA.

1987 A coup takes place in Fiji, aimed at curbing the influence of Indian migrants in government.

1990 Anti-Semitism resurfaces in France with the desecration of a Jewish grave at Carpentras cemetery.

BIRTHDAYS

Thomas Gainsborough 1727, English painter of sentimental rural genre scenes.

Otto Klemperer 1885, German conductor.

Bobby Darin 1936, American pop singer who reached the charts with "Mack the Knife".

FANATICAL MONK STABS KING

1610 France's Good King Henry IV was murdered today as he rode in his carriage in Paris. A fanatical Catholic monk, François Ravaillac, jumped on to the carriage wheel when the coach stopped in the traffic and plunged a dagger into the King's chest. Ravaillac's aim was to stop the King's planned war against Catholic Spain and Austria. Henry ended 50 years of religious war in France and won wide popularity through his reconstruction of the devastated country. He is succeeded by his 8-year-old son, Louis XIII.

Goldwyn back in the big time

1939 Hollywood film producer Sam Goldwyn took control of United Artists today after buying out Charlie Chaplin, Mary Pickford and Douglas Fairbanks, who founded the movie corporation in 1919 with director D. W. Griffiths. Goldwyn sold his interest in Metro-Goldwyn-Mayer (MGM) in 1924, and has since been an independent producer. He is currently producing *Wuthering Heights* with director William Wyler. A Polish immigrant, Goldwyn is famous for his unusual turns of phrase.

ISRAEL BORN IN FIRE

1948 With eight hours still to run before the British mandate in Palestine runs out, the torn nation's 400,000 Jews today proclaimed the Zionist state of Israel and threw open the doors to Jewish immigrants, banned since 1944. US president Harry Truman immediately recognized the Jewish state. Meanwhile battle raged on between Jews and Arabs in a civil war that has claimed thousands of lives this year. With Britain's troops withdrawing, the 30,000-strong Jewish defence, Haganah, is on a full-scale war footing.

• 1955 – EASTERN BLOC SIGNS WARSAW PACT • 1873 – *SKYLAB I* BLASTS OFF FOR ORBIT

GOVERNOR GEORGE GUNNED DOWN BY WHITE ASSASSIN

1972 George Wallace, Governor of Alabama, is fighting for his life in a Washington hospital after an assassination attempt earlier today. Wallace, known for his racist and segregationist policies, was campaigning for the Democratic Party's presidential nomination in Maryland when a young white man shouted "Hey George" – and fired five shots at him at close range. Wallace was hit in the stomach, leg and in the spine. Doctors are confident Wallace will survive the shooting, but fear his spinal cord may have been damaged and he could be paralysed. The gunman, Arthur Bremer, 21, was arrested at the scene.

1718 London lawyer James Puckle patents the machine gun.

1829 The US Congress designates the slave trade as piracy.

1895 Death of Joseph Whitaker, English publisher of *Whitaker's Almanac*.

1918 The world's first regular air mail service begins between Washington and New York.

1936 Amy Johnson arrives in England after a record-breaking return flight from London to Cape Town.

1957 Britain's first H-bomb is dropped on Christmas Island.

1987 American actress Rita Hayworth dies.

1988 The USSR begins evacuating troops from Afghanistan.

BIRTHDAYS

Frank Baum 1856, American children's author best-known for *The Wonderful Wizard of Oz*.

James Mason 1909, English actor who appeared in more than 80 films.

Mike Oldfield 1953, British composer and instrumentalist who had a big hit with "Tubular Bells".

MEDICS TAKE TO THE SKIES OF OZ

1928 Medical care went airborne in Australia today with the launching of a Flying Doctor Service. Dr K. St Vincent Welch of the Australian Inland Mission launched the service, to cover the vast area of Central Australia and Queensland. A DH50 aircraft and a pilot have been provided by QANTAS – the Queensland and Northern Territory Aerial Service. Dr Welch will be called to emergency cases by means of a radio transmitter-receiver with a 300-mile (482-km) range.

SOVIETS AND CHINESE THAW ICY RELATIONS

1989 Soviet leader Mikhail Gorbachev shook hands with China's leader Deng Xiaoping in Peking's Great Hall of the People today, breaking the ice in a long-standing quarrel between the two nations. But the historic occasion was upstaged by events that occurred just outside the Great Hall as half a million Chinese gathered in Tiananmen Square demanding democratic reform in China. The demonstrations, which started last month, are led by student protesters, some 3,000 of whom are on hunger-strike.

• 1862 – BROOKLYN OPENS BASEBALL GROUNDS • 1998 – FRANK SINATRA DIES

1703 Death of the French writer of fairytales Charles Perrault.

1888 Emile Berliner gives the first demonstration of a flat recording disc.

1983 Diana Ross reunites with Mary Wilson and Cindy Birdsong to appear as The Supremes during a celebration of Motown Records' 25th birthday.

1984 Death of American author Irwin Shaw.

1989 The first successful hole in the heart operation is carried out.

1990 American entertainer Sammy Davis Jr dies of throat cancer.

1997 The Mobutu regime in Zaire collapses.

BIRTHDAYS

Henry Fonda 1905, American actor whose most notable films include *On Golden Pond*, for which he was awarded a posthumous Oscar.

Woody Herman 1913, American jazz clarinettist.

Liberace 1919, American pianist and kitsch entertainer.

Olga Korbut 1955, Soviet gymnast who stole the show at the Munich Olympics in 1972.

EDITH FOR PM

1991 France has its first woman prime minister. Socialist president François Mitterand announced today that Edith Cresson will replace the unpopular Michel Rocard, who has been dismissed. Cresson was Minister for European Affairs, and previously for Trade. Cresson faces a recession and rising unemployment – and the task of rallying a sagging socialist vote before the next elections. But she appears to relish the prospect.

DERBY CROSSES ATLANTIC

1875 A large crowd watched jockey Oliver Lewis ride Aristides to victory today in the maiden event of a new annual race, the Kentucky Derby, held at Churchill Downs in Louisville. The organizers intend the Derby to be one of the premiere Thoroughbred races of the American season, along with the Preakness Stakes at Pimlico in Maryland, now in its third year, and the Belmont Stakes at Jerome Park, New York, running since 1867. Horse-racing, the ancient sport of kings, is now the most popular spectator sport in America.

VAN GOGH KNOCKED DOWN FOR HIGHEST EVER PRICE

1990 A Japanese businessman paid $82.5 million for a Van Gogh in New York today, the highest price ever paid for a painting at auction. Paper manufacturer Ryoei Saito was the successful bidder for *Portrait of Dr Cachet* at Christie's. It was one of Van Gogh's last paintings before he shot himself. Mr Saito has not yet finished his buying spree – he is planning to attend Sotheby's New York sale tomorrow, and is said to have his eye on Renoir's famous *Au Moulin de la Galette*.

• 1943 – BOUNCING BOMBS DESTROY GERMANY'S INDUSTRIAL HEART

BOTTICELLI DIES
UNSUNG

1510 The great Florentine painter Sandro Botticelli has died in his native Florence aged 65. At the height of his career in the 1490s, Botticelli was the foremost of a new wave of Italian artists. He was only 25 when he was noticed by Lorenzo de' Medici, under whose patronage he did some of his finest work, including *The Birth of Venus*. He was taught by master of perspective Fra Filippo Lippi and sculptor Andrea del Verrocchio. Botticelli had hardly painted in recent years, and died in poverty.

1890 *Comic Cuts*, the first weekly comic paper, is published in London.

1935 Death of Paul Dukas, French composer, teacher and critic.

1962 Hong Kong puts up its own "Berlin wall" to keep out migrants.

1964 Bob Dylan makes his first major UK appearance at the Albert Hall.

1969 Dubliner Tom McClean becomes the first person to cross the Atlantic in a rowing boat.

1993 Rebecca Stephens is the first British woman to climb Everest.

2003 Casablanca, Morocco, is ravaged by terrorist bombs.

BIRTH OF THE PACKAGE TOUR

1861 A party of British workers and their families set off from London for Paris today on a new kind of holiday. Overland travel, the Channel crossing, hotel accommodation and meals all come in one convenient "package", arranged by Thomas Cook of London. Packaged holidays, offered to groups, are cheaper – Cook buys the tickets and hotel coupons in bulk and passes on the discounts to clients.

MAFEKING RELIEVED - EUPHORIA IN BRITAIN

1900 Extraordinary scenes of rejoicing have swept across Britain as a cable from South Africa brought news that the 217-day siege of the British garrison at Mafeking has been broken. London's streets filled with crowds as the tide turned in the Boer War following a string of humiliating British defeats. Reinforcements under Lord Roberts attacked the Boers from two sides, overwhelming them. The hero of the day is cavalry officer Colonel Robert Baden-Powell, the British commander in Mafeking. His unyielding defence tied down thousands of Boer troops and he has truly captured the British imagination.

BIRTHDAYS

Maureen O'Sullivan 1911, Irish actress who played Jane in six Tarzan movies.

Birgit Nilsson 1918, Swedish operatic soprano.

Dennis Hopper 1936, American actor and director.

Grace Jones 1955, Jamaican-born model turned pop singer.

Sugar Ray Leonard 1956, American boxer and world champion.

• 1861 – FIRST COLOUR PHOTOGRAPH • 1973 – WATERGATE SECRETS GO PUBLIC

1652 Slavery is banned in Rhode Island.

1803 Britain declares war on France.

1909 Death of Isaac Albéniz, Spanish composer and pianist, best known for the 12-piece Iberia.

1954 The European Convention on Human Rights comes into effect.

1987 Iraqi Exocet missiles hit the US naval frigate *Stark*, killing 26 – Baghdad says it is an accident.

1991 Muriel Box, British writer, feminist publisher and director of many films dies aged 85.

BIRTHDAYS

Nicholas II 1868, Russian tsar who was forced to abdicate at the beginning of the Revolution and was subsequently executed.

Bertrand Russell, 3rd Earl Russell 1872, British philosopher, mathematician and pacifist.

Frank Capra 1897, Italian-American director whose films include the Oscar-winning *It Happened One Night*.

Dame Margot Fonteyn 1919, British ballerina and partner of Rudolph Nureyev.

MAHLER DIES

1911 Gustav Mahler, the inspired Austrian conductor and composer, has died of heart disease at a sanatorium in Vienna, Austria. He was 51. Mahler had been expecting to die since he learned of his condition four years ago, yet he kept up a busy touring schedule in Europe and in New York, where he is a favourite. His Ninth Symphony is so charged with emotion that many find the work overpowering. Mahler always tended towards the magnificent: his symphonies are long works requiring huge orchestras, music on a monumental scale not heard before. They are awe-inspiring, but only the Second Symphony has yet gained any popularity.

WOMAN TOPS EVEREST

1975 Unstoppable Japanese climber Junko Tabei was today the first woman to reach the summit of the world's highest peak, the treacherous 29,029-ft (8848-m) Mount Everest in Nepal.

This island is almost made of coal and surrounded by fish. Only an organizing genius could produce a shortage of coal and fish in Great Britain at the same time.

Anuerin Bevan, opposition Labour politician, in a speech at Blackpool, 1945

EAST AND WEST GERMANS UNITE OVER CURRENCY

1990 In the face of strong Soviet disapproval, West and East Germany took the first step towards unity today when their two finance ministers met in Bonn to sign a formal accord on monetary union. From July 1 the two countries will have one currency – West Germany's deutschmark.

ANNE BOLEYN GOES TO THE BLOCK

1536 Anne Boleyn, English King Henry VIII's second wife, was beheaded in London today. She was 29. She had been charged with incest with her brother and four counts of adultery, but her real crimes were to let the king tire of her, and to fail to bear him a male heir. She gave birth to a daughter, Elizabeth, soon after they were married three years ago. Earlier this year Henry had her arrested after the stillbirth of a boy. He had meanwhile become infatuated with Anne's lady-in-waiting, Jane Seymour, and with Anne out of the way, an immediate marriage is planned. Henry's first wife, Catherine of Aragon, died in January. When she failed to bear him a son he tried to have the marriage annulled, and when Pope Clement VII refused Henry broke with the Roman church so that he could marry Anne. In fact they had already married in secret.

The ballot is stronger than the bullet.

Abraham Lincoln, in a speech on this day, 1856.

1649 England is declared a Commonwealth by the Rump Parliament.

1802 Napoleon institutes the title *Legion d'honneur* – the highest honour awarded for civil and military distinction.

1906 The 12-mile (19-km) Simplon Tunnel linking Italy and Switzerland through the Alps is opened.

1971 Death of American humorist Ogden Nash.

1984 Poet Laureate Sir John Betjeman, 78, dies.

1991 Helen Sharman, the first Briton in space, blasts off with two Soviet cosmonauts for a rendezvous with the Soviet Mir space station.

2014 Australian racing driver Sir Jack Brabham dies, aged 88.

BIRTHDAYS

Dame Nellie Melba 1848, Australian operatic singer.

Ho Chi Minh 1890, North Vietnamese revolutionary leader.

Malcolm X 1926, American Black Muslim leader.

Edward de Bono 1933, British doctor who developed the concept of lateral thinking.

MT ST HELENS EXPLODES

1980 At least 15 people were killed today when a long-dormant volcano in the US exploded. About 400 people were evacuated earlier when Mt St Helens in south-western Washington State started smoking a few weeks ago, but geologists did not expect the sudden violence of today's eruption, which started fires, mudslides and floods in areas thought to be safe. About 120 square miles (310 sq km) are devastated. The volcano is sending up a huge column of smoke and ash, darkening the sky 100 miles (160 km) away. It last erupted in 1857.

• 2007 – NEW STADIUM OPENS AT WEMBLEY • 1994 – JACQUELINE KENNEDY ONASSIS DIES

MAY
20

BIRTHDAYS

William Thornton 1759, American architect who created the Capitol in Washington.

Honoré de Balzac 1799, French novelist whose life's work was the *cycle La Comédie Humaine.*

James Stewart 1908, American actor whose many films include the Oscar-winning *The Philadelphia Story.*

JET TRAVEL MURDERS ORIENT EXPRESS

1961 The "king of trains and the train of kings", the once-luxurious Orient Express, set off from Paris today on its final journey to Istanbul. From its inauguration in 1883 until World War II stopped the service, the Orient Express was renowned as the epitome of luxury travel. It was used as the background to Graham Greene's *Stamboul Train* in 1932, and two years later was the setting for one of Agatha Christie's famous murders. Sadly, since the route reopened after the war, the standard of service has not been that preferred by kings – and these days, they fly.

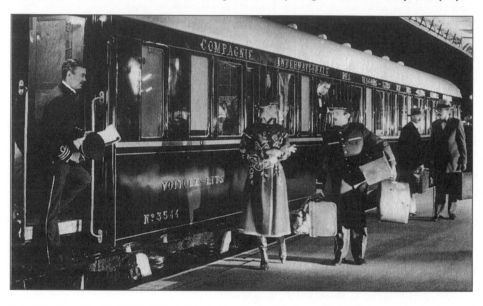

COLUMBUS STILL BELIEVED IN ASIA

1506 Christopher Columbus died today, virtually penniless, and still believing he had reached Asia. He was 55. Columbus spent seven years persuading Spain's Queen Isabella I to finance an expedition to search for a westward route to the Orient. Three months after leaving Europe his three ships reached the Bahamas. He sailed back and forth across the Atlantic on three further voyages, none successful. His discovery of favourable winds in both directions opened up the New World to Europe.

• 1910 – EARTH PASSES THROUGH THE FIERY TAIL OF HALLEY'S COMET

SOLITARY SPIRIT OF LINDBERGH

1927 Charles Lindbergh landed his plane in Paris this evening to win the $25,000 prize for the first solo flight across the Atlantic. A crowd of 100,000 turned out to welcome the 25-year-old American pilot in his specially-built plane, the *Spirit of St Louis*, as it landed at Le Bourget airport. Lindbergh took off from Roosevelt Field in Long Island early yesterday and was in the air for 33 hours and 40 minutes. He learned to fly five years ago and was flying a mail run between Chicago and St Louis when he heard about the prize money on offer. Now he is an international hero. US president Calvin Coolidge is sending a Navy cruiser to take him back to the US.

1471 King Henry VI of England dies in the Tower of London.

1618 Death of Italian physician Hieronymus Fabricius ab Aquapendente, who discovered one-way valves in veins.

1840 New Zealand is proclaimed a British colony.

1894 Queen Victoria opens the Manchester Ship Canal.

1975 The Baader-Meinhof terrorist gang goes on trial in Stuttgart.

1990 Ion Iliescu wins the first free elections in Romania.

2000 Sir John Gielgud, actor and director for 80 years dies aged 96.

2003 More than 2,000 people die as a massive earthquake hits Algeria.

Agincourt victor to rule France

1420 King Henry V of England is now ruler of France too, in terms of the Treaty of Troyes signed today. The agreement comes four years after Henry's spectacular victory at Agincourt. The treaty means that Henry can now marry the French princess Catherine de Valois, and that he will become king on the death of Charles de Valois.

The House of Lords is a model of how to care for the elderly.

Frank Field,
British politician,
1981.

RAJIV GANDHI ASSASSINATED

1991 Rajiv Gandhi is dead. The former prime minister of India was blown up by a woman terrorist suicide bomber at an election rally in South India this morning. He was 46. Gandhi's party, campaigning in the general election, had just arrived in the small town of Sriperumbudur, where a young woman knelt to kiss his feet. As Gandhi stooped to help her up, a bomb strapped to her body exploded, killing both of them. Sri Lanka's Tamil Tiger militants are suspected, but they have denied the charge.

Albrecht Dürer 1471, German painter, engraver, draughtsman and woodcut designer.

Henri Rousseau 1844, French naïve painter.

Thomas "Fats" Waller 1904, American jazz pianist and composer.

Andrei Sakharov 1921, Russian physicist and civil rights campaigner.

• 1966 – CASSIUS CLAY REMAINS UNBEATEN FOLLOWING CONTEST WITH HENRY COOPER

337 AD Constantine the Great is the first Roman emperor to convert to Christianity.

1455 The first battle of the English Wars of the Roses end with the Yorkists defeated by the Lancastrians at St Albans.

1885 French novelist, dramatist, poet and national literary hero, Victor Hugo dies in Paris, aged 83.

1981 Peter Sutcliffe, nicknamed the "Yorkshire Ripper" is found guilty at London's Old Bailey of the murder of 13 women and the attempted murder of seven others.

1990 New Zealand boats take the first three places in the Whitbread Round the World yacht race.

BIRTHDAYS

Richard Wagner 1813, German composer famed for the operatic cycle *Der Ring des Nibelungen*.

Sir Arthur Conan Doyle 1859, Scottish novelist who created the great detective Sherlock Holmes.

Laurence Olivier 1907, British actor, producer and director.

Rebels drive out Ethiopian president

1991 Ethiopian president Mengistu Haile Mariam fled to Zimbabwe today as rebel forces closed in on the capital, Addis Ababa. Mengistu's long civil war is largely held to blame for the environmental ruin which brought the famines of the 1980s. When Mengistu's Marxist regime came to power 40 per cent of Ethiopia was forested, but today only a tiny fraction of the trees are left and huge areas are uninhabitable. Mengistu spent $9 billion on Soviet arms to put down rebellions in Eritrea, Tigray and Oromo in the north, while only 3 per cent of the budget went to Ethiopia's farmers. The Ethiopian People's Revolutionary Democratic Front rebels now on the verge of victory, however, have worked with western agencies to help peasants and protect the environment in the areas they controlled.

US REBEL CHIEF TRACKED DOWN

1865 In the aftermath of the US civil war, Jefferson Davis, the fugitive president of the defeated Confederate states, was caught today by Union cavalry colonel Benjamin Pritchard in Irwinville, Georgia. He was disguised as a woman. There is the handsome reward of $100,000 for his capture to collect. President Andrew Johnson has publicly accused Davis of complicity in President Lincoln's assassination. Davis fled from Virginia last month as the confederacy collapsed, with the intention of organizing a government in exile. He is now awaiting indictment in prison at Fort Monroe.

WRIGHTS PATENT FLYING MACHINE

1908 Wilbur and Orville Wright patented their flying machine today, four years after their historic first powered flight at Kitty Hawk in North Carolina. That day the "Flyer I" made four flights, the longest lasting a minute and covering 852 ft (259 m). Today they still use the same machine, very much improved, to make flights of 40 minutes, travelling up to 25 miles (40 km)

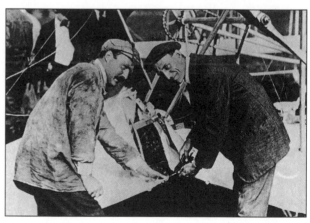

at altitudes of 150 ft (46 m) or more. Strangely the brothers are hardly known in America, except to a few hundred enthusiasts. But now their pioneering work is starting to bear fruit: last year the US Army Signal Corps contracted the Wrights to build a two-man aircraft capable of flying 125 miles (201 km), and later this year the brothers are to take their aircraft on tour in France – hence today's patent.

• 1792 – MUNGO PARK SETS OFF TO EXPLORE AFRICA • 1972 – NIXON VISITS THE USSR

VIOLENT END FOR CRIMINAL COUPLE

1934 The two bank robbers and cold-blooded murderers Bonnie Parker and Clyde Barrow died in a hail of bullets today when they drove their car straight into a police ambush in Louisiana. More than 50 bullets hit the pair, police said. Parker and Barrow have terrorized the southwestern states of America during the last four years, and have killed as many as 12 people in a series of brutal armed raids on small-town banks and gas stations. Clyde Barrow was 25 and Bonnie Parker just 23.

PIRATE HANGS

1701 Captain William Kidd was hanged for piracy and murder in London today. His trial and sentence were widely publicized in an attempt to deter other seamen from preying on merchant ships. Kidd, 56, was commissioned as a British privateer to wage war on Spanish and French ships. Five years ago he turned to piracy, taking rich prizes off the coasts of Africa. Thinking his commission would protect him, Kidd returned to Long Island with his fleet, but he was arrested in Boston shortly afterwards and brought to London for trial.

1498 Italian religious reformer Girolamo Savonarola is hanged and burnt at the stake for heresy.

1795 In Paris, troops put down an uprising caused by bread shortages.

1873 The North West Mounted Police are formed in Canada.

1887 The French crown jewels go on sale, raising six million francs.

1945 Heinrich Himmler, Adolf Hitler's minister of the interior, commits suicide.

1948 The *Empire Windrush* sets sail from Jamaica with the first boatload of West Indian migrants to the UK.

1991 Chinese authorities mark the fortieth anniversary of their "liberation" of Tibet with low-key celebrations.

BIRTHDAYS

Carl Linnaeus 1707, Swedish botanist who established the principles for classifying and naming plants and animals.

Sir Charles Barry 1795, English architect who designed the Houses of Parliament.

Anatoly Karpov 1951, Russian chess champion.

SEA SUCCESS FOR DA GAMA

1498 The Portuguese navigator Vasco da Gama arrived at Calicut on India's Malabar coast today, the first European to reach the Indies by sea. Da Gama sailed his four ships south from Lisbon to the Cape of Good Hope at the tip of Africa, and then up Africa's east coast. The sultan of Mozambique thought the voyagers were Muslims and gave them pilots for the journey north, but hostile Arabs attacked them at Mombasa. Da Gama's reception in Calicut could have been warmer: the gifts he took ashore today were more suited to Africa, and Calicut's ruler rejected them.

• 1863 – US FRONTIERSMAN KIT CARSON DIES • 1990 – US BOXER ROCKY GRAZIANO DIES

MAY
24

BIRTHDAYS

Gabriel Fahrenheit 1686, German physicist who invented the mercury thermometer.

Queen Victoria 1819, English monarch.

Bob Dylan 1941, American singer, songwriter and poet who became a cult figure.

MARX LUNACY GOES CELLULOID

1929 After six years on Broadway, the anarchic lunacy of the Marx Brothers now has movie audiences roaring. "Your eyes shine like the pants of my blue serge suit," leers Groucho Marx round his cigar in *The Coconuts*, premiered in New York tonight. Fast-talking Groucho (born Julius) with his bushy eyebrows and thick black moustache, Chico (Leonard), who mostly plays an Italian, Harpo (Adolph), who plays the harp but doesn't say a word, and fourth brother Zeppo (Herbert) who provides romantic relief, get full Marx for zaniness. The brothers are now making a film version of *Animal Crackers*, which opened on Broadway last year.

COPERNICUS TURNS HEAVENS UPSIDE DOWN

1543 As he lay dying today, Nicolaus Copernicus ,the canon of Frauenberg cathedral in Poland was brought the first copy of a treatise he has written that overturns church doctrine on man's place in the universe. His book, *On the Revolutions of the Heavenly Spheres*, claims – as Aristotle and Ptolemy claimed before him – that the Earth and the other planets revolve round the sun, which itself doesn't stay in one place. The universe, he says, is much bigger than was thought – and man's place in it is far from central. In fact Copernicus's scheme of things sounds very plausible, and the book is bound to cause immense controversy.

• **1941 – HMS *HOOD* SINKS WITH A LOSS OF 1400 LIVES** • **1974 – DUKE ELLINGTON DIES**

OWENS' RECORD BUSTING DAY

1935 Jesse Owens, a 21-year-old black student athlete from Alabama, set five new world records and equalled a sixth this afternoon – a world record in itself for a single day's achievement. He equalled the 100 yards record, then set new records for the long jump, 220 yards and 220-yard hurdles, relentlessly breaking the 200 metre records on the way.

1768 Captain Cook sets forth from England in his ship the *Endeavour* to explore the Antipodes.

1934 Death of Gustav Holst, British composer best-known for *The Planets*.

1950 French troops clash with Viet Cong guerrillas in Vietnam.

1961 The Ku Klux Klan clash with civil rights "Freedom Riders" in Montgomery, Alabama.

1965 Heavyweight boxer Cassius Clay knocks out Sonny Liston in the first round of their fight.

1986 South African troops drive 25,000 blacks out of Crossroads squatter camp.

AMERICANS TO DRAFT CONSTITUTION

1787 A special group met in the State House in Philadelphia today to set about writing a new constitution for the United States. They include George Washington, Philadelphia lawyer John Dickinson, President Benjamin Franklin, distinguished soldier, Alexander Hamilton and Virginia leader James Madison. The meeting was called because Congress faces bankruptcy and the states are alarmed by Shays' Rebellion earlier this year. The uprising by bankrupt farmers showed the need for a stronger central government, but under the Articles of Confederation the government has no control over commerce and cannot raise taxes or enforce its own laws.

BIRTHDAYS

Ralph Waldo Emerson 1803, American poet and essayist.

Miles Davis 1926, American trumpeter and composer who had a huge influence on jazz music.

Beverley Sills 1929, American operatic soprano who became director of the New York City Opera when she retired from singing.

Sir Ian McKellen 1938, British stage and screen actor.

THOR'S REED ADVENTURE

1969 Norwegian Thor Heyerdahl and his seven-man crew set sail today to cross the Atlantic in a reed boat named *Ra* after the Sun God of the Pharaohs. Heyerdahl, famed for his *Kon-Tiki* expedition across the Pacific in a balsa-wood raft the experts said would sink, now aims to prove that the ancient Egyptians sailed to America, which would account for the New World's pre-Columbian pyramids. His new craft was built by traditional boat-builders from Chad, using 12 tons of papyrus reeds. *Ra* sailed today from the old Moroccan port of Safi. Once again, the experts are predicting that the reed boat will sink.

• 1986 – WORLDWIDE, 30 MILLION PEOPLE RUN "A RACE AGAINST TIME" FOR SPORT AID

735 AD The Venerable Bede, English scholar, monk and historian, dies.

1660 King Charles II of England lands at Dover after a nine-year exile.

1791 The French Assembly forces Louis XVI to hand over the crown.

1805 Napoleon Bonaparte is crowned King of Italy.

1908 A major oil strike is made in Persia, the first in the Middle East.

1969 John Lennon and Yoko Ono begin a "bed-in" for world peace and invite the media to film them.

1988 Andrew Lloyd Webber's musical *Cats* opens in Moscow with a British and American cast.

BIRTHDAYS

Al Jolson 1886, American singer and entertainer, star of the first movie with sound, *The Jazz Singer*.

John Wayne 1907, American actor who appeared in more than 250 films.

Peggy Lee 1920, American singer-songwriter with a distinctive voice.

Stevie Nicks 1948, American singer-songwriter and member of Fleetwood Mac.

US CIVIL WAR OVER: HALF A MILLION DEAD

1865 The last organized resistance in the US civil war ended today when General Kirby Smith surrendered Confederate forces west of the Mississippi. Resistance east of the Mississippi ended on May 4, following General Robert E. Lee's surrender to Ulysses S. Grant at Appomattox on April 9. The Confederate navy still holds the port of Galveston in Texas. The war has torn America: half a million are dead and the South is crippled. President Lincoln's death is a severe loss to the post-war healing process; he called for generous reconciliation in his last speech, three days after Appomattox. President Andrew Johnson is instigating plans for amnesty and to bring the rebel states back into Congress.

MAKESHIFT NAVY EVACUATES BRITISH FROM DUNKIRK

1940 A strange armada of more than 700 boats set sail from Britain across the English Channel today as virtually everything that would float made for the beaches at Dunkirk in France to rescue 380,000 trapped Allied troops. The awesome Nazi war machine has taken just 10 days to sweep aside Allied defences in France and Belgium. In a lightning push through the Ardennes, German troops cut off the retreating British, French and Belgian armies now facing annihilation on the beaches. Helped by RAF air cover, the besieged troops are fighting a fierce rearguard battle to defend the beaches, but the makeshift flotilla of destroyers, ferries, fishing boats and pleasure craft are coming under heavy fire as they pick up the exhausted troops.

The history of the World is the World's court of justice.

Freidrich von Schiller, German dramatist, on this day, 1789.

• 1703 – DIARIST SAMUEL PEPYS DIES • 1923 – FRENCH WIN 1ST RACE AT LE MANS

KREMLIN TRIGGERS SHOPPING FRENZY

1990 The Kremlin announced its new economic package today – and provoked an unprecedented shopping frenzy in major towns across the whole Soviet Union. Hordes of panic buyers emptied shops of everything they could get their hands on, and many left with nothing. The reforms mean that the traditional food subsidies will be phased out to create what the Kremlin calls a "regulated market economy". Meat prices and sugar will double and bread will cost three times as much as it does currently. But the new package is not law until parliament approves it, and there may be a referendum.

1657 Lord Protector Oliver Cromwell refuses the title of King of England.

1851 Adolf Anderssen wins the first International Master chess tournament.

1900 Belgium becomes the first country to elect a government by proportional representation.

1963 Jomo Kenyatta becomes the first prime minister of Kenya.

1994 Novelist Alexander Solzhenitsyn returns to Russia after 20 years in exile.

BIRTHDAYS

James "Wild Bill" Hickok 1837, American frontiersman.

Amelia Bloomer 1818, American women's rights campaigner.

Isadora Duncan 1878, American dancer and pioneer of a hugely influential style.

Sam Snead 1912, American golfer who won 135 tournaments between 1936 and 1965.

Henry Kissinger 1923, German-born US secretary of state; shared the Nobel Peace Prize in 1973 with Le Duc Tho for his part in ending the Vietnam War.

JAPAN SINKS RUSSIAN FLEET

1905 Japan has won a great naval victory, annihilating the Russian Baltic fleet sent to relieve Port Arthur. Only three of the 38 Russian ships escaped from the straits of Tsushima in the Sea of Japan, while Japanese admiral Togo Heihachiro's fleet lost just three torpedo boats. Togo outmanoeuvred the Russians and sank all four Russian capital ships – including the Admiral Nakhimov, reputed to have been carrying $2000 million in gold and platinum. The Baltic fleet set sail 18 months ago for Vladivostok. It was too late to save Port Arthur, which surrendered to Japan on January 2 after a seven-month siege. On March 10 the Japanese routed the 200,000-man Russian army at Mukden. A humiliated Russia now has no choice but to concede defeat.

VIRTUOSO'S FINAL BOW

1840 The illustrious Italian violinist Niccolo Paganini went to his Maker today – although opinion may be divided on just which maker that might be. Many are convinced that the Devil himself played Paganini's violin for him. His skill was sheer wizardry – he could give stunning performances on only one string – and his music and dark good looks mesmerized his audiences, not least people's wives and daughters. Paganini died in Nice aged 58, and surely went to heaven.

There is no art which one government sooner learns of another than that of draining money from the pockets of the people.

Adam Smith, pioneering economist, 1776.

• 1564 – FRENCH PROTESTANT JOHN CALVIN DIES • 1949 – COMMUNISTS TAKE SHANGHAI

1891 The first world weightlifting championships are held in London.

1937 Death of Alfred Adler, Austrian psychiatrist.

1940 The Belgian army surrenders to the Nazis.

1967 British yachtsman Francis Chichester arrives in Plymouth 119 days after setting out on a solo round-the-world trip.

1972 The Duke of Windsor, English king who abdicated to marry American divorcee Wallis Simpson, dies in Paris.

2014 Maya Angelou, American poet and author, dies, aged 86.

BIRTHDAYS

Joseph Guillotin 1738, French physician and revolutionary who developed the guillotine.

William Pitt (the Younger) 1759, English statesman who became prime minister at 24.

Ian Fleming 1908, British novelist and creator of James Bond.

Edward Seaga 1930, Jamaican politician and prime minister.

Kylie Minogue 1968, Australian actress and pop singer.

DUTCH HOLD BACK NORTH SEA'S TIDE

1932 Dutch engineers completed the world's biggest dam today, claiming a major victory in their 800-year battle to push back the sea. The new dam wall, or dike, is 18 miles (29 km) long, and turns the Zuider Zee into a vast freshwater lake, called the Ijsselmeer. The dam cuts off the capital city of Amsterdam from the sea, and ships must now use the 14-mile (22-km) deep-water North Sea Canal, which was completed in 1876.

PARIS COMMUNE DROWNS IN BLOOD

1871 The Paris Commune collapsed today after a two-month siege, brutally suppressed by government troops in a week of bitter street fighting which has left 33,000 killed and part of the city in ruins. The communes at Lyons and Marseilles have already collapsed and the movement is dead. Backed by the National Guard, the communards set up a revolutionary municipal government in Paris in protest at the humiliating peace terms imposed by the victorious Prussian army, which had besieged the city for four months.

TEENAGER LANDS PLANE IN RED SQUARE

1987 A West German teenager's prank caused world-wide mirth today and seriously embarrassed the Soviet Union. Mathias Rust, 19, flew his light Cessna plane from Helsinki to Moscow, buzzed the Kremlin and landed in Red Square – evading the entire Soviet air defence system. He alighted to sign autographs for astonished Moscow passers-by before being taken away by bemused policemen. Extremely unamused are the hard men in the Kremlin, who are unlikely simply to dock Mathias's pocket money. The young prankster is in trouble.

• 1982 – MARADONA SELLS FOR £5 MILLION • 1985 – CYCLONE HITS BANGLADESH

EVEREST CROWNED BY HILLARY AND TENZING

1953 A British team has "crowned" Mount Everest, the world's highest peak, reaching the summit just four days before Britain crowns its new queen, Elizabeth II. New Zealand-born climber Edmund Hillary and the Sherpa guide Tenzing Norgay reached the 29,029-ft (8848-m) summit at 11.30 this morning. They stayed for about 15 minutes to take photos and plant the Union Jack, the Nepalese flag and the UN flag side by side in the snow, with biscuits and cake as a Buddhist offering. Then they began the downward climb, tired but elated at their success. For 30 years men have tried and failed to scale Everest – or "Chomolungma" as it is called in Tibetan, "goddess mother of the world". Hillary and Tenzing used up-to-date mountaineering equipment, including special nylon clothing and oxygen equipment, and expedition leader Colonel John Hunt planned the assault meticulously, making a close study of previous climbs. An attempt earlier this month failed in high winds, but today the weather was perfect.

1453 Constantinople falls to the Turkish army after a siege lasting for a year.

1795 Virginia Assembly opposes Britain's Stamp Act.

1914 Canadian Pacific liner the *Empress of Ireland* is wrecked in the St Lawrence River, drowning over 1000 people.

1972 Presidents Nixon and Brezhnev sign the first arms reduction pact.

1979 Abel Muzorewa becomes first black prime minister of Rhodesia.

1989 Boris Yeltsin is elected to the Supreme Soviet after popular protests at his exclusion.

2010 US actor Dennis Hopper dies, aged 74.

BIRTHDAYS

G. K. Chesterton 1874, English novelist, essayist and poet.

Joseph von Sternberg 1894, Austrian film director and actor whose innovative films include *The Blue Angel*.

Bob Hope 1903, English-born American comedian who won five Oscars.

John F. Kennedy 1917, American politician who was the youngest president ever elected.

The Queen is most anxious to enlist everyone who can speak or write to join in checking this mad, wicked folly of "Women's Rights", with all its attendant horrors, on which her poor feeble sex is bent, forgetting every sense of womanly feeling and propriety.

Victoria,
Queen of England,
in a letter, 1870.

EUROPEAN CUP VIOLENCE KILLS 41 AT HEYSEL

1985 Britain's soccer hooligans went on the rampage at Heysel Stadium in Belgium tonight, causing a riot which left 41 fans dead. Most of the casualties were Italian. Chanting hooligans from Liverpool charged Italian fans in the stands during the European Cup Final between Liverpool and Juventus, causing immediate panic as a wall and safety fence collapsed under the surge of people. The fighting went on as police struggled to rescue those who were trapped, with the hooligans using lethal iron bars and bottles as weapons. Bodies were being laid out in the car park as mounted riot police rode in to stop the fighting.

• 1660 – MONARCHY RESTORED IN ENGLAND, WITH CHARLES II AS KING

BIRTHDAYS

MARLOWE KILLED IN PUB BRAWL

1593 The English playwright Christopher Marlowe is dead, killed in a London tavern brawl after an argument over religion. He was 29, and had published only one of his plays. *Tamburlaine the Great* – already recognized as a classic. His *Doctor Faustus* remains unpublished. His work has greatly influenced his contemporaries Thomas Kyd and William Shakespeare. But last year Marlowe was arrested for counterfeiting, and earlier this month he was arrested again, accused of heresy.

GODDESS OF DEMOCRACY OUTFACES CHAIRMAN MAO

1989 A defiant Goddess of Democracy and Freedom confronted the huge portrait of Chairman Mao in Peking's Tiananmen Square this morning. The 30 ft (9 m) figure, modelled on New York's Statue of Liberty, was sculpted overnight by Chinese art students out of fibreglass and plaster. A million people flooded the square again today to demand democratic reform, defying the martial law declaration of 10 days ago in an awesome confrontation with authority. The campaign is now nationwide.

INDIANAPOLIS 500 IS FAST BUT SAFE

1911 The new face of high-speed motor racing made its debut today when Ray Harroun won a 500-mile (804-km) race held on a special 2.5-mile (4-km) brick-paved circuit at Indianapolis. Harroun, who came out of retirement to drive his Marmon Wasp to victory, covered the 200 laps at an average speed of 74.59 mph (120 kph). The prestige Vanderbilt Cup race on Long Island has now been banned since today's racing cars are too fast for safety on the open streets. The Indianapolis Motor Raceway's three-millon-brick track points the way forward – drivers may risk their necks but the spectators are safe. The Indianapolis 500 will be held every Memorial Day – the last Monday in May.

OUTGUNNED BOERS QUIT

1902 "With grief, South Africa's Boer generals formally surrendered to Britain tonight. The Boer War started with humiliation for the British – mere farmers overwhelmed the imperial forces in battle after battle. In the end 450,000 of Britain's elite troops were pitted against only 80,000 Boer fighters, who relied on mobility and expert guerrilla tactics. Britain's Lord Kitchener finally countered this by cordoning off the land

and herding the Boer women and children into concentration camps, where more than 20,000 – one in three – died of disease and malnutrition. The camps have caused deep dissent in Britain and outrage in Europe, where Britain has been dubbed the "Dirty Dog". The peace treaty provides for eventual self-rule for the Boer republics, with the issue of votes for natives to be dealt with after that.

1809 Death of Austrian composer Franz Joseph Haydn.

1939 Britain interns fascist leader Sir Oswald Mosley and other fascist sympathizers as the government consolidates emergency war powers.

1958 The Kremlin agrees to talks with the US on an atmospheric test ban treaty.

1962 Nazi war criminal Adolf Eichmann is hanged in Israel.

1965 British racing driver Jim Clark becomes the first non-American driver to win the Indianapolis 500.

1983 Jack Dempsey, American boxer who was world heavyweight champion, dies aged 87.

BIRTHDAYS

Walt Whitman 1819, American poet.

Walter Sickert 1860, British Impressionist painter.

William Heath Robinson 1872, English illustrator and cartoonist.

Clint Eastwood 1930, American actor and director who hit the big time with spaghetti westerns.

THE LAST MODEL T

1927 The last Model T Ford, No. 15,007,003, rolled off the assembly line today. It is to be replaced by the Model A. Retooling the Ford production lines will take six months and cost at least $200 million. Henry Ford has held on to the Model T too long, and has now lost first place to General Motors. Ford introduced the moving assembly line technique of mass production in the US. One result has been a drop in price – the first Model Ts cost $850 in 1908, but they now sell for under $300. But the thriving second-hand market has hit sales. Other companies are countering this by making their cars slightly different every year.

VENICE'S LITTLE DYER DIES

1594 The great Venetian painter Tintoretto died today at the age of 76. The "little dyer", nicknamed after his father, a "tintero", or dyer, combined Titian's brilliant use of colour with Michelangelo's draughtsmanship in some of the world's biggest paintings. Among his master works is the cycle of paintings in the Scuola of the Confraternity of San Rocco in Venice which took him six years working at great speed with a phalanx of assistants, including his two sons and daughter. Tintoretto's *Paradise*, the largest canvas in the world, measures 84 ft by 34 ft (25.5 m by 10.3 m). He will be buried in the church containing the 50 ft (15.2 m) painting *Last Judgement*.

• 1961 – SOUTH AFRICA DECLARES INDEPENDENCE • 1991 – CIVIL WAR ENDS IN ANGOLA

JUNE

PEPPER ASSAULT

1967 The Beatles, indisputably the foremost British pop group of the decade, today released their new album, *Sergeant Pepper's Lonely Heart's Club Band*. The new release – a distinctive blend of pop, symphonic and Indian musical forms – is the greatest achievement in their creative output so far, and looks set to become a Beatles classic. Over the eight years since their beginnings in Liverpool, the group have continued to experiment, producing ever more inventive and sophisticated work.

How reconcile this world of fact with the bright world of my imagining? My darkness has been filled with the light of intelligence, and behold, the outer daylight world was stumbling and groping in social blindness.

The deaf and blind author **Helen Keller,** who died today, 1968.

1815 Napoleon Bonaparte swears fidelity to the French constitution.

1831 Sir James Clark Ross locates the magnetic North Pole on his Arctic expedition with Admiral Parry.

1910 Captain Robert Falcon Scott sails out of London on the *Terra Nova*, bound for the South Pole.

1939 The Royal Navy submarine *Thetis* leaks carbon monoxide, poisoning 70 of its crew.

1942 Television licences are first issued in Britain.

1966 Bob Dylan uses an electric guitar for the first time in Britain – and is booed by purist folk fans.

1979 Rhodesia takes the name of Zimbabwe.

BIRTHDAYS

Marilyn Monroe 1926, American actress who led a turbulent life and became an icon after her death.

Edward Woodward 1930, British actor.

Pat Boone 1934, American singer.

Morgan Freeman 1937, American actor who won an Oscar in 2005 for his performance in *Million Dollar Baby*.

Royal family massacred in Nepal

2001 The kingdom of Nepal has been rocked by the murders of 11 members of the Royal Family during a banquet. Prince Dipendra, heir to the throne, has been named as the killer. It is believed he shot dead his parents and relatives, then turned the gun on himself. There has been no official word about what triggered the violence, though reports suggest the incident followed an argument about the Prince's choice of bride. Although the Prince is gravely ill in hospital, royal tradition means he is the rightful successor to the throne.

THE QUEEN CELEBRATES HER GOLDEN JUBILEE

2002 Wide-ranging celebrations marking the Queen's Golden Jubilee start today, with a classical prom in the grounds of Buckingham Palace. The People's Party begins on Monday with street parties and a three-hour concert at the palace. Irish band The Corrs will play at the Queen's Golden Jubilee concert with many other artists. On Friday, a fleet of warships sailed into Chatham Historic Dockyard to take part in the three-day maritime and military celebration attended by the Princess Royal. On Tuesday, there will be a ceremonial procession in central London, the day the Jubilee weekend celebrations come to an end.

• 1880 – FIRST PUBLIC TELEPHONE • 2004 – MANDELA ANNOUNCES HIS RETIREMENT

1868 Britain crushes the Marathas in India and annexes their lands.

1882 Italian nationalist leader Giuseppe Garibaldi dies aged 74.

1946 Italy's monarchy is abolished and the country becomes a republic.

1954 Jockey Lester Piggott wins his first Derby on Never Say Die.

1966 American automatic spacecraft *Surveyor* lands on the moon.

1985 English football clubs are banned from playing in Europe owing to hooliganism.

BIRTHDAYS

Marquis de Sade 1740, French writer who was imprisoned in the Bastille for his sexual perversions.

Thomas Hardy 1840, English novelist and poet whose books were set in imaginary Wessex.

Sir Edward Elgar 1857, English composer best-known for the Enigma Variations.

Lotte Reiniger 1899, German film animator who made the first full-length animated film in 1920 – *The Adventures of Prince Achmed*.

POLAND'S POPE COMES HOME

1979 An emotional welcome awaited Pope John Paul II as he set foot on the soil of his native Poland. Born 59 years ago in Wadowice and christened Karol Wojtyla, John Paul was only elected to office on October 16 last year – the first non-Italian to be elected Pope in 456 years. Although Poland is under Communist rule, much of the population remains true to its Catholic roots. The Pope's visit marks an opening-up in the relationship between the Church and the Communist Bloc.

MARCONI INVENTION: NO WIRES ATTACHED

1896 Italian-born physicist Guglielmo Marconi has taken out the first patent for a device that transmits spoken messages over long distances without the aid of cables. Using a transmitter and a receiver, Marconi's invention broadcasts sound by means of invisible electro-magnetic waves – a phenomenon first demonstrated by the German physicist, Heinrich Hertz. Although transmission is limited to a distance of under 12 miles (19 km), Marconi aims to extend its range still further, perhaps even to France.

VIVAT REGINA!

1953 The Archbishop of Canterbury solemnly lowered the Crown of St Edward on to the head of Princess Elizabeth Alexandra Mary, today, to make her Queen Elizabeth II of Great Britain and Ireland. Outside, in the cold and wet, thousands of spectators waited for the new Queen to emerge and make her journey to Buckingham Palace in the ceremonial golden coach. Black-market tickets for the event were going for as much as £50 ($92), while a balcony with a good view commanded up to £3500 ($6500). Those who could not make it were glued to the screens of a record two and a half million televisions.

• 1780 – FIRST-EVER EPSOM HORSE RACE • 1964 – PLO FORMS IN JERUSALEM

NEW SHIP-BASED PLANES FOR US TO CRACK JAPANESE

1942 The Midway Islands, some 1150 miles (1850 km) west-northwest of Hawaii, are the scene of a new kind of warfare – airborne attack between US and Japanese carrier-based planes. After last month's humiliating surrender of US troops under the command of General Jonathan Wainwright, the Americans hope that this bold, new-style offensive will help them to reclaim the Pacific islands from the Japanese, who have established a military presence there. If these hopes are fulfilled, the Battle of Midway – as it is being called – could prove a turning point for the Allies in the Pacific war.

1864 In the American Civil War, more than 6,000 Unionists are killed or wounded in less than an hour at Cold Harbor.

1875 Death of French composer Georges Bizet.

1964 The Rolling Stones begin their first US tour.

1972 In Cincinnati, Sally Priesand is ordained as the first woman rabbi.

2006 Montenegro declares independence from Serbia.

2013 Over one million people celebrate Queen Elizabeth II's Diamond Jubilee, witnessing a 1000-strong flotilla pass by the banks of the Thames.

BIRTHDAYS

Jefferson Davis 1808, American president of the Confederate states.

Tony Curtis 1925, American actor whose many films include *Some Like It Hot*, *The Boston Strangler* and *The Vikings*.

Allan Ginsberg 1926, American poet and leading light of the Beat movement.

Rafael Nadal 1986, Spanish world number one tennis player who won the French Open four years in a row from 2004.

LOVELORN ABELARD GUILTY OF HERESY

1140 The controversial views of leading French scholar Peter Abelard have landed him in serious trouble: in a dramatic verdict, a church court today has found him guilty of heresy. Abelard is no stranger to controversy and this is just one in a series of confrontations with the Church. Personal tragedy, too, has brought him fame of another kind, through his celebrated love affair with his beautiful pupil, Héloïse. The discovery of the couple's liaison so enraged Héloïse's uncle that he ordered Abelard's castration. After this brutal attack, the couple separated.

KAFKA'S LAST BREATH

1924 German novelist Franz Kafka died today in a sanatorium near Vienna after losing his seven-year battle with tuberculosis. With his pessimistic view of the world and of the despair and alienation of modern man, Kafka characteristically saw his illness as psychosomatic – a conspiracy between his head and his body to put an end to his internal anguish. Kafka was always reluctant to publish. Before his death he exacted a promise from his friend Max Brod not to allow the publication of any more of his writings.

Of course, I do have a slight advantage over the rest of you. It helps in a pinch to be able to remind your bride that you gave up a throne for her.

Ex-king Edward VIII, who married Mrs Simpson today, 1937.

• 1946 – THE FIRST BIKINI GOES ON SHOW • 1965 – FIRST AMERICAN TO WALK IN SPACE

1789 The Dauphin Louis, son of Louis XVI and heir to the French throne, dies at the age of seven.

1831 Prince Leopold,of the House of Saxe-Coburg-Gotha, becomes the first king of Belgium.

1941 Former German emperor Wilhelm II, forced to abdicate after World War I, dies in exile.

1944 Rome is liberated by the Allies.

1946 Juan Perón is elected president of Argentina.

1973 A Russian supersonic airliner explodes at the Paris Air Show, killing 33 people.

1988 Death of Sir Douglas Nicholls, governor of South Australia, the first aborigine to govern a state and to receive a knighthood.

2007 The war crimes trial of ex-Liberian president Charles Taylor opens in the Hague.

BIRTHDAYS

George III 1730, English monarch of erratic mental health.

Stephen Foster 1826, American composer of songs such as "Swanee River".

ITALIAN SEDUCER DIES

1798 Today sees the death, in Bohemia, of one of this century's most flamboyant characters, Giovanni Giacomo Casanova, Chevalier de Seingalt. Casanova was born in 1725 in Venice, the son of an actor. His expulsion from the Seminary of St Cyprian for "scandalous conduct" launched him on a varied and infamous career, in which he was writer, traveller, adventurer, soldier, spy, diplomat and dedicated ladies' man. One of the more daring exploits of this man of many parts was his escape from Venice's Piombi prison, where he was serving a five-year sentence after being denounced as a magician. Among his writings are *Icosameron*, a futuristic adventure fantasy, and his memoirs, *Histoire de Ma Vie*.

CHINESE ARMY BRUTALLY HALTS DEMOCRATIC REVOLT

1989 Up to 2600 people are thought to have been killed and 10,000 injured as soldiers opened fire on student demonstrators in Tiananmen Square, Beijing, it was reported today. Since the removal of moderate party chairman Hu Yaobang in 1987, the conflict between moderates and old-style Maoist hardliners has escalated to crisis point. In a massive demonstration for greater democracy, huge crowds of student protesters had, by last night, barricaded themselves into Tiananmen Square. In a show of force, the government ordered the army into action. Reaching the square from the Avenue of Eternal Peace, the troops showered the students with a hail of bullets, and their armoured vehicles crashed through the barricades. The square and surrounding city became a scene of horror and chaos. At one o'clock this morning, the soldiers – only a day ago hailed as "brothers and comrades" – made a final onslaught on those who were left. Marching forward, they shot indiscriminately into the crowd. In their wake came the tanks, mercilessly flattening all in their path.

• 1940 – DUNKIRK EVACUATION • 1989 – MASSIVE TRAIN EXPLOSION IN RUSSIA

BOBBY KENNEDY IS SHOT

1968 Doctors are fighting to save the life of 42-year-old Senator Robert Kennedy, who was shot in the head and shoulder just after midnight this morning. The shooting took place at the Ambassador Hotel in Los Angeles, where the Senator had been making a speech after winning the California primary election in his campaign for the Democratic presidential nomination. Kennedy has not regained consciousness since being rushed to hospital, and hopes for his recovery are not high. The alleged gunman, a Jordanian Arab by the name of Sirhan Bishara Sirhan, has since been arrested. The shooting comes five years after the assassination of Robert Kennedy's brother, President John Kennedy in Dallas, Texas.

REAGAN BOWS OUT

2004 Former American president Ronald Reagan died today, aged 93, after a long battle with Alzheimer's Disease. A former actor, Ronald Reagan served two terms as US president, from 1981–1989.

The great nations have always acted like gangsters, and the small nations like prostitutes.

Stanley Kubrick,
American film director, on this day, 1963

HOT AIR POWERS BALLOON BROTHERS TO SUCCESS

1783 Astonished local government officials in Annonay, France, today watched as a "hot air" balloon made by brothers Joseph-Michel and Jacques-Etienne Montgolfier slowly rose 6000 ft (2000 m) into the air, where it remained suspended for a full 10 minutes. The balloon, made of linen and paper, was "powered" by an ingenious method whereby heat from a fire on the ground warmed the air inside the balloon, thus causing it to rise. Today's demonstration is a culmination of earlier experiments by the brothers, working both together and independently, and is likely to rouse the interest of the Academy of Sciences.

1806 Louis Bonaparte is declared king of the Netherlands.

1826 German composer Carl Maria von Weber dies in London.

1972 The Duke of Windsor, briefly King Edward VIII of England, is buried at Windsor.

1988 Kay Cottee becomes the first woman to sail solo round the world non-stop.

1989 Solidarity beats the Communists in the first free Polish elections since World War I.

1990 Iran demands that British author Salman Rushdie is handed over to British Muslims.

1991 The so-called "pillars of apartheid":The Land Acts of 1913 and 1936 and the Group Areas Act of 1950, are nullified in South Africa.

BIRTHDAYS

John Couch Adams 1819, English astronomer.

Pancho Villa 1878, Mexican revolutionary.

Federico Garcia Lorca 1898, Spanish poet and dramatist.

Tony Richardson 1928, British film and theatre director.

• 1916 – LORD KITCHENER DROWNS AT SEA • 1967 – WAR ERUPTS IN THE MIDDLE EAST

1891 Death of Sir John Alexander Macdonald, first prime minister of Canada.

1933 The first drive-in movie opens at Camden, New Jersey.

1936 Gatwick Airport opens in Surrey, UK.

1956 Death of American archaeologist Hiram Bingham, who located the lost Inca city of Machu Picchu in Peru.

1976 American oil billionaire Jean Paul Getty, dies in England aged 83.

1984 Prime Minister Indira Gandhi orders the storming of the Golden Temple in Amritsar to arrest Sikh militants who have taken refuge there – 712 Sikhs and 90 soldiers die.

BIRTHDAYS

Aleksandr Pushkin 1799, Russian poet, novelist and dramatist.

Captain Robert Falcon Scott 1868, English explorer of the Antarctic.

Thomas Mann 1875, German novelist who wrote *Death in Venice*.

Björn Borg 1956, Swedish tennis champion who won the men's singles at Wimbledon five times.

ALLIES SEND A MILLION MEN TO FREE EUROPE

1944 As morning dawned today, five beaches on the northern French coast – code-named Utah, Omaha, Gold, Juno and Sword – became the scene of the largest military invasion in history. Under the supreme command of US General Dwight D. Eisenhower, one million men, in 4000 ships, began an assault on Rommel's "Atlantic Wall". The combined Allied troops were spearheaded by units of the US 82nd and 101st Airborne Divisions who landed near the town of Saint Mère-Eglise; British commandos took key bridges and knocked out Nazi communications. Plans for the Normandy Invasion have been underway since January, but were threatened by severe weather. Taking advantage of a lull, Eisenhower ordered the fleet to set sail. Four of the beaches surrendered early, but Omaha proved more of a problem. This evening, however, sizeable sections of all five landing areas are under Allied control. The final campaign to defeat Germany has begun.

MOURNERS TEAR OFF AYATOLLAH'S SHROUD

1989 There were scenes of hysteria at the funeral of Ayatollah Khomeini in Tehran, it was reported today. As the open coffin of the 87-year-old Iranian leader was borne over the heads of the crowd on its way to its resting place on the outskirts of the city, grief-stricken mourners clutched frantically at the body, unwrapping it and tearing up the shroud. Today's funeral ends a decade which, under the Ayatollah, has seen the revival of militant Islamic fundamentalism, of terrorism and war, and of hostility to the West, which came to a head with the seizure in Teheran of 52 US embassy staff, who were then kept hostage for 444 days.

THINKER'S THINKER DIES

1961 Carl Gustav Jung, the founder of analytical psychology, died today in Switzerland at the age of eighty-five. Jung's contributions to the study of the psyche include his division of personality types into introverted and extroverted, his ideas on the four functions of the mind – thinking, feeling, sensation and intuition – and his belief in a "collective unconscious" linking all mankind. A highly original thinker who loved the simple life, Jung spent his last years with his wife Emma in the house they had built by the shores of Lake Zurich.

• 1683 – OXFORD'S ASHMOLEAN FIRST PUBLIC MUSEUM • 1949 – ORWELL PUBLISHES *1984*

ISRAELI BOMBING RAID

1981 Israeli jets have carried out a bombing raid on a nuclear reactor near Baghdad, Middle Eastern sources claimed today. The raid succeeded in destroying the plant entirely. Prime Minister Begin justified the attack on the basis of the defensive "strike first" theory, saying that Iraq was planning to manufacture nuclear weapons to use against Israel.

HERO OF BANNOCKBURN DIES

1329 Scotland is in mourning today for the death of her king, Robert I. Seizing the throne in 1306, with his country under English domination, he was attacked and driven into hiding by English forces. He returned to earn a place in Scottish history with his legendary victory at the Battle of Bannockburn in 1314, when he routed the armies of Edward II and drove the English off Scottish soil.

1905 Norway declares independence from Sweden.

1933 The ballet *The Seven Deadly Sins* is premiered in Paris with choreography by Georges Balanchine and music and libretto by Kurt Weill and Bertolt Brecht.

1945 Benjamin Britten's opera *Peter Grimes* is premiered at Sadler's Wells Theatre in London.

1970 English novelist E. M. Forster, dies aged 91.

1977 Street parties are held all over Britain to celebrate Queen Elizabeth's silver jubilee.

1980 American novelist Henry Miller, author of *Tropic of Cancer*, dies aged 88.

1990 President de Klerk lifts the state of emergency in South Africa.

THE KING'S PALACE OPENS TO HIS PEOPLE

1982 The palatial mansion known as Graceland, in Memphis, Tennessee – home of rock superstar Elvis Presley, who died five years ago – today opens its doors to the public for the first time. Thousands of fans will now have a chance to see how their idol lived. After his first hit of 1956, "Heartbreak Hotel", Elvis dominated the pop music charts for the next 16 months. His gyrations during his performances drove teenage audiences wild and earned him the nickname "Elvis the Pelvis". With his blend of white country and western and black rhythm and blues, Elvis was one of the key figures in the development of rock 'n' roll. Those who make the pilgrimage to Graceland will be coming to honour the memory of a legend – a man who has become one of the lasting icons of the twentieth century.

Paul Gauguin 1848, French Post-Impressionist painter.

Pietro Annigoni 1910, Italian painter who is chiefly known for his portraits – and particularly that of Queen Elizabeth II.

Prince 1960, American singer and musician.

• **1712 – PHILADELPHIA BANS THE IMPORT OF SLAVES**

1376 Edward the Black Prince, son of Edward III of England, dies.

1847 In Britain, a new law limits women and children to a 10-hour working day.

1930 King Carol II of Romania is proclaimed king once more after returning from exile.

1969 Spanish dictator General Franco closes the border with Gibraltar.

1986 Kurt Waldheim becomes president of Austria despite evidence that he collaborated with the Nazis in World War II.

BIRTHDAYS

Robert Schumann 1810, German composer.

Sir John Millais 1829, English painter and one of the founders of the Pre-Raphaelite Brotherhood.

Frank Lloyd Wright 1867, American architect whose buildings include the Guggenheim Museum in New York.

Professor Sir Francis Crick 1916, British biologist who, with J. D. Watson, discovered the structure of DNA.

Nancy Sinatra 1940, American singer, daughter of Frank.

BRAINS BEHIND THE AMERICAN REVOLUTION

1809 Thomas Paine, guiding light of the American Revolution and one of the most influential thinkers of the age, died in New York City today. Through his writings, Paine inspired and revived the nation's morale during the dark days of America's fight for independence from Britain. His famous pamphlet *Common Sense*, published in 1776 and including the words, "The cause of America is in great measure the cause of all mankind" sold more than 100,000 copies in three months. *The American Crisis*, published later in the same year, is credited with contributing to American success at the Battle of Trenton. While in France, Paine wrote *The Rights of Man*, a defence of the French revolution that earned him the brand "traitor" in his native Britain. Although a supporter of the revolutionary cause, he was opposed to the execution of Louis XVI: this aroused radical suspicions and landed him in the Luxembourg Prison, where he worked on the statement of his religious beliefs, *The Age of Reason*, published after his release.

PROPHET'S BLISSFUL ABODE

632 Mohammed, prophet and founder of Islam, died today in Mecca. Mohammed took up his calling late in life: at 40, a revelation from Allah convinced him that he must spread the word of the one true god, and he began to forge the new religion. By the time of his death, and after several jihads (holy wars), most of the Arab peninsula had come to accept Islam, with Mohammed as its leader. Central to the Islamic message is a belief in the afterlife, in which the good will be rewarded by entry to Paradise: Mohammed will now pass into that "blissful abode – garden and vineyard" where there will be "girls with swelling breasts . . . and a brimming cup . . . a recompense from [the] Lord".

KING'S KILLER CAUGHT IN LONDON

1968 A man has been arrested in London for the killing of black civil rights leader Dr Martin Luther King last April. James Earl Ray, an escaped convict, is accused of firing the fatal shots that killed Dr King as he came out on to the balcony of his motel room in Memphis, Tennessee. Dr King was in the city to support a strike of local dustmen. Profoundly influenced by the teachings of Mahatma Gandhi, King insisted that protest should be non-violent, yet since he came to prominence in the civil rights movement in 1955 it was always on the cards that he himself would meet a violent end.

• 1914 – *PRINCE IGOR* STAGED IN LONDON • 1928 – CHIANG KAI-SHEK SEIZES PEKING

DESERTED NERO STABS HIMSELF

AD **68** Reports from Rome claim that the Emperor Nero has taken his own life. He is said to have stabbed himself in the throat with a dagger. The suicide occurred after Nero returned from Greece to find that he had been deserted by his Praetorian Guard. Resentment against the Emperor has been brewing throughout the Empire, with revolts in Africa, Spain and Gaul. High levels of taxation to fund Nero's excesses has been one cause of the hostility, as has his lack of interest in government. Leaving affairs of state to his advisers, Nero preferred to think of himself as a creative artist: "I have only to appear and sing to have peace once more in Gaul," he boasted.

LAST NUREMBERG NAZI HANGED

1951 The judgement of the Nuremberg court will be fulfilled today when the last Nazi is hanged for "crimes against humanity". The trials, which took place between November 1945 and October 1946, were conducted by four judges and four prosecutors from the US, UK, USSR and France. In all, 24 of Hitler's top men were accused on a number of different counts, including conspiracy to wage wars of aggression, killing of hostages and crimes against peace. Twelve men, including Goering, were given the death penalty.

1198 Otto of Brunswick is crowned German king and Holy Roman Emperor.

1898 China grants Britain a 99-year lease on Hong Kong.

1959 America launches the *George Washington*, the first nuclear submarine with Polaris missiles.

1967 Israel seizes the Golan Heights on the fifth day of war with Syria, Egypt and Jordan.

1975 First live transmission from the House of Commons.

1989 In China, show trials begin of the leaders of the demonstration in Tiananmen Square.

DICKENS DIES IN MID-CLASSIC

1870 Charles Dickens has died. He was engaged in his latest novel, *The Mystery of Edwin Drood*. The punishing schedule of Dickens' last few years affected his health badly, and is largely to blame for his sudden death. While continuing to write, he also made a series of tours of England and the United States in which he gave readings from his own works to enraptured audiences. Dickens' professional success was partly marred by personal unhappiness – he and his wife separated in 1859, and his sons failed to live up to his expectations. He died at Gad's Hill Place in Kent, the house he had loved from boyhood.

BIRTHDAYS

Peter I 1672, Russian emperor known as Peter the Great.

George Stephenson 1781, English engineer who developed greatly improved steam locomotives.

Elizabeth Garrett Anderson 1836, English physician who pioneered the admission of women to the medical profession.

Cole Porter 1891, American composer and lyricist whose musicals include *Kiss me Kate* and *Can-Can*.

• 1934 – DONALD DUCK MAKES FIRST APPEARANCE • 1964 – LORD BEAVERBROOK DIES

1727 King George I of England dies in Osnabrück.

1924 Italian socialist leader Giacomo Matteotti is assassinated by Fascists.

1926 Death of Spanish architect Antonio Gaudi y Cornet, who worked exclusively in Barcelona.

1934 British composer Frederick Delius dies.

1965 A British European Airways de Havilland jet airliner flying from Paris to London makes the first landing by automatic control.

1983 Mrs Thatcher's Conservative Party wins the British elections.

1986 Irish pop singer Bob Geldof and American philanthropist John Paul Getty II are given honorary knighthoods by Queen Elizabeth II.

BIRTHDAYS

Gustave Courbet 1819, French painter with an innovative naturalistic style.

Judy Garland 1922, American singer and actress best remembered for the film *The Wizard of Oz.*

Prince Phillip, Duke of Edinburgh 1921, Queen Elizabeth II's husband.

WITCH HUNT FEVER SWEEPS SALEM

1692 An ominous trial has been taking place in Salem, MA, and women found guilty of witchcraft were hanged today. It began when certain young girls from the area, after listening to the voodoo tales of a West Indian slave, Tituba, claimed that they were possessed by the Devil. The girls accused three women of witchcraft, and the hunt was on. In the wake of the accusations, a special court, presided over by judges Samuel Sewell, John Hathorne and William Stoughton, was set up to investigate the affair; although the court is a civil one, it has the full backing of the clergy. The trials began in May and are set to continue.

ISRAEL DOUBLES IN SIZE

1967 Six days of hostilities in the Middle East ended today with a victory for the Israelis, and a 200 per cent expansion in territory. The Six-Day War began on June 5, after Syria had asked for Egypt's help in withstanding threatened Israeli retaliation against Syrian border raids. Egypt's President Nasser called for the removal of UN peacekeeping forces at Suez, closed the Gulf of Aquaba, mobilized the army and moved troops into Sinai. Israel's answer was a burst of simultaneous air attacks on Syrian, Egyptian and Jordanian air bases that decimated its enemies' air capability. In the week that followed, Israel went on to defeat all enemy resistance.

DEMOCRATIC VICTORY

1990 Czechoslovak democrats have won a huge victory in the country's first genuine elections for 40 years, with Vaclav Havel's Civic Forum and its Slovak allies winning more than 170 seats out of 300. The new parliament must steer the country through tough economic reforms.

• 1829 – FIRST OXFORD-CAMBRIDGE BOAT RACE • 1865 – *TRISTAN UND ISOLDE* PREMIERES

80,000 CELEBRATE MANDELA'S BIRTHDAY

1988 A crowd of 80,000 packed London's Wembley Stadium today in what must be the biggest 70th birthday party ever. The only person unable to attend was the birthday guest himself – black South African leader Nelson Mandela, who has been in prison since 1964, serving a life sentence on a conviction of attempting to overthrow the state. In tribute to him, singers and musicians from all over the world, including South Africa itself, came to join in the day-long concert, which was televised and broadcast live to an estimated audience of 1 billion in 60 countries.

1727 George II of England accedes to the English throne.

1905 British golfer Harry Vardon wins his fourth Open golf championship.

1940 Italian dictator Benito Mussolini declares war on the Allies.

1970 Aleksande Feodorovich Kerensky, prime minister of Russia in 1917 until the Bolshevik Revolution, dies in exile in New York.

2010 The FIFA Football World Cup opens for the first time on the African continent in Johannesburg, South Africa.

YOUNGSTER CLAIMS TITLE

1989 At the tender age of 17 years and 109 days, Michael Chang of the United States today became the youngest-ever winner of the French Open tennis championships. He beat Stefan Edberg of Sweden to claim the title.

MERC GOES BESERK

1955 Horrified spectators saw the Le Mans racetrack in France become a scene of carnage today. One of the cars competing in the 24-hour Grand Prix – a Mercedes Benz – ran out of control and plunged into the grandstand, killing an estimated 80. The news has shocked the motor racing world. Questions will undoubtedly be asked about the safety of the sport, and tighter restrictions may be imposed.

BIRTHDAYS

Ben Jonson 1572, English dramatist and poet.

John Constable 1776, one of the greatest British landscape artists.

Richard Strauss 1864, German composer and conductor.

Jacques Cousteau 1910, French underwater explorer who invented a means of using television underwater.

Gene Wilder 1935, American actor best-known for comedy films such as *The Producers*.

EXIT "THE DUKE"

1979 John Wayne, veteran Hollywood star, died earlier today. Born Marion Michael Morrison in Winterset, Iowa in 1907, after a slow start he made his name as a genial tough guy and all-American hero in a series of westerns and war films, and became one of the best known and most successful actors in Hollywood. His first major screen appearance was as Ringo Kid in director John Ford's 1939 film *Stagecoach*, a part that set the tone for the rest of his film career.

• 1509 – HENRY VIII MARRIES CATHERINE OF ARAGON • 1946 – ITALY NOW A REPUBLIC

JUNE 12

1458 Magdalene College, Oxford, is founded.

1630 The fleet of the Massachusetts Bay Company docks at Salem with 700 Puritan colonists on board.

1667 Jean-Baptiste Denys successfully transfuses the blood of a sheep to a 15-year-old boy.

1963 Civil rights lawyer Medgar Evers is murdered by white segregationists.

1965 The Beatles are each awarded an MBE in the Queen's Birthday Honours List.

1982 Death of Dame Marie Rambert, Polish-born ballet dancer.

1997 The Globe Theatre opens its doors on the South Bank, London.

2003 Gregory Peck, Hollywood actor, dies.

BIRTHDAYS

Charles Kingsley 1819, English clergyman who wrote *The Water Babies*.

George Bush 1924, American Republican politician and president.

Anne Frank 1929, Dutch Jewish schoolgirl who, wrote her famous diary before going to her death in a Nazi concentration camp.

RUSSIANS GO TO VOTE IN FIRST DEMOCRATIC ELECTION

1991 Russia will make history today with the country's first-ever democratic elections. Frontrunner Boris Yeltsin is waiting to hear whether he has gained the 51 per cent share of the vote that he needs to make it through the first round. Yeltsin is one of six candidates. Individually, none of the others is likely to get a big enough vote to defeat him, but their combined share could present problems. Yeltsin supporters say that the other candidates have a subversive purpose in mind, and are standing to undermine his chances of success.

Once in the racket you're always in it.

Al Capone, Chicago gangster, charged today with 5000 prohibition offences, 1931.

NEW SPORT COULD CATCH ON IN USA

1839 A new kind of ball game was played today at Cooperstown, NY. Known as "baseball" because of its four-base infield, it is said to be the invention of Abner Doubleday, who is teaching local military cadets how to play. The game uses a soft ball to avoid injury – one way of putting out a player running from base to base is for a fielder to hit him with the ball. Although Cooperstown would like to claim all the glory for giving America a totally new sport, some have their doubts. Baseball bears a striking resemblance to the American children's game Old Cat and the English rounders, and may simply be an adaptation of these earlier forms.

INDIAN PM GANDHI MAY HAVE FIXED VICTORY

1975 A shock verdict in Allahabad, India has caused a scandal and a crisis of confidence in the country's leadership. A judge in Allahabad, home constituency of Prime Minister Indira Gandhi, has ruled that her landslide victory in 1971 was invalid because civil servants illegally aided her campaign. Mrs Gandhi, who came to power in 1966, is the daughter of Jawaharlal Nehru, India's first Prime Minister after the country gained independence from Britain in 1947. Today's verdict has brought calls for Mrs Gandhi's resignation, and she faces the biggest political storm of her career.

• 1809 – NAPOLEON EXCOMMUNICATED • 1917 – KING CONSTANTINE OF GREECE ABDICATES

WORKERS MARCH AGAINST POLL TAX

1381 A crowd of angry peasants marched on London today. The marchers, agricultural workers from Kent and Essex in south-east England, were led by Walter "Wat" Tyler. Similar protests are being launched in East Anglia. Although

economic unrest has been brewing since the 1350s, it is the unpopular new tax – "poll tax" – that finally brought matters to a head today. The protest took the government by surprise, and the peasants are in no mood to be ignored. There seems little doubt, however, that this "Peasants' Revolt" will be crushed – putting little pressure on the king to make changes.

So greatly did she care for freedom that she died for it. So dearly did she love women that she offered her life as their ransom.

Christabel Pankhurst on Emily Davison, who died protesting for her cause June 4, 1913.

---

323 BC Alexander the Great, King of Macedon, dies aged 33.

1842 Queen Victoria becomes the first British monarch to travel by train.

1893 The first women's golf championship is held at Royal Lytham in Britain.

1930 Sir Henry Segrave, who broke the British land and water speed records, is killed when his speedboat capsizes at 98 mph (158 kph) on Lake Windermere in northern England.

1956 Real Madrid win the first European Cup in Paris, beating Stade de Reims 4-3.

1989 Mikhail Gorbachev and Chancellor Kohl agree that East and West Germany should be reunited.

BIRTHDAYS

William Butler Yeats 1865, Irish poet, dramatist.

Elizabeth Schumann 1888, German-born soprano.

Dorothy L. Sayers 1893, English writer of detective stories.

Don Budge 1915, American tennis champion, the first amateur to win the Grand Slam.

BOXERS FIGHT FOR CHINA'S PRIDE

1900 A group of volunteer soldiers known as the Boxers went on the rampage through Peking today in protest against the "foreign devils" who have a hold on their country. Weakened by a century of conflict China has, over the years, agreed to a series of treaties that have given away large slices of territory to foreign powers, notably the US, Europe and Japan. Resentment against the terms of these treaties has, until now, only bubbled below the surface; events today, said to have been encouraged by the Chinese authorities, show just how deep Chinese anger really is.

• 1774 – RHODE ISLAND BANS IMPORT OF SLAVES • 1944 – DOODLEBUGS BATTER LONDON

1814 The Netherlands and Belgium are united by the Treaty of London.

1917 German planes bomb London for the first time.

1946 Death of John Logie Baird, British electrical engineer who invented an early form of television.

1964 Nelson Mandela is sentenced to life imprisonment.

1983 Protests erupt in Santiago against the regime of Chilean dictator General Pinochet.

1990 In Bucharest, Romania, street battles break out between students demanding democracy and miners providing support for the interim government of Ion Iliescu.

BIRTHDAYS

Harriet Beecher Stowe 1811, American novelist who wrote *Uncle Tom's Cabin.*

Sam Wanamaker 1919, American actor and director.

Che Guevara 1928, Legendary Argentinian-born revolutionary.

Steffi Graf 1969, German tennis star who won the Wimbledon women's singles title at 19.

CROMWELL LEADS DECISIVE VICTORY

1645 Parliamentary troops under the leadership of Oliver Cromwell are reported to have inflicted a heavy defeat on Prince Rupert's Royalist forces at Naseby, 20 miles (32 km) south of Leicester in the English Midlands. After a pursuit by Cromwell, the opposing armies took up positions on the ridges flanking the valley of Broad Moor – 10,000 Royalists facing 14,000 of Cromwell's men. The Royalists successfully attacked Cromwell's left wing, but then made the fatal error of pursuing the fleeing Parliamentarians. Cromwell seized his chance to regroup the right flank of his cavalry to make a crushing assault on the Royalist centre, routing Prince Rupert's army and scoring a decisive Parliamentary victory in the Civil War.

REAGAN KNIGHTED

1989 Former governor of California and US president Ronald Reagan today received a knighthood by Queen Elizabeth. As president of the United States, Reagan was one of the architects of the new cordiality between East and West, and has personally met Soviet leader Mikhail Gorbachev on several occasions to have talks on disarmament. During his 1988 visit to Britain, he called for "a newer world of freedom and individual rights for all".

BLIGH SPIRIT

1789 After drifting an incredible 3500 miles (5600 km) in an open boat, Captain William Bligh and 18 loyal crew members put ashore at the island of Timor today. Captain Bligh captained the 215-ton HMS *Bounty* on its voyage from Tahiti to the West Indies with a cargo of breadfruit trees. Tensions on board erupted when the vessel reached the Friendly Islands and large numbers of the crew, led by Fletcher Christian, mutinied.

• 1940 – GERMANS MARCH INTO PARIS • 1982 – ARGENTINA SURRENDERS OVER FALKLANDS

ALCOCK AND BROWN CROSS ATLANTIC IN ONE SWOOP

1919 Aviation history was made today as Capt. John Alcock and Lt Arthur Whitten Brown touched down on the green turf at Clifden, Ireland, thus completing the world's first non-stop flight across the Atlantic. Taking off from St John's, Newfoundland, yesterday, the two former World War I airmen completed their record-breaking flight – 1960 miles (3150 km) across the empty

expanse of the Atlantic Ocean – in only 16 hours 12 minutes. Their aircraft, a Vickers-Vimy bomber, was kept aloft by two 350-hp Rolls-Royce engines.

FRANKLIN'S KITE STUNT

1752 In a brave – or perhaps foolhardy – act, American founding father, diplomat and scientist Benjamin Franklin today flew a kite in a thunderstorm to prove his theory that electricity and lightning are the same phenomenon. He also believes that electricity is "an Element diffused among, and attracted by, other matter, particularly Water and Metals". If it is, it should be possible to harness its power.

BARON KNIGHTS SIGN DEAL

1215 King John and his barons met on the banks of the River Thames at Runnymede, near London, today to hammer out a new deal. The document signed is called the Magna Carta. Its effect will be a decentralization of power, taking total authority from the hands of the King and granting the people of England – particularly noblemen – basic rights and liberties.

1790 French Protestant militia massacre 300 Roman Catholics.

1813 Britain forms a new coalition with Prussia and Russia against Napoleon.

1846 The 49th parallel is proclaimed to be the border between the US and Canada.

1888 Emperor Frederick III of Germany dies.

1904 The paddle steamer *General Slocum* catches fire in New York Harbor, killing 693 people.

1933 China and Tibet end a two-year war with a treaty that agrees mutual respect for the pre-war border.

1934 Hitler and Mussolini meet for the first time.

BIRTHDAYS

Edward the Black Prince 1330, eldest son of Edward III of England.

Harry Langdon 1884, American silent film actor.

Erroll Garner 1923, American jazz pianist and composer.

Simon Callow 1949, British stage and screen actor.

Courtney Cox 1964, American actress who starred in the long-running TV series *Friends*.

• 1844 – VULCANIZED RUBBER PATENTED • 1860 – FIRST SCHOOL FOR NURSES OPENS

JUNE 16

1880 Salvation Army ladies wear their bonnets for the first time as they march in East London.

1948 The first air hijack occurs when Chinese bandits attempt to take over a Cathay Airways Catalina flying boat.

1958 Former prime minister of Hungary Imre Nagy is hanged for his role in the unsuccessful revolution of 1956.

1963 Valentina Tereshkova of the USSR Union blasts off in *Vostok 6* – the first woman in space.

1977 Death of Werner von Braun, German rocket pioneer.

1990 Belgian police arrest IRA members suspected of killing Australian tourists in Holland.

BIRTHDAYS

Gustav V 1858, Swedish monarch who reigned for 43 years.

Stan Laurel 1890, English-born comedian who went to the USA and formed a successful partnership with Oliver Hardy.

Tom Graveney 1927, British cricketer considered to be in the top 10 best British cricketers ever.

EUROPE BACK IN SPACE BUSINESS

1983 Everything went according to plan when the European rocket *Ariane 1*, blasted off from the French National Space Centre at Kouron, French Guiana today. *Ariane* launched the one-ton ESCI into an elliptical "transfer orbit". Early tomorrow the satellite's booster rocket will be fired to thrust it into "geostationary orbit" 22,000 miles (35,000 km) above the equator. Today's performance, means Europe is back in competition with the US for satellite contracts.

Napoleon's troops crush Prussia's

1815 After a bitter and bloody battle the French scored a resounding victory against the Prussians at Ligny, in Belgium, today. Napoleon opened hostilities at about 2.30 pm and by 3.15 pm the battle was fiercely engaged. At about 7.45 pm a contingent of elite French troops broke the Prussian centre. The Prussian commander of the Lower Rhine, Field Marshal Blücher, responded by leading his cavalry reserve to stem the French advance. By 9 pm it was all over. The Prussians lost an estimated 12,000 men, the French 8500.

BALLET STAR NUREYEV LEAPS TO FREEDOM

1961 A star dancer of the Leningrad ballet, forbidden at the last minute to fly to London with the rest of the troupe, has asked for political asylum. Rudolf Nureyev, 23, was waiting to board the London flight at Le Bourget airport in Paris today when officials from the Russian Embassy ordered him to return to Moscow immediately. He refused and ran to a police officer crying, "Protect me!" Nureyev was immediately taken to the police commissioner's office at Le Bourget where he made a formal request for asylum. He was later driven to the Ministry of the Interior.

BATTLE OF BUNKER HILL

1775 The second battle of the American revolution commenced just before dawn today at Bunker Hill and Breed's Hill, just north of Boston, Massachusetts. After an unsuccessful attack on the American left flank, British general William Howe ordered his men to storm the central redoubt defended by 1600 patriots under the command of Colonel William Prescott. The British were repulsed with blistering fire and only on their third attempt – reinforced with extra troops from Boston – did they succeed in capturing the position. Although the British gained the military victory, the moral victory belonged to the patriots for the courage and discipline they displayed under fire. The Americans lost around 400 men, the British 1000.

Don't fire until you see the whites of their eyes.

American revolutionary soldier **William Prescott** at the Battle of Bunker Hill, 1775.

1579 Francis Drake drops the *Golden Hind*'s anchor off the southwest coast of America.

1867 In Glasgow Royal Infirmary, Joseph Lister becomes the first surgeon to attempt any form of antiseptic treatment.

1944 Iceland becomes an independent republic.

1988 In Kingston, Jamaica, reggae poet Dennis Loban is found guilty of the murder of reggae star and ex-Wailer Pete Tosh and is sentenced to hang.

BIRTHDAYS

Edward I 1239, English monarch who encouraged parliamentary institutions and subdued Wales.

John Wesley 1703, English religious leader and founder of Methodism.

Igor Stravinsky 1882, Russian- born composer who first found fame with the ballet scores Diaghilev commissioned for his Ballets Russes.

Ken Loach 1936, British film director.

Barry Manilow 1946, American singer and songwriter of vast popularity.

BREAK IN AT WATERGATE HQ

1972 Five men have been caught snooping around the Washington complex of flats, offices and hotel known as The Watergate, in use by the Democratic Party as their headquarters during the election campaign. The men were all equipped with electronic eavesdropping equipment. It is rumoured that the men were in the pay of the Republican "Committee for the re-election of the President" (CREEP). A major political scandal is feared.

WORLD IN AIDS FIGHT

1991 Eight thousand scientists and researchers gathered today at Fortezza da Basso, Florence, for an international conference on AIDS. The disease has now spread across 163 countries and is rife in Africa. The World Health Organization estimates the true number of cases worldwide at more than 1.5 million, with a total number of people with HIV at between 8 and 10 million. WHO predicts that by the year 2000, 40 million people worldwide may be affected by HIV.

• 1950 – FIRST KIDNEY TRANSPLANT • 1970 – POLAROID CAMERA PATENTED

JUNE
18

1037 Renowned Persian philosopher and physician Avicenna dies.

1583 The first life insurance policy is issued in London.

1789 Austrian troops occupy Brussels.

1902 Death of Samuel Butler, British novelist who wrote *Erewhon*.

1936 Death of Maxim Gorki, Russian novelist and the first president of the Soviet Writers' Union.

1975 The first North Sea oil arrives on shore in Britain.

1977 Sex Pistol Johnny Rotten is attacked with razors in a London pub.

2000 At Dover, 58 Chinese immigrants are found suffocated in the back of a lorry while trying to enter Britain illegally.

BIRTHDAYS

Viscount Castlereagh 1769, British foreign secretary who played an important role at the Congress of Vienna which reconstructed Europe after the fall of Napoleon.

Paul McCartney 1942, ex-Beatle and major British pop musician.

FIRST WOMAN TO FLY ATLANTIC

1928 Thirty-year-old Amelia Earhart became the first woman to fly the Atlantic when the trimotor *Friendship*, in which she was a passenger, landed at Burny Port today. Miss Earhart, the daughter of a railroad attorney and graduate of Columbia University, is employed as a settlement worker in Boston. Aviation is a passionate hobby with her and she is a very accomplished pilot. A plucky girl, Miss Earhart also hopes to make a solo flight across the Atlantic herself one day.

GALLIC APPEAL

1940 Charles de Gaulle, founder of the Free French in England, made a radio appeal from London today urging his fellow countrymen to continue to resist the Germans. It was in response to Marshall Pètain's announcement yesterday that the French have approached the Germans with a request for an Armistice.

NAPOLEON BEATEN IN THE MIRE OF WATERLOO

1815 British and Prussian forces under the command of the Duke of Wellington and Field Marshall Blücher finally defeated Napoleon in a bloody battle at Waterloo, in Belgium, today. Fighting started at about 11.30 am, and raged ferociously all day. Napoleon's first decided advantage was gained at 6 pm, when Wellington's position fell into his hands. But the Iron Duke kept a cool head, quickly readjusting his lines and fortifying his torn centre. The desperate fighting was ultimately concluded by a British-Prussian victory.

• 1979 – SIGINING OF THE STRATEGIC ARMS LIMITATIONS TALKS (SALT)

SIR ROBERT TELLS LONDON POLICE: KEEP 'EM PEELED

1829 Home Secretary Sir Robert Peel founded the London Metropolitan Police today, modelled on the highly respected Irish constabulary. The measures Sir Robert is taking to reform the criminal law are earning him much praise. As one liberal Whig has said, Peel can rightly claim that all his legislation has sought "some mitigation of the severity of the criminal law, some prevention of abuse in the exercise of it, or some security for its impartial administration."

1790 The French Assembly abolishes hereditary nobility.

1935 The British government overrides the Treaty of Versailles by agreeing to allow Germany a massive increase in its naval strength.

1963 In Britain, the contraceptive pill is made available to women free under the NHS.

1967 The Monterey Pop Festival draws thousands of flower children to hear stars such as Jimi Hendrix, Janis Joplin and The Mamas and the Papas.

1993 Death of Sir William Golding, author of *Lord of the Flies* and winner of the Nobel Prize for Literature.

BIRTHDAYS

James I 1556, English monarch, son of Mary, Queen of Scots. The first Stuart king of England and Ireland and, as James VI, King of Scotland.

Blaise Pascal 1623, French mathematician, physician and theologian who invented the first calculating machine.

Joshua Nkomo 1917, Zimbabwean politician.

Salman Rushdie 1947, British novelist.

NO CLEMENCY FOR ROSENBERGS

1953 Thirty-five-year-old Julius Rosenberg and his wife Ethel, 37, were sent to the electric chair at Sing Sing tonight accused of passing atom bomb secrets to the Russians. While thousands worldwide continued to protest, President Eisenhower turned down a final plea for clemency. "They have received the benefit of our justice ... I cannot intervene," he said, adding that their crimes were "worse than murder". The Rosenbergs' guilt — which they have never admitted to — is seriously doubted throughout the world. Prison officials reported that they made no last requests, either for visitors or for a special last supper.

• 1846 – FIRST OFFICIAL BASEBALL MATCH • 1937 – J. M. BARRIE DIES

1789 In France, the Third Estate of the States General forms a National Assembly to oppose the aristocracy's domination of the proceedings.

1837 Eighteen-year-old Victoria accedes to the English throne on the death of her uncle, William IV.

1863 West Virginia, the Panhandle State, becomes the 36th state of the Union.

1960 American Floyd Patterson knocks out the Swede Ingmar Johansson to become the first boxer to regain the world heavyweight title.

1990 Nelson Mandela gets a ticker-tape welcome in New York.

BIRTHDAYS

Catherine Cookson 1906, British novelist, immensely prolific and popular.

Errol Flynn 1909, Tasmanian actor who specialized in swashbuckling roles.

Lionel Richie 1949, American singer and songwriter best-known for "Say You, Say Me".

Nicole Kidman 1967, Australian Oscar-winning actress.

BROADWAY HOT FOR SATCHMO AND FATS

1930 Fats Waller and Louis Armstrong took New York by storm tonight when their hit revue, *Hot Chocolates*, opened on Broadway. *Hot Chocolates* – which takes its title from the 12 gorgeous dancers who feature in the show – first opened at Connie's Inn in May 1929 and critics couldn't praise it enough. Armstrong is at his gravelly best singing "Ain't Misbehaving", while the pianist and vocalist Thomas "Fats" Waller takes credit for a number of the excellent songs.

FILM MURDER ANGERS U.S.

1979 American TV reporter Bill Stewart was gunned down by Nicaraguan National Guardsmen today as he walked towards a road block with a white flag in one hand and his official yellow press card in the other. The sequence was filmed and relayed on American TV, shocking the nation. It is expected that President Carter will review the question of American support to the regime.

BLACK HOLE HORROR

1756 Of the 146 British men thrown into Calcutta's notorious Black Hole prison today, only 23 have survived into the night. The Nawab of Bengal, Suraj ud-Daulah, attacked the English settlement in Calcutta because he feared invasion. Reports had reached him that the English in Bengal had fortified their settlements without his permission and were abusing the trading privileges granted by the Imperial firman of 1717. The Black Hole measures only 18 ft by 14 ft (5.4 m by 4.2 m) in size.

• 1819 – THE *SAVANNAH* IS THE FIRST STEAMSHIP TO CROSS THE ATLANTIC

FRENCH KING FOILED IN VAIN ESCAPE PLAN

1791 The escape plan of Louis XVI of France and his family was foiled as members of the National Guard caught the fugitive king at Varennes and brought him back to Paris today. He had been attempting to get away to safety across the country's eastern border. This final act of foolishness has undermined the King's credibility as a constitutional monarch, and the National Assembly have suspended his powers. Clearly underestimating the strength of popular demands for economic and administrative reforms, the King has allowed himself to be dominated by reactionary forces within the aristocracy. His reluctance to sanction the achievements of the National Assembly – such as the Declaration of the Rights of Man and of the Citizen, and the dismantling of the feudal regime – reveals a serious lack of foresight. The King is now in an extremely precarious position.

1377 Edward III of England dies.

1527 Italian political theorist Niccoló Machiavelli dies aged 58.

1675 Construction starts on Sir Christopher Wren's St Paul's Cathedral.

1868 Richard Wagner's opera *Die Meistersinger von Nürnberg* premieres.

1908 Death of Russian composer Nikolai Rimsky-Korsakov, best known for *Scheherazade*.

1908 A suffragette demonstration in London attracts 20,000 supporters.

1942 General Rommel's troops take 25,000 Allied prisoners at Tobruk, Libya.

1988 The Burmese government imposes a curfew as the regime totters in the face of student protests.

BIRTHDAYS

Jean-Paul Sartre 1905, French philosopher, novelist, dramatist and critic who propounded the philosophy of existentialism.

Mary McCarthy 1912, American novelist, critic and journalist, whose work includes *Memories of a Catholic Girlhood*.

IT'S A BOY!

1982 The Princess of Wales gave birth to a lusty, 7 lb (3.1 kg) blue-eyed prince in St Mary's Hospital, Paddington, today. Prince Charles, who emerged two hours later, described his son as having "sort of blondish hair, though it'll probably turn into something else later on". He said that both mother and baby were extremely well, but "the Princess is a little tired as it has been a long time". Diana, 21 next week, was in labour for just over 16 hours. The new prince is second in line to the throne after his father.

BRAZIL WINS SOCCER TROPHY FOR EVER

1970 Brazil carried off the third world cup in a thrilling match in Mexico today. Pele opened scoring with a header, but it was Gerson's goal in the 65th minute that triggered a dazzling display of Brazil's real talents. Pele, Tostao, Jairzinho and Rivelino all played with sublime artistry. When Carlos Alberto scored the last goal three minutes from time, the crowd responded with an ecstatic ovation. Brazil's third triumphant victory means the Jules Rimet Trophy has found a permanent home.

• 1788 – US CONSTITUTION COMES INTO FORCE • 1990 – EARTHQUAKE SMASHES IRAN

1377 Richard II accedes to the throne of England.

1906 President Roosevelt sues John D. Rockefeller's Standard Oil company for operating a monopoly.

1940 France accepts the armistice terms of Germany and Italy.

1941 Germany invades the USSR.

1989 The captain of the capsized cross-Channel ferry *Herald of Free Enterprise* is charged with manslaughter.

1989 In China, seven students involved in the Tiananmen Square protests are shot after televised show trials.

BIRTHDAYS

George Vancouver 1757, explorer after whom Vancouver Island and Vancouver are named.

Billy Wilder 1906, Austrian-born film director and writer whose string of hits includes *Sunset Boulevard*.

Kris Kristofferson 1936, American singer, songwriter and actor.

Meryl Streep 1949, American actress whose films include *The French Lieutenant's Woman*.

FRENCH SURRENDER

1939 Today, eight days after German troops entered Paris, the French formally surrendered to Germany. President Pétain's request for an armistice was transmitted to Hitler on the night of June 16. Hitler's terms were delivered to the French envoys two days later. Talks between the two countries took place while German troops continued to advance through the Loire. On June 22, however, the French bowed their heads and accepted all of Hitler's terms. The bitter event took place in Marshall Foch's old railway carriage in the forest of Compiègne – the same used by the French to humiliate the Germans when they accepted their surrender in 1918.

MAGIC BULLETS TARGET SEX DISEASE

1910 Paul Ehrlich, the German bacteriologist and immunologist, announced the definitive cure for syphilis today. The renowned scientist, winner with Elie Metchnikov of the 1908 Nobel Prize for physiology, has discovered that certain substances are capable of functioning as "magic bullets", attacking specific bacteria in the body while leaving the rest of the organism unharmed. The "magic bullet" against syphilis micro-organisms is an arsenical compound called Salvarsan. Mr Ehrlich was appointed director of the Royal Institute for Experimental Therapy at Frankfurt in 1906.

EXPLORER CAST ADRIFT TO DIE

1611 Early this morning the explorer Henry Hudson was bundled into a shallop by his mutinous crew and set adrift without food or water to die in the open sea. This act was the barbaric conclusion of Hudson's fourth attempt to find the North-west Passage to the Orient. Hudson left England on April 17, 1610 in the sailing ship *Discovery*. His roughneck crew were troublesome and rebellious – particularly during the hardships of the bitter Arctic night when the ship went into winter quarters in James Bay, Canada. Hudson's eldest son was set adrift with him.

• 1814 – FIRST CRICKET MATCH PLAYED AT LORD'S • 1960 – JUDY GARLAND FOUND DEAD

Quaker Penn seeks peace with Indians

1683 William Penn, the English Quaker and advocate of civil and religious liberty, signed a treaty with chiefs of the Lenni Lenape Tribe today in a bid to ensure the peace of his colony. Penn was granted a huge tract of land in the New World by King Charles II, which he subsequently named "Pennsylvania". Since arriving from England in September 1682, Penn has gone all out to establish friendly relations with the Indian tribes in the area.

Surely the right course is to test the Russians, not the bombs.
British Labour politician **Hugh Gaitskell,** in the *Observer*, 1957.

1757 British troops defeat the Nawab of Bengal, making possible the British annexation of Bengal.

1796 Pope Pius VI signs an armistice with Napoleon.

1980 Sanjay Gandhi, son of Indira Gandhi and next in line for political power, is killed in an air crash.

1980 Death of Olivia Manning, British novelist best known for her Balkan Trilogy.

1991 The International Monetary Fund agrees to offer associate membership to the Soviet Union.

2002 A fire in a youth hostel kills 15 backpackers in the town of Childers, Australia.

BIRTHDAYS

Empress Josephine 1763, Martinique-born wife of Napoleon Bonaparte.

Edward VIII 1894, British monarch who abdicated in order to marry the divorcee Mrs Simpson.

Alfred Kinsey 1894, American zoologist and sociologist.

Alan Mathison Turing 1912, British mathematician and computer expert.

EMPIRE CELEBRATES GVR

1911 Thousands turned out to celebrate the coronation of King George V in London today. Twelve thousand members of the Metropolitan Police lined the route where crowds waited for the moment when the robed and crowned King and Queen would drive by. Seven thousand people attended the ceremony, including representatives from all over the world. It has also been a day of rejoicing for the Empire, which has joined with the Mother Country in rendering homage to the new King.

• 1848 – SAXOPHONE PATENTED • 1956 – NASSER BECOMES PRESIDENT OF EGYPT

JUNE
24

1509 Henry VIII of England is crowned.

1947 A pilot sees nine unidentifiable circular objects in the sky above Washington state.

1948 The Berlin airlift begins after the Soviets blockade the city.

1953 Jacqueline Bouvier announces her engagement to US senator John F. Kennedy.

1978 Twelve white missionaries are massacred in Rhodesia's bush war.

1985 Keith Hardcastle, Britain's longest surviving heart transplant patient, dies six years after receiving his replacement heart.

BIRTHDAYS

Horatio Herbert, Earl Kitchener 1850, British secretary of state for war in 1914.

Jack Dempsey 1895, American heavyweight boxing champion.

Professor Fred Hoyle 1915, British astronomer and notable science-fiction writer.

Claude Chabrol 1930, French film director who is credited with beginning the *nouvelle vague*.

CUSTER'S LAST STAND

1876 General Custer and his men were defeated today in a bloody battle with the Indian chief Crazy Horse and his Sioux warriors. Custer had been ordered to take his regiment up the Rosebud Creek and into the valley of the Little Bighorn River to ferret out the hostile Indians believed to be camping there. Early this morning Custer spotted a large Indian village and, unaware that it was harbouring more than 1500 fighting men, decided to attack at once. With Custer's army totalling about 650 men, it was a lost battle from the start. He was unable to penetrate with mounted troops, and his cavalry were forced to dismount and fight on foot. The 225 officers and men of Custer's battalion were overwhelmed and every last one was killed.

WOMEN ORDAINED ANGLICAN PRIESTS

1990 For the first time in the history of Europe two women deacons have been ordained priests of the Anglican Church. The historic ceremonies were conducted by the Bishop of Connor and took place in St Anne's Cathedral, Belfast, today. The women are Kathleen Young, a 50-year-old physiotherapist of Carrickfergus, Co. Antrim, and Irene Templeton, 49, from Belfast.

CABOT TAKES MAINE CHANCE

1497 John Cabot sailed into Maine today, just 35 days after leaving Bristol in his ship *Matthew*. Armed with letters patent from King Henry VII authorizing him to discover and possess lands "unknown to all Christians", he immediately went ashore and finalized ownership. Cabot – real name Giovanni Caboto – is a Venetian explorer in the service of the English crown.

• 1314 – BATTLE OF BANNOCKBURN • 1983 – FIRST AMERICAN WOMAN IN SPACE

SLOVENIA AND CROATIA DECLARE INDEPENDENCE

1991 Yugoslavia plunged deeper into political crisis as Slovenia and Croatia declared their independence today. Despite warnings from the EC and the US that they would not be recognized, the two key republics voted overwhelmingly to "disassociate" from Yugoslavia, annul federal laws and gradually sever ties with the other republics. Croatian officials said that although the republic would consider itself part of Yugoslavia for the time being, it wants to negotiate with other republics to form an alliance of sovereign states. Slovenia's Interior Minister, Igor Bavcar, announced that a formal ceremony proclaiming independence will be taking place tomorrow. Faced with the break-up of the country, Yugoslavia's federal parliament called an emergency session and asked for army intervention to prevent any border changes. EC foreign ministers have agreed not to recognize the declarations of independence by the two republics and to freeze contacts with their leaders.

WAR IN KOREA

1950 Open hostilities began today between Communist North Korea and the Republic of Korea in the South. There has been constant tension in the country since the end of World War II, when the USSR established a puppet government in the Russian-controlled sector and militarized the line of the 38th parallel. A United Nations commission was established to oversee free national elections, but North Korea refused to allow the delegates in. On August 15, 1948 the Republic of Korea was proclaimed in the south and Syngman Rhee was elected President. This was followed on September 9 by the formal establishment of the Democratic People's Republic in the north. Unrest, subversion, and border incidents began almost immediately and today's clash seemed inevitable. The North Korean army and air force total some 127,000 men, while the South Korean army numbers approximately 98,000.

1788 Virginia becomes the tenth US state.

1870 Queen Isabella II of Spain abdicates.

1925 The first car telephone is exhibited in Germany.

1932 The Indian cricket team play their first Test against England at Lord's and lose by 158 runs.

1975 Mozambique gains independence after 400 years of Portuguese rule.

1987 Joan Collins obtains a 45-second divorce from husband Peter Holm.

1997 Death of Jacques Cousteau, French underwater explorer and aqualung diver.

BIRTHDAYS

Louis, 1st Earl Mountbatten of Burma 1900, supreme Allied commander in south-east Asia in World War II.

George Orwell 1903, British novelist whose books include *Nineteen Eighty-Four*.

Carly Simon 1945, American singer and songwriter best known for "You're So Vain".

George Michael 1963, British pop musician.

• 1867 – BARBED WIRE PATENTED • 2009 – MICHAEL JACKSON DIES

1794 The French defeat the Austrians at the Battle of Fleurus.

1830 King George IV of England dies.

1857 The new military honour the Victoria Cross is awarded by Queen Victoria to 62 servicemen in a ceremony in London.

1913 Emily Dawson becomes the first female magistrate in London.

1959 Ingemar Johansson becomes the first Swedish heavyweight boxing champion.

1990 The IRA bomb the Carlton Club in London, a popular haunt of Conservative MPs.

2007 UNESCO designates the Galapagos Islands an endangered heritage site.

BIRTHDAYS

Willy Messerschmitt 1898, German aircraft designer best-known for his World War II planes.

Peter Lorre 1904, Hungarian-born actor whose many films include *The Maltese Falcon* and *Casablanca.*

Laurie Lee 1914, British poet and author of the autobiography *Cider with Rosie.*

CONQUISTADOR DIES

1541 The Spanish conqueror of Peru, Francisco Pizarro, was attacked and killed in his house in Lima today. His assassins were followers of fellow adventurer, Diego de Almagro, with whom Pizarro had quarrelled and whom he later had executed. Pizarro's conquest of Peru was funded by the Spanish emperor Charles V. He will be remembered as a ruthless man who played a major part in crushing the fabled Inca Empire.

HUMAN GENOME DRAFT COMPLETED

2000 Scientists announce that they have completed a draft of the human genome. Researchers have worked for over a decade to decipher the biochemical instructions required to build and maintain the human body. Now, they have determined the exact sequence of the three billion individual chemical building blocks that make up DNA, the double-stranded molecule hidden in the nuclei of nearly all cells.

JFK CHARMS THE SOCKS OFF BERLIN

1963 A million and a quarter West Berliners turned out to give a tumultuous welcome to President Kennedy today. It was a triumphant eight-hour tour during which the whole city was gripped by a frenzy of jubilation. John F. Kennedy appeared confident and relaxed. Addressing the 120,000-strong crowd in Rathaus Square, he declared, "Two thousand years ago the proudest boast in the world was '*civis Romanus sum*'. Today, in the world of freedom, the proudest boast is '*Ich bin ein Berliner*'." He concluded his speech by saying, "All free men, wherever they may live, are citizens of Berlin, and, therefore, as a free man, I take pride in the words '*Ich bin ein Berliner*'."

CALIFORNIA DREAMS THWARTED

1989 Another wave of refugee boats from Vietnam has hit Hong Kong, whose closed refugee camps are already bulging with 45,000 "boat-people". They are fleeing poverty and believe they are bound for California. But there is talk of sending them back to Vietnam. Hong Kong is complaining that the western nations' low refugee quotas mean that Hong Kong must do more than its fair share to help, with scant resources. In fact Hong Kong is wealthy, and has hundreds of square miles of rural land, but it doesn't want the refugees competing for its people's jobs, homes and school places.

1693 The first magazine for women, the *Ladies Mercury*, is published.

1939 Pan-American Airlines operates the first scheduled transatlantic air service.

1954 The first nuclear power station is opened at Obninsk in the USSR.

1976 Six Palestinians hijack an Air France Airbus from Athens.

1988 British mountain climbers Dave Hurst and Alan Matthews become the first blind climbers to reach the summit of Mont Blanc, Europe's highest mountain.

BIRTHDAYS

Louis XII 1462, French monarch whose reign was dominated by the wars his father, Charles VIII, had initiated.

Charles IX 1550, French monarch who ordered the massacre of the Huguenots on St Bartholomew's Day in 1572.

Charles Parnell 1846, Irish politician who led the Home Rule party in the House of Commons.

Helen Keller 1880, American blind, deaf and mute teacher, social worker and writer.

LIBERTY BELL PEALS AGAIN FOR AMERICAN FREEDOM

1778 Today the Liberty Bell has been returned to Philadelphia after spending a year hidden under the floorboards of the Zion Reformed Church in Allentown, Pennsylvania. It was taken there as a precautionary measure when the city was threatened by the British one year ago. Cast by Thomas Lester's London foundry, it bears the biblical inscription "Proclaim Liberty throughout the land unto all the inhabitants thereof." It was rung on July 8, 1776 to proclaim the Declaration of Independence, and has been a symbol of American Independence ever since.

No man knows my history . . . If I had not experienced what I have, I could not have believed it myself.

Joseph Smith, Mormon founder, who was murdered today, 1844.

• 1871 – YEN INTRODUCED IN JAPAN • 1990 – QUEEN MOTHER CELEBRATES 90 YEARS

BIRTHDAYS

Henry VIII 1491, English monarch famous for his rebellion against the Roman Catholic church.

Sir Peter Paul Rubens 1577, Flemish Baroque painter.

Jean-Jacques Rousseau 1712, French philosopher and writer.

Mel Brooks 1926, American producer, director and writer.

PEACE TREATY SIGNED AT VERSAILLES

1919 The peace treaty officially ending four years of devastating war was finally signed by the Germans today. The treaty was first presented to the six chief German delegates at the historic conference in the Trianon Palace Hotel at Versailles on May 7, 1919. The Germans considered the terms excessively harsh – they include demands for massive reparations – and refused to sign. They quickly changed their minds, however, when threatened with an occupation by Allied troops.

All the world over, I will back the masses against the classes.
British statesman **William Ewart Gladstone,** in a speech at Liverpool, 1886.

DE GAULLE RESISTS NAZIS

1940 Britain gave its formal recognition to General Charles de Gaulle as leader, in exile, of the French nation. De Gaulle had been in London when France fell to the Germans and believed that they had given in too easily. In his radio broadcasts, remembered as the voice of honour and freedom, de Gaulle rallied the country in support of the Resistance.

IRAQIS HANDED BACK POWER

2004 The US-led coalition formally handed power back to Iraq, seven years after the invasion of Iraq which toppled Saddam Hussein's regime. At a surprise low-key ceremony in Baghdad, US administrator Paul Bremer transferred sovereignty to an Iraqi interim government led by Iyad Allawi, from the majority Shia community, in a move that was widely welcomed around the world.

• 1838 – QUEEN VICTORIA CROWNED • 1914 – ARCHDUKE FRANZ FERDINAND ASSASSINATED

MARADONA ON A ROLL

1986 Argentina took the World Cup again today – thanks to Maradona, who was indirectly responsible for all the goals. The West Germans did their best to keep him in check with Matthaus marking Maradona, shoulder to shoulder, so closely attached that they might have been a honeymoon couple on the dance floor. It was a thrilling game and Maradona was the undisputed star of the show.

TOBACCO TREAT FOR VIRGINIA

1620 The UK government has today banned the growing of tobacco in Britain. A tobacco-growing monopoly has instead been granted to the colony of Virginia, at a tax of one shilling per pound. Colonists have been using the leaf as their main exchange commodity in return for manufactured goods from Europe. *Nicotiana tabacum*, named after the French ambassador to Lisbon who is said to have sent seeds to Catherine de Medici, is of American origin, smoked by the Indians. But King James I of England denounced it as a health hazard in 1604.

48 BC Julius Caesar becomes absolute ruler of Rome.

1801 The first census is carried out in Britain.

1855 The *Daily Telegraph* is first published in Britain.

1864 Samuel Crowther, Bishop of Niger, becomes the first black Church of England bishop.

1905 The Automobile Association is founded in Britain.

1940 Death of Swiss painter and graphic artist Paul Klee.

1965 The first US military ground action begins in Vietnam.

1967 American actress Jayne Mansfield is killed in a car crash.

1974 Isabel Perón takes over the presidency of Argentina.

1990 Lithuania to suspend declaration of independence for 100 days.

SOUTH AFRICA IMPOSES NEW RACIST LAWS

1925 The South African government today adopted racial inequality as a political policy, passing an act which bars black South Africans from holding skilled or semi-skilled jobs. Job inequality between blacks and whites has its roots in the gold-mining industry of the last century when mining bosses had an almost limitless pool of cheap, unskilled labour in the native population. Skilled labour, however, had to be attracted from overseas by the lure of high wages. By the 1900s blacks had acquired the necessary skills for promotion, but white employees refused to be ousted from their positions. Today's legislation marks the rise of a new oppression of the majority black population.

ATLANTIC CONQUEROR

1986 Pop and airline millionaire Richard Branson, and the crew of Virgin *Atlantic Challenger II*, beat the Atlantic crossing record by slicing two hours and nine minutes off the time set in 1952. They arrived at Bishop's Rock lighthouse, off the Scilly Isles, at 7.30 this evening.

BIRTHDAYS

Antoine de Saint-Exupéry 1900, French novelist and aviator best known for *The Little Prince*, a children's fable.

Rafael Kubelik 1914, Czech conductor and composer.

• 1603 – LONDON'S GLOBE THEATRE BURNS DOWN • 1976 – SEYCHELLES INDEPENDENCE

1789 The revolutionary mob in Paris attacks Abbaye Prison.

1822 In Spain, rebels take King Ferdinand VII prisoner.

1919 Death of British physicist Lord Rayleigh, who was awarded the Nobel Prize in 1904 for his discovery of argon gas.

1971 Three Russian astronauts are found dead after a record-breaking 24 days in space which ended in oxygen failure.

1974 Russian ballet dancer Mikhail Baryshnikov defects to the West while on tour in Canada.

1994 Tonya Harding is banned for life and stripped of her national championship title for an attack on her rival figure skater Nancy Kerrigan.

BIRTHDAYS

John Gay 1685, English poet and playwright best known for the ballad opera *The Beggar's Opera*.

Susan Hayward 1918, American actress who won an Oscar for *I Want to Live*.

Mike Tyson 1966, American and world heavyweight boxing champion.

TIGHTROPE THRILLS AS BLONDIN WALKS OVER FALLS

1859 Crowds held their breath in stunned admiration as a daring Frenchman crossed the 167 ft (51 m) high Niagara Falls balanced on a tightrope today. The whole extraordinary feat took just five minutes. Thirty-five-year-old Charles Blondin, whose real name is Jean François Gravelet, is an acrobat and tightrope walker of world renown. Born at St Omer and trained at Lyons, he is currently engaged in a tour throughout the United States.

AZTEC KING SLAIN BY SPAIN

1520 The Aztec sovereign of Mexico, Montezuma II, was killed today by the Spanish conqueror Hernando Cortez who had overthrown his empire and taken him prisoner. Misled by the ancient prophecies of his race, Montezuma II and his people received Cortez and his men as divinities when they first arrived at the Mexican capital, Tenochtitlan. Montezuma II was a successful conqueror until overthrown by Hernando Cortez.

HONG KONG IS GIVEN BACK

1997 Against a backdrop of celebrations all over China, the region of Hong Kong in the South China Sea, has been handed back to the Chinese after 99 years of British administration. Attending the ceremony are Prince Charles and Prime Minister Tony Blair, as well as Chinese President Jiang Zemin who has promised to govern Hong Kong by the principle of "one country, two systems".

SUPERMAN SIGHTED

1938 Thanks to Action Comics, a new super crime fighter from the distant planet of Krypton has made his appearance among us today. He can leap taller than the highest building, run faster than a speeding train, is invulnerable and possesses the strength of 200 men. Most of the time his true identity is hidden behind the mild, unassuming persona of Clark Kent, a reporter on the *Metropolis Daily Globe*. But when action calls he quickly materializes in a blue catsuit and red cape, with a big "S" emblazoned on his enormous chest. And what's his name? Why, Superman, of course!

• 1934 – NIGHT OF THE LONG KNIVES • 1936 – *GONE WITH THE WIND* IS PUBLISHED

1894 Amidst much celebration, the Tower Bridge was opened by H. R. H. The Prince of Wales. His cavalcade made a double crossing before the bascules were raised to allow an impressive procession of boats to sail down the Thames.

• 1997 – *HARRY POTTER AND THE PHILOSOPHER'S STONE* IS PUBLISHED

JULY

DARWIN PRESENTS THEORY OF EVOLUTION

1858 Amidst controversy, eminent British scientist Charles Darwin has presented his views on evolution and the principles of natural selection to the Linnean Society in London. Churchmen are concerned that Darwin's theory refutes the Book of Genesis. Darwin has based much of his work on observations made while serving as a naturalist on the brig-sloop HMS *Beagle* between 1831 and 1836. During this time his observations convinced him that species evolved gradually and that natural selection is responsible for changing the genetic constitution of a species in favour of particular genes carried by successful individuals.

WAR ENDS IN ALGERIA

1962 After eight years of war between the Algerian nationalist population and the French army and settlers and 132 years of French rule, Algeria looks set to gain independence. A referendum held in Algeria today has almost unanimously backed de Gaulle's independence plan. A ceasefire called in March prompted by the intensification of terrorist activity in the country during the early months of this year, has allowed discussions between the French government and the National Liberation Front's (FLN) provisional government to take place. In spite of the talks, acts of terrorism continued and a mass exodus of Europeans began as the prospect of a new Muslim state became more likely.

1847 First adhesive stamps go on sale in the US.

1860 Death of American Charles Goodyear, pioneer of rubber processing.

1916 Coca-Cola launches its distinctively shaped bottle.

1916 The Battle of the Somme begins with heavy casualties.

1937 The 999 emergency telephone call comes into force in Britain, the first of its kind in the world.

1941 The first-ever television commercial is shown in New York, advertising a Bulova clock.

1990 The Deutschmark becomes the official currency of both East and West Germany.

BIRTHDAYS

Charles Laughton 1899, English actor whose most famous performance was in *The Hunchback of Notre Dame*.

Olivia de Havilland 1916, American actress who won Oscars for *The Heiress* and *To Each His Own*.

Carl Lewis 1961, American athlete who won four gold medals in the Los Angeles Olympic Games in 1984.

• 1969 – CHARLES INVESTED AS PRINCE OF WALES • 2004 – MARLON BRANDO DIES

1644 In the English Civil War, the Battle of Marston Moor turns the tide in Oliver Cromwell's favour.

1778 Swiss-born French philosopher Jean-Jacques Rousseau dies.

1951 The worst floods in US history leave 41 dead and 200,000 homeless in Kansas and Missouri.

1964 President Johnson signs the US Civil Rights Bill, which prohibits racial discrimination.

1990 A hundred Muslim pilgrims die of suffocation in a tunnel in the Holy City of Mecca.

1997 Death of James Stewart who won an Oscar for *The Philadelphia Story*.

BIRTHDAYS

Thomas Cranmer 1489, English cleric who was consecrated Archbishop of Canterbury for his support of Henry VIII in the latter's divorce dispute with the Pope but was burnt at the stake as a heretic during the reign of Queen Mary.

Hermann Hesse 1877, German novelist.

Patrice Lumumba 1925, Congolese statesman and prime minister from 1960–61.

WILLIAM BOOTH ESTABLISHES CHRISTIAN "ARMY"

1865 British evangelist and itinerant preacher William Booth today founded the Christian Mission in Whitechapel, one of London's worst slums. Thirty-six-year-old Booth from Nottingham has been a minister of the Methodist New Connection church for some years but the church has been reluctant to accept his poor converts. As a result, he has established his own mission along military lines, with military titles, hierarchy and uniforms. More than a Christian evangelical church, Booth's "Salvation Army" acts as a social service and reforming organization for the most destitute members of society. He works with his wife, Catherine, a public preacher.

GOODBYE TO GROMYKO

1989 Russia's longest-serving foreign minister, Andrei Gromyko, has died in Moscow today aged 79. Foreign minister for 30 years, he was also president of the Supreme Soviet for three years. He became notorious in western diplomatic circles for his austere and humourless manner, pursuing the Cold War relentlessly.

VIETNAM REUNIFIED

1976 North and South Vietnam were reunified today in the aftermath of the fall of Saigon and the tragedy of the Vietnam War. The division 22 years ago into separate states resulted in continuous fighting and massive loss of life: the Communist Vietcong within South Vietnam attempted to seize power from the government, aided by North Vietnam and China. The US provided military support to South Vietnam for a number of years, during which time the war escalated. Unpopular with Americans for its part in the war, the US withdrew in 1973 in the most humiliating political defeat it has ever suffered. A peace treaty was signed between North and South Vietnam in the same year, but in March last year North Vietnam invaded South Vietnam and Saigon fell in April. The resulting Socialist Republic of Vietnam proclaimed today faces enormous economic and social problems.

• 1900 – FIRST ZEPPELIN FLIGHT • 1973 – HOLLYWOOD STAR BETTY GRABLE DIES

SWEDE BECOMES YOUNGEST WIMBLEDON CHAMPION

1976 Twenty-year-old Swedish tennis player Bjorn Borg became the youngest ever men's singles winner at Wimbledon today defeating Ilie Nastase of Romania 6-4, 6-2, 9-7. A talented all-round sportsman, Borg showed early promise at tennis and at 11 won his first tournament. He has been in Sweden's Davis Cup team since he was 15. His superb athleticism and sportsmanlike temperament helped him win the Wimbledon Junior championship at 16 and the French championship at 18. Borg looks set to carry on for many seasons to come.

HERO OF CHERNOBYL DIES

1990 Anatoli Grishchenko, the Russian who braved radioactive fallout at Chernobyl to avoid an even worse catastrophe, died of leukemia today. Grishchenko flew a helicopter over the damaged reactor and dropped the loads of sand and concrete needed to seal the plant and prevent meltdown. The disaster occured in April 1986 when fire broke out at the reactor causing the worst ever nuclear accident to date.

CONFEDERATES ROUTED AT GETTYSBURG

1863 With more than 51,000 dead and wounded, the Battle of Gettysburg is over and the Confederate Army has been routed. Superior numbers and strong defensive positions helped General George Meade's Union Army to defeat General Robert E. Lee just outside the market town of Gettysburg, Pennsylvania. This may prove to be a turning point in the grim and bloody struggle between the North and South.

1898 Captain Joshua Slocum becomes the first solo round the world sailor.

1905 In Odessa, Russian troops kill over 6000 to restore order during a strike.

1962 French property in Algeria is taken over as the country gains its independence.

1971 Jim Morrison, lead singer with the Doors, dies of a heart attack in Paris.

1988 The USS *Vincennes*, based in the Gulf during the Iran-Iraq war, shoots down an Iranian airliner in error, killing 286 people.

BIRTHDAYS

Robert Adam 1728, Scottish architect and designer with an influential style.

Franz Kafka 1883, Czech writer best known for the novels *The Trial* and *The Castle*.

Ken Russell 1927, British film director with an idiosyncratic and controversial style.

Tom Stoppard 1937, Czech-born playwright known for *Rosencrantz and Guildenstern are Dead*.

Tom Cruise 1962, American actor who starred in *Top Gun*, *Magnolia* and *Mission Impossible*.

• 1608 – CHAMPLAIN FOUNDS CITY OF QUEBEC • 1928 – FIRST TV SET GOES ON SALE

JULY 4

BIRTHDAYS

Giuseppe Garibaldi 1807, Italian soldier who played a major role in the unification of Italy.

Thomas Barnado 1845, Irish philanthropist who founded homes for destitute children.

Louis B. Mayer 1885, Russian-born co-founder of MGM.

Louis Armstrong 1900, Legendary American jazz musician.

Neil Simon 1927, American playwright of enormous popularity.

CONGRESS ACCEPTS DECLARATION OF INDEPENDENCE

1776 In an historic session today the Continental Congress accepted, with minor amendments, the Declaration of Independence written by Thomas Jefferson under the instructions of a five-member committee. Although Congress voted on July 2 to declare independence, the declaration passed today formally severs American links with Britain. It has come about largely as a result of the War of Independence, which has raged for over a year.

HOSTAGE ORDEAL ENDS AS ISRAELI COMMANDOS SWOOP

1976 A crack force of 200 Israeli commandos has made a daring raid of Entebbe airport, freeing all but three of the 98 hostages held by Palestinian terrorists since June 27. The commandos arrived in three Hercules C-130 transport planes and took just 53 minutes to complete their mission. The drama began when Palestinian terrorists hijacked an Air France A 300-B airbus after take-off from Athens airport and demanded to be flown to Uganda. The passengers, a mix of Israeli and other nationalities, have been pawns in an international drama, now thankfully over.

SUFFRAGETTE APPEARS IN TROUSERS

1853 Controversial and outspoken suffragette Amelia Jenks Bloomer shocked her audience in Connecticut today by appearing in trousers while she delivered a speech denouncing the requirement that women should cover their legs. Mrs Bloomer has been appearing in this attire – a knee-length skirt combined with loose trousers bound in at the ankle and dubbed "bloomers" – since 1849 as a form of protest. The issues of women's rights in general and the issue of dress reform in particular are ones that Mrs Bloomer holds dear. She is the publisher of a magazine devoted to temperance and literature, entitled *The Lily*.

• **1848 – COMMUNIST MANIFESTO PUBLISHED** • **1881 – BILLY THE KID SHOT DEAD**

DIVA SAYS FAREWELL TO COVENT GARDEN

1965 In a stunning final performance, soprano Maria Callas tonight bade farewell to the operatic stage and her numerous fans at Covent Garden, some of whom had queued for 48 hours for tickets. In a voice noted for its fine range and gift of expression, Callas sang *Tosca* before a packed house. She has sung all of the most exacting soprano roles, excelling particularly in the *bel canto* style of the pre-Verdian Italian opera.

TEMPERANCE TURNOUT BOOSTED BY RAIL EXCURSION

1841 The temperance movement got a boost today as Thomas Cook, entrepreneur and ardent temperance supporter, organized the first special rail excursion to transport the faithful to meetings. Today's excursion from Leicester to Loughborough and back again was pronounced a great success by Mr Cook. "All went off in the best style and in perfect safety we returned to Leicester," he said.

STONES GIVE FREE CONCERT IN HYDE PARK

1969 Two days after the death of guitarist Brian Jones, the Rolling Stones gave a free concert in Hyde Park attended by a record 250,000 people. Policed by the London branch of Hell's Angels and recorded for television, the concert was a great success. During the evening Mick Jagger paid tribute to Jones by reciting Shelley while clouds of white butterflies were released over the stage.

1811 Venezuela declares independence from Spain.

1830 The French capture Algiers and seize its ruler's fabulous jewellery collection.

1975 Arthur Ashe beats Jimmy Connors to become the first black men's singles champion at Wimbledon.

1975 The Cape Verde Islands gain independence from Portugal.

1989 Colonel Oliver North is fined $150,000 (£95,000) and given a suspended prison sentence for the role he played in the Iran-Contra affair.

BIRTHDAYS

Phineas Barnum 1810, American showman.

Cecil Rhodes 1853, English-born colonialist and statesman in Southern Africa.

Dwight Davis 1879, American tennis player and founder of the Davis Cup.

Jean Cocteau 1889, French poet and artist, best-known for *Orphée* and *Les Enfants Terribles*.

Georges Pompidou 1911, French statesman and president from 1969 until his death in 1974.

• 1817 – FIRST GOLD SOVEREIGNS ISSUED IN BRITAIN • 1977 – BHUTTO OUSTED IN PAKISTAN

1189 French-born Henry II of England dies.

1801 The English and Spanish fleets are defeated by the French off Algeciras.

1809 Pope Pius VII is arrested for excommunicating Napoleon.

1892 Dadabhai Naoroji becomes Britain's first non-white MP.

1893 French author Guy de Maupassant dies.

1928 The *Lights of New York*, the first all-sound feature film, is premiered.

1960 Death of Aneurin Bevan, British Labour politician who, as minister of health from 1945 to 1951, created the National Health Service.

1973 Otto Klemperer, German-born conductor, dies at the age of 88.

BIRTHDAYS

Bill Haley 1925, American rock 'n' roll star.

Dalai Lama 1935, Tibetan spiritual leader in exile.

Vladimir Ashkenazy 1937, Russian pianist and conductor.

Sylvester Stallone 1946, American actor best known for the "Rocky" movies.

GIBSON MAKES HISTORY

1957 Sporting history was made today as American Althea Gibson became the first black Wimbledon champion beating fellow American Darlene Hurd 6-3, 6-2. An outstanding player, 30-year-old Gibson hasn't lost a single set throughout the entire fortnight's play.

Musicians don't retire; they stop when there's no more music in them.

Louis Armstrong, jazz trumpeter, who died today of a heart attack, aged 71.

NATO SEEKS A NEW ROLE

1990 In the wake of the momentous events in Eastern Europe in recent years, and the drive towards reunification by East and West Germany, NATO (the North Atlantic Treaty Organization) has declared that the Warsaw Pact is no longer a military threat to the West, and so must now seek a new role for itself in the 1990s. This declaration in London comes hard on the heels of the announcement in May by NATO defence ministers of major cuts to budgets. It is understood that NATO will now become a primarily political organization.

SIR THOMAS MORE EXECUTED

1535 Distinguished politician and author Sir Thomas More was executed today at the Tower of London after being found guilty of high treason. Formerly a favourite of King Henry VIII, More refused to take an oath of supremacy to the king as head of the Church in preference to the Pope, so was charged and found guilty of high treason. He has been held in the Tower for a year in hope that he would recant. Sir Thomas is greatly respected in the country and has had a most distinguished political and diplomatic career. London born, he studied at Oxford under Linacre and his religious beliefs were strongly influenced by Colet. More entered parliament in 1504 and from 1509, when he enjoyed the favour of the King, was employed on various foreign missions. He was appointed Speaker of the Privy Council in 1518 and became Speaker of the House of Commons in 1523, during which time he was knighted. Against his own strongest wishes he succeeded Wolsey as Lord Chancellor in 1529 and resigned in 1532 over King Henry VIII's ecclesiastical policy and his marriage to Anne Boleyn. As a devout Catholic, More refused last year to recognize the King as head of the Church and hence he lost his own head today.

LONDON ATTACKED IN THE RUSH HOUR

2005 Fifty-two people were killed and around 700 injured as four co-ordinated suicide bombers set off devices on London's transport system during the morning rush-hour. Three bombs exploded on London Underground trains within 50 seconds of each other, followed by another on a bus in Tavistock Square an hour later. The homemade, organic peroxide-based devices were packed into rucksacks carried by four British-raised muslims. Two of the bombers made video tapes, broadcast by Al Jazeera and featuring al-Qaeda members, citing Britain's forces in Afghanistan and Iraq, and its financial and military support of America and Israel, as their reasons for the bombings.

1307 English king Edward I, conqueror of the Welsh, dies on his way to Scotland to fight Robert the Bruce.

1937 The second Sino-Japanese war breaks out.

1950 The first airshow is held at Farnborough in Surrey, UK.

1970 Death of Sir Allen Lane, founder of Penguin and the first publisher to promote the paperback.

1988 An 11-year-old American boy pilot takes off from San Diego, bound for Le Bourget in Paris.

1990 Martina Navratilova makes Wimbledon history by winning her ninth title.

BIRTHDAYS

Joseph-Marie Jacquard 1752, French silk weaver and inventor of the Jacquard loom.

Gustav Mahler 1860, Austrian composer and conductor.

Marc Chagall 1887, Russian painter and designer who spent most of his life in France.

Vittorio de Sica 1901, Italian film director who is best-known for *Bicycle Thieves*.

Ringo Starr 1940, drummer with The Beatles.

US TAKES OVER OCCUPATION OF ICELAND

1941 President Franklin D. Roosevelt today ordered American troops to occupy Iceland, in a move to release British forces from Iceland and deter any attack from the Nazis. Although Iceland is an independent country, Britain occupied it earlier this year to prevent Germany from turning it into a base from which to further threaten British shipping. Although the United States is not at war with Germany at this point, the country is as committed to the Allied cause as is possible without actually declaring war on Germany. Roosevelt continues to stress that the US must remain an "arsenal of democracy".

JAPAN OPEN TO TRADE AFTER 250 YEARS OF ISOLATION

1853 US Naval officer Commodore Matthew Perry today persuaded Japan to unlock its doors to trade with the rest of the world. Backed by armed ships in Edo Harbour, Perry convinced the current shogun that the Japanese should treat shipwrecked sailors with more consideration, that American vessels should be allowed to purchase coal and that American merchants should be allowed to trade in at least one port. Japan effectively closed its doors to the western world when it expelled the Spanish in 1624 and the Portuguese in 1639.

• 1985 – BORIS BECKER BECOMES YOUNGEST-EVER WIMBLEDON MEN'S SINGLES CHAMPION

1497 Portuguese navigator Vasco da Gama sets sail from Lisbon to find a sea passage to India.

1905 American tennis player May Button becomes the first foreigner to take a Wimbledon title.

1933 Death of novelist Anthony Hope, author of *The Prisoner of Zenda*.

1965 Starting gates for horse-racing are used for the first time at Newmarket in Britain.

1967 British actress Vivien Leigh, star of *Gone With the Wind*, dies of tuberculosis aged only 53.

1990 One billion television viewers watch West Germany defeat Argentina to win the World Cup.

BIRTHDAYS

Joseph Chamberlain 1836, English politician who advocated free education.

Count Ferdinand von Zeppelin 1838, German aircraft manufacturer.

John D. Rockefeller 1839, American multimillionaire and founder of the Standard Oil Company.

Sir Arthur John Evans 1851, English archaeologist.

SHELLEY DROWNED

1822 Leading figure in the Romantic movement Percy Bysshe Shelley drowned today in the Bay of Spezia, when his small boat foundered in a storm. He had just visited the poets Byron and Leigh Hunt at Leghorn and was returning home. A somewhat controversial figure, Shelley nevertheless has contributed enormously to English literary and intellectual life, leaving behind an impressive legacy of poetry, essays, pamphlets and letters. A great rebel and anarchist, his life and work reflect his intellectual courage, his keen sense of injustice and sharp sense of humour.

TENSION IN THE MIDDLE EAST HEIGHTENS

2014 Amid growing tensions between Israel and Hamas following the kidnapping and murder of three Israeli teenagers in June and the revenge killing of a Palestinian teenager in July, Israel has launched Operation Protective Edge on the Palestinian Gaza Strip, starting with numerous missile strikes. The military campaign has been criticized by human rights groups in Palestine and the US as "collective punishment." Israeli leaders are saying that the current military operation won't be short. According to a senior official "The prime minister's instruction by the end of the meeting was to prepare for a thorough, long, continuous and strong campaign in Gaza. A ground offensive is on the table."

ZIEGFELD GLORIFIES THE AMERICAN GIRL

1907 With the flashing of legs and the twitching of ostrich plumes, the Follies hit Broadway today. The theatre manager and producer Florenz Ziegfeld has brought an All-American version of the Folies Bergère of Paris to the New York stage, using that magic combination of beautiful girls, semi-nudity, great pageantry and comedy to ensure success; his theme – "Glorifying the American girl". Although less risque than the original, Ziegfeld's Follies are bound to cause a stir. Ziegfeld is no stranger to the art of dramatic promotion and has in the past managed Sandow the famous strong man, as well as French actress Anna Held.

• 1945 – FRENCH RESISTANCE LEADER JEAN MOULIN EXECTUED BY NAZIS

SANDINISTAS OVERTHROW SOMOZA

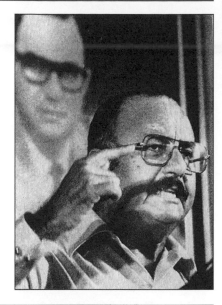

1979 The civil war in Nicaragua is over – the Sandinista rebels have overthrown General Somoza, prompting his resignation. The bloody conflict between the Sandinista rebels and Somoza's army has cost the lives of thousands of Nicaraguans. Somoza's downfall was inevitable after he lost the support of conservatives, the business community and his biggest ally, the US. In fact the US has been instrumental in helping to work out a plan to replace Samoza. The man who will take Nicaragua through the transitional period is the new president Francisco Malianos.

1810 Argentina proclaims independence from Spain.

1850 Death of Zachary Taylor, 12th US president.

1922 Eighteen-year-old American swimmer Johnny Weissmuller swims the 100 metres in 58.6 seconds.

1925 In Dublin Oonagh Keogh becomes the first female member of a stock exchange.

1943 British and US forces begin the invasion of Sicily.

1990 Nairobi is closed down on the third day of rioting in Kenya.

1990 A 15-mile (24 km) stretch of the Cumbrian coast in northwest England is declared unsafe after items contaminated by the leaks from Sellafield nuclear plant in 1983 are washed up on the beach.

CRIME WRITER JAILED FOR CONTEMPT

1951 American crime writer Dashiell Hammett was jailed today for contempt of court when he refused to testify before the House Un-American Activities Committee. Senator Joe McCarthy's crusade against communism has led to the blacklisting of many in public life and the arts who are on the left of the political spectrum. Hammett has virtually given up the writing on which his reputation depends (his crime classics include *The Maltese Falcon* and *The Thin Man*). His partner, playwright and author Lillian Hellman, is also expected to be called before the Committee to testify.

BIRTHDAYS

Elias Howe 1819, American inventor of the sewing machine.

Edward Heath 1916, British Conservative politician, prime minister 1970–4.

David Hockney 1937, British artist of great repute.

SWEET DREAMS

1902 A German pharmaceutical company has today taken out a patent on a new compound which will alleviate insomnia. The company claims that barbaturic acid can be used as a sleeping aid, as an anaesthetic for surgery and to help control epilepsy.

The greater the power, the more dangerous the abuse.

Edmund Burke, British political philosopher, who died today, 1797.

• 1938 – 35 MILLION GAS MASKS ON SALE • 1989 – US PRESIDENT BUSH TOURS EUROPE

BIRTHDAYS

Camille Pissarro 1830, French painter who was a central figure of the Impressionist group.

James McNeill Whistler 1834, American painter and graphic artist.

Marcel Proust 1871, French novelist.

Carl Orff 1895, German composer, teacher and conductor best-known for the oratorio *Carmina Burana*.

EL CID DIES OF GRIEF

1099 The famed Spanish warrior Rodrigo Diaz de Bivar, or El Cid as he was more commonly known, has died today in Valencia, apparently of grief at the defeat of his forces against the Moors. His great achievement has been the capture of the Muslim city of Valencia, after a siege of nine months, which he has ruled absolutely for the past five years. It seems certain that with his death and the defeat of his forces, his wife Ximena will be unable to withstand the onslaught of the Moors and Valencia will be abandoned, once again becoming a Muslim city. Born at Burgos around 1043 of a noble Castilian family, El Cid rose to fame for his successes in the war between Sancho of Castile and Sancho of Navarre. El Cid became a combination of *condottiere* and compatriot at the tender age of 22 and has been fighting constantly since that time, sometimes for the Christians and sometimes for the Moors. He has served many rulers but none more faithfully than Alfonso VI of Castile, in spite of being exiled by the jealous king.

GOODBYE AND GOOD RIDDANCE

2011 British tabloid newspaper *News of the World* published its last edition after 168 years in the wake of a phone hacking scandal, with a front cover that read "thank you and goodbye". A public backlash and withdrawal of advertising forced the closure of the newspaper.

A BLOWN UP IN NEW ZEALAND

1985 The Greenpeace protest ship *Rainbow Warrior* sank today in Auckland harbour after two explosions tore the hull apart below the waterline. A Portuguese photographer was killed in the blast, but nine other people on board escaped uninjured. There are suspicions that French secret agents are behind the explosions – *Rainbow Warrior* was preparing to lead a flotilla of seven peace vessels into the French nuclear testing site of Muroroa Atoll in the Pacific to coincide with Bastille Day. The international implications of French Secret Service involvement in the *Rainbow Warrior* sabotage plan would be serious.

CHINESE UNEARTH A TERRACOTTA ARMY

1975 Archaeologists in China today unearthed a vast army of 8000 terracotta figures, sculpted and fired in the shapes of warriors, chariots and horses all drawn up in battle formation. Found near the ancient Chinese capital of Xi'an, they were created more than 2000 years ago for Qin Shi Huangdi, the first emperor to unite China. He created the first totalitarian society and ruled it with efficiency and utter ruthlessness. The figures are a mile (1.6 km) from the emperor's tomb and look as if they are guarding it. They range in height from 5 ft 8 inches (173 cm) to 6 ft 5 inches (195 cm), and are highly individual in their appearance. They reveal the enormous skill of the artisans who created this spectacular memorial. Their reward was to be walled up inside the emperor's tomb, so that the secret of the army would die with them.

1789 The Marquis de Lafayette, presents the Declaration of the Rights of Man to the National Assembly.

1937 Death of George Gershwin, the American composer best known for *Rhapsody in Blue* and *Porgy and Bess*.

1941 Sir Arthur Evans, the British archaeologist who excavated Knossos in Crete, dies just three days after his 90th birthday.

1979 US *Skylab* burns up on re-entering the Earth's atmosphere after six years in space.

1990 Police and Mohawk Indians fire at each other near Montreal over a land rights dispute.

BIRTHDAYS

Robert I 1274, Scottish monarch known as Robert the Bruce.

Yul Brynner 1915, American film actor, one of Hollywood's most magnetic stars.

Gough Whitlam 1916, Australian statesman and Labour prime minister 1972–75.

Leon Spinks 1953, American boxer who took the world heavyweight title from Muhammad Ali.

JAMES II DEFEATED

1690 Deposed Roman Catholic King of England James II met defeat today at the hands of the current king, William III or William of Orange, on the banks of the River Boyne in Ireland. James had recently raised a French/Irish army from his exile in France and landed in Britain intending to retake the crown. James was deposed in June 1688 shortly after the birth of his son when parliament became concerned about the possibility of a Catholic succession to the throne.

Acting is a masochistic form of exhibitionism. It is not quite the occupation of an adult.
Laurence Olivier, the British actor, who died today, 1989.

• 1776 – CAPTAIN COOK SETS SAIL TO FIND THE NORTH-WEST PASSAGE

1789 Fire sweeps Paris after two days of rioting.

1799 Britain passes the Combination Act, which bars any combination of working men trying to improve working conditions in an attempt to prevent the spread of revolutionary ideas from France and the formation of trade unions.

1944 The RAF becomes the first air force to use jet aircraft in operational service.

1952 Dwight D. Eisenhower resigns from the army in order to begin a presidential campaign.

1982 Hostilities between Britain and Argentina over the Falkland Islands are officially ended.

BIRTHDAYS

Julius Caesar 100 BC, Roman general and statesman and dictator.

Josiah Wedgwood 1730, English potter and industrialist.

Henry Thoreau 1817, American naturalist and writer.

George Eastman 1854, American inventor of the Kodak camera.

Amedeo Modigliani 1884, Italian painter and sculptor.

FIRST BRITISH PILOT IS KILLED IN CRASH

1910 British aviation claimed its first victim today when Charles Stewart Rolls, partner in the Rolls Royce car firm, crashed his Wright biplane at a flying competition in Bournemouth. According to one spectator, the rudders of the biplane seemed to break during a tilt, causing the machine to nose-dive into the ground. Rolls was still in his seat after the crash, but all attempts to revive him failed.

I have a Catholic soul, but a Lutheran stomach.

Erasmus, on why he failed to fast during Lent – he died today, 1536.

SUNDAY TIMES IN COURT OVER SPYCATCHER

1987 The *Sunday Times* newspaper found itself in the dock today over the controversial book *Spycatcher*, written by former MI5 agent Peter Wright, which reveals the innermost workings of the agency. The government has stopped publication of the book in England and is attempting to prevent publication in Australia. The *Sunday Times* has gone against the government's injunction and has published excerpts of the book. The political implications are embarrassing for the present government, which insists that the book is a breach of confidentiality.

BRADMAN'S SCORE BREAKS ALL RECORDS

1930 Australia's Don Bradman broke all Test cricket records today with a score of 334 runs against England at Leeds, breaking R. E. Foster's record at Sydney 27 years ago. He also set a record for the number of runs scored in a single day of play – 309 of his 334 runs were hit today.

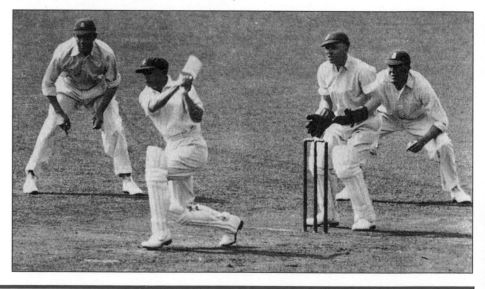

• 1878 – TURKEY CEDES CYPRUS TO BRITAIN • 1920 – PANAMA CANAL OPENS

GENERAL TOM THUMB DIES

1883 Circus midget General Tom Thumb has died today aged 45. Part of P. T. Barnum's Greatest Show on Earth since the age of four, Charles Sherwood Stratton was 25 inches (62 cm) tall when Barnum found him, and over the course of his life reached a height of 40 inches (102 cm). As well as touring extensively with the circus, Tom Thumb performed at the American museum owned by Barnum. A master at massive public campaigning, Barnum made a fortune out of the likes of Tom Thumb and Swedish opera singer Jenny Lind.

1878 The Congress of Berlin ends with the European powers limiting Russian naval expansion, permitting Austria-Hungary to occupy Bosnia-Herzegovina and gaining Turkish recognition of the independence of Serbia, Romania and Montenegro and of Bulgarian autonomy under Turkish suzerainty.

1957 Elvis Presley gets his first UK No. 1 with "All Shook Up".

1980 Death of Sir Seretse Khama, president of Botswana, who married Englishwoman Ruth Williams, as a result of which he had to renounce his chieftaincy of the Bamangwato tribe.

1990 The Italian port of Brindisi witnesses the arrival of 4500 Albanian refugees.

2014 Death of Nadine Gordimer, South African political activist.

YELTSIN RESIGNS FROM COMMUNIST PARTY

1990 President of the Russian republic Boris Yeltsin resigned from the Communist Party today. This final severance with the Party concludes a process that has been going on since he was sacked by Gorbachev in 1987 for his impatience with economic reforms. Gorbachev, then as now, continues to walk a tightrope between hardliners and reformers. Yeltsin was a strong Gorbachev supporter for some time but has now emerged clearly in opposition to him, a position that was highlighted after demonstrations in Moscow by his supporters in March 1989. This support helped Yeltsin win a seat in the first election of a multi-candidate system later that month. In May of the same year he was elected to the Supreme Soviet. Continuing economic problems and trouble in the republics dog Gorbachev's administration, although his international stature is high.

Sir George Gilbert Scott 1811, English architect who was an advocate of the Gothic revival style.

Harrison Ford 1942, American actor whose films include *Star Wars* and *Witness*.

MARAT STABBED TO DEATH IN HIS BATH

1793 Leading figure in the French Revolution, Jean Paul Marat, has been stabbed in his bath by Charlotte Corday, a Girondist supporter. Although popular for his compassion for the poor and his concern for social justice, he may not be too sadly missed as he is largely responsible for denouncing deputies, ministers and kings, calling for innumerable executions. His paper *L'ami du peuple* provoked hatred but made him popular with the "scum" of Paris; it also gave him enormous power. Marat was elected a deputy of the Convention but was one of the most unpopular men in the House. He became involved in the Jacobin struggle with the Girondists and his death seems to be a further escalation of this violent struggle for supremacy. There are fears that the Jacobins will use his death as an excuse for a reign of terror.

• 1930 – FIRST WORLD CUP SOCCER CONTEST HELD • 1947 – MARSHALL PLAN ACCEPTED

JULY
14

BIRTHDAYS

Emmeline Pankhurst 1858, English suffragette.

Woody Guthrie 1912, American folk singer, guitarist and composer.

Ingmar Bergman 1918, Swedish film and theatre director whose influential films include *The Seventh Seal*.

Arthur Laurents 1918, American playwright and librettist who wrote *West Side Story*.

MOB STORMS THE BASTILLE

1789 Two days of rioting in Paris have culminated in the storming of the Bastille prison by a mob demanding munitions stored within its walls. Commander Marquis de Launay, who has been holding the prison with his men, refused to surrender the arms to the mob, fearing the volatile atmosphere throughout the city would be further heightened by weapons. The building has been stormed by the crowd, the munitions taken and the seven prisoners within have been released. The Bastille was built in 1370 as part of the defences of the city of Paris, but by the 17th century it had become a symbol of French absolutism, a prison which held political prisoners. There are fears that this civil unrest may be the beginning of a revolution.

KING FEISAL IS MURDERED

1958 King Feisal, his uncle the Crown Prince Abdul Illah and the Prime Minister Nuri el-Said were murdered in Iraq during a coup today. The coup has implications for the whole region. President Chamoun in nearby Lebanon has demanded aid from the West. The US is expected to respond by sending marines to Beirut – a move certain to be criticized as interventionist by the Soviet Union.

MATTERHORN CONQUERED BY BRITISH TEAM

1865 The formidable Matterhorn has been conquered by an expedition led by British explorer Edward Whymper. Scaling the third highest peak of the Alps has not been without its price, though. During the descent four of the seven climbers in his team were killed. Situated in the Alps on the border between Switzerland and Italy, the Matterhorn is a comparatively low mountain at 14,700 ft (4480 m) but is extremely difficult to climb.

• 1867 – 1ST DEMONSTRATION OF DYNAMITE • 1959 – 1ST NUCLEAR WARSHIP LAUNCHED

CRUSADERS TAKE JERUSALEM

1099 Jerusalem, long under Muslim rule, has been seized by Christian Crusaders led by Godfrey of Bouillon. The capture of this ancient city and the massacre of its Jewish and Muslim citizens is the culmination of the first armed pilgrimage organized by Pope Urban II to recapture places sacred to Christians. The army of French and Norman knights assembled in Constantinople, and proceeded to march through Anatolia, capturing Antioch on June 3 last year before moving on to Jerusalem. The massacre of the Muslim and Jewish inhabitants will further harden Muslim feeling against the Christians. Jerusalem is an important city to all three religious groups: for Jews, it is the focus of religious reverence and nationhood; for Christians, it is significant as the scene of Christ's final agony and triumph; and for Muslims, Jerusalem was the goal of their prophet's mystic night journey and is the site of the third most sacred shrine in Islam. The city has been under Muslim rule since the 7th century, with access to religious sites freely open to other groups until the recent takeover of Jerusalem by Seljuk Turks. The Seljuks have forbidden pilgrimages — hence Pope Urban's armed crusade.

NEW RECORD FOR ROUND-THE-WORLD FLIGHT

1938 A new world record for round-the-world flight has been set by millionaire Howard Hughes and his crew of four. Flying a twin-engined Lockheed, Hughes and his men completed the journey around the world in just three days, 19 hours and 17 minutes after take off from Brooklyn airport. This cuts by half the previous record set by Wiley Post five years ago, with a time of 7 days, 18 hours. Hughes' 14,824-mile (23,718 km) flight via Paris, Moscow, Omsk, Yakutsk, Fairbanks and Minneapolis was made at an average speed of 208 mph (333 kph). He and his crew have been greeted in New York with a ticker tape parade.

1795 "The Marseillaise", written by Claude Rouget is officially adopted as the French national anthem.

1857 As the Indian Mutiny continues, 200 Britons are chopped up and thrown down a well at Cawnpore.

1916 Edward Boeing sets up the Pacific Aero Products Company.

1930 The British government orders 1000 Spitfire fighter planes.

1976 Death of American novelist Paul Gallico.

1989 Eleven people are killed and 127 injured in clashes between Georgians and Abkhazians in the Abkhazia enclave of Soviet Georgia.

1990 In Colombo, capital of Sri Lanka, Tamil Tigers massacre 168 Muslims.

BIRTHDAYS

Inigo Jones 1573, English architect.

Rembrandt van Rijn 1606, Dutch painter and etcher.

Iris Murdoch 1919, British novelist whose books include *A Severed Head*.

Julian Bream 1933, British guitarist and lutenist.

• 1904 – ANTON CHEKHOV DIES • 1954 – BOEING 707 MAKES MAIDEN FLIGHT

1791 Louis XVI of France is suspended from office until he agrees to ratify the French constitution.

1945 The first atomic bomb is exploded on the White Sands Missile Range in New Mexico, USA.

1951 King Leopold III of Belgium abdicates.

1967 The Biafran War begins as Nigerian troops march into the oil-rich secessionist region of Biafra.

1990 At least 100 people die in an earthquake in the Philippines.

BIRTHDAYS

Sir Joshua Reynolds 1723, English painter and leading portraitist of his day.

Mary Baker Eddy 1821, American founder of the Christian Science movement.

Roald Amundsen 1872, Norwegian explorer who was the first to reach the South Pole.

Ginger Rogers 1911, American actress and dancer who partnered Fred Astaire in ten musical films.

Margaret Court 1942, Australian tennis player who won the Grand Slam in 1970.

RUSSIAN ROYALS SLAUGHTERED

1918 The Tsar of Russia, Nicholas II, and his family were murdered today in the cellar of the house in Ekaterinberg where they had been confined since May. Their bodies were then burned and thrown into a disused mine shaft. The local Bolshevik commander is thought to have ordered the killings when it became apparent that his men could not hold Ekaterinberg against the approaching White Russian forces and prevent the family's rescue. The Petrograd Soviet and the Revolutionary Workers' and Soldiers' Council insisted that the family be sent to an area where Bolshevik sentiment is blood red rather than be allowed to leave the country.

CURE FOR KILLER DISEASE FOUND

1885 French chemist Louis Pasteur, 63, has confounded his critics by proving beyond doubt that his ideas on the best way to tackle the killer disease rabies are correct. Nine-year-old rabies victim Joseph Meister is now making a rapid recovery thanks to receiving a weakened strain of the virus administered by Pasteur ten days ago. This latest success for Pasteur was only made possible by his previous research into disease-inducing micro-organisms such as anthrax and cholera. The vaccine for rabies is obtained from the dried tissues of animals infected with the virus.

• **1867 – REINFORCED CONCRETE PATENTED** • **1965 – MONT BLANC ROAD TUNNEL OPENS**

"LADY DAY" FINDS PEACE

1959 Billie Holiday, considered by many aficionados to be one of the greatest jazz singers of all time, died at Metropolitan Hospital, New York, today. She was 44. Born in Baltimore of unmarried teenage parents, "Lady Day", as she would become known, started her singing career in Harlem clubs aged 15 after several years as a prostitute. By the mid-30s she was an established artist, performing with the cream of musicians from the big bands. She formed a unique partnership with tenor saxophonist Lester Young, whom she nicknamed "the President".

By the 1950s her health and vocal performance were beginning to show signs of the alcohol and narcotics to which she had become accustomed. She was admitted to hospital shortly after performing at the Phoenix Theatre in Manhattan. Holiday died as she had lived – the victim of a catalogue of personal disasters including rape, racism, imprisonment and unhappy love affairs.

If you have to ask what jazz is, you'll never know.

Louis Armstrong, jazz trumpeter – the first Newport Jazz Festival took place today, 1954.

AEROPLANE SHOT DOWN

2014 Malaysia Airlines Flight 17 crashes in Ukraine, after being shot down by a missile. Fifteen crew members are among the 298 people killed. The plane's flight path took it over Donetsk in the troubled region of eastern Ukraine – a route some airlines had chosen to avoid. Footage later emerged of the crash site in this territory controlled by pro-Russian separatists, and witnesses spoke of dozens of bodies on the ground.

LONDON'S NEW WEEKLY

1841 The first issue of a weekly newspaper called *Punch* was published in London today. The idea for the paper came from engraver Ebenezer Landells, who suggested to journalist Henry Mayhew that a publication along the lines of Philippon's audacious *Paris Charivari* would go down well in London. Mayhew and his fellow joint-editors Mark Lemon and Joseph Stirling Coyne hope to provide an entertaining mix of satiric humour, cartoons and caricatures.

1453 The Hundred Years' War ends.

1794 The Commune of Paris, set up in May 1791, is suppressed.

1815 Napoleon surrenders to the British at Rochefort.

1951 The Abbey Theatre in Dublin, founded in 1907 by poets Lady Augusta Gregory and W. B. Yeats, burns down.

1969 *Oh! Calcutta*, the show devised by influential critic Kenneth Tynan and condemned by many in Britain as obscene on account of its profanity and nudity, opens in New York.

1981 More than 100 people die when suspended walkways in the lobby of the new Hyatt Regency Hotel in Kansas collapse.

• 1790 – FIRST SEWING MACHINE PATENTED • 1968 – *YELLOW SUBMARINE* PREMIERES

1721 French rococo painter Jean Antoine Watteau, best known for his *fetes galantes*, dies.

1877 Thomas Edison records the human voice for the first time.

1925 Adolf Hitler publishes *Mein Kampf.*

1936 Under the command of General Franco, the Spanish army rises up against the Republican government.

1996 TWA flight 800 explodes over Long Island, New York, killing all 228 passengers.

2003 Dr David Kelly, who wrote a dossier on Iraq's military capabilities for the UK government, is found dead.

BIRTHDAYS

Dr William Gilbert Grace 1848, English cricketer who scored 54,896 runs and took 2876 wickets in his illustrious career.

Vidkun Quisling 1887, Nazi collaborationist who led the occupation government in Norway in World War Two.

Nelson Mandela 1918, South African politician and outstanding black leader.

AGGRO ARTIST DIES

1610 The Italian artist Michelangelo Merisi da Caravaggio has died in exile in Porto Ercole at the age of 39. Caravaggio won fame and notoriety in Rome for his rejection of Renaissance ideals and insistence on painting directly onto the canvas. His use of low-life models, even in large religious works, caused much offence. Caravaggio fled Rome four years ago after killing a companion over a game of racquets. After a brief stay in Naples he moved on to Malta, but soon fell foul of the Order of St John by assaulting the highest grade of knight. Agents of the Order were sent after the fleeing Caravaggio and remained hard on his heels until the end. The violent temper of the peripatetic artist got him into trouble in Naples where he was wounded in a tavern brawl, forcing him to move on again. Alighting in Porto Ercole, a Spanish enclave on the Tuscan coast, he found himself the victim of wrongful arrest. On release, he made frantic efforts to catch up with a ship which he thought had all his belongings on board; these were, in fact, in Porto Ercole. This exertion brought on a fever to which he succumbed.

TSAR ASSASSINATED AFTER ABDICATING

1762 The former Tsar of Russia, Peter III, has been assassinated at the village of Ropsha eight days after abdicating. He was being held in custody by Grigori Orlov, one of the ringleaders of the recent coup to oust the unpopular Tsar in favour of his wife, Catherine.

750,000 WAR DEAD COMMEMORATED

1920 A new national monument dedicated to the "Glorious Dead" of the Great War was unveiled in Whitehall today. Designed in Portland stone by the distinguished architect Sir Edwin Lutyens, it replaces the temporary plaster monument erected for the Allied Victory Parade last year. The only adornments on the new Cenotaph – from the Greek words *kenos* and *taphos*, meaning empty tomb – are the flags of the three armed services and the Merchant Navy. The new monument will be the focal point at the Armistice Day commemoration in November. Londoners are already treating it with suitable reverence, by doffing their hats on passing.

• 1817 – DEATH OF JANE AUSTEN • 1955 – DISNEYLAND OPENS IN CALIFORNIA

TWO-WAY RELUCTANCE IN POLAND

1989 General Wojciech Jaruzelski, the man who imposed martial law eight years ago, was voted in as Poland's first president today. The general won the required 50 per cent majority of valid votes cast by a mere one vote. Four Solidarity representatives declined to participate in the election, declaring it unlawful because Jaruzelski was the only candidate. The problems facing the new president are daunting: a bankrupt economy, no effective government and a resentful and cynical population. Jaruzelski was reluctant to offer himself for election, but to have turned his back would, in his words, "contradict the duties of a politician and soldier and also the logic of my public service in recent years".

NAZI STYLE RULES

1937 Those wishing to discover what constitutes art in Hitler's Third Reich should make their way to the Bavarian capital, Munich, where two strikingly different exhibitions have been mounted for this purpose. What the Führer describes as "true German art" is of lofty subjects such as patriotism and family life and rendered in a stiff, academic style. "Degenerate, Bolshevik and Jewish art", on the other hand, is all modern art. Artists whose works are classified as "degenerate" include Beckmann, Chagall, Dix, Grosz, Kandinsky, Klee, Kokoschka and Modersohn-Becker. In 1933 Goebbels ordered that "all artistic productions with cosmopolitan or bolshevist tendencies" should be removed from German museums and galleries. The examples of "degenerate" art currently on show have been taken from a stockpile of about 20,000 modern works seized at that time. According to one SS officer, the steel helmet is the most perfect object ever created.

1545 King Henry VIII's battleship the *Mary Rose* sinks in the Solent.

1799 The Rosetta Stone is discovered in Egypt.

1821 George IV is crowned King of England.

1848 The first women's rights assembly begins at Seneca Falls, NY.

1849 Founder of the Bathai religious sect, Sayid Ali Mohammed, is executed in Persia by order of the Shah.

2001 Novelist Lord Archer is sentenced to four years in prison for perjury.

2014 US actor James Garner dies, aged 86.

BIRTHDAYS

Samuel Colt 1814, American inventor of the six-shot revolver.

Edgar Degas 1834, French Impressionist painter.

Charles Horace Mayo 1865, American physician, member of a family of physicians who set up the Mayo Clinic in Rochester, Minnesota.

George Hamilton IV 1937, American country and western singer.

Ilie Nastase 1946, Romanian tennis player noted for his erratic behaviour on court.

PRINCE ALBERT LAUNCHES WORLD'S LARGEST SHIP, THE *GREAT BRITAIN*

1843 The Prince Consort of the United Kingdom, Albert, was at Wapping Dock today to launch the world's largest ship, the 3270-ton, 322-ft (98 m) long Atlantic liner *Great Britain*. The all-metal vessel was originally designed by Isambard Kingdom Brunel (right) as a paddle steamer. She has since been fitted with screw machinery, supplemented by sails on six masts.

• 1870 – NAPOLEON DECLARES WAR ON PRUSSIA • 1997 – IRA CEASEFIRE ANNOUNCED

1629 English adventurer Sir David Kirke seizes Quebec from the French.

1937 Italian physicist Guglielmo Marconi, inventor of radio telegraphy, dies aged 63.

1951 King Abdullah of Jordan is shot dead outside a mosque.

1979 The Sandinista National Liberation Front takes power in Nicaragua.

1982 An IRA bomb explodes outside the Horse Guards barracks in London's Knightsbridge, killing two guardsmen and seven horses.

1999 Death of King Hassan II of Morocco, prompting mourning in the Arab world.

BIRTHDAYS

Sir John Reith 1889, Scottish engineer who became Director General of the BBC.

Sir Edmund Hillary 1919, New Zealand mountaineer and explorer who, along with Sherpa Tenzing, was the first to reach the summit of Mount Everest.

Diana Rigg 1939, British actress who partnered Patrick MacNee in the Avengers television series.

BEATLES ROMANCE OVER

1968 Actress Jane Asher stunned listeners to the BBC radio programme *Dee Time*, hosted by Simon Dee, today with the news that her engagement to Beatle Paul McCartney is off, marking the end of a five-year relationship.

SHOOTING TRAGEDY AT BATMAN FILM

2012 Filmgoers in Aurora, Colorado, were watching the new Batman film, *The Dark Knight Rises*, when a gunman entered the theatre and opened fire. James Eagan Holmes, who was 25 years old at time of the shooting, is the latest in a long line of young, socially awkward Americans to use relaxed gun laws and acquire deadly equipment. In this latest attack, 12 people were killed and 58 more injured. Holmes told the police he was the Batman character 'Joker.' President Obama is under pressure to tighten the restrictions on gun ownership.

BRUCE LEE FOUND DEAD

1973 Kung fu film star Bruce Lee was found dead in the bathroom of actress Betty Ting Pei in Hong Kong yesterday. He was 32. Reputedly the fittest man on earth, San Francisco-born Lee (real name Lee Yuen Kam) is thought to have died of a swollen brain, possibly caused by an allergic reaction to aspirin. Lee's martial arts films – *Fists of Fury*, *Enter the Dragon*, *Way of the Dragon* and *Game of Death* – won him a large following. Many fans are refusing to believe that Bruce Lee is really dead, suggesting that cult status is not far off for the former king of kung fu.

• 1944 – HITLER BOMB PLOT FAILS • 1976 – US SPACECRAFT *VIKING* LANDS ON MARS

TREASURE HUNT BRINGS MILLIONS

1985 A 20-year search for gold, silver and jewels in the wreck of a Spanish galleon has ended in triumph for chicken farmer-turned-treasure hunter Mel Fisher. His divers have found about half the original $400 million-worth (£217 million) of booty, in the wreck of *Nuestra Senhora de Atocha*, 40 miles (64 km) west of Key West, Florida. The galleon was one of nine Spanish ships sunk by a hurricane in 1622.

THE EAGLE LANDS

1969 US astronauts Neil Armstrong and Edwin Aldrin completed the most breathtaking and perhaps the most hazardous part of the historic Apollo 11 space mission today. Michael Collins remained in the command-service part of the spacecraft, known as *Columbia*, while his two colleagues manoeuvred the lunar module, called *Eagle*, onto the surface of the Moon. Six-and-a-half hours after landing, Armstrong began the first Moon walk in human history. He stepped onto the fine and powdery surface with the words, "That's one small step for a man, one giant step for mankind".

ROBERT BURNS DIES IN HARDSHIP

1796 Scotland's unofficial Poet Laureate, Robert Burns, has died in Dumfries at the age of 37. His premature death from rheumatic heart disease is being attributed to the privations and hardship of his years as a struggling tenant farmer. Burns' success as a poet began on publication of his first volume, entitled *Poems, Chiefly in the Scottish Dialect*. Country people and Edinburgh sophisticates found much to admire in the book's blend of social satire, verse letters, nature poems and high-minded idealization of family life. Burns' low social status, however, prevented him from truly finding his niche, despite his undoubted intellectual abilities. He spent the last seven years of his life collecting and providing words for traditional Scottish tunes as well as working for the excise service.

1798 Napoleon defeats the Mamelukes at the Battle of the Pyramids.

1904 The Trans-Siberian railway is completed.

1954 Britain, the US and the World Bank turn down Nasser's plea for aid to build the Aswan Dam.

1960 Mrs Sirimavo Bandaranaike, widow of the murdered prime minister of Sri Lanka, Solomon Bandaranaike, becomes the first woman prime minister in the world.

1994 Tony Blair is elected leader of the Labour party in Britain.

2008 Former Bosnian Serb leader Radovan Karadzic is arrested in Serbia.

2011 NASA's Space Shuttle program ends.

BIRTHDAYS

Baron Paul Julius von Reuter 1816, German-born founder of the Reuter's telegraph office, London.

Ernest Hemingway 1899, American novelist whose macho image was reflected in his books.

Karel Reisz 1926, Czech-born film director best-known for *Saturday Night and Sunday Morning*.

• 1897 – TATE GALLERY OPENS IN LONDON • 1988 – END OF THE IRAN-IRAQ WAR

1790 The French clergy are removed from the control of Rome and property is nationalized.

1932 Death of American impresario Florenz Ziegfeld, founder of the Ziegfeld Follies.

1969 Spanish dictator General Franco names Juan Carlos, grandson of King Alfonso XIII, as his heir apparent.

1976 Death of Sir Mortimer Wheeler, British archaeologist.

2003 Saddam Hussein's two sons Qusai and Udai are killed as American soldiers storm a house in the northern city of Mosul following a tip-off from an Iraqi source.

BIRTHDAYS

Philip I 1478, Spanish monarch.

Gregor Mendel 1822, Austrian monk and botanist who discovered the fundamental principles governing the inheritance of characters in living things.

Selman Abraham Waksman 1888, Russian-born microbiologist whose work led to the discovery of actinomycin and streptomycin.

91 KILLED IN JERUSALEM BOMB EXPLOSION

1946 A bomb planted in part of the King David Hotel in Jerusalem has left 91 people dead and 45 injured. The target of the terrorists — most likely the Jewish extremist organization Irgun Zvai Leumi — was the British military HQ and the civil secretariat. The extremist campaign against British administration in Palestine seems set to intensify, assisted, either actively or passively, by the great majority of the Jewish population. The long-awaited report by the Anglo-US committee of enquiry regarding the problems of European Jewry and Palestine recently concluded that any attempt to establish an independent state or states in the area would result in civil strife and that the mandate should be maintained.

Picnickers watch Confederates triumph in battle

1861 The first major set-to in the American Civil War ended yesterday in a somewhat bloody nose for the Union army under General Irvin McDowell. Forced by his political masters into launching a premature attack against the Confederate forces holding Bull Run (or Manassas), General McDowell found himself outnumbered by an enemy that had already received advance information of his battle plans. The Confederates were only marginally more competent in battle than their adversaries, however, and had it not been for the resolution of General Jackson's brigade all might have been lost for the southerners. Confusion and an air of unreality were intensified by the presence of Washington sightseers, picnicking while watching the action.

A NEW HEIR IS BORN

2013 Prince William and Catherine Middleton, the Duke and Duchess of Cambridge, have announced the birth of their first child. George Alexander Louis was born at St. Mary's Hospital in London at 16.24 BST, and weighed 8 pounds 6 ounces (3.8kg). Both mother and child are said to be doing well. As per tradition, a formal bulletin announcing the royal birth was mounted on an easel, and displayed outside Buckingham Palace.

• 1957 – BP AND SHELL QUIT ISRAEL • 1969 – APOLLO 11 LEAVES THE MOON

WHO DO YOU THINK YOU'RE KIDDING, MR CHURCHILL?

1940 The auxiliary force raised in Britain at the beginning of the French campaign last month has been given a new name. The Local Defence Volunteers are from now on to be known as the Home Guard. The one million-strong force, which has many WWI veterans in its ranks, is intended to protect Britain against German invasion. The men who form Britain's last line of defence may have been bemused as much as encouraged by prime minister Churchill's proposed slogan "You can always take one with you" – wags may feel tempted to suggest the insertion of the word "home". Weapons are scarce and it is doubtful whether enthusiasm alone could offer effective resistance to Adolf Hitler's men.

1757 Death of Domenico Scarlatti, Italian composer of 400 innovative harpsichord sonatas.

1858 In Britain, the Oath of Allegiance is modified to allow Jews to sit in Parliament.

1916 Death of Sir William Ramsay, Scottish chemist who isolated neon, xenon and krypton.

1951 Philippe Pétain, French general and statesman who headed the collaborationist Vichy government in WWII, dies.

2011 Grammy award-winning singer Amy Winehouse dies, aged 27.

I brought it all to life. I moved the whole world onto a 20-ft [6.5-m] screen. I was a greater discoverer than Columbus. I condensed history into three hours and made them live it.

D. W. Griffith, pioneer US film-maker who introduced the techniques of flash-back, crosscut, close-up and longshot, and who died today, 1948.

FREUD DOMINATES INTERNATIONAL PSYCHOANALYTIC ASSOCIATION

1914 The resignation of the president of the International Psychoanalytic Association, Carl Gustav Jung, seems to have secured the future of the Freudian movement. The Vienna-based doctor has circulated to all members of the association a paper highlighting that the ideas of Jung do not square with Freudian theory. Perhaps the most contentious issue has been the definition of the term "libido", which for Freud signifies sexual energy, but for Jung also a mental energy. The departure of Jung and others leaves the association in the hands of men dedicated to Freud's ideas.

Raymond Chandler 1888, American novelist with a distinctive and much-imitated style.

Haile Selassie I 1892, Ethiopian emperor who led the resistance to the Italian invasion in 1935.

Richard Rogers 1933, British architect best-known for the Pompidou Centre in Paris and the Lloyd's building in London.

Daniel Ratcliffe 1989, English actor who was cast as Harry Potter in 2000, aged 11.

• 1803 – IRISH REBELLION IN DUBLIN FAILS • 1986 – PRINCE ANDREW MARRIES FERGIE

1704 Britain captures Gibraltar from Spain.

1824 The world's first public opinion poll is carried out in Delaware.

1925 The first successful insulin treatment is carried out on a six-year-old girl at Guy's Hospital in London.

1936 In Spain, General Mola sets up a Falangist government at Burgos.

1967 *The Times* carries a full-page advertisement advocating the legalization of marijuana signed by, among others, the Beatles.

2010 Northern Irish snooker legend Alex 'Hurricane' Higgins dies, aged 61.

BIRTHDAYS

Simon Bolivar 1783, South American soldier and statesman who liberated Colombia, Venezuela and Ecuador from Spanish rule.

Alexandre Dumas père 1802, French novelist and dramatist best-known for *The Three Musketeers*.

Frank Wedekind 1864, German dramatist, actor, singer, poet and essayist.

Amelia Earhart 1898, American aviator and the first woman to fly solo over the Atlantic.

MORMONS FIND THEIR PLACE

1847 Mormon leader Brigham Young (pictured below with his many wives) and his party of 147 members of the Church of the Latter-Day Saints reached the safety of the Salt Lake valley today. The exodus from Nauvoo, Illinois, to a "land that nobody wanted" began early last year. The hazardous journey has claimed many of his people's lives, despite Brigham Young's excellent organization and preparation for the trip. Crops are already being planted on this day of their arrival. The Mormon appetite for hard work has not won them acceptance in any community, nor has their doctrinaire interpretation of God's word. They can make this new land their own, however, and all who enter it will have to conform to the Mormon way of life.

TURKEY AND GREECE END TERRITORIAL DISPUTE

1923 The Treaty of Lausanne signed by Greece and Turkey today concludes the peace settlement begun at the end of the Great War but aborted by Kemal Ataturk's nationalist overthrow of the Ottoman dynasty. Acceptance of the original Treaty of Sévres would have reduced Turkey to a small area around Constantinople extending 25 miles (40 km) into Europe, and Anatolia (excluding Smyrna). Ataturk has surrendered all claim to territories of the Ottoman empire occupied by non-Turks and confirmed Greece in possession of all Adriatic islands (except Imbros and Tenedos, which are to be returned to Turkey). These concessions have been made so that the ancient commercial port and religious centre of Smyrna, and Eastern Thrace, may be restored to Turkey.

This is the greatest week in the history of the world since the creation.

Richard Nixon, US president, on the landing of men on the moon, three days earlier, 1969.

JAPAN'S PM RESIGNS

1989 Japan's Liberal Democratic Party has suffered its first defeat in 30 years, forcing the resignation of the prime minister, Sosuke Uno. The LDP had seemed to be on the road to political recovery under the premiership of Uno after the Recruit scandal claimed his predecessor. However, last month Uno's former mistress slung mud at his name, ruining his chances.

• 1567 – MARY QUEEN OF SCOTS ABDICATES • 1980 – PETER SELLERS DIES

DANCE TO DEATH

1917 In peace time the French public might have raised a collective wry smile at the spectacle of a femme fatale dancer and courtesan called Mata Hari being charged with employing her sexual charms to weaken French Army officers into betraying their country. The exotic-sounding Mata Hari is a 41-year-old Dutch woman, Margaretha Geertruida MacLeod, who agreed to spy for the French in enemy-occupied Belgium despite already working for the German consul in The Hague. Apart from MacLeod's own admission that she had on one occasion passed out-of-date information to the Germans, the prosecution

could produce no firm evidence of her spying activities. The trial ended today with the military court at Vincennes finding her guilty as charged. She is to be shot by firing squad.

You cannot control a free society by force.

Robert Mark, British police commissioner, 1976.

COAL IS TRANSPORTED BY LOCOMOTION

1814 Killingworth is the latest colliery to experiment with locomotives for transporting coal out of mines. Their chief mechanic, George Stephenson, has built an engine that can draw eight loaded carriages bearing 30 tons of coal at four miles per hour (6.4 kph). Stephenson got the idea for *Blucher* after seeing the "steam

boiler on wheels" built by Matthew Murray for John Blenkinsop in operation at a neighbouring mine. *Blucher* is an adhesion machine with vertical cylinders. A chain drive leads to the front tender wheels to increase grip. Stephenson is convinced that *Blucher*'s power can be further increased, and is to continue experimenting with the engine.

1554 The Catholic Queen Mary of England marries Philip II of Spain.

1835 Death of Samuel Taylor Coleridge, English poet and critic.

1909 French aviator Louis Blériot becomes the first man to fly the Channel, travelling from Calais to Dover in a Blériot XI.

1956 Fifty lives are lost when an Italian ocean liner SS *Andrea* sinks off the Massachusetts coast after colliding in fog with a Swedish liner MS *Stockholm*.

2009 The last British veteran of the Western Front in World War I, Harry Patch, dies, aged 111, a week after the oldest veteran Henry Allingham, 113.

BIRTHDAYS

Arthur James Balfour, 1st Earl 1848, British statesman and Conservative prime minister and foreign secretary from 1916 to 1919.

Johnny "Rabbit" Hodges 1907, American jazz saxophonist.

Steve Goodman 1948, American songwriter whose "The City of New Orleans" gave Arlo Guthrie a hit.

• 1587 – CHRISTIANITY BANNED IN JAPAN • 1943 – MUSSOLINI FORCED TO RESIGN

1788 New York becomes the 11th state of the Union.

1863 Death of Sam Houston, American soldier, president and Texan leader.

1953 In Cuba rebel leader Fidel Castro leads an unsuccessful attack on the Moncada barracks and is imprisoned by dictator Fulgencio Batista.

1956 President Nasser nationalizes the Suez Canal.

1977 Israeli prime minister Menachem Begin orders more settlements to be built on the West Bank.

2004 The Frozen Ark project is launched to preserve the DNA of endangered species.

BIRTHDAYS

George Bernard Shaw 1856, Irish dramatist and one of the founding members of the Fabian Society.

Carl Jung 1875, Swiss psychiatrist and pioneer psychoanalyst.

Stanley Kubrick 1928, American film director whose works include *Dr Strangelove*.

Mick Jagger 1943, British pop singer and founder member of the Rolling Stones.

ARGENTINA CRIES FOR "EVITA"

1952 Eva Perón, the wife of the President Argentina, Juan Perón, died in Buenos Aires today after a long illness. She was 33. Senora Perón wielded enormous influence in public affairs. One of her main achievements was to win the vote for Argentinian women. "Evita", as she was known to Argentina's 18-million population, was recently proclaimed the "spiritual chief of the state" by Congress. That same body is expected to pass a bill ordaining that "for the rest of history" July 26 will be a day of national mourning for Argentina. Senora Péron's body will lie in state until August 8 in the Ministry of Labour and Social Welfare.

TWENTY-SIX DIE IN RAILROAD STRIKE MAYHEM

1877 An America-wide railroad strike has brought mayhem and violence in Pittsburgh, Buffalo, St Louis and Chicago. The strike is in support of better pay and conditions for railroad workers. Some bosses regard the unrest as politically inspired by revolutionaries bent on the destruction of capitalism. Unionization is one of their chief bogeymen. Train crews are increasingly becoming unionized. Now other members of the railroad work force, which has grown rapidly since 1870, are similarly seeking to protect their interests.

It is uncertain whether the development and spread of electronic and computer technology will increase the spread of literacy or diminish the need for it and result in an oral culture overwhelming the present written one.

Eugene Radwin, US educationist, 1990.

CHARLES V SANCTIONS NEW PIZARRO EXPEDITION

1529 Francisco Pizarro's decision to ask the Spanish Emperor Charles V to sanction another expedition to the wealthy kingdom south of Panama has paid off. The Council of the Indies has granted the 54-year-old soldier and explorer of South America the right of conquest, the governorship of the new lands and the title of Captain General for life. Last year Francisco Pizarro returned to Panama with gold, llamas and a few Indians as evidence of the riches that he believes are there for the taking. However, no funds appear to have been provided for the new expedition, nor have the contributions of Pizarro's partners, most notably Diego de Almagro, received recognition.

ROBESPIERRE SLIPS IN HIS OWN BLOODBATH

1794 In an historic vote today the Convention in Paris decided to arrest the chief architect of the "Reign of Terror", Maximilien François Marie Isidore de Robespierre, and his supporters. They have become increasingly hostile to the 36-year-old lawyer and his aims, and yesterday were alarmed by his demand for a carte blanche regarding future use of the guillotine. Robespierre spoke in such menacing terms that few present could have doubted that their own necks might yet feel the kiss of that steely Madame. When Robespierre attempted to address the Convention he was drowned out with cries of "Down with the tyrant". Support from the troops of the Commune, Robespierre's principal power base, was not forthcoming, and he was lost. Robespierre is now in custody awaiting execution.

SPINOZA CHALLENGES SCRIPTURE

1656 The Jewish religious authorities in Amsterdam have decided to excommunicate 24-year-old student Benedict Spinoza for failing to modify his unorthodox interpretations of Scripture. The civil authorities have also taken action by banishing him from Amsterdam for a short period. Neither bribes nor threats have persuaded Spinoza to change his contention that there is nothing in the Bible to support some orthodox views – for example, that God has no body, that angels exist or that the soul is immortal. The budding philosopher is said to be dismayed by the reaction to his ponderings.

WAR ENDS IN KOREA

1953 The Korean War formally ended today with the signing of a peace pact at Panmunjom. Lieutenant General William H. Harrison signed for the UN forces and General Nam Il for the Chinese people's volunteers and North Korean forces. The armistice negotiations have taken just over two years, in which time the two sides have met 575 times. The three-year conflict has cost an estimated five million lives.

Democracy passes into despotism.

Plato, Greek philosopher. Today military leaders in Greece handed power to civilian government, 1974.

1789 Thomas Jefferson heads the new US dept of Foreign Affairs.

1921 Sir Frederick Banting and Charles Best isolate insulin at the University of Toronto.

1946 American novelist and poet Gertrude Stein dies in Paris.

1985 Ugandan president Milton Obote is overthrown by a military coup.

1986 American cyclist Gregory James LeMond becomes the first non-European to win the Tour de France.

1996 A nail bomb explodes at the Olympics in Atlanta, killing two people.

BIRTHDAYS

Hilaire Belloc 1870, English poet, novelist and essayist best known for his light verse.

Anton Dolin 1904, British ballet dancer who with Alicia Markova founded London's Festival Ballet.

Bobbie Gentry 1942, American singer of "Ode to Billy Joe".

Christopher Dean 1958, British ice-skater who, with his partner Jayne Torvill, won an Olympic gold medal for ice dancing.

• 1941 – JAPAN INVADES INDO-CHINA • 1980 – SHAH OF IRAN DIES IN CAIRO

1741 Death of Antonio Vivaldi, Italian composer.

1868 A treaty is signed allowing Chinese immigration to the USA.

1914 Austria-Hungary declares war on Serbia.

1935 The Boeing B-17 *Flying Fortress* bomber makes its first flight.

1965 President Lyndon Johnson sends 50,000 US ground troops to Vietnam.

1987 Golfer Laura Davies becomes the first Englishwoman to win the US Women's Open.

2004 Francis Crick, co-discoverer of DNA structure, dies, aged 88.

BIRTHDAYS

Beatrix Potter 1866, English children's author and illustrator.

Marcel Duchamp 1887, French artist who became the leader of the New York Dada movement.

Sir Garfield Sobers 1936, Barbadian cricketer who scored a record 365 runs against Pakistan in the 1957–8 Test series.

Riccardo Muti 1941, Italian conductor and artistic director of La Scala in Milan.

NEW "POTATO" PLANT MAY PROVIDE ANIMAL FODDER

1586 A new type of plant has been introduced into Ireland by some explorers associated with Sir Walter Raleigh. Called *Solarium tuberosum*, or the potato, it is a perennial herb thought to originate from the Andes region of South America. The tubers of the plant are eaten by the South American Indians. Sir Walter plans to plant some tubers on his estate at Youghall, near Cork, with a view to feeding the crop to his livestock.

EQUAL RIGHTS

1868 The Fourteenth Amendment of the US Constitution was formally ratified today. The main purpose of this latest addition to the US statute book is to extend to the four and a half million or so black Americans the same personal and property rights enjoyed by other citizens of the United States. The Fourteenth Amendment builds on the provisions of the Thirteenth Amendment abolishing slavery by defining, for the first time, national citizenship and unequivocally including black Americans within that definition.

NORTHERN IRELAND: PEACE AT LAST?

2005 The Provisional IRA announced an end to its 36-year campaign of armed struggle in Northern Ireland, saying it would use "purely political and democratic programmes through exclusively peaceful means" to bring about a united Ireland and remove Northern Ireland from British hands. The group was responsible for the deaths of around 1,800 people during its campaign of terror – some 1,100 members of the British security forces and 630 civilians. The group itself lost 275–300 of its 10,000 members. A ceasefire had been in place since 1998 when the British government demanded the disarmament of the IRA before allowing Sinn Fein, the political party linked to the IRA, into multi-party talks on the future of Northern Ireland.

• 1750 – **DEATH OF J S BACH** • 1945 – **B-25 BOMBER CRASHES INTO EMPIRE STATE**

GERMAN COMPOSER ROBERT SCHUMANN DIES

1856 The avant-garde German composer Robert Schumann, husband of the celebrated pianist Clara Schumann, has died in a private asylum at Endenich, near Bonn, at the age of 46. Schumann gave up studying law in order to devote himself to a career in music. He has left a large body of work ranging from piano pieces and songs to chamber music, choral works and symphonies. Schumann's music has not found wide acceptance among audiences and appreciation of it has been largely confined to a small clique of professional musicians and composers.

750 MILLION WATCH ROYAL WEDDING

1981 The heir to the British throne, Prince Charles, married Lady Diana Frances Spencer in front of 750 million people today. The ceremony in London's St Paul's Cathedral was televised live throughout the world. A note of discord was sounded about the event by the King and Queen of Spain who declined their invitation to the wedding because the royal couple's honeymoon plans include picking up the royal yacht *Britannia* in Gibraltar, a long-standing bone of contention between Britain and Spain.

1830 French liberals opposed to Charles X's new laws seize Paris.

1833 Death of William Wilberforce, prime mover in the British anti-slavery campaign.

1948 The first Olympic Games since World War Two opens at Wembley in London.

1968 The Pope condemns all birth control.

1974 Cass Elliott, singer with pop group the Mamas and the Papas, dies in London of a heart attack.

1983 Actor David Niven, the quintessential English gentleman, dies of motor neurone disease.

BIRTHDAYS

Alexis de Tocqueville 1805, French political scientist, historian and politician.

Benito Mussolini 1883, Italian founder of the Fascist Party and ally of Hitler in World War Two.

Sigmund Romberg 1887, Hungarian-born composer who wrote *The Student Prince*.

Dag Hammarskjöld 1905, Swedish politician and second secretary general of the United Nations.

SPANISH INVASION RECEIVES CALM BRITISH RECEPTION

1588 The armada of 130 ships sent by King Philip II of Spain to attempt an invasion of England was sighted today off Cornwall. The English fleet under Charles Howard, Baron Howard of Effingham, is confident of success, however. Howard has 197 ships with about 16,000 men, most of them seasoned sailors, at his disposal. His commanders seem equally nonchalant. Sir Francis Drake was playing a game of bowls on Plymouth Hoe when he received news of the armada's approach. He finished the game before making for the fleet assembly point at Portsmouth. Factors that may tell against the Spanish in battle include the lack of experience of their new commander, the Duke de Medina Sidonia, and the lack of pace and manoeuvrability of their ships.

• 1890 – VINCENT VAN GOGH DIES • 1900 – KING UMBERTO I OF ITALY SHOT DEAD

1718 Death of William Penn, Quaker founder of Pennsylvania.

1930 In the first ever World Cup final, Uruguay beats Argentina 4–2.

1958 A left-wing coup that overthrows the monarchy in Iraq arouses Western fears of a Middle Eastern domino effect.

1963 British double agent Kim Philby turns up in Moscow, seven months after his disappearance in Beirut.

1980 The New Hebrides, in the south-west Pacific, gain independence from Britain and France, taking the name Vanuatu Republic.

2007 Veteran film directors Michelangelo Antonioni, 94, and Ingmar Bergman, 89, die within hours of one another.

BIRTHDAYS

Giorgio Vasari 1511, Italian painter, architect and writer.

Emily Brontë 1818, English novelist, author of *Wuthering Heights*.

Henry Ford 1863, American car manufacturer.

Henry Moore 1898, English sculptor and graphic artist.

SPEKE NAMES LAKE VICTORIA

1858 British explorer John Manning Speke, 31, has named the great lake he found in the heart of Africa today after Queen Victoria. He has until recently been exploring the region with Richard Burton. Speke's claim that in Lake Victoria he has found the source of the Nile is unlikely to be accepted by Burton, nor by many others in the scientific community. Speke developed an interest in exploration while serving with the British Army in India. His chance to join a pukka expedition came three years ago when he became a member of Burton's abortive attempt to explore Somaliland. Speke was badly wounded in the attack by Somali natives that put paid to the expedition.

IRA murder top UK politician

1990 Ian Gow, chairman of the Conservative backbench Northern Ireland committee and one of the most outspoken critics of IRA terrorism, was killed by a bomb concealed beneath the chassis of his car. The 5 lb (2.25 kg) bomb exploded at 8.39 am as Mr Gow prepared to drive out of the carport adjoining his East Sussex home. He knew his name was on an IRA hit list found last year.

England on top of the world

1966 England won the World Cup of football, at Wembley this afternoon after an epic tussle with West Germany. It looked as though England were home and dry with a 2-1 victory, but West Germany snatched a last-minute equalizer. Before the start of extra time, manager Alf Ramsey coolly told his exhausted players: "Well you've won it once. Now you'll just have to do it all over again, and you will." They did do it again, thanks to two goals by striker Geoff Hurst.

• **1898 – DEATH OF OTTO VON BISMARCK, FIRST CHANCELLOR OF THE GERMAN EMPIRE**

FIRST SUCCESS FOR RANGER PROGRAMME

1964 NASA scientists are on the brink of answering many questions about the composition of the Moon. They have landed a camera-equipped spacecraft on the surface of the earth's only satellite. The *Ranger 7* probe reached its target area, the Mare Nubium, some 68 hours after blast off. The craft is fitted with six cameras, one covering a wide field of view, the other five taking close-ups of smaller areas. The pictures sent back reveal that part of the Moon is not covered with a deep layer of dust, as had been supposed. The surface material seems to have a spongy texture and is very different in composition from the rock found on Earth.

1556 Death of Ignatius Loyola, Spanish cleric who founded the Jesuit order to propagate the Roman Catholic faith.

1914 Kaiser Wilhelm II of Germany rejects a British offer of mediation in the Austro-Serbian crisis as "insolence".

1932 The Nazi Party doubles its representation in the Reichstag.

1975 Irish pop group the Miami Showband is ambushed and murdered by Protestant gunmen.

1979 Nigeria seizes British oil installations in a bid to persuade Margaret Thatcher to take a tough line on apartheid.

1990 In Trinidad, Muslim rebels release prime minister A. R. Robinson but continue to hold their other hostages in Port of Spain's television station.

BIRTHDAYS

Milton Friedman 1912, American economist and advocate of the free market economy.

Lynne Reid Banks 1929, British author best-known for *The L-Shaped Room*.

J. K. Rowling 1965, British author who created the Harry Potter books.

TIBETANS REBEL AGAINST CHINA

1958 Kham tribesmen in Tibet are reported to be increasing their guerrilla activity against Chinese troops. The armed resistance to the Chinese presence in Tibet is not as yet on the same scale witnessed last year in Kham province when tribesmen breached part of the main China-Tibet highway. But if the unrest spreads it may give the Chinese authorities an excuse to crack down. Under the terms of the 1951 agreement Tibet supposedly enjoys full autonomy. In reality Peking makes all decisions relating to domestic and foreign affairs.

KIDNAPPED US MARINE HANGED

1989 The Organization for the Oppressed of the Earth, a group of Shi'ite Muslim extremists closely linked with the pro-Iranian Hezbollah (Party of God), announced today that they had executed Lieutenant Colonel William Higgins, the US Marine abducted in Lebanon in February 1988. The group also released a video showing a bound and gagged man revolving slowly at the end of a rope. Close examination of the grisly low-quality tape has led the CIA to believe that William Higgins may have been killed at a much earlier date.

• 1919 – WEIMAR REPUBLIC ESTABLISHED • 1965 – BRITAIN BANS CIGARETTE ADS ON TV

AUGUST

ENOLA GAY

NO S

JESSICA ENNIS

LONDON 201

ENNIS

London 2012

adidas

OLYMPI CHAMPI

BRITONS NEVER NEVER SHALL HAVE SLAVES

1833 In a momentous move, Britain has ended its 400-year involvement in slavery. The act passed by parliament today frees all slaves in the nation's territories after a five- to seven-year apprenticeship. A sum of £20 million ($37 million) has been earmarked to compensate slave-owners. Today's news marks a victory for the Anti-Slavery Society (formed in 1823) and their parliamentary leader, Thomas Fowell Buxton, who have campaigned hard for this amendment. It also completes the work begun some 40 years ago by William Wilberforce.

LAUDA NEAR DEATH AFTER INFERNO

1976 A 40-second inferno has left world motor racing champion Niki Lauda fighting for his life. The accident happened on the second lap of the German Grand Prix, when Lauda's car spun out of control, bounced off a safety barrier and exploded. Lauda has suffered injury to his lungs as a result of inhaling raw, unvaporized petrol.

RUSH HOUR COLLAPSE

2007 Thirteen motorists died when a road bridge over the Mississippi river collapsed during the evening rush hour in Minneapolis, USA. The entire 150 m (500 ft) span of steel and concrete collapsed, hurling around 50 cars into the river 20 m (65 ft) below. A report by the National Transportation Safety Board found a design fault was to blame: metal plates used in the construction were not thick enough to bear the combined weight of the bridge and cars.

1714 George Louis, Elector of Hanover, accedes to the British throne as George I.

1778 The first savings bank opens in Hamburg, Germany.

1798 Nelson attacks and annihilates the French fleet at Aboukir Bay.

1969 The first pictures of the planet Mars are beamed back to earth.

1985 America agrees to sanctions against South Africa in protest against apartheid.

2005 US astronomers claim to have discovered a 10th planet.

BIRTHDAYS

Claudius I 19 BC, Roman emperor who invaded Britain in AD 43.

Jean Baptiste de Lamarck 1774, French zoologist who coined the term vertebrate and invertebrate.

Francis Scott Key 1779, US poet, attorney and author who wrote "The Star Spangled Banner".

Sam Mendes 1965, English stage and film director who received an Oscar in 1999 for *American Beauty*.

• 1774 – OXYGEN DISCOVERED • 1914 – GERMANY DECLARES WAR ON RUSSIA

1589 Henry II, the last Valois king, is stabbed to death by a mad Dominican monk.

1830 Charles X of France is overthrown and abdicates.

1834 The South Australian Association gains a charter to found a colony.

1945 The Potsdam Conference ends.

1948 "Reds under the Bed" in the US – politician Alger Hiss testifies to the McCarthy hearings.

1964 US involvement in Vietnam escalates after a torpedo attack on the navy ship Maddox in the Tonkin Gulf: President Lyndon B. Johnson orders a retaliatory strike.

1980 A right-wing Italian terror group bombs Bologna railway station in Northern Italy, killing 84.

BIRTHDAYS

Sir Arthur Bliss 1891, English composer and Master of the Queen's Music from 1953.

James Baldwin 1924, American author known for *Another Country*.

Peter O'Toole 1932, Irish actor, most famous for his role in *Lawrence of Arabia*.

NELSON CATCHES FRENCH NAPPING

1798 A 14-vessel naval squadron commanded by Rear Admiral Horatio Nelson has scored a brilliant tactical victory over a 17-strong French fleet in the Mediterranean. The wily Nelson caught the French with their ensigns down – at anchor in Aboukir Bay, north of the River Nile in Egypt. Most of the French ratings were ashore getting water, leaving their commander de Breuys with 120 guns but no one to fire them. As Nelson's fleet sailed into the attack on both sides of the anchored French men-of-war, de Breuys could not launch the classic response, a broadside. The battle, which started yesterday afternoon at around 4.30, did not end until early this morning. The French are reported to have lost 11 ships of the line and two frigates, 1700 of their men are dead, 1500 wounded and 3000 captured. The victorious British, whose losses amounted to only 1000 dead and wounded, aim to take home six of the captured vessels as prizes.

"FASTEST GUN" HAS NO CHANCE

1876 The man billed in his colourful shows as the "fastest gun in the West", "Wild Bill" Hickok fell victim to an assassin's bullet today. Hickok, 39, was playing poker in the saloon in Deadwood when killer Jack McCall struck, shooting the unsuspecting ex-lawman in the back from a vantage point behind the bar. As a federal marshal Hickok (real name James Butler Hickok) single-handedly tamed the notoriously rough frontier towns of Hays City and Abilene.

SADDAM SNATCHES OIL-RICH KUWAIT

1990 Saddam Hussein today made good Iraq's claim to the oil-rich state of Kuwait by invading it. Thousands of heavily armed Iraqi troops quickly cut through the paper-thin defences of their tiny Gulf neighbour and are now firmly in control of its capital, Kuwait City. The Al-Sabah family, which has ruled Kuwait for more than two centuries, has fled to Saudi Arabia. Tensions between the two countries have been high for several weeks since Saddam accused Kuwait of deliberately over-producing oil, thus depressing prices and damaging Iraq's fragile economy. Iraq's action has been condemned by world leaders, most forcibly by British PM Margaret Thatcher and US president George Bush who have not ruled out a military response to the crisis.

• 1865 – LEWIS CARROLL PUBLISHES *ALICE'S ADVENTURES IN WONDERLAND*

NEXT STOP – INDIA

1492 Shortly before sunrise today a flotilla of three ships set sail from the Spanish port of Palos de la Frontera in search of a land called India. The leader of the expedition, Cristobal Colon (Christopher Columbus) has spent the last eight years trying to get the project off the ground. The latest hitch came just seven months ago when his patrons, King Ferdinand and Queen Isabella of Spain, were told of Colon's price for undertaking the trip: a knighthood, the ranks of Grand Admiral and Viceroy (these to become hereditary) and 10 per cent of the receipts from his admiralty. The stunned monarchs dismissed Colon, but later recalled him and met all his demands. Colon claims to have received divine guidance in his career to date. He will need every iota to see him safely through the perilous adventure ahead.

216 AD Battle of Cannae, in which Carthaginian general Hannibal defeats the Romans.

1460 Scottish King James II is killed during the siege of Roxburgh Castle.

1792 Death of Sir Richard Arkwright, the Englishman who invented the water-powered spinning frame.

1924 Death of Joseph Conrad, Polish-born British novelist.

2008 Russian writer and dissident Alexander Solzhenitsyn dies, aged 90

2010 President Obama announces the official end of US combat in Iraq.

BIRTHDAYS

Stanley Baldwin 1867, British Conservative prime minister.

Haakon VII 1872, Norwegian monarch who refused to surrender to the Germans in World War II.

Rupert Brooke 1887, British war poet.

P. D. James 1920, British crime writer.

Leon Uris 1924, American author famous for *Exodus*.

Martin Sheen 1940, American actor, known for his roles in *Catch 22* and *Apocalypse Now*.

SIR ROGER HANGS FOR TREASON

1916 One of Britain's most distinguished civil servants, Sir Roger Casement, was hanged in London today for his involvement in the Easter Uprising in Dublin. The former consul in Portuguese East Africa was an Ulster Protestant whose sympathy with the predominantly Catholic Irish nationalists led him to seek aid for their cause in Germany and the United States. His attempt to recruit Irish prisoners-of-war to a German brigade that would play a key role in the planned uprising was unsuccessful. Casement returned from the failed mission in a German submarine and was arrested by British forces soon after landing.

FARGO'S FINAL JOURNEY

1778 William George Fargo, the wealthy pioneer of the long-distance express service, has died at his home in Buffalo, New York, aged 65. Fargo was already established in the freight forwarding business when he hit upon the idea of offering a transcontinental express service from east coast to west coast between New York and San Francisco. The service went into operation in 1852 with hired stagecoaches. Their cargo was protected by armed guards on the long and perilous journey between the east and west coasts. In time Wells Fargo also offered a banking service to the many miners among its clientele, buying the miners' gold dust in exchange for cash.

• 1778 – TEATRO ALLA SCALA OPENS IN MILAN • 1926 – LONDON'S 1ST TRAFFIC LIGHTS

AUGUST
4

1578 The Portuguese king and his court are killed in a failed crusade to Morocco.

1954 Britain's first supersonic fighter plane makes its maiden flight.

1987 Death of the "Vamp", Polish-born silent movie star Pola Negri.

1990 A counterfeiting ring is smashed after a man is arrested in London with printing plates for producing dollar notes and enough security paper to print $25 million.

1990 Iraq installs a nine-man puppet government in Kuwait and sets up a new People's Army.

2002 One of the largest manhunts ever known in the UK is launched after two Soham schoolgirls disappear.

BIRTHDAYS

Percy Bysshe Shelley 1792, English lyric poet.

David Russell Lange 1942, New Zealand Labour politician and prime minister 1984–9.

Barack Hussein Obama 1961, elected the 44th President of the United States in 2009, and the first African-American to hold the office.

FAIRYTALE ENDING

1875 The death was announced in Copenhagen today of Hans Christian Andersen, famed the world over for his fairy tales and stories. He was 70. Andersen was born into poverty in Odense, the son of a cobbler and a woman who was both superstitious and illiterate. At the age of only 14 he left his job as a tailor's apprentice and went to Copenhagen to seek his fortune on the stage. The director of the Royal Theatre, Jonas Collin, took an interest in the boy, sending him to grammar school and eventually to university. His first book of fairy tales, published in 1835, soon became a bestseller throughout the world. His timeless tales do not pander to wish-fulfilment and leave the reader wiser rather than happier.

We draw the sword with a clear conscience and with clean hands.

Kaiser Wilhem II, in a speech in Berlin, 1914.

TEAM GB'S SUPER SATURDAY

2012 Great Britain enjoyed its single most successful Olympic day in 104 years, with gold medals in six events, including three in a remarkable hour in the Olympic stadium. Jessica Ennis, Mo Farah and Greg Rutherford added track gold to the ones won in cycling and rowing earlier in the day. Ennis smashed her own British record in winning the heptathlon, while Farah has the opportunity to go for double glory when he attempts the 5,000m in two days' time.

• 1955 – BECKETT'S *WAITING FOR GODOT* PREMIERES • 2000 – QUEEN MOTHER IS 100

BRILLIANT OWENS BLOWS ARYAN MYTH

1936 German Chancellor Adolf Hitler today turned his back on a living refutation of his theory of Aryan superiority. As 23-year-old black American athlete Jesse Owens was acknowledging the cheers of the vast crowd after his gold-medal triumph in the 200 metres final of the 11th Olympiad, the Führer left the stadium. The multi-talented Owens has turned the Führer's rascist philosophy on its head by winning a gold in the 100 metres, 200 metres and the long jump. A fourth gold medal, in the 4 x 100 metres relay, is almost a certainty, too. The Führer's pique at having a "black mercenary" – the name given to black Americans by propaganda minister Josef Goebbels – threaten his party to glorify the Third Reich is not spoiling the genial American athlete's fun, however. He is revelling in the warmth of the Berlin crowds.

UNDERWATER TRIUMPH

1958 The US nuclear-powered submarine *Nautilus*, under Commander William R. Anderson, has completed an historic 2000-mile (3200-km) underwater journey from Point Barrow in Alaska to the Greenland Sea. The 319-ft (97-m) craft passed directly under the North Pole during its five-day voyage. The achievement makes an appropriate finale to the 1957–8 International Geophysical Year.

US-UK LINK-UP

1858 The completion today of the world's first transatlantic telegraph cable is a dream come true for American financier Cyrus West Field, 39, who has sunk considerable financial resources and mental energy into this monumental project. The cable, which runs between Ireland and Newfoundland, was laid jointly by the naval vessels USS *Niagara* and HMS *Agamemnon*. Later this month Queen Victoria and US President Buchanan will inaugurate the line by exchanging messages.

• **1861 – NATIONAL INCOME TAX IS INTRODUCED IN THE US, TO FUND THE CIVIL WAR**

1497 Italian-born English explorer John Cabot returns to London after discovering what he thinks is Asia but what is in fact Cape Breton Island off the coast of Canada.

1806 Holy Roman Emperor Francis II abdicates.

1962 Jamaica becomes independent after 300 years of British rule.

1988 The Russian ballerina Natalia Makarova dances with the Kirov Ballet for the first time since she defected 18 years previously.

2003 Gene Robinson becomes the first openly gay bishop.

BIRTHDAYS

Alfred, Lord Tennyson 1809, English poet famous for "The Charge of the Light Brigade".

Alexander Fleming 1881, Scottish scientist who discovered penicillin.

Lucille Ball 1911, American comedienne who starred in the series *I Love Lucy*.

Andy Warhol 1928, American artist whose self-portrait sold for £1.8 million in 2011.

ATOM BOMB WIPES OUT HIROSHIMA

1945 At around 8.15 this morning an atomic bomb, dubbed "Little Boy", was released by a B-29 of the US Air Force, the *Enola Gay*, above the central Japanese city of Hiroshima. Two-thirds of the city has been destroyed and at least 140,000 people have been killed. Few people in the immediate vicinity of the epicentre are thought to have survived the blast. US President Harry Truman was made aware of the bomb's destructive capabilities three weeks ago. His decision to use it was made in the face of a terrible conundrum: how to end World War II. The Japanese military are committed to a fight-to-the-death policy and it would take a further half million American lives to force them into surrender by conventional means.

US WOMAN SMASHES CHANNEL RECORD

1926 Sports star Gertrude Ederle put in a record swim today in the English Channel. The 20-year-old New Yorker, Olympic gold medallist (1924) and women's freestyle world record-holder, completed the 35 miles (56 km) that separate Cap Gris-Nez and Dover in a lung-bursting 14 hours 31 minutes.

I am become death, the destroyer of worlds.

Robert J. Oppenheimer, nuclear physicist who developed the atom bomb, quoting Vishnu, 1945.

YACHTING NEWS

1971 A gauntlet of 200 yachts and an enthusiastic crowd greeted the return to the Hamble of round-the-world yachtsman Chay Blyth today. The 30,000 mile (48,000 km) voyage took Blyth just 292 days – beating the existing record by 21 days. The 31-year-old former paratrooper is no stranger to sea adventure – five years ago, he and fellow para John Ridgway rowed across the Atlantic.

• 1890 – ELECTRIC CHAIR USED FOR THE FIRST TIME • 1962 – MARILYN MONROE FOUND DEAD

CENTRAL COOLING

1987 The leaders of Nicaragua, El Salvador, Guatemala, Honduras and Costa Rica signed a peace plan in Guatemala City today which aims to settle 10-year-old conflict in the region. The plan, the brainchild of Costa Rica's president Oscar Arias, calls for a ceasefire in Nicaragua, El Salvador and Guatemala, an end to all foreign involvement in the region, including US sponsorship of the Nicaraguan Contra guerrillas, and an amnesty for political prisoners.

SAY BYE BYE TO LITTLE SOOTY SWEEPS

1840 The British Parliament has passed a law forbidding the indenturing of child sweeps. Supporters of the bill have waged an emotive campaign against the practice, citing the appalling conditions in which climbing boys live and work. In addition to the risk of serious accident and misshapen limbs from climbing chimneys, the boys are also liable to suffer respiratory disease and cancer of the groin as a result of the fumes and soot. Some masters, it is claimed, deliberately starve their lads to keep them undersized, and reluctant climbing boys are driven up narrow flues by pricking or scorching the soles of their feet. Until an efficient sweeping machine is patented, however, there is every likelihood of the trade continuing unabated.

US EMBASSIES IN AFRICA BOMBED

1998 At least 200 people have been killed and over 1,000 injured in explosions at the US embassies in Kenya and Tanzania, which took place within minutes of each other. No one has claimed responsibility for the blasts but US officials believe the attacks were the work of Osama bin Laden, an Islamic Muslim fundamentalist. The first blast occurred in the Tanzanian capital Dar es Salaam and caused widespread devastation. The second, five minutes later, was in Nairobi, the capital of Kenya. The explosion demolished a five-storey office block, which crashed down onto the US embassy next door, ripping off its bomb-proof doors. Two passing buses were also wrecked. Volunteers have worked hard to pull survivors from the rubble.

1556 A UFO appears above Basle in Switzerland.

1830 Louis Philippe is proclaimed King of France.

1888 A killer, "Jack the Ripper" murders a London prostitute.

1913 American aviator Samuel Cody becomes Britain's first air fatality.

1929 The *Graf Zeppelin* airship takes off for a trip around the world.

1931 Legendary jazz pianist, trumpeter, cornet player and composer Bix Deiderbecke dies.

1938 Death of Konstantin Stanislavsky, the influential Russian theatre director, actor and pioneer of "method" acting.

BIRTHDAYS

Louis Leakey 1903, Kenyan paleontologist who uncovered crucial evidence of man's early evolution, including a 1,750,000-year-old skull.

Ralph Johnson Bunche 1904, American diplomat who became the first Black American to hold an important position in the State Department.

Walter Swinburne 1961, Irish jockey who won the Derby in 1981 on Shergar.

• 1957 – DEATH OF OLIVER HARDY • 1987 – DAVID OWEN RESIGNS FROM BRITISH SDP PARTY

1576 Work begins in Denmark on the first purpose-built observatory.

1588 The Spanish Armada is finally defeated by the British.

1900 The first Davis Cup tennis tournament begins at Longwood, in Boston, MA.

1963 The US, Britain and the USSR sign the nuclear Test Ban Treaty in the Kremlin.

1973 American vice-president Spiro Agnew goes under investigation for tax evasion.

1991 British journalist John McCarthy is freed by the Lebanese terrorist group who have been holding him hostage.

BIRTHDAYS

Ernest Lawrence 1901, American physicist.

Jimmy Witherspoon 1911, American blues singer.

Dino De Laurentis 1919, American producer of *La Strada* and many other films.

Esther Williams 1923, American actress and former champion swimmer.

Dustin Hoffman 1937, American actor whose films include *Midnight Cowboy*.

MONT BLANC CONQUERED

1786 Mont Blanc, at 15,771 ft (4807 m) the tallest peak in Europe outside the Caucasus, has been conquered at last. Twenty-five years ago a scientist from Geneva named Horace Benedict de Saussure offered prize money for the first ascent of this glory in the alpine chain. The prize has today been claimed by a local man, Doctor Michel Gabriel Paccard of Chamonix, who completed the climb with his porter, Jacques Balmat.

WORLD HEALTH SCARE

2014 The West African Ebola outbreak has been categorized as 'a public health emergency of international concern' by the World Health Organization (WHO). At least 3,000 people have been infected with the virus, but the WHO has warned that more than 20,000 people are likely to be infected. *Medecins san Frontier* head Joanne Liu has emphasized the scale of the crisis by explaining "it is impossible to keep up with the sheer number of infected people pouring into our facilities". In a damning criticism of world leaders, the charity says the global response has so far been "lethally inadequate".

NIXON QUITS

1974 Richard Nixon made history today as the first US president to resign his office. In an emotional television address to the nation, Mr Nixon admitted to errors of judgement which he said demanded that he stand down. Only four days ago the beleaguered president was forced to own up to his complicity in the break-in by members of his re-election committee to the Democratic Party Committee's HQ in the Watergate building, Washington, in June 1972. Evidence of political espionage and a dirty tricks campaign against his opponents had been mounting. The resignation will take effect as of noon tomorrow, when Nixon's deputy, Gerald Ford, will be sworn in as the 38th president of the United States.

• 117 AD – HADRIAN BECOMES EMPEROR OF ROME • 1963 – THE GREAT TRAIN ROBBERY

CREEK TRAGEDY

1814 A settlement of the dispute between the US government and the Creek Indians was formally concluded today with the signing of the Treaty of Fort Jackson. Under the terms of the treaty the Indians are to lose 23 million acres (9.3 million hectares) of land, comprising over half of Alabama and part of southern Georgia, to the US. The war flared up last August with the Creeks' fears about losing traditional hunting grounds to white settlers. Their first foray ended in the massacre of frontierspeople at Fort Minis, on the lower Alabama River. The response from the US authorities was swift. A 5000-strong militia under General Andrew Jackson wiped out two Indian villages and this spring, at the Battle of Horseshoe Bend, killed more than 800 warriors and took 500 women and children prisoner. The Indians' campaign was chaotic, for at no time were all 50 Creek towns united in aim, and some towns chose to fight with the US.

1867 John Harrison Surratt is arrested as an alleged conspirator in the assassination of American president Lincoln.

1919 Death of Ruggiero Leoncavallo, Italian composer best known for the opera *I Pagliacci*.

1942 Mahatma Gandhi is arrested in Britain for his "Quit India" campaign.

1965 Singapore becomes an independent state within the Commonwealth of Nations.

1975 Death of Russian composer Shostakovich.

REAL-LIFE DRAMA

1967 The bizarre life of playwright Joe Orton, 34, came to a bizarre end today. In a tiny Islington bedsit, police found Orton with his skull smashed in and his flatmate Kenneth Halliwell, 40, dead from an overdose. A note written by Halliwell read "If you read his diary all will be explained". Orton shot to fame in 1964 with the success of his first play, *Entertaining Mr Sloane*. This was followed in 1966 by *Loot*. Orton's unique brand of anarchic humour both shocked and entertained audiences. In his personal life, too, Orton challenged conventional morality, revelling in the danger of anonymous sexual encounters in public lavatories.

BIRTHDAYS

Thomas Telford 1757, famous Scottish bridge engineer.

Leonide Massine 1896, Russian ballet dancer and choreographer.

Robert Aldrich 1918, American film director whose films include *The Dirty Dozen*.

Philip Larkin 1922, British poet.

Rod Laver 1938, Australian tennis star who won the singles at Wimbledon four times.

Whitney Houston 1964, American singer and actress.

GRACE STUMPED BY HOBBS

1930 Surrey and England batsman Jack Hobbs notched up another milestone in his illustrious career today by scoring even more runs than cricketing giant W. G. Grace. In a perfectly judged 40 against Middlesex at the Kennington Oval, London, Hobbs overtook the great doctor's aggregate record of 54,896 runs. Five years ago Hobbs broke another of W. G. Grace's records, by exceeding 125 centuries. Hobbs is so thrilled that he intends inscribing his bat as a reminder of his historic achievement today.

• **1945 – US HYDROGEN BOMB EXPLODES OVER JAPANESE CITY OF NAGASAKI**

843 AD The Treaty of Verdun divides the Frankish empire.

1846 The Smithsonian Institution for scientific research is established in Washington with a bequest from English scientist James Smithson.

1885 The first Promenade Concert, organized by Sir Henry Wood, is held at Queens Hall in London.

1913 The Treaty of Bucharest is signed, ending the second Balkan War and partitioning Macedonia.

1966 The first American moon satellite, *Orbiter I*, is launched.

BIRTHDAYS

Count (Camillo Benso) Cavour 1810, Italian statesman who played a large role in the unification of Italy and became prime minister in the new kingdom.

Herbert Hoover 1874, American Republican president 1929–33 with a belief in individual freedom that led him to reject federal relief for unemployment during the Depression and lost him the 1932 election to Franklin D. Roosevelt.

HarmonIOUs

1788 August 10 seems a propitious day for Wolfgang Amadeus Mozart. Last year on this day the prolific Salzburg-born composer completed *Eine Kleine Nachtmusik*, a tuneful little piece, and today he finished his "Jupiter" symphony. Despite his almost constant composing, however – three complete symphonies since June 26 this year – and his appointment as Kammermusicus to write music for court balls, the 32-year-old Mozart is deeply in debt with no relief in sight.

US WHITEWASH

1900 Torrential rain brought the first international tennis competition, the Davis Cup, to a premature close at Longwood, Boston, today. The United States held an unassailable 3-0 lead over the challengers, Great Britain, when the match was abandoned. The three-day competition is the brainchild of US doubles champion Dwight Davis, who has also donated the tournament trophy, a massive gold-lined solid silver punchbowl valued at $1,000 (£544). The winning team comprised Davis himself, M. D. Whitman and Holcombe Ward. With the three top British players unavailable, Arthur Gore, Ernest Black and H. Roper Barrett could only struggle manfully against seemingly overwhelming odds. These included a heat-wave on the first two days, grass twice as long as they are used to in England, a net that sagged 2-3 inches (5-7.5 cm) and tennis balls likened to "animated egg-plums".

USAIN BOLT DEFENDS SPRINT TITLES IN STYLE

2012 Breaking records is becoming a habit for Usain Bolt. The Jamaican has become the first man in history to defend his two Olympic sprint titles. Having retained his 100m title in an Olympic record time of 9.63 seconds – in a final where only one runner failed to break the 10-second barrier – he went on to beat fellow Jamaicans Yohan Blake and Warren Weir in the 200m in a time of 19.32 seconds to complete a remarkable clean sweep. Though he failed in either event to break his own world records the man himself was clearly delighted with his achievements, modestly declaring himself as a 'living legend' of the Olympics.

• 1889 – SCREW-TOP BOTTLE PATENTED • 1961 – BRITAIN APPLIES TO JOIN EEC

JACKSON POLLOCK KILLED

1956 Avant-garde artist Jackson Pollock was killed today when his car hit a tree near East Hampton, New York. He was 44. Pollock was recognized as a major talent, although recognition in some quarters was accompanied by derision in others. His search for a process by which he could transfer his personality into his art led him to develop "drip painting" – pouring paint on to a flat canvas in a seemingly haphazard manner. According to Pollock, this demanded a great deal of mental preparation first. Pollock the man was plagued by alcoholism and psychiatric problems for much of his adult life. Only through his art, it is said, did he achieve equilibrium.

HEATH TAKES THE HELM

1971 British PM Edward Heath proved his abilities as a team captain at sea today by leading the British contingent to victory in the 605-mile (973-km) Fastnet race for the Admiral's Cup. Heath, 55, will need all his skills at the political rudder if he is to steer his government's policy on Northern Ireland into calmer waters. So far measures have produced an escalation rather than a reduction in violence.

1853 A French protectorate is established in Cambodia, following years of attacks by the Thais and Vietnamese.

1932 US president Herbert Hoover says it is time to scrap Prohibition.

1952 Crown Prince Hussein of Jordan is named successor to his father King Talal.

1990 Forty Britons trapped in Kuwait by the Iraqi invasion celebrate their freedom.

2004 The first licence for the cloning of human embryos is issued in the UK.

2014 Robin Williams, star of many films, including *Mrs Doubtfire,* dies age 63.

STEEL MAN'S GOLD HEART

1919 Andrew Carnegie, the steel baron, has died at his home in Lennox, Massachusetts. He was 84. Andrew joined the Penn Railway Co. and worked his way up to Superintendent. He first struck oil on his own land and invested in iron manufactures. By the turn of the century 25 per cent of steel output in the USA was produced by Carnegie-owned companies. In his lifetime he set aside $350 million (£189 million) for philanthropic purposes. Foundations such as the Carnegie Corporation of New York will ensure he is not forgotten.

BIRTHDAYS

Richard Meade 1673, English physician to royalty and pioneer of preventative medicine.

Hugh MacDairmid 1892, Scottish dialect poet and founder of the Scottish National Party.

Enid Blyton 1897, British author of children's books.

Alex Haley 1921, American author of *Roots,* which traced his ancestors from Africa to slavery.

• 1942 – LENINGRAD SYMPHONY PREMIERES • 1962 – CHAD BECOMES INDEPENDENT

1791 African slaves on Hispaniola, mount a revolt against plantation owners.

1848 Death of George Stephenson, who invented the "Rocket" locomotive.

1955 Death of German novelist Thomas Mann, author of *Death in Venice*.

1964 Ian Fleming, creator of secret agent James Bond 007, dies.

1980 The first giant panda born in captivity is delivered safely in Mexico.

1983 In Santiago, Chile, 17 people are killed in a demonstration against military dictator General Pinochet.

2000 Russian nuclear submarine *Kursk* sinks during training in the Barents Sea.

2014 American actress Lauren Bacall, star of *The Big Sleep*, dies aged 89.

BIRTHDAYS

George IV 1762, English king.

Robert Southey 1774, English poet and writer.

Cecil B. De Mille 1881, American film director.

Mark Knopfler 1949, British guitarist with Dire Straits.

FORD JUMPSTARTS MASS MOTORING

1908 The car that some are predicting will revolutionize motoring started rolling out of the factory today. The car in question is the Model T from the Ford Motor Company, a sturdy black four-cylinder number that comes in two versions, tourer and roadster. Both are retailing at incredibly low prices: the roadster at $825 (£445) and the tourer for just $25 (£13) more. The key to Ford's low pricing policy is volume production. The company intends concentrating its manufacturing muscle on the Model T, enabling it to utilize standardized parts and employ an assembly-line method of production.

KEEPING BACTERIA AT BAY

1865 During an operation at Glasgow Royal Infirmary today British surgeon Joseph Lister, 38, demonstrated a method of preventing infection of an operation wound. It involves the use of carbolic acid as an antiseptic to protect the patient against microorganisms. Lister hopes that his method will lead to a drop in the current 50 per cent mortality rate among amputation cases.

Tiger! Tiger! burning bright
In the forest of the night,
What immortal hand or eye
Could frame thy fearful symmetry?

William Blake, English poet and artist, dies, 1827.

TRUTH WILL OUT

1990 The Communist Chinese government's attempt to restore its tarnished image after the slaughter in Tiananmen Square has received a severe setback. Official documentation from the riots that broke out last March in the Tibetan capital Lhasa have revealed that more than 450 were killed, the majority by bullets, 750 injured and 3000 detained. More embarrassing still for Beijing is the revelation that the riots were provoked by members of the People's Armed Police. Dressed as Tibetans, these *agents provocateurs* attacked and burned shops, offices and food stores, providing the authorities with the excuse they needed for cracking down on a native population whose resentment against Chinese rule was reaching boiling point.

• 1883 – DEATH OF THE LAST QUAGGA • 1960 – *ECHO* SATELLITE LAUNCHED

CHURCHILL'S GLORY DAYS

1704 The allied armies of the Grand Coalition won a resounding victory today over a numerically superior Franco-Bavarian force at Blenheim, north of the Danube. Led by John Churchill, Duke of Marlborough, and his "twin-captain", Eugene, Prince of Savoy, the allied army of 52,000 men mounted a surprise attack on the 56,000-strong enemy force. By the end of the afternoon the enemy had been routed. The victory has saved Vienna from imminent capture by the French. Recognition of Churchill as a soldier of genius also seems assured.

EXPLOSIVE ATTACK

1978 A building which served as the Beirut HQ of the Palestine Liberation Front and contained the offices of their rivals, Al-Fatah, was ripped apart by a bomb today, leaving an estimated 150 people dead. Soon after the attack the pro-Iraqi PLF accused the pro-Syrian Popular Front of the Liberation of Palestine of attempting to annihilate its leadership. Later, however the PLF blamed "American and Israeli intelligence agents" instead.

1814 The British take over the colony at Cape of Good Hope from the Dutch.

1910 Death of nurse Florence Nightingale.

1946 Death of the British novelist H. G. Wells, whose books include *The Time Machine*.

1962 East-German, Peter Fechter, is shot and bleeds to death while trying to escape over the Berlin Wall.

1971 American saxophonist King Curtis is stabbed to death in New York.

1989 Twelve people are killed in Australia when two hot air balloons collide in the worst-ever hot-air balloon disaster.

DEATH OF MILLAIS

1896 Sir John Everett Millais, the President of the Royal Academy, died today. An infant prodigy, Millais caused a scandal in 1850 with his painting *Christ in the House of His Parents*. The art-loving public was outraged by the artist's realistic depiction of the Holy Family and especially by the revelation that the initials "PRB" stood for Pre-Raphaelite Brotherhood, a group of artists who considered their work to be superior to that of Raphael and all who succeeded him. Millais soon turned his back on the Brotherhood and, in 1885, became the first artist to receive a baronetcy.

John Logie Baird 1888, Scottish electrical engineer who invented television.

Jean Borotra 1898, the first Frenchman to win Wimbledon.

Alfred Hitchcock 1899, English film director.

Archbishop Makarios III 1913, Cypriot churchman and president of Cyprus 1960–77.

Fidel Castro 1927, Cuban revolutionary who became socialist president in 1959.

• 1876 – BAYREUTH FESTSPIELHAUS OPENS • 1991 – UK DANGEROUS DOGS ACT IN FORCE

1922 Death of Lord Northcliffe, founder of the *Daily Mail* and the *Daily Mirror* newspapers.

1947 Pakistan becomes independent from India.

1949 Konrad Adenauer becomes chancellor of West Germany.

1951 Death of Randolph Hearst, king of America's yellow press.

1956 Death of Bertolt Brecht, Marxist German playwright and poet.

1986 Benazir Bhutto is jailed by Pakistani dictator General Zia.

1994 Venezuelan terrorist "Carlos the Jackal" is arrested in Sudan.

BIRTHDAYS

Richard von Krafft-Ebing 1840, German psychiatrist who published his pioneering studies of sexual aberrations in *Psychopathia sexualis*.

Dave Crosby 1941, British guitarist with the Byrds and founder member of Crosby, Stills and Nash.

Halle Berry 1966, American actress who was the first African-American female to win the Best Actress Oscar for her role in *Monster's Ball* in 2001.

CLOSE ENCOUNTERS FOR THE RAF

1956 Royal Air Force personnel were last night involved in an extraordinary game of cat-and-mouse with several UFOs. One of these was tracked by ground radar and also seen with the naked eye by operators in the radar tower at RAF Lakenheath as a bright light passing overhead. An RAF pilot reported seeing the object streak beneath his aircraft. After detecting a stationary target that suddenly raced northwards at 600 mph (965 kph), a second station called in an RAF fighter to investigate. The pilot made airborne radar contact with the object, only to have it move behind his fighter. Despite the pilot's best efforts, the object could not be shaken off. A second aircraft was called in, at which point the object moved off and all radar contacts were lost.

NEW COLONY GOES LEGAL

1619 The colony established in the New World in 1607 by the Virginia Company of London held its first legislative assembly in Jamestown today. The historic assembly was made possible by charters secured last year, which transferred the government of the colony from the Crown to the Company. The first of its kind in the New World, it may point the way forward to new colonies as and when they become established. Under the chairmanship of Governor Sir George Yeardley, the new assembly passed laws against drinking and gambling.

TRAGEDY AT SEA

1979 The classic Fastnet Race ended in tragedy today when a Force 10 gale and mountainous seas claimed the lives of 15 sailors from competing yachts. Of the 306 yachts that lined up at the start of the race three days ago, only 177 completed the 605-mile (973-km) course; 23 sank or were abandoned and scores of others were disabled, a high number with broken rudders. Sailors had no advance warning of the severity of the storm, which changed dramatically from a bumpy but manageable Force 8 to a rough, howling Force 10.

• 1969 – BRITISH TROOPS ENTER NORTHERN IRELAND • 2006 – PLUTO LOSES PLANET STATUS

HORSE ATTITUDES

1991 Tomorrow's Siena palio goes ahead amid adverse publicity. French film star Brigitte Bardot, a fervent animal rights campaigner, started a row when she denounced the 800-year-old horse race as a cruel tradition. The mayor of Siena, Pier Luigi Piccini, has denounced Bardot as a "publicity seeker". The Sienese will fight to keep the palio and the tourism it attracts, despite allegations of routine doping and fatal injuries incurred.

TIVOLI'S GARDEN OF DELIGHT

1843 The Tivoli Gardens in Copenhagen were opened today by George Carstensen. They provide a much-needed meeting place for the citizens of Copenhagen and are expected to attract visitors to the city from all over the world. Laid out on part of the city's old defence works, the gardens offer a range of amenities and are illuminated by thousands of gas lights at night, creating a magical atmosphere.

WOODSTOCK 'N' ROLL

1969 An estimated 300,000 people are expected to attend the three-day Woodstock Music and Art Fair which opened at Bethel, in upstate New York, today. The outdoor rock concert has attracted many leading performers, including Jimi Hendrix, Joan Baez, Ravi Shankar, Janis Joplin, Santana, The Grateful Dead, The Who, Joe Cocker and Jefferson Airplane. The thousands of young people fighting their way through the traffic jams to savour hippie culture may find the real thing a salutary experience. The hard facts of the peaceful communing are water and food shortages and a sky full of large threatening clouds.

1057 The Scottish King Macbeth is killed.

1955 Twelve Indian protesters demanding the return of Goa are killed by Portuguese troops.

1965 Twenty thousand National Guards are called in to control the race riots in the Watts area of Los Angeles, California.

1989 Giant mutant trees are found growing around the damaged Soviet nuclear reactor at Chernobyl.

1990 One hundred and fifty people are killed during clashes in the townships outside Johannesburg.

BIRTHDAYS

Napoleon Bonaparte 1769, Corsican military man and Emperor of France 1804–15.

James Keir Hardie 1856, Scottish politican and founder of the British Labour Party.

T. E. Lawrence 1888, English soldier and writer known as Lawrence of Arabia.

Robert Bolt 1924, English playwright who wrote *A Man for all Seasons*.

Oscar Peterson 1925, Canadian jazz pianist and composer.

• 1914 – PANAMA CANAL OPENS • 1947 – INDIA GAINS INDEPENDENCE FROM BRITAIN

1886 Death of Ramakrishna, the Indian Hindu saint and religious educator who taught the essential unity and truth of all religions.

1886 Death of Ned Buntline, the American author who pioneered the dime novel.

1949 Margaret Mitchell, the author of *Gone with the Wind*, dies after being hit by a car.

1979 Death of John G. Diefenbaker, Canadian statesman and Progressive Conservative prime minister who opposed nuclear weapons in Canada.

2009 Jamaican sprinter Usain Bolt breaks the 100m world record at the World Championships in Berlin. Two days later he would break the 200m record.

BIRTHDAYS

Charles Bukowski 1920, American poet, short-story writer and novelist.

Shimon Peres 1923, Polish-born Israeli statesman and prime minister of Israel 1984–86.

Ted Hughes 1930, British Poet Laureate.

Madonna 1958, American pop singer and actress.

BABE STRIKES OUT

1948 "Babe" Ruth, the most famous baseball player of all time, died in New York today aged 53. Baltimore-born Ruth (real name George Herman Ruth) will be chiefly remembered for his ability as a batsman. He broke the major league home-run record in three consecutive seasons (1919-21), and again in 1927 with a staggering score of 60.

IDI AMIN DIES

2003 The notorious former Ugandan president Idi Amin died today. Amin gained control of Uganda in 1971 after overthrowing the government in a military coup and soon after announced plans to expel 50,000 Asians from Uganda. By 1977 he was coming under increasing pressure from around the world amid accusations of mass murder, including that of the Anglican Archbishop of Uganda. He headed a bloody incursion into Tanzania the following year but fled from his country a few months later when 45,000 Tanzanian troops invaded Uganda in revenge, ending his regime of terror.

BLOOD SPILT FOR SUFFRAGE

1819 An orderly political reform meeting held in St Peter's Fields, Manchester, broke up in confusion and violence today, leaving 11 dead and some 400 injured. Magistrates, alarmed by the 60,000-strong crowd that had turned out for the event, ordered the Manchester yeomanry to seize the speakers, including fiery orator Henry Hunt. When the yeomanry also started setting about those carrying "revolutionary" banners, the chairman of the bench of magistrates ordered the 15th Hussars and the Cheshire Volunteers to clear the crowd. The incident is sure to aggravate the ill-feeling that exists between radicals and the Tory establishment. The rally itself was intended as a high point in the political campaign for universal suffrage.

• 1960 – CYPRUS IS A NEW REPUBLIC • 1977 – ELVIS PRESLEY DIES

PAKISTAN PRESIDENT BLOWN OUT OF THE SKIES

1988 General Zia ul-Haq, Pakistan's iron-fisted ruler for the past 11 years, died today when the camouflaged C-130 Hercules plane in which he was travelling crashed shortly after take-off. Zia, 64, was on his way back to Islamabad after watching a demonstration of the capabilities of the US M1A1 Abrams tank at an army testing range near the airport of Bahawalpur. Among the 30 people on board were the US ambassador to Pakistan, Mr Arnold Raphael, and the US embassy's military liaison officer, Brigadier General Herbert Wassom. Intelligence officers suspect that the aircraft may have been downed by a bomb or ground-to-air missile.

PUGILIST'S CHARTER

1743 True to his word, champion bare-knuckle fighter Jack Broughton has published a set of rules to control boxing. He is said to have been determined on this course since Yorkshireman George Stevenson died of injuries sustained in a gruelling bout with him two years ago. Past practices now forbidden under the new rules include hitting an opponent when he is down, kicking, gouging, head butting and grasping an opponent below the waist. Broughton is also responsible for introducing 10-oz (300-g) gloves, called mufflers, to protect the hands and face from bruising during training. His gymnasium is among the many boxing establishments to benefit from the innovation, which has encouraged interest in the sport.

1896 The first pedestrian to be killed by a car is knocked down in Croydon, England.

1945 After Japanese occupation during World War II, Indonesia declares itself a republic.

1983 Death of Ira Gershwin, brother of George, who collaborated on songs such as "Lady be Good".

1987 Donald Harvey, a former nurse's aide, is charged with the murder of 28 people in Ohio, having admitted to more than 50 murders.

1989 An Australian airliner becomes the first commercial plane to fly non-stop from London to Sydney.

BIRTHDAYS

Davy Crockett 1786, American frontiersman and politician.

Mae West 1892, American comedy actress, scriptwriter and international sex symbol during the 1930s.

V. S. Naipaul 1932, Trinidadian writer and novelist.

Robert De Niro 1943, American actor, star of many films.

ANOTHER BRICK IN THE WALL OF ISOLATION

1961 There seems little doubt now that the East German authorities are intent on erecting a permanent barrier between the Eastern and Western sectors of the city. On August 13 the East German police began to string barbed wire and set up road blocks along the inner boundary of the eight districts of the Soviet sector of Berlin. This temporary barrier is now

being replaced with a 9-ft (2.7-m) cement wall topped with barbed wire, complete with armed sentries in watchtowers. The decision to build the wall was taken by Communist leader Walter Ulbricht, with the backing of the Soviet Union, in the light of the continuing massive exodus of East Germans to the West, estimated to be running at around 2000 people a day.

• 1896 – GOLDEN STRIKE ON THE KLONDIKE • 1999 – TURKISH EARTHQUAKE KILLS 14,000

1823 Death of André Jacques Garnerin, French balloonist and parachutist.

1850 Death of the French novelist Honoré de Balzac.

1984 South Africa is banned from taking part in the Olympic Games.

2002 Pope John Paul II draws crowds of two million at a Papal mass in Krakow.

BIRTHDAYS

Virginia Dare 1587, American colonist, the first child of English parents to be born in the New World.

Meriwether Lewis 1774, American explorer who was joint leader with William Clark of the first overland expedition to the Pacific Northwest.

Franz-Joseph I 1830, Austro-Hungarian emperor who invaded Serbia and helped initiate World War I.

Caspar Weinberger 1917, American statesman and secretary of defence for Ronald Reagan.

Roman Polanski 1933, Polish film director who has worked in Europe and the USA.

Robert Redford 1937, American actor whose films include *Butch Cassidy and the Sundance Kid.*

SPAN-TASTIC

1930 After seven years in the making the huge steel arch of the new Sydney Harbour Bridge has been completed. Some 38,390 tons of riveted, high-tensile silicon British steel has gone into the 1650-ft (503-m) arch, one of the largest in the world. Sydney Harbour is so deep that the bridge's British designers, Dorman Long of Middlesbrough, had to find a novel way of supporting the structure. The two halves were built out as cantilevers and supported by wire-rope anchorages situated on either side of the harbour.

Protestant women may take the pill. Roman Catholic women must keep taking the Tablet [a British Roman Catholic paper].

Irene Thomas, British writer. The first oral contraceptive was marketed today, 1960.

LEGACY OF BRUTALITY

1227 The Mongol ruler Genghis Khan, conqueror of an empire that extends from the Pacific to the Dnieper River, died today after falling from his horse. The son of Yesugei, a member of a royal Mongol clan, Genghis succeeded in uniting the Mongol tribes of nomadic horsemen and harnessing them into a terrifyingly effective war machine. The name Genghis Khan became synonymous with brutality as he pursued his goal of world conquest. Mongol leadership has now passed to Ögodei Khan.

RED GUARDS PLAY MAO'S GAME

1966 The first of eight huge demonstrations by semi-military groups called Red Guards took place in China's capital, Peking, today. These young radicals have poured into the capital from all over China to answer Mao's call for the denunciation and removal of senior officials held responsible by Mao for dampening down revolutionary ideals among his countrymen.

• **1939 – THE WIZARD OF OZ MOVIE IS RELEASED IN NEW YORK**

HITLER GETS THE "JA" VOTE

1934 The German people went to the polls today to give their verdict on Adolf Hitler's assumption of the titles Führer and Reich Chancellor. Of the 45.5 million eligible to vote, 38 million have voted "Yes", 4.25 million "No" and 870,000 spoilt their ballot papers. This is an impressive majority for the new German head of state, who announced on August 2, the day that President von Hindenburg died, his intention of merging the office of president with that of Chancellor.

PASCAL DIES

1662 Blaise Pascal, the French mathematician, physicist and religious philosopher, died in Paris today, aged 39. Pascal pursued his intellectual enquiries with an all-consuming passion. In November 1654 he experienced the "night of fire" that changed his life, and he temporarily abandoned the world of science – and inventions such as a calculating device, the syringe and the hydraulic press – to go in search of religious truth among the austere moral precepts of Jansenism taught in the convent of Port-Royal. Thereafter, he wrote only at the convent's request and never again under his own name. *Les Lettres provinciales*, his most popular work, is a beautifully written defence of Jansenist Antoine Arnaud, who believed that no amount of Communion could wash away sins not truly repented. At the time of his death Pascal was working on a treatise of spirituality.

If you want people to think well of you, do not speak well of yourself.

Blaise Pascal, French philosopher and mathematician, who died today, 1662.

HUNGERFORD MASSACRE

1987 A lone gunman went on a six-hour rampage through the small British town of Hungerford, on the Wiltshire-Berkshire borders today, leaving 14 dead, including the gunman's mother, and a further 14 maimed from gunshot wounds. The man, ex-paratrooper Michael Ryan, 27, eventually turned his gun on himself. Ryan was said to have been deeply depressed by the death of his father two years ago. He had a passion for guns and had collected a vast personal arsenal.

14 AD Death of Augustus, the first Roman emperor.

1929 Death of Sergei Pavlovich Diaghilev, founder of the Russian ballet company Ballets Russes in Paris.

1960 The Soviets sentence U-2 spy plane pilot Gary Powers to 10 years' detention.

1979 Pol Pot, ex-dictator of Cambodia, is sentenced to death for genocide.

1990 Iraqi leader Saddam Hussein offers to release all Western hostages in exchange for a US withdrawal from the Gulf.

BIRTHDAYS

John Dryden 1631, British poet and critic.

Orville Wright 1871, American aviation pioneer, who, with his brother Wilbur, made the first powered and controlled flight.

Coco Chanel 1883, French fashion designer who revolutionized women's clothing.

Ogden Nash 1902, American humorist.

Willy Shoemaker 1931, American jockey who rode a record-breaking 7000 winners.

• 1936 – FEDERICO GARCIA LORCA SHOT DEAD • 1977 – GROUCHO MARX DIES

1912 Death of William Booth, the British founder of the Salvation Army.

1913 Adolphe Pégond becomes the first person to parachute from a plane.

1924 British sprinter Eric Liddel refuses to run in the 100m at the Paris Olympics on religious grounds.

1940 Radar is used for the first time by the British during World War Two.

1956 The first nuclear power in Britain is generated at Calder Hall power station in Cumbria.

1988 A ceasefire between Iran and Iraq takes effect.

2012 Tony Scott, British director of films such as *Top Gun* dies, aged 68.

BIRTHDAYS

Benjamin Harrison 1833, American Republican president.

H. P. Lovecraft American science-fiction author of macabre tales.

Jack Teagarden 1905, American jazz trombonist, singer, composer and bandleader.

Robert Plant 1948, English singer and songwriter, best known as the vocalist of the rockband Led Zeppelin.

RAF INVINCIBLE IN BATTLE FOR SKIES

1940 The offensive launched by Germany on August 13 in preparation for an invasion of the British Isles is being met with strong resistance and considerable victory by the RAF. Southeast England has borne the brunt of the attacks from fleets of bombers protected by fighter aircraft. So far 236 German aircraft have been downed for the loss of just 95 British, with the RAF's efforts concentrated on destroying the Luftwaffe's bombers. A switch of German tactics may well be on the cards as Luftwaffe supremo Hermann Goering searches for a way of cracking the British fighter command nut and winning air superiority.

AXE FALLS FOR TROTSKY

1940 Leon Trotsky, a leader of the Russian Revolution in 1917, was stabbed to death at his home in Coyoacan, near Mexico City today. He was 61. Ramón Mercader, a Spanish communist, has been charged with murder. Trotsky had lived abroad since January 1929, when Stalin lost patience with the steady stream of criticism issuing from the Ukrainian's place of exile at Alma-Ata in Central Asia and banished him from Soviet soil. His fall from grace in the Soviet hierarchy came swiftly after the death of Lenin in 1923. Outmanoeuvred by the wily Stalin, he found himself first ousted from the Politburo, then the Party, and finally the Soviet Union itself.

DAGUERRE CAPTURES THE REAL WORLD

1839 The Académie des Sciences heard yesterday of a revolutionary new photographic process. The process records an image by exposing to light a copper-coated silver plate sensitized by iodine which is then developed by bringing it into contact with heated mercury vapour. The image produced is of an exquisite tonal quality, however, so damages easily and cannot generate duplicates. The way ahead seems to be the negative-positive process of photography developed by Englishman Henry Fox Talbot, announced in February.

• **1913 – FIRST STAINLESS STEEL IS CAST** • **1989 – THAMES *MARCHIONESS* TRAGEDY**

ANTI-GORBY COUP FLOPS

1991 President Mikhail Gorbachev arrived back in Moscow today after the collapse of the attempt by hardliners to depose him. All but one of the eight ringleaders of the plot have been rounded up. Gorbachev seems deeply saddened by the fact that several of his closest and most trusted colleagues, including the Kremlin chief of staff and the head of the KGB, were involved in the plot. Gorbachev's steadfast refusal to be coerced into resigning was echoed by mass demonstrations against the coup by the peoples of Moscow and Leningrad. There was also a disinclination on the part of many in authority – notably in the armed forces – to behave unconstitutionally. Russian Federation president Boris Yeltsin has identified the Communist Party as a stumbling block to further reform.

THINK CADILLAC

1902 Manufacturer Martin Leland has honoured Detroit's founding father, Antoine de la Motte Cadillac, by naming his new automobile after the French colonial administrator. The new Cadillac car is lightweight and has a single cylinder engine. Beautifully designed and finished, the Cadillac aims to carve a niche for itself as the Rolls-Royce of the American motor industry.

SARIN GAS ATTACKS

2013 Around 1,429 people, including many children, are killed in chemical attacks in the suburbs of Damascus, apparently involving sarin gas. Opposition groups blame the Assad regime.

1951 Death of Constant Lambert, English composer and conductor.

1959 Death of Sir Jacob Epstein, American-born sculptor.

1961 Britain releases nationalist Jomo Kenyatta, former president of the Kenya African Union who was imprisoned for his part in the Mau Mau rebellion.

1988 British licensing laws are amended to allow pubs to stay open 12 hours a day, except on Sundays.

1989 The American fashion journalist Diana Vreeland dies.

BIRTHDAYS

William Murdoch 1754, Scottish engineer who pioneered the use of coal-gas for lighting.

William IV 1765, English monarch known as "the sailor king" because he joined the Royal Navy at 13.

Aubrey Beardsley 1874, English illustrator who played a leading part in the Aesthetic movement.

Princess Margaret 1930, English royal, sister of Queen Elizabeth II.

Usain Bolt 1986, celebrated Jamaican sprinter.

BENIGNO'S CORAZON TAKES HEART

1984 A massive demonstration was held in Manila today to mark the first anniversary of the murder of Benigno Aquino, the leader of the anti-Marcos faction in the Philippines. Aquino was gunned down as he stepped on to the tarmac at Manila airport after returning from a three-year sojourn in the United States. The chant of "enough is enough" directed at the regime of Ferdinand Marcos is getting louder. The people of the Philippines are looking to Aquino's widow, Corazon ("Cory"), for a new champion who will challenge Marcos for the presidency he has held by force since 1972.

• 1959 – HAWAII BECOMES 50TH US STATE • 1986 – VOLCANIC GAS WREAKS HAVOC

1849 Amaral, the Portuguese governer of Macao, is assassinated for anti-Chinese politics.

1868 Ten thousand Chinese plunder the China Inland Mission.

1940 Death of Sir Oliver Lodge, English physicist who pioneered wireless telegraphy.

1953 Iran's Shah returns to the Peacock Throne and Mossaddegh is jailed after a military coup.

1978 Death of Jomo Kenyatta, the first president of Kenya.

1989 British Telecom launch the world's first pocket-phones which operate within 100 yards of a public base station.

BIRTHDAYS

Claude Debussy 1862, French composer.

Jacques Lipchitz 1891, Lithuanian-born US sculptor.

Dorothy Parker 1893, American writer, critic and humorist who was a founder member of the Algonquin Round Table.

Henri Cartier-Bresson 1908, French photographer, considered one of the greatest.

RED ROSE FLOWERS AGAIN

1485 The 30-year struggle between the houses of Lancaster and York for the throne of England ended today in victory for the Lancastrians. The decisive blow was dealt at Bosworth Field, 12 miles (19 km) west of Leicester, where key noblemen such as the Stanley brothers deserted Richard at his hour of greatest need to swing the battle Henry Tudor's way. Richard III fought on bravely before being killed. The 1000 or so mercenaries supplied by King Louis XI of France were a major factor in Tudor's success. Opposition to the 28-year-old usurper, who will be known as Henry VII, is likely to continue, however, until a way can be found of reconciling the white rose and the red, the well known emblems of the houses of York and Lancaster.

CHARLES CHALLENGES THE COMMONS

1642 The divide separating King Charles I from the English Parliament seems to be hardening into a battle line. The King has raised his military standard in Nottingham town. It is almost certain that he will be able to count on the support of many peers and gentry who fear the consequences of a parliament infiltrated by the "common people". Three days ago both houses of parliament issued a joint statement denouncing as traitors any who join the King's cause. A parliamentary army of 10,000 has been mobilized.

I have recently been all round the world and have formed a very poor opinion of it.

Thomas Beecham, British conductor, 1946.

HALF-SMILE HALF-INCHED

1911 The world's most famous painting, Leonardo da Vinci's *Mona Lisa*, was stolen during the night from the Louvre Museum in Paris. Museum officials are embarrassed by the loss of their most prized exhibit, which is one of the few works that the great Leonardo actually completed. Police do not have any clues as to the identity of the thief, or thieves, and seem to be banking on the *Mona Lisa* recovering herself. Just a glimpse of her smile should give away the whereabouts of the painting, said to represent the mystery of existence.

• 1985 – FIFTY-FOUR DIE AS BOEING 747 CATCHES FIRE AT MANCHESTER AIRPORT

FRINGE SUCCESS

1960 A new type of show is the talk of this year's Edinburgh fringe: *Beyond the Fringe*, the work of Alan Bennett, Peter Cook, Jonathan Miller and Dudley Moore, brings political satire to intimate revue. Critics are hailing it as the best thing to hit Edinburgh for many a year.

PREJUDICE THREATENS TRUE JUSTICE

1927 In one of the most controversial cases in American legal history, Nicola Sacco and Bartolomeo Vanzetti went to the electric chair today. In July 1921 a jury found the men guilty of the murders of a factory paymaster and a guard during a robbery in South Braintree, Massachusetts. The guilty verdict was challenged on the grounds that the judge and jury had been prejudiced against the two political anarchists who were

also immigrants. Calls for a retrial were denied, even when in 1925 condemned criminal Celestino Madeiros gave evidence that the murders had in fact been committed by the Morelli Gang. Governor A. T. Fuller refused clemency for the two Italians, supported by an independent committee inspecting the case. For many, questions concerning the administration of justice in this case remain to be answered.

GOTHS GATECRASH ROME

410 The disintegration of the once-mighty Roman Empire is continuing apace with the fall of Rome to the Visigoths. Alaric, King of the Visigoths, ordered his men to storm the city after the refusal by the Roman emperor of the West, Honorius, to agree to his terms. The citizens of Rome are paying the price for their emperor's delusions of power. While he remains in the safety of his new and impregnable capital, Ravenna, they are being sacked. Two years ago, when Alaric first threatened the city, the Roman authorities contemplated offering sacrifices to the gods as a means of keeping the Visigoths at bay. On this occasion, the authorities needed only to offer land and subsidies. Fortunately for those who treasure Rome's beauty, first reports of the sack suggest that booty rather than wholesale destruction is the main aim of the invaders. The biggest loss from the fall of the capital is to Roman prestige.

93 AD Death of Gnaeus Julius Agricola, Roman general.

1305 Sir William Wallace, Scottish patriot, is hung, drawn and quartered.

1680 Death of Captain Blood, who tried to steal the Crown Jewels from the Tower of London in 1671.

1940 German bombers begin night raids on London.

1944 Pro-Nazi dictator of Romania, General Ion Antonescu is overthrown.

1990 The German states choose October 3 as the date for reunification.

BIRTHDAYS

Louis XVI 1754, French monarch responsible for the Revolution and the last king of France.

Gene Kelly 1912, American dancer, choreographer, singer, actor and director who starred in Hollywood musicals.

Peter Thomson 1929, Australian golfer who won numerous major victories at home and overseas.

Willy Russell 1947, English playwright from Liverpool whose plays include *Educating Rita*.

• 1818 – STEAMSHIPS RUN ON THE GREAT LAKES • 1926 – RUDOLPH VALENTINO DIES

1690 Job Charnock establishes a trading post on behalf of the English East India Company in Kalikata, West Bengal.

1906 Kidney transplants are carried out on dogs at a medical conference in Toronto, Canada.

1940 *The Lancet* reports the first purification of penicillin by Howard Florey and Ernest Chain.

1975 Annabel Hunt gives the first official nude opera performance in Britain in *Ulysses*.

1990 The Irish hostage Brian Keenan is released from Beirut.

BIRTHDAYS

George Stubbs 1724, English animal painter and engraver, celebrated as the greatest of all horse painters.

William Wilberforce 1759, English philanthropist and anti-slave-trade campaigner.

Sir Max Beerbohm 1872, English caricaturist, writer and wit.

Jorge Luis Borges 1899, Argentinian author who dictated *The Book of Imaginary Beings* having gone blind.

PRESSURE PUSHES POET TO POISON

1770 Poet Thomas Chatterton, 17, fatally poisoned himself with arsenic today at his lodgings in London. He had become increasingly depressed by lack of recognition. Chatterton's enthusiasm for recreating the medieval world, in his "Rowley" poems, came at the wrong time. He was denounced as a "forger" in the mould of James Macpherson, whose "rediscovery" of the works of the third-century Gaelic bard, Ossian, became the literary sensation of the 1760s.

BITTER BRITISH TORCH WASHINGTON

1814 The small but very bitter war currently being fought by Britain and America is continuing in a punitive vein. The latest target is Washington, which has been burnt by a 4000-strong British force of Peninsular War veterans under General Ross. The army, which was brought to the Washington approaches by ships of Admiral Cochrane's fleet, defeated local defence forces at Bladensburg before entering the capital and putting it to the torch. Among the casualties is the US president's official residence, the White House.

SPANIARDS FIND WOMEN WARRIORS

1542 The Spanish explorer Francisco de Orellana has discovered new lands east of Quito. Last April, he and a group of 50 men were sent ahead of the expedition, led by Gonzalo Pizarro to gather provisions. Instead of returning, Orellana was

persuaded to push on and explore the great river system that lay before them. The men drifted with the current and eventually reached the mouth of the river. They are said to be full of fantastic tales of treasure and, most curiously of all, tribes of women warriors resembling Amazons. Orellana is keen to return to his "Amazon River" in order to exploit its wealth further. This may prove problematical, however, because Spain and Portugal are in dispute over ownership of the territory.

• AD **79** – MOUNT VESUVIUS ERUPTS • **1959** – THE MAU MAU REBELLION BEGINS

TSAR PUNISHES *POTEMKIN* REBELS

1905 Eight of the mutineers from the Russian battleship *Potemkin* who recently returned to Russia after fleeing to Romania at the end of June have been sentenced to death. The remainder have been imprisoned. The mutiny, in which several officers were killed, was part of the nationwide campaign against the government of Tsar Nicholas II. Heavy taxation, the Tsar's refusal to introduce constitutional government and defeat in the Russo-Japanese War are the main issues fuelling the present wave of social unrest.

VIVE LA FRANCE!

1944 The four-year long ordeal that Paris and her citizens have suffered at the hands of the Nazis is almost over. With the forces of General Leclerc approaching the city and Resistance fighters continuing to attack from the centre, liberation is almost complete. Parisians owe thanks to the Kommandant of Paris, General von Choltitz, who gave himself up today rather than carry out his Führer's order to blow up the capital's bridges and principal buildings to halt the advance. Tomorrow Free French leader General Charles de Gaulle will attend a liberation procession through the streets of Paris and a service of thanksgiving in Notre Dame cathedral.

WEBB CRACKS THE CHANNEL CHALLENGE

1875 Englishman Matthew Webb made history today by becoming the first person to swim the English Channel. The 27-year-old master mariner from Shropshire set off from Admiralty Pier, Dover, yesterday. Swimming breaststroke, he covered the 21-mile (34 km) stretch to Calais in 21 hours 45 minutes, emerging on the French side tired but triumphant. His plans as a professional swimmer look set to continue.

1819 Death of James Watt, English inventor of the steam engine.

1830 A revolution begins in Belgium.

1837 Henry William Crawford of London patents a process for producing galvanized iron.

1841 Three graduates from Oberlin Collegiate Institute, Ohio are the first women to earn degrees.

1867 Death of Michael Faraday, English chemist and physicist.

2009 Veteran US senator Edward Kennedy dies.

BIRTHDAYS

Ivan the Terrible (Ivan IV) 1530, Russian tsar who executed more than 3000, including the royal heir.

Leonard Bernstein 1918, American composer and conductor.

Sean Connery 1930, Scottish actor who played the leading role in seven James Bond movies.

Wayne Shorter 1933, American saxophonist with Art Blakey's Jazz Messengers.

Elvis Costello 1954, British singer and songwriter.

• 1919 – THE FIRST SCHEDULED INTERNATIONAL AIR SERVICE BEGINS

1748 The first Lutheran synod is founded in the American colonies.

1789 The French Assembly adopts the *Declaration of the Rights of Man*.

1952 The first Intercontinental Ballistic Missile (ICBM) tests have taken place in the USSR.

1958 Death of English composer Ralph Vaughan Williams.

1970 A national women's strike causes chaos in New York.

1988 American swimmer Lynne Cox crosses the 11-mile (17.5 km) wide Lake Baikal in Siberia in 4 hours, 20 minutes – the first long swim in a cold water lake.

BIRTHDAYS

Joseph Michel Montgolfier 1740, French inventor and pioneer of the hot air balloon with his brother Jacques Étienne Montgolfier.

Prince Albert 1819, Bavarian-born consort to Queen Victoria.

Lee De Forest 1873, American radio and television pioneer and inventor of the Audion vacuum tube, which made broadcasting possible.

US WOMEN VOTE

1920 The US legislature today ratified the Nineteenth Amendment giving American women the right to vote. The Amendment was bitterly opposed by some members of the Senate before eventually being submitted to the legislature in June last year. That American women now have equality with their sisters in Britain, Germany and Russia is largely due to the efforts of the two-million-strong National American Woman Suffrage Association which has been campaigning for votes for women since 1869.

Anyone who wants to carry on the war against the outsiders, come with me. I can't offer you either honours or wages; I offer you hunger, thirst, forced marches, battles and death. Anyone who loves his country, follow me.

Guiseppe Garibaldi – he was defeated by the Austrians at Morrazone today, 1848.

FRENCH SETBACK AT CRÉCY

1346 An English army under Edward III has won an overwhelming, and unexpected, victory at Crécy today. This latest phase in hostilities between France and England – which the pessimists say looks set to last 100 years – opened when King Edward III, accompanied by his eldest son, Prince Edward, landed in Normandy last month. Their army sacked Caen and threatened Rouen before being pursued northwards by a large French force, estimated at around 50,000, under Philip VI. Battle was joined at Crécy-en-Ponthieu. Although numerically outnumbered by a ratio of 2 to 1, the English proved to have superior weaponry. Philip's 6000 Genoese crossbowmen were simply no match for Edward's 7000 well-trained longbowmen and the short-barrelled bombards aimed at the French ranks. For his battle performance, King Edward's 16-year-old son was awarded spurs and ostrich plumes and with them the mottoes *Homout* (Courage) and *Ich dene* (I serve).

TV TRANSMISSION IN BRITAIN

1936 The first high-definition television programmes seen in Britain were transmitted today from the BBC studios at Alexandra Palace, London, to the Radio Show at Olympia (Radiolympia). A regular service is due to open next November. Six weeks ago in New York the RCA station W2XBS started transmitting experimental high-definition television programmes.

• 1989 – MINI CELEBRATES 30 YEARS • 2012 – NEIL ARMSTRONG DIES

KRAKATOA BLOWS ITS TOP

1883 The most catastrophic volcanic eruption witnessed by man reached its climax today on the Indonesian island of Rakata. In May the 6000 ft (1800 m) high Krakatoa volcano, which has its base 1000 ft (300 m) below sea level, began to show signs of rousing from its 200-year slumber. Activity died down only to resume again in June and become more terrifying in its effects. At 10 am this morning Krakatoa erupted with a fury that was heard in Australia, more than 2200 miles (3540 km) away. Debris has been tossed 50 miles (80 km) into the atmosphere, blotting out the sun and plunging the region into darkness. Gigantic tidal waves up to 120 ft (36 m) high have devastated the coastal towns of Java and Sumatra, leaving an estimated 36,000 people dead.

IRA MURDER MOUNTBATTEN

1979 Lord Louis Mountbatten was murdered today by an IRA bomb as he and members of his family enjoyed an outing on his 30-ft (9-m) fishing boat, *Shadow V*. The bomb exploded five minutes after the party had left the picturesque harbour of Mullaghmore in the Irish Republic. Killed with the 79-year-old former admiral and viceroy of India were his grandson, Nicholas Knatchbull, 14, local boy Paul Maxwell, 17, and Lady Brabourne. Later in the morning the IRA murdered 18 British soldiers at Warrenpoint in Northern Ireland.

COKE WAR IN COLOMBIA

1989 The proposed clampdown by the Colombian government on the Medellin drug-trafficking cartel has received a blunt response. "Total and bloody war" has been declared on the government of President Virgilio Barco. The cocaine-smugglers are particularly perturbed by the reinstatement of extradition to the United States, a process which bribery and threats of violence had forced the Colombian Supreme Court to abandon. Eduardo Martinez Romero, the cartel's leading money launderer, has already been arrested as part of the clamp-down. The traffickers have repeatedly said that they would "prefer a grave in Colombia to a prison cell in the US" – not surprisingly, as the last drugs baron to head reluctantly northwards, Carlos Lehder, received a life sentence on arrival. The traffickers have offered to give up the trade in return for immunity from prosecution.

1783 Jacques Alexandre César Charles makes the first hydrogen balloon ascent.

1813 Napoleon defeats the allied army at Dresden.

1910 Thomas Edison shows "talking pictures" for the first time.

1919 Death of Louis Botha, first prime minister of South Africa.

1928 Members from 15 nations sign The Kellogg-Briand Pact, an international agreement to condemn all war as a means of settling disputes.

1951 US jets arrive in Britain to set up an air base at Greenham Common.

1975 Death of Haile Selassie, deposed emperor of Ethiopia.

BIRTHDAYS

Sam Goldwyn 1882, Co-founder of MGM.

Lyndon Baines Johnson 1908, American president following Kennedy's assassination.

Mother Teresa of Calcutta 1910, Yugoslavian-born missionary dedicated to the poor and sick.

Bernhard Langer 1957, German two-times Masters winning golfer.

• 1576 – VENETIAN PAINTER TITIAN DIES • 1859 – WORLD'S FIRST OIL WELL DRILLED

1850 Franz Liszt conducts the first performance of *Lohengrin* by his friend Richard Wagner, who has fled Germany to escape arrest for his role in the Dresden uprising.

1850 The Channel telegraph cable is finally laid between Dover and Cap Gris Nez.

1862 Garibaldi's army land at Calabria in their march to Rome.

1967 Death of Charles Darrow, American inventor of Monopoly.

1988 Death of American film director John Huston whose films include *The Maltese Falcon*.

BIRTHDAYS

Johann Wolfgang von Goethe 1749, German poet, novelist, playwright.

Count Leo Tolstoy 1828, Russian author of novels such as *War and Peace*.

Peter Fraser 1884, Scottish-born New Zealand prime minister 1940–49.

Sir Godfrey Hounsfield 1919, British inventor of the EMI medical scanner.

Lindsay Hasset 1913, Australian cricket captain.

AGE OF THE MILE

1981 Sebastian Coe proved last night that he is presiding over a golden age in middle-distance running. In the aptly named Golden Mile at the Heysel Stadium in Brussels, Coe regained the world record he had lost only two days ago to his great rival Steve Ovett. Seb slashed Ovett's time by 1.07 seconds, completing the four-lap race in an incredible 3 minutes 47.33 seconds.

KING'S AMERICAN DREAM

1963 The eloquence for which civil rights leader Martin Luther King Jnr has become renowned reached new heights today. The occasion was the interracial march on Washington, a peaceful demonstration by 200,000 people committed to the civil rights cause. Standing by the Lincoln Memorial, King gave his vision for America. "I still have a dream. It is a dream chiefly rooted in the American dream. I have a dream that one day this nation will rise up and live out the true meaning of its creed. We hold these truths to be self-evident, that all men are created equal."

THUMBS DOWN FOR THE CHALLENGE OF STEAM

1830 Inventor Peter Cooper's latest creation, a steam-driven locomotive called *Tom Thumb*, was today outstripped by the oldest kind of traction in the world – horse power. Since its inception three years ago the Baltimore and Ohio Railroad has relied on horse traction. Now it is looking to the future. On today's showing, though, the horse looks to be the more reliable of the two. After racing neck-and-neck for much of the race, the belt slipped from the loco's drum, the steam pressure dropped and the contraption slowed down. Cooper is sure that the technical hitch which handicapped *Tom Thumb*'s performance today can be overcome. Race watchers agree that *Tom Thumb* completed the race looking fresher than the horse.

• 1988 – COLLISION AT GERMAN AIR DISPLAY • 1996 – CHARLES AND DIANA DIVORCE

KATRINA DEVASTATES NEW ORLEANS

2005 Hurricane Katrina hit the Gulf coast of the USA killing 1,836 people and causing $90 billion of damage in the country's worst-ever natural disaster. The costliest hurricane in US history formed over the Bahamas, then travelled across Florida. It intensified quickly as it passed over the Gulf of Mexico, with wind speeds increasing to 175 mph (280 kmh). The worst damage was caused by widespread flooding to coastal towns. The greatest number of fatalities occurred in New Orleans where 80 per cent of the city flooded.

1835 John Batman and associates officially establish Melbourne.

1877 Death of Brigham Young, Mormon leader and founder of Salt Lake City.

1885 The first motorcycle is patented by Gottlieb Daimler in Germany.

1918 More than 6,000 British policemen go on strike for better pay.

1975 Death of Eamon de Valera, three times Irish prime minister and president from 1959–73.

1987 American actor Lee Marvin dies.

1990 The blockade of a bridge over the St Lawrence river in Canada by Mohawk Indians ends.

GANDHI COMES TO LONDON

1931 The Indian nationalist leader Mohandas Gandhi arrived in London today to attend the second Round Table Conference at St James's Palace. He is the sole representative of the Indian National Congress party. That Gandhi has agreed to call off the campaign of civil disobedience and attend the meeting is thanks largely to Lord Irwin, the former viceroy of India, who has publicly stated his commitment to India being accorded dominion status.

I do not mind what language an opera is sung in so long as it is a language I don't understand.

Edward Appleton, British physicist, 1955.

BIRTHDAYS

Maurice Maeterlink 1862, Belgian poet and playwright.

Elliot Gould 1938, American actor who starred in *M*A*S*H*.

James Hunt 1947, British world champion racing driver.

Richard Gere 1949, American actor who first rose to fame with *Yanks* and *American Gigolo*.

Michael Jackson 1958

ONE-WAY TRAFFIC AT ST LOUIS OLYMPICS

1904 Christmas came early this year for the US Olympic team. Out of a total of 23 track and field events, US athletes collected 21 gold medals. The major reason for the supremacy of the home team is that few European athletes came to St Louis – fewer than a twelfth of the competitors attending the Games were non-Americans. Apart from the cost and effort of attendance, overseas competitors were put off by the decision to make the Games part of the postponed Louisiana World Fair.

• 1831 – FIRST ELECTRIC TRANSFORMER DEMONSTRATED • 1842 – OPIUM WAR ENDS

1860 The first trains in Britain begin running.

1862 "Stonewall" Jackson leads the Confederates to victory against the Union army at the second Battle of Bull Run in Virginia during the American Civil War.

1901 The vacuum cleaner is patented by Scotsman Hubert Cecil Booth.

1937 Joe Louis flattens Britain's Tommy Farr to win the heavyweight boxing title at Madison Square Gardens in New York.

1939 Children start being evacuated from cities as war between Germany and Britain seems imminent.

1941 The Germans surround Leningrad.

BIRTHDAYS

Jacques Louis David 1748, French court painter whose paintings include *The Rape of the Sabines*.

John Gunther 1901, American author and journalist who wrote *Inside USA* and *Inside Russia Today*.

Ernest Rutherford 1908, New Zealand physicist who led the way for modern atomic science at Cambridge.

ALL FOR LOVE

30 BC Roman leader Mark Antony, has committed suicide at the court of his Egyptian lover, Cleopatra. He was 52. Antony's political demise was signalled last year with his defeat by Roman emperor Caesar Augustus at the battle of Actium. The beautiful Queen Cleopatra was the cause of the break-up of the triumvirate Antony had formed with Augustus and Lepidus (the ruler of Africa) 10 years ago. Antony's loyalty to Rome was called into question after he made gifts of land to the Egyptian queen. Cleopatra is understood to be attempting face-to-face negotiations with the resolute Augustus. If she fails to mollify him, as seems likely, she will doubtless share a similar fate to Mark Antony.

AYATOLLAH'S REGIME SHAKEN BY BOMB

1981 A wave of anti-government violence has culminated in the murder in Teheran of the president of Iran, Muhammad Ali Rajai, and his prime minister, Muhammad Javad Bahonar – victims of a bomb planted in the premier's office. The government of Ayatollah Khomeini has been subjected to a series of violent attacks since the dismissal of president Bani Sadr two months ago. The dismissal was seen as a victory for religious forces over secular politics in Iran. A speaker of the Iranian Parliament said today that it was up to the Iranian people to ensure the revolution continues as planned.

EAST-WEST HOTLINE

1963 A telephone line between the White House and the Kremlin became operational today. The agreement to have a "hotline" linking the US President with his opposite number in Moscow was struck in April. It may prove to be a lifeline, preventing delays in diplomatic communication that can lead to misunderstandings between the two super-powers – as occurred last year during the Cuban missiles crisis.

During the last few weeks I have felt that the Suez Canal was flowing through my drawing room.

Clarissa Eden, wife of British prime minister Anthony Eden, as British and French troops sailed for Suez, 1956.

THE GREAT GRACE DECLARES AT SIXTY

1908 W. G. Grace, who celebrated his sixtieth birthday last month, has decided to retire from first-class cricket. In a first-class career spanning 43 years, Grace has scored a phenomenal 54,896 runs, notched up 126 centuries, knocked 2879 wickets and grabbed 871 catches. Such is his love of the game that Dr Grace intends to continue playing in minor cricket. His enormous success as a cricketer, and indeed his cricketing longevity, is put down to the solid technique instilled in him by his indomitable mother. A stickler for the straight bat, she coached him out of making loose shots during his formative years in county cricket.

MIXED REVIEWS FOR WEILL'S LATEST

1928 The taste of the critics and the Berlin public are poles apart if the reception given to Kurt Weill's *Threepenny Opera* is any guide. The audience loved its jazz rhythms but Berlin's most influential critics hated it, especially the libretto by Bertold Brecht. Any good words were reserved for the music.

DIANA DIES IN PARIS CAR CRASH

1997 Diana, Princess of Wales, has been killed in a car crash in Paris. The accident happened after the princess left the Ritz Hotel in Paris with her companion Dodi Fayed, son of Harrods owner, Mohamed Al-Fayed. Dodi Fayed and the car's chauffeur were also killed in the crash which happened in a tunnel under the Place de l'Alma in the centre of the city. The princess' Mercedes was apparently being pursued at high speed by photographers on motorbikes when it hit a pillar and smashed into a wall. Tributes to the princess have been pouring in from around the world.

1688 Death of John Bunyan, English author of *The Pilgrim's Progress*.

1900 Coca-Cola goes on sale in Britain.

1957 Malaya achieves independence from Britain.

1962 The former British possessions of Trinidad and Tobago become independent.

1963 Death of Georges Braque, French Cubist painter.

1972 US swimmer Mark Spitz wins five gold medals in the Munich Olympics.

1994 IRA announces a "complete cessation of military activities".

BIRTHDAYS

Caligula 12 AD, Roman emperor remembered for his murderous reign.

Maria Montessori 1870, Italian educationist.

Sir Bernard Lovell 1913, English astronomer.

Van Morrison 1945, Irish-born international singer whose songs include "Moondance" and "Gloria".

Edwin Moses 1955, American athlete who made a world record when he ran in the 400 metre hurdles in 1976 – his first Olympics.

• 1422 – DEATH OF ENGLISH KING HENRY V • 1900 – COCA-COLA ON SALE IN BRITAIN

SEPTEMBER

SUN KING ECLIPSED

1715 France's Sun King, Louis XIV, died today at 76. He had ruled France for 72 years. A cultural extravaganza blossomed for 20 years at Louis' magnificent palace at Versailles, accompanied by an economic boom and French domination of the world stage. However, Louis' brutal suppression of the Protestant Huguenots was a disaster, and a long succession of wars sapped France's strength. His second wife, Madame de Maintenon, persuaded him that his sufferings were God's punishment for the blood he had spilled. On his deathbed he counselled his five-year-old heir Louis XV to avoid wars and extravagance.

1920 The French create the state of Lebanon, with Beirut as the capital.

1923 A massive earthquake in Japan kills more than 300,000 people.

1948 Chairman Mao sets up a provisional government in China.

1951 The Anzus Treaty, a mutual defence treaty between Australia, New Zealand and the United States, is signed.

1969 Libyan Colonel Muammar al-Gaddafi seizes power after the monarchy is overthrown.

BIRTHDAYS

Amilcare Ponchielli 1834, Italian composer of the opera *La Gioconda*.

Sir Roger Casement 1864, Irish nationalist and British diplomat, sentenced to death by the British after he attempted to arrange for Irish World War One prisoners in Germany to take part with him in a Republican rebellion.

Edgar Rice Burroughs 1875, American novelist who created the fictional character Tarzan.

Rocky Marciano 1923, US heavyweight boxer.

FISCHER REELS IN TITLE

1972 Bobby Fischer became the first American world chess champion today. The temperamental 29-year-old boy wonder from Brooklyn finally triumphed over defending champion Boris Spassky of the USSR after a marathon two-month struggle, which also established Fischer as one of the world's unreasonable people. Fischer, who was US champion at 14 and an international grandmaster at 15, sailed undefeated through the qualifying matches to face Spassky, and then argued with the champion over petty details for months before agreeing to play. The showdown in Reykjavik in Iceland drew avid media attention – Fischer's constant tantrums made riveting viewing. The two men played in an atmosphere boiling with resentment, yet the chess was brilliant.

BLIND, DEAF AND DUMB BUT BRILLIANT

1904 A young woman who has been both blind and deaf since the age of two graduated from college today, with honours. Helen Keller, 24, now holds a doctor's degree from Radcliffe College in Cambridge, Massachusetts. When she was an infant a brain fever left her in a silent, dark world. She was confined to hysterics, screams and tantrums until an inspired teacher, Anne Mansfield Macy, helped her to read braille and write using a special typewriter. Two years ago Helen published her autobiography, *The Story of My Life* – but her story is far from over.

• 1939 – GERMANY INVADES POLAND • 1951 – BRITAIN'S FIRST SUPERMARKET OPENS

SEPTEMBER 2

1834 Death of Thomas Telford, Scottish engineer and bridge builder.

1865 Boundary disputes end between the British settlers and the Maori Kingitanga in New Zealand.

1937 Death of Baron Pierre de Coubertin, founder of the modern Olympic Games.

1942 The German SS destroys the Warsaw Ghetto, killing 50,000 Jews.

1958 South Africa's new premier Hendrik Verwoerd promises to strengthen apartheid.

1976 The European Court of Human Rights says that the British torture Ulster detainees.

1988 Chilean exiles led by Salvador Allende's daughter return to Santiago.

BIRTHDAYS

John Howard 1726, English prison reformer who campaigned for sanitary improvements and wages for gaolers.

Jimmy Connors 1952, American tennis player.

Lennox Lewis 1965, British former undisputed World Heavyweight champion boxer.

VIET MINH BOSS GOES FOR BROKE

1945 Nationalist leader Ho Chi Minh proclaimed the independent Democratic Republic of Vietnam in Hanoi today, with himself as its first president. Ho's Viet Minh guerrilla army marched into the capital last week when the Japanese withdrew from Vietnam after four years of occupation. Ho and other nationalists formed the Communist Viet Minh – the League for the Independence of Vietnam – in 1941, and have fought alone against the Japanese. Trained in Moscow, Ho was a founding member of the French Communist Party and founded the Indo-Chinese Communist Party in 1930. The British arrested him in Shanghai, and he plagued the French colonial government in Vietnam before the war. Ho Chi Minh has wide public support, but France has no intention of giving up Indochina and is unlikely to recognize the new republic.

WORLD'S WORST WAR ENDS

1945 Japan has formally surrendered to Supreme Allied Commander General Douglas MacArthur. The frock-coated Japanese foreign minister signed the unconditional surrender announced by Emperor Hirohito last month after US atomic bombs obliterated the cities of Hiroshima and Nagasaki. The capitulation is almost as humiliating for Japan as her defeat – according to the martial code of *bushido*, only cowards surrender; warriors choose.

WARRING DERVISHES MOWN DOWN AT WILL

1898 General Sir Herbert Kitchener's 25,000-man Anglo-Egyptian army slaughtered a huge Mahdist dervish army at Omdurman in Sudan today. At least 10,000 dervish warriors were killed. They fought bravely but were simply mown down by Kitchener's Maxim machine guns. Kitchener lost 500 men. Thus ends 14 years of dervish rule after the Mahdi, Muhammad Ahmad, massacred General Charles Gordon and his entire garrison at Khartoum in 1885.

PRUSSIAN BLUES

1792 More than a thousand people died in Paris today as fear of the advancing Prussian army degenerated into a drunken orgy of killing. The mob set out to execute alleged traitors and royalists, still held in prison. Prisons were sacked and the inmates ruthlessly hacked to death. Most of the victims have been ordinary criminals. The rioting continues tonight.

• 1858 – *YELLOW ROSE OF TEXAS* COPYRIGHTED • 1973 – J. R. R. TOLKIEN DIES

LIONHEART GRABS ENGLISH THRONE

1189 Richard the Lionheart received his father's crown at Westminster today and became King Richard I of England. Richard's first royal act was to free his mother, Eleanor of Aquitaine, from the tower where King Henry II imprisoned her 16 years ago for supporting their warring sons in a rebellion against their father. Richard, Duke of Aquitaine in France, rebelled again, forcing the ailing Henry to conclude a humiliating peace earlier this year. Henry's favourite son, John, was amongst the rebels, and in July Henry died, brokenhearted. Richard, a petty and quarrelsome man, is looking to his new kingdom to finance a third Christian crusade to the Holy Land.

1650 The Scots are defeated by the English at Dunbar.

1651 The army of Charles II of England is beaten by Oliver Cromwell's army in a battle at Worcester.

1939 New Zealand, Australia, Britain and France declare war on Germany.

1950 The first world driving championship is won by Nino Farina of Italy at the Monza Grand Prix.

1969 Ho Chi Minh, president of North Vietnam during the Vietnam War, dies after a heart attack.

1976 The US spacecraft *Viking II* lands on Mars.

1980 The opening night of the tragedy *Macbeth* at London's Old Vic, starring Peter O'Toole, receives deep criticism.

BIRTHDAYS

Matthew Boulton 1728, English engineer who invented and manufactured the steam engine with James Watt.

Sir Frank MacFarlane Burnet 1899, Australian virologist who was awarded the Order of Merit in recognition of his work on diseases such as influenza, polio and cholera.

AMERICA UNITED IN STATE OF FREEDOM

1783 Britain recognized an independent United States of America today. The Treaty of Paris marks the end of the American Revolution following two years of negotiation. In an unprecedented war, Britain sent an army of 60,000 to fight a well-armed people on their own ground. However France, Spain and Holland sided with the rebels. The decisive blow came when rebel commander-in-chief George Washington trapped Lord Cornwallis's army in Yorktown, forcing him to surrender. The war lingered on, but the colonies were already severed from the empire. The new nation has emerged from its revolution with a burgeoning sense of freedom and purpose.

CHECHEN SEPARATISTS HOLD SCHOOL HOSTAGE

2004 Russian forces stormed a school in Beslan, North Ossetia, where Chechen separatists were holding more than 1,000 people hostage. The Islamic terrorists had taken the school two days earlier, demanding an end to the Second Chechen War. The hostages were held in a small gym and surrounded by mines and bombs. A series of explosions shook the school, leading to a devastating fire and a chaotic gunbattle as the Russian security forces stormed in. There were 186 children among the 331 people who died. The government has been criticised for its ineffectual negotiations, its use of excessive force and its repression and censorship of the media.

• 1658 – OLIVER CROMWELL DIES • 1930 – FIRST NONSTOP FLIGHT FROM PARIS TO NEW YORK

1797 A French army coup disposes of British-backed royalists in Paris.

1821 Tsar Alexander closes Alaska to shipping.

1870 Napoleon Bonaparte's nephew, Emperor Napoleon III, is deposed and the Third Republic is declared in France.

1923 *Shenandoah*, the first rigid airship to be built in the United States, is launched.

1948 Queen Wilhelmina of The Netherlands abdicates.

1989 Death of Georges Simenon, Belgian novelist of world-wide acclaim who created the fictional detective Maigret.

2014 Death of Joan Rivers, US actress, writer and comedian, aged 81.

BIRTHDAYS

Dawn Fraser 1937, Australian swimmer and one of the greatest ever – she broke the 100 metres freestyle record nine successive times.

Tom Watson 1949, American golfer and five-times winner of the British Open, also winning the US Masters in 1982.

KIROV STAR SEEKS ARTISTIC FREEDOM

1970 Leningrad's famous Kirov Ballet, currently in London, lost its brightest star today when Natalia Makarova defected. Widely considered the perfect ballerina, she told reporters today that Russian ballet is stifled by politics and she is seeking artistic freedom in the west. The Kirov's artistic director, Konstantin Sergeyev, is reported to be furious at losing Makarova and is threatening to resign.

TEENAGER PUNISHED

1987 Mathias Rust, the West German teenager who flew his light plane from Poland straight through the Russian air defence system and landed in Moscow's Red Square on May 28, will have plenty of time to think about his extraordinary prank. Today a Soviet court sentenced him to four years in a labour camp.

How can you bear to go further, selling products injurious to others in order to fulfil your insatiable desire?

Lin Ze-xu, Chinese imperial commissioner, in a letter to Queen Victoria complaining about the opium trade, 1839.

MAKE LIGHT WORK

1881 The best-lit factory in America opened in New York today. The Edison Electric Light Company's new "central power station" in Pearl Street generates enough electricity to light up 7000 of Thomas A. Edison's new incandescent lamps. Edison's carbon-filament lamp burns for more than 40 hours and is cheaply replaced. The company is now offering electricity for sale – power cables lead from the new plant's 900-horsepower steam-driven generators to the premises of 85 paying clients, and there is plenty of spare capacity.

• 1966 – JACK BRABHAM WINS THE ITALIAN GRAND PRIX AT MONZA

BLACKEST SEPTEMBER AT MUNICH OLYMPICS

1972 Eleven Israeli athletes died when Palestinian terrorists struck at the Munich Olympics early today. Eight hooded Black September terrorists broke into the Olympic Village and attacked the sleeping Israelis in their dormitories. Two athletes died in a hail of bullets while 18 escaped, and the remaining nine were taken hostage. The Games were stopped and 12,000 police surrounded the village. The

terrorists demanded the release of 200 Palestinians held in Israel and safe passage out of Germany. The German leaders agreed and the gang and their hostages were taken to Munich airport. In a tragic blunder police sharpshooters opened fire, and all nine athletes were killed in the ensuing battle, as well as four terrorists and one policeman. Three of the gang were captured and one escaped. The Games will continue, albeit under a cloud.

DEATH FIRE HOT ON HEELS OF PLAGUE

1666 The massive, city-wide fire that has raged in London for a number of days started at Pudding Lane bakery in London's East End. The flames quickly spread next door to a tar store, which exploded, igniting the neighbourhood. The next morning, as fire gripped the city, thousands of families fled their homes to seek safety in small boats on the River Thames and in the fields outside the city. Today the blaze was at last halted by Navy teams who blew up a swathe of buildings in the path of the flames. More than 13,000 homes and 90 churches have been destroyed, and 400 acres (162 hectares) of the city, from the Tower to the Temple, are reduced to smouldering rubble – yet only nine lives were lost. London was still reeling from last year's great plague, which cost 75,000 lives.

1569 Death of Pieter Breughel the Elder, Netherlandish painter.

1800 French troops occupying Malta surrender to the British.

1922 American aviator James Doolittle makes the first American coast-to-coast flight.

1969 Death of American blues singer and guitarist Josh White.

1980 The world's longest road tunnel is opened in Switzerland between Goshenen and Airolo.

2008 Both the North-west Passage and the North-east Passage are clear of sea ice for the first time in recorded history.

Giacomo Meyerbeer 1791, German composer, notably of operas such as *Les Huguenots*, *L'Africaine*.

Jesse James 1847, American outlaw.

Darryl F. Zanuck 1902, American film producer.

Arthur Koestler 1905, Hungarian-born writer, best known for the novel *Darkness at Noon*.

Freddie Mercury 1946, British lead singer of the band Queen.

• 1991 – THE USSR CEASES TO EXIST • 1997 – MOTHER TERESA OF CALCUTTA DIES

1879 The first British telephone exchange opens in Lombard Street, London.

1936 British aviator Beryl Markham flies solo across the Atlantic.

1940 King Carol II of Romania is forced to abdicate by pro-German Ion Antonescu.

1968 The kingdom of Swaziland in Southern Africa gains independence.

1987 The historic Venice regatta is held without the city's gondoliers, who are on strike to protest against the damage to the city caused by powerboats.

1988 Eleven-year-old Thomas Gregory from London is the youngest to swim the English Channel.

2007 Italian tenor Luciano Pavarotti dies, aged 71.

BIRTHDAYS

Marquis de Lafayette 1757, French statesman and soldier who fought with the American colonists for independence, and was a major figure in the French Revolution.

Joseph Kennedy 1888, American founder of the dynasty that gave rise to the first Catholic American president.

SOVIETS ADMIT THEIR JETS DOWNED KAL 007

1983 Soviet military chiefs called a highly unusual press conference in Moscow today to explain why a Soviet jet fighter shot down a South Korean airliner last week, with the loss of 269 lives. The Soviets maintain that flight KAL 007 was on a spying mission for the US. The night flight was far off course – it was shot down near secret Soviet military installations on the island of Sakhalin off Siberia, north of Japan. The Soviets say it refused to answer signals and was flying without navigation lights. Tonight the Soviet leaders expressed sympathy for the bereaved.

Drugs have taught an entire generation of American kids the metric system.

P. J. O'Rourke, US journalist: today President Bush announced he would halve the US drug problem, 1989.

ARCHITECT OF APARTHEID

1966 Coloureds danced in the streets of Cape Town today after South African prime minister Dr Hendrik Verwoerd was assassinated in parliament. The grand architect of the white racist apartheid system was stabbed four times in the chest by a white parliamentary messenger wielding a stiletto – because the government "didn't do enough for whites". Since 1950, Verwoerd, 65, a socio-psychologist, has sub-divided the country's 73 per cent black majority into ethno-linguistic minorities, each with its pseudo-independent "homeland" (totalling only 13 per cent of the country), effectively exporting them from South Africa and leaving the whites as the majority. Millions of blacks have been forcibly relocated to the poverty-stricken homelands, which serve as cheap labour pools. Untold numbers now live illegally in what used to be their own country, at the mercy of the police. The hard-line minister of justice and police, B. J. Vorster, will succeed Dr Verwoerd.

• 1566 – DEATH OF SULEIMAN THE MAGNIFICENT • 1914 – BATTLE OF THE MARNE BEGINS

TUTU IS ARCHBISHOP

1986 Bishop Desmond Tutu, the black general secretary of the South African Council of Churches, was today enthroned as Archbishop of Cape Town, the leader of two million South African Anglicans. He is the church's first black leader. Tutu was awarded the Nobel Peace Prize in 1984 for his opposition to South Africa's racist apartheid regime. He has condemned the state of emergency imposed in June to suppress the uprising in the black townships, and defies the emergency laws in calling for economic sanctions against South Africa and for foreign investors to leave.

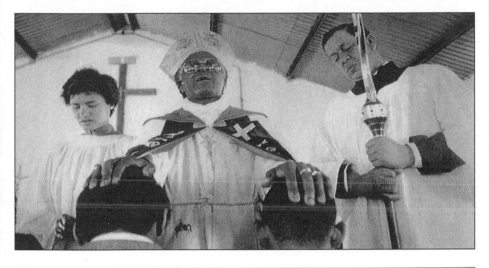

This is the historic hour when our air force delivers its blows right into the enemy's heart.

Hermann Goering, Nazi field marshal, unleashing the Luftwaffe bombers on British cities, 1940.

MOON FINALLY GOES TO THE DARK SIDE

1978 Keith Moon, rock drummer with The Who, died today in his London flat of an overdose of drugs prescribed to combat his alcohol problem. The stick-twirling virtuoso has been described as one of the most talented of contemporary rock drummers. Moon and the band's guitarist Pete Townshend are famed for their on-stage violence – most performances end with guitars and drums smashed in a fury of destruction.

1812 Napoleon's forces defeat the Russians at the Battle of Borodino.

1848 The Vienna assembly abolishes serfdom.

1901 The Boxer Uprising in China ends with the signing of the Peace of Peking.

1910 Death of William Holman Hunt, English Pre-Raphaelite painter.

1910 Polish chemist Marie Curie announces she has isolated pure radium.

1940 Romania returns southern Dobruja to Bulgaria.

1981 Death of Christy Brown, severely handicapped Irish author of the autobiographical *Down All our Days*.

BIRTHDAYS

Elizabeth I, 1533, English monarch, daughter of Anne Boleyn and Henry VIII.

Elia Kazan 1909, Turkish-born Broadway director who co-founded the Actors Studio, which trained many stars.

Anthony Quayle 1913, English actor of stage and screen.

Buddy Holly 1936, American rock singer killed in an aircrash, aged 23.

• 1571 – TURKISH OTTOMAN FLEET IS ROUTED • 1940 – FIRST NIGHT OF THE BLITZ

1900 More than 5,000 lives are lost when a hurricane strikes the city of Galveston in Texas, USA.

1916 US President Woodrow Wilson promises women the vote.

1968 Britain's Virginia Wade beats Billie Jean King to win the first US Open Tennis Championships.

1974 US President Gerald R. Ford pardons Richard Nixon for his part in the Watergate affair.

1990 Northern and Southern Korean delegates meet on the border for the first talks in 45 years.

2002 Pete Sampras wins a record 14th Grand Slam title at the US Open, Flushing Meadow.

BIRTHDAYS

Richard I 1157, King of England known as "the Lion Heart" who began a crusade in 1190.

Antonin Dvorak 1841, Czech composer.

Siegfried Sassoon 1886, English war poet.

Hendrik Frensch Verwoerd 1901, South African prime minister and pioneer of apartheid.

Peter Sellers 1925, great English comic actor.

MICHELANGELO'S DAVID FACES MODERN GOLIATHS

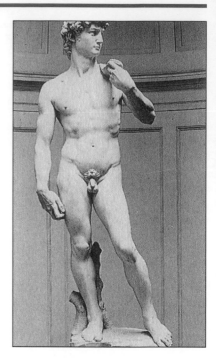

1504 Florence unveiled a magnificent symbol of its independence from its powerful neighbours today. The 29-year-old Florentine sculptor Michelangelo Buonarotti allowed nobody to see his enormous 13-ft (4-m) marble statue, which has taken him three years to carve, until it was unveiled. It is a wonderful figure of David, standing relaxed, his sling over his shoulder, about to face Goliath in battle. The statue was to have adorned the facade of the Cathedral of Florence, which commissioned it, but Michelangelo and the grand council of the new Florentine republic have placed it instead at the main entrance to the Palazzo Vecchio, the seat of the city's government, where its message is clear.

MONTREAL GIVES IN

1760 French forces at Montreal surrendered to British General Jeffrey Amherst today, ending 70 years of conflict during which the American colonies were caught up in Europe's wars. Britain declared war on France in 1756 as part of the Seven Years' War in Europe, and suffered a series of defeats in America until General Amherst's forces overwhelmed the French fortress at Louisbourg in 1758. General Amherst went on to conquer Ticonderoga and Crown Point, opening the way to Montreal. General James Wolfe then defeated the French garrison at Quebec, with both General Wolfe and the French commander-in-chief the Marquis de Montcalm dying in the battle. Today General Amherst attacked Montreal from three directions, forcing the French to surrender.

PENGUIN CHARGED FOR *LADY CHATTERLEY*

1960 A bid by Penguin Books to publish D. H. Lawrence's notorious novel *Lady Chatterley's Lover* has brought the publishers a charge of public obscenity. Penguin will stand trial at London's Old Bailey next month. The book was first published privately in Italy in 1928. Lord Chatterley, an industrialist paralyzed below the waist in the war, symbolizes the impotence of the upper classes; his wife Constance seeks solace in the arms of Mellors, His Lordship's gamekeeper. The prosecution says it contains 13 sexually explicit episodes with heavy use of certain Anglo-Saxon terms. Penguin, however, argue differently, saying the book is great art.

• 1888 – FIRST ENGLISH LEAGUE FOOTBALL • 1943 – ITALY SURRENDERS TO THE ALLIES

RACE STIRS RIOTS IN LONDON

1958 Notting Hill in north London has been torn by three nights of race riots, with serious injuries and more than 150 arrests. The fighting was provoked by whites – police say extreme right-wing activists were at work here. It started when white youths beat up five blacks, leading to petrol bombings and street battles between gangs of up to 2000. Meanwhile in Nottingham a television director was accused of starting a race riot by reconstructing a previous clash between black and white youths. The mock fight exploded into battle. A magistrate today jailed five rioters – and condemned the media.

ISRAELI WHIZKID HACKED PENTAGON SECRETS

1991 During the Gulf War, a teenager hacked into Pentagon computers to find out how top-secret Patriot anti-missiles worked. When he tired of browsing military secrets he turned to Visa, finding his way into the customer files. He provided details to an international network of hackers, who promptly went on a spending spree. Six of them were arrested in North America, and named 18-year-old Deri Schriebman of Israel as the source. Today he showed awed detectives how he did it, as well as how to make free long-distance telephone calls. "He's the most talented hacker we've ever seen," experts said.

STUNTED ARTIST FELLED BY LOW LIFE HE PAINTED

1901 Henri de Toulouse-Lautrec, Post-Impressionist artist and chronicler of Paris low-life, died today following a paralytic stroke. He was 36. Toulouse-Lautrec was a master draftsman and observer. Born an aristocrat, he smashed both thighs in a fall from a horse when he was 14, and bone disease left him horribly stunted. The young Toulouse-Lautrec haunted the Montmartre red-light district in Paris and produced stylish Art Nouveau posters for nightclubs and performers, and charming, if cynical, paintings of his friends the Montmartre prostitutes.

1513 King James IV, King of Scotland, dies at the Battle of Flodden Field.

1911 The first airmail service in Britain begins, operating between Hendon and Windsor.

1948 North Korea claims its independence.

1963 Twenty-seven-year-old Jim Clark from Scotland is the world's youngest motor racing champion, driving Colin Campbell's Lotus.

1978 Eighteen-year-old Czech tennis player Martina Navratilova defects to the West and asks the US for political asylum.

BIRTHDAYS

Cardinal de Richelieu 1585, French statesman and chief minister to Louis XIII from 1624, who crushed all opposition to the monarchy.

Cesare Pavese 1908, Italian poet and novelist who was imprisoned for his anti-fascist views in 1935.

Otis Redding 1941, American singer and songwriter known.

Hugh Grant 1960, English actor famous for his performance in *Four Weddings and a Funeral*.

• 1087 – DEATH OF WILLIAM THE CONQUEROR • 1976 – MAO TSE-TUNG DIES

1919 The allies sign the Treaty of Saint Germain with Austria at the Paris Peace conference.

1945 Nazi collaborator Vidkun Quisling, premier of Norway during World War II, is sentenced to death.

1962 Australian Rod Laver completes the Grand Slam after winning the US Tennis Championships.

1965 Yale University publishes a map showing that the Vikings discovered America in the 11th century.

1979 The Lancaster House conference on the future of Rhodesia opens.

1983 Death of Balthazar Johannes Vorster, former pro-Nazi prime minister of South Africa.

BIRTHDAYS

Sir John Soane 1753, English neo-classical architect.

Mungo Park 1771, Scottish surgeon who explored the true course of the River Niger in Africa.

Robert Wise 1914, American film director whose productions include *West Side Story*.

Arnold Palmer 1929, American golfing champion.

PICASSO'S PICTURE OF PAIN COMES HOME TO SPAIN

1981 *Guernica*, Pablo Picasso's picture of pain, returned to Spain today after four decades in exile. *Guernica* is Picasso's vision of the appalling destruction of the Basque capital by German bombers in 1937 during the Spanish civil war. In 1940 Picasso sent the painting to New York for safekeeping during the war, and later refused to allow it to be shown in Spain until General Franco's Fascist rule ended and democracy was restored. Picasso died, in 1973, before that happened. Today his masterpiece took its rightful place in the Prado Museum in Madrid.

CONGRESS BACKS MAHATMA GANDHI

1920 The Indian National Congress voted today to adopt Mahatma Gandhi's campaign of non-cooperation with the British colonial government. "Non-cooperation is our only weapon," he said, and promised the campaign would lead to victory within a year. He has managed to unite the rival Hindu and Muslim parties in protest.

WHAM SLAM DANKE MAM

1988 Steffi Graf, the 19-year-old West German tennis star, was today the third woman in history to win the Grand Slam – the Australian, French, Wimbledon and US open singles titles in the same year. Graf beat Gabriela Sabatini 6-3, 3-6, 6-1 to win the US Open. Last year she won 11 of her 13 tournaments, 75 of 77 matches and the French Open. This year she lost only one set in the entire Grand Slam – the second set against Sabatini today.

• 1989 – HUNGARY LIFTS RESTRICTIONS ON ITS BORDER WITH THE WEST

NAZIS FLEE AS US TROOPS ENTERS GERMANY

1944 With the Nazis in retreat throughout Europe, the first Allied forces entered Germany today when the US First Army under General Omar Bradley crossed the German border at Eupen. Bradley's forces were with the Free French soldiers who liberated Paris on August 25. Last week British and US troops freed Brussels and Liège in Belgium and advanced on the Siegfried Line, Germany's main defence. The Line is under heavy US assault in the south near Nancy, the lynchpin in Adolf Hitler's southern defences. German soldiers are fleeing en masse.

CROMWELL SOAKS IRELAND IN BLOOD

1649 Oliver Cromwell today had 1500 Irish rebels put to the sword. When the city of Drogheda rejected his offer to surrender, Cromwell's Roundhead troops sacked the city. Ireland has been in turmoil since the insurrection of 1641. The English Civil War left Parliament on a weak footing, with the Royalist Marquis of Ormond controlling most Irish fortresses. He rebelled, claiming the exiled Charles II as king. Cromwell landed near Dublin with 16,000 troops, and his terror tactics have turned the tables. Today's massacre has left the remaining Royalist strongholds anxious to surrender.

AMERICA UNDER SIEGE

2001 The United States has become the victim of the worst terrorist attack ever launched. A hijacked American Airlines Boeing 767 crashed into the North Tower of the World Trade Center in New York, killing all passengers and causing an enormous explosion. Fifteen minutes later, a second hijacked plane crashed into the South Tower. A third plane was flown at the Pentagon in Washington and a fourth crashed in Pennsylvania after the hijackers were overpowered. Both towers of the World Trade Center collapsed and the number of dead has been estimated at 3,000.

1777 Washington's troops defeated at The Battle of Brandywine Creek in the American War of Independence.

1948 Death of Muhammed Ali Jinnah, first governor-general of Pakistan.

1950 Death of Jan Smuts, the Boer guerrilla leader who became a British field marshal and a world statesman.

1971 Former Soviet premier Nikita Khrushchev dies, aged 77.

1987 Pete Tosh, Jamaican reggae star and former member of The Wailers, is shot dead.

2003 Swedish foreign minister Anna Lindh is murdered.

BIRTHDAYS

James Thompson 1700, Scottish poet who wrote "Rule Britannia".

D. H. Lawrence 1885, British novelist who examined human sexuality and social conditions in industrial society.

Ferdinand Marcos 1917, Filipino president whose corrupt rule came to an end when he was deposed.

• 1915 – OPENING OF THE FIRST BRITISH WOMEN'S INSTITUTE

1878 Cleopatra's Needle, the obelisk of Thothimes III, is erected on London's Thames Embankment.

1910 The world's first policewoman is appointed by the Los Angeles Police Department.

1935 American millionaire Howard Hughes achieves an aviation record.

1936 British tennis champion Fred Perry becomes the first non-American winner of the US Tennis championships.

1953 Nikita Khrushchev is elected first secretary of the Soviet Communist Party.

2005 Israel completes its withdrawal from the Gaza Strip after 38 years of occupation.

BIRTHDAYS

Herbert Henry Asquith 1852, British Liberal Prime Minister.

Louis MacNeice 1907, Irish poet, playwright and broadcaster.

Jesse Owens 1913, American track and field athlete who won four gold medals at the Berlin Olympics in 1936.

Hans Zimmer 1957, Oscar-winning German film score composer.

POLICE BRUTALIZE BIKO

1977 The South African Black Consciousness activist Steve Biko has died after six days in police detention. There is little doubt that he was beaten to death and the news has sparked international outrage. Biko, 30, is the latest in a long line of deaths in custody. He was detained under Emergency powers in Port Elizabeth and interrogated for five days. Guards found him unconscious in his cell yesterday, foaming at the mouth, and he was then driven 750 miles (1207 km) to Pretoria, naked and handcuffed, to die in a prison hospital.

RELIEF WALTZES IN TO SAVE VIENNA

1683 The two-month siege of Vienna ended today when the Turkish Ottoman army surrounding the city was routed by a European relief force. Grand vizier Kara Mustafa had led his army into Hungary and then turned towards Vienna, the main Christian bastion against Muslim Ottoman expansion. However, poor tactics cost Mustafa the battle, opening the way for a Christian attack on the Ottoman empire.

WALKER'S RUIN

1860 William Walker, American filibuster and ex-president of Nicaragua, was shot today by a firing squad in the Honduras. Walker, 36, a soldier of fortune, landed in the Honduras last month on a military escapade, but was captured by government forces, court-martialled and sentenced to death. Three years ago, Walker took advantage of a civil war in Nicaragua to seize control and set himself up as dictator. But he argued with his business backers, who had him overthrown and expelled.

• 1953 – JFK AND JACQUELINE LEE BOUVIER MARRY • 1974 – HAILE SELASSIE DEPOSED

PEACE IN THE MIDDLE EAST

1993 In a ceremony on the lawn of the White House, Israeli premier Yitzhak Rabin and PLO leader Yassir Arafat have signed a peace accord after months of secret negotiations. President Clinton was there to host the ceremony, which was attended by 3,000 dignitaries. The agreement makes provision for a transition to complete Palestinian autonomy in the Gaza Strip and West Bank. The accord, however, has many dissenters.

AIDS IS GLOBAL

1985 The World Health Organization announced in Geneva today that AIDS is now a worldwide epidemic. While virtually every major drugs company has joined the race to find an effective treatment, the WHO is coordinating a global AIDS prevention and education effort. But many traditional societies that are now affected have strong taboos against the open discussion needed, and even Western societies resist the implications.

1907 The British liner *Lusitania* arrives in New York at the end of her maiden voyage.

1955 Little Richard records a sanitized version of "Tutti Frutti" in LA.

1957 The 1998th performance of *The Mousetrap* makes it UK's longest-running play.

1970 In Mexico for the World Cup, England football captain Bobby Moore is accused of stealing a diamond bracelet.

1989 A British banking computer error gives customers £2 billion ($3.7 billion) in just half an hour.

WOLFE SCALES NEW HEIGHTS

1759 A British expedition today defeated the French forces at Quebec. James Wolfe, the young general who led the attack, was killed in the battle – but he lived long enough to hear that he had won. The French commander, the Marquis de Montcalm, was fatally wounded. Wolfe led 5000 men up the St Lawrence River, intending to meet up with General Amherst's land forces, but Amherst did not arrive and Wolfe continued alone. He laid siege to Quebec in May, but was unable to break the French resistance until today, when he and his men scaled the cliffs behind Quebec and surprised the French on the Plains of Abraham. Wolfe has died a hero – Quebec is the key prize in the French and Indian war, now in its third year.

PROTEST FOR EQUALITY

1989 South Africa's biggest anti-apartheid demonstration in 30 years took place today in Cape Town. Twenty thousand people of all races marched to the City Hall in protest against the police killings of 23 protesters during the whites-only election last week.

People think we do not understand our black and coloured countrymen. But there is a special relationship between us.

Elize Botha, wife of South African president P. W. Botha, 1988.

• 1598 – KING PHILIP II OF SPAIN DIES • 1788 – NEW YORK IS FEDERAL CAPITAL OF THE US

1791 Louis XVI swears allegiance to the French constitution.

1803 British General Lake captures Delhi in India.

1960 The Organization of Petroleum Exporting Countries (OPEC) is created by Iran, Iraq, Kuwait, Saudi Arabia, and Venezuela.

1962 Distillers Company agrees to pay £14 million ($26 million) compensation to thalidomide victims.

1975 Elizabeth Ann Bayley Seton, canonized by Pope Paul VI, becomes the first American saint.

1988 On route to Sydney, a six-man expedition arrives in New Delhi in a London taxi; its meter is running at London rates and shows a fare of £13,200 ($24,300).

BIRTHDAYS

Baron von Humboldt 1769, German scientist who explored Central and South America.

Charles Dana Gibson 1867, American artist who created the Gibson Girl.

Jack Hawkins 1910, British actor whose films include *The Bridge on the River Kwai*.

TRAGIC BUFFALO SLAYING

1901 US president William McKinley died early this morning in Buffalo, New York, eight days after being shot by an anarchist. He was 58. Vice-President Theodore Roosevelt took the oath this evening. McKinley was greeting visitors at the Pan-American Exposition in Buffalo when Leon Czolgosz, a young Pole, shot him twice in the stomach at point-blank range. President for five years, McKinley followed a foreign policy that turned the US into a world imperial power. He annexed Hawaii, conquered Spain in a two-year war, winning Puerto Rico, Guam and the Philippines, and sent troops to China to quell the Boxer Rebellion. At 43, Roosevelt is the youngest president yet. He returned a hero from the war in Cuba as a leader of the Rough Riders and was elected Governor of New York.

LUNAR LANDING

1959 Man reached out and made contact with the moon today. *Lunik II*, a Soviet spacecraft, crash-landed on the moon after a two-day journey. It sent back a stream of scientific data during the trip. The Soviets are preparing a further space shot, *Lunik III*, set to fly round the moon and photograph the "dark side" which no man has yet seen.

LIFE TAKES A FATAL TWIST

1927 "Goodbye, my friends, I go to glory," the American dancer Isadora Duncan called out as she set off for a drive near Nice in France. Seconds later she was dead. The end of her shawl had caught in the rear wheel of her Bugatti sports car, breaking her neck as the car pulled off. She was 49. Isadora Duncan revolutionized the world of ballet, winning worldwide acclaim for her free, barefoot interpretations of classics. She largely inspired Serge Diaghilev's spectacular Paris Ballets Russes.

• 1851 – DEATH OF THE DUKE OF WELLINGTON • 1868 – FIRST RECORDED HOLE IN ONE

DEFECTOR POISONED

1978 A Bulgarian defector has died in hospital in London four days after being stabbed with a poisoned umbrella tip. Georgi Markov was a broadcaster on the BBC's foreign service. He was standing at a bus stop on Tuesday evening when he was jabbed in the leg from behind. He never saw his assailant. Later he collapsed in a coma and did not recover consciousness.

1821 San Salvador declares its independence.

1859 Death of Isambard Kingdom Brunel, the great British engineer.

1871 The Army and Navy Cooperative begins the first mail order service to meet the needs of its members in Britain and abroad.

1928 Britain's first robot is demonstrated at the Model Engineering Exhibition in London by inventors Captain Rickards and A. H. Renfell.

1966 Britain's first nuclear submarine, HMS *Resolution*, was launched by the Queen Mother.

1975 Civil war begins in Beirut between the Christians and Muslims.

WATERGATE BURGLARS ARE NIXON AIDES

1972 Seven men were indicted in Washington today in connection with the break-in at the Democratic National Committee headquarters at the Watergate office building in Washington on June 17. They were charged with burglary, conspiracy, and wiretapping. Five of the seven were arrested at the scene, attempting to instal secret bugging devices. They were all members of the Republican committee to re-elect president Richard Nixon. The other two men were former White House aides Howard Hunt and Gordon Liddy, members of the same committee.

ROCKET TRAGEDY

1830 William Huskisson, British MP and former cabinet minister, today became the first person to be killed by a train. Huskisson, head of the Board of Trade, fell under the wheels of George Stevenson's "Rocket" steam engine as it departed on the inaugural run of the Liverpool and Manchester Railway. He was crossing the track to greet the prime minister, the Duke of Wellington, who opened the new passenger line.

GLOBAL MELTDOWN

2008 "Meltdown Monday" saw the collapse of Wall Street giant Lehman Brothers, the fourth-largest investment bank in the US. The biggest bankruptcy in US history dealt a blow to already-fragile global finances. When the dust settled, global stock markets were down 40 per cent, and the world had entered a deep recession, with rising unemployment and a collapse of house prices.

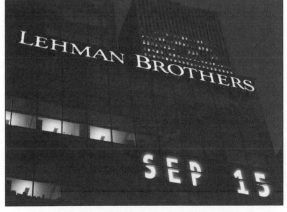

BIRTHDAYS

Titus Oates 1649, English Anglican priest who successfully created anti-Catholic feeling by inventing a "Popish plot".

Agatha Christie 1890, English crime writer.

Jean Renoir 1894, French film director.

Prince Henry of Wales 1984, the second son of Prince Charles and Diana, Princess of Wales.

• 1916 – TANKS DEPLOYED ON THE SOMME • 1917 – RUSSIA PROCLAIMED A REPUBLIC

1498 Death of Tomas de Torquemada, principal architect of the Spanish Inquisition.

1824 Death of King Louis XVIII of France.

1959 Charles de Gaulle, French President of the new Fifth Republic and former head of the committee of National Liberation in Algiers, offers Algeria a referendum on independence.

1963 Malaysia becomes independent and a mob of more than 100,000 burns down the British Embassy in celebration.

2010 Pope Benedict XVI begins the first papal visit to Britain since Henry VIII's split with Rome.

BIRTHDAYS

Henry V 1387, English king who defeated the French at Agincourt.

Sir Alexander Korda 1893, Hungarian-born film producer.

Lauren Bacall 1924, American actress who made her debut in *To Have and Have Not.*

Charlie Byrd 1925, American jazz guitarist.

B. B. King 1925, American blues guitarist.

PILGRIMS SEEK FREEDOM IN NEW WORLD

1620 A group of Puritan separatists set sail from Plymouth today in the *Mayflower*, bound for the New World and religious freedom. The group, most of them uneducated farmers, fled to Holland in 1608 to escape King Charles I's religious oppression. They settled in Leyden, free to follow their beliefs, but they were poor, and could not adapt to Dutch society. Church elder William Brewster went to London and found a sponsor for the voyage to America in Sir Edwin Sandys, treasurer of the Virginia Company. Sandys arranged a plantation grant and financing through London merchants hoping to profit from the venture. Another elder, John Carver, chartered the 180-ton *Mayflower* at Southampton, which sailed today with 102 passengers.

TREATY TO SAVE THE OZONE LAYER

1987 Seventy countries signed an agreement in Montreal today to curb the threat to the ozone layer. The ozone layer absorbs ultraviolet radiation from the sun that would harm all life if it reached the Earth's surface. Three years ago a seasonal "hole" in the layer was discovered over Antarctica, thought to be caused by chlorofluorocarbons (CFCs), gases used in aerosols and as refrigerants. CFC use will be frozen at current levels and reduced by half within 12 years.

PRIEST USES PULPIT TO PREACH REVOLUTION

1810 A rural Mexican priest ended his Sunday sermon today with the fiery war-cry: "Death to the Spaniards!" and set a revolution in motion. Father Miguel Hidalgo y Costilla, the pastor of Dolores, is now leading a ragged army of more than 10,000 Indians and peasants against the Spanish colonial government. Hidalgo was sent to the provinces's when his his liberal attitudes enraged both the government and the Inquisition.

• 1908 – GENERAL MOTORS IS ESTABLISHED • 1977 – T REX STAR MARC BOLAN DIES

FIRST AIR DEATH AS ORVILLE WRIGHT CRASHES

1908 A American army officer was killed today when Orville Wright's flying machine broke a propeller in mid-air and plunged 150 ft (46 m) to the ground. Wright was badly injured, but his passenger, Lieutenant Thomas W. Selfridge, was killed – the first passenger to die in an aircraft accident. Orville Wright made the first-ever powered flight in 1903.

HONG KONG SEES SWING TO LIBERALS

1991 With six years left before China takes over Hong Kong, the British colony today held its first direct elections – and liberals swept the board. Seventeen of the 18 seats contested went to candidates who are strongly opposed to both the Hong Kong and Chinese governments. The outspoken United Democrats won 12 seats. Conservative business-backed candidates, who are pro-China, were left out in the cold. Less than a third of the seats in the legislature were elected.

1701 Death of King James II of England.

1877 William Henry Fox Talbot, British pioneer of photographic techniques, dies aged 77.

1941 Reza Pahlavi sacks his unpopular father and becomes Shah of Iran.

1944 "Operation Market Garden" begins as British airborne forces land at Arnhem, Holland, aiming to secure a bridge over the Rhine to facilitate an invasion of Germany.

BIRTHDAYS

William Carlos Williams 1883. American poet and physician who wrote "Journey to Love".

Sir Francis Chichester 1901, English yachtsman and aviator who was knighted for sailing round the world solo in *Gypsy Moth IV*.

Sir Frederick Ashton 1906, British dancer, choreographer and director.

Anne Bancroft 1931, American actress who made her name on Broadway in *The Miracle Worker*.

Maureen Connolly 1934, American tennis player known as "Little Mo".

UNITED STATES COMPOSE BRAND NEW CONSTITUTION

1787 George Washington, leader of the Philadelphia Convention, was today presented with a new Constitution for the United States of America. Thirty-nine delegates representing 12 of the 13 states (all but Rhode Island) signed the document after months of debate. The difficulty was to balance a strong central government with both democratic principles and adequate representation of the states. The result is mixed government: representatives in the lower house will be elected by popular vote, the states will have equal representation in the upper house and each state will decide how to choose its presidential electors. The public has its say in the ratification of the new Constitution by the states as the supreme law of the land. The constitution's lack of a bill of rights is already being criticized. The Convention's Federalists say no such bill is needed, but the Anti-Federalist faction strongly disagrees.

• 1792 – CROWN JEWELS STOLEN IN PARIS • 1931 – FIRST LP RECORDS DEMONSTRATED

96 AD Roman Emperor Domitian is murdered by assassins in the pay of his wife, Domitia.

1759 French forces at Quebec surrender to the British.

1914 Irish Home Rule Bill is given Royal Assent.

1955 Four years after they fled to Russia, the British government admits Donald Maclean and Guy Burgess really were Soviet spies.

1967 Death of Sir John Cockroft, English nuclear physicist who first split the atom.

1981 Under President Mitterand, France abolishes the guillotine.

1988 The military seize power in Burma.

BIRTHDAYS

Samuel Johnson 1709, English lexicographer and celebrated conversationalist.

Greta Garbo 1905, Swedish-born Hollywood film legend.

Kwarne Nkrumah 1909, Ghanaian prime minister and then president.

Lance Armstrong 1971, American Tour de France champion charged with doping offences.

NO HELP FOR DESPERATE HENDRIX

1970 Early this morning rock superstar Jimi Hendrix left a message on the answering machine of ex-manager Chas Chandler: "I need help bad." But Chandler was out and no help came. Hendrix was pronounced dead on arrival at St Mary's Hospital at 11.45 am, killed by an accidental overdose of sleeping pills. He was 27. Jimi Hendrix is probably the most powerful thing that ever happened to the guitar – a rock 'n' roll genius with a solid background in the blues. He was the highest-paid act at Woodstock Festival last year and the star of the Isle of Wight Festival last month. But he has been beleaguered by lawsuits over royalties and contracts, squabbling managers and bands that broke up around him.

What dreadful hot weather we have! It keeps me in a continual state of inelegance.

Jane Austen, British novelist, in a letter, 1796.

TSAR'S PM GUNNED DOWN

1911 Russian premier Pyotr Stolypin died today after being shot in Kiev last week by a police double agent. It took a true statesman to hold down Stolypin's job in the turmoil of today's Russia, and he held it for six years. He even achieved something with his reforms, but his tactics were ruthless. Faced with a reluctant Tsar, reactionary civil servants and the socialists in the Duma legislative assembly, nothing short of ruthlessness would have worked; but it won him few friends. Recently he fell out with the Tsar, his council of ministers and the Duma. Now he has been removed.

• 1851 – **FIRST EDITION OF** *THE NEW YORK TIMES* **IS PUBLISHED**

DISNEY SPEAKS MICKEY SQUEAKS

1928 Hollywood artist Walt Disney today released the first sound cartoon film, *Steamboat Willie*. The film features Mickey Mouse and Disney himself provides his squeaky voice on the soundtrack. Mickey – originally Mortimer Mouse when he was conceived in Disney's animation studio last year – is a clever caricature of an impish child. Disney and his chief collaborator Ub Iwerks are working on more cartoon characters.

UNION REMAINS INTACT

2014 Scotland has voted to stay in the United Kingdom after voters decisively rejected independence. With the results in from all 32 council areas, the "No" side won with 2,001,926 votes over 1,617,989 for "Yes". Prime Minister David Cameron said he was delighted the UK would remain together and that commitments on extra powers would be honoured "in full".

BP IN DEEPWATER OVER SPILL

2010 The Deepwater Horizon oil well was finally capped after spewing millions of barrels of oil into the Gulf of Mexico, following an explosion in April. The well had been temporarily sealed on 3 June while a relief well was dug, allowing workers to start pumping in the cement to create a permanent "kill". Top US federal official, Coastguard Admiral Thad Allen, said the well was now "effectively dead". "Additional regulatory steps will be undertaken but we can now state definitively that the Macondo Well poses no continuing threat to the Gulf of Mexico," Admiral Allen went on. A pressure test showed the cement plug put in place by BP was holding. The US Government has named BP as the responsible party, and officials have committed to holding the company accountable for all cleanup costs and other damage.

SEPTEMBER 19

1356 Led by the Black Prince, Edward, the English defeat the French at the Battle of Poitiers.

1881 Death of James Abram Garfield, 20th US president who was shot on July 2 having been in office just four months.

1905 Death of Thomas Barnardo, British doctor, philanthropist and founder of homes for destitute children.

1994 US troops arrive in Haiti after long negotiation and a mounting tide of refugees floods out of the Republic; the aim is to return the ousted President Aristide to power.

BIRTHDAYS

Sir William Golding 1911, British author best known for *The Lord of the Flies*.

Zandra Rhodes 1940, British fashion designer.

"Mama Cass" Elliot 1943, large American who began as singer of The Mamas and the Papas.

Jeremy Irons 1948, British leading actor of stage and screen.

Twiggy (Lesley Hornby) 1949, British actress and singer who first found fame as a model in the 60s.

• 1876 – CARPET SWEEPER PATENTED • 1955 – JUAN PERON OUSTED IN ARGENTINA

1792 France's untried army defeats the Duke of Brunswick's, attacking Prussian troops at Walmy.

1946 The first Cannes Film Festival opens.

1959 America's Disneyland refuses a visit by Soviet prime minister Nikita Khruschchev for security reasons.

1961 Argentinian Antonio Albertondo begins the first non-stop swim across the Channel.

1961 Rhodesian premier Ian Smith bans the black opposition party.

1984 Forty die as a suicide bomber attacks the US Embassy in Beirut.

2005 Veteran Nazi-hunter Simon Wiesenthal dies.

BIRTHDAYS

Sir George Robey 1869, English comedian and star of the music hall.

Jelly Roll Morton 1885, American pianist, singer and composer and one of the first jazz musicians, who made his first recording in 1923.

Kenneth Moore 1914, English actor who played World War II fighter pilot hero Douglas Bader in *Reach for the Sky*.

DRAKE BOWLS ROUND WORLD

1580 Francis Drake returned to England today, his ship laden with treasure. Drake, the first captain to sail round the world, has captured tons of silver, gold, coins and jewels from Spanish galleons in the Americas. Spain wants him hanged for piracy, but Drake is a public hero – and Elizabeth herself backed his expedition. Drake set off three years ago with five small ships, but only his *Golden Hind* reached the Pacific. His first prize was a Spanish treasure galleon and others followed. Drake landed at San Francisco Bay and claimed it for England, then crossed the Pacific to trade in the Spice Islands before setting course for home, via the Indian Ocean and the Cape of Good Hope.

VIOLENCE THREATENS PEACE ACCORD

1991 President F. W. de Klerk, ANC leader Nelson Mandela and the ANC's arch-rival, Chief Mangosuthu Buthelezi, head of the Zulu Inkatha movement, signed a "national peace accord" last Saturday after a week of violence that claimed 120 lives nationwide. It is hoped the agreement will be the basis of further negotiations on a new constitution. But the two most extreme black parties refused to sign, and the heavily armed far right-wing white groups refused even to attend. They have accused de Klerk of treachery and are threatening a new "Boer War".

DACKO KOS BOKASSA

1979 Africa's most bizarre dictator, self-styled Emperor Jean Bedel Bokassa of the Central African Empire, was overthrown today in a coup by his cousin, David Dacko. Dacko was president until Bokassa, then an army colonel, overthrew him in 1965. Bokassa has terrorized his people, tortured and murdered, and sacked the poverty-stricken country's coffers to support his grotesque pretensions. He crowned himself emperor two years ago, donning a $2 million (£1.1 million) crown and ascending a massive golden throne. Now Bokassa has fled to France – amid horrifying accusations of child cannibalism in the palace.

• **1519 – FERDINAND MAGELLAN SETS SAIL TO CIRCUMNAVIGATE THE WORLD**

KING IN POKER GAME

1327 England's King Edward II has been murdered in prison. Fearful shrieks from the dungeons broke the silence in Berkeley Castle in the early hours today, and this morning the citizens of Bristol were called to look on the horribly distorted face of the dead king. It is believed he was killed with a red-hot poker. Many think Edward's queen, Isabella of France, and her lover Roger de Mortimer plotted the murder to ensure the succession of the King's son, 15-year-old Edward – under Isabella's regency. Edward II was a weak and foolish king whose lavish treatment of his favourites raised the ire of England's nobles.

SACRED STONES SOLD

1915 Stonehenge was sold today for £6600 ($12,210), bought with the surrounding fields by a local farmer. The finest and most elaborate of Europe's prehistoric megaliths, the concentric circles of standing stones are a powerful mystery. The antiquarian William Stukeley said 150 years ago Stonehenge was a Druid temple, but it is now known that it was already ancient when the Druids arrived in England and dates back to before Christ. In 1136 Geoffrey of Monmouth wrote that the stones had magical healing powers. How they were transported also remains a mystery.

HURRICANE HUGO IN A HUFF

1989 Hurricane Hugo, the worst storm this decade, hit the US coast last night and left widespread destruction in South Carolina and Georgia. Charleston is badly damaged. Hugo's 140-mph (225-kph) winds swept through the Caribbean, leaving death and chaos in Puerto Rico, the Dominican Republic and the Virgin Islands – where riots and looting followed the storm. Whole towns are wrecked, with many killed or injured.

1745 Bonnie Prince Charlie wins the Battle of Prestonpans in Scotland.

1857 British forces retake Delhi from Indian mutineers.

1903 The first recorded Western film opens in the US, titled *Kit Carson* – it is 21 minutes long.

1944 US general Douglas MacArthur returns to the Philippines, attacking the Japanese near Manila.

1993 Russian President Boris Yeltsin dissolves the Russian Parliament pending elections to a new legislative body.

BIRTHDAYS

H. G. Wells 1866, English author who pioneered science fiction when he wrote his first work, *The Time Machine*.

Gustav Holst 1874, British composer and teacher whose best-known work is *The Planets*.

Sir Allen Lane 1902, English publisher who founded Penguin Books.

Leonard Cohen 1934, Canadian poet and singer whose gloomy songs and growling delivery won him a cult following in the 1960s and 70s.

• 1792 – FRENCH MONARCHY ABOLISHED • 1981 – BELIZE GAINS INDEPENDENCE

1860 China's Emperor flees Peking as Anglo-French forces advance.

1862 President Abraham Lincoln issues his Preliminary Emancipation Proclamation freeing slaves in the South.

1972 Idi Amin gives the 80,000 Asians in Uganda 48 hours to leave.

1986 The youngest heart and lung transplant patient, a two-and-a-half-month-old baby, is given new organs at the Harefield Hospital, Middlesex, UK.

BIRTHDAYS

Michael Faraday 1791, English physicist who invented the dynamo.

Erick von Stroheim 1885, Austrian-born Hollywood film director and actor whose eccentric leather-clad image and autocratic ways won him the title "The Man You Love to Hate".

John Houseman 1902, Romanian-born producer, writer, stage director and founder, with Orson Welles, of the famous Mercury Theatre in New York.

Fay Weldon 1931, English author whose novels include *The Life and Loves of a She-Devil*.

OUTRAGE IN NZ AS FRANCE ADMITS TO *RAINBOW* BOMBS

1985 French prime minister Laurent Fabius today admitted that the *Rainbow Warrior* was sunk by French agents. A crew member was killed when the Greenpeace ship was rocked by two explosions in Auckland Harbour, New Zealand, on July 10. She had been due to lead a flotilla of peace ships into the French nuclear test zone at Muroroa Atoll in French Polynesia in a protest action. The incident brought international condemnation. The French defence minister has resigned amid a storm of protest and demands for the head of the secret service to be sacked.

THE ZULU NAPOLEON

1828 Shaka, King of the Zulus, was murdered today at Dukuza, his capital in Natal, by his half-brothers Dingaan and Mhlangana. Dingaan has taken the throne. The Zulu were a small clan when Shaka became their chief, but through bloody conquest he welded them into the mightiest nation in Southern Africa. Shaka abandoned the traditional light throwing spear and adopted a short, broad-bladed stabbing spear for his regiments, along with a tall shield of tough hide. Ardent disciplined warriors, his troops ran barefoot into battle, the flanks separating to attack from three sides. Shaka's revered mother, Nandi, died last year, and the grief-stricken king lost his mind. Thousands of Zulus have been executed for showing insufficient grief. Now the bloodbath has ended.

POLAND'S WORKERS FOUND SOLIDARITY UNION

1980 Polish workers today exercised a new freedom to form an independent labour union. The new Solidarity union's leader, electrician Lech Walesa, led the Gdansk inter-factory committee which coordinated the massive shipyard strikes this summer. The wave of work stoppages forced the government to concede, allowing independent unions, freeing jailed dissidents and lifting press censorship.

I only regret that I have but one life to lose for my country.

Nathan Hale, hero of the American Revolution, in a speech before being hanged by the British as a spy, 1776.

• 1792 – FRANCE BECOMES A REPUBLIC • 1989 – IRA TARGETS ROYAL MARINES MUSICIANS

CONFRONTING ISIS

2014 The US and five Arab allies have launched the first strikes against a Sunni militant group called the Islamic State in Iraq and the Levant (also known as the ISIS or ISIL). The Pentagon said warplanes, drones and Tomahawk missiles were used to target several areas including ISIS stronghold Raqqa. The US has already launched about 190 air strikes in Iraq since August. However, Monday's action expands the campaign against the militant group across the border into Syria. Syrian President Bashar al-Assad said he supports any international efforts to combat "terrorism" in Syria, state media reports.

ASTRONOMERS ROW OVER NEW PLANET

1846 Two German astronomers have discovered another planet, the eighth in distance from the Sun, about a billion miles beyond Uranus. Johann Galle and Heinrich d'Arrest of the Berlin Observatory were told just where to look by the young French astronomer Urbain Le Verrier. He had concluded that the irregular orbit of Uranus could only be explained by the gravitational pull of another planet, and calculated its position to within one degree. The announcement has brought a protest from 24-year-old English astronomer John Adams, who claims he made the same prediction nine months ago, and the credit should be his. British scientists scoffed at his findings at the time. Further controversy surrounds a name for the new planet. Le Verrier wants to call it "Leverrier", but others favour Neptune.

SILENT U-BOATS ARE NEW LETHAL WEAPON

1914 The German submarine U-9 has sunk three British cruisers off the Dutch coast, with 1500 lives lost. The war at sea started in earnest on August 28, when a British fleet raided the Heligoland Bight and sank four German ships. Today's battle off Holland shows the new shape of sea warfare: powerful warships were helpless against the silent attack of one small submarine. The German fleet is outnumbered and blockaded in the North Sea, but the U-boats are not so easily stopped. German mines have claimed several British ships.

KEYSTONE COPS

1912 King of comedy Mack Sennet's new slapstick short *Cohen Collects a Debt* was released today and was an instant success. The film features policemen known as the Keystone Cops, whose antics had the audience in stitches.

1942 Australian troops under US general Douglas MacArthur start an offensive in New Guinea to drive back the Japanese.

1974 The world's first Ceefax teletext service begins on BBC television in Britain.

1987 Death of Bob Fosse, American dancer director of the autobiographical film *All that Jazz.*

2000 Rower Steve Redgrave wins his fifth Olympic Gold medal in the coxless 4's during the Sydney Olympics.

2010 The world's biggest wind farm is inaugurated off the UK coast in Kent.

BIRTHDAYS

Gaius Octavius Caesar 63 BC, first Roman emperor.

Armand Hyppolyte 1819, French physicist.

John Coltrane 1926, American saxophonist.

Ray Charles 1932, American singer of classics like "I Can't Stop Loving You".

Julio Iglesias 1943, Spanish popular romantic singer.

Bruce Springsteen 1949, American singer-songwriter who achieved success with his album *Born to Run.*

• 1940 – GEORGE CROSS INSTITUTED FOR CIVILIANS • 1939 – DEATH OF SIGMUND FREUD

1852 A hydrogen-filled airship, the first of its kind, makes its maiden flight at Versailles.

1941 The Siege of Leningrad begins: the British RAF support the Red Army.

1960 The first nuclear-powered aircraft carrier, the USS *Enterprise*, is launched at Newport, Virginia.

1975 The first all-British team reaches the summit of Mount Everest, having also made the first ascent of the steep south-west face of the mountain.

1983 Italy jails chemicals executives responsible for the Seveso dioxin disaster, when a poisonous gas cloud contaminated a wide radius of land.

BIRTHDAYS

F. Scott Fitzgerald 1896, American novelist and short story writer.

Svetlana Beriosova 1932, Russian prima ballerina with the Grands Ballets de Monte Carlo and the Sadler's Wells Ballet.

Linda McCartney 1942, American photographer married to Paul McCartney and campaigner for animal rights.

WAR IN THE GULF

1980 Iraq invaded Iran in force today and destroyed the huge oil refinery at Abadan as months of border incident flared into full-scale war. Iraq, taking advantage of the domestic chaos in fundamentalist Iran, is hoping for a quick victory over its bigger neighbour. The prize is dominance in the Persian Gulf.

OLD-STYLE SAMURAI MEET BRUTAL REALITY

1877 Japan's modern army today crushed a rebellion by 40,000 feudal samurai warriors fighting for their old way of life and their honour. The Meiji Restoration of 1868 broke the closed military rule of the Shoguns as Japan moved to transform itself into a modern world power. The samurai armies and their *bushido* code of honour were an anachronism. The new Meiji government cut their pay, stopped them carrying swords – and refused to invade Korea. At this the incensed samurai rebelled. Today their leader committed ritual suicide amidst the fallen; many of the survivors followed suit.

1200 REFUGEES SLAUGHTERED ON TRAIN

1947 A trainload of Muslim refugees fleeing to Pakistan has been massacred by Sikhs at Amritsar in the Punjab, with at least 1200 defenceless people shot and hacked to death. This is the worst single incident so far in the communal violence that has swept the sub-continent since the partitioning of India on August 15. Some say as many as 15 million refugees caught on the wrong side of the Hindu-Muslim divide are trying to flee to safety.

BLACK FRIDAY AS GOLDEN BUBBLE BURSTS

1869 Panic hit Wall Street today as the bottom fell out of the gold market – and the entire stock market followed. Thousands of speculators led the plunge towards bankruptcy. The blow fell when President Ulysses S. Grant told the US Treasury to release its gold. The sudden glut knocked the price down, killing a bid by financiers Jay Gould and James Fisk to corner the market. They had said they'd succeeded in stopping the president selling government gold, But Grant had simply been slow to react.

• 1930 – COWARD'S *PRIVATE LIVES* PREMIERES • 1973 – PERON RE-ELECTED IN ARGENTINA

BANDARANAIKE CUT SHORT BY BUDDHIST MONK

1959 Sri Lankan prime minister Solomon Bandaranaike has been assassinated. Bandaranaike led the People's United Front leftist alliance which won the 1956 election. His Sinhalese nationalism has angered the large Tamil Hindu minority – Sinhalese is now the sole national language. Yet he was shot by a Sinhalese Buddhist monk. He is to be succeeded by his wife, Sirimavo Bandaranaike, a radical socialist.

Women and small people are the most difficult to deal with.

Confucius (551-479 BC), Chinese sage and founder of Confucianism.

1932 Catalonia in Spain becomes autonomous: it has its own parliament, language and flag.

1954 "Papa" Doc wins the presidential elections in Haiti.

1960 Death of Emily Post, American columnist and writer on etiquette.

1970 Death of Erich Maria Remarque, German author of *All Quiet on the Western Front*.

1986 In Wales a British police constable is jailed for biting off part of a colleague's ear during a rugby match.

2000 Cathy Freeman races to victory in the 400-metre race in front of her home crowd at the Sydney Olympics.

TURIN UNVEILS "SHROUD OF CHRIST"

1933 Church custodians at Turin cathedral in Italy today showed the famous Turin Shroud to the public for the first time in 400 years. The stained, 14-ft (4.2-m) long cloth is believed to have been the burial shroud of Jesus Christ. At the cathedral today it was impossible not to be moved by the cloth's imprint of a body, front and back, and the clear picture of a man's face, eyes closed. Scientific opinion is that the image is the actual imprint of the body of a man. Today's crowd had no doubt about whose face it showed.

BIG GUNS MAKE LITTLE ROCK RESPECT BLACK STUDENT RIGHTS

1957 Protected by a thousand army paratroopers, nine black children took their places in the all-white Central High School in Little Rock, Arkansas, today. The Federal district court in Little Rock ruled that the nine students be admitted to the Central High following a Supreme Court ruling that segregated schools contravene the Fourteenth Amendment. But Arkansas Governor Orville Faubus flouted the order. When the black children arrived at the school they were barred by armed National Guardsmen. In an unprecedented move, President Eisenhower removed the National Guard from Faubus's control and sent in the 101st Airborne Division. Furious Southern governors have demanded their withdrawal.

BIRTHDAYS

William Faulkner 1897, American novelist and winner of the 1949 Nobel Prize for Literature.

Dmitri Shostakovich 1906, Russian 20th century composer.

Sir Robert Muldoon 1921, New Zealand prime minister from 1975 to 1984.

Michael Douglas 1944, American actor and son of Kirk.

• 1818 – FIRST HUMAN BLOOD TRANSFUSION • 1977 – ITALIAN RACER AGOSTINI RETIRES

1815 The Holy Alliance is signed by Tsar Alexander I of Russia, Francis I of Austria (formerly Holy Roman Emperor Francis II), and Frederick William III, King of Prussia.

1903 Women get the vote in the Connecticut state elections.

1907 New Zealand becomes a Dominion.

1945 Hungarian composer Béla Bartok dies.

1957 The first performance of *West Side Story* is given in New York.

1984 Britain and China agree that Hong Kong will revert to Chinese rule when the lease expires in 1997.

1989 Vietnamese troops pull out of Cambodia.

BIRTHDAYS

T. S. Eliot 1888, American-born poet, playwright and highly influential critic.

George Gershwin 1898, American composer who worked with his brother, lyricist Ira Gershwin.

Bryan Ferry 1945, British pop singer, who was lead singer of Roxy Music.

Olivia Newton-John 1948, Australian star of the film *Grease*.

BESSIE DIES SINGING MISSISSIPPI BLUES

1937 The Empress of the Blues is dead. And Bessie Smith's friends are saying she would still be alive if she'd been white: Miss Smith was hurt in a car smash today in racist Mississippi, and bled to death waiting for an ambulance. She was 43. Bessie Smith learnt to sing in a gospel church in Tennessee, and started her singing career in honky tonk bars. She got her big chance in 1923 when she went to New York to make a "race record" for sale in the black communities. She was an instant sensation and is now a household name, her records are landmarks of blues singing. Now she has died, a victim of prejudice and stupidity. That's how the blues were born, and that's why people like Bessie sing them.

JOHNSON RUNS INTO DRUG SHAME

1988 Canadian sprinter Ben Johnson flew home in disgrace from the Seoul Olympics today, stripped of his gold medal after failing a drugs test. Two days ago Johnson was a hero after winning the 100 metres with a new world record. But tests proved that he'd taken anabolic steroids to boost his strength. The scandal hit the world's front pages today, but Johnson isn't the only one to have failed the drugs tests – so have nine other athletes. Following the US-led boycott of the Moscow Olympics in 1980 and the inevitable Eastern-bloc boycott of the 1984 Games in Los Angeles, this is the first Olympics since 1976 where east and west have met, and the west has not shone. Russia has swept up the most medals, and the heroes are the East German swimmers and African long-distance runners.

TEMPLE OF WAR TAKES DIRECT HIT

1687 The masterpiece of ancient Greek architecture, the Parthenon, has become a casualty of war. Turkish forces that have besieged the Acropolis of Athens were using the old temple as a powder magazine, and today the attacking Venetian army scored a direct hit on it with a mortar bomb. The powder exploded, blowing off the roof, ruining the frieze-covered walls and damaging much of the marble sculpture. But still the battle continues. The Parthenon is the temple of Athena, Goddess of War. It was designed by Ictinus and Callicrates under the direction of the great sculptor Phidias and completed in 432 BC. Phidias's huge image of Athena was destroyed by the Crusaders. Over the years the Parthenon has been used as a Catholic church, a mosque and a harem.

• 1983 – AUSTRALIA WINS AMERICA'S CUP • 2008 – DEATH OF PAUL NEWMAN

SLAVES BY THE SHIPLOAD

1672 A British company chartered today has been given a monopoly of the African slave trade. The Royal African Company is now arranging shipments of slaves from the African coast to the markets in the Americas. A healthy slave costs less than £20 ($37) on delivery in America. The new company's chief competition is the Dutch West India Company, which has had a monopoly of the West African slave trade for 50 years. Britain and France are at war with Holland, and last month a Dutch fleet attacked New York. Regardless of European hostilities, the number of slave ships plying the Atlantic is bound to grow. The New World plantations cannot operate without slaves and enormous profits are to be made from the trade in "black gold".

1791 Jews are granted French citizenship.

1917 Death of Edgar Degas, French painter and sculptor.

1921 Death of Engelbert Humperdinck, German composer.

1922 Constantine I, King of Greece, abdicates following the Greek defeat in Turkey.

1960 Europe's first "moving pavement", the travelator, is opened at Bank Underground Station in London.

1979 Death of Dame Gracie Fields, singer and entertainer whose songs include "Sally".

2002 A Senegalese ferry sinks with 1,000 fatalities.

TOP MODEL CAN'T MARRY AS SHE WAS BORN A HE

1990 Glamorous British model Caroline Cossey has failed to overturn a law that won't let her get married – because her birth certificate says she's male. And so she was, until a sex-change operation 15 years ago transformed her into the beautiful and successful model "Tula". She appealed against the ruling in terms of the European Convention on Human Rights, but the European court today upheld the British law.

Samuel Adams 1722, American revolutionary involved in planning the Boston Tea Party.

George Cruikshank 1792, British political cartoonist.

Louis Botha 1862, South African prime minister, the first of the Union of South Africa.

Vincent Youmans 1898, American composer of popular music whose hits included "Tea for Two".

TOKYO JOINS BERLIN-ROME AXIS

1940 Imperial Japan signed a 10-year economic and military alliance with Nazi Germany and Fascist Italy in Berlin today. The Tripartite Pact pact is a coup for Nazi leader Adolph Hitler, whose policy of *Blitzkrieg* in Europe has gained him conquests, but no allies other than Italy and an increasingly reluctant Spain. Japan is also a useful buffer against the United States. Japan and Russia, however, have been bitter enemies since their war over Manchuria in 1905, and the peace treaty that was signed by Russia and Germany a year ago is looking ever more shaky.

REGGAE LEGEND HITS UK

1975 Jamaica's big reggae stars, Bob Marley and The Wailers, have a first European hit as "No Woman No Cry" enters the UK Charts.

• 1930 – AMERICAN BOBBY JONES COMPLETES THE FIRST-EVER GOLFING GRAND SLAM

1868 Rebel generals oust Queen Isabella in Spain.

1891 Death of Herman Melville, American author of *Moby Dick*.

1895 Death of Louis Pasteur, French chemist and micro-biologist.

1978 John Paul I is found dead after only 33 days as Pope.

1986 British welterweight boxer Lloyd Honeyghan becomes world champion in just six rounds with US boxer Donald Curry.

1989 Ferdinand Marcos, ex-President of the Philippines, dies in exile.

BIRTHDAYS

Caravaggio 1573, Italian baroque painter.

John "Gentleman" Jackson 1769, English pugilist who managed to get boxing accepted as a legitimate sport.

Georges Clemenceau 1841, French prime minister from 1917 to 1920.

Al Capp 1909, American cartoonist who drew the "Li'l Abner" strip.

Brigitte Bardot 1934, French actress and international sex symbol.

MARINES ENTER BEIRUT AFTER LEBANESE MASSACRE

1982 US president Ronald Reagan has sent marines into Beirut on a peace-keeping mission. They will be joined by Italian and French contingents, and Reagan said both Syrian and Israeli forces would leave the Lebanon. This follows the massacre of hundreds of Palestinian civilians 10 days ago by Israeli-backed Lebanese Christians in the Sabra and Chatila refugee camps in West Beirut. The massacre was the Christians' revenge for the assassination four days earlier of Lebanese Christian president-elect Bashir Gemayel, now replaced by his brother, Amin.

PTOLEMY KILLS POMPEY CAESAR NOT IMPRESSED

48 BC The Roman general Pompey the Great has been stabbed to death in Egypt. Caesar defeated Pompey at Pharsalus last month, forcing him to flee to Egypt. Egyptian king Ptolemy XIII granted him refuge, but then had him killed, seeking to curry favour with Caesar. Caesar, however, is furious at the ignoble end of his adversary and is now leading an expedition to Egypt.

DIRTY TRICKS SULLY PRISTINE WHITE SOX

1920 Eight members of the Chicago White Sox were indicted today on charges of taking bribes to lose last year's World Series to the Cincinatti Reds. Baseball fans are appalled – the national game is highly revered and the World Series, first played in 1903, is the game's main celebration.

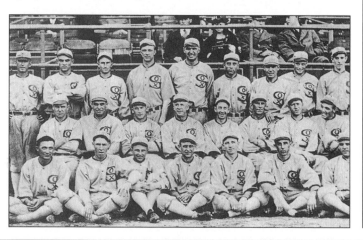

The workers have nothing to lose in this revolution but their chains. They have a world to gain. Workers of the world unite!

Karl Marx and Friedrich Engels, the closing words in *The Communist Manifesto*, 1848.

DAY OF DEATH AS NAZIS SHOOT 30,000 JEWS

1941 A special Nazi death squad has murdered thousands of Russian Jews in Kiev, machine-gunning them systematically in Babi Yar ravine. The shooting continued all day, and more than 30,000 men, women and children are feared dead. Nazi Gestapo secret police chief Heinrich Himmler sent four *Einsatzgruppen* (strike squads) into Russia behind the advancing German war machine with the express mission of exterminating Soviet Jewish civilians and other "undesirables". Kiev fell to the Nazis 10 days ago, and Leningrad is under siege.

1902 French writer Emile Zola dies.

1911 Alleging mistreatment of Italians in Libya, Italy declares war on the Ottoman Empire.

1930 George Bernard Shaw refuses a peerage.

1952 John Cobb, British and world waterspeed record holder, is killed on Loch Ness in Scotland.

1987 John M. Poindexter officially resigns from the US Navy over the Iran-Contra scandal.

2010 Death of US movie star Tony Curtis, aged 85.

ATHENS WREAKS REVENGE ON PERSIA

480 BC Though outnumbered two to one, the Greeks today routed a huge Persian war fleet in the straits of Salamis. Themistocles of Athens led the Greek fleet and won with a strategy of feints that left the Persian fleet divided and exposed. The lines of Greek ships, each propelled by 200 oarsmen, ploughed into King Xerxes' Persians with devastating effect, sinking scores of galleys. After fierce fighting, the remnants of the invading Persian fleet fled, leaving more than 200 wrecked galleys and thousands of casualties. The Greeks lost 40 ships. Three years ago, with today's battle in mind, Themistocles persuaded Athens to use the profits of a new silver mine to build the biggest fleet in Greece. Without naval support, the Persian army's chances of conquering the Greeks are slim.

BIRTHDAYS

Tintoretto 1518, Italian painter, one of the most important of the Venetian school.

Miguel de Cervantes 1547, Spanish playwright best known for his novel *Don Quixote*.

Viscount Horatio Nelson 1758, British naval commander and national hero.

Gene Autry 1907, American singing cowboy who wrote and recorded more than 200 songs.

Stanley Kramer 1914, American film producer and director.

ULSTER PROTESTANTS VOW TO FIGHT HOME RULE

1913 The Protestant majority in Ulster province vowed today to fight rather than be ruled by Catholic Dublin. At a meeting in Belfast, the Ulster Unionist Council agreed to set up a provisional government if the British parliament approves Irish home rule. Under pressure from nationalist leader John Redmond, British prime minister Herbert Asquith introduced the Irish Home Rule Bill in parliament last year. But Ulster's Protestants are committed to British rule to avoid becoming a small minority in an Irish state.

• 1938 – MUNICH CONFERENCE BEGINS • 1950 – FIRST TELEPHONE ANSWERING MACHINE

1630 John Billington is executed in New Plymouth for murder – the first capital crime in America.

1792 French troops take Speyer in the Rhineland.

1882 Water power is first used to produce electricity at a plant on the Fox River near Appleton, Wisconsin.

1931 Pay cuts in the British Navy prompt mutinous protest by 12,000.

1933 Franklin D. Roosevelt announces his New Deal.

1949 Mao Tse-tung formally becomes chairman of the Peoples' Republic of China.

1993 An earthquake claims the lives of 10,000 villagers in western and southern India.

BIRTHDAYS

Lewis Milestone 1895, Russian-born American film director who won an Oscar for *All Quiet on the Western Front*.

Truman Capote 1924, American novelist and short story writer.

Johnny Mathis 1935, American ballad singer.

Marc Bolan 1947, British lead singer of T-Rex.

AVIAN FLU EXPLODES

2005 The global spread of highly pathogenic H5N1 influenza in birds is considered a significant and imminent pandemic threat. Today the UN has issued a warning to the world that an outbreak of avian influenza, or "bird flu" as it is more commonly known, could kill between 5 and 150 million people. David Nabarro, the newly appointed Senior United Nations System Coordinator for Avian and Human Influenza, made this announcement after it was confirmed that the virus had spread to migratory birds making Africa and the Middle East highly susceptible to infection. Scientists fear the virus could evolve into a form which could be passed from human to human after deaths among those working closely with infected birds in Asia. Several countries are stock-piling anti-viral supplies.

RIPPER STRIKES WITH CLINICAL PRECISION

1888 Jack the Ripper murdered two more prostitutes in the streets of London's East End early this morning. His first victim was Liz Stride, in her late 30s. Her body was found at 1 am. The mad killer had left her with a cut throat. An hour later he struck again a mile away, killing Cathy Eddows, also in her 30s. The Ripper slit her throat expertly and then performed his dreadful ritual on the corpse, disembowelling her with all the skill of a surgeon. This morning's victims were his third and fourth. London is aghast at the latest killings, and the city's prostitutes are terrified. There seems no doubt that unless he is caught the maniac will strike again. The police have made little headway in the case. The murderer's surgical skills suggest an upper class background, and dark rumours are circulating of conspiracy in high places.

CHAMBERLAIN "PEACE WITH HONOUR"

1938 British prime minister Neville Chamberlain has returned from Munich tonight, where he and French premier Edouard Daladier met with Germany's Adolf Hitler and Italian premier Benito Mussolini to discuss the Czechoslovakian crisis. Chamberlain has agreed to Hitler's demands for German occupation of the Sudetenland in Czechoslovakia in return for Hitler's promise that this would be his last bid for more territory. Tonight Chamberlain called the agreement "peace with honour". The Czechs, however, are calling it treachery.

• 1791 – *DIE ZAUBERFLÖTE* PREMIERES • 1927 – BABE RUTH HITS 60TH HOME RUN

1955 Screen rebel James Dean has been killed in a car crash. The 24-year-old star died like he lived – too fast. He crashed his high-powered Porsche sports car while on his way to compete in a motor race. Dean's role as the misunderstood teenager in *Rebel Without a Cause*, released this year, instantly made him the object of mass teenage adulation and his death has caused widespread heartbreak.

• 1970 – BRITAIN SWAPS HOSTAGES FOR TERRORIST LEILA KHALED

OCTOBER

SIAMESE CATHARSIS

1868 Mongkut, king of Siam, has died in Bangkok. In 17 years as ruler he implemented sweeping political, economic and social change. Mongkut's decision to reverse centuries of isolation was formulated during the 27 years he spent as a Buddhist priest. Widely travelled, he saw that radical steps were needed to solve the country's problems. Siam had one commodity to offer the US in return for all their advice – elephants. These, Mongkut thought, could be used in the development of the USA. Siam's experience of imperialism was soured last year when France forced him to relinquish his vassal state, Cambodia, and make it a French protectorate.

1880 The Edison Lamp Works manufactures the first electric light bulbs.

1903 European railways link with Russia.

1918 British officer T. E. Lawrence (Lawrence of Arabia) and the Arab forces of Emir Faisal capture Damascus from the Turks.

1936 The BBC begins regular TV broadcasts from Alexandra Palace, London.

1938 German forces enter Sudetenland, once part of Czechoslovakia.

1974 The Watergate trial begins.

1987 Forty-eight-year-old surrogate grandmother Mrs Pat Anthony gives birth to triplets in South Africa.

BIRTHDAYS

Stanley Holloway 1890, English actor who was Oscar-nominated for his role in *My Fair Lady*.

Vladimir Horovitz 1904, Russian concert pianist.

Jimmy Carter 1924, American president who was instrumental in Israel and Egypt signing the Camp David agreement.

Julie Andrews 1935, British film and stage actress, famous for her role in *The Sound of Music*.

CHINA TO BE MAO'S REPUBLIC

1949 China has been proclaimed a People's Republic under the leadership of Mao Tse-tung, as Chairman, and Chou-En-Lai, as Prime Minister. The defeat of the Nationalist forces of Chiang Kai-shek leaves the Communists with a clear path for the implementation of their radical social and economic policies. One of the primary objectives of Chairman Mao is the industrialization of his Republic, which he hopes will raise China to the status of a great power.

FRANCO RULES

1936 General Francisco Franco Bahamonde, 44, was today proclaimed "Chief of the Spanish State" by the nationalist military junta that is trying to seize power in Spain. His elevation comes a month after the death in a plane crash of the former leader, General Sanjurjo. The nationalists are looking for a speedy end to the chaos gripping the country – unlikely because the capital, Madrid, and the east of the country are firmly in control of government forces.

• 1969 – CONCORDE BREAKS THE SOUND BARRIER • 1987 – EARTHQUAKE SHAKES LA

322 BC The great Greek philosopher Aristotle dies.

1780 British officer John André, who negotiated with the treacherous American revolutionary General Benedict Arnold for the surrender of West Point, is executed as a spy.

1871 Mormon leader Brigham Young is arrested for bigamy.

1935 Italian forces invade Abyssinia – Mussolini's bombers have already pounded border towns.

1987 Death of Sir Peter Medawar, biologist and Nobel prize-winner.

2003 J. M. Coetzee wins the Nobel Prize for Literature.

BIRTHDAYS

Mohandas Karamchand Gandhi 1869, Indian leader who used civil disobedience in his campaign for Indian independence.

Roy Campbell 1901, South African poet whose vigorous and satirical work includes *The Flaming Terrapin*.

Graham Greene 1904, British novelist, playwright, short story writer and *Times* journalist.

FRENCH STRENGTHEN HAND AT SPANISH COURT

1700 The death was announced today of the Spanish king, Charles II. He was 39. Alarm bells will have rung in England, Austria and Holland with the announcement that before his death, Charles, who leaves no heir, named Philip, Duke of Anjou, as his successor. Two years ago the nations with an interest in the succession agreed that Joseph Ferdinand, the electoral prince of Bavaria, should get the crown. Spanish territory would be ceded to pay off the rival French and Austrian claimants – Philip, the second grandson of Louis XIV, and the Archduke Charles, the second son of the Hapsburg emperor Leopold I. This ingenious plan went awry when Joseph Ferdinand inconveniently predeceased Charles, leaving the physically and mentally handicapped Spanish monarch susceptible to the blandishments of the French party at his court. War looks inevitable.

There are many reasons why novelists write, but they all have one thing in common – a need to create an alternative world.

John Fowles, British novelist, 1977.

TEXANS UP IN ARMS AGAINST MEXICO

1835 Texan-Americans today struck the first blow for an independent Texas by staging an armed uprising against the centralist government of Antonio de Santa Anna in the town of Gonzales, 67 miles (108 km) east of San Antonio. American immigrants, with their slaves, first settled here in 1825 when Texas was largely undeveloped and there was little interference from the Mexican government. Santa Anna's bid to change Mexico from a federation of states into a centralized system with himself as undisputed head is popular with the army but has little support among the general population, especially the Texan-Americans who have a great deal to lose from Santa Anna's policy. The situation may prove to be a heaven-sent opportunity for America to expand westwards.

• 1950 – *PEANUTS* APPEARS FOR FIRST TIME • 1985 – ROCK HUDSON DIES OF AIDS

BERLIN BACKS WILLY BRANDT

1957 The Berlin city assembly made history today by voting in its youngest ever *Oberburgermeister*, or Mayor. The man entrusted with his difficult office is 44-year-old Willy Brandt. He was elected unopposed by 86 out of the 118 members who voted. Herr Brandt's Social Democratic Party (SPD) was the only party to put up a candidate. Speculation that he would face a challenge by fellow SPD politician Willi Kressmann proved groundless. The composition of the Berlin senate remains unchanged, with the SPD maintaining its one-seat advantage over the Christian Democratic Union party.

BRITISH NUKE OWN WARSHIP

1952 The first British atomic weapon was exploded today off the Monte Bello Islands, west of Australia. The test was designed to assess the effect of an atomic bomb exploding in a harbour. The ship in which the weapon was exploded, the 1370-ton frigate HMS *Plym*, vapourized except for a few fragments which landed on the nearby islands and started fires in the vegetation. Watching newsmen felt the force from 65 miles (104 km) or so away.

I don't want art for a few, any more than education for a few, or freedom for a few.

William Morris, British designer, who died today, 1896.

1226 Death of St Francis of Assisi, founder of the Franciscan order.

1867 Death of Elias Howe, who patented the sewing machine and made $2 million (£1.1 million).

1959 Post codes are introduced in Britain.

1967 Death of Sir Malcolm Sargent, hugely popular British conductor perhaps best-loved for his Promenade concerts.

1967 Woody Guthrie, American singer and songwriter of "This Land is Your Land" dies from Huntington's Chorea.

1987 Death of French dramatist Jean Anouilh, whose works include *Antigone* and *L'Alouette*.

BIRTHDAYS

Pierre Bonnard 1867, French painter mainly of Paris scenes.

Gore Vidal 1925, American satirical author and critic.

Eddie Cochran 1938, American singer whose hits include "Summertime Blues".

Chubby Checker 1941, American singer whose "The Twist" became an international dance hit.

OJ SIMPSON ACQUITTED OF MURDER

1995 OJ Simpson has been found not guilty of the murders of his ex-wife Nicole and her companion Ronald Goldman. The jury took just a few hours to reach a unanimous decision in the trial that has gripped America. Nicole Brown Simpson and Ronald Goldman were stabbed to death outside her Brentwood house on June 12. Former American football star Simpson was arrested soon after but insisted he was innocent. Simpson's fate has become essential television viewing ever since 95 million Americans watched police give chase on the day of his arrest.

• 1906 – SOS BECOMES THE INTERNATIONAL DISTRESS CALL

1859 Death of German publisher of travel guides, Karl Baedeker.

1883 In Glasgow, Sir William Alexander Smith founds the Boys' Brigade.

1895 The first European edition of *The New York Herald* is published.

1895 American Horace Rawlins wins the first US Open Golf tournament.

1910 Portugal is proclaimed a republic.

1952 The first use of an external device called a pacemaker to control heartbeat.

2010 British actor and comedian Norman Wisdom dies, aged 95.

BIRTHDAYS

Giovanni Battista Piranesi 1720, Italian architect and engraver.

Jean-François Millet 1814, French painter, chiefly of scenes of peasant life.

Rutherford B. Hayes 1822, American statesman and Republican president from 1877–81.

Buster Keaton 1895, American actor, director and screenwriter of Hollywood comedies such as *The Navigator*.

RUSSIAN REBELS SURRENDER IN WHITE HOUSE SIEGE

1993 Troops and tanks loyal to President Yeltsin have opened fire on the White House in Moscow and finally put an end to the pro-Communist rebellion. The rebels were occupying the building and had attempted a partial take-over of the national television centre. The siege followed escalating battles between the pro-Communists and the security forces loyal to President Boris Yeltsin in Moscow. The protests have been sparked by President Yeltsin dissolving parliament and calling for fresh elections on 21 September. Vice President Alexander Rutskoi, a key player among the hard-line communists and nationalist parliament rebels, called on people to take to the streets and urged police officers to switch their allegiance. Several people were injured in clashes between riot police and the 600 demonstrators. An estimated 146 people have died in the struggle. President Yeltsin has pardoned the ringleaders.

Janis ODs

1970 Rock singer Janis Joplin was found dead today in Hollywood. She had taken an overdose of heroin. Joplin, 27, was known for her uninhibited singing style. She routinely drank a bottle of Southern Comfort on stage to improve her performance. Recently, though, she had eschewed this method of getting "high", relying instead on the music, and had fought her heroin addiction.

RUSSIA WINS FIRST HEAT OF SPACE RACE

1957 The Russians have launched the world's first artificial satellite, *Sputnik I*. The 22-inch (53 cm), 185-lb (84 kg) disc of *Sputnik I* is at this moment circling the Earth at an estimated 18,000 mph (29,000 kph). On each 96-minute orbit, *Sputnik* comes to within 143 miles (231 km) of the Earth at one extreme of its trajectory and to within 584 miles (942 km) at the other. It is expected to continue sending signals from its two radio transmitters until early next year.

IRA CALLS OFF DEATH STRIKE

1981 The IRA has called off the seven-month old hunger strike that has cost the lives of ten republicans held in H-block of the Maze prison in Belfast. The Maze became the focus of interest for the world's media after the first batch of hunger strikers died. The men in the Maze wanted the British government to give them the status of political prisoners.

• 1669 – DEATH OF REMBRANDT • 1824 – MEXICO BECOMES A REPUBLIC

MILOSEVIC TOPPLED

2000 Slobodan Milosevic has finally been swept from power as President of the Federal Republic of Yugoslavia amid gathering protest nearly two weeks after he failed to acknowledge defeat in the general elections of September 24. Crowds stormed the parliament building and state-owned television station in Belgrade in protest. Finally Vojislav Koštunica has been able to claim the presidency.

TEA-TIME

1952 Her majesty's government has taken a significant step towards reviving the nation's addiction to tea by removing it from the list of rationed commodities. The British people's burden remains great, however – meat, bacon, sugar, butter, margarine, cooking fats, cheese, eggs, sweets and chocolates are all still subject to strict rationing.

1880 Death of Jacques Offenbach, French composer who wrote *The Tales of Hoffman*.

1908 Bulgaria declares its independence from Turkey.

1930 The R-101 rigid airship crashes on the edge of a wood near Beauvais, France, killing 48 passengers including Air Minister Lord Thompson, who may well have contributed to the disaster by bringing luggage on board equivalent to the weight of about 24 people.

1994 Fifty members of the Solar Temple cult are found dead in Switzerland.

1999 A train crash near London's Paddington station kills 31 people.

SPAIN RISKS IT ALL

1796 Spain signed the Treaty of San Ildefonso with France today. Many Spaniards are hostile to the alliance. The man most in favour of it is Manuel de Godoy, Spain's Prime Minister. By backing France, however, he is weakening Spain's dwindling imperial clout. Spain will now be on the opposite side of the fence from her natural allies, the anti-Revolutionary coalitions engineered by Britain. She will also lose her markets in America.

BIRTHDAYS

Chevalier d'Éon 1728, French spy who conducted missions for his country disguised as a woman.

Vaclav Havel 1936, Czech playwright and human rights spokesman who became the nation's president in 1989.

Bob Geldof 1954, Irish pop musician who was lead singer with The Boomtown Rats and the instigator of Live Aid.

JARROW'S UNEMPLOYED MARCH WITHOUT FOOD

1936 A British workers' movement has hit on the idea of hunger marches as a way of bringing public attention to the plight of the unemployed in depressed areas of the country. In the formerly prosperous Tyneside shipbuilding town of Jarrow, which now has a permanent jobless rate of two-thirds of its population, 200 unemployed were given a rousing send-off. They are taking with them on a long march to London a petition with more than 11,000 signatures. The government's attempt to revive the four areas of the country officially recognized in November 1934 as depressed – including Tyneside – has failed. The marchers believe the capitalist system has broken down.

• 1989 – MOULIN ROUGE CELEBRATES 100 YEARS • 2011 – APPLE'S STEVE JOBS DIES

1536 English reformer and Bible translator William Tyndale is strangled and burnt at the stake.

1807 Sir Humphrey Davy discovers a new metal, and names it potassium.

1860 The Franco-British force captures Peking.

1892 Death of Alfred, Lord Tennyson, great English poet.

1902 A 2000-mile (3200-km) railway line running from Cape Town in South Africa to Beira, Mozambique, is completed.

1968 British drivers Jackie Stewart, Graham Hill and John Surtees come first, second and third in the US Grand Prix.

BIRTHDAYS

Jenny Lind 1820, Swedish operatic soprano dubbed the "Swedish Nightingale".

Le Corbusier 1887, French architect born in Switzerland who promoted the idea of the house as "a habitable machine".

Thor Heyerdahl 1914, Norwegian explorer who led an expedition from the western coast of South America to the islands east of Tahiti.

CAMP DAVID AVENGED

1981 The president of Egypt, Anwar Sadat, was assassinated today while attending the military parade marking the anniversary of Egyptian successes in the 1973 Yom Kippur War. Sadat, 62, was rushed to the Maadi Armed Forces Hospital, south of Cairo, but died soon after arrival. Sadat and other ministers were watching a fly-past when men dressed as soldiers opened fire with grenades and automatic

weapons from a truck that had stalled in front of the reviewing stand. Seven other senior Egyptian officials and guests were also killed. Sadat's signing of the Camp David treaty with Israel in 1979 won him a host of enemies in the Arab world. Chief among these was the exiled opposition leader Lieutenant General Saad El-Shazli, who is thought to have masterminded the killing.

You ain't heard nothin' yet, folks.

A line from the film **The Jazz Singer**, the first picture with sound, which hit the screen today, 1927.

BYZANTINE BASIL BLINDS BULGARIANS

1014 The Byzantine emperor Basil II has brought his country's 28-year-war with Bulgaria to an end with an act of unprecedented savagery. Tsar Samuel's defeated army of 15,000 men has been blinded. One eye has been left to each 100th man to ensure that the army finds its way back to the Tsar. Meanwhile, Basil is looking for further lands to incorporate into his empire. Sicily, now in the hands of the Arabs, is next on his list of military conquests.

ARABS ATTACK AS ISRAEL PRAYS

1973 One of the holiest days in the Jewish calendar, Yom Kippur ("Day of Atonement"), has turned into one of the bloodiest. A joint Egyptian-Syrian invasion force has attacked Israel on two fronts and the Israeli defence force has been mobilized. The Arabs are unlikely to win this latest round of hostilities on the battlefield, such is Israel's military superiority. The wily Egyptian leader Anwar Sadat believes that a bloody nose might persuade Israel to negotiate seriously over the Arab territory lost during the 1967 Six-Day War.

• 1807 – POTASSIUM DISCOVERED • 1928 – CHIANG KAI-SHEK MADE PRESIDENT OF CHINA

US TO ROOT OUT TERRORISTS IN AFGHANISTAN

2001 Today President George Bush announced the start of Operation Enduring Freedom whose aim is to root out al-Qaeda members, particularly Osama bin Laden, from Afghanistan. US and UK troops will join with those of the Northern Alliance, a federation of groups opposed to the Taliban regime in Afghanistan. The terrorists, who were behind the September 11 attacks, are thought to be hiding out in caves in the Afghan White Mountains.

Decades of pain and humiliation – that is precisely what differentiates Central European countries from their Western counterparts.

Czeslaw Milosz,
Polish novelist and 1980 Nobel Prize for Literature winner, 1991.

1908 Crete revolts against Turkish domination, seeking unity with Greece.

1919 Holland's first airline, KLM, is established.

1959 Pictures of the far side of the moon are relayed back to Earth for the first time.

1985 Italian cruise liner the *Achille Lauro* is seized by Palestinian terrorists.

1988 An international rescue operation seeks to free grey whales trapped in ice in Alaska.

2006 Russian journalist Anna Politkovskaya is murdered in Moscow.

ARNIE ELECTED GOVERNOR

2003 Hollywood film star Arnold Schwarzenegger has won the race for governor of California, ousting the Democrat incumbent Gray Davis. It is the first time that Californians have voted to sack their governor mid-term. With almost all the votes counted, Schwarzenegger – running as a Republican – has secured almost 48%. In a victory speech, Mr Schwarzenegger thanked the people of California for giving him their trust.

BIRTHDAYS

Heinrich Himmler 1900, German head of the Gestapo.

Reverend Desmond Tutu 1931, South African archbishop of Cape Town who was awarded the Nobel Peace Prize in 1984.

Thomas Keneally 1936, Australian author whose novel *Schindler's Ark*, based on a true story, won him the Booker Prize.

Vladimir Putin 1952, elected as Russian President in 2000.

Jayne Torville 1957, British ice-skating champion.

TURKS INVINCIBILITY BLOWN AT LEPANTO

1571 A Holy League of naval forces from Spain, Venice and the Vatican has exploded the myth of Turkish military invincibility by annhilating their fleet at the battle of Lepanto in the eastern Mediterranean. The Turkish commander, Ali Pasha, was killed in the fray along with 25,000 of his men. The fleets were evenly matched with about 200 galleys and 80,000 men on either side. Christian galley slaves accounted for half of the Turkish manpower; 12,000 of them have been freed. Turkish galley-losses are estimated at about 150 to the allies' 15. The architect of the Holy League's victory is the dashing Don John of Austria, 24, who has managed to weld disparate fleets into an effective force.

1805 The outnumbered French troops defeat the invading Austrians at Ulm.

1809 Metternich is appointed Austrian foreign minister.

1952 A rail crash in Harrow, Britain involving three trains kills 112.

1965 Britain's tallest building to date, London's Post Office Tower opens.

1967 The first British speeding motorist is breathalysed, in Somerset.

1973 The first legal commercial radio station in Britain opens as LBC (London Broadcasting) goes on the air.

BIRTHDAYS

Sir Alfred Munnings 1878, English artist, critic and president of the Royal Academy.

Juan Perón 1895, Argentinian general and president.

Cesar Milstein 1927, British molecular biologist who in 1984 shared the Nobel Prize for Medicine for his work.

Reverend Jesse Jackson 1941, American politician and black civil rights campaigner.

HAITIAN DESPOT TAKES OWN LIFE

1820 Henri Christophe, the Haitian leader who believed that despotism was the only form of government for his people, has shot himself. He was 53. A former slave, Christophe rose to prominence as a military commander during the war against the French in 1791. After 1806, when his efforts to become overlord of the entire country had been thwarted, Christophe established his own fiefdom in northern Haiti. He built a fortress, Citadelle Laferrière, south of his capital, Cap-Haitien. His people have been in revolt for the past two months – since hearing that their despotic ruler, now calling himself King Henri I, had suffered a stroke. Christophe could expect no mercy.

DOW JONES TRACES UPS AND DOWNS

1897 A New York news agency has come up with the novel idea of charting the general trends in the trading of stocks and bonds on Wall Street. The company, Dow Jones & Co, Inc, computes a daily industrials average by using a list of 12 stocks and dividing their total price by 12. The creator of this unique statistical measure is the highly respected financial journalist Charles Henry Dow, 46, the founder and editor of *The Wall Street Journal*.

MULTI-MILLION BULLION RESCUED

1981 Treasure worth £45 million ($83 million) which has lain in the Barents Sea for almost 40 years was retrieved last night. For the past three weeks a team of 10 divers has been working round the clock to recover 431 gold bars, weighing 23 lb (10.5 kg) apiece, from the hull of the British cruiser, *Edinburgh*. In May 1942 the ship was transporting the bullion from Russia to Britain when she became involved in a running battle with German destroyers and a U-boat and was eventually sunk. The companies involved in the salvage operation, Wharton Williams and Jessop Marine Recoveries, will receive 45 per cent of the value of the gold. The British and Soviet governments will receive the rest.

• **1871 – WELLINGTON INVADES FRANCE** • **2005 – INDIAN EARTHQUAKE KILLS 73,000**

KILLER FIRE SWEEPS THROUGH CHICAGO

1871 Fire has devastated Chicago. The inferno began yesterday in the southwestern part of the city and quickly spread north. The recent long spell of dry weather rendered the city's many wooden buildings into ideal tinder. About 300 people are estimated to have lost their lives, and a further 90,000 their homes. In all, four square miles of the city have been destroyed, including the business sector, at a cost of $200 million (£108 million). Improved safety standards are expected to be the priority of any reconstruction programme for the city.

1192 King Richard the Lionheart abandons the Holy Land after an unsuccessful Crusade.

1962 Uganda receives formal independence.

1963 Three thousand lives are lost when the Vajont Dam in the Alps is wrecked by a rock slide.

1973 Elvis Presley divorces Priscilla.

1987 Death of Clare Boothe Luce, former US congresswoman, ambassador, novelist, editor and playwright who wrote *The Women*.

BIRTHDAYS

Camille Saint-Saens 1835, French composer and pianist who is perhaps best known for his opera *Samson and Delilah*.

Jacques Tati 1908, French actor, film director and screenwriter.

John Lennon 1940, English pop singer, musician and songwriter who rose to fame with the Beatles.

Steve Ovett 1955, British middle-distance runner who won the gold medal at the Moscow Olympics in 1980.

NOBEL PROBLEMS FOR SOLZHENITSYN

1970 The winner of this year's Nobel Prize for Literature, dissident Soviet writer Aleksandr Solzhenitsyn, has excused himself from attending the award ceremony in Stockholm in December, for "personal reasons". It is unclear whether the Soviet authorities refused to permit him to leave the USSR or whether Solzhenitsyn declined to go for fear that he would not be re-admitted. The championing of Solzhenitsyn in the West has made life difficult for him with the Soviet authorities, who view the award as provocation. Last year he was expelled from the Soviet Writers' Union.

CHE SHOT DOWN ON THE JOB

1967 Ernesto "Che" Guevara, the Argentine-born revolutionary who helped Fidel Castro win power in Cuba, has been shot dead after being captured by Bolivian Army troops. He was 39. Che Guevara was in Bolivia as part of a Cuban-sponsored expedition to topple the military government of President Barrientos and export Fidel Castro's brand of Communism to other Latin American countries. The struggle in Bolivia is expected to be carried on under the leadership of Inti Peredo, although without the charismatic Che Guevara the prospects of the movement do not look good.

• 1984 – JORDAN RESUMES DIPLOMATIC RELATIONS WITH EGYPT

1794 The Russians crush the rebel Polish army, taking its leader prisoner.

1903 British suffragette Mrs Emmeline Pankhurst forms the Women's Social and Political Union in Manchester to fight for female emancipation.

1911 The Chinese revolution breaks out at Wuchang in Central China.

1940 A German bomb destroys the high altar of St Paul's Cathedral in London.

1954 Ho Chi Minh returns to Hanoi as the French evacuate.

1957 A major radiation leak is detected at the Windscale atomic power station in Cumbria following a nuclear accident on October 7.

1985 Death of Yul Brynner, bald-headed American actor.

BIRTHDAYS

Antoine Watteau 1684, French rococo painter of the famous in rural backgrounds.

Giuseppe Verdi 1813, Italian romantic opera composer.

Thelonius Monk 1920, American jazz pianist and composer.

CITIZEN WELLES

1985 Orson Welles died at his Los Angeles home today, aged 70. Wisconsin-born Welles (real name George Orson) knew success early in his career. In 1938, when he was only 23, he came to the attention of Hollywood with his radio production of H. G. Wells' *The War of the Worlds*, which had several million Americans believing that Martians had landed in New Jersey. His first film, *Citizen Kane*, which he directed, produced, wrote and starred in, was highly praised. But there was no way but down from this pinnacle of perfection. Disillusioned, he left Hollywood after the war to act in Europe. Eventually Welles drifted into television, providing voice-overs for commercials, most notably Carlsberg beer.

Music creates order out of chaos; for rhythm imposes unanimity upon the divergent, melody imposes continuity upon the disjointed, and harmony imposes compatibility upon the incongruous.

Yehudi Menuhin, violinist, 1976.

YALE BREAK AT NEW HAVEN

1718 Puritan leader Cotton Mather definitely seems to have the Lord on his side. He has received a generous response to his request for further assistance for the Saybrook School from its principal benefactor, wealthy British trader Elihu Yale. Mr Yale responded with gifts worth £800 ($1470). The money from the sale of these items – which included a portrait of George I – will be used to construct a building, to be called Yale College, at the university's new home in New Haven. The university's curriculum emphasizes classical studies and rigid adherence to orthodox Puritanism. Mather and his fellow Congregationalists determined from the outset that their college would not be based on the Harvard model – that bastion of learning is also a hotbed of religious dissent.

• 1935 – *PORGY AND BESS* OPENS IN NEW YORK • 1975 – BURTON AND TAYLOR REMARRY

ALGERIA STRICKEN

1980 The Algerian city of El Asnam was hit by an earthquake of catastrophic proportions yesterday. Algerian radio said that 80 per cent of the city was destroyed. Twenty thousand are feared dead. The first shock wave registered 7.5 on the Richter scale. El Asnam (formerly Orleansville) had to be almost totally rebuilt after the last earthquake, in 1954, which damaged an area of 30 square miles (78 sq km). The city stands on a section of an unstable fault zone stretching from Gabes, Tunisia to Agadir, Morocco. President Chadli Bendjedid has proclaimed a week's national mourning.

JODRELL REACHES FOR THE STARS

1957 The world's largest steerable radio-telescope went into operation at the Jodrell Observatory today. The instrument, which has a 250-ft (81-m) diameter parabolic bowl, is mounted on a trunnion 180 ft (58 m) above ground level. The telescope's designer, Bernard Lovell, has completed his project in time for tracking the first Sputnik, launched one week ago.

Tact consists in knowing how far we may go too far.

Jean Cocteau,
who died today, 1963.

1809 Death of Meriwether Lewis, American explorer.

1919 The first in-flight meals are served on board a London to Paris flight.

1961 Death of Leonard "Chico" Marx.

1976 The widow of Mao Tse-tung, Qiang Qing, is arrested in Berlin for attempting to seize power on Mao's death.

1980 Soviet cosmonauts return to earth after a record 185 days in space in the craft *Salyut 6*.

Sir George Williams 1821, English social reformer who founded the YMCA.

Eleanor Roosevelt 1884, American writer and civil rights campaigner who was married to US president Franklin D. Roosevelt.

François Mauriac 1885, French novelist, dramatist and critic.

Art Blakey 1919, American jazz drummer and leader of the Jazz Messengers.

Robert "Bobby" Charlton 1937, English footballer, who in 1966 won the World Cup and was named European Player of the Year.

SEARCHING FOR NESSIE

1987 The latest in sonic wizardry has been brought in to settle the long dispute over the existence of the Loch Ness monster. "Nessie" was first sighted by an unimpeachable source – St Columba – back in 565. Since then there have been numerous claims of sightings, including photographic evidence. Today's trawl of the loch by some 24 boats fitted with sophisticated sonic detectors revealed a large moving object at a depth of around 180 ft (58 m). A positive identification of the object has yet to be made, however.

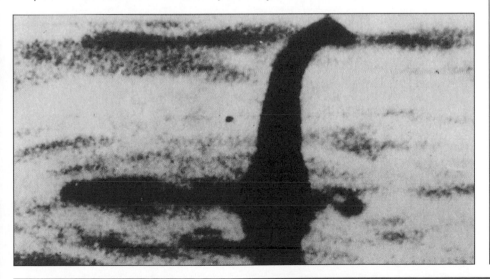

• 1727 – GEORGE II CROWNED IN ENGLAND • 1968 – LAUNCH OF *APOLLO 7*

1609 "Three Blind Mice" is the first known secular song to be published.

1845 Death of Elizabeth Fry, English social and prison reformer.

1924 Death of Anatole France, French writer and Nobel Prize winner.

1928 The first "iron lung" is used at the Boston Children's Hospital in Massachusetts.

1964 Death of Ian Fleming, the English creator of the fictional character James Bond.

2002 Nearly 200 people are killed when a bomb explodes inside a nightclub in Bali, Indonesia. Muslim groups linked to Al-Qaeda are blamed.

BIRTHDAYS

Edward VI 1537, English monarch, the son of Henry VIII and Jane Seymour.

Ramsay McDonald 1866, Scottish statesman and first Labour prime minister of Britain.

Jaroslav Drobny 1921, Czech tennis champion who defected to the West.

Luciano Pavarotti 1935, Italian tenor of huge popularity.

CAVELL PAYS HIGH PRICE FOR HUMANITY

1915 The German authorities in Belgium have executed British nurse Edith Cavell, 50, for her role in an underground operation to help Allied soldiers escape from Belgium to the Netherlands, a neutral country. Cavell had confessed to providing shelter for escapees at the Berkendael Institute in Brussels, a Red Cross hospital of which she was matron. There the men received money and guides from Philippe Baucq, who was arrested and subsequently shot with Nurse Cavell. Reports suggest that responsibility for her death lies solely with the occupation administration in Belgium, which committed the deed before telling the Berlin authorities.

BOERS GET FIRST STRIKE

1899 The Boer states have responded to Britain's dispatch of troops to South Africa by issuing a declaration of war, and they have already drawn first blood. The British military garrison at Mafeking, under Colonel Robert Baden-Powell, is currently under siege by Boer forces. If the siege drags on, and it seems likely to do so, it may become a symbol of the wider struggle between a colonial power intent on defending its commercial rights and Dutch Boers who resent British inroads in South Africa.

TERRA FIRMA IS NOT A MIRAGE

1492 Following a month in which he has experienced many mirages of land, intrepid explorer Christopher Columbus and his three ships have finally sighted terra firma. The sighting took place at the crack of dawn this morning. Columbus went ashore and took possession of the island in the name of his patrons, Isabella and Ferdinand of Spain, but is already keen to set sail again, to find the Island of Cipango.

• 1901 – WHITE HOUSE OFFICIALLY NAMED • 1984 – IRA BOMB THATCHER IN BRIGHTON

TURIN SHROUD A FORGERY

1988 The Turin Shroud, for centuries regarded as the burial cloth of Jesus Christ, is believed to be a fake. The results of exhaustive carbon dating tests, carried out on the shroud at laboratories in Oxford, Zurich and Arizona, were revealed today. Speaking at a press conference in London, Professor Edward Hall, the head of the Oxford team, said that the data showed with 95 per cent certainty that the 14 ft (4.5 m) linen cloth dated from between 1260 and 1390, a period when forgery was rife. The Catholic Church, which has consistently expressed caution over the shroud's origins, accepts the findings, but one regular visitor to the Turin Cathedral chapel, Signora Angela Bosso, 72, remarked: "I don't believe in those scientists."

MINING NIGHTMARE DRAWS TO A CLOSE

2010 The last of 33 Chilean miners who spent 69 days in a collapsed copper and gold mine, is winched to safety. The miners were trapped 700 m (2,300 ft) below the surface when part of the San José mine collapsed on 5 August. A new shaft had to be made with specially designed drilling equipment to free the trapped men.

TWELVE GOOD MEN UNITE JEWRY

1843 Twelve men met in a café on New York's Lower East Side today to establish a new fraternal order of Jews in the USA. Their aim is to bring a sense of community to the 15,000 Jewish people living in the United States. They plan to concentrate initially on arranging private rituals and providing assistance to the elderly, widows and orphans and victims of tragedy and persecution. The name of the new organization is B'nai B'rith. meaning "Sons of the Covenant".

My definition of a free society is a society where it is safe to be unpopular.
Adlai Stevenson, US politician, 1952.

1399 Coronation of Henry IV, the first King of the House of Lancaster.

1792 US President George Washington lays the foundation stone of the White House.

1904 *The Interpretation of Dreams* by Austrian psychoanalyst Sigmund Freud is published.

1988 The Law Lords lift an injunction and allow British newspapers to print extracts from Peter Wright's book *Spycatcher*.

BIRTHDAYS

Lenny Bruce 1924, American social satirist who was arrested and charged with obscenity on several occasions.

Margaret Thatcher 1925, British Conservative politician and prime minister from 1979 to 1990.

Paul Simon 1941, American pop singer, songwriter and musician who, as part of the duo Simon and Garfunkel, produced big hits such as "Mrs Robinson".

Ian Thorpe 1982, swimmer who has won five Olympic golds, more than any other Australian.

• AD 54 – ROMAN EMPEROR CLAUDIUS I DIES • 1857 – US HORSE WINS AT NEWMARKET

1791 The Society of United Irishmen is set up in Belfast to demand rights for Catholics.

1912 President Theodore Roosevelt is shot in an attempted assassination.

1939 The Royal Navy battleship *Royal Oak* is torpedoed and sinks in Scapa Flow with a loss of 810 lives.

1976 Death of Dame Edith Evans, Britsh stage actress.

2010 French-American mathematician and father of fractal geometry Benoît Mandelbrot dies, aged 85.

BIRTHDAYS

William Penn 1644, English Quaker leader who founded the American Quaker colony of Pennsylvania.

Eamon de Valera 1882, American-born Irish politician who was president of the newly declared Irish Republic from 1919–22, three times Irish prime minister and subsequently president from 1959–73.

Dwight D. Eisenhower 1890, American military commander and twice US president after the war.

HAROLD FALLS AT HASTINGS

1066 The dispute over who should succeed the late Edward the Confessor as king of England was settled in a battle near Hastings today. On his deathbed Edward is thought to have named Earl Godwin's son, Harold, his successor in order to prevent bloodshed between two other claimants, William, Duke of Normandy and Harald Hardrada, king of Norway. When the two heard that Harold had been crowned, they joined forces and set sail for England. Harold threw back the challenge from the north, killing his Norwegian namesake. But today the English peasant army lost heart soon after their leader fell, mortally wounded. The Normans are heading for London, to secure William's position.

HUMAN BREAKS SOUND BARRIER

2012 Austrian skydiver Felix Baumgartner became the first human to break the sound barrier without mechanized propulsion after jumping from a platform 39 kilometres above the Earth. Baumgartner hit estimated speeds of 1357.64 km/h (843.6 mph), or Mach 1.25 during his descent, which lasted over four minutes. He landed in eastern New Mexico. His suit was specially designed to withstand the varying pressures during his descent, and was responsible for ensuring his blood didn't boil or lungs explode. Baumgartner was reflective in his post-jump comments, saying "Sometimes you have to go up really high to see how small you are."

NEW HOPE FOR BURMA

1991 This year's Nobel Peace Prize has been awarded to the Burmese opposition leader Aung San Suu Kyi. Daughter of the martyred General Aung San, she returned to Burma in 1988, after an absence of 28 years, founding the political party, the NLD (National League for Democracy). She denounced the government and in July 1989 was put under house arrest and barred from participating in the May 1990 elections. Despite winning only 10 out of 485 seats, the military refused to hand over power to the NLD, which won 81 per cent of the seats they contested. The Peace Prize may be seen as part of an international effort to win her release.

• 1913 – **BRITAIN'S WORST MINING DISASTER** • 1944 – **FIELD MARSHALL ROMMEL DIES**

MILLIONS MARCH TO END VIETNAM WAR

1969 The biggest anti-war demonstration in America's history was staged today. Millions of Americans took part in organized rallies and marches to register disapproval of their country's continuing involvement in the Vietnam War. The protesters want a moratorium, an end to the war that has, after eight years of US involvement, cost the lives of 40,000 US servicemen.

1821 The Central American Federation wins independence from Spain.

1927 Britain's Public Morals Committee attacks the use of contraceptives.

1945 French politician Pierre Laval, who led the Vichy government in World War Two, is executed.

1964 Harold Wilson wins the British elections for the Labour Party.

1997 *Thrust* sets the first supersonic land speed record, breaking the sound barrier at 766 mph (1226 kph).

BIRTHDAYS

Virgil 70 BC, Roman epic, didactic and pastoral poet.

Evangelista Torricelli 1608, Italian mathematician who invented the barometer.

Friedrich Wilhelm Nietzsche 1844, German philosopher who developed the idea of the *Ubermensch*.

P. G. Woodhouse 1881, English author of more than 90 books who created the famous butler Jeeves.

C. P. Snow 1905, British author and parliamentary secretary to the Ministry of Science and Technology.

GREGORIAN YEAR

1582 Pope Gregory XIII has decreed that 10 days should be dropped from the annual calendar. The Julian calendar calculated a year as 365¼ days, overestimating it by 11 minutes 14 seconds. The equinox this year fell on March 11, 14 days earlier than in Caesar's time. By losing 10 days this month and counting years ending in hundreds as leap years only if they are divisible by 400, the new calendar should now work.

MULTI-RACIAL VICTORY

1993 ANC leader Nelson Mandela and President F. W. de Klerk of South Africa have today been jointly awarded the Nobel Peace prize, as an acknowledgement of their commitment to build a peaceful, multi-racial South Africa. The prize comes after years of negotiations between the two men.

I'm not interested in the bloody system! Why has he no food? Why is he starving to death?

Bob Geldof, Irish rock musician, in Ethiopia during the famine, 1985.

• 1928 – *GRAF ZEPPELIN* MAKES 1ST ATLANTIC CROSSING • 1964 – COLE PORTER DIES

1906 British New Guinea becomes part of Australia.

1975 GOES I (Geostationary Operational Environmental Satellite) is launched.

1978 Polish cardinal Karol Wojtyla is elected Pope, the first non-Italian pope since 1542.

1989 A committee of the Convention in International Trade in Endangered Species meeting in Lausanne, Switzerland, votes 76–11 in favour of a ban on the trade in ivory.

BIRTHDAYS

Noah Webster 1758, American lexicographer responsible for the first American dictionary.

Oscar Wilde 1854, Irish-born writer and wit whose work includes the play *The Importance of Being Earnest*.

David Ben-Gurion 1886, Polish-born first Israeli prime minister who was the leading force in the creation of the state.

Eugene O'Neill 1888, American dramatist whose finest plays include *The Iceman Cometh*.

Günter Grass 1927, German novelist, author of *The Tin Drum*.

WORST STORM, BUT NO WARNING

1987 The London Weather Centre is battening down its hatches to meet a deluge of criticism after failing to alert southern England to the imminent arrival of the worst storm to hit Britain in 300 years. The violence of the Force-11 storm brought down roofs, chimneys, trees and power lines, claimed the lives of 18 people and caused an estimated £100 million ($184 million) of damage. Life was brought to a halt on land and sea as police advised people to stay at home rather than add to the chaos. Sevenoaks in Kent has lost six of the giant oak trees which gave the town its name, while experts at Kew Gardens said that it would take about 200 years to replace some of the trees lost from their arboretum. The Met Office is blaming a computer error for its miscalculation.

PINOCHET ARRESTED

1998 The former Chilean military dictator Augusto Pinochet has been arrested in London in the first step of extradition proceedings. Spain has applied to have Pinochet brought to justice on human rights charges relating to the war that followed the overthrow of President Allende in 1973. His arrest has caused much controversy around the world, with some saying the former dictator should have immunity from prosecution.

JUSTICE WROUGHT IN NUREMBERG

1946 Ten leading Nazis found guilty of crimes against humanity by the International War Crimes Tribunal a fortnight ago were hanged at Nuremberg prison today. Hermann Goering chose to exit via a different door, taking poison less than two hours before he was due to be executed.

• 1793 – EXECUTION OF MARIE-ANTOINETTE • 1964 – FIRST CHINESE ATOM BOMB TESTED

ITALY'S ACHILLE'S HEEL

1985 The Italian government under Bettino Craxi fell from power today as a consequence of its handling of the *Achille Lauro* affair. The cruise ship *Achille Lauro*, carrying 454 passengers, was hijacked by Palestinian terrorists ten days ago. They threatened to blow it up if 50 Arab prisoners held in Israel were not released. After tortuous negotiations the release of the ship and its passengers, minus one elderly man, Leon Klinghoffer, whom the terrorists had murdered, was secured and the Palestinians promised its safe passage to Tunis. On the orders of President Reagan, US jet fighters intercepted the terrorists' plane, forcing it to land in Sicily. The US were keen to apprehend Mohammed Abbas, the mastermind of this

hijack. US forces and Italian Carabinieri then clashed over who had the right to arrest the hijackers. The US bowed to Italian sensitivities. Abbas was arrested and then allowed into neighbouring Yugoslavia by the Italian authorities.

1651 Defeated by Oliver Cromwell at Worcester, Charles II of England flees to France.

1806 The tyrannical Emperor Jacques I, first ruler of independent Haiti, is assassinated.

1985 The House of Lords votes to allow doctors to prescribe contraceptives to girls under the age of 16 without parental consent, ending a campaign by Catholic mother Mrs Victoria Gillick against such action.

1988 Beethoven's Tenth Symphony is performed for the first time in London.

BIRTHDAYS

John Wilkes 1727, English journalist and political agitator who campaigned for press freedom.

Baroness Karen Blixen 1885, Danish author of *Out of Africa*.

Rita Hayworth 1918, American actress and dancer who often partnered Fred Astaire.

Montgomery Clift 1920, American actor usually given introspective roles.

Ernie Els 1969, South African golfing champion known as "the Big Easy".

OIL COUNTRIES BLACKMAIL WEST

1973 The ten Arab members of Opec announced an enormous 70 per cent hike in oil prices and a cutback in production in response to America's support for Israel in the Yom Kippur War. President Nixon had proposed a $2200 million aid package to the beleaguered nation. Western Europe will be particularly hard hit by the decision because it relies on the Arab producers for 80 per cent of its oil. Inflation and petrol rationing are expected. The Arabs' policy is likely to drive a wedge between the US, on whom an oil embargo has also been imposed, and Europe, which is fearful of further retaliatory measures for America's support for Israel.

PERÓN WOOS ARGENTINA

1945 Tonight Domingo Perón addressed a 300,000-strong crowd from the balcony of the presidential palace in Buenos Aires, and told them of his desire for a just and strong nation. In his speech, ex-military man Perón promised that he would lead the people to victory in the forthcoming presidential election. Two weeks ago Perón's ambition to become undisputed leader of the Argentinian people received a severe setback when he was ousted from his positions of vice-president and minister of war. His re-emergence is due largely to his politically astute wife, Eva Duarte, who helped rally support.

• 1849 – FREDERIC CHOPIN DIES • 1956 – BRITAIN OPENS FIRST NUCLEAR POWER STATION

1865 Lord Palmerston, twice British prime minister, dies.

1898 The US takes possession of Puerto Rico from Spain.

1907 The first plans are announced for an International Court of Justice to be set up in the Hague.

1966 The Queen grants a royal pardon to Timothy Evans, who was hanged for the murder of his wife and child in West London.

1968 John Lennon and Yoko Ono are remanded on bail for possession of cannabis following a police raid at their flat in Montague Square, London.

BIRTHDAYS

Canaletto 1697, Italian painter best remembered for his views of Venice.

Pierre de Laclos 1741, French author of *Les Liaisons Dangereuses*.

Chuck Berry 1926, American rock and roll pioneer whose hits included "Maybelline".

Martina Navratilova 1956, Czech-born American tennis champion who won the Wimbledon women's singles title nine times.

END OF AN ERA

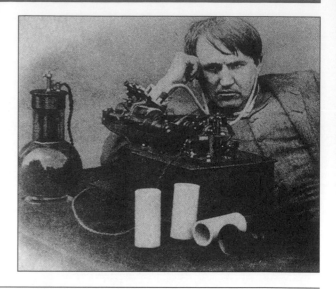

1931 America's most prolific inventor, Thomas Alva Edison, has died at the age of 84. Edison's lack of formal education proved no handicap to him: his inventions include the phonograph, microphone and the kinetoscope. He designed a complete electrical distribution system for lighting and power.

HARDLINER SIDELINED

1989 Erich Honecker, East Germany's hardline ruler, has been ousted from the job he has held for the past 18 years. His economic chief, Günter Mittag, and minister for propaganda and agitation, Joachim Herrmann, have also been forced to quit. The unsmiling, bureaucratic Honecker, 77, had failed to respond to the desire among East Germans for change. The new ruler the 21-man Politburo are pinning their hopes on is the youthful Egon Krenz, 52. Reform groups are not convinced that Egon Krenz, formerly head of internal and external security, will set the wheels of reform moving. In their eyes he is closely associated with the policies that have created the discontent.

ORDEAL OVER AS HOSTAGES FREED

1977 The five-day ordeal of passengers aboard a German Lufthansa jet hijacked by Palestinian terrorists ended today when a squad of crack troops stormed the aircraft at Mogadishu airport when it became likely that passengers would be killed. Three of the four Palestinians were killed in the shoot-out. The terrorists had already killed the pilot, Jurgen Schumann. The hijack was in support of the left-wing Baader-Meinhof urban terrorist group.

FRENCH SUFFER BRAIN DRAIN

1685 The French king Louis XIV has turned the screw still further on Protestants by revoking the Edict of Nantes. In 1598 Henri IV issued this edict to safeguard the civic and religious rights of French Protestants – Huguenots – and to usher in a new age of toleration. Thousands of Protestants are expected to respond to today's action by fleeing. Some warn of dire consequences to the French economy as a result of such a skills drain.

• 1873 – RULES OF AMERICAN FOOTBALL FORMULATED • 1995 – RED RUM DIES

NIGHTMARE ON WALL STREET

1987 Wall Street has experienced the worst day in its history, with the Dow Jones Industrial Average plummeting a record 508.32 points, wiping $500 billion (£270 billion) off the value of shares. The percentage decline was 22.6, almost 10 per cent higher than the big crash of 1929. Last Friday a record 338.5 million shares changed hands as wave after wave of sell orders hit traders. The dramatic sell-off has hit stock markets around the world. In London the FT index fell 250 points, responding to the overnight collapse in Tokyo and other Far Eastern markets and slashing more than £50 billion ($92 billion) off share values. There was no sign, however, of the panic selling that has turned Wall Street from a bull to a bear market

almost overnight. The change in mood has been caused by fears about America's persistent trade deficit, now $15.7 billion (£8.4 billion), a 40 per cent depreciation in the value of the dollar over the past year and the spectre of further increases in interest rates.

You cannot shake hands with a clenched fist.
Indira Gandhi, on this day 1971, at a press conference in New Delhi.

NO WAY OUT FOR BRITISH

1781 British commander General Charles Cornwallis, 46, delivered his 8000 troops into the hands of the besieging American forces at Yorktown today. Two days ago Cornwallis had signalled his willingness to come to terms. He had been hemmed in by superior forces on land and at sea for the past three weeks with no relief in sight. All he could do was surrender, allowing General Washington finally to win the War of Independence for the colonists.

1860 The first company to manufacture internal combustion engines is formed in Florence.

1901 Brazilian aviator Alberto Santos Dumont circumnavigates the Eiffel Tower in his airship to win the first aviation prize.

1950 The North Korean capital of Pyongyang falls during the Korean War.

1987 One of Britain's finest cellists, Jacqueline du Pre, dies.

2000 The oldest ever cave painting is discovered near Verona.

2003 Mother Teresa of Calcutta is beatified.

BIRTHDAYS

Alfred Dreyfus 1859, French army officer who was falsely accused of treason.

Auguste Lumière 1862, French moving picture pioneer who, with his brother Louis, developed and manufactured the cinématographe.

John Le Carré 1931, British novelist whose job in the British Foreign Service influenced his writing.

Evander Holyfield 1962, US boxing champion.

• 1864 – BATTLE OF CEDAR CREEK IN THE AMERICAN CIVIL WAR

BIRTHDAYS

Sir Christopher Wren 1632, English architect famous for many major English buildings including St Paul's Cathedral in London.

Dame Anna Neagle 1904, British actress and former chorus dancer who starred in many films.

Danny Boyle 1956, English filmmaker who directed *Trainspotting* and won an Oscar in 2008 for *Slumdog Millionaire*.

MAO'S MARCH OF DESTINY

1935 Three hundred and sixty-four days ago military pressure by the Nationalist army of Chiang Kai-Shek forced the evacuation of Kiangsi Province, where the Communists, under Mao Tse-tung had established their Chinese Soviet Republic. An estimated 90,000 people began the migration to the relative safety of Shensi Province on the Yellow River. Today the survivors of that long and arduous march through difficult mountain terrain reached their destination. More than half the marchers perished during the 6000-mile (9600-km) journey. The first task for Communist leader Mao Tse-tung will be to organize a strong defensive position. Shensi has the potential to provide a more secure power base for the Communists, but only if its defences can thwart future Nationalist attacks.

A CHANCE TO SERVE

1915 Less than three months after 30,000 women marched down Whitehall shouting the slogan "We demand the right to serve", Prime Minister David Lloyd George has granted them their wish. The war now raging in Europe has left Britain with a labour shortfall and given women the opportunity to step into the breach. Government departments have vacancies for 200,000, private offices for about half a million, and agriculture and engineering a million between them. Trams and buses up and down the country are to team a male driver with a female conductor. Trade unionists fear the move may depress wages.

One starts to get young at the age of sixty and then it's too late.

Pablo Picasso, 1963.

BEGINNING OF THE END FOR GERMANY

1944 The US First Army, commanded by General Hodges, has announced that the German city of Aachen is now firmly in its control after a battle lasting over a week. More than 10,000 prisoners have been taken. The city is the first major German centre to fall to the Allies in its attempted push through the Siegfried Line. Much of the ancient city has been destroyed.

• 1822 – 1ST EDITION OF *THE SUNDAY TIMES* PUBLISHED IN BRITAIN

OPERA HOUSE'S VERY OWN DRAMA

1973 The Sydney Opera House was opened today by Her Majesty the Queen. The unique design of the building caused costs to soar, from an estimated A$7 million (£3 million) to an astronomical A$100 million (£43 million) plus. The most striking features of the house are its three sets of roof shells. These contain about 2000 panes of glass.

HUGE RIVER OF COAL CRUSHES ABERFAN

1966 The tiny Welsh coalmining community of Aberfan was hit by disaster today when a 500-ft (162-m) coal tip slipped, crushing Pantglas Junior School, a row of cottages and a farmhouse. The death toll of 144 people includes 116 children aged between seven and eleven years old. One eyewitness described the river of coal sludge that buried the village as "a black flood with a noise like thunder". The cause of the disaster is to be established by a special tribunal. The safety procedures operated by the National Coal Board, who run the Merthyr Vale colliery, are expected to come under close scrutiny.

NELSON TRIUMPHS

1805 Admiral Sir Horatio Nelson has clashed with French Admiral Villeneuve for the last time. After four hours of fierce exchanges off the southwest coast of Spain – and superlative manoeuvring by the British commanders –the Allied Fleet was finally beaten, losing 18 ships – more than half its strength. The worst blow of all, however, was the loss of Admiral Nelson, who was mortally wounded by a French sniper as he stood on the deck of his flagship *Victory*. The Battle of Trafalgar will be remembered as his finest victory.

1789 Martial law is imposed in France.

1923 The world's first planetarium opens in Munich.

1952 President of the Kenya African movement Jomo Kenyatta is arrested as Britain crushes the Mau Mau rebels.

1967 Norman Mailer is arrested in an anti-Vietnam peace demo.

1969 Willy Brandt is elected Chancellor of West Germany.

1979 In Britain unions agree to suspend *The Times* newspaper strike.

BIRTHDAYS

Katsushka Hokusai 1760, Japanese painter, engraver and printmaker.

Samuel Taylor Coleridge 1772, English poet.

Alfred Nobel 1833, Swedish industrialist and chemist who invented dynamite and founded the Nobel Prize.

Dizzie Gillespie 1917, American trumpet player and band leader.

Carrie Fisher 1956, American novelist, whose books include *Postcards from the Edge*.

• 1858 – *ORPHEUS IN THE UNDERWORLD* PREMIERES • 1969 – DEATH OF JACK KEROUAC

1835 Sam Houston is sworn in as president of the Texas republic.

1934 The American gangster Charles Arthur "Pretty Boy" Floyd is killed by FBI agents.

1962 ANC leader Nelson Mandela goes on trial for treason in South Africa, pleading not guilty.

1975 Death of Arnold Toynbee, historian and philosopher whose Study of History explores patterns of growth and decay of civilizations.

1987 The first volume of the Gutenberg Bible fetches $5.39 million (£3.26 million) in New York auction rooms.

BIRTHDAYS

Franz Liszt 1811, Hungarian composer of Romantic music and creator of the symphonic poem.

Sarah Bernhardt 1844, French stage actress who was hugely successful.

Joan Fontaine 1917, British actress who won an Oscar for her role in *The Constant Nymph*.

Catherine Deneuve 1943, French actress whose films include *Belle de Jour*.

SUPERSPY SCRAMBLES OUT OF SCRUBS TO FREEDOM

1966 KGB master spy George Blake has escaped from the maximum security wing of Wormwood Scrubs prison in West London. Blake, a former MI6 officer, had spied for the Russians for 12 years, revealing Britain's spy ring in East Berlin to the KGB and also the location of the tunnel from where US and British intelligence agents tapped Warsaw Pact communications. The sentence meted out to him in 1962 was the longest ever: 42 years, one year for each of the lives that Blake's treachery is estimated to have cost. Blake used a home-made rope ladder to scale the Scrubs' high perimeter wall. The media are pointing the finger at the KGB as his likely rescuers, although they can put forward no sound reason for Russian involvement in such a high-risk enterprise since the man is of no further use to them.

THE WINDSORS DROP IN ON HITLER

1937 The Duke of Windsor, former heir to the British throne, and his wife, Wallis, rounded off their tour of Germany today with a visit to Adolf Hitler's mountain eyrie at Berchtesgaden in Bavaria. The Führer and all the top Nazi officials were there to meet the Windsors, who are said to be enthusiastic supporters of the Nazi regime. The Nazi achievements which have particularly impressed the Duke are full employment and workers' housing. The unofficial tour has caused consternation in British government circles and the Duke had been advised to avoid such visits because of the adverse criticism they would attract.

I dedicate this prize to all those who suffer in public and in private and who never give up dreaming.

Ben Okri, Nigerian author of *The Famished Road*, on winning the Booker Prize, 1991.

KENNEDY EYEBALLS KRUSHCHEV OVER CUBA

1962 US president John F. Kennedy has made a move in the showdown with the USSR over the building of ballistic missile sites in Cuba. In a live broadcast the president said that he would take whatever steps were necessary to force the removal of weapons and installations from Cuban soil. Cuba will be placed under a naval "quarantine" – a blockade – until the Soviets remove them. Kennedy also said that the launch a missile against any nation in the western hemisphere would be viewed by his administration as a declaration of war on the US. Flights by U-2 spy planes recently confirmed the presence of a ballistic missile at a launch site in Cuba, one of many shipped from the USSR as part of Krushchev's promise to defend the fledgling communist state against further Bay of Pigs-type attacks by the US.

• 1906 – ARTIST PAUL CEZANNE DIES • 1917 – TRANS-AUSTRALIAN RAILWAY OPENS

SEXUAL SLAVERY NO LONGER LEGAL

1991 A husband's immunity from a charge of rape under British law was consigned to the dustbin of history today. Five Law Lords have ruled that the statement by 18th-century Chief Justice Sir Matthew Hale that "by their mutual matrimonial consent and contract the wife hath given herself in this kind unto her husband which she cannot retract", forms no part of English law.

NY OPERA LOVERS BUILD OWN THEATRE

1883 A small group of wealthy New Yorkers realized their dream last night at the opening of the new Metropolitan Opera House at Broadway and 34th Street. Frustrated at not being able to get boxes for the opera season at the Academy of Music, they decided to finance their own opera house. Last night's musical offering was Gounod's *Faust*, with Christine Nilsson in the role of Marguerite.

For the really keen cricket fan it's when you discover that your wife left you in May.
Denis Norden, British humorist, 1977.

TB PIONEER WINS NOBEL PRIZE

1952 The Ukrainian-born microbiologist Selman A. Waksman has been awarded the Nobel Prize for Medicine or Physiology for discovering the antibiotic streptomycin, an agent effective in the treatment of tuberculosis. A naturalized US citizen, Waksman, 64, has spent most of his career at Rutgers University. He and his team succeeded in extracting streptomycin from soil cultures in 1944. Subsequent clinical trials confirmed their belief that it would be effective against the micro-organism that causes tuberculosis.

EIGHTH ARMY NEWS

1942 The British Eighth Army today opened a massive offensive against Field Marshall Rommel's Afrika Korps at El Alamein. British field commander General Bernard Montgomery has targeted Rommel's gun emplacements, which

have been pounded with air and artillery fire. Since the inconclusive first battle of Alamein in July, the British have been resupplied and brought up to strength (230,000). The Axis forces number just 80,000.

1642 Charles I's Cavaliers clash with Oliver Cromwell's Parliamentary Roundheads in fierce fighting at the Battle of Edgehill in the Cotswolds.

1915 Death of legendary English cricketer W. G. Grace.

1921 Death of John Boyd Dunlop, Scottish veterinary surgeon who invented the pneumatic bicycle tyre.

1950 Death of American entertainer Al Jolson.

1989 The Lebanese parliament signs an agreement to distribute power equally between the Muslims and Christians.

BIRTHDAYS

Pierre Larousse 1817, French lexicographer and encyclopedist.

Robert Bridges 1844, English poet, playwright and prose writer.

Johnny Carson 1925, American entertainer and leading chat show host.

Diana Dors 1931, British actress and post-war sex-symbol.

Pelé 1940, Brazilian football player who began playing internationally at the age of 16 and scored more than 1000 goals.

• 1926 – LEON TROTSKY IS EXPELLED FROM THE COMMUNIST PARTY

OCTOBER
24

1537 The third wife of Henry VIII, Lady Jane Seymour, dies shortly after giving birth to a son.

1648 Treaty of Westphalia is signed, ending the Thirty Years' War.

1937 New Zealand aviator Jean Batten breaks the record, flying from Australia to England in just five days, 18 hours and 18 minutes.

1989 Fake American television preacher Jim Bakker is sentenced to 45 years in jail.

2005 Rosa Parks, 'the mother of the civil rights movement' dies aged 92.

BIRTHDAYS

Antonie van Leeuwenhoek 1632, Dutch microscopist who was the first man to see bacteria.

Dame Sybil Thorndyke 1882, English actress who gave her finest performance as George Bernard Shaw's *Saint Joan.*

Moss Hart 1904, American playwright and lyricist who wrote comedy hits.

Bill Wyman 1936, British bass guitarist and founder member of the Rolling Stones.

COAST TO COAST

1861 The successful completion of the first transcontinental electric-telegraph has forced the closure of the Pony Express service between St Joseph and Sacramento. The telegraph will be a boon to all citizens and business people east and west. The military are also said to be interested in its uses at a tactical level in the battlefield.

A business that makes nothing but money is a poor kind of business.

Henry Ford. Today the New York stock exchange crashed, 1929.

HUNGARIAN POWDER KEG ABOUT TO GO OFF

1956 Yesterday thousands of Hungarians took to the streets to demonstrate against the reimposition of strict Communist control over their lives under the new Hungarian hardline leader, Ernö Gerö. He responded with a bruising speech that heightened tensions still further. Taking their cue from Gerö, the police fired into the crowds and what was a peaceful demonstration may turn into a revolution.

CONCORDE FLIES FOR THE LAST TIME

2003 Concorde is making its final flights today, after 27 years of supersonic travel. Celebrities will experience the last of three flights, as the plane completes the last leg of a return flight to New York carrying about 100 people. Thousands of people are expected to gather at Heathrow airport to see the three planes touch down. British Airways chief executive officer Rod Eddington said the company was feeling a "mixture of sadness and celebration" about the retirement of Concorde.

• 1945 – VIDKUN QUISLING EXECUTED • 1957 – DEATH OF CHRISTIAN DIOR

GLORIOUS, BUT TOTALLY POINTLESS

1854 A misunderstanding has resulted in heavy British losses for no strategic gain in the Crimea. The incident occurred at Balaclava where the Russians were attempting to disrupt the siege on Sevastopol by attacking the British lines of communication. After the British had repulsed the move, their commander. Lord Raglan, noted that the Russians were trying to evacuate some British-made Turkish guns. He sent instructions for the Light Brigade to capture them. Visibility was very poor and the only guns that Lucan, the divisional cavalry commander, could see were in the main Russian battery

at the end of the North Valley. Believing this to be the objective, he ordered his brother-in-law, Lord Cardigan, to lead the Light Brigade in the charge against it. Despite suffering high casualties – 247 men killed or wounded and 475 horses lost – the Brigade succeeded in reaching the battery and scattering the Russian gunners. The cavalrymen's gallant but futile action was summed up neatly by General Bosquet: "C'est magnifique, mais ce n'est pas la guerre".

CHAUCER TAILS OFF

1400 Geoffrey Chaucer, the courtier, diplomat, civil servant and poet, has died at his home in the gardens of Westminster Abbey. He started writing in the 1380s when the pressures of the unsettled political situation in England encouraged him to seek relief in that direction.

The much-praised love poem *Troylus and Cryseyde* dates from this period. At the time of his death Chaucer was working on a poem about a group of pilgrims journeying to the shrine of Thomas á Becket at Canterbury who pass the time by telling stories.

SATIRISTS CELEBRATE

1986 The British satirical fortnightly magazine *Private Eye* celebrates its 25th birthday today. Originally a magazine filled with jokes and parodies, it broadened its content two years after its launch in 1961. Editor Richard Ingrams decided to unearth and print the scandal and gossip that other papers would no doubt love to, but dare not. This decision has won the magazine mixed reactions from victims and critics.

1556 Charles V, King of Spain and Holy Roman Emperor, retires to a Spanish monastery.

1760 Death of King George II of England.

1839 The world's first railway timetable is published in Manchester.

1900 The British annexe the mineral-rich territory of the Transvaal.

1936 A radio station in Berlin broadcasts the first radio request programme.

1952 The US blocks Communist China's entry to the UN for the third time.

1971 Taiwan is expelled from the UN so that the People's Republic of China can join.

1976 The Queen opens the National Theatre on London's South Bank.

BIRTHDAYS

Johann Strauss the Younger 1825, Austrian composer best known for his waltzes.

Georges Bizet 1838, French composer of the internationally famous opera *Carmen*.

Pablo Picasso 1881, Spanish and one of the greatest and most versatile 20th-century artists.

• 1452 – BATTLE OF AGINCOURT • 1825 – ERIE CANAL OPENS IN NORTH AMERICA

1860 Victor Emmanuel is named King of Italy.

1955 The underground American newspaper *Village Voice* is first published, backed by Norman Mailer.

1958 Pan American Boeing 707 jets and BOAC Comet airliners start flying regular jet services across the Atlantic.

1973 President Nixon prepares to launch World War III after hearing that the Russians are sending arms to the Middle East.

1986 Jeffrey Archer resigns as deputy chairman of the British Conservative Party following allegations that he paid a prostitute to make her leave the country in order to avoid a scandal.

1988 Soviet leader Mikhail Gorbachev promises to free all political prisoners by the end of the year.

BIRTHDAYS

Leon Trotsky 1879, Russian communist leader who was forced into exile by Stalin, sentenced to death in a Soviet court and later murdered in Mexico.

François Mitterand 1919, French president from 1981, founder of the French Socialist Party.

MOSCOW THEATRE SIEGE ENDS IN TRAGEDY

2002 The Moscow theatre siege has come to an end with the deaths of most of the rebels and more than 100 of the hostages. On the day the rebels were due to start executing hostages, Russian special forces pumped a paralysing gas into the auditorium. The authorities have declined to identify the gas. Chechen separatist rebels stormed the building three days ago and have since held the 850-strong audience hostage, threatening to blow up the building unless the Russian authorities called an end to the war in Chechnya.

In free society art is not a weapon . . . Artists are not engineers of the soul.

John F. Kennedy,
US president, 1963.

DOUBT OVER SERIAL KILLINGS

1440 One of the most extraordinary trials in French history, saw nobleman Gilles de Rais, 36, sent to the gallows in Nantes today. He was charged with crimes by two courts: satanism and heresy were levelled against him by a Church court; abduction, torture and murder by a civic court. His 140 or so alleged victims were children. The courts were told that despite inheriting great wealth and extensive lands, Rais' extravagant lifestyle had landed him in financial difficulties. Rais turned to alchemy and satanism in the hope that these would help him secure more riches. The accused changed his plea to guilty under the threat of torture. Some observers believe that the case against Rais was only slim and was brought because of pressure from the powerful Duke of Burgundy, who had a financial stake in his ruin.

GUNFIGHT AT OK CORRAL

1881 The gunmen's cemetery of Boot Hill in Tombstone, Arizona, received three more inmates today, courtesy of the Earp brothers, Wyatt (see right), Morgan and Virgil, and their sidekick, the tubercular gambler and gunslinger John H. ("Doc") Holliday. The streets were clear as the Earps and the "Deadly Dentist" began their walk to the OK Corral. Waiting, lined up against the adobe wall of the Assay Office backing on to the Corral, were Ike and Billy Clanton, the two McLowery brothers, Tom and Frank, and Billy Claiborne ...The fight was short and bloody. Within a minute the McLowerys and Billy Clanton fell, fatally wounded, and Virgil and Morgan Earp were wounded. Ike Clanton and Billy Claiborne survived the carnage.

• 1905 – NORWAY GAINS INDEPENDENCE • 1965 – BEATLES AWARDED MBES

REAGAN DEFENDS GRENADA INVASION

1983 US President Ronald Reagan has defended his decision to send a 2000-strong force of Marines and Army Rangers into the Caribbean island of Grenada. The invasion, he said, had saved the country from becoming a "Soviet-Cuban colony". A spokesperson for the Organization of Eastern Caribbean States said that concern about the military build-up in Grenada prompted the member states to ask the US for help. The further destabilization caused by the overthrow of Grenada's PM Maurice Bishop earlier this month was the final straw. Beyond the Caribbean the invasion is seen as a violation of international law.

QUAKERS CAN'T SHAKE OFF PERSECUTION

1659 If the Quakers hoped to find respite from persecution in the New World, they must be deeply disappointed. The latest arrivals have been flogged from settlement to settlement. Four Quakers, including a woman, Mary Dyer, were hanged in Boston today. So deep is the antipathy towards the sect's non-conformist religious beliefs and social customs that the only answer would seem to be for them to live in their own separate part of the country.

I want to take this occasion to say that the United States will never again seek one additional foot of territory by conquest.
Woodrow Wilson, US president, 1913.

COMMONS VOTES FOR EURO-VISION

1971 Ten years of campaigning to persuade Britain that future prosperity lies within the European Economic Community are beginning to bear fruit for PM Edward Heath. The House of Commons backed his decision to apply for membership of the Community by a margin of 132 votes. The EEC aims to promote the social and economic integration of Western Europe by working towards the elimination of all trade barriers and the establishment of common price levels and monetary union.

1505 Death of Ivan the Great (Ivan III), the first Tsar of Russia.

1953 British gunboats foil a leftist coup in British Guiana.

1971 The Republic of the Congo changes its name to the Republic of Zaire.

1986 The deregulation of the money market brings about a "big bang" in the City of London.

BIRTHDAYS

Captain James Cook 1728, English navigator.

Niccolò Paganini 1782, Italian virtuoso violinist and composer.

Theodore Roosevelt 1858 American statesman and president.

Dylan Thomas 1914, British poet whose first work was *Under Milk Wood.*

Roy Lichtenstein 1923, American painter and pioneer of Pop Art.

Sylvia Plath 1932, American poet who wrote the semi-autobiographical *The Bell Jar.*

John Cleese 1939, British comedian who established himself as a cult figure with the Monty Python team.

• 1764 – DEATH OF WILLIAM HOGARTH • 1904 – FIRST SUBWAY OPENS IN NEW YORK

1746 An earthquake completely destroys Lima and Callao in Peru.

1899 Death of Otto Morgenthaler, German inventor of the Linotype machine.

1958 The state opening of British parliament is televised for the first time.

1982 Forty-year-old Felipe González becomes Spain's first Socialist prime minister with a landslide victory.

BIRTHDAYS

Robert Liston 1794, Scottish doctor who performed the first operation in Britain on an anaesthetized patient.

Evelyn Waugh 1903, British journalist and satirical novelist.

Francis Bacon 1909, British painter with no formal art training.

Sir Richard Doll 1912, British cancer researcher who proved the link between cigarette smoking and lung cancer.

Bill Gates 1955, American businessman who founded Microsoft in 1975.

Julia Roberts 1967, American film actress famous for her role in *Pretty Woman*.

ELECTRIFYING LEAP

1831 The physicist and chemist Michael Faraday has succeeded in inventing a device that converts mechanical energy into electrical energy. After discovering that a current of electricity could be generated by plunging a magnet into a coil of wire, he set about trying to generate a steady current. He achieved this by spinning a copper disc between the poles of a magnet. The 40-year-old Englishman left school at 14 and was offered, a job by Humphrey Davy, director of the Royal Institution's laboratory.

KRUSHCHEV FORCED TO BLINK BY JFK

1962 It was confirmed today that the Soviet leader, Nikita Krushchev, had informed US President Kennedy that work on the missile sites under construction in Cuba would now be halted and that the missiles already delivered would be shipped back to the USSR. Krushchev has also offered to allow the UN to carry out on-the-spot inspections to check that the installations have been removed. The US will no doubt rely on its own U-2 spy planes for such confirmation. The US has been on a war footing for the past week, underlining Kennedy's determination not to allow alien missiles on America's doorstep.

HARVARD GRANT TO SET UP AMERICAN OXBRIDGE

1638 The future of the college established in Cambridge, Massachusetts, by Puritan emigrants from England two years ago has been assured by a generous bequest. The college is to receive 400 volumes and £779 17s 2d (approximately $1440) from the estate of Mr John Harvard, assistant pastor of the First Church of Charleston, who died last month. The donation will certainly help the college fathers towards achieving their aim of providing an education that is the equal of Oxford or Cambridge in England. On October 28, 1636 the General Court of Massachusetts founded the college on the comparatively modest sum of £400 ($740). Harvard's generosity is worth a lasting gesture of thanks.

NEW YORK BANKS TRY TO STEM WALL STREET PANIC

1929 The crisis of confidence that has hit the New York Stock Market has reached epic proportions. By the end of trading 16,410,030 sales had taken place, driving the Dow Jones index down rapidly a further 43 points and wiping out the stock market gains of the past year. Investment trusts have suffered most. Financial leaders had hoped that by pooling resources they could arrest the decline. Yesterday, however prices began to slide steeply again. Out-of-town banks are estimated to have withdrawn over $2 billion (£1 billion) from Wall Street. The nerves of the New York banks are strengthening – they have increased their lending by some $1 billion (£540 billion) to prevent a money panic.

DINGO BABY VERDICT

1982 Lindy Chamberlain, the mother whose baby daughter was supposedly snatched by a dingo, was found guilty of murder by a court in Darwin today. Mrs Chamberlain, 34, who is expecting her fourth baby, was sentenced to life imprisonment with hard labour. A murder charge was brought after British forensic expert Professor James Cameron examined the jumpsuit recovered seven days after Azaria's disappearance in 1980, from which he concluded that the baby's throat had been cut. At the trial itself scientific opinion on key parts of the evidence was divided. No motive for the murder was established by the prosecution. No body has ever been found.

HURRICANE SANDY CAUSES DEVASTATION

2012 Hurricane Sandy stormed up the US east coast today, causing millions of dollars worth of damage and further increasing the death toll. In total 133 people have been killed by the Category 3 storm. Especially hard hit were the islands of Cuba and Haiti, but the storm also swamped Jamaica, the Dominican Republic, Puerto Rico and the Bahamas. President Obama has called the storm "heartbreaking for the nations."

It's not the bullet with my name on it that worries me. It's the one that says "to whom it may concern".

Resident in Belfast, Northern Ireland. 1991.

1927 The tomb of Genghis Khan is discovered by Russian archaeologist Peter Kozlov.

1956 Israeli forces cross into the Sinai Peninsula, pushing towards the Suez Canal.

1964 Tanganyika and Zanzibar unite to form Tanzania.

1987 Multi-adaptable boxer Thomas "Hit Man" Hearns wins the world middle-heavyweight title .

1998 The Truth and Reconciliation Commission, set up to investigate the causes and results of Apartheid, reports after two years of hearings.

1998 Death of Ted Hughes, Poet Laureate for 14 years.

BIRTHDAYS

Jean Giradoux 1882, French author, diplomat and playwright.

Fanny Brice 1891, American Broadway star whose life story was immortalized in the musical *Funny Girl*.

Joseph Goebbels 1897, German Nazi propaganda chief.

Richard Dreyfuss 1949, American film star.

• 1618 – SIR WALTER RALEIGH EXECUTED • 1863 – RED CROSS FOUNDED

1823 Death of Edmund Cartwright, whose invention of the power loom contributed to the Industrial Revolution.

1974 Muhammad Ali knocks out George Foreman in the eighth round in Kinshasa to regain his title as world heavyweight boxing champion.

1979 Death of British aircraft designer Sir Barnes Neville Wallis, whose invention of "bouncing bombs" played a key part in World War Two.

2009 French cultural anthropologist Claude Levi-Strauss dies, aged 100.

BIRTHDAYS

John Adams 1735, American statesman and second president who signed the Declaration of Independence.

Richard Brinsley Sheridan 1751, Irish dramatist whose plays include *School for Scandal*.

Alfred Sisley 1840, French Impressionist painter.

Louis Malle 1932, French director whose films include *The Lovers*.

ORSON: THE MAN WHO PANICKED AMERICA

1938 A 23-year-old actor-director succeeded in taking millions of Americans across the narrow line that divides fact from fiction tonight with his gripping radio dramatization of H. G. Wells' sci-fi thriller, *The War of the Worlds*. Despite several reminders that the CBS presentation by Orson Welles and the Mercury Players was pure fantasy and that New Jersey was not really being invaded, thousands of New Yorkers panicked. Police switchboards were packed with anxious callers seeking information and advice, and roads and churches were jammed by people desperate to escape the clutches of the menacing Martians.

COMMUNIST CRITIC KILLED

1984 Kidnapped 12 days ago, the pro-Solidarity priest, Father Jerzy Popieluszko, was found dead in Wloclawek Reservoir in Poland today. Three secret police officers have been charged with abduction, but the Polish government claims that other, more important people ordered the killing. Hardline opponents of PM Wojciech Jaruzelski are thought to be most likely.

WED-IN BELLS RING FOR 13,000 MOONIES

1988 The head of the Unification Church, Rev. Sun Myung Moon, today presided over a mass wedding ceremony in South Korea. The identically clothed brides and grooms paraded before their Moonie master. The 6516 couples had all been personally matched by the controversial cult leader. In some cases the two sides were meeting for the first time. The newly-weds will spend the next 40 days getting to know each other – and, in a few instances, each other's language – before being allowed to consummate their vows.

• 1485 – YEOMAN OF THE GUARD ESTABLISHED • 1925 – FIRST PERSON CAPTURED ON TV

SUEZ CANAL SPLITS ATLANTIC ALLIANCE

1956 A bitter row has erupted between Washington and London and Paris over the bombing of Egypt by Anglo-French aircraft. The attack follows an ultimatum by Britain and France that Israel and Egypt should withdraw their forces from the Canal zone. Two days ago Israeli forces moved into the Sinai Peninsula, ostensibly in retaliation for Egyptian attacks on Israel. The alacrity with which the British and French produced the 12-hour ultimatum and then brought their military forces into play suggest that the timing of the Israeli action came as no surprise. It came as a great surprise to President Eisenhower, who finds himself in the Soviet camp on this issue. Anglo-French thinking is that the Suez Canal – nationalized by Nasser in July – must be kept open to international traffic, thereby securing Europe's supply of oil. President Eisenhower regards the action as a threat to world peace and wants an immediate ceasefire.

Gentlemen, it was necessary to abolish the fez, which sat on the heads of our nation as an emblem of ignorance, negligence, fanaticism and hatred of progress and civilization, to accept in its place the hat, the headgear worn by the whole, civilized world.

Kemal Ataturk, Founder of the Turkish Republic, 1927.

BODYGUARDS KILL GANDHI

1984 The Indian prime minister Mrs Indira Gandhi was shot dead today as she walked in the garden of her home in New Delhi. She was 67. Ironically her killers were the men detailed to protect her, constable Satwant Singh and sub-inspector Beant Singh. The two men, both Sikhs, had riddled Mrs Gandhi with bullets before police loyal to the prime minister intervened, shooting dead Beant Singh. Mrs Gandhi had ignored repeated warnings about the potential danger of keeping Sikh bodyguards. Three months ago Mrs Gandhi outraged Sikh feelings by ordering the Army to storm the holy Golden Temple of Amritsar. Her assassination is almost certainly linked to that act. Rajiv Gandhi is expected to be sworn in as his mother's successor to the post later today.

1517 Martin Luther nails his 95 theses against the corruption of the papacy in Rome to the church door at Wittenberg.

1864 Nevada becomes the 36th state of the Union.

1958 Nobel prize-winning author Boris Pasternak is expelled from the Soviet Writers' Union and is likely to be exiled for *Dr Zhivago*.

1958 The first internal heart pacemaker is implanted by Dr Åke Sonning in Stockholm.

1971 An IRA bomb explodes at the top of London's Post Office Tower.

BIRTHDAYS

Jan Vermeer 1632, Dutch painter of realistic scenes of domestic life.

John Keats 1795, English Romantic poet for his "Ode to a Nightingale".

Sir Joseph Swan 1828, English chemist credited with Edison for inventing the electric lamp.

Chiang Kai-shek 1887, Chinese leader of the Nationalist People's Party, exiled after being ousted by the Communists.

Eddie Charlton 1929, Australian snooker champion.

• 1888 – PNEUMATIC TYRE PATENTED • 1940 – BATTLE OF BRITAIN ENDS

NOVEMBER

VICTORIA PROCLAIMED INDIA'S RULER

1858 The East India Company's long reign over India came to an end today when the administration of the country passed to Queen Victoria. The East India Company, formed in 1600 to exploit trade with the East, has acted as an agent of British imperialism since the early 18th century. The Company's influence has finally been broken, however, by the violent and bloody events of the Indian Mutiny, which developed from a revolt of Indian sepoys in Bengal into a widespread uprising against British rule in India. Although British reconquest was completed with the relief of Lucknow in March of this year, reform was inevitable.

DE-STALINIZATION OF RUSSIA

1961 The Soviet Communist Party Congress's "de-Stalinization" theme has had a dramatic result: during the night Stalin's body was removed from the mausoleum in Red Square. Even Stalingrad, one of the most resonant names from Russia's struggle against the Nazis, has been renamed Volgograd.

A lie can be half-way round the world before the truth has got its boots on.

James Callaghan. British prime minister, 1976.

BILKO DEAD

1985 Comedian Phil Silvers died today aged 73. His showbiz career started on the vaudeville stage, and his many films include *Cover Girl*, *It's a Mad, Mad, Mad World*, *A Funny Thing Happened on the Way to the Forum* and *Buona Sera, Mrs Campbell*. He will be remembered worldwide for his role as Sergeant Bilko in the TV series *You'll Never Get Rich* (later retitled *The Phil Silvers Show*) between 1955 and 1958. The adventures of the crooked but lovable King of the Motor Pool and his sidekicks as they sought ever-more ingenious ways of subverting military authority (and making a buck) endeared him to millions, and are still popular today.

1814 The European Congress opens in Vienna.

1895 The first motoring organization, the American Motor League, is founded.

1922 First radio licences go on sale in Britain.

1950 US President Truman survives an assassination attempt.

1954 Algerian nationalists begin a war of independence against the French.

1967 *Rolling Stone* magazine makes its debut.

1972 American poet Ezra Pound dies aged 87.

1984 Rajiv Gandhi is sworn in as India's premier.

BIRTHDAYS

Spencer Perceval 1762, British prime minister from 1809 who was assassinated in the House of Commons.

Benvenuto Cellini 1500, Italian sculptor and goldsmith.

Stephen Crane 1871, American author of The *Red Badge of Courage*.

L. S. Lowry 1887, English painter of distinctive matchstick figures.

Gary Player 1935, South African golfing champion.

• 1755 – EARTHQUAKE DESTROYS LISBON • 1993 – BIRTH OF EUROPEAN UNION

1899 The Siege of Ladysmith in Natal begins as Boers encircle the town.

1920 KDKA in Pittsburgh becomes the world's first regular broadcasting station.

1953 Pakistan is to adopt Islamic law.

1957 Elvis Presley sets an all-time record with eight simultaneous UK Top 30 entries.

1963 Death of Ngo Dinh Diem, first president of the Republic of South Vietnam.

1984 Joseph Stalin's daughter Svetlana Alliluyeva goes home to Moscow 17 years after she went into exile and was stripped of her Soviet citizenship.

1990 Ivana Trump files for divorce from Donald.

BIRTHDAYS

Daniel Boone 1734, American frontiersman who was captured and adopted as a son of the Indian Shawnee chief Blackfish before returning to his settlement in Kentucky.

Burt Lancaster 1913, American Hollywood actor and former circus acrobat whose films include *From Here to Eternity*.

HAILE SELASSIE I CROWNED EMPEROR

1930 Ras ("Duke") Tafari, King of Ethiopia, was crowned Emperor Haile Selassie I in Addis Ababa today, amid immense pomp and splendour. Thousands of tribesmen in lionskin cloaks, waving spears and shields, lined the streets as the Emperor drove past in the ex-Kaiser's coronation coach. His accession follows the death of Empress Zauditu, with whom he has shared power since 1928. He has been regent and heir apparent since 1917; his liberal, westernizing influence acted as counterbalance to the conservatism of war minister Hapta Giorgis, and he secured Ethiopia's admission into the League of Nations in 1923. Haile Selassie (his name means "Might of the Trinity") intends to give Ethiopia her first written constitution. Ethiopia and Liberia are currently the only countries in Africa with black rulers.

SPRUCE GOOSE TAKES TO THE AIR

1947 In California the world's largest aircraft, the Hughes Hercules flying-boat, or "Spruce Goose", flew for the first time today. It has a wingspan of 319 ft 11 inches (97.51 m), is 218 ft 8 inches (66.64 m) long, has eight 3000 hp engines and seats 700 passengers. The brainchild of millionaire Howard Hughes, it has been under construction in Culver City since 1942 and cost $40 (£22) million to build.

CARTER GOES TO WASHINGTON

1976 The Democratic outsider Jimmy Carter, former Governor of Georgia, defeated the incumbent Republican Gerald Ford to become the 39th President of the United States today. Carter and his running mate, Senator Walter Mondale of Minnesota, won by the narrow margin of 297 electoral votes to 241, capturing 51 per cent of the popular vote. The 52-year-old from Plains, Georgia, is a liberal and a populist, and a symbol of the "New South"; he has received support from prominent blacks such as Representative Andrew Young of Georgia. He intends to institute an energy conservation programme, to reduce the wastefulness of government bureaucracy, and to appoint women to his cabinet.

• 1903 – *DAILY MIRROR* FIRST PUBLISHED IN BRITAIN • 1936 – THE TV AGE BEGINS

GRANT IS 18TH US PRESIDENT

1868 General Ulysses Simpson Grant, Commander-in-Chief of the Union armies in the Civil War, was elected President of the United States today on the Republican ticket. Grant's aggressive tactics in the early battles of the Civil War earned him the

nickname of "Unconditional Surrender" Grant. His inadequate preparations almost lost him the Battle of Shiloh, and he was criticized for his apparent indifference to heavy loss of life, but his victories at Chattanooga and Appomattox, and the subsequent Confederate surrender, proved the correctness of his strategic thinking. Before now Grant was unconcerned with politics, but his unanimous nomination by the Republican convention persuaded him to stand.

Russians and Italians sing like birds, with enormous pleasure and excitement. The English are locked more inside. Every Englishman has in his heart a Chubb lock.

Mstislav Rostropovich, 1991.

1706 Fifteen thousand people die as the town of Abruzzo in Italy is destroyed by an earthquake.

1903 Panama proclaims its independence from Colombia.

1926 Death of Annie Oakley, legendary American shooter.

1942 British field marshall Bernard Law Montgomery's troops break through commander of the Afrika Corps Erwin Rommel's front line in Africa and capture 9000 prisoners.

1954 Death of the French painter and sculptor Henri Matisse.

1992 Bill Clinton is elected President of the United States of America.

BIRTHDAYS

Karl Baedeker 1801, German publisher famous for his guide books.

Vincenzo Bellini 1801, Italian opera composer whose work includes *Norma*.

Alfredo Stroessner 1912, Paraguayan dictator.

Charles Bronson 1921, American actor who appeared in films such as *Death Wish*.

RUSSIAN DOG IN SPACE

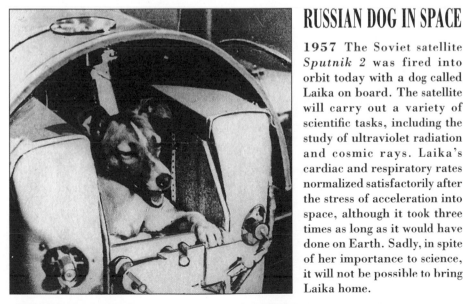

1957 The Soviet satellite *Sputnik 2* was fired into orbit today with a dog called Laika on board. The satellite will carry out a variety of scientific tasks, including the study of ultraviolet radiation and cosmic rays. Laika's cardiac and respiratory rates normalized satisfactorily after the stress of acceleration into space, although it took three times as long as it would have done on Earth. Sadly, in spite of her importance to science, it will not be possible to bring Laika home.

• 1875 – FIRST UNDERWATER OIL PIPELINE OPENED • 1984 – INDIRA GANDHI CREMATED

1847 German composer and pianist Felix Mendelssohn dies.

1890 The Prince of Wales travels on the Underground from King William Street to the Oval to mark the opening of the first electrified underground railway system.

1914 The first fashion show is held at the Ritz-Carlton Hotel in New York, organized by Edna Woodman Chase of *Vogue*.

1921 Japanese prime minister Hara Takashi is assassinated by a Korean.

1980 Ronald Reagan is elected 40th US president.

1987 Millionaire Peter de Savary buys Land's End, Cornwall, the southernmost tip of the British mainland.

BIRTHDAYS

William III 1650, Dutch-born King of England, Scotland and Ireland.

Walter Cronkite 1916, American award-winning journalist, newsreader and commentator with CBS.

Art Carney 1918, American actor of stage and screen who starred in the Broadway play *The Odd Couple*.

OBAMA MAKES HISTORY WITH ELECTION VICTORY

2008 Barack Hussein Obama was elected 44th President of the USA and the first African American to hold the office. Many world leaders welcomed the election of Senator Obama as the first black president and voter turnout was reported to be "unprecedented". Mr Obama delivered his victory speech in Grant Park, Chicago, to tens of thousands of supporters, "If there is anyone out there who still doubts that America is a place where all things are possible, who still wonders if the dream of our founders is alive in our time, who still questions the power of our democracy, tonight is your answer."

NELSON CLIMBS HIS COLUMN

1843 In Trafalgar Square today the monument in honour of Lord Nelson, to commemorate his last and greatest victory at the Battle of Trafalgar, was finally completed after four years' work. The 17-ft (5.5-m), 16-ton statue, the work of E. H. Bailey, was hauled up the column in two pieces and placed on a capital cast in bronze from guns taken from the *Royal George*. The 184-ft (60-m) column cost £50,000 ($92,000), nearly-half of which was contributed by Parliament, the balance by public subscription. Last weekend the statue was viewed by 100,000 people, not all of them admirers: one critic compared it to a ship's figurehead, and claimed that it displayed "a daring disregard of personal resemblance".

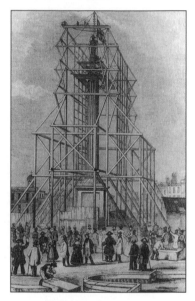

ROOSEVELT ENDS ARMS EMBARGO

1939 President Roosevelt signed an amendment to the Neutrality Act into law today, repealing the US embargo on arms sales to foreign powers. Arms can now be shipped to belligerent powers provided they pay cash and use non-US ships for transport. The beneficiaries will be Britain and France, thus effectively ending US neutrality in the war. It is hoped this will mean that the Allies will be able to win without active US involvement.

RABIN ASSASSINATED

1995 Israel is in shock after the assassination today of Prime Minister Yitzhak Rabin. Mr Rabin was addressing a peace rally in the Square of the Kings in Tel Aviv when a 27-year-old law student, a right-wing Jewish extremist, emerged from the crowd and killed him. The Prime Minister has been deeply unpopular with some Israelis since he shook hands with Yasser Arafat, the PLO leader, at the White House.

• 1946 – UNESCO IS ESTABLISHED • 1979 – US EMBASSY IN TEHRAN SEIZED

BOY EMPEROR EXPELLED FROM FORBIDDEN CITY

1924 The last Manchu emperor, 18-year-old Pu-yi, was forced to leave his palace in Peking today by Christian warlord Feng Yuxiang, who has taken control of the city. He was compelled to abdicate in 1912 by the revolutionary government in Nanking after the Wuchang uprising, ending 268 years of Manchu rule and over 2000 years of imperial tradition. The abdication agreement allowed him to live in the Forbidden City and retain all privileges. He was returned to the throne by General Xun's coup in 1917, but was dethroned again after only 12 days.

1854 The combined British and French forces defeat the Russians at the Battle of Inkerman during the Crimean War.

1912 The British Board of Film Censors is appointed.

1919 The great American screen lover Rudolph Valentino marries actress Jean Acker and is locked out on his wedding night.

1956 Soviet tanks crush the Hungarian revolt.

1979 Death of American cartoonist Al Capp, who created Li'l Abner.

2003 *Voyager I* becomes the first man-made object to leave the solar system.

BIRTHDAYS

John Haldane 1892, English physiologist and geneticist.

Roy Rogers 1912, American actor known as "King of the Cowboys".

Vivien Leigh 1913, British actress best known for her Oscar-winning role as Scarlett O'Hara in *Gone with the Wind*.

Art Garfunkel 1942, American singer who rose to fame with Paul Simon with hits such as "The Sound of Silence".

PLOT TO BLOW UP PARLIAMENT FOILED

1605 There was great rejoicing today at the narrow escape of His Majesty James I and Their Lordships, after a plot to blow up the Houses of Parliament was discovered late last night. Lord Monteagle, a Catholic peer, received a letter recently, warning him to stay away from today's State Opening. The letter also hinted at an explosion. On investigating the cellars beneath the House of Lords, Monteagle and the Lord Chamberlain discovered a man piling wood who gave his name as Guy Fawkes, and claimed that the wood belonged to his master, Lord Percy. They let Fawkes go on his way, but on further investigating the pile of wood, they discovered 36 barrels of gunpowder at the bottom. Fawkes, a 35-year-old Yorkshireman, was arrested when he returned at midnight to make the final preparations. It appears that this was a plot hatched by Catholics, headed by Robert Catesby, who were acting in protest at increasingly oppressive treatment of members of their faith by the King and his ministers. The band of plotters had tunnelled into the cellars from a house adjoining the Parliament buildings. They had then recruited Guy Fawkes, who is noted for his particular coolness and bravery. At the time of recruitment, Fawkes had been in the Netherlands, where he was serving in the Spanish Army.

• 1914 – CYPRUS ANNEXED TO BRITAIN • 1991 – DEATH OF ROBERT MAXWELL

NOVEMBER 6

1429 Henry VI is crowned King of England.

1656 Death of King John V of Portugal.

1813 Mexico is proclaimed independent from Spain.

1956 The construction of the Kariba High Dam on the Zambezi River begins.

1984 A Dublin High Court judge freezes striking British mineworkers' money after a High Court decision that the strike, now in its 35th week, is illegal and that the union must pay a fine in 14 days or have its assets seized.

2003 Michael Howard becomes the new Conservative party leader.

BIRTHDAYS

James Gregory 1638, Scottish mathematician and astronomer.

Adolphe Sax 1814, Belgian inventor of the saxophone.

James A. Naismith 1861, American inventor of basketball.

Sir John Alcock 1892, English aviator.

Mike Nichols 1931, American director of *The Graduate*.

GERMAN INFLATION SOARS

1923 The German mark reached the incredible figure of 4.2 trillion to the US dollar today, as against 4.2 to the dollar ten years ago. German workers can be seen taking their wages home in wheelbarrows and crates – worthless Monopoly money in a country where a loaf of bread costs as much as 200 million marks.

COMMNUNIST PARTY BANNED

1991 Boris Yeltsin, President of the Russian Federation, today issued a decree banning the Communist Party of the Soviet Union (CPSU) and the Russian CP, and nationalizing their property. He said that the Party's role in the failed coup of last August proved that the CPSU was not a legitimate political party but a "special mechanism for exercising political power".

Every Communist must grasp the truth,
"Political power grows out of the barrel of a gun".

Mao Tse-tung, Chinese Communist leader, 1938.

RAF'S NEW FIGHTER

1935 The Hawker Hurricane, the RAF's first monoplane fighter, flew for the very first time today and inaugurated a new era in military aviation. Heavily armed, with four machine-guns in each wing, it is claimed to be the fastest interceptor in the world, with a top speed of 325 mph (520 kph) at 20,000 ft (6500 m).

• 1860 – ABRAHAM LINCOLN BECOMES US PRESIDENT • 1893 – DEATH OF TCHAIKOVSKY

BOLSHEVIK REVOLUTION IN RUSSIA

1917 Vladimir Ilyich Ulyanov, known as Lenin, and his Bolsheviks successfully made a bid for power in St Petersburg today. Armed workers, soldiers and sailors began to take over various points throughout the city this morning, and by evening the Red Guards had seized the Winter Palace. The Council of Commissars has confirmed Lenin as its head, with Leon Trotsky as Minister of Foreign Affairs. The Bolsheviks' immediate task is to make good their promise of "Peace, Land and Bread", and it is their intention to conclude a peace treaty with Germany as soon as possible.

1659 The Franco-Spanish war ends.

1865 The Repeating Light Company of Springfield, MA, manufactures the first pocket lighter.

1916 Jeanette Rankin of Montana becomes the first woman member of the US Congress.

1960 In Moscow missiles appear for the first time at the annual parade in Red Square.

1961 Konrad Adenauer is elected German chancellor for the fourth time.

1980 Death of American actor Steve McQueen, whose films include *The Great Escape*.

BIRTHDAYS

Marie Curie 1867, Polish-born physicist.

Herman J. Mankiewicz 1897, American screenwriter who collaborated with Orson Welles on *Citizen Kane*.

Albert Camus 1913, French author associated with Existentialism who won the Nobel prize for Literature in 1957.

Dame Joan Sutherland 1926, Australian operatic soprano.

CANADA'S GOLDEN SPIKE

1885 The coast-to-coast Canadian Pacific railway was completed today. The government of British Columbia had made it a condition of joining the Confederation, rather than be annexed to the US, that they be linked to the rest of the country by a railway by 1891. The work is complete five years early, thanks to the efforts of Cornelius van Horne and his team, and enthusiastic backers like Donald A. Smith. It was Mr Smith who drove in the final "golden" spike (actually iron) at 9.22 Pacific time near Craigellachie, in the Rockies.

MUSSOLINI IS "II DUCE"

1921 Benito Mussolini became official leader of the 35 parliamentary members of the National Fascist Party. Before World War One he was a socialist, editing the Milan Socialist Party newspaper *Avanti*, but moved to the right during and after the War, eventually involving himself in the foundation of the Fascists. He is a fanatical supporter of the nationalist poet Gabriele d'Annunzio in his struggle to annexe the port of Fiume and pre-empt the Paris Peace Conference; his "squadristi", or black-shirts, have been active in anti-Bolshevik riots in Bologna, Florence and Milan. Mussolini's proud boast is that Fascism is both "aristocratic and democratic, reactionary and revolutionary".

• 1805 – LEWIS AND CLARK SIGHT THE PACIFIC • 1862 – GATLING GUN PATENTED

1793 Royal art collection in the Louvre is open to the public for the first time.

1827 *The Canton Register*, the first English language newspaper in the Far East, starts publication.

1987 A man serving 17 years for murder in a California prison decides to sue a juror for $24 million (£13 million) for sleeping through most of his trial and contributing towards what he claims was an incorrect conviction.

1988 Republican candidate George Bush wins the US presidential elections comfortably, carrying 40 states against only ten for his Democratic opponent, Michael Dukakis.

1989 In Virginia, Douglas Wilder becomes the first black state governor in the US.

BIRTHDAYS

Edmond Halley 1656, English astronomer and mathematician.

Christiaan Barnard 1922, South African surgeon and heart transplant pioneer.

Margaret Mitchell 1900, American author of *Gone with the Wind*, her only book.

FIRST BLACK SENATOR ELECTED

1966 Former Massachusetts Attorney General Edward Brooke became the first black senator in US history today, elected to the Senate with a majority of more than 500,000. Born in Washington DC in 1919, Brooke took his BSc at Howard University in 1941, and his LIB at Boston in 1949, in between winning a Bronze Star with the Infantry in Italy in World War II. He served as Chairman of the Boston Finance Commission from 1960 to 1962. Elected as Attorney General in 1962, he was re-elected in 1964 by the largest majority in State history, and during his term of office indicted more than a hundred officials, private citizens and corporations on graft and bribery charges.

I know it does make people happy, but to me it is just like having a cup of tea.
Cynthia Payne, London housewife, after her acquittal in the "sex-for-luncheon-vouchers" prostitution case, 1987.

REMEMBRANCE DAY BLAST KILLS 11

1987 A huge bomb went off today in Enniskillen, County Fermanagh, as marchers were gathering for a Remembrance Day parade. The bomb, which had been placed in a disused school building, claimed the lives of 11 people, including three married couples, and injured 63, some critically. The IRA admitted responsibility for placing the device, but blamed the British army for having triggered the explosion with a high-frequency scanning device. Gordon Wilson, 60, was buried in the wreckage with his daughter Marie, a nurse, who died. The distraught father still had the generosity to say of her murderers, "I shall pray for those people tonight and every night."

• **1932 – LANDSLIDE VICTORY PUTS FRANKLIN D. ROOSEVELT IN THE WHITE HOUSE**

NIGHT OF TERROR IN GERMANY

1938 The Jewish community in Germany endured a night of terror when Nazi thugs went on the rampage, attacking Jewish businesses, synagogues and property. Thirty-six people were killed during the night, and 20,000 arrested; more than 7000 shops were looted and 267 synagogues burnt down. Dr Goebbels, Minister of Public Enlightenment and Propaganda, claimed that the violence was a "spontaneous reaction" to the assassination in Paris of Ernst von Rath, a German diplomat, by a young Polish Jew. There is no doubt, however, that the pogrom was carried out on the instructions of the Gestapo. So that the insurance companies are not bankrupted by state hooliganism, the Nazis have declared their intention to confiscate insurance payouts and return them to the insurers. The huge amount of glass broken has led to the night being dubbed "Kristallnacht"; replacement glass will have to be imported and paid for in foreign currency.

BONAPARTE TAKES REINS OF POWER

1799 Thirty-year-old Corsican General Napoleon Bonaparte became France's new leader today. Bonaparte's rise to the top has been rapid. He made his name by his daring defeat of the British fleet at the Revolt of Toulon in 1793; his defence of the Tuileries against the mob in 1795 made him the hero of Paris. His exploits in Italy and Egypt – despite the shattering of his fleet by Admiral Nelson at Aboukir Bay – made him world-famous. Ironically, Corsica was only ceded to France by Genoa in 1768; had Bonaparte been born a year earlier he would not be French.

HIGH FLIER

1988 The Pentagon took the wraps off the Air Force's new attack plane today. A sinister, all-black aircraft, the Lockheed F-117A employs the latest stealth technology – radar-absorbent materials and a "faceted" surface that deflects radar signals at odd angles. The aircraft's key feature is that it can supposedly arrive undetected over a target.

1794 The Russians enter Warsaw, ending Polish rebellion.

1937 Ramsay MacDonald, formerly Britain's first Labour prime minister dies on a voyage to America.

1940 Death of former British prime minister Neville Chamberlain, who advocated a policy of appeasement towards the fascist powers in Germany but was forced to abandon this policy after Hitler's invasion of Czechoslovakia.

1970 Death of the French president Charles de Gaulle.

BIRTHDAYS

Ivan Sergeyevich Turgenev 1818, Russian writer whose work includes *Fathers and Sons*.

Dr Herbert Thomas Kalmus 1881, American inventor of Technicolor.

Katherine Hepburn 1909, American actress who won four Oscars.

Hedy Lamarr 1913, Austrian-born American actress who was billed as the most beautiful woman in the world.

Ronald Harwood 1934, South African-born playwright, novelist and television writer and presenter.

• 1922 – SS IS FORMED IN GERMANY • 1960 – JFK BECOMES PRESIDENT OF THE US

1913 Battersea elects the first coloured mayor in Britain, John Archer.

1914 The Australian cruiser *Sydney* sinks the German cruiser *Emden* off Sumatra.

1918 The German emperor Kaiser Wilhelm II appears at the Dutch frontier having abdicated.

1952 The 77-year-old doctor-philosopher Albert Schweitzer, who devoted the first 30 years of his life to himself and the rest to mankind, is awarded the Nobel Peace Prize for his humanitarian work in Africa.

2007 Innovative American author Norman Mailer dies, aged 84.

BIRTHDAYS

Martin Luther 1483, German religious reformer who began the Reformation.

William Hogarth 1697, English painter and engraver.

Richard Burton 1925, British stage and screen actor.

Sir Timothy Rice 1944, English lyricist, famous for works with Andrew Lloyd Webber such as *Evita*.

FLANDERS CARNAGE HALTED – FOR NOW

1917 British General Douglas Haig's grandiose plan of smashing through the German lines and on to the Channel was finally abandoned today, after 156 days and anything up to 250,000 casualties. The battle – the third on the Ypres Salient – started in June with the mining of the Messines Ridge, but the wettest August in living memory turned the ground to a quagmire. Allied troops were faced with the choice of paths under a constant barrage of fire from the Germans, or death by drowning in the mud. The damning verdict of British prime minister Lloyd George is succinct: "The most grim, futile and bloody fight in the history of war".

BERLIN WALL BREACHED

1989 A million East Germans poured into West Berlin early today, free at last to leave their country. East German leader Egon Krenz appealed to his fellow citizens to stay, promising multi-party elections, freedom of speech and a new criminal code, but since the borders with Hungary and Czechoslovakia were opened 167,000 have already left. On November 4, one million East Berliners marched for reform, gathering in Alexanderplatz, shouting "Egon, here we come." Two days later, half a million marched in Leipzig. This has been the biggest show of opposition in East Germany since Soviet tanks crushed a workers' revolt in 1953.

This is not the end. It is not even the beginning of the end. But it is, perhaps, the end of the beginning.

Winston Churchill refers to the Battle for Egypt, 1942.

STANLEY FINDS LIVINGSTONE

1871 "Doctor Livingstone, I presume?" were the first words spoken by Henry Morton Stanley to David Livingstone when Stanley tracked down the missing explorer on the shores of Lake Tanganyika. "Yes," said the Doctor. Livingstone, a 58-year-old Scot, is famous as the explorer of the Zambezi and discoverer of Victoria Falls, and as the first European to cross the continent from coast to coast. His search for the sources of the Nile and Congo rivers has occupied him to the point of obsession for some years. Stanley, also an explorer of some note, was commissioned to find Livingstone by James Gordon Bennett, proprietor of the *New York Herald*, although it is a moot point whether he was actually "missing" or merely out of reach.

• 1928 – HIROHITO BECOMES EMPEROR OF JAPAN • 1982 – DEATH OF BREZHNEV

GREAT WAR ENDS

1918 After four years and 97 days the guns finally fell silent today. In a carriage of Marshal Foch's train in the Forest of Compiègne, Foch, General Weygand and British Admiral Sir Rosslyn Wemyss accepted the German surrender from a civilian, Reichstag Deputy Matthias Erzberger, and two junior generals. The Kaiser abdicated and fled to Holland yesterday. The number of lives lost in the War is thought to be around 9 million, with another 27 million injured. It has been the most destructive war the world has ever seen.

1855 Death of Søren Kierkegaard, Danish philosopher.

1880 Australian bank robber Ned Kelly goes to the gallows two years after becoming an outlaw.

1920 The bodies of unknown British and French soldiers are buried at Westminster Abbey and the Arc de Triomphe respectively.

1921 The British Legion holds its first Poppy Day to raise money for the wounded of World War I.

1987 Van Gogh's painting Irises is sold in New York for $53.9 million (£29.3 million).

1995 Dissident writer Ken Saro-Wiwa and eight human rights activists are executed in Nigeria.

2000 A fire on a funicular railway in the Austrian resort of Kaprun leaves 155 holidaymakers dead.

PLO WOES

2004 Yasser Arafat, chairman of the Palestine Liberation Organization (PLO), has died at the age of 75. A controversial figure, Arafat spent much of his life fighting Israel in the name of Palestinian self-determination.

SMITH DECLARES UDI

1965 Ian Smith today declared Rhodesia an independent state, underlining his party's opposition to sharing power with the black majority in the country. The UN and Black African and Commonwealth leaders have all condemned the declaration.

BIRTHDAYS

Fyodor Mikhailovich Dostoyevsky
1821, Russian novelist whose major works include *Crime and Punishment*.

Leonardo DiCaprio
1974, American actor and producer, as well as an environmental campaigner.

JEEP LAUNCHED

1940 The Willys-Overland Company launched its new general-purpose vehicle for the US Army today. The 4-wheel drive vehicle, named "Jeep" for GP (general purpose), is in competition with a prototype from Ford. Trials will be carried out to decide which is to be selected.

• 1923 – MUNICH BEERHALL PUTSCH • 1975 – ANGOLA GAINS INDEPENDENCE

1035 Death of Canute II, Danish King of England.

1859 French trapeze artist Jules Leotard makes his debut at the Cirque d'Eté in Paris.

1901 Gales sweep Britain, killing 200.

1905 The Russian occupation imposes martial law on Poland.

1988 In Sydney, West Indies cricket captain Viv Richards scores his 100th century.

1990 A demonstration in Paris by over 200,000 French schoolchildren demanding better education turns into a riot.

2001 A passenger plane crashes in New York; 260 people die.

BIRTHDAYS

Auguste Rodin 1840, French sculptor.

Grace Kelly 1929, American actress who was arguably the most beautiful of her day.

Neil Young 1945, Canadian singer-songwriter widely regarding as one of the most influential musicians of his time.

Nadia Comaneci 1961, Romanian gymnast and Olympic gold medalist.

BROTHERS SET OFF FOR AUSTRALIA

1919 Two Australian brothers, Captain Ross and Lieutenant Keith Smith, set off from Hounslow, Middlesex, today, in an attempt to make the first flight from the UK to Australia. Their converted Vickers Vimy bomber, with its two Rolls-Royce Eagle engines (the same type as that in which Alcock and Brown flew the Atlantic in June), must carry the Smiths and their two mechanics the 11,130 miles (17,912 km) to Darwin in less than 30 days. Their planned route will take them through Cairo, Karachi, Calcutta, Bangkok and Singapore. If they make it they will win the prize of £10,000 ($18,400) put up by the Australian government. It is said that the registration of their aircraft, G-EAOU, stands for "God 'elp All of Us".

TIRPITZ SINKS IN NORWAY

1944 *Tirpitz*, the last survivor of Hitler's fleet of "unsinkable" battleships, is lying at the bottom of Tromsø Fjord today. She had been lurking in Norwegian waters for several years. Lancaster bombers of 617 Squadron, the famous Dambusters, sank her with direct hits from three 12,000-lb (5500-kg) "Tallboy" bombs, dropped from 14,000 ft (4500 m) right on to her decks. Incredibly, a squadron of German fighters assigned to protect the ship did not even take off. Over 1000 of the ship's crew were entombed below decks as she turned turtle.

YELTSIN FIRED

1987 Moscow Communist Party boss Boris Yeltsin has been fired by President Gorbachev after Yeltsin had the temerity to criticize him for the slow pace of *perestroika* (reconstruction). Yeltsin, an enthusiastic supporter of reform, also attacked Yegor Ligachev, number two in the Kremlin, for opposing Gorbachev's initiatives. He accepted criticism of what was termed his "political errors" and "personal ambition", and was replaced by Lev Zaikov.

• **1847 – FIRST DEMONSTRATION OF CHLOROFORM** • **1903 – DEATH OF CAMILLE PISSARRO**

DE GAULLE ELECTED

1945 By a unanimous vote General Charles de Gaulle was elected President of the French Provisional Government today. After the fall of France in 1940 de Gaulle carried a torch of hope for his countrymen, providing a rallying point for Free French forces. On many occasions, however, his pride and prickly temperament made him a difficult ally for Roosevelt and Churchill. The Pétain regime condemned him to death in his absence, but de Gaulle, who had served under Pétain in World War I, spared his old commander's life when he was in his turn sentenced to death for treason last year.

FREEDOM FOR AUNG SAN SUU KYI

2010 Burmese pro-democracy leader, Aung San Suu Kyi, was released after spending 15 of the previous 21 years under house arrest. Suu Kyi became an international symbol of peaceful resistance in the face of oppression and was awarded the Nobel Peace Prize in 1991, a year after her National League for Democracy won an overwhelming victory in an election that the Burmese junta later nullified.

THOUSANDS FEARED DEAD IN COLOMBIA

1985 Nevado del Ruiz, the 17,717-ft (5,400-m) Colombian volcano dormant since 1845, erupted in a ferocious explosion today. Melted snow swept down the mountain in huge torrents, creating a mud avalanche which completely buried the town of Armero huddled below. There are very few survivors from the town's 25,000 population. A 28-inch (71 cm) layer of ash and rock has covered a 70-sq-mile (181 sq km) area around the volcano, 80 miles (128 km) west of Bogota. Expert warnings of an imminent eruption were ignored and there was no attempt to evacuate the area, which has now become a sea of mud in which thousands of people are entombed for ever.

1851 A telegraphic service between London and Paris comes into operation.

1909 Two bombs are thrown at the Viceroy of India, the Earl of Minto.

1920 The first full session of the League of Nations begins in Geneva.

1923 In Italy, Benito Mussolini introduces a bill granting women the vote in national elections.

1925 The South African government calls for more segregation of blacks.

1973 Death of Italian fashion designer Elsa Schiaparelli.

1974 Death of Vittorio de Sica, Italian neo-realist film director.

2001 Kabul, the capital of Afghanistan, falls to the Northern Alliance.

BIRTHDAYS

Edward III 1312, English monarch who was defeated at Bannockburn by Robert the Bruce.

Charles Frederick Worth 1825, Anglo-French fashion designer.

Robert Louis Stevenson 1850, Scottish author whose classic tales include *Treasure Island*.

• 1914 – FIRST "BRASSIERE" PATENTED • 1941 – SINKING OF HMS *ARK ROYAL*

1900 Dr Karl Landsteiner of the Pathological and Anatomical Institute in Vienna announces the discovery of three different blood groups.

1908 Foul play is suspected on the death of Tsu-Hsi, Dowager Empress of China.

1915 Death of black leader Booker T. Washington.

1918 Tomas Masaryk is elected first president of Czechoslovakia.

1989 After five days of voting in Namibia's first elections, the South West African People's Organization (Swapo) is declared the largest party.

1990 In New Zealand, a gunman kills 11 of the 50 inhabitants of Aramoana.

BIRTHDAYS

Claude Monet 1840, French painter who was one of the pioneers of Impressionism.

Jawaharlal Nehru 1889, Indian statesman, first prime minister of independent India.

Joseph McCarthy 1908, US senator who led the Senate inquiry into alleged communists in the 1950s.

COVENTRY BLITZED

1940 The Luftwaffe visited Coventry last night in one of the most destructive raids of the Blitz so far. Making use of a "bomber's moon", 449 bombers dropped 503 tons of bombs and 881 incendiaries, turning the city into a raging inferno, killing 554 people and seriously injuring 865. The medieval cathedral, one of the city's glories, was almost completely destroyed.

IT'S THE TOP TEN

1952 Britain's first pop chart was published in the *New Musical Express* today. It contains three discs by Vera Lynn, "Homing Waltz", "Auf Wiedersehen" and "Forget Me Not", while Jo Stafford's "You Belong to My Heart" is No. 2, and Nat "King" Cole's "Somewhere Along the Way" is at No. 3. And Britain's first Number One? "Here in My Heart", by Al Martino.

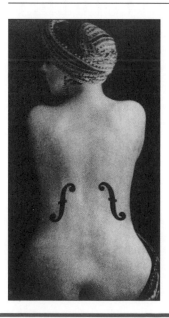

SURREALIST EXHIBITION IN PARIS

1925 A controversial exhibition of art by a group known as the Surrealists has opened at the Galerie Pierre in Paris today. Those featured include Joan Miró, Georgio de Chirico, Paul Klee, Hans Arp, Man Ray, Pablo Picasso and Max Ernst. Although Surrealism is primarily a literary movement, developed out of Dadaism by André Breton (author of the *Surrealist Manifesto*) and Paul Eluard, the visual arts have never been far behind. Ernst's *Reunion of Friends*, André Masson's *Trees* and Miró's *Ploughed Land* and Harlequin's *Carnival*, all of which are on display in the exhibition, illustrate well the Surrealist theory – primarily that art should be "uncontrolled by reason and independent of all aesthetic and moral preoccupation".

• 1948 – BIRTH OF PRINCE CHARLES • 1983 – WORLD'S LARGEST AIRPORT OPENS IN SAUDI

THE BELLS RING OUT

1918 Today was Victory Day in Britain as a war-weary nation celebrated the peace. At 11 am, to the accompaniment of church bells and fireworks, the all-clear was sounded for the last time. Factories closed, and there were scenes of unprecedented public revelry and rejoicing as what seemed to be the entire population took to the streets, waving flags and raising servicemen shoulder-high. Big Ben struck one for the first time in four years. Huge crowds gathered outside Buckingham Palace to sing "God Save the King" and "Rule Britannia", and later the King and Queen drove to Hyde Park. Hundreds thronged to Downing Street to hail the Prime Minister, Lloyd George.

SHERMAN BURNS ATLANTA

1864 General Sherman and his army set out for Savannah on their March to the Sea today, leaving Atlanta a smoking ruin behind them. An important strategic strongpoint for the Confederates, Atlanta had been in Sherman's hands since General Hood had given up resistance on September 1. Sherman, determined that the Confederates should have no further use of it, gave orders that all public buildings, machine-shops, depots and arsenals should be burnt, all civilians having been evacuated. To the accompaniment of military bands and the din of exploding ammunition, spectacular destruction was achieved.

1901 An electrical hearing aid is patented by Miller Reese of New York.

1913 In Mexico, rebel leader Pancho Villa takes Ciudad Juarez.

1922 The first scheduled broadcast is made from London's Marconi House.

1956 Elvis Presley's first film, *Love Me Tender*, is premiered in New York.

1965 Craig Breedlove of the USA sets a world land speed record of 613 mph (986 kph) in his jet engine car *Spirit of America*.

2003 Twenty-five people die in an explosion in a synagogue in Istanbul; Muslim fundamentalists claim responsibility.

2008 Somali pirates hijack a Saudi Arabian oil supertanker off the Somalian coast.

Queen Elizabeth docks for the last time

1968 The largest passenger liner in the world, Cunard's flagship *Queen Elizabeth*, docked in Southampton today at the end of her last transatlantic voyage. She was launched in September 1938 as a sister ship to the *Queen Mary*, but the war broke out before she went into service. She spent the war as a troopship, based in Sydney, and did not leave Southampton for her first commercial voyage until October 1946. Since then she has crossed the Atlantic hundreds of times, carrying thousands of passengers in unparalleled luxury. Sadly the jet age has overtaken her, and she can no longer compete economically. Her future is uncertain, although a group of Florida businessmen have expressed interest in her as a tourist attraction. Cunard's new liner, *Queen Elizabeth II*, will carry twice as many passengers and will be used mainly for cruising.

BIRTHDAYS

Gerhart Hauptmann 1862, German dramatist.

Erwin Rommel 1891, German general, commander of the Afrika Corps in North Africa during World War II.

Daniel Barenboim 1942, Israeli musical director of the Orchestre de Paris since 1975.

• 1837 – PITMAN'S SHORTHAND PUBLISHED • 1985 – THE ANGLO-IRISH AGREEMENT

1724 Highwayman Jack Sheppard is hanged at Tyburn in front of an audience of 200,000.

1797 Death of the Prussian king Frederick William II.

1907 In Britain, militant suffragettes shout down Chancellor of the Exchequer Herbert Asquith in Nuneaton.

1928 An obscenity trial begins in London over the publication of Radclyffe Hall's lesbian novel *The Well of Loneliness.*

1940 Marshal Pétain takes over the French government.

2010 Prince William and Catherine Middleton announce their engagement, eight years after meeting at Edinburgh University.

BIRTHDAYS

Tiberius 42 BC, Roman emperor whose days ended on the Isle of Capri.

Paul Hindemith 1895, German composer and viola player whose work was banned by the Nazis.

Frank Bruno 1961, British boxer who put the British and European heavyweight titles under his belt.

KING OF HOLLYWOOD IS DEAD

1960 Clark Gable, known the world over as "The King of Hollywood", died today aged 59. In a career that spanned nearly 30 years he made dozens of movies, from *The Painted Desert* in 1930 to his last, *The Misfits*, earlier this year. In the 1930s he starred with Garbo in *Susan Lenox*, Jean Harlow in *Red Dust* and Claudette Colbert in *It Happened One Night*, for which Gable won an Oscar. But it is for his portrayal of the arrogant Rhett Butler in *Gone with the Wind*, playing opposite the young Vivien Leigh, that he will always be remembered. Gable served with distinction as a documentary film-maker in the US Army Airforce during World War Two. The fact that he was married five times did nothing to dent his popularity with his female fans, who were captivated to the end by his easy manner and impudent grin on screen.

Force is not a remedy.
John Bright, British politician, in a speech. 1880.

BRITAIN TO BUILD AIR-RAID SHELTERS

1937 The House of Commons voted in favour of a national programme of air-raid shelter construction today. The Labour Party, concerned at the possible cost to the taxpayer, voted against the motion, but Sir Winston Churchill described the move as "indispensable", and claimed that once the nation was thus protected an enemy would find it "not worthwhile" to mount air-raids.

BRITAIN BLOCKADES LONG ISLAND SOUND

1813 Britain's mastery of the sea in the war of 1812 was further emphasized today when a mixed force of Royal Navy ships under the general command of Admiral Warren, including frigates, sloops and 74-gun ships of the line, took up positions in a blockade of Long Island Sound. All major American routes to the sea, including Chesapeake and Delaware Bays, the ports of New York, Charleston, Port Royal and Savannah, and the Mississippi, are now denied to US ships, and the blockade is beginning to cause severe economic losses.

• **1917 – BOLSHEVIKS TAKE MOSCOW • 1988 – ESTONIA CALLS FOR SELF-DETERMINATION**

BENAZIR BHUTTO WINS

1988 Benazir Bhutto became the first woman leader of an Islamic country today in the first democratic elections in Pakistan for 11 years. Her Pakistan People's Party, while falling short of an absolute majority, requires the backing of only 12 out of the 40 independent MPs to form a government. Benazir's father, Zulfiquar Ali Bhutto, was the country's leader from 1971 until he was deposed by a military coup headed by General Zia in 1977; two years later he was hanged. His daughter inherited the People's Party leadership, and was a thorn in the side of the military regime until Zia's death in an air crash last August. She has promised democratic reform.

CATHERINE THE GREAT DIES

1796 Russia's "enlightened despot" died of a stroke today at the age of 67. During her reign she made Russia a force to be reckoned with in European politics, and by her expansionist policies added more than 200,000 square miles (320,000 sq km) to her territory. Her court attracted the greatest minds of Europe, such as Voltaire and Diderot, who heavily influenced her thinking. She could also be ruthless, however. In 1762 she overthrew her husband, Peter III – and quite possibly connived at his subsequent assassination – and there is no doubt that lot of the serfs deteriorated significantly during her reign.

1603 Sir Walter Raleigh goes on trial for treason.

1880 The first three British female graduates receive their BA degrees from London University.

1913 The steamship *Louise* becomes the first ship to travel through the Panama Canal.

1922 Siberia votes for union with the USSR.

1990 A mass grave, believed to be that of WWII prisoners, is discovered by the bridge over the River Kwai, Thailand.

2010 Scientists at the CERN Large Hadron Collider, Geneva, trap anti-matter for the first time.

BIRTHDAYS

Louis XVIII 1755, French monarch, the first to take the throne after the fall of Napoleon.

Sir Charles Mackerras 1925, Australian conductor.

Rock Hudson 1925, American film star whose successes included light romantic comedies with Doris Day.

Martin Scorsese 1942, American film director whose films include *Taxi Driver*.

NEW FORMULA ONE RECORD BREAKER

2013 Sebastian Vettel wins a record-breaking eighth consecutive Formula One race in the 2013 United States Grand Prix. It was his 38th triumph, his 12th of the season, and it shattered the record of seven consecutive victories in one season previously held by Michael Schumacher and Alberto Ascari.

• 1869 – SUEZ CANAL OPENS • 1970 – SOVIET *LUNA 17* LANDS ON THE MOON

1626 St Peter's in Rome is consecrated.

1910 Suffragettes attack the House of Commons.

1922 Death of Marcel Proust, author of the seven-volume *Remembrance of Things Past.*

1977 President Sadat becomes the first Egyptian leader to visit Israel.

1988 A million Serbs demonstrate in Belgrade to demand independence.

1991 Gustav Husak, former president of Czechoslovakia who crushed the Prague Spring in 1968, dies, aged 78.

2004 The Civil Partnership Bill, enabling registered unions for same-sex couples, receives royal assent in the UK.

BIRTHDAYS

Louis Daguerre 1789, French pioneer of the photographic process.

Ignacy Paderewski 1860, Polish pianist, composer and statesman who was the first prime minister of the newly independent Poland.

Sir Alec Issigonis 1906, Turkish-born British car designer who created the Mini.

WOMEN'S CHRISTIAN TEMPERANCE UNION IS FORMED

1874 Cleveland, Ohio, today saw the foundation of the Women's Christian Temperance Union under the secretaryship of the charismatic Miss Frances Elizabeth Caroline Willard, president of the Evanston College for Ladies. The aims of the WCTU are to protect the home and develop Christian citizenship through individual commitment to abstinence and the abolition of the liquor trade. Its formation is a consequence of the Women's Temperance Crusade of 1873–4, in which militant women frequently invaded saloons to sing hymns and kneel in prayer; indeed there is a political element to the Union's aims, since insobriety and the ill-treatment of women so often go hand in hand.

WAITE AND SUTHERLAND RELEASED

1991 The Briton Terry Waite and the American Thomas Sutherland were released today by the pro-Iranian Islamic Jihad for the Liberation of Palestine, as part of a UN-brokered three-way exchange of Western hostages, Arabs held by Israel and Israelis missing in Lebanon. Terry Waite, the Archbishop of Canterbury's special envoy, was kidnapped on January 21, 1987, while on a mission to secure the release

of other hostages. His release immediately revived speculation about his links, involuntary or otherwise, with Colonel Oliver North and the Iran-Contra affair. It has been claimed that he had nearly 20 meetings with North between 1985 and 1987, and that three US hostages, in whose release he had been involved, had in fact been traded for arms. Thomas Sutherland, Dean of Agriculture at the American University in Beirut, was kidnapped on June 9, 1985.

• **1904 – GOLD FOUND IN RHODESIA** • **1987 – KING'S CROSS UNDERGROUND INFERNO**

PILGRIM FATHERS LAND AT CAPE COD

1620 The *Mayflower* made landfall at Cape Cod today, just over two months after setting sail from Plymouth. The passengers, 87 members of a separatist Protestant sect founded in Northamptonshire by William Brewster, intend to start a new life in America. Having received from the Virginia Company a charter to found a trading post in that territory, to land outside the northern limits seemed at first sight disastrous, but after discussion the group have decided to settle without rights in Massachusetts Bay. They are drawing up a preliminary plan of government.

DEATH OF FRANZ SCHUBERT

1828 One of the world's greatest musical geniuses, Franz Schubert, died today aged 31. Worn out by overwork, delirious from the syphilis he contracted in 1822, he expired at 3pm in a damp room in the Neue Wieden suburb of Vienna, attended by his devoted brother Ferdinand and stepsister Josefa. In a furious burst of activity over the past few months he had completed three piano sonatas, a string quintet, and a number of songs. Schubert had been confined to his room for over a week, his only occupation the correction of the proofs of his recent song cycle, *Winterreise*.

1905 British steamer *Hilda* is wrecked off St Malo, France, drowning 128.

1914 In Britain, Austrian and German internees riot at a detention camp on the Isle of Wight.

1917 A Revolutionary Diplomatic Committee is established in Petrograd headed by Leon Trotsky.

1920 One hundred thousand White Russian refugees from the Crimea arrive in Constantinople.

1988 Death of Christina Onassis, Greek shipowner and daughter of Aristotle Onassis.

BIRTHDAYS

Charles I 1600, English monarch who lost his head after the Civil War.

Viscomte Ferdinand de Lesseps 1805, French diplomat who supervised the building of the Suez Canal.

Hiram Bingham 1875, American senator and archaeologist who discovered Machu Picchu.

Indira Gandhi 1917, Indian politician, prime minister 1966–77 and 1980–4.

Calvin Klein 1942, American fashion designer.

MEXICAN GAS TRAGEDY

1984 Ten tanks of liquid gas blew up at a chemical factory in Mexico City today. Flames shot 300 ft (100 m) into the air, showering surrounding areas with burning debris and a cloud of poisonous gas. More than 500 people lost their lives and some 10,000 homes were destroyed. Firemen fought for 18 hours to bring the fire under control.

LINCOLN MAKES MASTERFUL SPEECH AT GETTYSBURG DEDICATION

1863 "Four score and seven years ago our fathers brought forth on this continent, a new nation, conceived in liberty and dedicated to the proposition that all men are created equal . . ." So began a two-minute speech by President Lincoln at the dedication of the cemetery where the dead of the Battle of Gettysburg are buried. His 15,000 listeners were exhausted by a two-hour oration full of learned detail from noted orator Edward Everett. The President was disappointed by their lack of enthusiasm, but Everett said admiringly, "I should be glad if I could flatter myself that I came as near to the central idea of the occasion in two hours as you did in two minutes."

• **1925 – ENGLAND IMPOSES A FOUR-MONTH PRISON SENTENCE FOR DRINK DRIVING**

1805 The first performance of Beethoven's opera *Fidelio* is staged in Vienna.

1925 In Italy, a law is passed banning the Freemasons and other secret societies.

1929 Salvador Dali holds his first lone show in Paris.

1985 American company Microsoft releases Windows 1.0 for PCs.

2003 Controversial pop star Michael Jackson is arrested on charges of child molestation but pleads his innocence.

BIRTHDAYS

Sir Samuel Cunard 1787, Canadian-born shipowner who established the Cunard line in Britain.

Alistair Cooke 1908, English-born journalist and broadcaster best-known for his radio programme *Letter from America*.

Nadine Gordimer 1923, South African novelist, anti-apartheid campaigner and winner of the Nobel Prize for Literature in 1991.

Robert F. Kennedy 1925, American politician and Democratic Attorney-General, brother of JFK.

POMP AND SPLENDOUR IN THE RAIN

1947 Princess Elizabeth, heir presumptive to the British throne, married Lieutenant Philip Mountbatten today amid scenes of pomp and splendour not seen since before the war. Undeterred by the rain, the crowds slept overnight in the streets to secure the best view, and were standing 50 deep in the Mall and Whitehall to cheer the King and his daughter on their way to Westminster Abbey. The Princess's ivory dress, covered with flowers of beads and pearls, and her tulle veil with a circlet of diamonds, were designed by Norman Hartnell. Her new husband was created Prince Philip, Duke of Edinburgh, by the King at a private ceremony at Buckingham Palace this morning.

BRITAIN'S EMPIRE DIMINISHED

1926 At the Imperial Conference in London today the oldest colonies of the British Empire – Canada, Australia, New Zealand, South Africa and Newfoundland – were granted the status of self-governing dominions and of equal status with Great Britain. The Irish Free State is also to become a dominion outside the United Kingdom, and the King is no longer its sovereign; the status of India is unchanged.

Something that everybody wants to have read and nobody wants to read.

Mark Twain defines a classic of literature, 1900.

NUCLEAR SCIENTIST JOINS PEACE CAMPAIGN

1972 One of Soviet Russia's prominent nuclear physicists, Andrei Sakharov, who was involved in the development of the Russian H-bomb, today put himself on a collision course with the authorities in Moscow. He joined 50 other civil rights campaigners and liberal intellectuals, including world-famous cellist Mstislav Rostropovich, in urging the Kremlin to abolish the death penalty and to free all political prisoners. Sakharov, 51, co-founded the Moscow Human Rights Committee in 1970, but as early as 1963 his concern about the threat of nuclear war led him to use his influence on Khrushchev to persuade him to negotiate a partial ban on nuclear testing.

• 1818 – VENEZUELA DECLARES INDEPENDENCE • 1992 – FIRE AT WINDSOR CASTLE

JUNK BOND KING GETS 10 YEARS

1990 Michael Milken, the so-called "Junk Bond King" was sentenced to 10 years in jail today after pleading guilty to violating federal tax and securities laws. Charges against him included manipulating stock prices, bribery and insider trading. In a plea bargain with the federal authorities back in April Milken also agreed to pay $200 million (£109 million) in fines and $400 million (£217 million) in restitution. Milken's huge success as head of the "Junk Bond" department at Wall Street finance house Drexel Burnham Lambert – in 1987 he earned $500 million (£272 million) – made him the personification of the predatory financial ethics of the 1980s.

SUPER POWERS REACH AGREEMENT

1985 The so-called "Fireside Summit" between presidents Reagan and Gorbachev, their first, ended today with a broad measure of agreement to work for a 50 per cent cut in their respective strategic nuclear arsenals. A range of other issues was also discussed, such as the emigration of Soviet Jews and the need to avoid a repetition of the Korean Airlines tragedy.

FRANCIS XAVIER RETURNS

1551 Papal legate Francis Xavier and his fellow Jesuits returned from their two-year journey to Japan today, the first missionaries to attempt baptism in this eastern country. The trip has been a moderate success – Francis has left behind 2000 Christians who, it is hoped, will form a thriving community. The latest mission found favour with the Mikado who at first, unimpressed with Francis's humble dress and bearing, refused to see him; but when Francis returned suitably dressed and bearing gifts, he gave his support.

1695 Death of Henry Purcell, English composer and organist.

1791 French navigator Etienne Marchand arrives in China after a record Pacific crossing of 60 days.

1913 Death of Tokugawa Keiki, last of the Japanese shoguns who controlled the country from 1603 to 1867.

1916 Death of Emperor Franz Josef, ruler of the Austro-Hungarian Empire since 1848.

1934 Cole Porter's musical *Anything Goes* opens in New York.

1964 The Verrazano-Narrows Bridge across New York harbour is opened – the longest single-span bridge in the world.

BIRTHDAYS

Voltaire 1694, French philosopher, scientist and moralist.

Harpo Marx 1888, American comedian who, as one of the Marx Brothers, remained entirely mute.

René Magritte 1898, Belgian Surrealist painter.

Coleman Hawkins 1904, American jazz saxophonist.

• 1783 – MONTGOLFIER BALLOON MAKES FIRST FLIGHT • 1910 – LEO TOLSTOY DIES

1900 Death of Sir Arthur Sullivan, composer of the Savoy Operas with librettist W. S. Gilbert.

1902 Fire destroys the Williamsburg Bridge over the East River in New York.

1907 The Cunard liner arrives in New York, completing her maiden voyage.

1916 Death of American novelist Jack London.

1980 Mae West, American film star, dies aged 88.

1989 A remote-control bomb kills Lebanon's president René Moawad and 23 others.

2010 347 people die in a stampede at the Khymer Water Festival in Phnom Penh, Cambodia.

BIRTHDAYS

Thomas Cook 1808, English travel agent who pioneered the concept of the package tour.

Benjamin Britten 1913, British composer whose works include the opera *Peter Grimes*.

Billie Jean King 1943, American tennis player and winner of 20 Wimbledon titles.

Boris Becker 1967, German tennis star.

KENNEDY ASSASSINATED

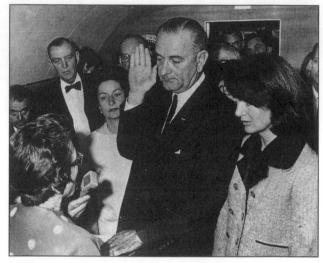

1963 President John F. Kennedy has been shot and killed in Dallas, Texas. The 46-year-old President and Mrs Kennedy were on the latest leg of a tour of the southern states to gather support for the Democratic Party. The shooting occurred this morning as the presidential motorcade swept through Dealey Plaza in downtown Dallas. Witnesses claim to have heard one or more shots from several directions, and a high-powered rifle was found in an upstairs room of the Texas School Book Depository, overlooking Dealey Plaza. Lee Harvey Oswald has been arrested and charged with the murder. Vice-President Lyndon B. Johnson was sworn in as President on the flight back to Washington.

BLACKBEARD MEETS HIS MATCH

1718 The notorious English pirate Edward "Blackbeard" Teach met his death today in hand-to-hand combat with Lieutenant Robert Maynard of HMS *Pearl*. For the past five years Teach has been the scourge of shipping off the coast of Virginia and the Carolinas. The *Pearl* was one of two British frigates sent by Virginia governor Alexander Spotswood to bring to an end Teach's long reign of terror.

VICTORY FOR ENGLAND

2003 In a moment of glory, the England team have achieved victory by winning the Rugby World Cup 2003. Sports fans have described the win as England's greatest sporting triumph since 1966. England fly-half Jonny Wilkinson made a last-minute drop kick to win England the game. The team was led by England rugby captain Martin Johnson who was euphoric at the 20-17 win over Australia.

• 2005 – ANGELA MERKEL BECOMES GERMANY'S FIRST FEMALE CHANCELLOR

RUSSIAN CONTROVERSY

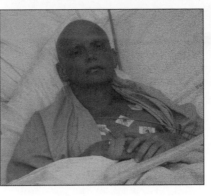

2006 Russian dissident and former KGB bodyguard Alexander Litvinenko died a slow and painful death in a London hospital after drinking tea laced with polonium-210. Litvinenko was a fierce critic of Russia's government and was reported to have fallen out with Russian President Vladimir Putin in the late 1990s. British investigators suspected former KGB agent Andrei Lugovoi of murdering Litvinenko with the lethal radioactive substance, stating there were "very strong indications it was a state action", and demanded his extradition from Russia. The denial of their request led to the expulsion of four Russian diplomats from Britain amid rumours of spying.

POST TO COLLECT

1852 Britain's first pillarboxes were introduced today in St Helier, Jersey. The six-sided boxes are of cast iron, 4 foot (1.3 m) high and painted red. They are the brainchild of Anthony Trollope, a surveyor for the Post Office and part-time novelist, who noticed while on a trip to the Channel Islands that there were many places for buying stamps but only one place to post letters.

US CASH SQUEEZE FORCES UK OUT OF SUEZ

1956 Under intense pressure from the US, the British government has agreed to begin a military withdrawal from the Suez war zone, following the ceasefire on November 8. Foreign Secretary Selwyn Lloyd said that troops will leave as "an act of faith" in UN undertakings to ensure the reopening of the Canal. The hostility of President Eisenhower and Secretary of State John Foster Dulles to the Anglo-French invasion has caused a run on the pound, and the US Treasury has made it clear to British Chancellor of the Exchequer Harold Macmillan that financial help in preventing a collapse of sterling depends on a UK withdrawal. Many senior Tories are critical of the government's handling of the Suez Crisis.

NOVEMBER
23

1499 Perkin Warbeck, a Flemish-born impostor is hanged after two attempts to escape from the Tower of London.

1670 Moliére's play *Le Bourgeois Gentilhomme* is premiered in Paris.

1921 In the US, President Harding bans doctors from prescribing beer.

1956 Petrol is rationed in Britain and driving tests are suspended as a response to the Suez crisis which threatens oil supplies.

1988 Sumo champion Chiyonofuji becomes the first sumo wrestler to win 50 consecutive matches.

2010 North Korea shells the South Korean island of Yeonpyeong in the most serious incident since the Korean War.

BIRTHDAYS

William Bonney (Billy the Kid) 1859, US outlaw.

Valdemar Poulson 1869, Danish inventor of the tape recorder.

Boris Karloff 1887, English actor who specialized in horror roles.

Sir Peter Saunders 1911, British impresario who staged Agatha Christie's *The Mousetrap*.

• 1889 – WORLD'S FIRST JUKEBOX UNVEILED • 1963 – *DR WHO* PREMIERES ON BBC TV

1572 Death of John Knox, Scottish Protestant reformer.

1859 Charles Darwin publishes his book *Origin of the Species*.

1902 The world's first conference for professional photographers opens in Paris.

1934 Swedish tenor Jussi Björling makes his debut at the Metropolitan Opera House in New York.

1979 Saudi Arabian troops storm the Great Mosque in Mecca to oust Iranian religious fanatics.

1990 White extremists attack 300 black children in a park in Louis Trichardt.

BIRTHDAYS

Laurence Sterne 1713, Irish novelist best-known for *Tristram Shandy*.

Frances Hodgson Burnett 1849, English novelist famous for *The Secret Garden*.

Henri de Toulouse-Lautrec 1864, French artist who turned his back on his aristocratic background to live among the cafés of Montmartre.

Scott Joplin 1868, American ragtime pianist and composer.

FREDDIE MERCURY DIES OF AIDS

1991 Freddie Mercury, one of rock's most flamboyant characters, has died of AIDS at the age of 45. Yesterday Mercury issued a statement confirming rumours that he had the disease. Mercury and his group, Queen, hit the music world in the 1970s with a teasing mixture of transvestism and original rock. Throughout the '70s and '80s the effervescent Mercury kept fans royally entertained with "Bohemian Rhapsody", "Crazy Little Thing Called Love"', "We Are the Champions" and many more. The fans loved him, his songs and the way he sang them. He was a mesmerizing performer, uninhibited and totally involved.

OSWALD SHOT

1963 Lee Harvey Oswald, the man charged with the assassination of President John F. Kennedy, was himself shot and killed today. While being transferred under police custody to the County Jail he was approached in the underground carpark of the Dallas Police Headquarters by Jack Ruby, a Dallas strip-club owner, who was immediately arrested in his turn.

A piece of each of us died at that moment.

Michael J. Mansfield, US senator, on the assassination two days ago of John F. Kennedy, 1963.

US TROOPS TAKE LUZON

1899 The US Expeditionary Force made an advance in its struggle against insurrectionist leader Emilio Aguinaldo today when it gained control of the Philippines largest island, Luzon. The roots of the struggle go back to the country coming under US control after the Spanish-American War. Bitterly disappointed, Aguinaldo declared the Malolos Republic last year has waged a guerrilla campaign since. Today's defeat is a setback for him, but he has vowed to continue the struggle.

• **1989 – THE ENTIRE GOVERNMENT OF COMMUNIST CZECHOSLOVAKIA RESIGNS**

BAND AID RECORD FOR ETHIOPIA

1984 When Boomtown Rat Bob Geldof watched a BBC TV report on the famine in Ethiopia he was so appalled at what he saw that he resolved to do something about it. The results of that something were seen today when an extraordinary gathering of British rock stars gathered at Sarm Studios in London to record "Do They Know It's Christmas?" Those who turned up free of charge to sing the song, written by Geldof and Ultravox member Midge Ure, included Phil Collins, Sting, George Michael, Bono and Boy George. The single will be released on December 7, and all of the proceeds will go directly to Ethiopian famine relief.

"HOLLYWOOD TEN" BLACKLISTED

1947 The so-called "Hollywood Ten" today refused to testify before the House UnAmerican Activities Committee enquiry into possible communists in the movie capital – on the grounds that the enquiry is unconstitutional. The ten screenwriters and directors – Alvah Bessie, Herbert Biberman. Lester Cole, Edward Dmytryk, Ring Lardner Jr, John Howard Lawson, Albert Maltz, Samuel Ornitz, Adrian Scott and Dalton Trumbo – face a professional ban and jail sentences for their continued lack of cooperation.

CEASEFIRE IN FORMER YUGOSLAVIA

1995 A ceasefire has been declared in the former Yugoslav republics of Bosnia, Serbia and Croatia following a peace agreement signed by the republics' leaders in Dayton, Ohio. The Dayton Peace Agreement comes after a summer of military operations which have left the Bosnian Serbs politically and militarily weakened. The United States and NATO have been threatening direct military action if the fighting does not stop. The deal provides for Bosnia to become a single state comprising the Muslim-Croat Federation and the Serb Republic. Sarajevo will once again become a unified city, and the central Bosnian government will have jurisdiction over trade, monetary policy and foreign affairs.

1913 In Natal, police open fire on demonstrators protesting against the imprisonment of Mahatma Gandhi, killing two and wounding another 20.

1935 The monarchy is restored in Greece.

1963 Assassinated president John F. Kennedy receives a state funeral.

1974 Death of U Thant, Burmese diplomat and secretary general of the UN 1962–72.

1989 The New Zealand All-Blacks' celebrate an unbroken run of 46 victorious rugby matches.

1993 Death of novelist Anthony Burgess.

2005 George Best, British soccer legend, dies age 59.

BIRTHDAYS

Andrew Carnegie 1835, Scottish-born American industrialist and philanthropist.

Karl Friedrich Benz 1844, German engineer and car manufacturer.

General Augusto Pinochet 1915, Chilean dictator who instituted a repressive military junta.

Joe DiMaggio 1914, American baseball star who married Marilyn Monroe.

• 1970 – ACCLAIMED JAPANESE WRITER, YUKIO MISHIMA, COMMITS RITUAL SUICIDE

BIRTHDAYS

Cyril Cusack 1910, Irish actor who made his film debut at the age of seven and went on to appear at the Abbey Theatre, Dublin.

Eugéne Ionesco 1912, French dramatist who initiated the Theatre of the Absurd.

Charles Schultz 1922, American cartoonist who created the *Peanuts* strip.

Tina Turner 1939, American singer who had hits such as "River Deep, Mountain High" with her husband Ike before gaining massive success as a solo artist in her own right.

ROOSEVELT COMES HOME

1906 President Theodore Roosevelt has returned to Washington from Central America, having made history by being the first US President to travel abroad while in office. His 17-day trip aboard the battleship *Louisiana* took him to Puerto Rico and then on to Panama to see for himself the building work on the canal he did so much to promote – or "to see how the ditch is getting on", as he put it. The cab of a 95-ton steam shovel made an excellent vantage point for the President as he viewed the awe-inspiring work of engineering, which will reduce the voyage between the Atlantic and Pacific by around 7000 miles (11,200 km).

NEW YORK GETS STREETCARS

1832 New York's public transport system was inaugurated today when Mr John Mason's horse-drawn streetcars, the city's first, went into operation between Spring and 14th streets.

I think Prohibition a piece of low, provincial persecution of the dirtiest and most dismal sort. I defy anybody to say what the rights of a citizen are if they do not include the control of his own diet in relation to his health.

G.K. Chesterton, writing in the *Illustrated London News*, 1921.

UK'S BIGGEST GOLD ROBBERY

1983 A daring and efficient gang of thieves pulled off Britain's biggest-ever robbery today: £25 millions' ($46 million) worth of gold bullion. They coolly broke into the Brinks-Mat security warehouse at Heathrow Airport, neutralized the alarm system and tied up six guards. They then spent an hour loading the gold, which weighed 25 tons, into a truck before making their getaway.

• **1922 – INSIDE OF TUTANKHAMUN'S TOMB SEEN FOR THE FIRST TIME**

CUSTER KILLS CHIEF BLACK KETTLE

1868 Blood flowed on the Washita River in western Oklahoma today when Lieutenant Colonel George Custer and his 7th Cavalry attacked and burned the village of Cheyenne chief Black Kettle. The Cheyenne have been bitterly resisting the building of the railroad in their territory, but it seems that Black Kettle had been negotiating for peace at the time of his death. The 29-year-old Custer is a controversial figure – his daring, reckless style attracted attention at the Battle of Gettysburg and he has only recently been restored to active duty following a court-martial for unauthorized absence from his command and for mistreating deserters. Within an hour after the dawn attack, 103 warriors were dead, according to Custer's unverified estimate. The 23 US dead, among them Major Joel Elliott, were slaughtered while in hot pursuit of a group of fleeing Indians.

FIRST WOMEN ON THE BEAT

1914 The first policewomen in Britain to complete their official training and assume active duty, Misses Mary Allen and E. F. Harburn, were patrolling the streets of Grantham, Lincolnshire, today. Reporting to the Provost Marshal of the county, the women are at present unpaid. They are in Grantham in response to a request from the military authorities – there is a military camp containing 18,000 soldiers just outside town (only 2,000 fewer than the population of Grantham), and it is felt that the women's presence on the streets could help to reduce tension. Wartime demands on manpower are expected to lead to the recruitment of more women to the force.

NZ WOMEN VOTE FOR THE FIRST TIME

1893 New Zealand went to the polls today, and for the first time in a national election anywhere in the world women voted too, a female suffrage bill having been passed in parliament by just two votes. The women of New Zealand owe this advance to the flamboyant Liberal leader Richard John Seddon, known as "King Dick", whose unwillingness to alienate a powerful feminist-temperance alliance helped force the measure through parliament, albeit with so narrow a margin. The women returned the favour by electing Seddon and the Liberals to power.

1875 Britain buys shares worth £4 million ($7.4 million) in the Suez Canal Company.

1895 Death of Alexandre Dumas fils, French novelist.

1942 The French fleet is scuttled by its crews six hours after German tanks arrive in Toulon.

1967 President de Gaulle turns down British entry into the Common Market.

1970 The Gay Liberation Front holds its first demonstration in London.

1991 A 15th-century Bible is sold at Christie's, London for £1.1 million ($2 million).

BIRTHDAYS

Anders Celsius 1701, Swedish astronomer who invented the Celsius temperature scale.

Alexander Dubcek 1921, Czechoslovakian politician who, as secretary of the Czechoslovak Communist Party in 1968, instigated the liberal reforms that led to the "Prague Spring" crushed by the Soviets in August of that year.

Jimi Hendrix 1942, American singer whose hits include "Purple Haze" and Bob Dylan's "All Along the Watchtower".

• 1919 – HUGE METEOR LANDS IN LAKE MICHIGAN • 1953 – DEATH OF EUGENE O'NEILL

NOVEMBER
28

1907 King Leopold II of Belgium hands over control of the Congo to the Belgian government.

1919 Nancy Astor becomes Britain's first woman MP.

1945 Death of Dwight F. Davis, founder of the Davis Cup tennis tournament.

1967 All horse-racing is banned in Britain owing to an outbreak of foot and mouth disease.

1971 In Rome, 100,000 demonstrators march against fascism.

1978 Iranian government bans religious marches.

2002 Suicide bombers target an Israeli-owned hotel in Mombasa, Kenya, killing 13.

BIRTHDAYS

Jean Baptiste Lully 1632, French composer and violinist to King Louis XIV.

William Blake 1757, English visionary poet, painter and engraver.

Friedrich Engels 1820, German socialist who wrote *Condition of the Working Class in England* in 1844.

Claude Lévi-Strauss 1908, French anthropologist whose books include *Structural Anthropology.*

CHINESE ENTER KOREAN CONFLICT

1950 The Korean War took a devastating new turn today when an estimated 200,000 Chinese troops poured over the River Yalu. Chou En-lai, the Chinese foreign minister, had repeatedly warned that his country would resist if US forces crossed the 38th Parallel into North Korea, but his warnings were ignored by the West. Now the US Eighth Army, along with large forces of Marines and South Koreans, is in humiliating retreat in appalling weather.

RIP VAN WINKLE'S CREATOR IS DEAD

1859 Washington Irving, the first successful American-born writer, died at his Tarrytown, New York, home today, aged 76. In 1820 he published *The Sketch Book of Geoffrey Crayon, Gent*, a collection of amusing stories that included "Rip Van Winkle" and "The Legend of Sleepy Hollow". The book launched him as a writer, which was all he had ever wanted to be, although he never quite reproduced its success.

MUMBAI UNDER SEIGE FOR TWO DAYS

2008 After two days of carnage, Mumbai security services have secured all but one of the locations where Islamic terrorists carried out a series of coordinated shooting and bombing attacks, leaving 183 people dead and wounding over 300. The 10 gunmen had launched attacks on two luxury hotels, a busy railway station and other major landmarks across India's biggest city on 26 November. Fighting continued until the following morning in the Taj Mahal Palace hotel, which gunmen had seized as people sat down for dinner, opening fire indiscriminately. India has accused Pakistan-based fighters from the banned militant group Lashkar-e-Taiba of carrying out the attacks. US intelligence agencies agree. After initial denials, Pakistan has conceded the attacks were partly planned on its soil.

A new scientific truth does not triumph by convincing its opponents and making them see the light, but rather because its opponents eventually die out, and a new generation grows up that is familiar with it.

Max Planck,
German physicist,
1934.

• 1948 – POLAROID CAMERA GOES ON SALE • 1990 – MARGARET THATCHER RESIGNS

DEATH OF EMPRESS MARIA THERESA

1780 Maria Theresa, Archduchess of Austria, Queen of Hungary and Bohemia, widow of Holy Roman Emperor Francis I has died. A key figure in politics, she has been described as "the most human of the Hapsburgs". An enlightened ruler, she introduced compulsory primary education and a rudimentary penal code, and encouraged the eminence of Vienna as a centre for the arts.

IRAQ MUST WITHDRAW FROM KUWAIT

1990 Following intensive diplomacy from President Bush and Secretary of State James Baker, the UN Security Council today approved Resolution 678, authorizing member governments to use "all necessary force" to ensure Iraq's complete withdrawal from Kuwait by January 15 next year. This is the first authorization of force by the UN since the Korean War.

ALLIED LEADERS MEET IN TEHRAN

1943 The first summit conference between Joseph Stalin, Franklin D. Roosevelt and Winston Churchill opens today in Tehran. The intention is to discuss the progress of the war and to plan for the future – in particular the coordination of the Normandy landings planned for June 1944 with a simultaneous Russian attack on Germany from the east. Also on the agenda are the possibilities of Russia entering the war against Japan and the post-war foundation of a United Nations organization.

1924 Death of Italian composer Giacomo Puccini.

1971 The British government announces a fund of £3 million ($5.5 million) for the victims of the drug thalidomide.

1974 German terrorist leader Ulrike Meinhof is jailed for eight years.

1986 Death of debonair British-born actor Cary Grant.

1989 Romanian gymnast Nadia Comaneci defects.

1994 Russian aircraft launch a bombing raid on Chechen capital, Grozny.

1999 The Northern Ireland power-sharing executive is formally set up.

BIRTHDAYS

Louisa M. Alcott 1832, American novelist best-remembered for *Little Women*.

C. S. Lewis 1898, Irish scholar and writer of science fiction.

Berry Gordy 1929, American songwriter and record producer who founded Tamla Motown.

Jacques Chirac 1932, French politician who served as president from 1995–2007.

• 1641 – FIRST ENGLISH NEWSPAPER PUBLISHED • 2001 – DEATH OF GEORGE HARRISON

1925 The US sends warships to Hankow, China, to prevent Communist attacks on foreigners.

1956 American boxer Floyd Patterson becomes the youngest boxer to win the world heavyweight title.

1983 Dutch brewery millionaire Alfred Heineken is kidnapped in Amsterdam.

1988 PLO leader Yasser Arafat is refused a visa to enter the US in order to address the UN General Assembly in New York.

1989 Germany's left-wing terrorist group the Red Army Faction blow up Alfred Herrhausen, the head of Deutsche Bank.

1989 In the Philippines, rebels attack Cory Aquino's presidential palace.

BIRTHDAYS

Andrea Palladio 1508, Italian architect whose neo-Classical style was much imitated throughout Western architecture.

Mark Twain 1835, American author of *The Adventures of Tom Sawyer*.

Sir Winston Churchill 1874, English statesman who, as prime minister, steered Britain through World War Two.

CRYSTAL PALACE DESTROYED BY FIRE

1936 One of London's landmarks, the Crystal Palace, burned down this evening. Designed by Joseph Paxton, the Duke of Devonshire's head gardener, the huge glass building, 1848 ft (600 m) long by 408 ft (132 m) wide, was originally constructed in Hyde Park to house the Great Exhibition of 1851. Six million people passed through the building during the Exhibition; When the Exhibition closed the building was dismantled and rebuilt on a hill in Sydenham, South London, where it was still a great draw – one-and-a-quarter million Londoners visited it in 1854. The flames were first noticed at 8 pm, and by 8.30 the entire centre transept was ablaze, with flames shooting 300 ft (100 m) into the sky. Visible from all over the city and as far away as Brighton, the blaze attracted a huge crowd of sightseers and special trains were laid on from Central London. Five hundred firemen fought to save the building, but in vain.

The legal profession is a kind of prostitution: lawyers are paid to find intellectual justifications for other people's actions.

Lisa Forrell, lawyer and dramatist, 1991.

REAGAN'S MEN DISMISSED

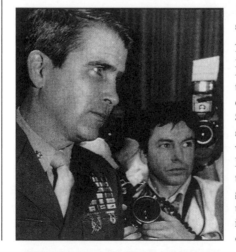

1986 The rapidly developing Iran-Contra scandal has claimed two prominent heads: Admiral John Poindexter, President Reagan's National Security Advisor, and Lieutenant Colonel Oliver North (left) of the National Security Council staff, a much-decorated ex-Marine. It has emerged that the $30 million (£16 million) profits from secret sales of embargoed arms to the Iranians were passed on to the US-backed Contras in Nicaragua to finance their struggle against the democratically elected Sandinista government. President Reagan has come under intense pressure over the extent of his involvement in the affair, but the sacrifice of his two aides is likely to defuse the crisis.

• 1900 – DEATH OF OSCAR WILDE • 1919 – FRENCH WOMEN VOTE FOR THE FIRST TIME

British actress Deborah Kerr today celebrates her birthday. Born in 1921, her films include *From Here to Eternity* and *The King and I*, in which her performances brought her two of her six Oscar nominations.

• 1979 – DEATH OF ZEPPO MARX, ONE OF THE FOUR MARX BROTHERS

DECEMBER

TREATY PRESERVES ANTARCTICA FOR SCIENCE

1959 Twelve countries today agreed to preserve Antarctica for peaceful scientific research in the first international agreement of its kind. The Antarctic Treaty was signed by the US, the Soviet Union, Britain, France, Belgium, Norway, Australia, New Zealand, Chile, Argentina, South Africa and Japan. It freezes all territorial claims on the last unexploited continent, throws the continent open to all scientists, and bans military bases, nuclear explosions and the dumping of nuclear wastes. Antarctica is the coldest place on Earth. If it melted, the oceans would rise 200 ft (65 m).

1640 Portugal expels the Spanish and regains its independence.

1908 Italy demands that Austria pay compensation for the annexation of Bosnia-Herzegovina.

1918 The Danish parliament passes an act giving independence to Iceland.

1973 Death of David Ben-Gurion, Israel's first PM.

1987 Death of James Baldwin, black American writer whose works include *Go Tell It on the Mountain*.

1989 A historic meeting in Rome between Pope John Paul II and Mikhail Gorbachev ends 70 years of mutual hostility between the USSR and the Vatican.

1989 The East German Communist Party votes to end its monopoly of power.

1990 Food rationing is imposed in Leningrad.

BOERS OUTRAGED AS SLAVES FREED

1834 The slaves of the British Cape Colony were emancipated today. Their freedom has caused a deep split in Cape society, with Dutch-speaking Boer farmers in outlying districts threatening to rebel. The issue has become the focus of Boer resentment of the harsh British rule. Labour shortages caused by Britain's abolition of the slave trade in 1807 have driven the Boers ever further into the hinterland. Raising beef makes more profit and needs less labour than raising crops, and the Boers graze their cattle over large areas. Their expansion has brought them into constant conflict with the black tribes. To the Boers, blacks are savage heathens or slaves. British Governor Sir Benjamin D'Urban is unsympathetic to their grievances. Some Boers are talking of leaving the Cape for the unexplored north.

Woody Allen 1935, American comedian, screenwriter, actor and director.

Lee Trevino 1939, American golfer who was the first to win the US, British and Canadian opens in the same year.

EUROPE AND BRITAIN JOINED

1990 Today the two halves of the Channel Tunnel were joined under the sea. A joint British-French effort, excavations for the high-speed rail tunnel were started from both the French and British sides of the English Channel. This morning the two construction teams broke through to meet in the middle.

• 1939 – *GONE WITH THE WIND* PREMIERES IN NEW YORK

1547 Death of Hernan Cortés, conqueror of Mexico for Spain.

1697 Christopher Wren's St Paul's Cathedral is opened in London.

1900 The US Supreme Court declares that Puerto Ricans do not qualify for American citizenship.

1908 Pu Yi succeeds to the throne of China.

1911 Chinese republicans capture Nanking.

1988 A 110-mph (177-kph) cyclone in Bangladesh kills thousands and leaves five million homeless.

2001 US energy giant Enron files for bankruptcy, raising questions about big business and politics, as President Bush had received large payments from the company.

BIRTHDAYS

Georges Seurat 1859, French painter who pioneered the technique of Pointillism.

Maria Callas 1923, Greek operatic soprano renowned for her dramatic interpretations.

Britney Spears 1981, American recording artist and entertainer.

A UNITED GERMANY VOTES FOR KOHL

1990 West German chancellor Helmut Kohl has won the first all-Germany election since 1933. Kohl's Christian Democratic Union and their allies have won more than half the vote, with a 20 per cent lead on the Social Democrats. East Germany's communist ex-rulers won a few seats in the new united German parliament.

"HANDS OFF" MONROE TELLS EUROPE

1823 US President James Monroe today warned Europe to keep its hands off *both* American continents. In his annual message to the US Congress, Monroe defended the newly-won independence of the Spanish colonies in Latin America and said the American continents were no longer subjects for European colonization. The warning follows concerted moves by US secretary of state John Quincy Adams and British foreign secretary George Canning to head off reported French plans to send troops to help Spain regain her New World colonies.

As I write, they are leading old John Brown to execution . . . This is sowing the wind to reap the whirlwind, which will soon come.

Henry Wadsworth Longfellow, American poet, today, 1859.

JOHN BROWN HANGED FOR TREASON

1859 The radical abolitionist John Brown was hanged today for treason against Virginia. Three years ago Brown and his sons murdered five pro-slavery settlers in Kansas. On October 16, Brown and 21 armed men attacked Harpers Ferry in

West Virginia, seized the federal arsenal and occupied the town. Federal troops commanded by Robert E. Lee recaptured the town the following morning and Brown was charged with treason. His trial was a sensation: Brown played on abolitionist sympathies in the North, where he is being hailed as a martyr, but his extremism has horrified the South, where he is seen as a murderous traitor. The whole affair has served to widen the rift over abolition.

• 1901 – SAFETY RAZOR MARKETED • 1927 – FORD'S MODEL A CAR GOES ON SHOW

JACKSON IS PRESIDENT

1828 John Quincy Adams lost the US presidential election to his arch-rival Andrew Jackson today. He is backed by the new Democratic Party, supported by southern farmers and northern workers. A noisy crowd of farmers and other supporters invaded the White House in Washington tonight to celebrate Jackson's victory.

3000 KILLED IN BHOPAL PESTICIDE SPILL

1984 More than 3000 people are feared killed and hundreds of thousands injured in the world's worst-ever industrial accident following a chemical spill at a pesticide factory in India. A storage tank at the Union Carbide plant in Bhopal, central India, began leaking just after midnight. In three hours the tank leaked more than 30 tons of the chemical gas methyl isocyanate (MIC). Most of those killed suffocated. Many survivors have suffered severe lung damage, while others are blinded. The plant was shut down as soon as the spill was discovered and the city declared a disaster area. Union Carbide has pledged to compensate victims as if the accident had happened in the US.

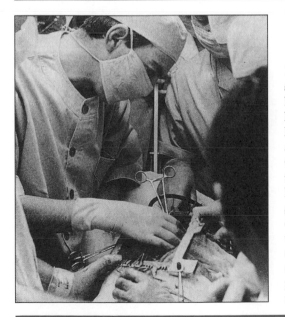

SURGEONS GIVE MAN NEW HEART

1967 A South African heart surgeon, Dr Christiaan Barnard, has successfully performed a human heart transplant operation. Leading a large team of surgeons at Groote Schuur Hospital in Cape Town, Barnard replaced the mortally diseased heart of Louis Washkansky, a 53-year-old grocer, with the healthy heart of a 25-year-old motor accident victim, Denise Darvall. Barnard said the main problem was not the operation itself but persuading the patient's immune system not to reject the new heart.

1894 Death of Scottish novelist Robert Louis Stevenson, author of *Treasure Island*.

1905 British troops put down a riot in Georgetown, British Guiana.

1910 France occupies the Moroccan port of Agadir.

1925 In New York, police smash the biggest bootlegging ring since Prohibition began and arrest 20 people.

1926 British novelist Agatha Christie disappears from her home in Surrey.

1989 In India, 800 people are arrested during a demonstration to commemorate the fifth anniversary of the Bhopal chemical disaster.

1990 Argentinian president Carlos Menem foils an attempted coup.

BIRTHDAYS

Joseph Conrad 1857, Polish-born English author whose books include *Heart of Darkness*.

Walt Disney 1901, American film producer and film animator.

Jean-Luc Godard 1930, French film director, one of the pioneers of the *nouvelle vague* of French cinema.

• 1919 – DEATH OF AUGUSTE RENOIR • 1989 – THE END OF THE COLD WAR

1154 Nicholas Breakspeare becomes the first English Pope.

1732 Death of John Gay, English poet and dramatist.

1791 In Britain, the *Observer Sunday* newspaper is first published.

1912 Turkey reaches an armistice with all Balkan allies except Greece.

1915 Georgia officially recognizes the Ku Klux Klan.

1937 In Britain, *The Dandy* comic is published for the first time.

1992 28,000 US troops land in Somalia to aid the relief effort as hundreds of thousands face starvation due to civil unrest.

2009 The UK's Ministry of Defence closes its special unit for monitoring UFO sightings after 50 years.

BIRTHDAYS

Samuel Butler 1835, English satirical novelist best known for *Erewhon*.

General Francisco Franco 1892, Spanish dictator from 1939 until his death in 1975.

Jeff Bridges 1949, American actor who won the Best Actor Oscar in 2010 for his performance in *Crazy Heart*.

Mystery of the *Marie Celeste*

1872 The American brigantine *Marie Celeste* has been found adrift in the Atlantic, her captain and crew mysteriously missing. The British brigantine *Dei Gratia* came upon the ship and boarded her when she failed to respond to their signals. The ship was deserted and the lifeboat was missing. The rigging was slightly damaged, but the cargo of 1700 barrels of alcohol was untouched. The *Marie Celeste* sailed from New York on November 7 bound for Genoa, commanded by Captain Benjamin S. Briggs and carrying a crew of eight and the captain's wife and daughter. They left no message aboard and there is no indication of what can have happened to them.

KRENZ OUSTED AS COMMUNIST RULE CRUMBLES

1989 East Germany's head of state, Egon Krenz, was forced to resign today only six weeks after he replaced a beleaguered Erich Hoenecker. With communist rule crumbling about him, Krenz had agreed to free elections and opened the Berlin Wall. New revelations, however, have linked him to large-scale corruption. Liberal Democrat leader Manfred Gerlach is acting head of state for the time being.

KING'S CARDINAL DIES

1642 Armand du Plessis, Cardinal Richelieu, who has ruled France for his king for 18 years, died today, aged 57. Louis saw Richelieu for what he was: a brilliant man, totally dedicated to France. In 1624, he made him chief of the royal council and gave him total authority. Richelieu has ruled ever since, with an iron hand and unerring skill. As a result, Louis has survived the Thirty Years' War, and France is at the forefront of European power – to the cost of her enemy, Spain. With Richelieu dead, King Louis has lost his right arm.

• 1947 – *A STREETCAR NAMED DESIRE* PREMIERES • 1974 – DEATH OF BENJAMIN BRITTEN

US CELEBRATES END OF PROHIBITION

1933 The US is celebrating the end of 14 long years of Prohibition. Utah became the last state to ratify the 21st Amendment, which effectively nullifies the 18th Amendment of 1919 prohibiting the "manufacture, sale, or transportation of intoxicating liquors". The 18th Amendment was the result of long campaigning by the Temperance Movement and the Women's Christian Temperance Union – boosted unexpectedly by the World War One grain shortage. The "Noble Experiment" just did not work. Americans did not stop drinking – the law simply pushed the lucrative liquor trade into the hands of criminals. Enforcement proved impossible. Anti-Prohibition "wets" have now won their campaign for freedom of choice.

1792 George Washington is re-elected US president.

1870 Death of Alexandre Dumas, père, author of *The Three Musketeers*.

1904 The Japanese destroy the Russian fleet at Port Arthur.

1906 Russian admiral Niebogatov goes on trial accused of surrendering ships to the Japanese.

1912 Italy, Germany and Austria renew the Triple Alliance.

1977 President Sadat of Egypt severs links with Syria, Libya, Algeria and South Yemen.

1978 The USSR signs a 20-year treaty of friendship with Afghanistan.

CONTROVERSIAL EXPULSION

1906 Episcopalian rector the Rev. Algernon S. Crapsey of Rochester, New York, was today convicted of heresy. The church had charged that Crapsey, influenced by the writings of Karl Marx had questioned the divinity of Christ. The case has created widespread controversy on both sides of the Atlantic.

BIRTHDAYS

George Armstrong Custer 1839, American cavalry commander.

Otto Preminger 1906, Austrian film director.

Little Richard 1935, American pioneer of rock 'n' roll.

Jose Carreras 1946, Spanish operatic tenor.

Ronnie O'Sullivan 1975, gifted English snooker champion.

DEATH OF MAN WHO DREW THE WORLD

1594 The great Flemish cartographer Gerardus Mercator has died, aged 82. He was at the centre of the great advances in mapmaking technique made this century. His method of depicting the world's curved surface on flat paper using straight lines of longitude and latitude soon became standard practice. Mercator designed a map of the world in 1538, and three years later a globe based on maps and descriptions by Ptolemy, Marco Polo and the Spanish and Portuguese navigators. In 1569 he published a series of world maps for use by navigators.

• 1791 – DEATH OF WOLFGANG AMADEUS MOZART • 1956 – FIRST BRITISH FEMALE JUDGE

1774 Austria becomes the first nation to establish a state education system.

1889 Death of Jefferson Davies, former president of the Confederate States of America.

1905 Norwegian explorer Roald Amundsen lands at Fort Egbert, Alaska, after a 2½ year voyage along America's Arctic coast.

1911 Mongolia is declared a Russian protectorate.

1914 The Germans capture the Polish city of Lodz.

1988 American rock 'n' roll singer and songwriter Roy Orbison dies.

1989 In Colombia, more than 40 are killed by a bomb at the headquarters of the security police.

1990 Saddam Hussein announces that all 3400 foreign hostages held in Iraq since the invasion of Kuwait are free to leave.

BIRTHDAYS

Ira Gershwin 1896, American lyricist who, with his brother George, wrote such hits as "Lady be Good" and "I Got Rhythm".

Dave Brubeck 1920, American jazz pianist and composer who had a big hit with "Take Five".

MURDER AT ALTAMONT

1969 An 18-year-old black youth was murdered in front of the stage while the Rolling Stones performed at a free concert at Altamont Speedway in California today. Meredith Hunter was stabbed to death by Hell's Angels bikers when he pulled out a gun during a confused scuffle at the stagefront. The whole incident was recorded by the crew filming the concert. Shocked and frightened, the Rolling Stones rushed through the rest of their numbers before escaping in a helicopter. This was the final performance of their US tour.

CROMWELL PURGES PARLIAMENT

1648 Oliver Cromwell's troops surrounded Parliament at Westminster today and refused to admit 200 Presbyterian MPs, purging the majority that opposes Cromwell's Independents. The remaining 50 MPs, all Independents, voted hearty thanks to Cromwell and moved on to discuss the fate of King Charles, who Cromwell is holding captive on the Isle of Wight.

IRELAND SPLIT AS FREE STATE IS BORN

1921 Ireland's 26 southern states gained independence from Britain today. Six of the eight Protestant-majority counties in the north will remain part of the UK. The agreement was signed in Downing Street this morning following negotiations between Prime Minister David Lloyd George's team and the rebel Irish nationalist leaders. Both sides would prefer a single Irish parliament in Dublin, but Ulster's Protestant leaders refuse to bow to the Catholic South.

• 1926 – DEATH OF CLAUDE MONET • 1991 – FRANCE WINS THE DAVIS CUP

JAPAN ATTACKS PEARL HARBOR

1941 A Japanese task force has launched a massive surprise attack on the US base at Pearl Harbor in Hawaii. Five US battleships and 14 other ships have been wrecked or sunk, 200 aircraft destroyed and 2,400 men killed. Intelligence reports had warned of Japanese fleet movements in the Hawaii area, but the US base was wholly unprepared.

America is outraged at the news, announced by the White House within hours. Japan and the US are not even at war – the attack comes during negotiations between the two governments. Yesterday President Franklin D. Roosevelt made a personal appeal to Japan's Emperor Hirohito to avoid war. In spite of strong isolationist opposition, the US now has no choice but to declare war on Japan, and thus on her allies, Nazi Germany and Fascist Italy.

1817 Death of Rear-Admiral William Bligh, captain of the *Bounty* when its crew mutinied.

1917 In Washington, President Woodrow Wilson declares war on Austria.

1982 Charles Brooks Jr., a Death Row prisoner at Fort Worth Prison in Texas, becomes the first American to die by lethal injection.

1988 President Gorbachev announces that Soviet military strength is to be cut by ten per cent.

1989 A revolt in the Philippines ends as 400 rebel troops abandon their siege of Manila's business centre.

1989 A gunman shoots 14 women in Montreal.

1995 A link is revealed between the cattle disease BSE and CJD, a brain disease in humans.

PITT IS PRIME MINISTER AT 24

1783 William Pitt has been made British prime minister and chancellor of the exchequer, at the age of only 24. He replaces the Duke of Portland, dismissed after just eight months when King George III persuaded the House of Lords to reject his Indian government bill. Pitt is already acknowledged to be one of the ablest statesman of the day, but he has a formidable task before him. In parliament he faces a large and hostile majority led by experienced tacticians, and he has no able speakers on his side.

Praise the Lord and pass the ammunition.

Howell Forgy, US naval lieutenant, when Japan attacked Pearl Harbor, 1941.

BIRTHDAYS

Gian Lorenzo Bernini 1598, Italian sculptor and architect.

Pietro Mascagni 1863, Italian composer best-known for the one-act opera *Cavalleria Rusticana.*

Eli Wallach 1915, American actor specializing in tough-guy roles.

SERBS BOMBARD BESIEGED DUBROVNIK

1991 Following a 67-day siege, Yugoslavian forces have wrecked Dubrovnik's historic Old Town in a savage two-day bombardment. Many people have been left dead or homeless. Some 50,000 civilian refugees were sheltering in the Old Town because the army had so far avoided shelling the historic area. The Croats held free elections last year in a bid for an independent Croatia, which is rejected by Yugoslavia's Serbian majority. The resulting war has been rife with atrocities, mostly against Croatian civilians by federal troops and Serbian irregulars.

• 43 BC – CICERO EXECUTED • 1988 – ARMENIAN EARTHQUAKE KILLS 100,000 PEOPLE

1847 An international convention of the Communist League adopts the principles of Karl Marx.

1864 Isambard Kingdom Brunel's Clifton Suspension Bridge at Bristol is opened.

1911 Richard Strauss's opera *Salome* receives its British premiere in London.

1941 Britain, Australia and the US declare war on Japan.

1949 Chiang Kai-shek's Nationalist government flees from China to Taiwan.

1988 New Pakistani prime minister Benazir Bhutto releases 1000 political prisoners.

BIRTHDAYS

Mary, Queen of Scots 1542, Scottish queen forced to abdicate in favour of her son.

James Thurber 1894, American humorist, writer and cartoonist whose satires on intellectual fashions appeared in the *New Yorker* over many years.

Sammy Davis Jr. 1925, American actor, dancer, singer and comedian.

Jim Morrison 1943, American singer with cult rock group The Doors.

JOHN LENNON SHOT DEAD

1980 Forty-year-old ex-Beatle John Lennon was murdered in New York tonight. Lennon and his wife Yoko Ono were walking into their apartment building when a man approached and shot Lennon five times. Police said the killer, Mark Chapman, 25, had shadowed Lennon since arriving from Hawaii three days ago. Earlier today he asked Lennon for his autograph, and Lennon obliged. Chapman offered no explanation for the shooting.

IVORY BAN FLOUTED

1991 Wildlife investigators have uncovered an illegal scheme to sell 15,000 elephant tusks worth £6 million ($11 million) to ivory dealers in defiance of the international trade ban on ivory. The 83 tons of poached tusks, the world's largest ivory stockpile, have been bought from the government of Burundi by two South African businessmen. They plan to fly the ivory out of Burundi and sell it in secret in the Far East. Four-fifths of Africa's elephants have been slaughtered for their tusks in the past 10 years.

SUPERPOWERS AGREE TO DESTROY MISSILES

1987 The US and the USSR have agreed to dismantle all 2611 medium- and short-range nuclear missiles based in Europe – the first agreement to cut the nuclear arsenals. President Ronald Reagan and General Secretary Mikhail Gorbachev signed the Intermediate-Range Nuclear Forces (INF) treaty in Washington today at the end of what was clearly a cordial summit meeting. The treaty provides for full on-site verification. It must be ratified by the US Senate before it becomes effective.

• **1863 – WORLD'S FIRST HEAVYWEIGHT BOXING CHAMPIONSHIP**

WALESA IS POLAND'S PRESIDENT

1990 The Solidarity trade union founder and leader Lech Walesa was elected president of Poland today in the country's first ever direct presidential elections. Ten years ago Walesa led Solidarity in a workers' confrontation with the communist regime. Initial concessions were followed by a severe crackdown, and Walesa was jailed for nine months. In 1983 he was awarded the Nobel Peace Prize. Again in 1988, Walesa led a wave of strikes which forced the regime to negotiate. Elections followed in June 1989, and Solidarity candidates won easily. August Mazowiecki became PM. Early this year the Communist Party was finally dissolved, and in May Solidarity candidates won majorities in the first local council elections. Walesa has played a major role throughout. But as president he will not have it all his own way: with the communists gone, divisions are appearing in the Solidarity movement as a democratic opposition begins to emerge.

MAPPING VENUS

1978 A better picture of the planet Venus emerged today after two US Pioneer spacecraft launched earlier this year reached it. Pioneer *Venus 1* went into orbit round the planet four days ago, probing the atmosphere and the surface with radar. Pioneer *Venus 2* had meanwhile launched four probes which descended into Venus's atmosphere today. One of the probes survived the landing and transmitted data from the surface for an hour. The orbiter has mapped mountains higher than Everest, and the solar system's biggest canyon.

We know what happens to people who stay in the middle of the road. They get run over.

Aneurin Bevan,
British Labour politician,
1953.

1783 London's Newgate Prison sees its first executions.

1910 The Turks suppress an Arab uprising in Palestine.

1917 The British capture Jerusalem from the Turks.

1955 Sugar Ray Robinson regains the world middleweight boxing title by knocking out Carl Olson.

1967 Nicholae Ceausescu becomes president of Romania.

2008 Scientists confirm the existence of a black hole at the centre of the Milky Way galaxy.

MILLIONS MISSING FROM MAXWELL PENSIONS

1991 At least £420 million ($773 million) is missing from pension funds controlled by billionaire Robert Maxwell. Maxwell died at sea a month ago, apparently after falling naked from the deck of his luxury yacht in the middle of the night. Sensational revelations have followed as the Maxwell empire collapsed amid massive debts and evidence of shady deals to prop up share prices. Maxwell's younger son Kevin is tonight fighting a court order stopping him and his brother Ian leaving Britain. This follows evidence that money continued to flood out of the Mirror Newspaper Group pension fund even after Maxwell's death. The court order also freezes Kevin Maxwell's assets worldwide.

• **1641 – DEATH OF SIR ANTHONY VAN DYCK • 1992 – CHARLES AND DIANA TO SEPARATE**

1910 Puccini's opera *La Fanciulla del West* is premiered in New York.

1978 Millions of Iranians demonstrate, demanding the abdication of the Shah and an end to the month-old military government.

1984 In Oslo, Desmond Tutu, Anglican Bishop of Johannesburg, is kept waiting 20 minutes for his Nobel Peace Prize owing to a bomb threat.

1990 The Serbian republic in Yugoslavia the Communist Party wins a free election.

1990 Australia's oldest newspaper empire, the Fairfax Group, goes into receivership with debts of A$1500 million (£660/$1222 million).

BIRTHDAYS

César Franck 1822, Belgian composer who developed a "cyclic form".

Emily Dickinson 1830, American poet who wrote over 1700 poems.

Olivier Messiaen 1908, French composer whose works include the symphony *La Turangalîla*.

Kenneth Branagh 1960, English actor and film director.

PEACE PRIZE FOR MOTHER TERESA

1979 Calcutta's Mother Teresa has been awarded this year's Nobel Peace Prize for her ceaseless work helping the destitute. Born in Albania in 1910, she joined a convent at 18 and taught in her order's school in Calcutta. In 1946 she heard "a call within a call" to help the desperately poor people around her, and was given permission to leave the convent. She found people dying in the streets and took them into a home to die in dignity, rescued orphans and cared for them. Other women joined her, and in 1950 she formed the Missionaries of Charity, dedicated to the destitute. Today they run 700 shelters and clinics. Calcutta is the world's most crowded place, with millions living in grinding poverty. The "living saint" and her sisters in Christ are often their only hope of survival.

FIRST NOBEL PRIZES AWARDED

1901 The man who invented the most powerful explosives the world has ever seen hoped that they would put an end to war. "On the day two army corps can annihilate each other in one second all civilized nations will recoil from war in horror," the Swedish chemist Alfred Nobel wrote to the Peace Congress in 1892. It was dynamite that Nobel had invented, and he made a fortune from the explosives factories he established. When he died in 1896, he left most of that fortune to a foundation to award annual prizes

"to those who, in the preceding year, shall have conferred the greatest benefit upon mankind". The first Nobel Prizes, worth $30,000 (£16,300) each, were awarded in Oslo and Stockholm today, the fifth anniversary of Alfred Nobel's death, for literature, chemistry, physics, medicine and for peace. The first-ever Peace Prize was shared by Jean Henri Dunant, founder of the Red Cross, and Frédéric Passy, founder of the French Society of the Friends of Peace.

We must use time as a tool, not as a couch.
John F. Kennedy, 1961.

• 1869 – WYOMING GIVES WOMEN THE VOTE • 1902 – ASWAN DAM COMPLETED

KING RENOUNCES THRONE FOR LOVE

1936 Britain's King Edward VIII has abdicated, less than one year after his accession to the throne. The king ended months of rumour and controversy tonight in a radio broadcast that he made to the nation from Windsor Castle. "I have found it impossible to carry the heavy burden of responsibility and to discharge my duties as king as I would wish to do without the help and support of the woman I love," he said. After the broadcast he boarded a Royal Navy destroyer in Portsmouth, taking him to exile in France to join the twice-divorced Mrs Wallis Simpson. Edward's younger brother has now become King George VI. Edward and Mrs Simpson first met in 1931 but their love affair did not begin until 1934, since when they have been inseparable. Edward's resolve to marry her could not be shaken even by the combined forces of the royal family, the British cabinet and the church. Prime Minister Stanley Baldwin finally told the king to choose between his throne and Mrs Simpson. The king chose Mrs Simpson.

MARTIAL LAW IN IRELAND

1920 Britain today declared martial law in large parts of Ireland in a bid to contain the Irish Republican Army's rebellion. Britain has over 40,000 soldiers in Ireland, and 7000 of the hated Black and Tans (ex-soldiers serving as police), whose brutality has been much criticized in England. Their "retaliations"

in search of IRA gunmen has left whole villages ablaze. The IRA's hit-and-run tactics have tied the British forces in knots. The British brought in mainland experts to improve army intelligence, and two Sundays ago, in a series of dawn raids, the IRA killed 14 of the experts in their beds. By nightfall 14 Irishmen were dead at the hands of the Black and Tans. Tonight, towns are ablaze in the wake of a massive army clampdown.

1688 King James II of England flees the country.

1894 The first motor show opens in Paris.

1909 A 2147 mile (3455 km) section of the Cape-to-Cairo railway is linked up at the Sudan-Congo border.

1963 In Los Angeles, Frank Sinatra Jr. is set free after his father pays kidnappers $240,000 (£129,729).

1990 The British government announces it will award £42 million ($77.7 million) to British haemophiliacs who became infected with the HIV virus after being treated with contaminated inhibitor Factor VIII.

BIRTHDAYS

Alexander Solzhenitsyn 1928, Russian writer best-known for *The Gulag Archipelago*.

Jean-Louis Trintignant 1930, French actor whose films include *A Man and a Woman* and *My Night with Maud*.

Rita Moreno 1931, Puerto Rican actress whose career encompassed an Oscar-winning performance in *West Side Story*.

• 1769 – VENETIAN BLINDS PATENTED • 1914 – BATTLE OF THE FALKLANDS

1900 In London, the War Office announces that more than 11,000 British troops have so far lost their lives in the Boer War.

1906 In South Africa, the Transvaal is given autonomy with white male suffrage.

1907 Dinizulu, King of the Zulus, surrenders to the commandant of the Natal forces, Colonel Sir Duncan Mackenzie.

1911 George V is crowned Emperor of India and founds New Delhi as the capital to replace Calcutta.

1990 US president George Bush agrees to send a $1000 million (£540 million) food aid package to the USSR.

BIRTHDAYS

Gustave Flaubert 1821, French novelist whose first book was *Madame Bovary*.

Edvard Munch 1863, Norwegian artist.

Edward G. Robinson 1893, American actor who was a heavy in films such as *Key Largo*.

Frank Sinatra 1915, American popular singer par excellence.

Emmerson Fittipaldi 1946, Brazilian motor-racing champion.

PLANE OR A BOAT?

1955 British electronic engineer Christopher Cockerell today patented a new kind of vehicle, half-ship and half-aircraft. His "hovercraft" floats on a cushion of air produced by fans, and is pushed forward by air propellers. Attempting to gain funding from the military, Cockerell has stumbled over whether the vehicle is best used as a plane or a boat.

VOYAGER CIRCLES EARTH WITHOUT REFUELLING

1986 The super-light experimental aircraft *Voyager* touched down today to complete its extraordinary nonstop flight round the world without refuelling. It took nine days, and pilots Richard Rutan and Jeana Yeager broke the endurance record as well as the distance record. *Voyager*'s hollow plastic body holds four tons of fuel. She has a truly original design, with two engines, propellers fore and aft, very long wings and huge double fins, on a strange three-pod body quite unlike that of former spacecraft. Modern superstrong, ultralight materials have opened up new vistas in flying, including a host of do-it-yourself options with advanced designs developed with computer models on PCs.

RUSSIA VOTES TO SCRAP USSR

1991 The Russian parliament today voted overwhelmingly in favour of replacing the Soviet Union with a loose Commonwealth of Independent States. Russia immediately withdrew its MPs from the Kremlin in a boycott supported by Ukrainian and Byelorussian MPs. This left the Soviet parliament without a quorum, and it adjourned. Soviet general secretary Mikhail Gorbachev is left with his job, but no apparent function. Russia, the Ukraine and Byelorussia reached agreement on the Commonwealth plan last week, and Russian president Boris Yeltsin, architect of the plan, is due to meet the five Muslim Central Asian leaders this weekend. There are already rifts in the new Commonwealth before it has been born, with new demands from the Byelorussian opposition, and radical Ukrainian amendments to the text of the agreement. However, the Soviet Union has no option left but a transfer of power.

• **1901 – MARCONI SENDS RADIO SIGNAL ACROSS THE ATLANTIC OCEAN**

IRISH BOMB KILLS 12 IN LONDON

1867 Irish bombers blew up the outer wall of Clerkenwell prison in London today in a bid to rescue a jailed comrade. The blast demolished the wall, as well as several nearby houses, killing 12 people and injuring more than 100. But the bombers failed to rescue the jailed Irishman. No arrests have yet been made. Police said the bombers are members of the Fenians, or Irish Republican Brotherhood, founded 10 years ago with the help of Irish Americans to overthrow British rule in Ireland. The Fenians are in open rebellion in Ireland and have mounted a number of attacks upon British property.

If a man had time to study one word only, "wit" would perhaps be the best word he could choose.

C. S. Lewis, 1960.

1784 Death of Samuel Johnson, English poet, critic and lexicographer.

1904 The first electric train comes into service on London's Metropolitan Railway.

1909 British explorer Ernest Shackleton is knighted.

1967 King Constantine of Greece flees his country after an unsuccessful attempt to topple the Greek military junta.

1988 In Brazzaville, South Africa signs an accord granting independence to Namibia.

1989 In South Africa, Nelson Mandela meets President F. W. de Klerk for the first time.

1989 The first Vietnam refugees are repatriated from Hong Kong.

"WE GOT HIM"

2003 Ousted Iraqi President Saddam Hussein is in custody following capture by US forces. "Ladies and gentlemen, we got him," US administrator Paul Bremer told journalists today. Saddam Hussein was found in a cellar at a farmhouse about 15 km (10 miles) south of his hometown Tikrit. British Prime Minister Tony Blair has welcomed the news, saying it "removes the shadow" hanging over Iraq. Saddam was the most wanted man by US authorities but had not been seen since Baghdad fell to US forces in April.

Heinrich Heine 1797, German poet and writer.

Sir Laurens van der Post 1906, South African novelist, travel writer and conservationist.

Christopher Plummer 1929, British stage and screen actor whose films include *The Sound of Music*.

GRANDMA MOSES DIES AT 101

1961 Grandma Moses, the American primitive painter, has died at the age of 101. Self-taught, Anna Robertson Moses only began painting in her 70s. Her bright pictures of American rural life were discovered by a New York art dealer, who exhibited them in his gallery in 1940. The following year one of her paintings, *The Old Oaken Bucket*, won her the New York State Prize, and in 1949 President Truman presented her with the Women's National Press Club award for her achievements in art.

• 1294 – POPE CELESTINE V ABDICATES • 1907 – THE LINER *MAURETANIA* RUNS AGROUND

1837 British troops crush rebellion in Canada.

1861 Prince Albert, consort of Queen Victoria, dies of typhoid.

1927 In China, Chiang Kai-shek's Nationalist forces put down an attempted communist coup.

1962 US *Mariner II* sends the first close-up photos of the planet Venus.

1973 Teenager John Paul Getty II is set free by his Italian kidnappers after his oil tycoon grandfather pays a ransom of $750,000 (£405,400).

1988 PLO leader Yasser Arafat announces that he accepts Israel's right to exist within secure borders.

1988 Eight million workers in Spain go on strike against government economic policies.

1990 ANC president Oliver Tambo returns home to South Africa after 30 years of exile.

BIRTHDAYS

Nostradamus 1503, French astrologer and physician who, in *Centuries*, made a number of prophecies.

George V 1895, English monarch.

PLANCK FINDS BUNDLES OF ENERGY

1900 The German physicist Max Planck today unveiled a completely new theory of energy. Up to now science has assumed that energy flows in a continuous stream. Planck's theory says energy is not continuous, it exists in tiny, indivisible bundles, or "quanta", almost like the atoms of matter. And it doesn't flow in a stream, nor in waves. What it does do is more like climbing a flight of steps. A "bundle" can only increase its energy level by absorbing exactly enough energy to "jump" to the next step, or quantum. In between the two steps, it simply does not exist. Planck's theory upsets Isaac Newton's orderly world – but it explains anomalies in physics which no other theory can account for.

CONNECTICUT SCHOOL SHOOTING

1894 Twenty children and six adults were killed today while attending primary school in the US state of Connecticut by a lone gunman. The shootings have prompted renewed debate about gun control in the United States, coming so soon after the Aurora shootings on 20 July. The killer was revealed to be 20-year old Adam Lanza. Lanza killed himself after committing the massacre. President Obama spoke of using "whatever power this office holds" to prevent further tragedies and a petition with 100,000 names signed a petition for renewed debate within days of the shooting. Whether this is a watershed moment for the debate remains to be seen, but that will be scant consolation for the grieving parents of Sandyhook, Connecticut.

POLAR VICTORY

1911 Norwegian explorer Roald Amundsen was today the first man to reach the South Pole, way ahead of the British team led by Captain Robert Scott. Amundsen's five-man team used dog sleds, crossing the 2000 miles (3200 km) of ice without difficulty, while Scott's motorized team has floundered. Amundsen planted a Norwegian flag and left a sympathetic note for Scott before starting back.

• 1799 – GEORGE WASHINGTON DIES • 1906 – 1ST GERMAN SUBMARINE ENTERS SERVICE

700,000 DEAD AT VERDUN

1916 The nine-month Battle of Verdun is finally over, at appalling cost and with little gain. The lines are more or less where they were in February – and more than 700,000 soldiers are dead. Meanwhile the Somme offensive has ended in a deadlock, again with little gained. It has cost the British 420,000 men, the French 195,000 and the Germans 600,000.

SIOUX CHIEF KILLED

1890 Chief Sitting Bull of the Sioux Indians is dead. He fled to Canada after his victory over General Custer at Little Bighorn in 1876 and was jailed for two years on his return in 1881. His people's suffering drove him to join the new Ghost Dance cult, dedicated to destroying the whites and restoring the Indians' vanished world. The government sent troops to arrest the Sioux leaders and suppress the cult, and Sitting Bull was shot in the skirmish that followed. He was 69.

1904 British statesman Joseph Chamberlain calls for curbs on immigrants from Europe.

1913 The world's biggest battle-cruiser, HMS *Tiger*, is launched in Glasgow.

1918 Portuguese president Sidonio Paes is assassinated.

1943 Death of Fats Waller, jazz pianist and composer.

1989 In Colombia, police kill Gonzalo Gacha, one of the leaders of the Medellin cocaine cartel.

1989 In Bulgaria, 50,000 demonstrators demand the end of communist rule.

1991 A ferry sinks in the Red Sea, drowning 476 people, mainly Egyptians returning from pilgrimage or work in Saudi Arabia.

BIRTHDAYS

Alexandre-Gustave Eiffel 1832, French engineer who built the Eiffel Tower in Paris.

Jean Paul Getty 1892, American oil billionaire and founder of the J. Paul Getty Art Museum in Malibu, California.

Alan Freed 1922, American disc jockey who first coined the phrase "rock 'n' roll".

US BILL OF RIGHTS RATIFIED BY STATES

1791 The Virginia state legislature today ratified the Bill of Rights and the Bill's 10 amendments became part of the United States Constitution. Unlike the Declaration of the Rights of Man and of the Citizen adopted in France in 1789, the US Bill of Rights provides specific protection for the basic rights of the individual to free expression and association, privacy and justice.

WALT DISNEY DIES

1966 Walt Disney has died at the age of 65. Disney's Mickey Mouse is possibly the most famous character in the world, fictional or living. He first appeared in 1928 in *Steamboat Willie*, the first sound cartoon film, and he was soon joined by Donald Duck and the rest of the Disney stable. In 1938 another world first, the feature-length *Snow White and the Seven Dwarfs*, was a phenomenal success. Disney also made live films such as *Treasure Island*, and beautifully photographed full-length nature films like *The Living Desert*, winning 30 Oscars for his film work.

• 1920 – AUSTRIA AND CHINA ADMITTED TO THE LEAGUE OF NATIONS

1850 The first immigrant ship, the *Charlotte Jane*, arrives in New Zealand.

1902 An earthquake in Turkestan, Central Asia, kills 4000.

1909 US marines force the resignation of President Jose Zelaya of Nicaragua.

1921 French composer, pianist and organist Camille Saint-Saëns dies aged 86.

1922 Polish president Gabriel Narutowicz is assassinated after only two days in office.

1965 British novelist and playwright William Somerset Maugham dies in Nice at the age of 91.

1991 In London, the new director-general of the security service MI5 is officially named for the first time – Stella Rimington – who becomes the first-ever female boss of the agency.

BIRTHDAYS

Jane Austen 1775, English novelist whose major works include *Emma*.

Sir Noel Coward 1889, English playwright, composer and actor.

Liv Ullman 1939, Norwegian actress who has appeared most notably in Ingmar Bergman films.

OPERATION DESERT FOX

1998 American and British forces have launched air-strikes against Iraqi military installations. The action, code-named Operation Desert Fox, comes after the Iraqi authorities suspended co-operation with UN weapons inspectors. Detractors are criticising the action as it has not been sanctioned by the UN. The air-strikes have provoked a storm of reaction in the Arabic-language and Middle East press, ranging from outright condemnation of the US and UK in many regional dailies to the analytical approach of the London-based Arabic press.

SOUTH AFRICA UNVEILS NATIONAL SHRINE

1949 The Voortrekker Monument commemorating South Africa's Boer pioneers has been unveiled in Pretoria. Today is a religious holiday in South Africa. On December 9, 1838, Boer commander Andries Pretorius and his 460 men vowed to observe an annual day of thanksgiving if God granted them victory over the Zulus. Seven days later they defeated 10,000 Zulu warriors in battle, with only two Boers injured. Pretorius thanked God, and kept his promise. In 1864 the Boer Transvaal Republic proclaimed December 16 a religious holiday. In 1877 Britain annexed the Transvaal, and on December 9, 1880, the anniversary of the vow, 9000 armed Boers vowed to fight for their freedom – and won it when 75 Boers routed 700 British soldiers at Majuba. Again, they thanked God. The foundation stone of the Voortrekker Monument was laid on December 16, 1938. Last year the right-wing Afrikaner National Party won the South African elections, and today the Boers thanked God for it.

TEA PARTY IN BOSTON

1773 A band of colonists thinly disguised as Indians boarded three ships in Boston harbour tonight and emptied 342 chests of tea worth £9000 ($16,500) into the sea. This latest protest against the Tea Tax is a deliberate challenge to Crown authority. In 1765 Britain's Stamp Act imposed new taxes on the colonies to help pay for the costs of the Seven Years' War. The taxes met with protests, boycotts and violent rejection, and the Act was repealed – to be replaced by the Townshend Acts' new taxes on tea, lead, glass, paper and paint. Protests swelled to a rejection of all forms of taxation, and colonists started to form defence associations. In 1770 the Townshend Acts were repealed, except for the Tea Tax, which was renewed this year to rescue the East India Company from bankruptcy.

• 1653 – CROMWELL MADE LORD PROTECTOR • 1944 – GLEN MILLER LOST AT SEA

AUSTRALIAN PM DISAPPEARS WHILE SWIMMING

1967 The Australian prime minister Harold Holt has disappeared and is presumed to have drowned near his holiday home at Portsea, Victoria, some 30 miles (48 km) from Melbourne. Although Holt, 59, is a strong swimmer and diver, it is understood that he almost drowned under similar circumstances just a few weeks ago. Military and civilian divers and search teams are hunting for him and the search will continue for some time. In the meantime, an interim prime minister will to be appointed. Holt was Minister of Labour from 1940 to 1941, then again from 1949 to 1958 and Federal Treasurer from 1958 to 1966 when he succeeded Sir Robert Gordon Menzies as prime minister.

1909 Death of King Leopold II of Belgium.

1987 In Britain, Davina Durbin becomes the world's first heart, lungs and liver transplant patient.

1989 In Romania, as many as 2000 anti-government protesters are massacred in the city of Timisoara.

1990 Radical priest Jean-Bertrand Aristide is elected president of Haiti.

1991 Joseph Robert Smallwood, Canadian politician, dies.

BRAZIL CHOOSES NEW PRESIDENT IN FREE ELECTIONS

1989 In the first free elections for 29 years, Brazilians have chosen Ferdinand Collor de Mello as president. He faces enormous problems, not least of which is the servicing of massive foreign debt. Interest payments on loans use up 40 per cent of the country's export income. The International Monetary Fund has forced the government to impose austerity measures to try to guarantee that the loans are repaid. Consequently prices have risen, wages have been cut and the annual inflation rate is around 700 per cent. It was the 80s economic decline that increased demands for democracy.

The airplane stays up because it doesn't have the time to fall.

Orville Wright explains, after making the world's first powered flight, 1903.

BIRTHDAYS

Sir Humphrey Davy 1778, English chemist who invented the safety lamp.

William Lyon Mackenzie King 1874, Canadian politician, Liberal prime minister three times.

Erskine Caldwell 1903, American novelist and journalist best-known for *Tobacco Road*.

Willard Frank Libby 1908, American chemist who developed radio-carbon dating.

Paula Radcliffe 1973, English long-distance runner, who broke her own world record at the 2003 London Marathon.

BRITAIN FACES A THREE-DAY WEEK

1973 Prime Minister Edward Heath's confrontation with striking miners as part of his campaign to control inflation has provoked a crisis for the economy. Miners have continued their overtime ban and as a result coal supplies to power stations are down by 40 per cent. As of today, industry and commerce will only be allowed five days' electricity in 14 until December 30, then will be allowed three days' worth a week in the New Year. Television will shut down at 10.30 pm throughout the country. The government is cutting £1200 million ($2208 million) from public spending in response to the crisis. The chancellor has also imposed tighter credit controls and tax on developmental gains are up from 30 per cent to 50 per cent.

• 1830 – DEATH OF SIMON BOLIVAR • 1939 – *ADMIRAL GRAF SPEE* SCUTTLED

1825 Tsar Nicholas I succeeds to the Russian throne.

1924 Pope Pius XI denounces the USSR.

1980 Death of Ben Travers, British novelist and comic dramatist.

1980 Death of Soviet statesman Alexei Kosygin, prime minister of the USSR 1964–80.

1987 In South Korea, Roh Tae Woo is declared the winner of the first presidential election to be held for 16 years but students riot, claiming electoral corruption.

1990 French cellist Paul Tortelier dies aged 76.

BIRTHDAYS

Joseph Grimaldi 1779, English clown who created the white-face make-up.

Paul Klee 1879, Swiss painter and etcher.

Willy Brandt 1913, chancellor of West Germany 1969–74.

Steven Spielberg 1947, American film director of hugely successful films, including *Close Encounters of the Third Kind*.

Brad Pitt 1963, American actor, star of *Fight Club* and *Ocean's Eleven*.

INTERNATIONAL PROJECT TO SAVE BRAZILIAN RAINFOREST

1991 The first international project to help save rainforests was launched today when the World Bank, the European Commission and the Group of Seven leading industrialized nations granted Brazil $250 million (£136 million) for conservation work in the Amazon basin. Of that sum, at least $100 million (£54.5 million) will go to scientific research. The money will also fund the establishment of national parks, tribal reserves, and the creation of new zones for non-destructive use of the rainforest's resources such as rubber tapping and collecting brazil nuts. All such projects must be approved by the World Bank and Brazil itself will have no control over how the money is spent.

END TO SLAVERY SECURED

1865 More than two years after Lincoln's Emancipation Proclamation theoretically abolished slavery, the dream has become a reality with the 13th Amendment. The earlier proclamation in January of 1863 applied only to areas not under Union control.

I don't mind your being killed, but I object to your being taken prisoner.

Lord Kitchener, British field marshal, answers the Prince of Wales' request to go to the World War One frontline, 1914.

BRITISH RAILWAYS AND PORTS TO BE NATIONALIZED

1946 Clement Attlee's Labour government has won the vote on state ownership and it looks like railways and ports will be the first industries to be nationalized. Despite the prospect of severe economic handicaps, Attlee has committed himself to a vigorous programme of reform. The Bank of England has already been nationalized and coal mines, civil aviation, cable and wireless services, railways, road transport and steel will follow. The British National Health Act came into force in November, providing comprehensive medical care for every member of society. Attlee also has ideas of giving India and Burma their independence.

• 1737 – ANTONIO STRADIVARI DIES • 1989 – EEC SIGNS 10-YEAR PACT WITH USSR

HONG KONG'S FATE SEALED?

1984 Britain and China have signed an agreement settling the fate of Hong Kong when the 99-year lease expires in 1997. Britain is to return all of its holdings in return for assurances that Hong Kong's social and economic freedom will be preserved for at least 50 years after China takes control. Hong Kong is to become a special administrative region within China, with its own laws, currency, budget and tax system. It will retain free port status and the authority to negotiate separate trade agreements. Whether China will honour these commitments remains uncertain. The Hong Kong community feels that Britain has betrayed its responsibilities. Although the New Territories were secured by Britain on a 99-year lease in 1898, both Hong Kong Island and Kowloon Peninsula were already in Britain's possession.

KASPAROV KEEPS WORLD CHESS TITLE

1987 Gary Kasparov, the reigning world chess champion from the USSR, retained his crown today in Seville against former champion and fellow countryman Anatoly Karpov. Although the series was tied at 12 games each, Kasparov as challenger wins the title under current international rules. He first took the title from Karpov in 1985. Karpov had held the title from 1975 to 1985.

For my name and memory, I leave it to men's charitable speeches, and to foreign nations, and the next ages.

Francis Bacon, English philosopher, in his will, published on this day, 1625.

1154 Henry II accedes to the throne of England.

1848 Emily Brontë, English author, dies of tuberculosis, aged 30.

1905 The first-ever motorized ambulance service for road accident victims is set up in London.

1927 In China, 600 communists are executed by the Nationalists.

1988 Violence erupts during the presidential elections in Sri Lanka.

1991 The Australian Labour Party caucus deposes prime minister Bob Hawke after eight years in office and replaces him with his treasurer, Paul Keating.

2011 North Korean leader Kim Jong-il dies of a heart attack at the age of 69.

BIRTHDAYS

Leonid Brezhnev 1906, Soviet statesman and president of the Soviet Union 1977–1982.

Jean Genet 1910, French novelist and dramatist whose autobiographical *A Thief's Journal* recounts his life in prison.

Edith Piaf 1915, French chanteuse with a haunting and powerful voice.

• 1851 – DEATH OF J M W TURNER • 1991 – GORBACHEV RESIGNS

1828 The Cherokees cede lands in Arkansas to the US and agree to migrate west of the Mississippi.

1968 Death of American novelist John Steinbeck.

1989 Troops surrender to demonstrators in the Romanian city of Timisoara after 4000 are killed.

1990 The UN passes a vote of censure against Israel for the killing of 21 Arab rioters on Temple Mount in October 1989.

1990 Soviet foreign minister Eduard Shevardnadze, one of Gorbachev's allies, resigns.

1991 President Boris Yeltsin announces that Russia wants to join Nato.

1991 It is announced that American and Egyptian archaeologists have discovered 500-year-old ships buried 8 miles (13 km) from the Nile.

BIRTHDAYS

Sir Robert Menzies 1894, Australian statesman, prime minister as leader of the United Australia Party and then the Liberal Party.

Errol John 1924, Trinidadian dramatist and actor who wrote *Moon on a Rainbow Shawl*.

BIGGEST LAND DEAL IN HISTORY SETTLED

1803 The United States and France have concluded the biggest land deal in history – some 831,321 square miles (2,153,121 sq km) called The Louisiana Purchase have been bought from France for a mere $15 million (£8.2 million). Uncertainty regarding the whole region began three years ago, when New Orleans, Louisiana, was transferred from Spain to France. Alarmed at the prospect of an ambitious Napoleon, the Americans began negotiations to buy New Orleans with very little success. US president Thomas Jefferson was prepared to ally himself to his old enemy Britain in order to get the French out of the New World, but France's capitulation marks the end of Napoleon's plans for an empire and makes the US one of the largest countries.

ALLIES RETREAT FROM THE DARDANELLES

1915 The Allies are retreating from the Dardanelles after the Gallipoli campaign under Sir Ian Hamilton attempted and failed to force the narrows and link up with Russia, costing the lives of 25,000 men. In the April 25 landing at Gallipoli many thousands of Australian and New Zealand troops were lost. The Turkish strait connects the Sea of Marmara with the Aegean Sea, and its shores are formed by the Gallipoli peninsula to the northwest and the Turkish mainland in Asia to the southeast. The Turks, with German backing, have been able to seal off the Russians in their Dardanelle ports and it looks as if this situation will remain.

A bill of rights is what the people are entitled to against every government on earth, general or particular, and what no just government should refuse to rest on inference.

Thomas Jefferson, US statesman, in a letter, 1787.

AMERICA'S FIRST MILL

1790 American industrialist Samuel Slater opened a cotton mill in his native country today, the first of its kind. The mill has 250 spindles which are powered by water and will be operated by a child labour force. Slater was previously apprenticed to a partner of British water frame inventor Richard Arkwright, during which time he learnt his trade.

MOSLEY'S CURE FOR DEPRESSION

1930 The former British Labour government minister, Oswald Mosley, has published a set of policy proposals that provide an answer to the country's present economic ills. He is advocating a firmer governmental hand on the economic tiller, to plan foreign trade, direct industry and use public finances to promote expansion. These proposals have already been rejected by Ramsay MacDonald and his Cabinet – whose response to the Depression has been to blame the capitalist system.

1375 Death of Giovanni Boccaccio, Italian writer and poet who wrote the *Decameron*.

1935 Walt Disney's *Snow White and the Seven Dwarfs* premieres.

1940 Death of F. Scott Fitzgerald, US author.

1964 Britain bans the death penalty.

1988 Soviet cosmonauts Musa Manarov and Vladimir Titov return to Earth after a record 365 days in space.

1989 American troops invade Panama and oust dictator Manuel Noriega.

2007 Queen Elizabeth II becomes the oldest reigning monarch in British history.

PAN AMERICAN FLIGHT CRASHES AT LOCKERBIE

1988 A Pan American jumbo jet blew up and crashed in the Scottish border town of Lockerbie this evening killing all 259 passengers on board and at least 11 people on the ground. En route from London Heathrow to New York, the jumbo disappeared from radar screens at 7.19 pm as it exploded in the air. The wing of the plane came down in a residential part of Lockerbie, destroying six houses. The nose of the plane with the dead crew still inside has been found about three miles (5 km) from the town. Dozens of fires have been burning in the town and the RAF has flown medical teams to assist the emergency services. American embassies were warned that a Pan Am flight would be targetted. No group has claimed responsibility for what was probably a bomb – Arab extremists are suspected.

BIRTHDAYS

Anthony Powell 1905, British novelist best known for the novel sequence "The Music of Time".

Heinrich Böll 1917, German Nobel Prize-winning novelist.

Jane Fonda 1937, American actress whose many fine films include *On Golden Pond*.

Frank Zappa 1940, American rock musician and singer.

• **1846 – ANAESTHETIC USED FOR THE FIRST TIME IN A BRITISH HOSPITAL**

INDEX

INDEX

INDEX

ACKNOWLEDGEMENTS

Aquarius Aug 15
Allsport Ltd Jul 30b (Pressens Bild); Aug 29b
American Heritage Publishing Co Mar 27b
Associated Press Jan 28t/Jan opener; Feb 1; Feb 2t; Feb 15; Mar 8b; Mar 25t; Mar 28b; Mar 31; Apr 20b; Apr 22b; May 18; May 25b; May 27; May 30t (Jeff Widener); Jun 7 (Mark Humphrey); Jun 12; Jun 17; Sep 12; Sep 21b/Sep opener; Sep 28t; Oct 14t; Nov 18b; Nov 23b; Dec 1b; Dec 8b; Dec 17
BBC Jul 24b
Boy Scouts of America Feb 8b
Bridgeman Art Library Feb 18/Feb opener; Apr 8t/Apr opener; May 16b/May opener; May 17t; Aug 13/Aug opener; Aug 22b; Sep 8; Nov 18t
British Pathe News Apr 4/Apr opener; Apr 19b; Apr 26
Allan Cash Ltd Aug 8t/Aug opener
Camera Press Mar 18b/Mar opener
Colorsport Feb 13b
Corbis Jan 10b, Jan 16th, Jan 24th, Feb 10t & b, Feb 22, Mar 15, Mar 28b, Mar 29, Apr 3t/Apr opener, Apr 25, May 25t/Intro, Jun 20t/Jun opener, Jul 9t, Aug 16, Aug 26, Sep 30t, Nov 7b, Nov 26b, Dec 5t/Dec opener, Apr 11 (Bettmann/UPI); May 12t; Jul 15; Dec 8t (Bettmann/UPI)
Culver Pictures Inc, N.Y. Nov 3t
Don Morley International Sports Sep 25b
Zoe Dominie Sep 4
E.T. Archive/Documentation Photographique de la Reunion des Musees Nationaux Mar 1b
Mary Evans Picture Library Jan 6t; Jan 20t; Jan 31 (Alexander Meledin Collection); Feb 3/Feb opener; Feb 4; Feb 12; Mar 3; Mar 4; Mar 7t; Mar 13b; Mar 16; Mar 17; Mar 22b; Apr 20t/Apr opener; Apr End; Jun 5; Jun 8; Jun 10t; Jun 13t/Jun opener; Jun 17; Jun 18b; Jun 20t; Jun 21; Jun 22; Jun 23t; Jun 26t; Jul 6; Jul 7; Jul 8t; Jul 14/Jul opener; Jul 19 (Institute of Civil Engineers); Jul 23b (Sigmund Freud Copyrights/W.E. Freud); Jul 25t; Jul 26; Jul 27; Jul 28t; Aug 1t; Aug 3; Aug 5b; Aug 10; Aug 16/Aug opener; Aug 18t; Aug 19; Aug 22t; Aug 24t/Aug opener; Aug 24b; Aug 25b; Aug 30; Sep 3; Sep 20; Sep 22; Sep 29; Oct 14t; Oct 19b/Oct opener; Oct 21b; Nov 19; Nov 21b; Nov 29t; Dec 5b; Dec 10b; Dec 23; Dec 27t; Dec 29t; Dec 29b
John Frost Newspapers Oct 9t
Ronald Grant Archive Jan 24; Mar 14; Apr 9; Apr 15; May 24t; Aug 31b
Giraudon/Louvre Aug 22b
Robert Harding Picture Library Mar 29b; July 11
Getty Images Jan 1t; Jan 2; Jan 3t; Jan 3b; an 4; Jan 5b/Jan opener; Jan 7b/Jan opener (Kaku Kurita/Gamma); Jan 9t; Jan 11; Jan 13; Jan 14/Jan opener; Jan 17/intro/Jan opener; Jan 22t; Jan 23; Jan 25b; Jan 26b; Jan 27; Feb 2b; Feb 5/Feb opener; Feb 9/Feb opener; Feb 11t; Feb 14; Feb 16; Feb 17; Feb 19 (Bloomberg); Feb 21; Feb 25b; Feb 26; Feb 27; Mar 5b/Mar opener; Mar 8t; Mar 9t; Mar 12t/Mar opener; Mar 14/Mar opener; Mar 18t; Mar 20; Mar 24t; Mar 25b; Mar 30; Mar 31/Mar opener; Apr 3b/Apr opener; Apr 7b &t; Apr 8b; Apr 9 (AFP); Apr 12t; Apr 13b; Apr 14 (Philip Ojisua); Apr 16 (Washington Post); Apr 17; Apr 18t/Apr opener; Apr 19 (AFP); Apr 21; Apr 24/Apr opener; Apr 28t; Apr 29t (UPI); May 3b; May 6b/May opener; May 7b; May 9; May 10t; May 10b/May opener; May 12 (China Photos); May 13b; May19; May 21t; May 22b; May 26t; May 28; May 31; Jun 10b; Jun 14t; Jun 19t; Jun 23b; Jun 26b; Jun End; Jul 1t; Jul 2; Jul 3t; Jul 5t/Jul opener; Jul 8b; Jul 9t; Jul 12; Jul 16b; July 17/Jul opener (Bob Willoughby); Jul 20t; Jul 24; Jul 25; Jul 28b (Phil Sheldon); Jul 29/Jul opener; Jul 30t; Jul 31; Aug 2/Aug opener; Aug 4t; Aug 5t; Aug 7; Aug 9; Aug 11t; Aug 14b; Aug 17; Aug 18b; Aug 21; Aug 27; Aug29t; Sep 6; Sep 10b/Sep opener; Sep 13; Sep 15 (Mario Tama); Sep 18b; Sep 19 (Jeff J Mitchell); Sep 21t; Sep 23 (Aris Messinis); Sep 30 (Keystone); Oct 1b; Oct 2; Oct 7t; Oct 8; Oct 9b/Oct opener; Oct 15/Oct opener; Oct 20; Oct 21t/Oct opener (Reuters); Oct 27; Oct 29; Oct 30t; Oct 31; Nov 4; Nov 7t; Nov 10/Nov opener; Nov 13 (AFP); Nov 15; Nov 17 (Jewel Samad); Nov 22b; Nov 23 (Natasja Weltsz); Nov 27; Nov 30t/Nov opener; Dec 3b/Dec opener; Dec 4b; Dec 6b; Dec 11t & b; Dec 12; Dec 13b; Dec 14t; Dec 19b; Dec 20; Dec 22b; Dec 24; Dec 26t; Dec 27 (AFP); Dec 28t &b; Dec 30t; Dec 31
Kobal Collection Mar 22t; July 20b; Sep End; Oct 10/Oct opener; Nov 16t; Dec 15b; Dec 27b/Dec opener; Dec 30b
London Features International Jun 11b; Sep 27b
Magnum Photos Ltd Nov 27 (Leonard Freed);
National Baseball Library, Cooperstown, N.Y. Sep 28b
National Film Archive, London Mar 1t
Peter Newark's Pictures Jan 1b; Jan 20b; Jan 22b; Jan 26t; Jan 28b; Jan 29; Feb 11b/Feb opener; Feb 23; Feb 24; Feb 28; Mar 6/Mar opener; Mar 11/Mar opener; Mar 12b; Mar 21; Mar 23; Apr 5/Apr opener; Apr 6; Apr 6t; Apr 8b; Apr 10; Apr 18b; Apr 22t; Apr 27; May 1; May 8b; May 22t; May 23t; May 30b; Jun 13b; Jun 24/Jun opener; Jul 4; Jul 13; Jul 18; Jul 23t; Aug4b; Aug 6t/Aug opener; Aug 11b; Aug 12; Aug 20t; Aug 31t; Sep 5/Sep opener; Sep 10t/Sep opener; Sep 14t; Sep 16; Sep 17; Oct 18; Oct 23; Oct 24t; Oct 25t; Oct 25b; Oct 26; Oct 28; Nov 5t; Nov 6b; Nov 11b; Nov 26t; Dec 2b; Dec 4t; Dec 7/Dec opener; Dec 16; Dec 25/intro/Dec opener; Dec 26b
Robert Opie Collection Jan 18b
Pictorial Press Jun 1
Press Association Jun 29
Reed International Books Ltd May 20b; Sep 24/Sep opener; Nov 14b "Ingres' Violin" 1924, Man Ray (C ADAGP, Paris and DACS, London 1992)
Photoshot Mar 24b (Fiona Simon/Retna); Oct 4 (Stevenson/Retna)
Rex Features Jan 19; Mar 9b; Mar 20; May 15; Jun 27; Aug 14t; Nov 8b; Nov 13b; Dec 21/Dec opener
Robert Opie Jan 18b
Roger Viollet Jan 19b
Royal Geographical Society May opener
Royal Photographic Society/Antoine Claudet Aug 20b
Roger Saunders Oct 5b
Science Museum Dec 17t
Syndication International Oct 3/Oct opener (Aldus Archive/Nat, Collection of Fine Arts, Smithsonian)
Times Library/Sporting Pictures (UK) Ltd Aug 1b
TopFoto Jan 4b; Jan 5t; Jan 8b; Jan 9b; Jan 12; Jan 15t; Jan 15b, Jan 16b, Jan 21 (AP); Jan 25t; Jan 30; Feb 6/Feb opener; Feb 7 (PA); Feb 8; Feb 13 (AP); Feb 14; Feb 20; Feb 25t; Feb 29; Mar 2 (AP); Mar 5t; Mar 7t/Mar opener (AP); Mar 10; Mar 13t; Mar 19; Mar 26; Mar 28t; Apr 1t; Apr 1b; Apr 2 (AP); Apr 11; Apr 12b; Apr 13t; Apr 14t; Apr 16; Apr 23 (AP); Apr 28b; Apr 29b; May 2/May opener; May 3t/May opener; May 4/May opener (AP); May 5; May 6t; May 7t; May 8t; May 12b; May 13t; May 14; May 16t/May opener; May 20t; May 21b (AP); May 23b; May 26b; May 29; Jun 2/Jun opener; Jun 3; Jun 4t; Jun 4b (AP); Jun 6/Jun opener; Jun 8; Jun 9; Jun 11t; Oct 30b/Oct opener; Nov 1t; Nov 1b (AP); Nov 2/Nov opener; Nov 3b/Nov opener; Nov 4/Nov opener (AP); Nov 5t; Nov 8t; Nov 9/Nov opener; Nov 11t; Nov 12/Nov opener; Nov14t, Nov 20, Nov 21t (AP); Nov 22t/Nov opener; Nv 24; Nov 25; Nov 28 (AP); Nov 29; Nov 30b; Dec 2t (AP); Dec 3t; Dec 6t; Dec 9t , Dec 10t (AP); Dec 14b; Dec 15t/Dec opener; Dec 16; Dec 18; Dec 19t, Dec 22t, Dec 23 (AP)
U.S. Signal Corps Dec 13t/Dec opener
Victoria & Albert Museum Nov ending
Wellcome Institute Library, London May 24b
Reg Wilson Photography Jun 16/Jun opener
Whitworth Art Gallery Aug 12

1715 James Edward Stuart, son of James II, lands in northeast Scotland to lead a Jacobite rebellion.

1880 Death of George Eliot (Mary Ann Evans), English novelist.

1894 In France, Captain Alfred Dreyfus is found guilty of treason and sent to Devil's Island.

1917 The Bolshevik government begins peace talks with Germany at Brest-Litovsk.

1921 The US Congress sets up a $20 million (£10.8 million) fund to aid the 20 million Soviet citizens facing starvation.

1984 Dom Mintoff resigns as prime minister of Malta.

1988 South Africa, Angola and Cuba sign treaties for the withdrawal of Cuban troops from Angola.

BIRTHDAYS

Giacomo Puccini 1858, Italian composer of operas such as *La Bohème*.

Dame Peggy Ashcroft 1907, English stage and screen actress.

Maurice and Robin Gibb 1949, English-born pop musicians and singers who, as the Bee Gees, had massive hits in the 1970s.

PETER RABBIT'S CREATOR DIES

1943 Beatrix Potter, the creator of Peter Rabbit and many other well loved children's book characters, has died today. Born an only child of wealthy parents, Miss Potter was never sent to school and as a result led a lonely life as a child. To amuse herself, she taught herself to draw and paint small natural objects. Her first book, the *Tale of Peter Rabbit*, was written for the son of her former governess in 1893, in the form of letters. Beatrix Potter illustrated the book herself and went on to write many more books. She lived at Sawrey in the Lake District from 1905 and in 1913 married William Heelis, a solicitor in the area. The rest of her life was chiefly devoted to her farms and to the newly established National Trust which aims to preserve Britain's heritage.

You mustn't think I advocate perpetual sex. Far from it. Nothing nauseates me more than promiscuous sex in and out of season.

D. H. Lawrence, British novelist, refers to *Lady Chatterley's Lover*, 1928.

FIRST US SOLDIER DIES IN VIETNAM

1961 US soldier James Davis today became the first American to die in Vietnam since America's involvement in the conflict. At the moment US involvement is limited to military advisers – some 200 Air Force members are joined by 700 Army training personnel in providing military advice, including bomber training. However, President Kennedy has just announced that the US will increase the number of advisers by as many as 16,000 over the next two years, giving rise to fears that American participation in the war will become entrenched and that direct military activity will soon follow.

• 1975 – 70 HOSTAGES SEIZED IN VIENNA • 1989 – CEAUCESCU OVERTHROWN

ROYAL FAMILY RETURNS TO ITALY

2002 Victor Emmanuel, the son of Italy's last king, has returned to Italy after more than 50 years in exile. He and his family attended a private audience with Pope John Paul II on Monday. Hours later the family left for Switzerland, and Emmanuel's decision visit the Vatican first has earned criticism. Sergio Romano, a former ambassador, described the decision as "a combination of arrogance, political insensitivity and bad upbringing". The visit was made possible by a reversal of the post-war ban on the royals' return. The family swore their loyalty to the Italian republic as part of the terms of the lifting of the ban on them returning to Italy.

GENERAL TOJO TRIES TO CHEAT EXECUTIONER

1948 A number of high-ranking Japanese war criminals have been executed today after standing trial for crimes against humanity. One of the most infamous of the lot, General Tojo, attempted suicide in the hope of regaining his self esteem: suicide is viewed as the only honourable course under the circumstances in Japanese culture. He was not successful. Tojo was Japanese PM from 1941 to 1944, during which time he became the chief instigator of the attack on Pearl Harbor, which brought the US into World War Two. After the war he was arrested, tried and sentenced.

1814 Andrew Jackson halts the British forces at New Orleans.

1985 In South Africa, six whites die in a bomb blast in Durban.

1990 In a Yugoslavian referendum, the republic of Slovenia votes in favour of becoming an independent state.

1997 Venezuelan terrorist "Carlos the Jackal" is sentenced to life imprisonment after being arrested in Sudan three years earlier.

AUTHOR WILLIAM THACKERAY DIES

1886 Author of the best selling novel *Vanity Fair*, William Makepeace Thackeray, has died in England at the age of 52. Although *Vanity Fair* is his best known novel, he wrote many other novels and lighter works. *Vanity Fair* first appeared in monthly installments illustrated by Thackeray himself. Born in Calcutta, his family sent him home to England to be educated at Charterhouse, then Trinity College, Cambridge. After university he studied law at Middle Temple, then art in Paris for a time. On his return to London, Thackeray began to work as a journalist, contributing to many publications, among them the magazine *Punch*.

BIRTHDAYS

Sir Richard Arkwright 1732, English inventor and industrialist.

Alexander I 1777, Russian tsar who defeated Napoleon's invasion of Russia in 1812.

Maurice Denham 1909, British stage and screen actor whose many films include *Sunday, Bloody Sunday*.

Yousuf Karsh 1912, Turkish-Armenian photographer who emigrated to Canada.

Helmut Schmidt 1922, German statesman, former chancellor of the Federal Republic of Germany.

• 1834 – "SAFTEY CAB" PATENTED • 1973 – SHAH OF IRAN DOUBLES OIL PRICES

1508 London houses receive piped water for the first time.

1851 Fire destroys part of the Capitol building in Washington.

1914 The first German bomb lands on British soil.

1943 President Roosevelt appoints General Dwight D. Eisenhower commander-in-chief of the invasion of Europe.

1989 Deposed Panamian leader Manuel Noriega gives himself up to the papal nuncio in Panama City.

1990 A cyclone sweeps the Queensland coast of Australia with wind speeds of 150 mph (241 kph).

BIRTHDAYS

John 1167, English monarch who was forced by his rebellious barons to sign the Magna Carta at Runnymede.

Kit Carson 1809, American frontiersman and Indian agent at Taos. 1910

Max Miedinger 1910, Swiss typeface designer who created Helvetica

Ava Gardner 1922, American actress who appeared in *The Sun Also Rises.*

BUSINESS AS USUAL

1814 In Ghent today representatives of Britain and America signed a peace treaty ending the two-and-a-half-year conflict between the two countries. The nub of the agreement is that the two sides are to stop fighting. This stalemate treaty is appropriate to the position on the ground in North America, where neither side has made gains. The issue of maritime rights, the main cause of the war, has been a dead letter since the ending of the Napoleonic Wars in Europe, hence British willingness to settle the dispute with America.

I am very sorry to know and hear how unreverently that most precious jewel, the Word of God, is disputed, rhymed, sung and jangled in every ale-house and tavern, contrary to the true meaning and doctrine of the same.

King Henry VIII comments on the translation of the Bible into English, 1545.

LIBYA DECLARES INDEPENDENCE

1951 King Idris I formally declared the independence of Libya, in North Africa in a broadcast from the balcony of the Mahara palace in Benghazi today. It is just over two years since the United Nations set the time limit

for Libya's independence at January 1, 1952. For the preceding six years, ever since the defeat of Axis forces in the area, the country had been administered by the French and the British governments: the Fezzan region by France and Cyrenaica and Tripolitania by the British. The new constitution of the federal democratic kingdom provides for two legislative chambers: one elected on a proportional representation basis, and the other nominated. Elections to the new parliament will be held early next year. King Idris, 61, was chosen as ruler of the new state by a Libyan National Assembly which met last year.

• **1871 – VERDI'S *AIDA* OPENS IN CAIRO • 1908 – FIRST INTERNATIONAL AVIATION SHOW**

CHRIST'S BIRTH DATE IS OFFICIAL

440AD The leaders of the Christian Church have decided that the date of the birth of Jesus Christ should be fixed. The date mooted is December 25, the day that the Romans celebrate the winter solstice. The Celtic and Germanic tribes as well as the Norsemen also hold this period dear. The Church authorities do not want their celebration to be tainted by an association with heathen customs, however, and are thought to be engaged in the task of creating rites that will underline the differences between their faith and any of an ungodly nature.

WILLIAM ORDERS DAY OF RECKONING

1085 King William I has ordered a complete survey of England. Several groups of commissioners will gather detailed information of the accounts of the estates of the King and of those who hold land by direct services to him in each county of the realm. The subjects of William's "description of England" are already referring to the impending investigation as "Domesday". From each manor information will be collected on the dimensions and the ploughing capacity of the land, the number of workers, and any extra amenities such as mills and fishponds. The King and his officers will then have an estimate of what every holder of land in the kingdom is worth.

DALAI LAMA FLEES LHASA

1950 The 15-year-old Dalai Lama is thought to have fled the Tibetan capital, Lhasa, to enlist help for his country's struggle to maintain its status as the only country in the world entirely under the control of priests. The crisis has deepened since October when China first invaded Tibet. Last month the Tibetan government took the unusual step of investing the Dalai Lama with full powers of office three years before he was due to receive them. It remains to be seen whether this further legitimization of his rule will deter the Chinese from "liberating Tibet by force".

800 AD Charlemagne is crowned Emperor of the West by Pope Leo III.

1066 William the Conqueror is crowned King of England.

1800 Britain's first Christmas tree is put up at Windsor by Queen Charlotte.

1914 British and German soldiers observe an impromptu truce on the Western Front.

1926 Hirohito accedes to the throne of Japan.

1972 Managua, capital of Nicaragua, is destroyed by an earthquake.

1983 Death of Spanish Surrealist artist Joan Miró.

1987 Israeli forces crack down on Arab rioters.

1989 President Ceausescu and his wife are executed by the Romanian army.

1991 French actress Orane Demazis, known for her roles in Marcel Pagnol's *Marseilles Trilogy*, dies.

BIRTHDAYS

Humphrey Bogart 1889, American actor whose legendary films include *The Maltese Falcon*.

Annie Lennox 1954, British pop singer, one half of the Eurythmics.

• 1950 – CORONATION STONE STOLEN • 1977 – DEATH OF CHARLIE CHAPLIN

BIRTHDAYS

Mao Tse-tung 1893, Chinese Communist statesman who proclaimed the establishment of the People's Republic of China in 1949.

Richard Widmark 1914, American actor whose films include *The Alamo*.

Phil Spector 1940, American songwriter and record producer whose distinctive sound was to be heard on many records of the 1960s.

BRITISH SINK MIGHTY GERMAN BATTLECRUISER

1943 The sea lanes of the North Sea have been made several degrees safer for Allied convoys by the sinking today of the mighty German battlecruiser *Scharnhorst*. The ship, commanded by Admiral Bey, left her lair in Altenfjord yesterday to attack convoy JW55B. Due to bad visibility *Scharnhorst* missed her prey and became separated from her escort of five destroyers. She continued the hunt alone, unaware that a Royal Navy long-range protection group comprising the battleship *Duke of York*, cruiser *Jamaica* and four destroyers was closing in fast. The convoy's cruiser and destroyer escort kept *Scharnhorst* at bay until the *Duke of York* could launch its attack.

GREAT ARCHAEOLOGIST DIES IN NAPLES

1890 The German archaeologist Heinrich Schliemann died yesterday in Naples. He was 58. Among his best-known discoveries is that of the great civilization at Hisarlik, Turkey, which he believed to be that of Homeric Troy. In 1876 he discovered a second civilization, at Mycenae in Greece.

TSUNAMI STORMS INDIAN OCEAN

2004 Nearly 300,000 people have died when a magnitude 9.3 earthquake in the Indian Ocean triggered one of the most destructive tsunamis in recorded history. The tsunami travelled across the Indian Ocean, wreaking havoc in countries as far apart as Indonesia, the Maldives, Thailand, Sri Lanka and Somalia. The western tip of the island of Sumatra, closest to the earthquake's epicentre, was worst hit and some coastal villages are thought to have lost more than 70 per cent of inhabitants.

• 1900 – *DANCE OF DEATH* PREMIERES • 1908 – JOHNSON WINS BOXING CROWN

WORLDWIDE SCIENTIFIC EXPEDITION SETS SAIL

1831 The Royal Navy vessel HMS *Beagle* under Captain Robert Fitzroy set sail from Devonport today on a five-year scientific expedition round the world. The purpose of the trip is to survey the coasts of Patagonia, Tierra del Fuego, Chile and Peru, to visit some Pacific islands and to set up a network of chronometrical stations. The official naturalist on board is recent BA graduate Charles Darwin, 22, whose task it will be to study the rocks and life of the places visited and to collect specimens. The post is unpaid but provides a unique opportunity for study.

1965 The *Sea Gem* oil rig collapses in the North Sea, drowning 13.

1983 Mehmet Ali Agca begs the Pope's forgiveness when the latter visits his would-be assassin in jail.

1980 Egypt and Syria resume diplomatic relations after a ten-year break.

1981 Death of American pianist and composer Hoagy Carmichael.

1984 In Poland, four policemen go on trial for the murder of Father Jerzy Popicluszko.

2008 Israel launches the largest offensive against the Gaza strip since 1967.

EVERY PICTURE TELLS A STORY

1968 The pioneering news photographer "Weegee" died at the age of 69. Born Usher H. Fellig in Poland, he emigrated to the US in 1910. The name Weegee was not adopted until about 1938, when his knack of arriving at the scene of an incident was so remarkable that people joked he must have access to a greater power through a clairvoyant's ouija board. In fact, he had a radio that picked up the emergency signals of the Manhattan police and firemen.

BIRTHDAYS

Johannes Kepler 1571, German astronomer who discovered that planetary orbits were elliptical.

Louis Pasteur 1822, French chemist and microbiologist whose many discoveries included the process of pasteurization.

Marlene Dietrich 1901, German actress who starred in Hollywood films such as *The Blue Angel*.

Gérard Depardieu 1948, French actor who came to international fame in the film *Green Card*.

BHUTTO ASSASSINATED

2007 Benazir Bhutto, twice prime minister of Pakistan, was assassinated as she left a Pakistan People's Party rally in the town of Rawalpindi where she had been campaigning for elections. An attacker opened fire as she stood in her armoured vehicle, then seconds later a bomb was set off, leaving 20 other people dead. An independent UN report concluded that insufficient security measures were taken by the government of President Pervez Musharraf and the police deliberately failed to investigate the murder as they feared intelligence agency involvement.

> *I am going to build the kind of nation that President Roosevelt hoped for, President Truman worked for and President Kennedy died for.*
> **Lyndon B. Johnson,** US president, 1964.

• 1904 – DUBLIN'S ABBEY THEATRE OPENS • 1904 – *PETER PAN* PREMIERES

BIRTHDAYS

Thomas Woodrow Wilson 1856, American statesman and Democratic president 1913–21.

Earl "Fatha" Nines 1905, American jazz pianist, composer and bandleader.

Maggie Smith 1934, British actress who won an Oscar for *The Prime of Miss Jean Brodie*.

COALITION PARTY WINS ELECTION

1918 The results of the General Election held in Britain on December 14 were announced today. They reveal that the Coalition Party under David Lloyd George has romped to victory, with a majority of 262 seats over all the other non-Coalition parties. It is the first election in which women have been allowed to vote, albeit not on an equal footing with men; only women of 30 years and older are eligible and those who have lived in the UK for six months. Of the 15 women candidates who stood for election only one, the notorious Sinn Fein leader Madame Markiewicz (Constance Gore-Booth), was elected. The Liberal Opposition under Herbert Asquith has been annihilated; only 26 Liberal followers of Asquith have been returned. The results are being read as a thumbs-up for the forces of stability and staunch nationalism.

TAY BRIDGE DISASTER

1879 Part of the Tay Bridge collapsed this evening as the 7.15 Edinburgh to Dundee train was passing. All 300 passengers and crew are feared dead. Gale-force winds are thought to have caused the collapse of 13 girders in the central part of the bridge. Early attempts to reach the train by steamboat have failed due to the severity of the weather. The bridge, at 10,612 ft (3442 m) the longest of its kind in the world, was hailed as a feat of engineering at its completion in May 1878.

SUKARNO MOVES INTO PALACE

1949 Ahmed Sukarno, the leader of the Indonesian Nationalist Party, has arrived in Batavia (Djakarta) to take up residence in the magnificent palace of the Dutch governors general. Since proclaiming Indonesia a republic after the Japanese surrender in 1945, Sukarno, 48, has defied all Dutch attempts to regain control of their former colony. Yesterday the Netherlands government formally signed the protocol transferring sovereignty to an Indonesia.

• **1908 – SICILIAN EARTHQUAKE DESTROYS MESSINA AND CLAIMS 150,000 LIVES**

ARCHBISHOP OF CANTERBURY MURDERED

1170 The Archbishop of Canterbury, Thomas à Becket, was murdered in Canterbury Cathedral this evening. The Archbishop had only recently returned from a six-year exile in France after incurring Henry's displeasure over the question of church versus crown rights in England. The tussle between the two had led to excommunication for the bishops Roger of York and Foliot of London, and the fear that the Pope might slap an interdict on England. Henry was the unwitting architect of the murder. It seems that his exclamation "Will no one rid me of this turbulent priest?" – uttered in extreme distress – was interpreted by the four knights who carried out the execution as a call to action.

SIOUX MASSACRED AT PINE RIDGE

1890 An attempt to disarm Miniconjou Sioux Indians on the Pine Ridge Reservation, South Dakota, ended in bloodshed today. About half of the Sioux casualties were women and children, lending weight to claims that the encounter was a massacre, not a battle.

BRITISH ADMIRALTY LAUNCHES SHIP OF IRON

1860 The world's first true ironclad warship, *Warrior*, was launched at Blackwall on the River Thames today. The British Admiralty first showed interest in the idea of iron-built warships as a consequence of the calamitous showing of wooden-built vessels during the Crimean War. The decision to build such a vessel was not taken until last year, however, when the launch of the French iron-clad *La Gloire* posed a threat to British naval supremacy. *La Gloire* is built primarily of oak but it has been fitted with a belt of iron extending from the upper deck to 6 ft (1.8 m) below the waterline.

1798 Britain, Austria, Russia, Naples and Portugal form a second alliance against Napoleon.

1911 Revolutionary leader Dr Sun Yat-sen becomes the first president of the Republic of China.

1926 Death of Austrian poet Rainer Maria Rilke.

1984 Rajiv Gandhi wins a landslide victory in the Indian general election.

1986 Harold Macmillan, 1st Earl of Stockton and former British prime minister, dies aged 92.

1989 Playwright Vaclav Havel is elected president of Czechoslovakia.

1989 Thousands of Vietnamese boat people battle with riot police in Hong Kong.

BIRTHDAYS

William Ewart Gladstone 1809, English statesman and Liberal prime minister.

Pablo Casals 1876, Spanish cellist of great stature who refused to live or play in Spain while Franco ruled the country.

Jon Voight 1938, American actor who found fame in *Midnight Cowboy*.

• 1924 – JOHN D ROCKEFELLER DONATES $1 MILLION TO NEW YORK'S MET

1903 A raging fire breaks out in the Iroquois Theatre in Chicago during a performance and kills 578.

1919 In London, the first female bar student is admitted to Lincoln's Inn.

1922 Soviet Russia is renamed the Union of Soviet Socialist Republics.

1968 Death of Trygve Lie, Norwegian politician and first secretary-general of the UN.

1988 In Moscow, Yuri Churbanov, son-in-law of former president Brezhnev, is sentenced to 12 years in jail for corruption.

1988 Colonel Oliver North subpoenas President Reagan and George Bush to testify in the Iran-Contra trial.

BIRTHDAYS

Rudyard Kipling 1865, English novelist and poet, most of whose works are concerned with India.

Sir Carol Reed 1906, British film director best-known for *The Third Man* and the Oscar-winning *Oliver!*

Bo Diddley 1928, American rhythm and blues singer.

RASPUTIN MURDERED

1916 The influential royal favourite Grigory Rasputin was murdered last night at the home of Prince Felix Yusupov in St Petersburg. He was 44. The behaviour of the Siberian peasant turned mystic had scandalized Russian society and seriously undermined the standing of the Russian royal family. Rasputin's influence over the royal family came about after he succeeded in easing the suffering of the Tsar's haemophiliac son, Aleksey Nikolayevich. Once established as a royal favourite, Rasputin lived up to his acquired name, which means "debauched one". The monk met his end at the hands of a group of Conservatives committed to saving Russia from his malign influence. Yusupov first plied the visiting Rasputin with poisoned wine and tea cakes. When this ploy appeared to be having no success, the noblemen shot him, then tied him up and threw his body into the freezing River Neva, where he finally died by drowning.

US RENEGOTIATES FOR NORIEGA

1989 Negotiations between Washington and the Vatican have restarted to bring an end to the refuge of the Panamanian dictator General Manuel Noriega in the Vatican embassy in Panama City. Noriega, who faces prosecution in the US on drug trafficking charges fled to the embassy on Christmas Eve to escape the clutches of the US marines sent by President Bush to arrest him.

RICHARD RODGERS DIES

1979 Richard Rodgers, one of this century's best-known composers of musicals, died in New York City today. He was 77. In a long and prolific career Rodgers formed long-standing working relationships with lyricists Lorenz Hart and Oscar Hammerstein II. Over the course of 17 years, Rogers and Hammerstein had an outstanding run of success with one hit after another, including *Carousel*, *South Pacific*, *The King and I* and *The Sound of Music*.

• 1880 – **THE TRANSVAAL BECOMES A REPUBLIC** • 2006 – **SADDAM HUSSEIN EXECUTED**

CAMBODIA BREAKS OFF RELATIONS WITH VIETNAM

1977 The Cambodian government announced today that it is breaking off diplomatic relations with neighbouring Vietnam. The two Communist countries are at loggerheads over which of them is to blame for the recent outbreaks of intense fighting along their borders. Much of the problem seems to have its roots in the movement of Cambodians across the frontier in the Mekong Delta soon after the fall of Saigon and before the North Vietnamese could establish full control in the area. The conflict is being exacerbated by ideological differences, with the Chinese-sponsored Cambodian regime laying claim to a more "revolutionary" outlook than that of Soviet-backed Vietnam.

1687 The first Huguenot emigrants to South Africa set sail from France, taking vines with which to start a wine industry in their new colony.

1922 The French government turns down a German offer of a non-aggression pact.

1986 Oil company Esso announces it is disinvesting in South Africa.

1988 In Islamabad, capital of Pakistan, prime ministers Rajiv Gandhi and Benazir Bhutto sign the first agreement between India and Pakistan in 16 years.

US TO OPEN IMMIGRATION DEPOT

1891 The new year will see the opening of the US government's new depot for handling immigrant arrivals to New York. Last year the government assumed sole responsibility for the screening of arrivals, a task formerly performed by the state of New York as the government's local agent. The new depot, on Ellis Island in the upper bay area, will be the nation's major immigration station. It is being trumpeted as a major improvement on the old facilities at the Battery on Manhattan Island and better able to cope with massive numbers of arrivals. The island is named after Samuel Ellis, who owned it in the 1770s.

BIRTHDAYS

Charles Edward Stuart 1720, Scottish royal aka Bonnie Prince Charlie.

Henri Matisse 1869, French painter and sculptor who initiated the vibrantly coloured style known as Fauvism.

George Marshall 1880, American statesman who, as secretary of state, devised the Marshall Plan for post-war economic recovery in Europe.

Ben Kingsley 1943, British actor best-known for his Oscar-winning performance as *Gandhi*.

GHANAIAN GOVERNMENT OVERTHROWN

1981 Former flight lieutenant Jerry Rawlings has overthrown the government of President Hilla Limann and seized power again in Ghana. In a radio broadcast to the nation, Rawlings claimed that Limann and his associates had brought about the country's "total economic ruin". Rawlings has given no indication of how long his Provisional Military Council will retain power, but he did remind his fellow citizens of the fact that he voluntarily returned the government to civilian rule three months after he toppled the military government of Lieutenant-General Fred Akuffo in June 1979.

1999 – BORIS YELTSIN RESIGNS, NOMINATING PRIME MINISTER PUTIN TO REPLACE HIM